THE DEVELOPMENT OF THE ENGLISH ECONOMY
TO 1750

To

Alper Mehmet
and to my
mother

THE
DEVELOPMENT
OF THE
ENGLISH ECONOMY
TO 1750

PETER KING, B.A., M.Litt.

Sometime Lecturer at Bristol Polytechnic.
History Master, The Manchester Grammar School

MACDONALD & EVANS LTD
8 John Street, London WC1N 2HY

1971

First published August 1971

©

MACDONALD AND EVANS LIMITED
1971

S.B.N.: 7121 0407 0

Printed in Great Britain by Clarke, Doble & Brendon Ltd,
Plymouth

PREFACE

Economic history is now an important subject in its own right—studied at schools, colleges of further education and universities throughout the country. Many books already cover the economic development of England from the Industrial Revolution to the present day, but few works cover the period before the middle of the eighteenth century. The purpose of this book is to give a detailed account of the origins and development of the English economy from the earliest times to the opening years of the eighteenth century. It is designed for the use of those taking "A" Level and degree examinations, although it is also of interest to the general reader. Attention has been focused on trends and problems, rather than on a strict chronology of events, but the factual details have been included in order to explain the intricacies of each period.

The study of the English economy during the medieval and mercantilist periods is a necessary prelude to understanding the modern industrial economy. Many features from the earlier periods persisted into modern times, because economic change is slow and piecemeal. The Industrial Revolution did not grow out of a primitive economy but from one which was the most sophisticated of its day. By the middle of the eighteenth century, English agriculture had outgrown in large measure the feudalism prevalent in Europe. Trade and finance were well organised and industry and transport growing rapidly. A study of the antecedents of those changes helps to explain what has been called the first industrial revolution. Economic philosophies and theories are often of long standing and much that passes today for radical or original is no more than re-advertising of past theories. For example, modern economic policy involves massive government interference and control, and this is in one sense neo-mercantilism, because it revives a policy common in the sixteenth and seventeenth centuries.

To some extent, the study of the past suffers from doubtful statistics, biased opinions and imperfect knowledge. Economic history is an ever-changing subject and fresh research adds almost daily to our understanding of the past. Every effort has been made to use the material available in specialised articles and to cite some of the leading names of those involved in matters where no final answer has been given. As far as possible, economic history has not been treated in isolation and made the prey of dull statistics and unenlightened writing. The subject has been placed in the

v

context of political changes and illustrated, where it is relevant, with accounts of social developments. In this approach, historians of earlier generations showed keener perception than some of their modern successors and thus their works have also formed an important foundation for the structure of this book.

Writing this work would have been impossible without the help of many people. The author readily acknowledges his debt to some fellow historians and masters. Mrs Jean Rock has done splendidly to type the work from a scarcely legible script in a short space of time. I should like to thank Susan Banfield and Catherine Bodman, who helped in their different ways to create this book when I was teaching in another place. Throughout the past year, my Sixth Form at The Manchester Grammar School have been constant in their attempts to improve my history and I think the book reveals to some extent my debt to them all. In particular, I should like to thank Colin Fairbrother for his help with proof reading and the index. Any mistakes which remain are, of course, my responsibility, although it is to be hoped that they are few in number.

June 1970   P.K.

CONTENTS

LIST OF ILLUSTRATIONS

LIST OF TABLES

CHAPTER 1

THE FOUNDATION OF THE ENGLISH ECONOMY

THE ENVIRONMENT OF THE ENGLISH ECONOMY

The English economy has always been an island economy, and this has shaped the pattern of life for the people and influenced the nature of their economic achievements. The resources on which the English population depended were principally located until the eighteenth century in their own island, and even after that time the island's agricultural capacity and mineral wealth provided for a great share of her needs. The British islands were established in the period 10,000 to 6000 B.C. when large parts of the continental shelf were submerged, and the North Sea and the English Channel were made by the inrush of the Atlantic Ocean.

Although the coastline then, and for many centuries afterwards, differed from its present form, its length and the large number of indentations made it of value for innumerable harbours. Twenty-three large river estuaries provided safe anchorages for ships of considerable size. It must be remembered that the absence of silting in many places now cut off from the sea combined with the shallow draught of early ships to make many places now regarded as inland towns into flourishing ports. Chester, Stamford, Ipswich, Canterbury and Winchelsea might be given as prominent examples. This long coastline of approximately 8,000 miles was of great importance because until the late eighteenth century seaborne trade was the main method of transportation for the internal as well as the external exchange of goods. For example, Newcastle coal went by sea to London, and West Country ports, and grain was brought in bulk to London by sea.

As long ago as 1450, the importance of England's coastline was mentioned by Sir John Fortescue, well known as the writer of a work on constitutional development and author of *The Commodities of England* (c. 1450). Fortescue did not share the pessimism of other fifteenth-century economic writers and he praised England's natural advantages for economic growth. The coastline was indented with the estuaries of many rivers, and these were referred to by Fortescue, as a second factor of importance. Rivers provided

1

one of the principal high roads of internal trade, being free in large part from internal tolls, and often navigable for considerable distances. In this respect the Severn and the Thames were the most important. Iron goods from the Forest of Dean and agricultural produce from Oxfordshire were the keys to the prosperity of many riverine ports. In the early eighteenth century, Daniel Defoe claimed there were 1,160 miles of navigable river in the country, and that no place was more than 15 miles from the coast or a river.

The insular position of England inevitably gave rise to shipping and fishing industries. It trained seamen who came to be the backbone of the Royal Navy. When, in the early sixteenth century, the discoveries of Columbus and others placed England in the middle instead of on the edge of the world, she was perfectly situated to embark upon her oceanic and commercial expansion and the development of an empire. The worst terrors of continental war were spared this country. Continental influences were slowed down and more carefully absorbed. A sense of continuity and insularity developed. Sheltered from foreign disturbance the island was the largest free trade area of the Middle Ages, and developed a strong central government earlier than most countries to protect merchants and their trade. Nevertheless the separation of England from Europe should not be exaggerated. The eastern tip of England, with London at the centre, and, to the north, the great fairs and the centres of the cloth industry; and, to the south, the Cinque Ports and Wealdan industries, pointed towards the Continent and the Low Countries. Up to 1066 a host of settlers came to England—Celts, Romans, Saxons, Danes and Normans. After that date, invasion was still possible, as the events of 1399 and 1485 were to prove. It was only with the defeat of the Armada in 1588 that England began a long period free from the threat of invasion, although as late as 1688 William of Orange succeeded. As seafaring folk the English found the Narrow Seas very little of a barrier. From 1066 to 1558, England held possessions in continental Europe and was often ruled by kings more foreign than English. Richard the Lion Heart was only in England for six months. Before 1066 the Roman and Danish empires had embraced the island. The international nature of feudal society and the Papal Church during the Middle Ages were further indications that national spirit was, to exaggerate, the "most defensive" as a barrier. "We are," said the philosopher Marquess of Halifax in the seventeenth century, "in an island, confined to it by God Almighty not as a Penalty but a Grace and one of the greatest that can be given to Mankind." Quite often it formed a bridge as well as a refuge for continental ideas and innovations.

Since England was mainly an agricultural primary producer for the greater part of the period covered by this book, topography, soil and climate are all key factors in determining the economic activity of the community. Without the great technical developments we have since achieved, the same factors were also bound to affect the pattern of settlement. In the earliest days the river valleys were barriers holding up communications and deterring agriculture with soils too heavy for Celtic ploughs. Then, and for centuries afterwards, the enormous expanses of forest and fen restricted settlement and limited the cultivable area of the country. At the height of agricultural expansion before the eighteenth century only half the country was cultivated. Ten out of thirty-nine million acres were calculated by Gregory King as late as 1696 to be "heaths, moors, mountains and barren lands," and one million under water or roadside. Population was largely restricted throughout the period to the east and south of the country and even in that area it tended to crowd along the coastline.

England may be divided broadly into two zones, separated by the 600 feet contour line. The highland zone consists of the uplands of the Celtic fringe of Scotland, Wales and Cornwall, and, in England, of the Cheviots, Pennines, Peak District, Welsh border hills and the uplands of Devon. In this region, from when the Romans regarded it primarily as hostile territory to be occupied militantly, conditions varied enormously from those in the other zone of lowland valley, downs and ridges. It was an area where cultural and economic ideas were retained long after they had altered further south. Throughout most of the period, the highland zone remained difficult to administer, hostile to settlement and of marginal use for agriculture. The whole population of Scotland, for example, had only reached one million by the eighteenth century. The lowland zone consisted of river valleys and coastal plains with intervening hilly regions largely composed of chalk downs and limestone ridges. Easy access from abroad and ease of communication by hill track or river voyage made the region congenial to settlement. At first, light-soiled areas were favoured, but with the slow improvement of the plough and of drainage techniques, heavy soils were frequented by the sixteenth century. Large areas of marshland in Kent, Essex and East Anglia added further fertile tracts during the great drainings of the twelfth to thirteenth, and sixteenth to seventeenth centuries, and the forests of the region in the Midlands and to the north and south of London were greatly reduced.

The concentration of economic activity in this region naturally followed these favourable conditions. It was the centre of both agriculture and industry. It was densely peopled, particularly in East Anglia, the London region and the Gloucester-Wiltshire-Dorset region. The focus of the area was London, whose disproportionate share of the national income was only being challenged at the end of the seventeenth century. Food for London came from places as far away as Lincolnshire, Cheshire, and Warwickshire. The capital's needs stimulated not only agriculture, but also the major industries. The cloth industry came to be situated in East Anglia and the iron industry in Kent by the fifteenth century with London as the main internal source of demand. The shipbuilding and leather industries were concentrated in the same region. Those historians who have been too closely preoccupied with fitting early economies into precise patterns often ignore the basic influence of climate and soils on the nature of man's various occupations. As an island separated from the land-mass of Europe, suitably cooled or warmed by the sea, and exposed to the path of the west winds and Atlantic cyclones, England is free from extremes of climate and, for its latitude, is surprisingly temperate. It is significant that the 40 inch isohyet roughly follows the 600 feet contour line and marks the limits of differing agricultural settlements. Drought is prevented by the transfer of water from the scarcely peopled west to the more populous east and by good surface drainage. Although humidity is high and sometimes enervating in the west, the climate is sufficiently temperate and variable to encourage work all the year round in the open air. The considerable varieties of climate conditioned the wide variety of agricultural systems that prevailed even at the height of the Middle Ages.

Fortescue drew attention to a "third commodity of this land which is that the ground thereof is so good and commodious to the sheep." The influence of the sedimentary deposits of the Ice Ages has been considerable, and the geological pattern of the country is immensely complicated. Flint, limestone, ragstone and Portland stone are among a number of regional varieties of stone that have influenced the building industry until the early-nineteenth-century growth of the brick industry. Certain rare commodities such as alum in the Isle of Wight, salt in the Wear Valley and Cheshire, and fuller's earth in Surrey and West Suffolk were to be of great value in industrial development. Although the precious minerals of silver and gold were nearly exhausted by the Romans, coal, tin and lead all produced extensive mining industries by the thirteenth century. The soils and climate helped the development of afforestation and the large forests of the country provided timber for the building and shipping industries and as a basic material for the iron industry's charcoal requirement. By the seventeenth century, their size had been greatly reduced and various fears for their future were being expressed.

It has been suggested that the Narrow Seas formed a link as well as a barrier to the Continent, and across them came the various races who were to make the English people. Moulded partly by the experience of places they left behind, and more by the influence of the island itself, a large number of different races formed an amalgam known as the English. Because they were few in number and lived in a small island, they quickly fused and created a national character. It is unfashionable today to even suggest that some nations possess talents superior to others. Yet England's reputation as a "nation of shopkeepers" and "the workshop of the world" was built up during long years of national development. Since economic history is the relationship of people to their environment, it is necessary to say something of the people themselves, for they made what they could of the geographical environment in which they found themselves. Others might not have reaped the same advantages.

With the earliest inhabitants of the island, the economic historian is little concerned. What are loosely called the Stone Ages, and should more accurately be referred to as the Palaeolithic, Mesolithic and Neolithic periods, lasted from about 25,000 B.C. to 10,000 B.C. Only at the end of this period, as the next section will indicate, could it be said that an economy was in being. The early dwellers in trees or caves were not without some refinements. Rough stone implements and bone tools helped the hunter and nomad. Fire and skins afforded warmth and protection from a hostile environment. During the Neolithic period, a fresh invasion occurred, the origins of which are not agreed upon by historians. Thus, waves of people came from the Eastern Mediterranean, settling in eastern and southern England about 2000 B.C. Because of their more sophisticated use of pottery and metals, they are referred to as the Beaker, or Bronze Age, Folk.

Bronze, an alloy of copper and tin, was of little use for weaponry and, with the invasion of the Celts in the last thousand years before Christ, a new and more warlike race occupied the country. The island was subjected to three invasions, although there is some dispute about their exact order. By the time Caesar arrived, the Celts were in occupation of most of the island. England was known as Albion (*albus* = white) or Cassiterides (*kassiteros* = tin). The Celts were a hardy, muscular, round-headed people, short and dark. When the Roman occupation occurred, some half to three-quarters of a million Romano-Celts appeared, but the inhabitants outside the towns were little influenced by the Romans. When the

Romans left in the fifth century, the Celts were again masters of the island.

Between A.D. 300 and 600 Europe underwent a period of racial strife and migrations which established the basis of the existing pattern of peoples. In England between 450 and 825, a group of German races, Jutes, Angles and Saxons succeeded in occupying most of the country. It has been established that the Celts offered vigorous and effective resistance to the Germanic peoples and migrated themselves. The Scots crossed from Ireland into Scotland and Wales, where the principality of Dyved was established. Gradually the Celts were driven back. In the West Country, the defeat of Deorham (577) started the conquest of the south-west which was completed by the subjection of Cornwall in 838. In Wales, Offa's Dyke marked the Saxon limitation of penetration but from 1070 the Normans were to embark upon conquests that extinguished the last Celtic kingdom in Wales as late as 1282 to 1284. It was not until 1018 that the eastern, and 1092 the western, parts of the Scottish border were stabilised, and after that there was a "Debateable" land for many years between the two countries.

Celtic influence on Saxon development was strong. By no means all enslaved or slaughtered, the Celts intermarried in large numbers. In the north, Celts outnumbered Saxons in the population. The realisation of Celtic survival makes the view that some Roman influence may have survived the invasions a little more tenable. Five Roman roads remained in regular use, three-quarters of the Roman towns became Saxon ones, and there is the undecided matter of the Roman influence on agriculture. Celtic influence was certainly part of the economic organisation of England well into the Middle Ages. Methods of ploughing and field allocation, systems of land tenure, and the work of metal and stone craftsmen are some of the indications of this survival.

At first, under the Saxons, England was again tribal. By 600 there were ten kingdoms, by 800 three and some under-kingdoms, and by 874 only one. Popular legend is correct in assuming Alfred was the first king of England with no Saxon rivals after Burghtred of Mercia submitted in 874. Alfred's immediate successors used the title King of England. Yet no sooner had the Saxon seafarers become agriculturists than the Danes from the east and the Vikings from the west invaded the country. From 787 to 1083, there were not many years when Danish incursions or threatened invasions did not harry the Saxons. The Western Isles of Scotland, large tracts of Ireland, the Isle of Man and Cumberland were all seized by the Vikings. In England, the Danes established three kingdoms in East Anglia, the Midlands and Northumbria after

Alfred had to admit partial defeat at their hands in 878. Danish kings ruled at York until 952 before their independent power was destroyed.

Danish influence, like that of the Celts, has in the past been underestimated. Wholesale settlement took place, occasioned by polygamy and poverty in Scandinavia. Danish economic and social influence was considerable. Again, land tenure and agricultural methods were affected. The close connection with the other shores of the North Sea stimulated trade. Warfare helped to promote the growth of "burghs" or fortified towns. The complex of cloth manufacturing towns and great international fairs of the Fenland region owed their inception to Danish trade. From 1016 to 1042, England was part of a Danish empire, and the Danes did not surrender their claim to the English crown.

In 1066 the last major settlement occurred as the result of a triangular contest between Saxons, Danes and Normans. The Danes were defeated at Stamford Bridge in Yorkshire, the Saxons at Hastings in Sussex, and William the Conqueror was crowned by the Archbishop of York on Christmas Day. At first, the Norman Conquest involved the displacement of the Saxon ruling class with another in which Normans, Bretons and Flemings were prominent. There was, however, some systematic movement of people. South Yorkshire, Wales and Ireland all felt the strong Norman yoke. After William devastated the north in 1069, sizeable settlements were made. Wales was subdued by its erstwhile military guardians, the Marcher Lords, and Ireland, or part of it at least, fell to Norman barons after 1169. During the Norman Conquest, the settlement of Jews was increased and many foreigners settled in the towns of eastern and southern England, particularly merchants from the Baltic region and Hanseatic towns. Not until the religious upheavals of the sixteenth century drove French and Dutch Protestant craftsmen with their agricultural and industrial skills to these shores, was there again to be any large-scale immigration.

Settlement in England was, therefore, a complicated process. Place names alone reveal the intricacies of the pattern. Added to the considerable divergences already produced by terrain, it led to an almost bewildering variety of dialects, customs, methods of holding and cultivating land, ways of carrying out agricultural occupations, and methods of industrial production. Weights, measures and values of coins varied from place to place. Thus, throughout nearly the whole period covered by this book events in one place must not be taken as representative of the whole. Slow communications, governmental fragmentation, and the prevalence of differing systems of law—all contributed to produce a varied

economic picture in which long-past traditions and coming innovations are found in practice side by side.

THE CREATION OF A PATTERN OF ECONOMIC ACTIVITY

In the economic development of England there have been two
events which might justifiably be called revolutions. It is important
to stress that economic revolutions evolve over a number of years
rather than in an instant of time in the way that political revolutions do. Nevertheless, in the far-reaching and fundamental impacts
of these two revolutions on the whole economic pattern for centuries
to come lies some justification for regarding them as unique. The
first revolution occurred at the end of the Stone Age and during
the Bronze Age. It formed the prelude to the Celtic economy and
laid the basis for the economic pattern of England throughout the
period covered by this book. It was the agricultural revolution
which made possible agricultural production. At the end of the
period covered by this book came the second revolution which
eventually changed the basis of economic organisation from that
of an agricultural to that of an industrial complex.

Thus, by about 500 B.C., an agricultural revolution had established in England a pattern of settlement. From caves and holes
in the ground, early man had moved into villages of conically
shaped wicker huts, and, in marshy regions, houses were erected
on stilts for the purposes of protection and to provide homesteads
for fishing communities. The agricultural revolution was based on
two factors. The first was the domestication of animals. From the
evidence of cave paintings it is clear that the dog was the first
domesticated animal. Basic requirements of food and clothing led
to the domestication of cattle and sheep, and the need for a beast
of burden, to that of oxen. It seems likely that the horse was the
last main animal to be adapted for man's use, and was only utilised
because of its value in warfare. Herding of cattle, pasturing and
the possession of flocks of sheep were well established by the time
of the Celtic invasions. The cattle herds had already produced
the earliest tracks along the upper slopes of the hills. Fishing was
widespread. Hollowed-out logs soon gave way to the curach, which
was a light inshore boat, and the coracle, which was a smaller
version suitable for rivers.

The second factor in this agricultural revolution was the creation
of a pattern of settled cultivation. As far as is known, it was in
the river valleys of the Middle East, favoured by river flood and
ripening sun, that settled agriculture was first established, and its
introduction to this country by the Beaker Folk would not, therefore,

seem unlikely. The need to stabilise the food supply in case of famine, the need to store food because of seasonal variations, and the rising population of herdsmen on the fixed and limited areas of cultivation led to the need to rely more on produced crops than on the random benefits of nature. In a very primitive way, agricultural technology was born in this revolution. Because of the lack of technical skill, only light soils could be used and thus cultivation was confined to the slopes of the hills. A simple one-field system of continuous cropping was used, but it was quickly realised that this could be improved upon by the alternation of two fields. The Celts definitely adopted the two-field system after 500 B.C. Hillside cultivation was subject to erosion and this was particularly so because the ploughing was done in strips along the sides of the hills. It became necessary to create terraces known as lynchets, of which an example may be seen today at Torwoodlee near Galashiels. The earliest form of plough was an antler or a simple hand-plough, later modified to be used by the foot. This primitive plough, called the caschrom, was still in use in eighteenth-century Scotland. By the time of the Celts, a foot-plough with a beam and coulter pulled by two oxen had been developed, still only suitable, however, for light soils.

Simultaneously with the agricultural revolution, there was economic development in other fields. The plough for agriculture and the boat for fishing were among the earliest technical innovations, and throughout much of the period covered by this book we shall be concerned with their steady improvement. Other implements were in use by the Beaker Folk during the Bronze Age. Flint axes and arrows, bronze sickles, and handmills for grinding corn were in existence. Moreover, man had already begun to produce for his comfort as well as for his necessity. Primitive weaving and ornaments of bronze and jade are evidence of this trend. By Celtic times, one of the most important of all industries, building, was creating a variety of domestic, military and religious constructions, many of which remain to this day. Industry, in the sense of mechanical production, was created soon after agriculture.

Even more surprising is the early existence of trade. When the enormous distances covered by migrating tribes are considered, it is obvious that the barriers to trade were not insuperable. The earliest trade was barter trade. This occurs when a sophisticated society meets a primitive one and is not confined solely to those early years. Slave traders in the seventeenth century obtained slaves in return for rum and beads. The acquisition of land in return for rifles was not uncommon in nineteenth-century imperial expansion. Barter trade is also caused by the absence of a numeraire or commodity in terms of which others can be valued for the purposes of trade. Such barter trade has been made familiar to many by the painting of Phoenicians exchanging pottery and Tyrian purple cloth for skins and huntings dogs, but such terms of pure barter are not likely to endure long. What economists call a double coincidence of wants is not readily available or even practicable. Numeraires are very soon created. Such commodities as shells, cattle or even wives, have served the purpose of a medium of exchange. It is only a short stage to the creation of money when a particular numeraire acquires fixed values and general acceptability. The evidence of coin distribution suggests that our earliest trade, which seems to have been with the Mediterranean region, was conducted both by barter and medium of exchange methods. Celtic trade was well organised, with a proper coinage.

THE ECONOMY BEFORE THE ROMAN CONQUEST

In the 500 years before the Roman Conquest of England, the island was occupied by the Celts and divided into a series of tribal areas. It is useful to consider England at this time as in many ways resembling a country before colonial occupation in the nineteenth century, and the Roman Conquest as the annexation of that country by a colonial power. Such a pattern is reflected in the economic changes of the two periods. Although the Celtic period may seem remote, the shallow impact of much that occurred in Roman times, meant that many Celtic practices survived to intermingle and coexist with the later Saxon innovations. Celtic agricultural systems, and methods of landholding survived in the upland region during the eighteenth century. Moreover, although very early in time, the Celtic economy cannot be regarded as primitive. It built on the existing foundations, so that barter had been largely replaced by a money economy, the self-sufficiency of local economic units had started to crack, and the rudiments of urban settlement and foreign trade had been established. The Celts were a race as well as a group of tribes and economic evidence shows that they were by no means parochial. Blue stones used at Stonehenge in Wiltshire came from Wales and the tin of Cornwall was exported from the Isle of Wight and even possibly from the Isle of Thanet.

Knowledge of Celtic economic conditions can be gathered from two main sources. The first and most important is archaeology with its associated arts of aerial photography and numismatism, but Classical writers provide considerable evidence about the structure of Celtic society. Pliny, Diodorus Siculus, Strabo, Ptolemy and Caesar—all discuss the Celt in England or France. Celtic society was tribal and warlike and the use of iron as the principal mineral invites a comparison with the Hittites of Asia Minor. Much iron manufacture was dedicated to the needs of war with the production of short swords, oval shields and the famous scythe-wheeled chariots, but there is evidence of its use for other purposes. An iron anchor and cable chain have been found near the Dorset coast.

The Celts occupied in the main the upland areas of the east and south or clustered in regions well defended by marsh and sea. They took over and developed the hill agriculture of the Beaker Folk. Agricultural limitations, particularly that of the plough, combined with the limited rise of the population in the face of great natural obstacles to prevent a shift to the valleys. The hazards of tribal warfare naturally made hills, with their possibilities for defence, the favourite sites for settlement. Stockaded villages with log cabins arose within massive earthworks, out of all proportion to the suggested population of the time. Caesar's account of the Veneti, a Celtic tribe in Gaul, showed that warlike considerations influenced their activity on the sea as well as the land. The Celts developed ships with sails and the connections across the Channel were the basis of developing trade as well as the cause of Caesar's invasions. Links with the Belgae and the Veneti of northern Gaul were particularly strong. The English Celts were clearly the most advanced group of their race, and the Celtic religion of the Druids had its centre in England, although it was widespread in Brittany and northern France.

Celtic agriculture was almost entirely subsistence agriculture, producing for the needs of the local community. Pastoral farming was widespread, particularly cattle rearing. There is considerable evidence of this in the form of dewponds and tracks for the movement of cattle, and some evidence from their export. England's earliest roads, known as the greenways, developed in this period, and although settlement and the importance of Stonehenge to Celtic religion should not be underestimated as reasons for their growth, the economic needs of cattle-drovers are of key importance. The three most important of these routes were the Harrow Way from Dover to Cornwall along the crest of the Downs, the Ridge Way and Icknield Way from the Wiltshire Downs across Berkshire and the Chilterns to Norfolk, and the Fosse Way from the Dorset Downs across the Cotswolds and eventually to the Lincolnshire Wolds and the Humber. Smaller roads sometimes called salt, tin or rush ways led off these main tracks.

By far the most important development in Celtic agriculture was the creation of a pattern of two-field farming. Since the early ploughs only had a coulter and no ploughshare, the farmer was forced to plough north–south and then west–east, and this tended to produce fairly small and roughly square fields. The simplest two-field system was merely to cultivate the two fields alternately leaving one fallow for a year, growing wheat or rye in one and barley in the other. The system adopted was, however, a little more complex than this. Although it was considered once to be solely Celtic, the existence of what is known as the infield-outfield system was widespread at the foot of the Alps and is found in upland, poor-soiled, exposed regions. The danger of associating the system solely with the Celts is an important reminder that economic organisation is not always directly related to the racial or political composition of a region. This is a point to bear in mind later when considering the more famous three-field system.

The infield-outfield system has a long history. It prevailed in the west and north of England throughout much of the Middle Ages and as late as the thirteenth century was found in the Midlands. An extreme case is its survival on a Norfolk farm as late as 1612. It was characterised by an infield, which was manured as frequently as possible and consisted of a number of irregular patches sown with wheat, oats, barley and bere (a coarse barley). There was no fallow and no rotation, and it was, therefore, an example of intensive low-yield cultivation. Accompanying this was a larger field or outfield which was only ploughed in part and otherwise used for grazing. This system clearly produced a very low yield and was suitable for thinly populated regions, where the extensive cultivation of the outer field was not supplanted by population pressure. Sometimes referred to as the run-rig system, this method of farming tended to keep the size of fields small averaging a half to one and a half acres. This smallness was intensified by the system of land tenure whereby the holdings were divided among the male survivors on the death of the owner. This practice was known as gavelkind and was a frequent method of land tenure in Scotland and Wales. Remarkably, it was also normal practice in Kent as late as the fifteenth century.

Just as aerial photography has provided much evidence for the lynchets and field pattern of Celtic times, archaeology has constantly increased our knowledge of other Celtic occupations. Subsistence farming was accompanied by the production of consumer goods. The Celts wore heavy cloth garments and sandals. The men wore trousers laced with leather thongs and a loose shirt. Armour was worn in battle, particularly helmets and breastplates. All these items were produced in the village by weavers and blacksmiths, and were by no means primitive. The use of dyestuffs for the cloth and embossing for the armour were commonplace. Even more luxurious items, such as bronze mirrors and jade and jet bracelets and necklaces from the Whitby region, have been found. Pottery was the chief manufacture of the Celts, made by hand without the wheel. Three main types of pottery are recognisable. Halstatt pottery is fairly rough and heavy. The earliest English pottery was discovered at Castle Hill, Scarborough, and is of this variety. The La Tène type characterised by intricate patterns of concentric lines is found in east Yorkshire and the Midlands. Aylesford ware and bead-rim pottery of a more refined kind is found in south-eastern England. Mining represented another important Celtic activity. Flint mines and works were extensively used, as the sites at Cissbury in Sussex and Grimes Graves in East Anglia show. Tin was mined in Cornwall and South Wales and is mentioned by Pytheas in 325 B.C. Iron was mined in the Weald and the Forest of Dean and lead in the Mendips. Gold and silver were mined in South Wales and the Mendips respectively and these metals were a further reason for Roman interest in the Celts.

The most impressive evidence of Celtic ability to conduct large-scale economic enterprises are the remains of the building activity of the period. Celtic buildings may be divided into three groups. The nature of domestic architecture can only be surmised from the foundations, but the existence of sizeable halls in many villages is certain. Because of the needs of warfare, villages of wood were easily sacrificed and the inhabitants retired to the hill fortresses. These remarkable interlocking earthworks mark the achievement of Celtic military architects and the labour of many hundreds for considerable periods of time. They represent, in the same way as the castles of Edward I at a later date, the development of sizeable economic resources. The fortresses proved capable of resisting Romans and Saxons and, together with cross-country walls of earth such as the Wansdyke and the Fossedyke, were barriers to invaders and protectors of settlement and trade. Among the most important of these fortresses to have survived are Cadbury (Somerset), Maiden (Dorset), Silbury (Wiltshire), and St Catherine's Hill (Hampshire).

The third group of buildings are the relics of pre-Christian religions. It is dangerous to assume that all the remains are connected with the Druids. We have little evidence of the earlier cults, which would most likely have followed the pattern of worshipping the forces of nature, common in agricultural communities. Although we have some account of the Druids from the hostile reports of Caesar, their tradition was oral and when they were exterminated in 61 their beliefs perished with them. The stone and earth edifices that remain over a wide area of western Europe might be more loosely classified as religious survivals of the worship of many different gods, to which legends, ruins and inscriptions of later times bear witness. What is clear is that either common architectural concepts or limitations of engineering skills led to great uniformity. Remains in Scotland, southern England, Brittany and the Île de France are very similar. Tombs take the form of long or round barrows of earth. There are small groups of stones, either a single upright or menhir, or a large slab of rock raised on two others called a dolmen. The most famous of these is Kit's Coty House, near Maidstone in Kent. Finally, there are arrangements of stones in circles or cromlechs and great lines or alignments. Although Stonehenge is the most famous of these stone circles, those at Avebury (Wiltshire), Bryn Mawr (Cumberland) and on the north-east coast of Scotland are larger. It is assumed that an elaborate system of rollers and earthworks was used to construct these buildings and that the materials were transported on river rafts. However they were constructed, they remain an important indication of Celtic engineering skill and evidence that even a simple rural economy had the means to promote sizeable undertakings.

The amount of Celtic agricultural and simple manufacturing activity combined with their European connections to provide a basis for the development of trade. England was, until the late fourteenth century, a primary producer. Her exports were either the marketable surplus or by-products of agriculture or the mineral resources of the country. Thus, although Celtic pottery and jewellery were exported, pottery and jewellery of finer types were imported, and European influence on design was considerable. The main exports were cattle, hides, hunting dogs, a little wheat and a few slaves, together with the products of tin, lead, iron, gold and silver mines. In return England received luxury items of amber and brass, finer cloths and the precious commodity of salt. It has been suggested that one reason why the Romans waited so long to embark on the final conquest of the island was that the receipts from customs duties on English exports were a considerable source of revenue to the Roman government of Gaul. To facilitate this trade, a flourishing coinage developed and minting was added to the list of manufactures. The earliest Celtic coins are known as Bellovaci coins and were in use from about 80 B.C. They were named after a chief of the Gauls who fled from Caesar in 57 B.C. English coins discovered so far are all located east of a line from Weymouth to the Yorkshire Wolds. There were small silver coins and later larger gold ones modelled on Roman and even Greek examples. The most detailed series of coins surviving come from the Catuvelauni tribe of Hertfordshire, and reflect the economic importance of St Albans and London.

Although there were no organisations which could technically be called towns in Celtic England, some of the villages had acquired the economic functions of being collecting places for trade and centres of population. This was true particularly of the tribal capitals, and it is significant that the Romans later recognised the site of fourteen large Celtic villages as being geographically and economically suitable for development into towns. This was partly done to placate the local population, but in such cases as Colchester and London it was a recognition of sizeable communities of some standing. The traditional claim for the foundation of London by a chief called Lud in 60 B.C. may contain a measure of truth. Tacitus later pointed out that, although the Romans had not given the city a high status, and it had suffered sack at the hands of Boadicea, it was "very celebrated for the number of its merchants and the abundance of its resources."

By the time that the Romans had decided to conquer England, the Celts had developed some measure of economic organisation. Subsistence agriculture was adequately, if crudely, organised. Simple manufactures of cloth, pottery, iron goods, jewellery and coins were established. Trade with Gaul and further afield was evidence of a small economic surplus and the imports added to the native means of embellishing the rude simplicity of tribal life among the richer Celts. Tracks linked together scattered villages and some larger concentrations of population. Simple engineers and slave labour had raised great fortifications and religious centres to serve as evidence for a building industry. The Roman impact was to be impressive but it could not eradicate many of the features of economic activity which the Celts had developed under the intense pressure of an environment which they had few means of resisting. Thus, such features as their infield-outfield system, their tracks and their attention to the island's mineral resources were to be at the basis of subsequent activity. In the same way as that of other colonial powers, Roman influence was in many respects to be superficial, the product of exploitation and occupation rather than of development and a consideration of the needs of the country.

CHAPTER 2

THE ENGLISH COLONIAL ECONOMY OF THE
ROMAN PERIOD

THE NATURE OF THE ROMAN IMPACT UPON THE ECONOMY

From Caesar's second invasion in 54 B.C. to the full-scale Roman
conquest of A.D. 43, Roman influence was slowly spreading in the
country. By 80 the conquest was complete and for two hundred
years Britannia was a peaceful Roman province. It was the last
major Roman province to be conquered, and it was one of the
first where Roman authority was challenged. From about 280, the
Romans succeeded for a hundred years in resisting invasion from
Scotland and across the North Sea and putting down numerous
internal rebellions. However, by 410 the legions had been withdrawn
and within about ten years England was the first major Roman
province to be abandoned.

Although it is dangerous to generalise in view of the small
amount of evidence for a 400-year occupation, it seems highly
probable that the Roman impact was not as great as used to be
thought in the last century. Only in the lowland zone was it other
than a military occupation. There was no large-scale immigration
because the climate did not favour the social and cultural traditions of the Romans. Although half a million Romano-Celts
existed, the rural Celts remained largely uninfluenced. City life
affected only a minority of the population. Only one *municipium*
(St Albans) was created in England, and Lipson has described
the towns as "the exotic product of an unstable civilisation." Some
historians, notably Seebohm, tried to argue that the impact of the
Roman Conquest was in many ways permanent. They pointed to the
future use of Roman urban sites and the influence of Roman roads.
But both the urban sites and roads were Celtic rather than Roman
in origin. Seebohm was particularly anxious to argue that Roman
agricultural methods replaced the existing Celtic system and were
the direct antecedents of the medieval manor. In this case it is
likely that Seebohm confused similarities imposed by economic
conditions with deliberate imitations or continuous development.
It will later be shown that any attempt to argue that the medieval
field system derived from the Romans rather than from the Celts

16

underestimates not only the Celts but also the impact of the subsequent Saxon invaders. It seems more likely that "being on the outer fringe of the Empire, and so near the still active forces of kindred barbarism, it is doubtful whether the English province was ever quite so efficiently and thoroughly Romanised as Gaul, for instance, or Spain."

This is not, however, to argue that the Roman period was without importance. On the contrary, it produced many changes in the economy of the country and marked a further stage in the exploitation of our resources. The Roman example set some sort of precedent and paved the way for the full introduction of Christianity by the Roman Church, whose earliest bishops adopted the sites of Roman cities as their sees. By the time England was conquered by the Romans, the Roman Empire was a vast military power controlling much of the known world. It was far from its simple agricultural origins, being by the first century A.D. a power concerned with the exaction of tribute, the running of state mines and the development of industry. Britannia thus immediately came to share in both the benefits and burdens of the fully developed imperial system. This conferred immense advantages. Linked together by the system of Roman roads created like Hitler's autobahns for military purposes, protected by an army of 300,000, free from internal tariffs, ruled by a vast imperial civil service and subject, by 211, to a common citizenship, the 80 million inhabitants of the Roman Empire lived peacefully and prosperously. A common language, currency and weights and measures, together with one rule of law and a code of commercial practice, facilitated economic growth.

Inherited from the Greeks was the Roman concept of civilisation being, in essence, urban. Roman cities could be merely vast grim barrack towns, but many were either thriving industrial centres such as Antioch, Damascus, Trèves and Lyons, or cultural centres such as Athens, Rome, Nîmes and Bath. The Romans lavished, perhaps too much, wealth on their cities and not enough on the countryside, but also there was a considerable measure of sophistication. Land was either *ager publicus*, owned by the state, or *latifundiae*, which were the large private estates where the *villae* were found. There were few *massa* or smallholdings. Agriculture was neglected. Absentee landlords, and the decline of the free workers into serfs introduced an atmosphere of cruelty and suppression. Crowded increasingly into towns and demanding to be fed, the population was subjected to famines. These alternated with the lavish free gifts of aspiring politicians to create an atmosphere of unrest. Poor food supply and slum conditions precipitated plagues.

It was ironic that the Romans who created the virtues of military honour, public service, civic dignity and respect for the law which lay at the very basis of much European development should have allowed them to decline. The simple pastoral society of Virgil's *Georgics* was to be the subject of Petronius' bitter description of a dying power. The collapse of Rome, which exercised the powers of Gibbon to account for it in terms of political collapse, was partially economic because the decline of agriculture was accompanied by the rise of a wasteful urban population reluctant to work or enterprise. It is true the imperial system collapsed. Inadequate emperors, sated with being worshipped as gods, followed one another in rapid succession. The Praetorian Guard of 9,000 men in Rome sometimes decided the succession. The army threw up rival emperors. Britannia with a garrison of 40,000 produced several, including the famous Constantine. It is also true that brutality and bestiality destroyed the Roman character. The obscene horrors of the games continued until 401, but by then their ritual murders and the slaughter of thousands of Christians had made their mark. Conspicuous consumption debauched the rulers. Profligacy and perversion were widely practised and the taint of Eastern cults made rancid the ideals of the empire. Vulgar ostentation, cheap triumph and crude imitation weakened the intellectual grasp of the nation of Cicero and Horace. Innovation was spurned. Such innovations as the steam engine of Hiero went unnoticed. No attempt to meet with the advanced civilisation of China was made. The power of the demagogue over the brutal urban mobs and the sway of the landlord over a degraded rural population of slaves left the empire without the means to recover itself.

Upon this shattered and demoralised empire there burst from 280 onwards a series of barbarian invasions. Britannia, menaced by the Picts and Scots and the Saxons, was typical of many provinces. Spasmodic attempts were made to recover the empire's lost prestige. Constantine cut the empire's losses by dividing it in two in 323, but still the barbarians came. Then the Romans invited the invaders to join with them and, having thus admitted the enemy within the walls, were subjected to 200 years of warfare across the breadth of Europe. Atrophied provinces sheltered for too long were unable to resist, and only in places such as England, where Roman power had been less pervasive, was resistance possible.

Britannia gained, at least temporarily, many benefits from Roman occupation, but these have to be set against the crushing burden of maintaining 40,000 troops, the heavy tribute, the exploitation of her mineral resources by forced labour, and the general effect of being involved in the period of imperial decline. The influences of the *villae* and the towns have been over-emphasised. At most there were 500 of the first and 60 of the second and they could not have exercised the influence some have attributed to them. Britannia was a frontier province. After a savage conquest, she was militarily occupied but never made really militarily secure, in spite of walls, roads and sea defences. Although the conquest ended tribal warfare and human sacrifice, the Romans practised infanticide until converted to Christianity and there is little evidence of any rapid rise in population which would suggest an expanding economy. Collingwood estimated the total population of the colony at a million, of whom half were Romano-Celts. This would appear to be rather high, for the evidence of tombstones suggests that it was mainly military veterans retired on the *ager publicus* who married and they would not tend to produce large families.

Roman influence was never as deep in England as it was elsewhere in Europe. Celtic institutions survived, modified but intact, and, after the Roman departure, met and mingled with the Saxons. The changes made in the economy were not long-lasting, and in many cases were detrimental to the country. Speaking of Roman London, J. A. Williamson said: "Merchants, slave dealers, financiers, land agents, economic adventurers of all sorts and races flooded in. London . . . sprouted as a mushroom city like Kimberley . . . in the nineteenth century." This description accurately conveys the situation in Roman Britain as far as the economic realities were concerned.

AGRICULTURE IN THE ROMAN PERIOD

In his agricultural poems, the *Georgics*, Virgil referred to Roman knowledge of drainage methods, and the first important consequence of the Roman occupation was the extension of the cultivable area. The Romans were concerned chiefly with the better exploitation of hill-based agriculture, but there is some evidence of a valley-wards shift made possible by the use of larger ploughs and drainage methods. Villas were more often found in the valleys as the Romans sought south-facing sheltered aspects for their country mansions. The most important extension of the cultivable area occurred in Cambridgeshire, where Car Dyke marked the beginning of the lengthy draining of the fens, and between Appledore, Romney and Hythe in Kent. There the Romans built the Dymchurch and Rhee Walls with sluices and a series of canals leading to them and began the task of draining Romney Marsh.

The Roman occupation led to increased pressure on agricultural resources. The influx of immigrants and others not concerned with agricultural production had to be catered for. The military establishment was large. Gradually the increasing number of towns became a fresh source of demand. Finally Rome demanded a tribute (*annona*) which had to be paid in corn. The export of corn particularly to the Rhineland was the key to Roman agricultural development. One writer (Zozimus) said 800 ships were involved in the corn trade. Besides cattle and sheep, pigs and geese were reared and three different breeds of hunting dog were known. Richborough in Kent became the centre for oysters, so famous that an English claimant for the imperial purple was called "that Richborough thief" at the end of the fourth century. Juvenal mentions British oysters. Besides developing existing commodities, the Romans increased the variety of British agricultural products. Probus gave permission for the commencement of viticulture in England. Pheasants and rabbits were introduced and also a number of fruits such as apples, pears and cherries.

In order to raise the production of wheat, the Romans temporarily modified the existing Celtic field system in three important ways. They introduced a new plough. They fostered the limited adoption of a three-field instead of a two-field system, and they encouraged the development of large estates (*latifundiae*), many of which were centred on a villa or great house. Those who claim that Roman influence on economic development was decisive argue that all three were permanent changes for the better, but a close examination suggests that, although Roman agricultural methods in England were normal in quality, they were defective in quantity. The Roman writer Pliny referred to the use of a heavier plough in Rhaetia (Switzerland). This was pulled by four or six oxen and was introduced into England along with the smaller plough or *aratrum*. The impact of the larger plough (*caruca*) was considerable because it changed the shape of the fields. Cross-ploughing was no longer necessary and the long furrow was made possible. The length of the furrow was about 220 yards and was the amount a team could work in one pull without pause. The width of the furrow was 22 yards and this produced the characteristic rolling nature of upfold and downfold, so very different from modern narrow furrows. Ploughing was done in units of an acre which seems to have been the amount of work that could be done in a day, because in the German region an acre was called a *morgen* or *tagewerk*. Thus, the fields became rectangles of at least an acre in extent rather than small Celtic squares. It is important to remember that no such plough has been discovered in England and that fields of a Celtic pattern survived over a wide area.

The adoption of a three-field rather than a two-field method of cultivation was claimed by Seebohm to be exclusively Roman because it was more sophisticated than either the existing two-field pattern or the method of common cultivation used by the Saxons. This rash assumption was based on the use of three fields in Italy, but it ignored the fact that hillside cultivators could not easily adopt it and the size of holdings would also have had to be considerably enlarged. In many ways the idea of using three fields and thus leaving only a third instead of a half of the land fallow logically developed from the use of the existing two fields. It did not require the particular genius of any nation but only the pressure on resources to stimulate the change. If it occurred, this change would have been largely confined to the large prosperous estates and, as they were among the first to suffer from pillage and defection, it is likely that the use of three fields would have been short-lived.

The *latifundiae* or large estates on which were situated the five hundred known English villas were largely concentrated in north-west Kent, west Sussex, Hampshire, and the Cotswolds. Collingwood regarded them as the key to the spread of Roman influence and if their example had been imitated their importance would have been immense. It seems more likely, however, that the villas were isolated examples of progressive holdings and that they degenerated into estates to be exploited by their owners. The villa was surrounded by an inner demesne cultivated by slave labour and an outer region worked by *coloni* or free cultivators. The villa was often an industrial unit with winepresses, cornmills and the means of manufacturing and dyeing cloth. Gradually the *coloni* ceased to be freemen, as they lost the right to divide or transfer their holdings, which became fixed at an area of roughly 30 acres called a virgate. It was this which possibly led Seebohm and others to imagine that the villa and the manor were directly connected, but it is clear that the villa was not conceived as a self-sufficient unit, dependent on the lord and subordinate to him. It lacked, therefore, the key characteristic of the manor, and was clearly a Roman institution which perished with the Romans.

The supplying of the villas with produce, luxury items and workers meant that they were of great importance in their own regions. They were large courtyarded houses with half-stone walls and timber uppers and roofs, and the number of rooms might vary from nine to fifty depending on the number of other buildings attached to the main house. The villas were remarkable for two things. Firstly, they revealed the highly skilled and luxurious nature of trade in their more exotic consumer requirements. Tessellated pavements, statues, fountains, sundials and pottery provided an embryo anticipation of that great host of auxiliary crafts that later went to support the medieval building industry. Secondly, the villas revealed the technological skill of the Romans. Piped water supply for baths and a central heating system (hypocaust) were luxuries which the rich were not to know again until the late nineteenth century.

INDUSTRY AND THE EXPLOITATION OF MINERALS

Mention of cloth making at some of the villas draws attention to the existence under the Romans of industries similar to those that had existed under the Celts. English cloth was well known in the Roman Empire. Periegetes, a geographer, made reference to its fine texture, and the market price of English cloth was mentioned in Diocletian's edict of prices. One historian, Haverfield, suggested that the town of Winchester was the centre of an imperial manufactory providing cloth for the emperor, but the more normal cloth works seem to have been in the villas. Traces of dye works have been found for instance at Silchester, Chedworth and Darenth. Lipson has claimed that there is evidence of fulling (a process whereby cloth is beaten in water to remove impurities and given a smoother finish) in Kent, Surrey and Gloucestershire.

Besides cloth making, pottery manufacture remained the other main industry. Celtic pottery was quickly swamped by exports and the home pottery industry contented itself with imitating continental styles, particularly Samian ware. Only towards the end of the period was there any revival of Celtic influence, as evidenced in pottery found in the New Forest and East Anglia. These regions together with the Thames Valley were the important manufacturing areas, the main centre perhaps being Caistor in Norfolk, where sizeable kilns and a large number of wharves provided for an export trade. It has been suggested that the introduction of the potter's wheel implied a measure of mass production and that this may well account for the decline in quality. England continued to produce iron goods, particularly in the London region, bronzework in the Severn Valley and pewterware (an alloy of tin and lead), after its production had declined in Gaul.

To the Romans, the exploitation of the mineral resources of the province was more important than the development of manufactures. All mines belonged to the state and were under the direction of the procurator or military ruler of the district in which they were found. Labour was provided by slaves, prisoners, forced labour and *laeti* (imported indentured workers). It had been the lure of precious metals that had helped to arouse Caesar's interest, and the Romans were responsible for intensively mining silver and gold. Gold was found in Wales, particularly at Dolaucothy in Carmarthenshire, and silver was mined in the Mendips. Sufficient silver was left for a small industry to survive until Tudor times, but the gold was exhausted. It has been suggested that the massive export of precious metals caused a shortage of coins and that this was one of the reasons why the Iceni were unable to meet interest on loans taken from moneylenders and were forced into rebellion under Boadicea.

Other metals were also mined. At first tin-mining declined in competition with the larger resources of Spain but by about 250 it had revived and both Exeter and Topsham show evidence of their use as Roman ports. Lead mines were particularly abundant in Derbyshire, Flintshire, the Mendips and Shropshire around Wroxeter where the Romans initiated development. Copper was mined in Shropshire and Angelsea and coal in Tyneside and Cumberland. Collingwood went so far as to suggest that "most modern seams" were used by the Romans but this is clearly an exaggeration. Iron was produced in the Forest of Dean, Warwickshire and the Weald of Kent and Sussex. The existence of the famous *pharos* or lighthouse at Dover (Dubris) and the great port of Pevensey (Anderida) suggest that there was a considerable export trade from this area. Tacitus was not mistaken when he referred to the minerals of England as the "profits of victory."

THE ESTABLISHMENT OF URBAN COMMUNITIES

Towns arose in the first place because they were provided with geographical advantages which made them nodal points for transport and focal points for trade and industry. Some of the Celtic villages where the tribal chiefs resided were towns in this sense although they possessed no distinctive form of organisation. No less than fourteen of these tribal capitals later became Roman towns in the process of pacification. Noviomagus, capital of the Regni of Sussex, became Chichester, Camulodunum, capital of the Trinobantes of Essex, became Colchester, and Verulamium, capital of the Catuvelauni of the Thames Valley, became St Albans. The first attempt of the Romans to create towns received a severe blow in Boadicea's revolt (A.D. 61) when London, Colchester and St Albans were destroyed. Roman towns were built as defensive posts, trading places and cultural centres, and they served to introduce the Celt to Roman life. To the Romans the city was the true centre of civilisation and it was the deliberate policy of

B

Agricola to introduce the Celt to civic life and induce them to support the régime. His policy of introducing Latin, encouraging the wearing of the toga, and building temples, baths and amphitheatres was designed to this end. The similarity of this to Western colonial methods might well have called forth today the remark made by Tacitus concerning the then policy in Britannia: "this among an ignorant people was called civilisation, while it was really an element of slavery."

Collingwood stressed that the villa was more important than the town as an agent of Roman civilisation, and it is easy to forget the smallness of these first towns. Altogether there were sixty Roman towns. One, St Albans, was a *municipium*; four, York (Eboracum), Gloucester (Glevum), Lincoln (Lindum) and Colchester, were *colonia* or places where veterans were settled, and the rest were *vici* or ordinary towns. In *colonia* the two town magistrates were elected, but in the *vici* they were appointed. None of the towns was particularly large. London covered 330 acres, St Albans 200 acres and Silchester 100 acres. The average population was 2,000 and only one Roman settlement approached our modern concept of a town. This was London with a population of 15,000. Our knowledge of Roman towns is extensive because in many cases settlement moved away to a nearby site, enabling excavations to be made. Perhaps the most important were those at Wroxeter (Uriconium) in 1912 and St Albans in 1930. Other Roman sites, such as Silchester, are also well preserved.

Although it is true that the Roman towns were found largely in the south, it would not be accurate to describe the occupation of the north as solely military. The three legions in England (there were four until one was exterminated in 117) were stationed at York (Ninth), Chester (Twentieth) and Caerleon-on-Usk (Second) and these three towns were important administrative and trading centres. Carlisle (Luguvallium), Corbridge (Corstopium), and Catterick (Caractonium) all had a sizeable civilian settlement. In the south, the places of entertainment and relaxation were naturally situated for the benefit of jaded Roman officials. Bath (Aquae Sulis), Buxton (Aquae) and Silchester (Calleva Atrebatum) were the most important. Round the coast were a chain of important ports such as Caistor (Venta Icenorum), Reculver (Regulbium), London, Richborough (Rutupiae), Dover, Lymne (Portus Lemmane), Pevensey, Portsmouth (Portus Magnus) and Southampton (Clausentum). Inland there were fewer towns although Winchester (Venta Belgarum), Cirencester and Old Sarum (Sorbiodunum) were important.

It is useful to realise that the period during which these towns flourished was shorter than that of the occupation. Thus, by 275 the walls of St Albans were in ruins. In 360 London was sacked so savagely by the northern Celts that, when its walls were rebuilt, it was renamed Augusta. The towns were not liked because they were the centres of Roman administration, symbols of the occupation and were bound to draw heavily on the limited resources of the surrounding countryside. By the time of the Saxon invasions, nearly all the town sites were deserted because the Celts did not keep them up when the Romans left. Although future towns were built on Roman sites, there was no attempt to copy the previous street plan and often the site chosen suggests not a conscious reoccupation but the influence of geographical factors which militated in favour of a town being built.

Clearly Roman towns were the focal points of economic development and, as new sources of demand, stimulated the economy. Through them filtered new ideas of which the most important was Christianity. This was established in Chichester, Canterbury, London and St Albans by 200 and was obviously brought into the country by poor converts. For the duration of the Roman occupation, the towns were set standards in organisation and convenience which were not to be seen again until the later part of the nineteenth century. Although it is true that continuous occupation of town sites was unlikely, the influence of Roman towns on urban development was perhaps greater than Lipson with his comment about "exotic" products would have allowed. There was the simple matter of civic tradition dating back to Roman times. The earliest Saxon towns were Canterbury, Winchester, Colchester and London, all Roman sites, and the establishment of these towns contrasts with the state of affairs in the Saxon homeland where, as late as the 770s, without Roman precedent there were no proper towns. When the Roman Church came in 597, the new bishops chose old Roman sites for their sees at Canterbury, Rochester and London. Even in the Middle Ages, when model towns were planned by such kings as Edward I, it was on the famous Roman "grid-iron" pattern that they were constructed.

THE FINANCES AND MILITARY ORGANISATION OF THE COLONY

Roman occupation was for the benefit of the empire rather than the province. From the first the Romans were concerned with the most decisive power of a colonial ruler—the right to tax. Caesar had obtained a tribute and refusal to pay it had been a technical reason for the Roman invasion in 43. The Regni of Sussex and the Iceni of East Anglia were compelled to pay tribute and it was the demand of Decianus and Seneca to call in arrears of this tribute that led to Boadicea's revolt in 61. Tribute continued to be levied in the form of wheat exports and the removal of pearls, gold and silver. The shortage of money caused by tribute and taxation led to the indebtedness of many Celts and it is significant that when Carausius raised the first major revolt against the Romans in 286 he abolished these taxes.

Britannia was ruled by a legate and a financial procurator who was directly responsible to the emperor. The Roman coinage replaced the Celtic one, although rival emperors and other rebels minted their own. By 290 the main mints were at London, Colchester and Wroxeter. The main taxes fell into five groups. There was a land tax from which it is claimed the carucage or medieval land tax was derived. There were levies in kind. There were occasional poll taxes. Slaves were subjected to special duties, and there were customs duties at the ports. Typical of the impact of the Roman tax system was the method adopted for the upkeep of the famous roads. Imperial roads, over which the postal service and diplomatic couriers started by Augustus travelled, were paid for out of the military budget. Lesser roads were looked after by a special official appointed by the *vicus* and were maintained either by a voluntary contribution or actual work on the road. It has been suggested that this was the origin of the *trimoda necessitas* of Saxon times, which was a set of obligations laid on all freemen, including the maintenance of roads, and the use of the Latin phrase suggests some connection.

Military occupation was the keynote of the whole province, and not merely the barren and largely deserted north, for in the south were the *colonia* of the veterans and from the south flowed supplies for the mighty military establishment. A large part of Britannia was a region which may be compared with the North-West Frontier Province of India between 1897 and 1947. The region was in reality the pivot round which the safety and prosperity of the rest of the country revolved. Large numbers were involved in the clerical and commissariat activities attendant on the army. Sizeable groups of *laeti* or foreign tribes, even possibly the earliest Saxons, swelled the population as did also the retired military settlers in the *colonia*. A considerable part of the production of goods and taxes went to support the army and, in a situation of scarcity, deprived the colony of further advantage. The army itself created demands for the building and engineering industries which made them among the most important of Roman activities. In many ways, the Roman army of occupation and the German army of the 1930s bear comparison, for they both had a privileged position and took a dispro-

portionate share of the national income, while at the same time
they stimulated economic activity.

Although the Roman army is justly famous and was the world's
first fully professional, regularly paid and pensionable army, information about its way of life rather than its campaigns is limited.
The main authorities are Marcellinus and Vegetius. There were
four main types of troops. There were legions of infantry, cohorts
of auxiliaries (those from Britannia serving on the Rhine and the
Danube), *turmae* and *alae* of cavalry, and an artillery of catapults
and *ballistas*. All these troops had to be supplied with equipment.
The leather industry was stimulated, since tents as well as clothes
and harness were made of the material. Corbridge in Northumberland was a flourishing centre of forges for the legions' weapons.
The legionary's diet was frugal—bread, soup and vegetables were
required—and granaries were established at Corbridge and Housteads for the needs of Hadrian's Wall. The main drink was a
mixture of vinegar and water. Hospitals were maintained at Housteads and Fendoch.

Supplying the needs of 40,000 troops was a key part of the everyday economy of Roman Britain. The long-term impact of this
occupation is to be found in three main types of construction:
forts, walls and roads. Northern England was held by a series of
rectangular fortresses, similar in pattern to a town, of which the
main ones were Chester, Caerleon-on-Usk, Manchester (Man-
cunium), York, Carlisle, Chesters (Cilurnum), Housteads (probably
Vercovicium) and Newstead (Trimontium). Besides these, there
were a hundred smaller forts in the province, and along the eastern
and southern coasts, as well as flanking the wall of Hadrian on
the shores of Cumberland and Northumberland, there were the sea
forts. On East Anglian coasts, there were Brancaster, Burgh and
Bradwell, and on the south coast, Reculver, Richborough, Dover,
Lympne, Pevensey and Porchester.

More famous than the forts are the walls. Built as legal boundaries and defensive networks, they stretched from Tyne to Solway
and Forth to Clyde. Hadrian's Wall was begun in 120 to 122 on
the site of a *vallum* possibly ordered by Trajan some years earlier.
This wall was restored in 211, 296 and 368 and abandoned by 400.
The Scottish wall lay on the line of forts started by Agricola. It
was first built by Lollius Urbicus in 143, restored by Antonius Pius
in 161 and abandoned by 197. Hadrian's Wall was 73 miles long
with seventeen forts, a mile-castle each mile and two turrets in
between each of these. It was on average 20 feet high and 10 feet
wide. Leonard Cottrell states that two million cubic yards of rock
and two million cubic yards of building stone were used in the

construction of this great work. The Romans also fortified their towns with walls, London having one with nine gates.

Neither fortresses nor walls were to have as much long-term economic significance as the network of 5,000 miles of Roman roads which were built partly on the routes of Celtic tracks and more often following the lines of military penetration. The roads were for imperial communications. Troops marching at four and a half miles an hour had to have a good surface to march on. Wagons and military equipment needed a broad road. The imperial post had to be swift. Although it is not true that the Roman roads were straight, because they avoided marshes and made for bridging points, nevertheless they tended to avoid centres of population and were to that extent less useful. However, they were focused on London, and became so much a part of the nation's transport system that, when trunk roads were classified in 1937, the framework used was still that of the Roman *viae publicae*.

Owing to imperial demands upon them the roads were built to a lavish standard. They were 16–24 feet wide and raised 6 feet above the existing countryside on an *agger* or embankment. The road was based on small squared stones sometimes set with mortar (*statumen*) on which was placed a ballast of small stones set with lime (*rudus*) capped with a covering of lime, chalk and broken tiles (*nucleus*). The surface was either of paving-stones or a mixture of gravel and lime. On these roads, Roman Britain saw a greater variety of transport than was to be seen again until the time of the Stuarts. Celtic chariots were famous and Cicero remarked "I hear that in Britain are most excellent chariots; bring me one for a pattern." The lightest was the single-horse *covinus*. More usual were the *cisium* or two-horse carriage and the *carpenta*, a heavy four-wheeled baggage cart drawn by oxen. To these the Romans added the light *currus* for races drawn by two horses, the more normal *carucca* and *pilentum*, usually for the nobility or women travellers, and the *plaustrum*, which was a heavy wagon.

The practice of giving names to Roman roads is of later inception, although it is convenient to use them. Perhaps the most famous was Watling Street from Dover through London to Wroxeter and thence to Chester. Ermine Street from London to Lincoln and Newcastle was the foundation for the Great North Road. Icknield Street stretched from the port of Caistor through Silchester to Dorchester. Cirencester was linked to Silchester by Akeman Street. The Fosse Way stretched from Exeter through High Cross to Lincoln and was linked to Doncaster by Ryknield Street. The great majority of the Roman roads lay to the south of the Fosse Way and there were only three major roads to the north of it stretching out towards Hadrian's Wall. Invaders found the roads as useful as the Romans themselves, and the Picts were able to advance on London in 368 down Ermine Street. Therefore, it seems unlikely that the Roman roads were completely neglected. A certain amount of decay was acceptable in view of the fall in the amount of traffic, but during Saxon times, the four roads where the royal "frith" or peace was held to protect travellers were Watling, Ermine and Icknield Streets, and the Fosse Way. This is at least one clear indication of the contribution made by the Roman occupation to the development of the economy.

THE COLLAPSE OF ROMAN INFLUENCE

Between 400 and 600, a complete change occurred in the distribution of the British population, and in the political organisation of the country. The hold of the Romans had been precarious and with the weakening of central authority the influence of the towns and villas contracted from the fourth century onwards. This process of decline was accelerated by military rebellions, starting with that of Carausius, who grasped the importance of a fleet, and was followed by several others. In the north, the Picts became increasingly bold and by 380 both walls were abandoned. Across the North Sea, encouraged by knowledge acquired through trading contacts and compulsory migrations, the German tribes began to find Britannia a profitable province to raid.

The Romans were not a maritime nation, although they had a Channel fleet which relied rather too much on galleys. From about 280 the coast of eastern and southern England was defended by a series of fortresses, paralleled by others in northern France. There has been considerable dispute about the origin of these forts. The normal explanation is that they were part of Diocletian's reforms and that the appointment of the Count of the Saxon Shore to oversee them marked a definite military reform. Others think they were started by Carausius to keep out the Romans and were later taken over by them. Naval defence by means of land fortresses was not a particularly wise move and, like another chain of fortresses erected by Henry VIII in the 1530s, proved to be of less value than expected. As they were built in isolated areas, their sea communications could be cut and the chain of command was weak. Such fortresses could be outflanked as the Romans themselves proved when Asclepiodotus defeated a rebel called Allectus in 296 by landing in a fog on the Hampshire coast. Nevertheless, it seems that some of these fortresses retained garrisons and both

Lympne and Pevensey put up considerable resistance to the German invaders.

As barbarian attacks on Rome increased, the attempt to keep England grew gradually weaker. The view that the province was suddenly deserted in 410 has now been abandoned. Each military rebellion had weakened the legions. Many were withdrawn in 410, but coins found at Richborough indicate later occupation and it has been suggested Roman troops were here as late as 428. Our evidence for events in this period is at its weakest. Continental writers caught glimpses of events here. Bede's famous history, based to some extent on the work of a Celtic monk, Gildas, is embroidered with legend. The *Anglo-Saxon Chronicle* begun in the late ninth century was chronologically inaccurate and set out to glorify Wessex at the expense of other kingdoms. Increasingly, historians have been forced to rely on the evidence of place names and burial sites. The investigation of the latter in 1938 showed a very different pattern of settlement from the one recorded in the written sources.

Two factors need to be stressed. Celtic civilisation was more resilient and better organised, and Roman penetration less thorough, than some have suggested. The likelihood of Roman survival is reduced by this, and also by the lengthy period of decay of at least 200 years. At its greatest extent, the colonial power had claimed the support of no more than an interested minority for their rule. Thus, the English conquest was not easy or comprehensive. Celtic ways influenced the invaders and it was Celtic rather than Roman agricultural methods, for example, that the Saxons adapted. Celtic resistance, based on the pre-Roman earthworks and forts, was strong. It took from 449 to 473 to subdue Kent. The penetration of Wessex was held up from 520 to 550 in the area of Salisbury Plain. The Celts were not finally beaten in Cornwall until 838. Intermarriage, rather than slavery, was the lot of the Celts and in some parts the Saxons formed a minority of the population. This period of settlement may be said to have been completed by 600 when there were about ten kingdoms established in Britain. It is important to realise that the traditional division of the settlers into Angles, Saxons and Jutes overemphasises the differences. In many ways, the invaders had much in common in attitude and institutions.

It would be wrong, therefore, to claim, as Green once did, that the Saxon invasion was the beginning of English history. The economic organisation of the Anglo-Saxons was derived from their experience in Germany, modified by their movement across the sea and influenced by the existing Celtic way of life. What have been called "the bones of shire and state" were laid on no exclusive Teutonic model. The Saxons established a framework of political and legal life within which economic activity was again possible with a degree of regularity. Yet Celtic two-field systems and primitive industries were the basis of Saxon activities. Roman roads carried their major communications, and by the eighth century, three-quarters of the Roman town sites were reoccupied. In some ways there was no break in economic development, but this does not substantiate the view that Roman institutions of land tenure and farming methods survived, for, in order that that might occur, the whole haphazard and brutal course of the invasion would have to be reassessed.

CHAPTER 3

THE ORGANISATION OF A PERMANENT ECONOMIC FRAMEWORK

THE ENVIRONMENT OF THE ANGLO-SAXON ECONOMY

The Saxon period was one in which England came to recognise the importance of the sea, and by the time of Alfred she possessed a fleet. During Alfred's reign, English seamen penetrated into distant waters. Othere reached Archangel and Wulfstan the eastern Baltic. The Saxons, and more particularly the Frisians, were seafaring people and came to this country in oak keels some 77 feet long and 11 feet wide, carrying perhaps forty people. Their boats were clinker-built with the planks of wood overlapping and nailed together, and this remained the normal method of construction until the late Middle Ages. Danish and Viking invasions renewed interest in the sea. Colonies of Frisians settled at York and their naval engineers were employed by Alfred. The Norsemen had two types of ship. The knarr was a shortish vessel weighing about 50 tons and used for trading whereas the longship was 80 feet long, weighed about 30 tons and carried forty people, as the discovery of the Gokstad ship in 1880 confirmed in detail.

It would be a mistake to regard the Channel as a barrier during this period. The close connection with the continent of Europe was never completely severed. Celts kept contact with Brittany from the shores of Cornwall, and their missionaries spread as far as Switzerland. Saxons and Frisians maintained friendly relations. The Danes succeeded eventually in uniting England to a North Sea empire, and the Norman conquest had been preceded by the peaceful penetration of Norman ideas. Both the Saxon and Danish invasions were large-scale emigrations. Bede referred to the deserted shores of the North Sea from whence the Saxons were forced by the slow subsidence of the land. Established in marshland colonies called *terpen*, they were compelled gradually to emigrate by coastal erosion culminating in the formation of the Zuider Zee at the end of the eighth century. The Danes found that the narrow coastlands of Scandinavia had been overpopulated due to polygamy, and life was rendered fruitless by almost ceaseless warfare. Links across the Channel were greatly increased by royal intermarriage, particularly with the royal house of Flanders, by pilgrimages under-taken by many Saxon monarchs, including Ine of Wessex and Cnut, and by missionary activity which, for example, led St Boniface from Devon to south Germany and to the dedication of Stavanger Cathedral in Norway to St Swithun of Winchester. Such contacts suggest that there was flourishing international trade in Saxon times, and that economic activity in England did not necessarily receive a massive stimulus from the Norman invasion.

Saxon England saw the establishment of settlement over a wider area than before, and, in particular, its extension into the river valleys and forest regions. Two types of land were still neglected: heavy clay soils, that could not be ploughed or drained, and breck-land with light sandy soils, such as parts of west Norfolk and Surrey. It was the main contribution of the Saxons, however, to make sizeable inroads on the forests. The availability of timber for houses, heating, utensils and the production of charcoal combined with the availability of pasture for pigs, with beechmast for them to eat, to provide cogent reasons for forest settlements. The amount of wood used by the Saxons was very considerable. One thegn or lesser noble near Rochester was taking ten cartloads a year from his property in 855. In some of the earliest laws, such as those of King Ine of Wessex (726), penalties were laid down for starting forest fires or felling large numbers of trees. Lawsuits over the right of pannage for pigs were of such importance that one at Sinton in Worcestershire was held before the King of Mercia in 825. Assarting, that is taking—in the forest, proceeded rapidly during Saxon times, unimpeded by restrictions. It is now clearly estab-lished that there were no Saxon forest laws, such as those intro-duced later by the Normans. The claim that Cnut introduced such laws was challenged as long ago as 1894, but only now have his-torians finally agreed on this matter. The amount of Saxon activity is best revealed by place names, and an examination of the map of modern Sussex and Kent for places with names including the suffixes -lea, -ly, -hurst, -field, -den and -dene will soon show the extent of settlement. According to Postan, in some parts of the country, such as south-east Leicestershire and west Northampton-shire, the area cleared for agriculture by the eleventh century was at its maximum extent and subsequently fell.

However, in spite of this movement, the great acreage of forest remained largely intact, and was to do so until Tudor times, when the constant demand for charcoal and timber for shipping and building combined with the spread of settlement to reduce their size. The most impressive of the forests was the Andredweald, esti-mated in the ninth century to stretch 120 miles across Kent, Sussex and Hampshire in a belt 30 miles wide. Such a forest was not impenetrable and was crossed by three Roman roads, one of which may still be seen at Holtye near East Grinstead. Later the forest became a key industrial region for iron and glass manufacture. North of London, through Essex stretched a belt of forest 40 miles wide, of which Epping and Hainault are the remains. Apart from Selwood, southern England was otherwise free from forests. In the Midlands, however, there were great tracts. In the west Midlands, Feckenham, Arden, Kinver, Morfe and Cannock stretched from the Severn to the Trent. In the east Midlands, Rockingham, Needwood, Charnwood, and Bruneswald (or Bromswold) were equally impressive. Further north, Sherwood (Nottinghamshire), Kesteven (Lincolnshire) and Galtres (Yorkshire) were the main forests.

In the same way as these forests, while impeding communications and limiting settlement, were made to serve the economy, extensive areas of marsh and fen were utilised in spite of their apparent inhospitality. Mention of Alfred on the Isle of Althelney, or Hereward the Wake on the Isle of Ely, is sufficient to indicate that regions of rich alluvial soil today were then marshy wastes. Marshes surrounded the mouth of the Thames on both sides. In Kent and Sussex the abandonment of the Roman defences led to the reappearance of marshes which were not settled until the ninth century. The coastline was further inland than today and the settlements occurred on islands at the estuaries of the Brede and Rother rivers. It was not until after the Norman Conquest that any attempt was made to reclaim this region. The other principal marshland region in the south was in Somerset where the whole area around Glastonbury was one of lagoons and islands, sheltering the possible sites of the earliest Christian church and the dwelling place of Arthur. Stretching from the Humber to Cambridge and beyond was the most extensive area of marshland, leaving Leeds an island, cutting off the uplands of Lincolnshire, and having within its confines numerous islands where the Church chose for security and peace to erect the great Benedictine abbeys of Peterborough, Ely, Crowland, Ramsey and Thorney. This wilderness was not unprofitable as fowling, fishing and eeling were carried out, and the presence of marsh tribes such as the Loidis, Spalde and Gyrwas shows that a living was to be made in the expanse of water and reeds.

One other aspect of Anglo-Saxon geography was also vastly different from what we would expect. The coastline from Norfolk to Dorset was subjected to extremes of erosion and deposition due to tidal movements, the wide variety of rock strata and the numerous estuaries. It was not until Tudor times that the modern coastline was completed and this process was under way during the Saxon period and for long afterwards. In Norfolk and the Fens, some towns, such as Wisbech, which we consider to be inland were then easy of access to the sea whereas some, such as Brancaster, a port in Roman times, became inland towns. Further south, deposition gradually silted the Yare so that Norwich was no longer accessible while denudation wore away the coast leaving the Saxon town of Dunwich and the Roman fort at Walton beneath the sea. Off the mouth of the Thames, the Channel between Kent and the Isle of Thanet began to fill. This was known as the Wantsum and had been navigated by the Romans who had marked its importance with the ports of Reculver and Richborough. Canterbury on the Stour had also been a port. Thanet was an island when Hengist and Horsa landed in 449 and the Danes wintered there in 855, but the building of a new port at Sandwich, 2 miles south of Richborough, which became the fleet headquarters of Ethelred II showed that silting was well in progress by then.

To the south again lay the Goodwin Sands. Legend has it that these were the submerged property of Earl Godwin, but it is more likely that they were formed as part of the process which was filling the Wantsum, although the legend may well be accurate as to the time when the sands became sufficiently prominent to be a danger to shipping. In the area where the Rother and Brede reached the sea and Winchelsea and Rye had appeared on islands by the eleventh century, the process was more complicated. Deposition from the east and west combined with the draining of the marshes to create the promontory of Dungeness during the Middle Ages. The nearby Sussex coast was a participant in this process, whereby the Roman port of Pevensey and the marshes which turned the site of the battle of Hastings into a place on a peninsula surrounded by the sea and the river Roar were filled in by deposition. Further west, the area round Selsey was heavily eroded. In Saxon times, therefore, many places were ports which were later inland towns, and rivers like the Roar, Brede or Rother had considerable importance. Some towns, such as Old Hastings and Old Winchelsea, existed which were later to be destroyed, and any study of the economic development of ports and trade in this region has to pay particular attention to the altered geographical circumstances which belie the evidence of today's maps.

ANGLO-SAXON AGRICULTURE

There is little agreement among historians on the total amount of land brought into use during the Saxon period although Postan's claim that the arable area reached an extent in the twelfth century greater than two centuries later is accepted. Seebohm gave a figure of 5 million acres and another historian, Maitland, one of 9 million. However much land was involved, one half to a third lay fallow every year and the yield of crops was very low. It has been estimated that it took 7 acres to feed one person compared with 2·5 acres today, not forgetting the vast rise in the standard of living. The great majority of the Saxons obtained their living on the land and resided in small village communities of about 200–300 people. They had started the attack on the forests and marshes which meant that "the Medieval landscape was in perpetual dissolution," and they had developed methods of farming and landholding so that the "rural England of 1066 was already an old country."

The important question to be answered is concerned with the method of cultivation and its origin. By the ninth century, when evidence is available, the Saxons were using the two- and three-field system of farming with common rights, agricultural planning, holding of equipment, and many of the features of what later became known as the "three-field system." The problem is to explain why and how the Saxons adopted this system of farming now that the "mark" theory has finally been discarded. Briefly this theory, advanced by historians such as Stubbs and Freeman in the 1870s, argued that the Saxons brought their agricultural methods with them from their German homelands. Imposing a false symmetry and presupposing an astonishing degree of democratic ardour among Teutonic backwoodsmen, these historians argued that the land was allotted by the village "moot" on the principle of fairness, so that all obtained shares of good and bad ground, held roughly equal holdings and farmed for the common good. This theory was dismissed by Maitland as a figment of German imagination, and a moment's thought will suffice to show that a system of farming is more likely to evolve from existing conditions and in response to demand and the environment. Nevertheless Lipson still held that, since the value of soil could be eight times in one place what it was in another, it was likely that some concept of communal fairness was involved, and he instanced contemporary (1915) examples in Palestine, India and Japan.

It seems more likely that, when a family settled in the forest with other families, they would take a small piece of land varying in size according to the fertility of the soil, the number of plough oxen available, the standard of living and the nature of the land customs which applied to that particular people. As the village grew, a fresh area would be taken from the forest and divided among the villagers, and in extreme cases three large fields would be so formed. In most cases, however, two fields was the normal number and in the thirteenth century a famous agricultural writer Walter of Henley, was to refer to their existence "in many places." With the division of holdings among relatives and by marriage, the strips would become more variegated and a pattern emerge of two fields full of strip holdings. The holding was loosely described as a hide, which was the possession of a family and therefore used as a unit for taxation purposes. Orwin pointed out that the hide could not be assumed as a regular unit of 120 acres because the calculation that eight oxen owned by four peasants would have a quarter each, *i.e.* a virgate of 30 acres, was too regular and was not based on any recognisable evidence.

The unit of landholding thus varied considerably. The virgate of 30 acres, known to the Saxons as a yardland, was found mainly in the Midlands and the south, and, although Seebohm claimed this was evidence of continuity from Roman times, it is more likely to be the same area because the acreage involved was manageable by a peasant and his family. In Kent the holding was larger and called the *sulung*, divided into four yokes, later called *iuja*, while in the north the unit was a ploughland divided into eight oxgangs, later called *bovates*. Thus, the use of the fields, and the acre itself varied considerably at first in relation to the amount of labour and later, as holdings became more stabilised, according to the nature of the tenure of the land.

Communal farming was practised on the scattered strips for equally practical reasons. Poverty compelled the Saxons to adopt the collective use of the land, particularly for ploughing, because ploughs were expensive items, and for harvesting, because it was a communal matter of life or death. It has been claimed that the Saxons used a heavy plough similar to the Roman one and drawn by eight oxen. It was fully developed with a coulter and mould-board. This view was based to some extent on literary sources such as the *Plough Riddle* or Aelfric's *Colloquies* and has been challenged. Hunter-Blair says there is no evidence that such a plough existed and Vinogradov argued that villeins could not afford so expensive a plough. Whatever the truth of this matter, within the holdings the furlongs continued to be ploughed 220 yards by 22 yards and this suggests that ploughs of the larger kind were in use, as there was no reversal to the smaller Celtic fields. Necessities and shortages produced the Saxon communal agricultural effort, and it was only later in the tenth century that these activities became formalised into customary obligations with the growth in the power of certain lords and changes in the concept of landholding.

Evidence for the practice of Saxon agriculture is forthcoming from a number of sources. The laws of the Saxon kings provide passing references, of which the most important are those of Ine of Wessex (726) showing that a communal duty of enclosing the fields existed at that time. The records of three estates have survived: Tiddenham, in Gloucestershire, Hurstbourne Priors in Hampshire and Cranborne in Dorset—all most probably from the tenth century. Lastly, there are two works written between 960 and 1060 which it is suggested are part of one comprehensive work. These are the list of duties performed by various kinds of agricultural labourer in the *Rectitudines Singularum Personarum*, and a record of a bailiff's or overseer's duties called *Be Gesceadwisan Gerefen*. None of these records can be taken as typical for the whole country and they doubtless convey degrees of regularity and uniformity beyond those in existence.

Broadly speaking there were three groups in the village: the lord and his retainers and assistants; the peasants; and the auxiliary workers on and off the land. The lord at first was distinguished by blood or by battle, later by the type of landholding. Known as hlaford or eorl, he might also be a special follower of the King or of a sub-king. Then he was known as a gesith or member of the war-band, sworn followers of the King who fell to a man as a personal bodyguard in battles like Nectansmere (685) or Hastings (1066); or followed him into exile. Such men swore a personal oath (hold-oath) to "love all that he loves, and hate all that he hates." A gift was given by the superior lord in return for services, most often in the form of the precious cattle of Saxon times and known as the heriot. Later lords were given land in return for services and by the tenth century were more often referred to as thegns. Thegnhood did not correspond to any later equivalent feudal rank, in spite of the formalisation of the heriot into a feudal obligation. Thegns were rewarded for past services, whereas feudal mesne tenants were appointed to provide future services. This is clearly shown by the admission to the rank of thegn of others besides nobles or royal servants. Saxon laws show that if a peasant came to possess five hides, or if a merchant made three trading voyages overseas, they could become thegns. Most Saxon thegns were poor and probably owned little more than the peasants, but there were exceptions to this state of affairs. In the early 1000s, thegns holding between fifteen and seventy-two estates existed and some of the more important thegns (particularly those with administrative roles as earls or sheriffs) had begun to exercise lordly rights. Godwin, for example, claimed the right of purveyance on his Gloucester estates at Berkeley. The lord's position was, however, still essentially personal and his rights were few and ill-defined.

It was the richer class of eorls or thegns that from the first prevented the village from being an entirely self-sufficient economic community. Descriptions in early poems such as *Beowulf* and the *Widsith* show that thegns were accustomed to quite a high standard of living. Usually the thegn would be the possessor of a hall, and in 1011 one thegn is spoken of who "afterwards adorns the house pleasantly." English tapestry was famous and on the Continent "opus anglicanum" was a synonym for the finest work. William of Poitiers referred to work in cloth of gold and elaborate embroidery was practised. Robes, gold and silverware, glass, furs, jewels and elaborate harness were all in use and would naturally have been imported into the village. Green in his great works *The Making of England* and *The Conquest of England* gave unrivalled descriptions of the life of thegns which deserve quotation:

> "The centre of the homestead was the hall, with the hearth-fire in the midst of it, whose smoke made its escape as best it could through a hole in the roof. . . . Here the board set upon trestles when needed, furnished a rough table for the family meal; and when the board was cleared away, the women bore the wooden beer-cups or drinking horns to the housemaster and his friends as they sat on the settles or benches ranged round the walls, while the gleeman sang his song or the harp was passed around from hand to hand. Here too, when night came and the fire died down, was the common sleeping place, and men lay down to rest on the bundles of straw which they had strewn about its floor."

Green drew attention to the growth of the nobles' wealth:

> "The thegn himself boasted of his gems, of his golden bracelets and rings; his garments were gay with embroidery and lined with costly furs, the rough walls of his house were often hung with silken hangings, wrought with figures or pictures. We hear of tables made of silver and gold, of silver mirrors and candlesticks; while cups and basins of the same precious metals were stored in the hoards of the wealthier nobles."

To supply such needs there were a large number of travelling chapmen or pedlars, first mentioned in the laws of Hlothere of Kent and Ine of Wessex at the turn of the eighth century.

Ordinary peasants were known as ceorls, a word unjustly translated as churl. From the earliest times, wergelds, or moneys to be paid in respect of injuries done, show that there were different sorts of ceorl. The lesser ceorls or laets were entitled to a wergeld four-fifths that of a ceorl. The ceorl himself had a wergeld which was equal to a sixth of that of an eorl. Throughout the Saxon period, it is clear that many ceorls became less free, for reasons to be explained in the following section, but it is important to realise that, at the time of the Norman Conquest, a considerable number of ceorls remained freemen answerable only in the courts of the hundred and shire and free to do as they wished with their land. It is far too easy to suggest that an automatic decline of free ceorls into the position of medieval villeins was taking place on a widespread scale. Sokemen (*sochemanni*), freemen (*liberi homines*) and payers of money rent (*censuarii*) made up 12 per cent of the population as late as 1086, even after a period when more precise legal definitions of status had reduced their numbers. In the *Rectitudines* three types of ceorl are mentioned, but these were not castes and the duties done by them, although obviously similar to those later done by villeins, were so varied that it is clear they were not fixed predial services but the performance of a necessary division of labour. Geneats paid rent in food (feorm) or money (gafol) and performed certain services for the thegn such as horse-watcher or hunting duties. It was a rank, not without honour, known in the Midlands as radcnihts. Geburs holding a yardland usually performed quite heavy services including two days on the lord's land and some boon services. Cotsetlas held much smaller amounts of land and performed even heavier services, but even they were told to perform these "as every freeman ought to do."

As an example of the distribution of these classes, Whitelocke quotes the estates of Edith, wife of Edward the Confessor, at Leominster in Herefordshire, where there were 8 geneats, 238 geburs, 75 cotsetlas and 82 slaves. At Hurstbourne Priors, the geburs paid 40*d.* a hide each autumn, and they were required to plough and sow three acres and wash and shear the lord's sheep. At Tiddenham, where there were nine hides belonging to the thegn and twenty-one to the ceorls, the geburs were required to provide rods and yarn for fishing and maintain weirs and nets in the Severn. Both feorm and gafol were paid and the services were described as "very heavy." Cranborne estate in Dorset was a more considerable affair with 3,000 acres of pasture, 6,000 of woodland, 1,200 of ploughland and 20 of meadow, two-fifths of which belonged to the lord and was serviced by week work and boon work on special occasions. The ceorl lived in a wooden cruck cottage of wattle and daub, which was usually one room in which the whole family and some animals lived. A hole sufficed for a chimney, a few more for windows, and the furniture would have been wood with straw for bedding. The needs of the ceorl were met almost entirely within the village.

Each village contained a large number of auxiliary workers. Green listed them as the blacksmith, ploughman, oxherd, cowherd, shepherd, goatherd, swineherd, hayward, woodward, beeward, carpenter, tailor, salter and baker, to which might be added the alehousekeeper and the miller. Dependent on the thegn were a further group including falconers, hawkers, dog-keepers, huntsmen and foresters. On women fell a considerable share of the work, including dairying, clothmaking and baking. Spinsters called in *Beowulf* "weavers of peace" provided the simple garments of the ceorl. Cornmills or querns and communal ovens provided various types of bread, the malthouse and brewery provided bright, mild and smooth varieties of ale, distinguished as early as the seventh century. In a very large number of villages there was a watermill, mentioned for the first time in eighth-century documents. By the time of *Domesday Book* (1086), the number of mills was 5,611, and these were highly concentrated in certain areas. In the six eastern counties, 964 mills served 2,784 settlements, and over 80 villages had more than 4 mills.

The main aim of agricultural production was self-sufficiency and lack of technical expertise combined with frequent war to make this difficult. It was always hard to keep a Saxon army together at harvest time when troops deserted for a more important task. But the village was never entirely self-sufficient. The needs of the richer owners and the more general need for such commodities as salt or iron meant that there would be imports. Village crafts were ample but not adequate and again there would have to be imports. Nor can it be said that the village did not provide a marketable surplus. The export from England of raw wool, cloaks, cheese, and hunting dogs showed that, as a primary producer, we utilised some of our agricultural production. The village was mainly concerned with the growing of crops, the herding of animals and the utilisation of wood. The *Gerefa* mentions over a hundred implements made with wood, and the *silva infructuosa* was of great value. The pig was the main meat animal, cattle being used for hides, oxen as beasts of burden and sheep for wool. Danish experts, examining grains of cereal imbedded in pottery, have shown that barley was the most important crop. In a sample of 101 specimens, 83 were barley, 14 were oats and only 4 wheat. White wheat bread was regarded as a delicacy for the lord or for use in the sacrament. Most people ate barley (or rye) bread. This is shown by the derivation of the word barn from *bere-aern*, and the word barton from *baer-tun*, both derivatives of *bere*. The poor quality of agricultural techniques most probably made it difficult to grow wheat and St Cuthbert failed to do so on Lindisfarne. Barley with honey was turned into mead or with malt into ale, wine being reserved for the sacrament and the use of the rich.

THE BONDS OF SOCIETY AND THE ORIGINS OF THE MANOR

As agricultural production was the main source of economic wealth and the greater part of the population was employed in agriculture, it is essential to grasp the nature of land tenure in the Saxon period and during subsequent centuries. In so far as it is possible, discussion of the method of production—the three-field system—and the unit of landholding—the estate or manorial system—have been separated from one another. In a few cases, fields, manor and even village coincided to provide that well-known abstraction, the "typical manor," but this was by no means always the case. The development of agricultural techniques, the changes in methods of land tenure and the pattern of village settlement were each influenced by many factors including economic ones. Having discussed the pattern of settlement which led to the creation of the Saxon "tuns" or villages, sometimes possessing a rudimentary council called a tun moot or later a tithing, and having discussed as well the method of agricultural production, it is necessary now to examine the way in which society had developed from a tribal state into a manoralised condition by the time of the Norman Conquest.

The earliest loyalty in the village community was to the lord and his successors. It has already been stressed that Saxon lordship was personal, based upon an oath holding one man to serve another in return for protection. In addition to this bond, the Saxons recognised loyalty to one's kin. In *Beowulf* there is a lament for a kinless man. The kin had many duties, such as presiding over the inheritance of land, the arranging of marriages and the perpetuation of a blood feud against the relatives of a killer of one's own kin. This state of affairs similar in many ways to the ways of Israel in the Old Testament, was frowned upon by the Church. Archbishop Theodore spoke against the blood feud in the 670s and both Alfred and Edmund sought to limit the practice. In this they were not noticeably successful, as a famous blood feud involving the chief nobles of Northumbria in the eleventh century showed. The blood of one's kin was so strong a factor that even illegitimacy was not regarded as a bar. Both Offa of Mercia and William the Conqueror were illegitimate but regarded as related to the "cynekin." Moreover, marriages were arranged within the prohibited degrees of the Church and even a king like Ethelbald of Wessex married his stepmother.

Gradually, during the tenth and eleventh centuries, the Saxons built up a third set of bonds which is referred to as "bohr and frankpledge." The idea was to combat crime and enforce simple civic duties by associating men in groups and making others responsible for them. At the lowest level, men were associated in groups of ten in the tithing. They were to be responsible for a man's army service in the fyrd, his appearance at court, and his payment of fines, including angylde for not supporting a hue and cry against a suspected criminal. Cnut's laws ordered all men to have "hundred and bohr" and "hundred and tithing"; that is, to be associated with one of these groups. Simple community responsibility had arrived. This involved service in the fyrd, participation in the processes of law, and possibly fulfilling the *trimoda necessitas*, which added duties of repairing bridges and the walls of fortified places to service in the fyrd.

Crime was apparently rife in the tenth century, and the laws of Athelstan and Edgar made much of the evils of cattle-stealing. A number of measures were taken to strengthen the severity of the penalties, to develop the hundred court and to make sure that every man was under a lord answerable for him. There has been much dispute about what constituted a hundred, but by the tenth century it was an administrative and legal unit concerned with minor offences, keeping the peace, organising the hue and cry and enforcing other communal duties. Its functions are made plain in the *Edict of Grateley* (c. 931), the *Ordinance of the Hundred* (940–6) and the *Wantage Code* (979–1016). The court was to be held every four weeks and at first proceeded entirely on oaths sworn by the accused. Before long, this was supplemented by the system of compurgators. By this, any number of men from twelve to forty-eight who were considered law-worthy swore to the innocence of the accused. Gradually these men ceased to be witnesses and became jurors, but what is important for our purposes is to realise that by the tenth century men were closely bound communally by the operation of a harsh penal code and the need for such sureties. The great majority of Saxons were free but subject to the close bonds of the hundred, and under an obligation to have a hlaford or lord.

It was in these circumstances that during the tenth and eleventh centuries a new form of landownership and jurisdiction began to grow. The older view that this organisation derived from the Roman *villae* was clearly mistaken because there is a gap of some 400 years between the departure of the Romans and the growth of the manor. Green's view, that by the tenth century "the bulk of English villages were now in demesne . . . the free ceorl had all but vanished," was the reverse of the truth. It is clear, as Lipson stressed, that at the time of the Norman Conquest many villages were still not affected by this new development. The essence of Saxon organisation was variety or as the *Rectitudines* said: "let him who is over the district take care that he knows what the old land-customs are and what are the customs of the people." The Norman Conquest imposed uniformity of terminology and of legal status on what was a growing and complex situation. The widespread existence of freemen, the frequency of money rents, the enormous varieties in agricultural services and the limited nature of the lords' jurisdictions—all point to a degree of growth involving a much later start to the evolution of the manor than Roman origins would suggest.

Lipson stressed that "the phenomena of economic life can seldom be traced to the agency of a single factor" and, therefore, "no theory of the manor is tenable which lays stress upon one aspect to the entire exclusion of the other." The manor evolved for a wide variety of reasons. In its essence, it was that part of the hundred which had passed into the private jurisdiction of a lord and was ruled in everyday life not by the hundred but by the manor court. In theory, all the land was the tribe's and thus, in practice, the king's. From the eighth century, a series of land grants including specific rights were made from this land. These grants are referred to as laen land or boc land and were made either to the Church or to the gesiths and thegns in return for service to the Crown. The rights involved varied and included sac and soc, toll and team, and infangentheof and utfangentheof. In effect these meant, respectively, control over jurisdiction, property and the administration of the criminal law. With the increasing stress on men placing themselves under a lord in the criminal code, the thegns developed their private jurisdiction to a point where rudimentary seigniorial status had been conceded. This was the essence of the manor, but the grants were not complete in the feudal sense. The workers remained, as we have seen, largely free, and they kept the wergelds of free men. They were allowed to attend the hundred and shire courts, and Maitland suggested that only a vague seigniorial jurisdiction existed by the time of the Conquest.

This development was only part of the process which created the manor. Economic necessity proved as powerful a force as legal and tenurial innovation. Saxon agricultural communities were subjected to great pressures and the Danish wars increased these to breaking point in some parts, when destruction and service in the fyrd added to the villagers' miseries. The government began a steady pressure to increase its revenue by augmenting fines and even by direct taxation known as the geld or carucage. Among the fines a villager might have to pay were wergeld (to relative of injured party), bot (to injured party), wite (to a man's lord), and oferhymes (to the king). In addition fyrdwite (for failing to attend the muster), brig bot and burgh bot (for failing to meet the *trimoda necessitas*) and angylde (for not joining the hue and cry) might be levied. Lastly, there was the feorm and gafol (food and money rents) to pay, and a steady growth in the Church's requirements. By the tenth century, plough alms fifteen days after Easter, tithe of young stock at Whitsun, tithes of the fruits of the earth on All Saints' Day, church scot at Martinmas, and soul scot (burial fees) were all being demanded. Combined with the increasing incidence of the geld, these financial pressures compelled ceorls to commend themselves to a lord who would, in return for their services, meet their financial obligations. The manor became, in Maitland's words, "a house against which geld is charged," and it was true that, in regions where geld had not been levied, the number of free ceorls was proportionately higher. This same process of commendation lay at the root of European feudalism, where the dangers were greater and the powers of the lords correspondingly wider.

Therefore, the two elements which went to create a manor were commendation and seigniorial jurisdiction. Both were established in England before the Norman Conquest and manors undoubtedly existed in considerable numbers in southern England. But there was no manorial "system." The institution was of comparatively recent growth, and was still subordinate in many ways to the older forms of Saxon justice. Generalisation from the evidence of church estates, such as the famous example of the estate of St Oswald of Worcester (c. 972), is unwise because such estates were usually better organised and more inclined to a strict interpretation of the law than ordinary secular estates. Many villages like Grantchester near Cambridge were quite free. At Hanningford near Ely in 1086, two men "held their land freely and were only commended to the abbot." This implies a temporary character in their commendation. The rights granted to Saxon thegns were personal gifts of the King in return for past services and they were not designed to create a territorial aristocracy even if they had the effect of so doing. The manor existed in 1066, but it was not a fully developed structure either in jurisdiction or organisation. Feudalism was to give it a new coherence.

THE ORIGINS OF THE TOWNSHIP OR BOROUGH

By nature the Saxons were not town-dwellers and earlier historians used to claim that it was the example of the Roman towns which led to the early establishment of English towns. This may have been so on the Continent, but no English town, with the possible exception of Exeter, can show continuous development during the 200 years of Saxon settlement. Some Roman towns, such as Silchester, Wroxeter and Pevensey, lost their importance and, when new towns were founded on Roman sites at places like St Albans or Colchester, no conscious effort was made to rebuild them on the exact Roman position. By the end of the eighth century, however, there is evidence that towns had reappeared. Bede referred to London as *emporium*, and Alciun to York and the Frisian colony in that city. The coming of the Roman Church led to the virtual refounding of Canterbury, Rochester and Winchester. Although many town charters were forged, it seems that Southampton's earliest charter dates from 720 and that of Canterbury from 786.

Towns arose where geographical advantages made them useful. Fords were important to cattle drovers and bridging points to travellers. River and sea communications influenced the growth of many of the earlier towns. Oxford, for example, grew in importance for this reason and the earliest churches of St Martin, St Mildred and St Ebbe prove that it was well established by the beginning of the ninth century. The repute of a local saint, Frideswide, added to its importance, and after the Treaty of Wedmore (878) with the Danes it became a border town and a fortified burgh. At Gloucester, the produce of the river with its sixty-five fisheries, including thirty-three for salmon on the neighbouring Wye, enhanced its position as a commercial centre. In 681 a nunnery was founded and soon after the great Benedictine monastery. Gloucester was also a border town as was Chester to the north. Established as a deep water port on the Dee, and fortified by Alfred's daughter, Ethelfleda, in 907, Chester traded in cattle, cheese, bread, fish and slaves. The foundation of St Werburgh's and St Olav's pointed to the joint influence of Saxons and Vikings on its growth. Coining was a further indication of a town's importance. Alfred's mint at Oxford is mentioned in Green's account of the town's growth and Bristol first rose to prominence in Cnut's time when two coiners Aegelwine and Aelfwine are mentioned in business there. The town had been established some time before that and the church of St Mildred suggested Mercian influence. Like Chester, it was a centre for the slave trade.

Natural advantages lay at the basis of urban development, as the origins of such varied towns as Cambridge, Aylesbury, Lincoln, Worcester, Sandwich and Yarmouth proved in Saxon times. Green rightly emphasised the importance of the Church as a factor in town development, pointing out how Church dedications mark influences exerted on a town's growth and help to trace the rise of the population. Throughout the Middle Ages, the Church was an immense economic force for good and ill, and from the earliest times the link of urban development with the building of monasteries or the veneration of saints and relics was a close one. At Abingdon ten traders dwelt "in front of the door of the church" and at Wells the local market grew up at the gate of the bishop's palace under his jurisdiction. Freeman stated that for all practical purposes Wells was a city "which exists only in and through its cathedral church . . . the history of the church is the history of the city." The shrine of St Swithun enhanced the early growth of Winchester. Boston became famous due to a local saint (St Botulf) and then took advantage of the silting of the Witham and Ouse to become a great port. A similar pattern of development was later discernible at St Ives in Huntingdonshire. Bishops were appointed to sees in old Roman cities and Canterbury became a port on the Stour after St Augustine had made it a bishop's seat. At Bury St Edmunds lay a King of East Anglia shot to death with arrows by the Danes in 870, and it was said that the visitors and traders in that town "daily wait upon the Saint and the Abbot and the brethren."

Assessing the total number of towns is not easy, because it depends upon the precise definition of a town, which historians have not yet agreed upon for this period. Size is a deceptive factor to judge by, even though rough calculations can be made from a document called the *Burghal Hidage* dating from the reign of Edward the Elder. Two sets of calculations are possible. Since the document lists the number of hides attached to each of the towns and maintains that each pole of the defending walls was to be manned by four men from the hides, it is possible to calculate the circuit of the town walls. Winchester was assigned 2,400 hides, which works out at 3,280 yards. This calculation compares well with the known length of the medieval wall of Winchester which was 3,300 yards. Based on the same calculation, Southwark (1,800 yards), Wareham and Buckingham (1,600 yards), Oxford and Chichester (1,500 yards), Cricklade and Wilton (1,400 yards), Lewes and Malmesbury (1,200 yards) were the chief towns at this time. By multiplying the number of burgage tenants by five (a figure considered too low by Whitelocke) a rough estimate of population may be made which gives populations of 8,000 for York, 6,600 for Norwich, 5,000 for Thetford, 3,500 for Oxford and 2,000 for Colchester. For London and Winchester, there are no figures but as the chief port, and the capital, they were clearly larger and may have approached 15,000 inhabitants. The number of mints is another indication of a town's standing since a law of Ethelred II divided towns into "principal" with three moneyers and "others" with one. In Athelstan's time London had eight, Canterbury seven and Winchester six moneyers. By the eleventh century London had twenty and York ten. London and Winchester were clearly the leading towns because when Edgar tried to establish uniform weights and measures he based them on the standards in force there. As to the total number of boroughs, the *Burghal Hidage* lists thirty. Forty-four places had mints by the end of Edward the Confessor's reign and Tait claimed that there were seventy-one towns which could be called boroughs in Saxon England.

The precise meaning of the word burgh or borough has long been the subject of argument. It is generally agreed that the tenth century saw the rapid rise of a considerable number of towns, but the reasons for this have been hotly disputed. On one side are Maitland, Ballard and Stephenson who have argued that the burgh was essentially an artificial military creation. On the other are Lipson, Darlington, Tait and Whitelocke who dispute this point, but are divided over the exact nature of the burgh. As with the origins of the manor, too much emphasis has been placed on legal niceties and oversimplified political reasons for boroughs which were, at bottom, economic organisations. The old theory was that, in the tenth century, burghs were founded by Alfred and Ethelfleda to protect trade and act as defensive posts against the Danes. Security and favourable tenures were used to attract settlers and the burghs became recognisable trading ports with the right to hold markets, to permit trade in the presence of witnesses and to be exempt from tolls. In return for these privileges, the tenants would keep up the walls and defend the post with or without the assistance of the fyrd. In some cases this theory fits the facts. The *Anglo-Saxon Chronicle* between 910 and 924 mentions the foundation of some burghs, and the *Burghal Hidage* is dated soon afterwards. At the same time, the Danes were creating fortified trading posts in their newly-won territory at Derby, Lincoln, Leicester, Stamford and Nottingham.

There are a number of difficulties in the way of accepting this viewpoint. It makes burgage tenure essentially military and dependent on participation in the defence of a burgh. But burgage tenure was more complex than this and was to be found in towns which are not mentioned as burghs in the *Burghal Hidage*. Burgage tenants held land in the town and outside it and some burgage tenants were directly appurtenant to landlords outside the town. This state of affairs is known as tenurial heterogeneity and suggests a rather different pattern of development. Some examples will illustrate the matter. Bishops of Worcester secured tenants in London in 857 and 889. The Archbishop of Canterbury leased six tenements in Wallingford, and even a lesser man like Aelfgar of Bishopsworth could lease ten burghal properties in Bristol. Several reasons are put forward for this state of affairs, some of which are not entirely convincing. It is suggested that the duty of maintaining the burgh was laid on the landowners, who let houses to tenants to discharge their responsibilities for them. Rising land prices in towns, such as those in Winchester indicated in a document of 975–8, may have induced landowners to buy up town properties as an investment. The close connection of local landowners with burgage tenures is weakened, however, by the presence of burgage tenures from manors some distance away. Moreover, the number of burgage tenures sometimes has little relation to the number of tenures appurtenant to the manor. At Dunwich there were 316 burgesses but only 80 were part-tenants of the local lord. In this situation we have evidence that, however burgage tenure originated, it became a useful and profitable form of landholding. By 1050 a charter shows that burgage tenure was heritable and could be mortgaged. Before long a legal distinction was drawn in documents between "burgh riht" and "land riht." The economic advantages of living in a town made the burgesses wealthy and independent men. At Ipswich the 538 burgesses held over 40 acres of land.

It may be tentatively suggested that burgage tenure arose for a number of reasons, of which Crown necessity and landlords desire for a profit were the key factors. Later, tenure by virtue of the collective importance of the burgesses acquired its privileged role, and the townsmen gradually threw off the control of the Crown and the local landlord. Burgage tenure and borough status have, therefore, no automatic connection although, if the burgesses were strong and independent, their collective action would soon give their town a status similar to a borough, and they would clearly attempt to regularise this by means of a charter. This raises the matter of the existence of merchant guilds in Saxon times. Tait firmly supported their existence while others such as Gros have denied their presence and claimed that the early charters were forgeries and that later charters too easily accepted claims of early Saxon privileges. Borough government emerged for a variety of reasons. There was a need to keep the peace and the earliest associations in towns are called cnicht or frith guilds, and were found in Cambridge, Dover, Winchester and London by the reign of Athelstan. Like dwellers in the hundreds, those in the towns were aware of the need to enforce the criminal law, and combined for that purpose. Coining was a serious offence punishable by mutilation and Athelstan and Ethelred II tried to regulate minting and confine it to particular towns. Trade with foreigners was often a matter of dispute and, from the time of Edward the Elder, attempts were made to ensure that transactions were only carried out in front of the port gerefa, and later in front of witnesses. Edgar arranged for bodies of men, numbering between twelve and thirty-six, to be appointed, and at least two of them were to be present at commercial transactions. This group of law-worthy men are in all probability the "lawmen" of Exeter or the "witan" of Lincoln mentioned at this time. Cnut re-enforced the system and required the lawmen to meet three times a year.

Trade needed regulation in many ways and the attempt to enforce uniform weights and measures by Edgar and Ethelred II would have again fallen on the burgesses or the law-worthy men. As trade increased, the profits from tolls grew at port and town gates and, where the town managed to secure the right of collection for itself by an outright money payment to the lord, as the practice was at Torksey or Dover, the town took over financial responsibilities. Darlington was right to argue that borough government developed from the need to protect trade, to levy tolls, regulate coinage and weights and measures, and to preserve law and order in the town. The court was naturally run by those with a stake in the trade and property of the town although at first all townsmen had a right to attend. Burgage tenure rather than residence gave a man a say in the running of the town. The earliest court known is that of London which could meet once a week or in full session three times a year. Mentioned first in the reign of Athelstan, this court was the direct predecessor of the present Common Council of the City of London, a body older than Parliament itself. Evidence for the meeting of courts is abundant by the beginning of the eleventh century. At Exeter, Totnes, Lydford and Barnstaple there were "witans," and at other places similar bodies existed: "iudices" at Chester, "lawmen" at Lincoln and Stamford.

If there were no merchant guilds in their fully organised state, and if it is doubtful whether privileges later claimed by boroughs were granted to them at this time, it is certain that the functions of the merchant guild were being carried out by organisations largely influenced by the burgesses and that the towns were starting to feel their way towards a more independent position. London had already played a decisive role in the choice of Edmund II and Cnut, although it was not the capital. Exeter with its continuous history claimed virtual independence and resisted the Normans for a year under the leadership of Harold II's mother in 1067. Along the south coast, the great confederation of the Cinque Ports was in its embryonic stage. Williamson writes that

"the Domesday survey in 108[6] shows that Dover, Sandwich and Romney had certain privileges, varying in each case, on account of rendering sea services to the Crown. It does not mention Hastings or Hythe. Among the services, Dover undertook to convey a messenger of the King across the Channel for twopence in summer and threepence in winter. Thus by the end of the Conqueror's reign The Crown had separate contracts with three ports of the Five who were to be the founder-members of the confederation. Rye and Winchelsea had not yet attained the same importance. Neither is mentioned in Domesday, but there is an un-named 'new burgh' in the region, which may be Rye. That town was a recognised borough in the middle of the following century. Of Winchelsea—the old Winchelsea on the now lost island—there is likewise no clear mention until 1130; although the King, returning from Normandy in 1067, landed at 'Vincenesium' which might be Winchelsea."

Thus, although the old claim that the Cinque Ports were created in the reign of Edward the Confessor may be discounted, the genesis of their independence had started before 1066.

London was by far the most impressive of Saxon towns. In one levy of the geld totalling £82,500 London paid £10,500. The respect paid to London by Edmund II, Cnut and William I, who was crowned there and gave it a Charter, were a measure of its importance. Edward the Confessor bypassed Winchester when he came to build the first Westminster Abbey on Thorney Island. London had grown from the founding of the see at St Paul's, with the bishopric of Ercewald (c. 676) and the ring of churches round St Paul's (St Augustine, St Gregory, St Benet and St Faith) which showed the rise in the population. Under the Mercian kings Ethelred and Offa, London became a thriving port, Frisian merchants settled there, and Offa, as well as living there, established a mint. Two churches dedicated to the Mercian St Mildred show this development. There is no evidence of a bridge until Edgar's reign, but there were clearly a number of wooden structures on the site of the Roman bridge at the junction of Ermine and Watling Streets. During the ninth century the area between the Fleet and Walbrook became thickly populated. Alfred secured the town's transfer to Wessex in 886 and it was made a fortified burgh. By Athelstan's reign, there were eight moneyers and the London frith guild was meeting at the east end of St Paul's. By the end of the tenth century, London had stretched out towards Aldermanbury and

Lothbury along Cornhill and East Cheap—as the churches of St Peter, Cornhill and St Swithun indicate. In Ethelred II's time, details of London port tolls and the use of her weights and measures as standard reflected her commercial growth and, with the increasing size of ships, Billingsgate and Queenhythe came into use. The effects of Danish attacks were quickly repaired and development spread from St Dunstan's in East Cheap out to St Botolph's at Aldgate and Bishopsgate. The presence of a sizeable Danish community, mentioned by William of Malmesbury, is proved by the existence of St Clement's Danes, St Olav's and St Magnus's on each side of the bridge. By the Norman Conquest, therefore, London with sixteen churches nearly occupied the whole space within the confines of the Roman wall and was ready for her rapid medieval growth.

INDUSTRY, TRADE AND FINANCE BEFORE THE CONQUEST

One mistake frequently made when studying economic history is to assume that there were periods in history when the government displayed no interest in the economy. These are looked back upon as golden ages, because it is easier to criticise governments that act than those that do not. Mid-Victorian England was one such period, and Saxon England was another. The view that the "Norman yoke" of firm government with central administration and harsh laws dealing, for example, with the forests, replaced a period of halcyon freedom is mistaken. From the earliest times, the government was involved in the economy, even if it was a small government. The royal household was a major source of demand for home produce, luxury imported goods and finance to support certain royal policies. The safety of the realm and the encouragement of trade by treaty and regulation was from the earliest time a government function, *ad hoc* and ineffective in execution, but nevertheless part of the functioning economy.

In theory, the Crown lived off the produce of the royal lands, receiving rent in the form of payment in kind and cash. The great bulk of rent was collected as feorm rather than gafol and the incidence was heavy involving a levy of ale, corn, malt, honey, dairy produce and livestock. From this the medieval right to purveyance stemmed, as well as royal rights over minerals and the wrecks of ships. Tribute was levied from under-kings and the Crown began to collect the profit of the courts (oferhymes) when the king's frith had been broken. As early as Offa's time, tolls were being levied by port gerefas on incoming goods. The Crown also received substantial sums for commuting its rights to collect dues in a town, or for granting privileges. One charter cost the Bishop of Worcester 300s. in 855. Coining and the profits thereof were a jealously guarded royal prerogative. The collection of the feorm was the responsibility of the scir reeve and the procedure for collecting it at the twice-yearly meeting of the shire court was detailed in Edgar's *Ordinance of Andover*. Gradually, the scir reeve replaced the ealdormen or local magnate and, by Ethelred II's time, presided over the shire court, as is indicated in the *Wantage Code*.

There was a rudimentary central administration based on the royal household, where a large number of thegns performed specialised tasks. Two government departments had appeared in a simple form. There was the Chamber, or camera, where royal jewellery was kept and this royal hoard was settled permanently at Winchester by the time of Cnut. It was the beginning of the Exchequer. The other government department was the Chancery, run from the first by priests, and dating possibly from the issuing of the earliest laws. The Chancery was mainly responsible for issuing charters and some 1,500 authentic Saxon charters have survived. The clerks evolved writs, short writs or breves, and indentures for the purpose of record and, following Papal example, initiated the use of the seal by Edward the Confessor's time, when the first chancellor, Regenbald, held office.

Thus, the Crown had the means to start direct taxation and, at the end of the tenth century, three direct taxes were levied. The main tax is more properly called the geld, although popularly known as the Danegeld. It was based on the hide, as this was the holding of the family and an assessment was made on units of a hundred hides and paid in practice by the manors and villages in proportions. Incidence of the tax was heavy. Taking the geld of 1084 as an example, William I levied a tax of 6s. a hide, and as a hide was worth 20s. a year, this was just over a quarter of its annual value. For comparison the price of an ox varied between 2s. and 2s. 6d. and was considered a very expensive item. Tributes had been raised on an *ad hoc* basis in the days of Alfred's wars, possibly for the first time in East Anglia in 865. Edred had left £16,000 to his people "that they may be able to buy relief for themselves from famine and the heathen army." In Etheldred II's reign, the idea of financing the tribute out of a general tax was accepted due to the advice of Sigeric the Archbishop and Leofsige, ealdorman of Essex, and a royal favourite.

Figures given in the *Anglo-Saxon Chronicle* for the levying of the geld are reproduced in Table 1.

Table 1—The Yields of Danegeld

991	£10,000
994	£16,000
1002	£24,000
1007	£30,000
1012	£48,000
1014	£21,000
1018	£82,500

Considering that large parts of the country were devastated by war throughout most of this period, and even allowing for the customary exaggeration of such figures, this represents a sizeable revenue from direct taxation, particularly when it is recalled that a geld under Henry I raised only £2,500. The incidence of the tax was a major factor in increasing the dependence of the ceorls on the richer lords, and it was responsible for widespread suffering. It was because Archbishop Alphege refused to add to the burden of the geld by asking for a personal ransom that he was pelted to death with bones by the Danes in 1012.

The other two taxes were more short-lived. Here geld was levied by Ethelred II to raise a new army in 1014 and was continued by Cnut to pay the salary of his personal guard of huscarls. With their disbandment, the tax ceased in 1051 and this was considered to be one of the benefits bestowed by St Edward. The Saxon fleet, commenced by Alfred, had fallen into decay, but in 999 Ethelred II decided to revive it in view of the Danish emergency, and in 1008 every 310 hides were made responsible for the provision of a ship. This became an annual levy used, for example, by Harthacnut in 1040, and the hundreds grouped themselves into threes to provide the tax. In 1012 a tax of eight marks (£4) to the rowlock was charged, but the tax declined with the laying-up of the fleet in the 1050s. Incidentally, those lands paying feorm seem to have been exempted from the geld, which is not surprising when the size of the feorm is realised. Oxfordshire paid £150, Warwickshire £65, and thirty-six sextares of honey. Green rightly commented, as long ago as 1883, that "all these [taxes] made a much larger sum than we commonly think of as royal revenue of the time."

Perhaps the most interesting interference by Saxon government in the economic affairs of the country was its attempt to control the slave trade. Slavery was a natural condition of ancient society, and it has been argued that the glories of Greece and Rome could not have been realised without the existence of a large labour force receiving virtually no wages. Such prominent examples as the kidnapping of St Patrick by slavers in his early life, or the Saxon boys on sale in Rome who drew the attention of Pope Gregory and led to St Augustine's mission in 597, indicate the prevalence of a slave trade. The slave, known as a theowa or thrall, was of two main types. There were the wealh or the descendants of the Celts, and there were slaves reduced to their servitude by punishment, or in war, or when they were given as a part of a tribute or even as part-payment of a debt. Law-worthiness was denied the slave, who had no wergeld and was as much the property of his master as the cattle or pigs. For disobedience, flogging and even the death penalty might be inflicted by a slave's master: "Herein is declared that Ediwic, the widow of Saewgels, bought Gladut Colewin for half-a-pound, for the price and the toll; and Aelword the port-gerefa took the toll."

Slaves were clearly good business, and they were traded at the ports of Chester and Bristol on the west coast, and at London and in the Cleveland and Humber regions of Yorkshire. Bede mentioned London as a slave market in the days of Ethelred of Mercia, the Frisians being active in pursuit of the trade there, as they were at York. The Danish invaders had always been slavers and even Olav Tryggvesson, King of Norway, had been sold in a slave market as a child. Chester was the centre for imports from Ireland and again Danish merchants played their part in building up the trade. Bristol rose slowly—and early in Edward the Confessor's reign was coupled with the manor of Barton in paying feorm to the king—but by the end of the reign, slavery had become of major importance coupled, according to William of Malmesbury, with a white slave traffic for the purposes of prostitution. A slave was worth sometimes as much as 20s., which was the value of eight plough oxen. Tolls levied on them were a lucrative source of income and the port reeve at Lewes in Sussex, while he received a farthing an oxen sold, received 4d. for every male slave. Slavery was widespread as the evidence of grants of freedom to slaves helps to illustrate. Such manumissions, as they are called, are found in places as far apart as Canterbury, Bath, Exeter, Lichfield and Durham. The numbers involved were quite considerable although they were to show a decline after the Norman Conquest. In Cornwall, 21 per cent of the population were calculated to be slaves as late as 1086, but by then a good deal had been done to reduce their numbers. On Edith's estates at Leominster where, it will be recalled, there were 82 slaves in 1050, there were only 25 in 1086. Similar figures for another estate at Barstable in Essex show a fall from 149 to 90 over a twenty-year period.

c

The Church led opposition to the slave trade, showing once again how considerable the impact of the Church on economic activity might be. Archbishop Theodore forbade Christian burial to kidnappers, and the sale of children over seven by their parents, although the later leader of a campaign against slavery, St Wulfstan of Worcester, found the practice still going on in 1014. Egbert, the first Archbishop of York, excommunicated parents for this practice. Other bishops set an example by freeing slaves they found on their estates. When St Wilfrid became Bishop of Selsey in 681, he freed 250 slaves, and in 786 at the Synod of Chelsea the bishops agreed to free all their slaves. The practice of freeing slaves spread, and found its way into the wills of the laity, although the freedom given was conditional, inasmuch as the owner retained his right to receive wergeld on behalf of his ex-slaves. Clerical opposition and personal philanthropy did not succeed in eliminating slavery. Athelstan, who is recorded by Whitelocke as freeing a slave soon after he became King, was responsible for a harsh law declaring that runaway slaves should be stoned to death and that slaves might carry no weapons.

Since the government was unable to stop the trade, it resorted to regulation in an attempt to improve the lot of the slaves. Moreover, since the Danes recognised thralldom, and England was divided by the treaty of 878, concessions had to be made. In a later treaty with the Danish leader Guthrum in 886, Alfred provided for the repatriation of slaves who had fled across the border, roughly marked by Watling Street. On the other hand, Alfred added four days, when the slave was free to buy and sell, to the traditional holy days when he did not have to labour. Athelstan, possibly worried by the number of slaves who would flee and become outlaws, also made concessions and allowed the slaves to join in the local tithing. Ethelred II's policy was equally equivocal, for while he renewed the treaty about fugitive slaves with the Danes in 994, he reasserted an old law forbidding the sale of slaves to heathens, a provision later repeated by Cnut. The failure to suppress the trade in slaves illustrated very early two important principles. One was that a social evil could not be redressed by voluntary means, particularly if it was tied to an economic interest. The other was that legislation was ineffective in suppressing an economic activity while there was profit to be made, and the learning of both lessons might have forestalled much pointless medieval legislation and economic argument concerning the evil of making a profit and the need for parliamentary and guild control of prices.

None of the ports engaged in the slave trade earned a living by this one import. Bristol, Chester and London were ports in their own right, engaged in a wide variety of trade. Internally, there were problems of communication in Saxon England, but these should not be exaggerated. Some of the Roman roads stayed in common use and there were also networks of hrycgweg or minor roads. Road-building was rare, although Cunningham pointed out the notable exception of the Celtic monks in Scotland, and the enforcement of the *trimoda necessitas* would have barely kept highways in repair. Ferries existed, however, on some of the rivers and those over the Humber at South Fernby and Barton-on-Humber brought in £3 and £4 a year respectively in tolls. Much trade was likely, therefore, to have been carried in light coastal shipping of various kinds. It has already been mentioned that internal trade depended upon chapmen and pedlars who provided luxury items and may have travelled with pack-horses. Humbler items such as salt were, no doubt, also conveyed in this way. Aelfric writing at the end of the tenth century referred to "purple robes and silk, precious stones and gold, rare apparel and spices, wine and oil, ivory and brass, copper and tin, sulphur and glass." Travelling on largely unpoliced roads, it was not surprising that chapmen often found themselves in trouble. In Alfred's laws it stated that "when they had need of more men with them on their journey, let them declare it." Assaults on travellers were common and in about 969 Edgar seems to have punished the inhabitants of the Isle of Thanet severely for an attack on Yorkshire merchants. The problem of protecting traders when localism was so strong was to become more serious during the Middle Ages.

It would be a mistake to imagine that Saxon trade lacked sufficient money, although its distribution and the lack of any form of credit facility strictly limited its use. The number of mints, the level of taxation, the demands of the Church, and the payment of cash rents (gafol) all point to the existence of a proper medium of exchange. Bronze coins or minimi circulated from the fifth century and by about 550, coins from the neighbouring state of Merovingian France, called tremisses, had appeared, and from these developed the first gold coins. Among the earliest identified are those of Penda of Mercia, and there were various regal issues. During the eighth century, a silver coinage replaced the gold one as a more convenient medium of exchange. These sceattas are found from Wisby on the Baltic to Marseilles on the Mediterranean and are good evidence for the widespread nature of Saxon trade. Offa of Mercia introduced a type based on the Frankish designs of the neighbouring realm of Charlemagne and coins of this pattern remained in use throughout the Saxon period. It is significant that when the Danes occupied Northumbria in the late 860s, they replaced the debased bronze pennies with sceattas, which they regarded as the best type of money for trade.

Saxon kings issued trade regulations of various kinds. We have noticed already the law of Athelstan concerning the right of a merchant to become a thegn, the laws regarding witnesses to trade transactions which affected the growth of towns, and the attempts to control and standardise the currency. Whitelocke summarised some of this intervention as follows:

"Kings issue trade regulations of various kinds. They may interfere to forbid the export of certain goods, as when King Athelstan forbids the export of horses and various kings prohibit the sale of men across the sea; they establish prices—a wey of wool is not to be sold at less than 120 pence according to Edgar's law; the same code standardises weights and measures as one observes in London and Winchester; a careful supervision of the mints is maintained; the Church's veto of trading on Sundays and certain festivals is enforced by the secular authorities. Precautions at the ports were necessary to prevent the entry of hostile ships; we know something of the arrangements at Chester, where a ship must await a licence to enter."

Among the most interesting evidences of royal concern with trade are, however, two treaties which concerned themselves with such matters and are the earliest evidence of our commercial relations with other powers. The first of these treaties was between Offa of Mercia and Charlemagne of France in 796. Offa had done much to establish London as a port and was clearly interested in trade. Between England and France there were close contacts, and at least one English merchant, Botta, lived at Marseilles. After a dispute over the quality of English cloaks, the French agreed to protect English merchants if they would not pass themselves off as pilgrims. Links with France grew throughout the ninth century, strengthened by monastic ownership on both sides of the Channel. For example, St Mary of Rouen had estates in Devon, and Lewisham Priory was owned by the monks of Ghent. By Ethelred II's time, we were importing wine and dried fish from Normandy, particularly Rouen, and pepper, tallow and wood from Ponthieu and Flanders.

The other treaty was made by Cnut on a visit to Rome when he secured the right of freedom of import to Englishmen in the Holy See. The treaty was with the Emperor of Germany and was most probably sealed in 1027. There had been trouble over the dues payable by English merchants in the empire and they were settled at £50 of silver, two greyhounds and two fur coats every three years. Cnut secured some reduction in these demands. Our trade with the German region was also quite extensive by the end of the tenth century. By Edgar's time, English wool was reaching the German states. We were receiving pottery, querns for corn-grinding, iron from Liège, glass and wine from the Rhineland, Flanders and the south; while from Baltic shores, furs, timber, oils, skins and eiderdown were brought from Wisby and Lübeck. Through German and north Italian markets, the Saxons also received luxury items such as spices, ivory and silverware from the Byzantine Empire lying round the shores of the Aegean. England's main exports remained those of a primary producer: wool, cloth, hides, greyhounds, cheese, fish and cattle, but these were supplemented by a small export trade in various craft products, noticeably embroidered tapestry, and metal work.

The fundamental reason for the growth of Saxon trade was the need of the isolated village community for materials and articles it could not produce itself and for which it was willing to exchange its small surplus. Three obvious commodities required by every village were salt, iron and wine and in each of these there was accordingly a considerable trade. Although Lipson described the salt industry as "fragmentary" there is considerable evidence of its growth and extent. There were mines at Droitwich in Worcester-shire which, with special tolls of 4d. an ox cart, had developed as a specialised community, with salt pedlars to deliver the commodity. Worcestershire was a region where there were considerable works and a grant of Ethelbald of Mercia in 716–7 refers to three salt "houses" and six furnaces. Kent was an important producing region where Egbert made a grant for some saltworks, which allowed them to take 120 loads of wood from the Andredweald. Most of the southern counties had salt pans. By the time of *Domesday*, there were seventy to eighty "saltmen" in Dorsetshire, and 285 salt-pans in Sussex. The Bishop of Sherborne received a private concession at Lyme Regis from Cynewulf of Wessex. Iron, although it was imported, was produced in Kent and Sussex, particularly around Mayfield, in smaller quantities in Northamptonshire, Lincolnshire and Yorkshire, and, most important of all, in the Forest of Dean. In this region, feorm was quite often rendered in "blooms" of iron, and at Hereford, by Edward the Confessor's reign, six smiths were producing 120 horseshoes a year for the king. Wine, it will be recalled, was largely imported.

Industry did not play a large part in the Saxon economy and was confined to a simple continuation of existing activities and the development of the crafts already mentioned. Milling was important throughout the country and even a county like Dorset had 272 mills. Some towns were milling centres, such as Derby with fourteen mills, and the concentration of large numbers of mills in the eastern counties has already been mentioned. Fishing was important and grew with the rise of Catholic rules of abstinence. The main fisheries were from herrings off the east coast where the catch at Dunwich, Southwold and Yarmouth was 60,000 a year. Further south, Dover, Sandwich and Southease netted 38,500. Eels were particularly important in the eastern fenlands and the town of Wisbech rendered 14,000 eels a year to the Bishop of Ely. Salmon were caught in the Wye, as was mentioned earlier, and the Dee was equally important. Chester once sent the local ealdorman, or royal official, 1,000 salmon a year. Lampreys were found in their thousands around Petersham in Surrey. Pottery was produced at Ipswich, Thetford, Stamford, St Neot's and York, but most other industries were more widely spread geographically. Leather, mentioned in Aelfric's *Colloquy*, was produced in many places, and the clothing industry, it will be recalled, was localised. As to mining, the Saxons were less ambitious than their Roman predecessors. Lead was the only mineral at all extensively mined in the Severn Valley and in Derbyshire. Towards the middle of the eleventh century, a small amount of quarrying had started. This was for millstone in Sussex or Essex, but stone was first starting to come into use as a building material, at least for the towers of churches. One church in Essex is described as being of "stone and lime" and Earl Harold's hall on the Bayeux tapestry is of stone. Building in stone was, however, the exception and Saxon development did not presage the great changes at the end of the eleventh century, when stone replaced wood in important parts of the building industry.

Saxon luxury industries were few, but of exquisite craftsmanship. Such evidence as the famous Alfred Jewel found at Athelney in 1693, or the Sutton Hoo burial ship (*c.* 700) show that, in spite of overall poverty, the Saxons possessed artistic talent even if they lacked certain basic skills. It is noticeable, for example, that their mathematical and surgical instruments were Roman in design, and that, although it possessed certain native features, architectural design was influenced by Celtic and Frankish example. Bede claimed that Benedict Biscop sent for glassmakers "a kind of worker hitherto unknown in Britain," and the request was renewed in 756. Later, Saxon glassware supplemented the normal horn and bone drinking cups. Church vestments were the starting point for the English embroidery industry and Aldhelm referred to this in the eighth century. The most famous example was the Bayeux tapestry, and although other items have perished, wills provide evidence of the existence of other tapestries. Illuminated manuscripts, of which the Lindisfarne Gospels are the most famous, were followed by books, among the earliest of which is the *Book of Cerne* from Lichfield in the early ninth century. Saxons designed large free-standing stone crosses, such as those at Bewcastle and Rothwell on the border, and the more delicate work of the Winchester school in the south. Roods or carved screens in places such as Romsey and Headbourne Worthy in Hampshire suggest a considerable artistic renaissance in the mid eleventh century after Celtic, Carolingian and Danish influences had been absorbed. It is the opinion of modern historians that the Anglo-Saxon Church flourished in the eleventh century, and this necessarily meant the steady creation of a series of craft traditions which were to lie at the basis of the future medieval craft industries.

If the crafts associated with church building underwent a steady improvement, the advance of Saxon architecture is less certain and it may be said that the technique of building large constructions so often associated with the Normans was not within the competence of the Saxons. At a meeting of the Witan or "close royal council" at Calne in Wiltshire in 978 the floor gave way, killing many of the council. Regarded at the time as divine intervention, such a collapse more accurately reflected human error, and it was not surprising that, during Edward the Confessor's reign, Normans brought over their own designers for castles and St Edward chose Frenchmen to build the first Westminster Abbey. Recent excavations at York and Winchester show that the preceding Saxon cathedrals were larger than originally thought, but they are not the products of great engineers and technicians, such as were to build England's medieval cathedrals. The tradition of using foreign masons was an old one. St Augustine brought Italian masons to England and so did St Wilfrid after his Roman visits. Benedict Biscop introduced French craftsmen. The influence of the Roman Church, and the travels of churchmen meant that the native style was influenced by Carolingian, Romanesque and even Byzantine styles. Typical of these wanderings by churchmen were those of Sigebert, Abbot of Sherborne, who was said to have visited Constantinople and India. English missionaries, such as St Boniface in South Germany, also brought foreign influence to bear on church design. Freeman noticed, for example, the similarity of church towers in western Switzerland, the Pyrenees and southern England. The native pride of such Saxon commentators as Wilfrid of Ripon, Acca of Hexham and Ethelwold of Winchester needs to be set against this background of growing continental influence. Even Saxons such as St Wulfstan decided to rebuild on coming into contact with Norman influence, and this circumstance, together with the fact that much Saxon building was wholly in wood or half-timbered, makes it difficult to assess the work involved, or the materials used.

Probably the earliest Saxon buildings to survive are Monkwear-mouth, Escomb and Jarrow in the north (c. 674 onwards), and Bradford-on-Avon church built by St Aldhelm between 675 and 709. Outstanding examples of Saxon churches include Earls Barton in Northamptonshire, Repton in Derbyshire, and a considerable number in the counties of Sussex, Essex and Gloucestershire. The tall, slender, low-spired church at Sompting is very reminiscent of such German examples as Coblenz, and Freeman pointed out that the famous "long and short" design on the tower of Earls Barton may also be seen in the amphitheatre at Verona in Italy. The main features of Saxon architecture were the large stones and heavy walls with small two-lighted windows heavily splayed inside and out, and with a semi-circular top, or even a triangular one. Towers were important, sometimes with open arcading, and often with "long and short" work. These towers continued to be built after the Conquest in such places as St Benet's, Oxford, or St Michael's, Cambridge. The overall plan of the church was normally long, narrow, high and square-ended, although Romanesque influence led St Ethelwold initially to build a rotunda at Abingdon and there was one at St Augustine's, Canterbury.

Stimulation of craft industry, the demand for luxury items, help to the wine and fish trades and a nascent building industry were some measure of the Church's influence on trade. A far more important influence was the Danish invasion and its consequences. In the 1920s and 1930s, a number of historians created something of a stir by asserting that the Danish impact on English society and economy had been underemphasised. The credit for realising this rests, however, with an earlier writer, Green, who spoke of a "social revolution" and "the development of English trade and commerce" as a result of Danish occupation of much of eastern England, and the later conquest by Cnut. Green made the mistake of claiming that it was only a settlement by conquerors rather than a migration, although he argued that the -by, -wick, -fell, -gate, -which, -thorpe, and -thwaite endings to place names indicated "new settlements." Green pointed out that at the time of *Domesday* twenty-three out of twenty-seven landowners in the Cleveland region were Danes and many of the peasants' names were Danish. The impact of the settlers upon agriculture has already been mentioned, and the way in which towns developed apace with the new trade. The Danes lived by the sea either as pirates or traders. Famous Danish rulers, such as St Olav, were partners in trading ventures, and Harold

Fair-Hair's son was known as Bjorn the Merchant. One saga referred to: "King Bjorn [who] had also merchant ships on voyages to other lands, by which he procured himself costly goods and such things as he thought needful, and so his brothers called him, the Freightman and the Merchant." Knowledge of Danish influence is gained from the work of St Godric of Finchale (a monastery in the Wear Valley), who visited Flanders and Denmark, and the writings of Aelfric of Eynsham called the *Colloquies*.

Evidence of the Danish impact may be seen in the growth of towns, particularly York with 2,000 houses and 10,000 inhabitants. The river Humber took its name from the sea god Oegir, and in the city of York the church of St Olav and Guthrum's Gate marked the influence. The five Danish Boroughs of the East Midlands became the centre of a network of fairs and inland ports connected to the Wash and its rivers. All five Danish towns became the centre of shires—Leicester, Lincoln, Stamford, Derby and Nottingham—and the area passed into settled organisation under the Danes. Grimsby grew as a rival port to York and Boston and appeared in a Norse saga in the twelfth century:

> "Unpleasantly we have been wading
> In the mud a weary five weeks;
> Dirt indeed we had in plenty
> While we lay in Grimsby harbour."
> (*The Orkneyinga Saga*)

In East Anglia, which was held by the Danes for the shortest time, this was sufficient to focus attention on the towns of Ipswich with 2,000 inhabitants and Norwich with 6,000 people by the eleventh century. As proof of its Danish connection, Norwich gave as part of its feorm in 1086 "a bear, and six dogs for the bear-baiting."

William of Poitiers commented on the capacity of the Danes for long voyages. Their settlement of Greenland, Iceland and almost certainly the east of America is well known. They developed the Baltic trade and visited Constantinople. Links with Ireland and with Norway and Denmark were strengthened by a people who saw nothing inconsistent in burying in the tomb of a Viking sea-lord his battle-axe and a pair of scales. The extent of imported luxuries by the Danes is even said to have considerably increased the amount of silver, and thereby the trading capacity, of Late Saxon England. Aelfric referred to silver in his list of imports.

Lastly, because the Normans were Northmen veneered with Christianity and feudalism, but more deeply attached to energetic strife on the field of battle, the Danes gave England a new unity

c*

in 1066. This point has been too often laboured. Southern England was united from Alfred's time, and the feudal jurisdictions and turbulent barons did not necessarily make it more united after 1066. Neither before nor after 1066 could a government in London control the north or the west, for administration was paralysed by distance and deference to the local lord. Least of all could it be said that a national economy had yet emerged. By 1066 a considerable number of features, which were to assume greater prominence in medieval times were in existence. Agriculture was organised to produce mainly for self-sufficiency. Industries and crafts were growing steadily and the spread of international trade was about to compel the medieval mind to take notice of the reality of credit and its possibilities. Sizeable towns were appearing. In the country, the manor, and in the town, the guild, had started to grow. All these activities were still local; local customs, wages, rates of feorm or gafol, weights and measures or prices all precluded the idea of a national economy. Government was small and tentative but already there was a rudimentary civil service. Direct taxation was developing. Some statesmen were aware of the need for economic controls of a wide variety of activities from buying and selling wool to buying and selling men. The Saxon economy was neither primitive nor sophisticated. It was the period in which the people adjusted to the new environment and saw, as William the Conqueror saw, that the land could be rich and yet was relatively poor. The Norman Conquest was presented to Europe as a crusade; its excuses were matters of honour and inheritance among princes, but the hope of gain could not have been far from the minds of those who had reached their limits of expansion in French territory. Thus, it might be said that the medieval economy developed during the ninth, tenth and eleventh centuries and the Norman Conquest decided the direction that development should take in common with the rest of feudal Europe. With some exaggeration, H. A. L. Fisher concluded:

"As the island was conquered bit by bit, the properties of the Saxon thegns were dealt out to the hard-headed gentlemen adventurers from abroad. A new French speaking aristocracy, in comparison with their Saxon predecessors most formidable, cruel and versatile, dragooned the wretched peasants to its imperious ends, dominated the countryside, and gave from its imposing castles a new impulsion to the national life. England became once more a province of the Latin world. . . . The Norman Conquest drew England once more into full communion with the inheritors of Rome, with their theology, their architecture, their poetical literature, their law, their social and political organisation, with all that was moving in the Roman Curia or in the law school at Pavia, or among the active monasteries of Normandy, Burgundy and Lorraine. . . . From the soil of the plundered country vast cathedrals rose to the heavens, erected by the labour of a subject peasantry."

The Normans were the catalyst, through their organisations and influence, which systematised and cosmopolitanised the weak and growing Saxon economic and social pattern and made it the basis of the medieval economy.

CHAPTER 4

THE ENVIRONMENT, CHARACTERISTICS AND ANALYSIS OF THE MEDIEVAL ECONOMY

THEORIES, TERMS, RECORDS AND STATISTICS

As long ago as 1882, Cunningham said that "the period of feudalism was not so stagnant as the nature of the system might have led us to suspect," but even today there are still some writers who argue that the basic characteristic of a period of nearly 400 years was "stagnation." Any study of the medieval period needs to start by clearing out the way certain misconceptions which have hampered an appreciation of an economy as subject to change under the influence of economic laws as any other. In one sense, there was no such thing as the medieval economy since it evolved from the Saxon antecedents already described and changed almost as imperceptibly into the mercantilist era of the Tudors. Although, for political historians, the Middle Ages may be safely defined as lasting from William I to Henry VII, this has not much relevance for the economic historian. He is concerned with the concept of economic growth which comes about slowly. The Norman Conquest or the accession of Henry VII do not mark economic changes, but merely change the framework within which the basic requirements of demand and supply are met. This is true equally during the course of the Middle Ages. Events such as the Black Death in 1348–50 may well have had immediate short-term economic consequences, but they serve also to accelerate or retard underlying economic changes, not to cause them. Economic change is piecemeal, closely following alterations in supply and demand. People produce for necessity or profit not according to a particular "system." In studying the Middle Ages, it is far too easy to speak of a feudal, manorial or guild system, and seek to incorporate the known facts within this framework. It has already been shown, in the cases of the manor and the guild, that variety rather than conformity was the keynote of development.

Consider as an example the medieval village communities where the majority of the population worked. Although the aim of production was primarily self-sufficiency, this did not prevent production of a surplus to export, or the need for trade to import all manner of commodities into the village. By the thirteenth century, led by the example of the very Church that opposed in theory the profit motive, many estates were being specifically exploited for profit. Villages were not isolated by poor communications. Jusserand long ago discussed the numbers of travellers on medieval roads and the Gough map of the fourteenth century shows a network of roads. Neither difficulties of communications nor the difficulties arising from outlaws and war had the effect of restricting trade in the way they were once thought to do. The Wars of the Roses, for example, involved armies at the most of about 30,000 men, and did far less damage to the economy than seems likely at first. Although the Church and to some extent other organisations, including the government and the guilds, opposed the profit motive, credit was available and widely utilised throughout the Middle Ages, and there was no such development as that of a money economy. It has been pointed out that, in the smallest villages, rents in cash, payments to the Church and feudal obligations were discharged in money. Although the majority of the people were agricultural labourers, this did not mean they were necessarily impoverished serfs. Many of them possessed, and later came to own, land and make a profit for themselves. Domestic industry was widespread and provided an additional source of income. Even if the methods of agricultural production were customary, inefficient and slow to change, they provided well enough for a smaller population. The existence of twelve to fifteen corn markets, corn dealers and corn carting services all "conflict with the generalisations commonly made as to the isolation and self-sufficing character of the old English village."

Each manor was different, and in each the pace of change was different. There were common characteristics which make it possible to generalise, but always with the proviso that every place and time produced varied economic responses. Methods of farming changed. Three fields rather than two fields became general, and enclosure developed. The area under cultivation changed with shifting population, the decay of tillage and the constant medieval attack on the waste by one means of enclosure or another. Methods of holding land altered with the constant growth of money rents, the consolidation of lords' demesnes and then of villeins' holdings and the appearance by the fourteenth century of copyholders and leaseholders. To suggest, therefore, as Seddon has, that "the complete acceptance of customary practice implied stagnation" is by no means to give a fair account of agricultural change in the Middle Ages.

Medieval towns were small. Early in the fourteenth century there were only forty with a population over a thousand, but this must not be taken as an indication of urban insignificance. *Domesday* showed 12 per cent of the people in towns which is slightly more than the number who nowadays live in the country, but it was significant that 20 per cent were engaged in industry which was diversified and domestic as well as town-based during the Middle Ages. Because of the overall limitation of the total population, towns of a smaller size were capable of exercising considerable influence particularly as they were jealous of their privileges. Towns with their local jealousies and guilds with their elaborate restrictions were, however, also necessary for the protection and regulation of a growing volume of trade. The local market was of prime importance and merely because it did not always embrace national proportions, its economic significance was not thereby reduced. The rise of the merchants' power as an estate of the realm, the steadily developing credit facilities and merchant class, and the increasing privileges of towns and guilds—all reflected the steady rise of trade requiring handling and capable of maintaining increasingly concentrated populations. In this connection, the larger churches and monasteries and some of the castles had the same economic influence on surrounding communities as towns because they set up new sources of demand by populations not directly engaged in agriculture. Change was slow in medieval times because population was small and did not often bring pressure to bear on resources other than agricultural land. The standard of living for the majority was low even if they were not penniless. Nevertheless, industry and mining made considerable technical progress in the medieval period. The rise of the cloth industry involving the spread of fulling-mills, the replacement of the distaff with the spinning-wheel, and the organisation of domestic production and the export facilities of the clothiers showed that change was as apparent in industry as in agriculture. The building industry with its technical improvements, the substitution of stone for wood, the development of the use of bricks, and the heavy capitalisation involved in cathedrals and castles might serve as another example. Merely because medieval and other industrialists and technicians were slow and organisationally simple, this does not mean that they were without the means for making changes.

Internal trade was matched by international enterprise. Although it is better to visualise medieval trade as between individual merchants and towns rather than between countries, the international nature of feudal society and the cosmopolitan influence of the Church meant that European trade flourished. The part played by aliens in the medieval economy was of major importance. Normans and Flemings, the settlements of Jews and Hanseatic merchants, and the activities of German and Italian bankers all affected the English economy. Our French possessions involved us during most of the Middle Ages in costly wars, but they brought with them the trade of northern and western France to which England was linked for long periods by common allegiance or by her conquests. English banking and shipping were in the hands of foreigners to an overwhelming extent until the late fourteenth century, and it might be argued that mecantilism contracted rather than expanded the international nature of trade from then onwards. Government supervision of trade for the purposes of revenue, to protect merchants or to influence political decisions was common throughout the Middle Ages and was not, as Cunningham argued, a deliberate policy started by Edward III.

Anxiety to systematise and simplify these complicated developments may be partly due to the lack of information on the medieval economy in past years, or to the mistaken assumption that medieval economic theories and practice coincided. It is also very easy to misinterpret the information we have. The most simple danger is forgery, which was not considered improper in the Middle Ages. Town charters and monastic deeds are obvious places for this to occur and it is on town and monastic records that so much economic information is based. Nor were medieval writers particularly concerned over the accuracy of figures. Deaths in battles or in plagues might be taken as an example, or the accounts given of depopulated villages as a result of enclosure for sheep farming. Units of measurement were not standardised in spite of attempts like those of 1197–8 and 1215. Thus, statutes relating to cloth sizes in 1465 and 1484 present the interpreter with an insuperable problem of arriving at the precise size of a "broadcloth." This has meant that Carus-Wilson has challenged statistics of the cloth trade, England's most important industry which have been based on the aulnage reports of government inspectors. Recently Bridbury has argued in favour of the relative accuracy of the aulnage accounts at least in the reign of Richard II. Even if the problem of the aulnage figures is resolved and we can have reasonably accurate figures for cloth exports, there are still no figures for total cloth production as domestic consumption remains unknown.

Customary valuations play an important part in adding to

difficulties. Custom duties were assessed at one date and remained unchanged, while the value of money altered considerably. In the countryside the real value of a holding might easily be concealed behind a customary rent or other payment. This was particularly true where services in the fields had been commuted for a money payment. Statutes and the restrictions of legal terminology quickly blind the reader to the immense variety of local practice. Statutes of the realm were far more announcements of intentions and declarations of ideal states of affairs than accurate reflections of economic reality. Words used by lawyers, writing in Latin, such as *manerium* or *villanus* were blanket-terms often later translated invariably as "manor" or "villein," and leading to too great an assumption of uniformity in economic matters. Other words, such as acre, hide, hundred or virgate, which imply a specific measurement, were in reality vague terms. The virgate may have been 30 acres in many cases, but it varied from 8 to 60 acres, and that variation is sufficient to include a number of different types of holding. Some medieval words mean the opposite of what they imply at first. *Libertas* were not liberties but privileges of freemen or barons, not the birth-rights of ordinary men and women. Words such as *communitas* have no exact translation and need most careful interpretation. It is easy to see how a careless or too comprehensive reading of evidence with as many pitfalls as this has led to arguments about medieval economic history, which might with a little care have been avoided. Nowadays historians are more aware of the problems and they are prepared to admit the large gaps in their knowledge, but as long as the gaps remain, the differences of interpretation will be many as attempts are made to assess small amounts of statistical material.

Information on medieval economic development is derived in the main from records, remains or writings which were not written by economists. There were writers on economic matters, and a host of Church theorists, but their works contain little to help build up a general picture. Archaeology and the associated work of the historical geographer provide some of the most interesting evidence. Beresford and Joseph have carried out an aerial survey of the country to discover the remains of medieval life and found a surprising amount of evidence. Beresford has made a careful study of the shifting pattern of villages in the Middle Ages. Other geographer historians have tackled medieval town planning, or the drainage of the Fens. Darby's *Historical Geography of England before 1800*, produced in 1951, was a model for such studies. There are also literary sources. Poetry supplies some interesting examples, such as a lengthy poem by Thomas Deloney on a clothmaking factory at Winchcombe, ballads relating to Robin Hood and the causes of social unrest, and poems of more considerable merit, such as Langland's *Piers Plowman*, or Chaucer's Prologue to the *Canterbury Tales*. Even writers on specific economic topics resorted to verse, of which Adam de Moleyn's (Bishop of Chichester), *Libel of English Policy* (*c.* 1436) is perhaps the most important. Chroniclers mixed accounts of national events with legend and details of local events. By far the most famous chronicles are monastic. St Alban's, the richest abbey in England, kept a chronicle from the time of Roger of Wendover (*c.* 1200) to that of Thomas of Walsingham (*c.* 1450). There were also lay chroniclers, the most famous of whom is Froissart, who wrote in the middle of the fourteenth century. Letters from the fifteenth century provide another readable source. Those of the Paston family, who rose from humble yeoman status in Richard II's reign to provide a Justice of the Common Pleas in Henry VI's time, are the most famous together with the Stonor letters. The Cely papers giving details of the activities of a clothier in the same period are also of great importance.

However, the bulk of information comes from records. National records are abundant. Some of them such as *Domesday Book* (1086) or the *Hundred Rolls* (1274) and *Extenta Manerii* (1275) are unique. Year in year out, great series of records were enrolled and the Rolls Series provides an invaluable record, from which Jusserand, for example, drew much information on economic affairs. Exchequer records are, of course, of particular importance as are the yearbooks of courts and the customs rolls form other important collections, together with the statutes of the realm and the parliamentary rolls. None of these records make for entertaining work, but from them an enormous amount of miscellaneous information may be obtained. This was demonstrated when Thorold Rogers composed his massive works on prices and wages in 1866 and 1890, which still remain the major works on these subjects. Local records, however, are of equal if not greater importance. They fall into three main categories, church, borough and manor records. Bishops and abbots were administrators of the largest and most efficient estates in the country and left behind them detailed records. Thus, the estates of the Bishop of Winchester or of the Abbey of St Augustine's at Canterbury provide much information. Church estates were not, however, typical of lay practice and generalisations have been drawn too often from their isolated example. Studies have now turned to individual manors, anticipated by Davenport's study of the manor in Forncett in Norfolk in 1906. From manor court and honorial court records much information can be obtained, and to these court rolls should be added records of property, such as wills, charters, writs, cartularies and registers, and manorial and household accounts. Special surveys and *inquisitiones post mortem* also yield information. Borough records include the customs accounts, the town records and the records of the various guilds.

Medieval economic history is not to be regarded as the fixed residuum of a number of systems remaining largely unchanged for many years. Economic development continued to reflect the laws of supply and demand rather than those of the Church, and there was an enormous difference between pronouncements of Parliaments or priests on economic matters and everyday practice. Limitations in the scope of sources prevent us from forming a complete picture of the medieval economy. To the extent that the overdrawn pictures of "Merrie England" or medieval "stagnation" must give way to a more tentative drawing, this is to the good. The medieval economy was too localised and divided to present other than a rather confusing pattern, but this is only made worse by trying to discern economic policies or systems, and then being forced to admit numerous exceptions to each of them. Statistics can help us, but they are still piecemeal and extracted from records written for other purposes than the recording of economic activity. The medieval economy was more concerned with the estate than the state. Foreigners were those from a neighbouring town or even a rival guild. Thus, it is possible to be reasonably precise about local economic conditions; less so about the national situation.

Although the political, social and religious structure of society was quite different from today, and the economy still in a fairly embryonic state, it was growing in economic terms. There were periods of expansion and depression. Prices and wages rose and fell. Credit dealings, commercial organisation and operations expanded as population and wealth increased. Local markets were of key importance. Self-sufficiency in a land menaced by famine was the main concern, but production in agriculture and industry of a surplus for profit and international trade was as much a feature of the medieval economy as the circulation of money and the accumulation of capital at all levels of society. The essentially capitalist nature of economic activity in the Middle Ages is strongly urged by Postan, and many historians have agreed with him. It was as much an era of competition as of co-operation. Wingfield-Stratford said as long ago as 1928 that by the middle of the fourteenth century "the capitalist had come to stay." He went on to discuss the replacement of foreign bankers by English financiers, including Walter de Cheriton, who financed the French wars at the time of

Crécy, and the rise of the de la Poles, merchants of Hull. Certainly the suggestion that the Middle Ages saw the development of capitalism has important consequences for the well-known argument about the Protestant religion and the rise of capitalism in the sixteenth century. Perhaps it is time that this myth, like that of the one of the money economy in the thirteenth century, is repudiated, and it is realised that market forces controlled barons, bishops, abbots, villeins and wool-broggers as much as they do present-day economic experts, planners and Treasury officials.

THE ECONOMIC VIEWPOINT OF THE MIDDLE AGES AND THE THEORIES OF THE CHURCH

The sources from which our knowledge of medieval economic history are drawn, it has been emphasised, are in the main not specifically economic documents. The Middle Ages, however, provided the first examples of writings specifically concerned with economic matters. These fall into a number of different groups. *Domesday Book* is unique and will be dealt with separately. The information provided therein about the economy of the later eleventh century is of immense importance. One other work stands by itself, and this is the *Dialogus de Scaccario*, written in 1177 by Richard Fitzneal, Treasurer under Henry II. This work has a three-fold importance. It gives an account of the working of the Exchequer, which was the main government financial department. It enables an assessment to be made of the sources of royal income, particularly the feudal incidents. Finally, it gives a survey of financial resources at a time when the Crown was about to resort to taxes on moveables as it found the traditional revenues inadequate.

Domesday Book was written by clerks working in the larger monasteries. Fitzneal was the illegitimate son of a Bishop of Ely, who rose to office as a clerk. It is not surprising that, in an age when literacy was largely confined to churchmen, they should produce many of the practical as well as the theoretical economic works. That they did so is a further indication of the immensely important role of the Church in the economy. In the fourteenth century there appeared a number of works connected with finance. Walter of Bardes, Comptroller of the Mint, wrote about the Exchequer in a period when it was declining, and also drew attention to the problem of maintaining the value of coins. His *Tractatus Novae Monetae* was the forerunner of a more important work by Nicholas Oresme, Bishop of Lisieux. This was *De Mutatione Monetarum*, written in 1373, and later translated into English. In this work a number of important monetary points are discussed. Oresme distinguished between ordinary or "artificial" wealth and real wealth. He advocated bimetallism, that is the use of both silver and gold for the currency standard, although he failed to decide the ratio of values between them. In particular, Oresme attacked the idea of devaluation or, as it was then known, debasement of the coinage, which had been used by Edward III to raise money quickly. This would only have the effect of making people hoard "good" money and upsetting international trade, according to Oresme.

Concern over the supply of money seems to have been one of the roots of mercantilism. Cunningham pointed out that this concept evolved during the fifteenth century and although the full implications will be discussed later, it is important to notice evidence for the medieval origins of what became the prevailing economic sentiment of Tudor and Stuart times. Pressures on the English economy, resulting from the prolonged wars with France, coupled with defeats to weaken our trading position and to encourage pessimists to criticise our economic strength. The most famous of these pessimists was Moleyns, but there is other evidence that the views expressed there were gaining ground. A petition to Parliament in 1444 complaining about the weaknesses of English shipping; the Yorkist pamphlet *Of England's Commercial Policy* (1452); a work called *The Debate of the Heralds*; and Sir John Fortescue's *Commodities of England*; all argued a similar case. This was in favour of national self-sufficiency in terms of treasure and food supply, necessitating control over shipping, and particularly the carrying trade. Thus, by the end of the Middle Ages, financial writings had given way to what might fairly be described as a consensus of opinion in favour of a particular economic policy.

Better known than these early financial works are those dealing with agriculture. The most important work was Walter of Henley's *Treatise on Husbandry*. Henley was a Dominican friar who wrote between 1230 and 1250 in French. This work was translated later into Latin and English and remained in use until it was replaced by Sir Anthony Fitzherbert's *Book of Husbandry* in the 1520s. Henley's work is important because his descriptions give valuable clues as to the nature of agricultural development by the thirteenth century. His advocacy of three-field instead of two-field production and of rents instead of labour services very much reflected a period of agricultural expansion. There were many lesser works, written by such men as Robert Grosseeste, Bishop of Lincoln, who gave the Countess of Lincoln twenty-eight practical maxims for running an estate. This is an interesting work as it is one of the earliest household books dealing with the running of an honour. One of the most famous of these was the Earl of Northumberland's *Household Book* for 1512. During the Middle Ages, the earlier work of Palladius on fruit farming was translated by a Colchester monk and formed the basis for the *Treatise of Planting and Grafting of Trees*. Another clergyman, Sir Richard de Benese, a canon of Merton, produced one of the earliest works on surveying: *The Book of Measuring Land* (1537). That the Church should take the lead in writing on agricultural matters was not surprising when the extent and efficiency of their estates is realised. The earliest set of continuous estate accounts start on Church lands at Winchester in 1208–9, and the Church early favoured double-entry bookkeeping.

On the other hand, the Church put out another set of economic works during the Middle Ages based upon different principles from their profitable agricultural and financial pursuits. The doctrines of the Church on economic matters were derived from many sources, but the principal one was the work of Aristotle and its later amplification by Thomas Aquinas. The fundamental idea was that money was a fungible good, that is to say, it was destroyed when it was exchanged and possessed no value in itself. Saving and taking interest were therefore wrong. This was defined in the Lateran Council of 1175 and re-affirmed at the Councils of Lyons (1274) and Vienne (1312). Aristotle put it this way: "Others maintain that coined money is a mere sham, a thing not natural, but conventional only, which would have no value or use for any of the purposes of daily life if another commodity were substituted by the users." Thus, as Aquinas maintained, "pecunia non parit pecuniam." These views were supported by the views of some of the early fathers of the Church, such as St Jerome. It is important to realise that this view of money as a fungible good, and not a strict interpretation of Christ's teaching concerning money, lay at the root of the Church's theory. Later writers have sometimes contrasted too favourably a non-materialistic, almost communistic, society placing little emphasis on money with the bankers and land speculators of post-Reformation times. Christ's views of holding property in common (Acts 2, 44–5), and surrendering private property (Acts 4, 37) lay at the basis of the monastic vows of poverty, and were not part of the doctrine, although in the condemnation of using money for a profit (Acts 5, 1–4) there was a measure of similarity.

To what extent was the theory that the taking of interest was immoral put into practice? The traditional view was that it was

regularly enforced, and that this helped to restrict usury, and led
to the establishment of the Jews as an international non-Christian
group specialising in credit dealings, until the breakdown of Papal
power early in the sixteenth century allowed credit dealings to
become widespread. Lady Stenton once said that "a few Christians
defied the Church and engaged in the trade, but they were not to
be found, like the Jews, in every town. Even in small towns, like
Windsor, where there was no permanent Jewry individual Jews
attended." Glanville, the twelfth-century lawyer, referred to laws
against usury and in certain cases, such as that of Ralph Corn-
waille in 1377, they were enforced. These laws were renewed under
the Tudors and, although a bill to abolish them was introduced in
1571, it was not until the ending of the Church court's authority
in 1641 that all prosecutions stopped. Practice seems to have differed widely from precept. Even in the twelfth century there is
evidence of a native credit class, including a financier like William
Cade, and during the next century this class continued to grow.
The view of Cunningham that "dealing for credit was little developed and dealing in credit was unknown" has now been replaced
by the view of Postan that "sale credits . . . in reality formed the
financial basis of medieval trade," and this point will be discussed
in detail in a later chapter. The Church itself needed money and
went to the Jews for it. Carlyle's famous account of Abbot Sampson
of Bury St Edmunds (1182) shows that he borrowed from the Jews,
and even the Pope was forced, according to Lipson, to contravene
the law of the Church on usury. Lady Stenton's claim that the Jews
alone handled credit in the twelfth and thirteenth centuries is wide
of the mark. Both the Flemings and the Italians were active by the
time of Richard I, and in England, improving landlords, and early
industrialists, used to deal freely in credit, giving interest and
making a profit. What possibly gave the Jews a more prominent
role was their relatively small numbers. They were compelled to
charge high rates of interest, amounting to 43 per cent, because
they were often the subject of persecution or repudiation of debts.
However, this was not exceptionally high as the ordinary rate of
interest charged at the French fairs reached 40 per cent in wartime
conditions. In England they obtained a privileged position as collectors of money and givers of credit to the Crown. They were
allowed their own laws and schools and synagogues in special
ghettos or Jewrys. The Jews were given specific royal protection
from 1194, and a special Exchequer of the Jews grew up. Forced
by the Crown to give large sums of money in return for this protection, the Jews ceased to have much value for ordinary merchants,
and they were eventually expelled in large numbers in 1290.

, By 1255, when they were used as the collateral for Richard of Cornwall, the Jewish community was worth only 5,000 marks.

Persecution was often the lot of medieval Jews, and in some cases this was activated by a desire to destroy records of debts incurred. They were often rich men, for one Jew was able to finance Strongbow's expedition to conquer Ireland in 1170. Certain Jews were very wealthy, such as Aaron of Lincoln, his son Elias; Josce of York (*d.* 1190), his son Aaron; and Jurnet of Norwich and his two sons. This wealth aroused resentment and gave rise to rumours and racial prejudice To this was added the teachings of the Catholic Church concerning the responsibility of the Jews for Christ's death. Schools for the conversion of Jews developed by Innocent III between 1205 and 1215 were set up, one on the site of the present Public Record Office in London and another in Bristol. If conversion failed, persecution was tried. In 1218 Jews were compelled to wear a distinguishing mark by Archbishop Langton. When a deacon married a Jewess in 1222, he was burnt to death by order of a church meeting at Osney-by-Oxford and a Jew was burnt for blasphemy in 1274. Accusations of coin clipping and ritual murder were added to the charge of being extortioners. As early as 1144, Jews in Norwich were accused of murdering a Christian boy by Thomas of Monmouth, a monk. It was even said that the earliest stone houses in England at Lincoln were built by Jews to protect themselves from the mob. Sometimes even stone walls did not protect them from prejudice. In 1256 the death of a child in Lincoln led to the execution of eighteen Jews and the imprisonment of seventy-three others. Jewish pogroms were initiated by Richard I in London during 1189 and by 1190 they had spread to Bury St Edmunds, Thetford, Norwich, King's Lynn, Stamford, Lincoln and York. Jews were accused of hoarding money needed for the Third Crusade, although they had already contributed a quarter of their moveables (a tax on personal property). Another medieval hero, Simon de Montfort, permitted similar outrages in 1265.

Jealousy and suspicion were added to religious prejudice and greed. The Jews made a considerable contribution to the development of medicine, and to literature, Lady Stenton draws attention to one particular family where Moses of London and his son Elias wrote important works of scholarship. But once the Jews had outlived their financial usefulness they were expelled. This particular move was made by another distinguished medieval king, Edward I. Pressed by the merchant community, Edward passed the Statute de la Jeuerie (1275) which allowed the Jews to charge 43 per cent for only three years, and imposed a poll tax of 3*d*. or 4*d*. on all Jews. It also forbade them to obtain more than half a man's chattels in recovery of a debt. The policy was part of a wider one including the Statute of Acton Burnell (1284) and De Falsa Moneta (1299) designed to protect the mechant community, but it had the effect of further weakening the Jews' usefulness. Severe penalties for coin clipping enacted in 1279 were also aimed at the Jews and 293 Jews were executed in London. Finally, in 1290 some 16,000 Jews were expelled from the country after being ruined by the heavy poll tax raised for the war in Gascony in 1286. This was accomplished with a good deal of barbarity but, as Roth has shown, did not lead to their complete removal. In 1282 synagogues were closed in Canterbury Province. In 1286 Honorius IV told the Archbishops it was wrong to allow them to remain in the country, and in 1287 Jewish physicians were forbidden to practise. They fled to France where, between 1306 and 1321 they were accused of spreading leprosy and forced to leave. Later in the fourteenth century, those Jews who had fled to Germany were accused of causing the Black Death, and they fled eastwards again—to Poland. Christian religious and financial prejudice had initiated a major and shameful theme of European development.

Another doctrine of the Church which met with the support of lay authorities for different reasons and had, therefore, a considerable impact, was that of the just price. King-Hall once said: "The price system of the economic world is at the centre of its being. It has been compared—but the comparison is incomplete—to the nervous system of the human body in so much as movements of prices indicate changes in economic conditions." Prices are ultimately determined by supply and demand in the operation of the market. In this way they may be determined unfairly to one part of the community or another, but any attempt to impose price levels related to other criteria must fail. This is what the Church and, to a certain extent, the government and guilds tried to do in the Middle Ages, and they failed. The slow rise of medieval prices was due to the rate of growth, not the operation of the doctrine of the just price. The idea of a just price evolved from the medieval acceptance of a law of natural justice, which supplies an ideal standard by which the equity of particular relations can be measured. The practical implication was that every commercial activity might be judged by a rule of right, independent of economic circumstances. Not to do so was to interfere with the operation of a Christian society, so that, in the words of John Wycliffe, "both men of law and merchants and chapmen and victuallers sin more in avarice than do poor labourers and this token thereof; for now be they poor, and now be they full rich, for wrongs that they [have] done." Tawney summarised the view of Aquinas on the matter of the just price as follows: "That prices, though they will vary with the varying conditions of different markets, should correspond with the labour and costs of the producer, as the proper basis of the communis estimatio, conformity with which was the safeguard against extortion."

If this viewpoint was firmly enforced, it meant that normal commercial practice would be at a standstill, and it is important to realise that prosecutions were in ecclesiastical not civil courts. Ordinary commercial practices were carried on in spite of opposition; the most common being engrossing, forestalling and regrating. Engrossing was cornering the market in view of impending shortage, forestalling was selling at a different price from the one prevailing to make a profit by, for example, selling more at a cheaper price, and regrating was buying wholesale and selling retail at widely different prices. Closely coupled with these activities were the giving of false measures by buying at one measure and selling at another; or by practising the usual commercial stratagems of false description and adulteration. Government legislation such as that of 1197, 1215, 1340 and 1361 was largely ineffective, and it was left to the local guilds to determine price and quality. This was one of their most important functions. With the rise of prices, including wages, in the fourteenth century, the government developed from 1350 a complicated series of measures to regulate prices and wages because the security of the realm was menaced, rather than because the natural order was being upset.

One other offshoot of the Church's views calls for some attention: the doctrine of the superfluum. Theologians justified the individual holding of property because men would waste communal property and be unable to divide it equitably among themselves. It was right for a man to seek such wealth as was necessary for a livelihood, but to do more was to be guilty of avarice, one of the deadly sins. Therefore, it followed, that holding property was a form of stewardship. Riches, as St Antoninio said, exist for man and not man for riches. Charity was enjoined on all men and the wills of medieval laymen included more than conventional distribution of wealth. It was a moral duty, but unfortunately one which was often broken. The most famous example was the acquisition of vast wealth by the higher clergy which so aroused the opposition of John Wycliffe. The Church was often paradoxically the recipient of the layman's surplus wealth, and Wycliffe's solution was even more paradoxical—to return the lands and wealth to secular ownership, a form of disendownment. His arguments are contained in

De Dominio Civili, written in the 1360s. A Papal Bull in 1377 compared Wycliffe with the well-known humanist Marsiglio of Padua, who had urged that the Church should be for social good and not for economic gain. Tawney pointed out a case in France where a usurer, on consulting the Bishop of Paris about his surplus wealth, was advised to spend it on the building of Notre-Dame. The chapter of the cathedral was, incidentally, lending money with interest at the time. By the fifteenth century, in the words of Wingfield-Stratford, "chantry chapels, opulent of detail and colouring were available for those whose means might run to some remission of a sentence in purgatory, or for devout guildsmen." In such cases the moral obligation was turned upside down.

Church doctrines were impracticable and they were defied by the Church as much as anyone. On the one side they came close to a primitive communism like that in the writings of Gratian: "communis enim usus omnium quae sunt in hoc mundo, omnibus hominibus esse debuit." There was little difference here from the preaching of radical friars like John Ball, who said "my good friends, matters cannot go on well in England until all things shall be in common." In popular rhymes the rich were consigned to Hell:

> "Rise up, rise up, brother Dives
> And go with us to see
> A dismal place, prepared in Hell
> To sit on a serpent's knee."

But the reality was otherwise. The Church itself was a capitalist institution and the forces of the market were stronger than the threat of Hell. Any attempt to confine usury to the Jews failed before Christian anxiety to make a profit. The gap between the communal Christ-like life of many medieval scholars, aesthetics and friars, and the activities of guilds and fairs was too great for one to much influence the other. The desire to serve God by glorifying Him in stone, glass, silver, metalwork and cloth was greater than the will to humbly serve him in sackcloth and ashes. The contemplation of a medieval cathedral brings this paradox very much to life.

POPULATION AND THE CHANGING ENVIRONMENT

The mainspring of economic development is demand, and this is produced to a large extent by the rise in population. Provided resources expand sufficiently to meet that demand, a rising standard of living will ensue with higher wages, although the distribution of this increased personal income will depend upon the social structure of the time. During the Middle Ages the rate of population growth was slow in comparison with the period from the sixteenth century onwards. At Taunton between 1209 and 1348, which were the years of high achievement for the medieval economy, the growth rate was 0·85 per cent per annum. Some places experienced a more rapid rate of growth, such as towns with changes in the amount of their trade, or very fertile lands brought quickly into cultivation. Thus, some fenland villages grew between 1086 and 1260 by as much as an eightfold increase. Unfortunately the mobile nature of parts of the population may have led to double counting and it is very difficult to give an estimate of the percentage increase for a whole county. Relying on even less trustworthy figures for the total population, Coulton suggested an increase of 0·147 per cent a year, which meant that it would take a village nearly seven years to raise its population from 300 to 301.

Estimates of the total population were based until recently on the work of Russell. His estimates were in turn based on *Domesday Book* and poll tax returns, and he suggested that the population rose from 1·75 million in 1086 to 3·5 million by the 1340s, and then, following the Black Death, fell to 2·25 million by 1377. But Russell's figures have been questioned. His *Domesday* numbers were based on the assumption that heads of households (between 280,000 and 290,000) multiplied by a figure of 3·6 would give the approximate population. It has been suggested that a figure of 5 might be more appropriate, and this would mean almost a 50 per cent increase in the total. Russell's poll tax figures have also been questioned in view of the evasion of poll tax by about 25 per cent of the population. Moreover, the claim that the Black Death was the beginning of the period of declining population is no longer accepted. Population was falling from early in the fourteenth century, and this fact together with the high mortality of the Black Death of 1348–50 suggest that the earlier expansion of population was considerably greater over a shorter period of time. Following the Black Death, there were frequent serious plagues, and if these and the normally high mortality rate (seventy to seventy-five per thousand) are taken into account, the capacity of the medieval population to renew itself was considerable. In 1938 Coulton suggested populations of 2·5 million at the Conquest and 5 million by Henry VII's death, and more recently Postan has suggested that "higher estimates may well appear to be more consistent with the economic and social conditions . . . at the end of the thirteenth century." Pressure on resources of land and labour during this period was so great that it could scarcely be met, and this was due in part to a sharp rise in population when a high death-rate and a higher birth-rate went hand in hand.

Although the total population, even on the highest estimate, did not exceed 5 million, its distribution meant that pressure on resources, and the growth of urban and, more important, semi-urban regions was greater than might at first be supposed. Over much of the country there was a very low population density. In the west, counties such as Shropshire, or in the north, one like Lancashire were thinly peopled. A figure of 2·5 persons per square mile has been given as the average density of population in the upland region, although some places reached 10 per square mile. That such a figure is not too extreme is illlustrated by the fact that Cheshire had only seventy-five medieval parishes. In the east and south matters were different. Villages averaged in size over a hundred inhabitants. Forty places had over a thousand inhabitants by the beginning of the fourteenth century. A density of population amounting to 40 to 50 per square mile has been suggested for this region, and may be an underestimate. Pressures to produce a surplus, to develop the best agricultural methods, or to employ the available labour in auxiliary industries were all actively at work. Parishes in the east and south were small and many, and *Domesday* surveyors in Kent even missed some of them. Many areas which were legally speaking not towns but villages had sizeable populations equivalent to those of a fair-sized town. In the fifteenth century, for example, while some towns experienced decline in population and industrial activity, places like Stroudwater, Lavenham and Hadleigh developed as "industrial villages."

Asessments of total population and its distribution are made particularly difficult by the mobility of settlement in the Middle Ages. This was produced in many ways, of which assarting the forest and inning the fens were the most notable; and the shifting of population on the coasts in response to silting and the alteration of river courses were perhaps, the most dramatic movements. Between 1100 and 1300, over one hundred places attained the rank of a town, all reflecting internal growth and migration from surrounding villages. Since towns were often dependent on a staple or single commodity, their population could fluctuate violently. Deliberate policies of re-settlement were initiated, of which the creation of the new town of Salisbury in the 1220s was the most famous. Such re-settlements were also carried out in the country-side as the movement of people from the traditional upland wold farming of Yorkshire into the Vales of Pickering and York in the 1070s indicated. Impoverishment of soil, the outbreak of plague, an alteration in ownership, or a change from arable to pastoral farming—all brought about the extinction of village sites and the creation of new ones, and, as Beresford said, "the medieval landscape was in perpetual dissolution." In Norfolk, for example, of the 726 settlements mentioned in *Domesday Book*, compared with a survey made in 1316, 70 new ones have appeared, 69 mentioned in 1086 are not mentioned in 1316 although they still existed, and 35 had already disappeared and were never mentioned again. Where land marginally useful for arable farming had been brought into use, it was liable, either because of declining usefulness or because it was turned over to sheep rearing, to experience a fall in population such as that in Devon and Cornwall during the fifteenth century. Thus, while the margin of cultivation was thrust forward at one point, it fell back at another, and there can be little doubt that less land was being cultivated for arable farming at the end of the Middle Ages than at the beginning.

All agriculturally based communities have not experienced such a slowly rising population. Ireland in the eighteenth century or India in the late nineteenth century might be given as pertinent examples. Ireland was Roman Catholic, as England was in the Middle Ages, and the views of that Church carried great weight in the two countries at the two different times. India was subjected to periodic epidemics and serious famines, such as those experienced in medieval Europe. Thus, Ireland and India suggest that neither the prevalent morality of Roman Catholicism, nor the sudden devastation and long-term debilitation of the population by plague and famine is likely to explain, by itself, the low rate of growth. Yet both of them may help to explain the matter. If the average village contained some 300 people, that is some 60–70 families, and there was strict control and considerable difficulty placed in the way of leaving a village, then marriage outside the prohibited degrees of consanguinity must have been difficult. Until 1215 it was forbidden to the seventh degree; after the Lateran Council of that year, to the fourth degree. The stigma of illegitimacy, the fine (leyrwite) for illegitimate children taken by the manor court, and the tendency towards abortion or flight and subsequent possible death must have been strengthened by this situation.

Plagues and sudden deaths were regarded as heavenly judgments. A Leicester chronicler speaking of "the general mortality throughout the world" in 1348, attributed it to what he regarded as the shameless conduct at a tournament of "forty to fifty ladies of the fairest and comeliest (though I say not of the best) among the whole kingdom." More serious was the opposition of the Church to the practice of medicine and "the belief that monks and friars were the doctors of the Middle Ages is a gigantic delusion." Barber-surgeons, or ordinary housewives, often punished as witches, performed most of the rudimentary medical activities of the period. Monks were prohibited from engaging in surgery in 1163, 1284 and 1300. Anatomy was forbidden altogether. Medical practice derived from the poorly translated works of the Arabs, or the remains of those of Galen and Hippocrates. Gerard of Cremona produced ninety-two volumes which were regarded as standard, and the earliest English writers on medical matters, John of Gaddesden (1316) and John Arden (1380) borrowed from Gerard's works. Chaucer's doctor had been "grounded in astronomy," and the connection of disease with the occult was believed to be too strong to allow any adequate diagnosis and cure. Midwifery and obstetrics must have been deplorable and in one work on the duties of a doctor he is advised: "Look he not over openly [at] the lady or the daughter or other fair women in great houses." Treatment under such circumstances was obviously difficult.

Finally in assessing the role of the Church, it must be remembered that large numbers of monks and nuns were in theory celibate, although not infrequently fathers and mothers. The withdrawal of 1 in 375 of the population from the lawful marriage market must have had an effect. The permitting of early marriages, which may have resulted in weak babies who died young, the swift exhaustion of fertility, or the appearance of multiple molar pregnancy, reduced the likelihood of healthy offspring. In the families of the rich, for which evidence has survived, a high birth-rate and high infant mortality are common, and could have been commoner among the poor. The forbidding of divorce by the Church and the cost of securing a degree of nullity again reduced the possibilities of successful child bearing in many marriages and prevented re-marriages. When it is remembered that women did a great deal of field work, were involved in the domestic production of cloth, and were, in fifteenth-century Coventry, for example, compelled to enter domestic service until they were married, and that it was an age where brutality to wives was permitted and condoned, the unhappy circumstances of many medieval women were likely to have reduced the chances of successful pregnancy or the happy rearing of children.

Living conditions on the whole were not conducive to a healthy life, particularly in towns, and it is significant that, by the Tudor period, plagues were largely concentrated in urban regions. In London there was one latrine to every ward and twelve dung-carts for the whole city. With some exaggeration Bindoff says "the standard of life achieved . . . was almost unimaginably low. Most Englishmen lived on a diet which was often meagre and always monotonous, and was little calculated to promote resistance to disease; wore coarse and ill-fitting clothes, which harboured dirt and vermin; and lived in hovels whose squalor would affront the modern slum-dweller. Theirs was, indeed, the margin of subsistence." It is certainly true that there is a relationship between bad harvests and death-rates in the period from 1290 onwards because the basis of the diet was bread. Thus, there was an excess of carbohydrate at the expense of protein. It is not clear whether eggs or peas or beans provided the main source of protein, but the latter were poor yielders of the substance anyway. Barley and oats were used in preference to wheat and an average family needed thirty-six bushels a year. On the other hand, since most ordinary villeins had a croft and owned some animals, this basic diet was nearly always supplemented. Onions, cabbages, beans, peas, various herbs, apples, pears, plums, cherries, and various wild fruits were among the vegetables and fruits eaten. Honey was often available, and pork was the staple meat. Mead and ale were plentiful and nutritious drinks. Considering villeins' houses: whereas the old view was that a cruck cottage like that at Didbrook in Gloucestershire was the best improvement on the single-room wattle and daub cottage and was still "dismal, depressing, unhealthy, foul-smelling and short of head room," this is no longer held to be the case. It is now clear that in the thirteenth century, the typical peasant house was more complex. In 1304, in the village of Cuxham in Oxfordshire, all the villein houses had more than two rooms, and more substantial houses called "long houses" were common in places as far apart as West Hartburn in County Durham and Hangleton in Sussex. There is substantial evidence of periodic rebuildings gradually increasing the amount of stone, but the absence of surviving examples makes generalisation difficult.

There were obvious dangers to health which must have led to high infant mortality and early death, if for no other reasons than the exposure to the elements and the hardness of the winter on a subsistence diet with little heating or protective clothing. The delight in spring which characterises so much medieval poetry was no mere poet's fancy. "When soft be the weather and every field is full of flowers," the long winter months with little fuel and salted meat or half-cured fish to eat were at an end for the time being. However, medieval society was rural and it had many advantages which modern town-dwellers might envy. At the lowest level, opportunities for promiscuity and the survival of pagan practices are recorded in court book after court book of the ecclesiastical courts. There were forty holy-days a year, many of which were public holidays, and the closely integrated village communities were able to celebrate full well. England was renowned for her love of outdoor sports. A description of London by Fitz Stephen, Thomas à Becket's chaplain, referred to those activities including "children's sports" and "battles on the water." "In the holy days all the summer," said Fitz Stephen, "the youth are exercised in leaping, dancing, shooting, wrestling, casting the stone and practising their shields; the Maidens trip in their Timbrels, and dance as long as they can well see." During the Crusades, the Saracen Turks were amused by the sporting activities of their Christian opponents, but they had their warlike side. From 1337 until 1597, archery was officially encouraged and legally enforced at the butts on the village green. Latimer, a famous preacher of Tudor times, once referred to archery: "It is a goodly art, a wholesome kind of exercise, and much commended in medicine . . . that it wrestles against many kinds of disease." Merry England was as much a myth as the idea that the Middle Ages were a time of unrelieved gloom. The spirit of early songs and carols or the wit of medieval stone-masons would disprove the one as much as poverty, poor diet and frequent illness could mitigate the spirit of:

> "Summer is i'cumen in
> Lude sing cuckoo!
> Groweth seed and bloweth mead
> And springeth the wood new."

The worst shadow which lay across so many men's lives was the plague. In the fourth century, plagues had contributed considerably to the decline of Rome. From the mid-fourteenth century until the early eighteenth century, there was a series of devastating plagues in Europe ending with the famous outbreak at Marseilles in 1721. It was after a series of bad harvests starting in 1272 and followed by those of 1277, 1283, 1292 and 1311 that the first serious outbreaks occurred in 1315–17, accompanying a famine when resistance was naturally lowered. The Black Death reached Europe in late 1347 from the Crimean and Bosphorus regions, whence it was brought by Italian traders. The summer of 1348 was exceptionally wet, and the plague found ready conditions to encourage its dispersal when it reached this country. By 1350 the plague had crossed the length of the country and entered Scotland. It was the first and most devastating of a series of plagues which, because they were separated by a time interval of nearly ten years, prevented the recovery of the population. The plague of 1361 attacked the newly born offspring of those that had survived 1348–50. On that account it was known as "la mortalité des enfants." It lasted into 1362, prolonged again by the appalling weather in January that year. Once more in 1368–9, the plague returned in full fury. Although it claimed only three bishops instead of the four who had succumbed in 1361–2, the plague of 1368–9 was a serious one, removing yet another generation of adults. The plague returned in 1375, 1382, 1390, 1406, 1438–9, and 1464–5, although by then it had considerably lessened in severity.

These plagues were bubonic, that is, they were the result of infection by fleas carried by the black rat. For ecological reasons, the black rat seems to have migrated into eastern Europe at the time of the Crusades, possibly helped by the presence of the Crusaders in their ships. This is substantiated by Lunn's contention in 1930 that the plague spread along navigable rivers and estuarine shores. Only in the 1720s, when the brown rat supplanted the black rat, did bubonic plague die out in Europe. But England experienced another type of plague called Sudor Anglicus or the sweating sickness. The earliest outbreaks were recorded in 1471 and 1478, and it returned in 1485, 1487, 1499, 1506 and 1517. These later plagues were largely confined to the towns, which were increasingly crowded within their medieval walls by the fifteenth century. In 1388 the first public health Act in English history was passed to clear the streets of Cambridge for the benefit of a Parliament. Other causes of the sweating sickness were, however, advanced by no less an authority than Erasmus. Writing in 1524 he complained about "thin-drawn air, sometimes somewhat pestilent," the dirty rushes and cesspits in people's houses and the public dirt in the gutters. In particular he referred to badly salted fish as a cause of the sweating sickness. Erasmus recommended that "the streets should be less defiled with filth and urine," that people should eat less salted food and enjoy more fresh air. Such reforms were long in coming.

Plagues were a major factor in repressing population growth, and it is significant that none were recorded in the expansionist thirteenth century. These epidemics were one of the main reasons for changes in settlement patterns because they either wiped out whole communities, or compelled villagers to migrate from land of marginal utility when they were deprived of a favourable labour situation. For example, after the Black Death, Tilgarsley in Oxfordshire, and Middle Carlton and Ambion in Leicestershire disappeared altogether. Seacourt in Berkshire gradually declined until it disappeared in the 1420s. At Bishopstone in Wiltshire, the old village was replaced by a new one. The statement of Briggs and Jordan about the population of the Middle Ages saying that it was "relatively static" is true inasmuch as large-scale or long-distance

D

migration was impossible, but to suggest that only villeins leaving the manor, or those affected by the growth of towns, moved is to underestimate the local fluctuations. In a way, one might describe these as the result of delayed shifting cultivation. Soil fertility declined, plague infested a village, a fire destroyed it, the lord of the manor took little interest, or the land was of insufficient value to maintain rents or an increased population. Villeins sought very much to buy their own land or to extend their smallholdings. The consequence of these changes was the "budding" of new villages—Greater or Lesser, Magna or Parva—or the location and settlement of new sites.

However, the most spectacular movements of population were brought about by the taking-in of forests and fens, and by the changes in coastal settlement which were caused by the effects of erosion and deposition. Forest clearing or assarting reached two peaks in the mid twelfth and the first half of the thirteenth century, and so great was the extension of the cultivable area that during the fifteenth century there was a sizeable contraction. This was due to the attempts to develop such areas as the thinly soiled downs of Wiltshire or the crowded parts of the Weald or the Midland forests. Assarting, known also as intaking, and creating purprestures or brecks, was done by efficient estate bailiffs or stewards, as well as by individual landowners. Thus, whereas forest clearance on the slopes of the Cotswolds was carried out on the eastern slopes by the Bishops of Winchester and on the western slopes by the Bishops of Worcester, in counties such as Devon (following a disafforestation charter in 1204), or Warwickshire in the Arden region, individual villeins were responsible for the assarting. The clergy was particularly active in the work of reclamation from forest, and fen waste. The Cistercians are well known for their work in such places as West Yorkshire, where villages such as Byland and Old Kirkstall were eliminated, but the work of the Augustinian Canons in north-east Yorkshire should not be neglected. The canons of St Paul's were busy reducing the size of Epping Forest in north Essex and east Hertfordshire. In the Midlands, Rockingham, Sherwood, Needwood and Charnwood forests were extensively cleared in the twelfth century and by 1300 Leicestershire had 400 villages in an area of half a million acres, many of which had been previously forested. In other places, such as the Weald of Kent and Sussex, the peak was reached in the thirteenth century.

There were limitations to this extension of the cultivable area. In the case of the true forests, this was due to the existence of special forest laws and to the power of the Crown. Forest was a general term for "woody grounds and fruitful pastures," but it was also used with specific reference to an area outside the normal ambit of the law. Royal forests covered much of the area west of London towards Windsor and Bagshot, the New Forest created in Hampshire from 1078, the Hay of Hereford, Rockingham, Shotover and Bernwood in the Midlands, Lonsdale and Amunderness in Lancashire, and Allerdale and Inglewood in Cumberland. The forests were valued by the Crown for hunting and the rights of warren. As late as John's reign, wolves were plentiful, and wild boar survived until the middle of the thirteenth century. The laws were strictly enforced by courts which were organised by the Assize of Woodstock of 1184 and the Charter of the Forests in 1217. William I introduced savage forest laws which included mutilation and even skinning alive, but these soon gave way to the more profitable practices of selling immunity to the laws to forest communities and fining those who encroached on the forests. Thus, Richard I began selling immunities in Surrey in 1190 and John continued the practice; in 1204, Essex paid 500 marks and Cornwall 2,200 marks. After investigations of the forests in 1167 and 1175, the forest eyre (or judicial visitation) was busy fining people in Berkshire for assarting the forests.

The area under jurisdiction of the Chief Forester and his subordinate wardens, verderers and foresters varied from reign to reign. Stephen gave up previous afforestations, but Henry II added considerably to the forests and his favourite residences were his hunting lodges at Clarendon and Woodstock. The severe measures of Richard I and John led to demands in Magna Carta for a widespread reduction in royal authority, but little was conceded. The Forest Charter of 1217 ended the severe penalties, but the forest courts of Regard, Swainimote and Attachment retained their powers to prevent pannage of pigs during the fawning season, for example, and continued to arouse resentment. Not until 1300 (Articuli super Cartas) were the powers of the Crown considerably reduced, but they were not fully abolished until 1641. Then the remaining royal forests were left as they had been in 1623. Forest jurisdiction was gradually eroded by the demands of landowners denied rights on their own lands and the ever-increasing number of villeins who wanted to expand into the forests with their smallholdings. After a series of disputes in Warwickshire and Worcestershire in the 1220s, the Statute of Merton was passed in 1236 to allow the enclosing of the waste rather than the forests. This statute stopped tenants from using a writ of *novel disseizin* to prevent a landlord enclosing waste and allowed enclosure, provided rights of common were left in sufficiency for the village. After this the law fluctuated, giving the landlord more power in 1289, but reducing it in 1305, when pasture rights were guaranteed. Lords, thus limited by law in enclosing waste, were still anxious to exploit forests as well, and obtained grants from the royal forests or reductions in royal power to benefit themselves.

Enclosure of forest and waste was laborious and litigious, and apart from the rapid development of monastic holdings in Yorkshire, was a slow and often piecemeal process. Reclamation of the Fens had to be more systematic since it involved a measure of capital outlay. Thus, it is usually the larger monasteries, or combined groups of villagers, that embarked upon the reduction of the large marshland regions of Saxon England, which so far had been only slightly affected by work at Glastonbury in the tenth century. Marshland was valuable for rights of turbary or turf gathering, fishing and fowling, eeling and later for sheep grazing. The rich soil and ready drainage were added advantages. Thus, some of the earliest enclosures for sheep were on the marshes, and not until the late fourteenth century was arable land of marginal value turned over to pasture on the slopes of the Downs and Wolds. Four main areas of marshland enclosing may be pointed out. In the West Country, the Glastonbury monks encroached on Sedgemoor around Mere marsh and, under such abbots as Michael Ambresbury and Roger Ford, developed the area during the thirteenth century. In Kent, the monks of St Augustine's Priory, Canterbury, took the lead in draining the Isle of Thanet in the late thirteenth century, and before that date they had embarked, in the Romney Marsh, on the drainage of the Denge and Welland regions west of Romney. In Lincolnshire, the gradual reduction of the marshland which had once stretched from the Humber to the Wash, was so extensive that by 1332 lowland regions paid more than upland regions in the subsidy of that year. By far the most considerable works were undertaken, however, in the area surrounding the Wash. Crowland, Thorney and Ramsey took a lead, although nearly all the religious houses were involved. Monastic clearances were large and rapid, and in 1189 there were riots at Crowland Abbey as a result. Richer villeins soon realised the advantage and communal inning occurred in Lincolnshire and Norfolk in the thirteenth century. However, with the decline in monastic activity in the late fourteenth century and a realisation that technical difficulties lay in the path of further drainage schemes, the attack on the Fens slowed down. Experiences such as that of the Canterbury manor of Ebony, which was reclaimed under the progressive Prior Henry of Eastry and was subjected to constant flooding, were an indication that a limit had been reached for the time being.

Movements of population in the coastal region were more rapid and made in response to the elimination of old ports, or the deliberate creation of new ones. These changes were most clearly to be seen along the coasts of Sussex and Kent during the Middle Ages. The movement to establish new coastal settlements was, however, as Beresford has shown, wider than this. Portsmouth was developed from the 1190s, with the decline of Portchester which had been a port since Roman times. Such a change is marked by the declining fortunes of Portchester Castle. Used by Richard I and John and repaired by their chief engineer, Elias of Oxford, the fortification soon became outdated, and although Richard II employed the famous Henry Yevele and a subordinate, Hugh Kynton, to increase the castle's defences, by 1441 it was described as "ruinous and feeble." Further north, the ports of the Humber underwent changes. Kingston-upon-Hull was established by Edward I on the site of Wyke and Hedon, and when Ravenser was lost by erosion, and the Wash ports silted as a result of inland reclamations, the port rose to fresh importance. The development was systematic and involved the purchase of 150 acres to be developed, the diverting of the Humber and the building of new roads. The town was given a charter in 1440. King's (then Bishop's) Lynn was developed by the Bishops of Norwich.

Geography's influence on the course of economic history was most clearly marked along the coasts of the Narrow Seas. Along the Sussex shore, Chichester took second place to Bosham as a port, Selsey declined after the bishopric was moved in 1075 and was gradually cut off from the mainland. Seaford at the mouth of the Ouse ceased to be a port during the fifteenth century as the marsh south of Lewes was inned, and the port of Newhaven began its slow growth. The Hastings of Saxon times disappeared beneath the sea and a new town (called Old Hastings) was established as the Roar river slowly eroded the chalk hills on which the first town was built. It is not clear when the change occurred but it seems that following the violent storms of the late thirteenth century there was a considerable decline in the fourteenth century. Hastings' contribution to the Cinque Ports fleet dropped from twenty-one to as low as three ships and there was a serious French raid in 1377. By far the most spectacular changes took place at Winchelsea. This port, on an island at the mouth of the Rother, was increasingly exposed to storm damage in 1250 and 1252 and in 1287 the whole town was destroyed by the inundations of the sea. By then, Edward I's town-building activities had started a new

Winchelsea further inland, on what was still a navigable lagoon. Edward had already undertaken planned economic development in Aquitaine where assarting and the development of vine growing was accompanied by the building of nearly a hundred bastides, some of which were "definite urban developments."

New Winchelsea was planned by Gregory of Rokesley and Henry le Waleys. Development took place in the form of a gridiron pattern of streets surrounding the church of St Thomas, and the construction of wharves for a harbour. For a time, with the help of Gervase and William Alard in the early thirteenth century, the new port flourished, but it never filled the original planned ninety acres, nor was St Thomas's ever completed. Gradually, inning of the marshes combined with the dumping of ballast to produce silting and by the reign of Richard II the town was in decay. By Henry VII's time, merchants were said to be leaving the town. Again, French raids had contributed to decline. Rye was destined to survive until the draught of ships became too great, but further east again, Romney suffered the same cycle of prosperity and decline. The inning of the lands of the Rother surrounding the present village of Brooklands started the difficulties, and the great storm of 1287 diverted the Rother from Romney to Rye. Then came a further extension of inning and by the fifteenth century Romney was no longer a port. Hythe suffered as well during the fifteenth century, but the more dramatic decline was that of Sandwich which was slowly replaced by Dover as the chief Narrow Seas port. Sandwich suffered from the silting of the Wantsum and her decline is marked by the failure of the annual fleet of Italian galleys to call there, as well as at London and Southampton, during the 1460s.

All these changes not only brought about the collapse of the Cinque Ports, but also increased the power of London and developed ports further west. Thus, it is clear that economic activities were affected closely by the environment in the Middle Ages. Population was subject to considerable local changes. On the land, particularly by forests or fens, and by the sea, spectacular alterations occurred, and over the whole country, the smallness and, often, the scattered nature of villages made it easy to grow from the nucleus or shift the nucleus of population. Population was thus subject to regional fluctuations and growth, although the overall growth rate was slow. The distribution of population combined with the limited resources, and the likelihood of a large increase in the twelfth and thirteenth century, to suggest that the growth rate need not necessarily be viewed disparagingly. Although plague was the key factor in reducing the growth rate, the net reproduction rate, mortality rates, and length of life were determined by more basic questions of health, hygiene, and the nature of the social structure with a poor standard of living and a degrading social position for women.

THE NATURE OF FEUDALISM

Although environment and the economic necessities of supply and demand did much to determine the framework of medieval economic activity, it was also influenced greatly by the type of society that existed in the Middle Ages. This was different in many respects from later societies. Relationships were based much more on land and its responsibilities than on any other social ties. Government was by landlords enfeoffed to govern and to run estates. The bonds of society were the operations of the land law through the processes of feudal organisation. Even central government was feudal in composition. Royal revenues were raised from royal estate in the first instance and William I retained a large amount of land in royal hands, where it remained until it was sold by the Tudors and Stuarts. The close advisers of the king were the greater barons and they owned particular types of estates known as honours, in which barons imitated the same organisations as the Crown possessed. For example, over a hundred lords on the Welsh Marches had their own chancerys. The local power of the landlord was often more effective than that of central authority.

When other bonds were formed in the medieval community, these were also in a sense feudal. They were concerned with jurisdiction, with the creation of a set of privileges *(libertas)* to be granted to a particular group *(communitas)*. Towns and guilds were obvious examples of this trend which was widespread. Both town and guild received charters of incorporation and burgesses or guildsmen were privileged individuals. At the same time as the growth of towns indicated a very slow shift away from the overpowering importance of land, it also showed that the change was made in a feudal context. The old view that freedom was to be found in towns was wide of the mark because all medieval communities paid respect to rank and rendered deference to privilege. When Parliament began to develop as an adjunct of government, it was on the basis of the gradual admission of new "estates" to the *communitas* of the realm. Such a development occurred simultaneously in Castile, France and England, and reflected the necessity to admit new and powerful groups to the privilege of government. Rights in the Middle Ages were not the individual's, but the community's, however small the community. Some like the Cinque

Ports or the guilds of masons, iron-workers or lead-miners were large organisations, while others like the local market or the jurisdiction of an honour could be very small, but nearly all medieval economic organisations were based on these concepts of the fraternity, guild or corporation.

In this context, the largest corporation of all, the Church, must be considered. Estimates vary, but they all suggest that the Church was an enormously wealthy corporation owning a seventh of England's wealth in 1086 and a fifth in 1485. In 1337 a third of the nation's property was said to be ecclesiastical, and a third of Kent and of Gloucestershire belonged to the Church. Worcestershire was largely owned by the Church which controlled 50,000 acres including the fifteen largest manors. The government of the country was run by clerks (churchmen) and the highest offices of state were almost entirely monopolised by them until the mid thirteenth century. Bishops, abbots and minor clergy all came together, or separately, to the early Parliaments. Church law, which was Roman law, operated over a wide sphere of matters including inheritance and wills as well as spiritual or moral offences. Bishops and abbots were landlords and among the most prosperous: they were, therefore, barons, and that is how they came to sit in the House of Lords. Churchmen controlled the fates of towns and fairs, regulated finance, spread investment, and by rearing the best sheep in the country came to be the very pivot of economic prosperity. Medieval society was regarded as a reflection of God's laws. In its highest form, this view implied the total unity of Christian Europe under the Pope and the Holy Roman Emperor as the spiritual and temporal "swords" that held society in awe and order. At the simplest level, it meant that the ordinary parish priest worked in the fields and the literate clerk in the government office. Some indication has already been given of the way in which the Church's theories influenced economic ideas. The Church's power affected the whole structure of society because the Church was not apart from the rest of the community. Parish priests, monks, nuns, friars, and members of fighting religious orders made up a sizeable proportion of the population. If lay brothers, palmers, pilgrims, pardoners, summoners and other court officials, who were hardly spiritual church officers, are added to the list the numbers involved in Church affairs were immense.

Feudal society was thus formed against a background of concepts which started with the local communities and developed up to the acceptance of a single united Christendom. In theory, feudal and Christian Europe were one doing homage alike to the Emperor and the Pope. Nationality had little influence, and it is best to visualise medieval Europe and for that matter medieval England as a group of *communitas* bound together by oaths of allegiance and acts of homage, and divided by acts of feudal defiance like *diffidatio* or renouncing one's allegiance. A whole host of different governments existed and it was only under particularly powerful or wilful kings that large areas were effectively subordinated to one ruler. Royal authority in England was always weak in the north and the west. Areas of special jurisdiction fell outside direct royal control. Large areas called palatinates might be as great as Cheshire, Kent or Durham. Smaller areas called honours, such as Richmond or Wallingford, existed in profusion. Over Church lands, authority was disputed, but not until near the end of the thirteenth century (Statute of Mortmain, 1279) did the state impose a serious check on the Church's right to hold land, and it was many years before Common Law replaced Canon Law in such places as Ely or Peterborough, which lay under the exclusive jurisdiction of the Church.

Such a confusion and multiplicity of organisations was a necessary prelude to more national concepts of government. While they lasted, economic affairs were dictated by the pattern of feudal politics and regulated by feudal organisations, but it is unwise to speak of a feudal economy. This is a source of much confusion. If it is remembered that the manor was formed before feudalism was organised, and that the system of agriculture, the duties and the ranks of the villeins, were all in existence before the introduction of fully developed feudalism in the period from 1072 onwards, then matters will be clearer. The introduction of feudalism was the alteration of the governing class and the subsequent development of feudal practice in wide areas of society. Feudalism affected the medieval economy, but it did not create it. Feudalism grew in response to the political conditions of the late eighth, the ninth and the tenth centuries in Europe. The use of the words "feudal system" is misleading, and it was once suggested sarcastically that a famous seventeenth-century legal writer, Sir Henry Spelman, invented the feudal system. Although the kind of feudalism introduced by the Normans was more rigid than existing practices of government and land tenure, it was by no means a uniform system. Feudalism has been traced to many different sources including the relationship of *clientes* and *patrones* in the Roman Empire, and the relationship of the *principes* and *comites* in Teutonic Europe, but it is more likely that such relationships were common to a particular stage of development. They were forms of lordship, that is of relations between superior and inferior ranks of society. Such lordship was not considered to create servility, but to be the

D*

natural order of a society in which each social group performed a specific function, so that the whole of society then functioned properly.

On the Continent, feudalism developed under the stress of constant war. It was necessary to provide for localised government and to secure the creation of a sufficiently large army. Kings made grants of land to nobles in return for specific services, and this process can be seen in France and Germany in the late eighth and early ninth centuries. These holdings were known as fiefs (*feodum* or *beneficium*) or marks, and gradually they acquired more permanent status. A capitulary of 877 in France recognised that fiefs could become hereditary; that is they were alodial tenures which could be inherited or extended as the lord wished. The lord was given seizin or possession of his land and invested by his superior lord, but the fiefs were *in hereditas* and inalienable, except when they were forfeited by treason or *diffidatio*. The lords of these great estates soon acquired semi-royal powers. They established courts, administrations and armies of their own, and by conquest or marriage added to their fiefs until they became great tracts of land. Typical of such a development was Normandy, itself given as a fief by the King of Paris to Rollo in 911, which became a great state in its own right. Feudal lords settled inferior tenants on their land, standing in the same relation to them as they did to their own lord. Such mesne tenants, as they were known, held land on the basis of a number of knights' fees (*servitium debitum*), each fee requiring the lord to return a certain number of knights (that is, armed horsemen not dubbed knights) who were usually calculated in fives or multiples of five. Feudalism was essentially, therefore, a system of landholding in return for military or other services, and a system of government based upon this military organisation and the principle of feudal allegiance. It is vital to grasp that barons and knights were not ranks of a peerage but types of landowner. Greater barons held estates which were honorial, that is they had a *caput* or headquarters, and had the right of immediate access to the king. Lesser barons and knights held estates of varying numbers of knight fees. Many greater barons were known as earls and, because they were the most powerful organisations, earldoms were the first estates to become great hereditary possessions. But earls, barons and knights had their status determined by the type of landholding, the nature of the oath of allegiance demanded, and the power or otherwise of the superior lord. It was not until the feudal organisation of England was declining that a series of hereditary nobles, ranging from dukes to viscounts, began to emerge. It must also be stressed that feudalism and chivalry were not directly connected. A society which placed such emphasis on military prowess or power, and whose Church was a warrior Church, soon came to elevate military honour to a high place. The horrors of medieval warfare were mitigated by a code of conduct. The knight's service as a squire, or his vigil in the Church overnight before he was dubbed, were parts of an elaborate ceremonial designed to render warfare dignified and Christian. The Crusades acceler- ated this development on the Continent, and in England the reign of Edward III is generally taken as being the age of chivalry—the epoch of the Black Prince and the Order of the Garter.

Feudalism clearly had many disadvantages. It depended too much on a series of downward pressures so that, if the king was not powerful, the greater tenants would exploit their position, and frag- ment the administration. Moreover, although it was designed to provide a feudal host, it did not succeed in doing so. England's feudal host was only some 4,200 knights, and by the thirteenth century there was great difficulty in raising a thousand. Tenants, were, on the other hand, provided with their own armies and, throughout the Middle Ages, rebellion and civil war were endemic. On the Continent, feudalism was systematically organised in a series of great fiefs. The amount of land available and the great distances involved facilitated such development, with contiguous fiefs growing more and more independent of central authority. In England the feudalism of Europe was considerably modified. For example, to supplement the feudal host, the kings kept the Saxon fyrd. To form a check on feudal courts, the shire courts under the sheriffs, and later a whole network of courts at Westminster Hall in London, preserved royal power and kept alive the earlier Common Law to develop alongside the more rigid Roman feudal law. Mesne tenants were equally responsible to the king as to their immediate lord. Whether or not this was the product of the Oath of Salisbury in 1086 is still uncertain, but it is clear that the English oath of fealty was not so exclusive as that on the Continent. Finally, although half of the land distributed to tenants-in-chief was in the hands of ten men in the 1080s, large estates were not usual. The Count of Mortain, William I's cousin, had his 793 knight fees scattered in different parts of the country, particularly in Cornwall and the North Riding of Yorkshire. This should not be regarded as a deliberate act of policy, and it did not apply among the Marcher lords of Wales, or the Norman conquerors of Ireland. Some tenants-in-chief had very large compact estates, such as that of the Earls of Gloucester with 300 knight fees which were worth £600 a year and covered 40,000 acres. Three other large estates occupied much of the remaining part of Gloucestershire which had not fallen to the Crown or the Church.

The introduction of feudalism meant, in the first place, the apportioning of England among a group of some two hundred tenants-in-chief, known as the "companions of the Conqueror." In their turn, these tenants-in-chief enfeoffed the mesne tenants until all the Saxon earls or thegns had been deprived. The Saxon nobility lost in the battles of 1066, by taking part in further rebellions and by fleeing abroad. William took a sixth of the available lands comprising 1,400 manors and dispossessed Saxons to obtain the best estates. Thus, Brichtric, lord of Tewkesbury in Gloucestershire, was deprived of 20,000 acres, although he later recovered a small part of his lands at Leckhampton and Woodchester. By 1086 there were only two large Saxon landowners left in the country—Thurkill of Arden and Colswein of Lincoln. The last of the higher Saxon nobility or earls, Waltheof, was executed in 1076. Eventually, all the Saxon bishops except Wulfstan of Worcester were removed, and by 1075, thirteen out of the twenty-three chief monasteries in England were in Norman hands. Church and lay ownership was on the same basis and very few church lands were held by tenure of frankalmoign (free alms), although Battle Abbey, built to commemorate Hastings, was a notable exception.

It used to be thought, on the evidence of a writer called Ordericus Vitalis, that the division of England among the Norman, Fleming and French followers of William was done systematically, the number of knight fees (approximately 60,000) being the basis for the division of the spoils. Now it is accepted that the movement was more *ad hoc*. At first, William was under considerable pressure to reward his followers and to garrison a country which experienced serious rebellion in every year until 1071, and then again in 1075–6. Lands were swiftly distributed to royal relatives and the most powerful lords were created, including a number of earldoms possessing palatine rights, although they were not called palatines until the fourteenth century. At first, Kent, Sussex and Hampshire, and Cornwall were made earldoms, followed by Gloucester, Shrewsbury and Hereford, and eventually by Chester, Durham and Lancashire. Chester was given to Hugh the Fat, Count of Avranches, and remained a powerful earldom, which negotiated its own Magna Carta, until it was incorporated into the royal estates under Henry III. Lancashire was in the possession of the Crown and only achieved palatine status for a time from 1351. Durham was granted to Bishop Walcher and remained under the jurisdiction of its Prince-Bishops until 1836. There were no members of Parliament for the county until 1675. None of the three southern earldoms survived. Cornwall was incorporated into the Crown lands, and Kent was deprived of its status after the revolt in 1082 of William's half-brother, Odo, Earl of Kent and Bishop of Bayeux. These earldoms along the Welsh border acquired lasting significance, because they formed the basis of defence against the Welsh and for the Norman settlement of Wales and Ireland. The earldoms of Gloucester, under William and then Roger FitzOsbern, and of Shrewsbury, under Robert Montgomery of Bellême, were to remain of great importance.

Once the larger estates had been disposed, it became possible to organise the knight fees. The first writ concerning the *servitium debitum* which has survived was sent in 1072 to Ethelwig, Abbot of Evesham, referring to five knights. A fee was worth £20 a year and provided one knight to serve for forty days, although this was not supposed to involve service overseas. By the reign of William II, it is fairly certain that the creation of knight fees was general, but the wide discrepancy between the number of knights and the number of fees suggests that the quantities involved varied enormously and that the process was never completed. The great majority of enfeoffments were for military service like those which have survived for Hereford in 1085 to 1086, but it is important to recognise that, almost from the first this was considered to be an uneconomic way of raising an army, and money payments were substituted. According to Chew, this began on monastic estates by the time of Henry I and by 1159 scutage or shield money was being regularly raised. There were other forms of tenure. Serjeanty was the holding of land in return for a special duty which was performed. Sometimes this would be of great importance such as being constable of a castle; at others the duties were more ceremonial: to be the King's Champion or look after the royal chess set. Cornage was a tenure that involved special defence duties, such as the blowing of horns, the sounding of bells, and the lighting of beacons. Lastly, there was socage, which was all that remained of the free tenures of Saxon eorls or ceorls. The services were fixed, the man owed fealty but no feudal incidents or aids, and very often paid a money rent. Burgage tenure was the free tenure in towns. Villein tenure applied to the land of those holding lands from a mesne tenant. The person who took possession of such land became a villein by tenure, as distinct from a villein by status. Villein tenure was not free inasmuch as duties in cash and kind were either unlimited, or largely fixed by the lords who determined the customs of the manor in a particular area.

Money was always involved in feudal relationships. At the lowest level, there was the customary rent (*redditus*) paid originally in kind but increasingly in money, as the *Boldon Book* of 1183 illustrates for the Bishop of Durham's estates. Free tenants in socage paid money rents and many knights paid a scutage of 40s. instead of a fully armed horseman. Henry II and Richard I took eleven scutages and John the same number. The Crown had the right to demand money payments, including taxes on moveables and tallages and benevolences. The feudal system lay at the basis of the country's finances because the main taxes were the feudal "incidents." Taxation such as the geld, or tax on moveables like the thirteenth taken by John in 1207, was regarded as exceptional, and it was expected that the Crown and the nobles should "live off their own." Custom fixed the feudal incidents at too low a figure for the Crown's liking, or too high a figure for the mesne tenants, and many medieval revolts involved issues concerning the incidents.

Aids (*auxilia*) were required for the knighting of the eldest son, the marriage of the eldest daughter and the ransoming of the lord's person. Aids were constantly abused by the lords and were sometimes onerous. The ransom for Richard I was a good example, requiring an aid of 20s. and a 25 per cent tax on moveables. Demands for limitation grew and, in Magna Carta, mesne tenants were forbidden to demand any irregular aids while additional aids were only to be raised by common consent of king and barons. In 1275 (Statute of Westminster) mesne tenants, aids were fixed at 20s. in the £, and this was extended to tenants-in-chief in 1351. Reliefs were duties paid on taking up a new estate and are sometimes confused with the pre-Conquest heriot. Heriots were given in gratitude for past services in giving the land. Reliefs allowed a man to obtain livery of seizin, that is, to enter on his lands. By clause 2 of Magna Carta, reliefs on larger estates (baronys or honours) were fixed at £100 and for knight fees at 100s. Prior to this, John had raised a relief of £6,000 on a £100 estate. Primer seizin was an additional relief taken from tenants-in-chief involving one year's profits from the lands. It was confirmed to the king by the Statute of Marlborough (1267). When the heir to an estate was under twenty-one if a man, or fourteen if a woman, the lord had the right to control the lands until the new heir came of age. Clauses 6 and 7 of Magna Carta sought to restrict wastage of land so held, but the prevention of abuse was difficult. In the case of women, the additional right to bestow them in marriage, provided there was no disparagement, was also acquired by the lord. By the time of Henry III this power had extended to male heirs as well. Any crime such as treason or felony which "corrupted the blood" was followed by the escheat of the estate, that is, it reverted to the lord.

As fiefs became heritable, it became increasingly difficult to divide them. Alienation was punished with fines. Alienation of property to religious houses which reduced feudal profits was restrained in 1279, and the alienation of land by sub-infeudation—that is by creating new lords—was forbidden in 1290. This was accompanied by the growth of entail and primogeniture which was marked by a statute in 1285. Entailed estates became homogeneous units, descending century after century to the same family, and were to be a key factor in stabilising and territorialising English landowner-ship, cutting down absentee landlords, preventing the excessive sub-division of property, and stimulating the younger sons to seek their fortune elsewhere. Feudal incidents continued for a very long time. Wardship was revived by the Tudors with a special Court of Wards in 1540. Feudal incidents and tenures were abolished in 1641 and 1646, and this was confirmed finally in 1660. But some rights survived. Escheat for treason or felony lasted, for example, until 1870. Moreover, the franchises continued and in 1836 there were still fifty-five medieval franchise courts, and they were not idle. Palatinate courts in Durham handled 150 cases in their last ten years. Secular powers were eliminated first. In 1536, for ex-ample, the customs of the Marcher lords was abolished in 136 lordships, but the Church retained the power in the Isle of Ely, the Isle of Peterborough, and Bury St Edmunds, until 1888. As late as 1921, baronial councils still conducted business at Lancaster and St Albans, and the law courts recognised feudal tenures until 1925, when the last manorial rights were abolished.

Feudalism was never comprehensive in England. The strong system of Saxon government and the comparatively late introduc-tion of feudal military service meant that English feudalism was always compounded of Common and Roman law. England was too small a country for large fiefs to develop completely out of the authority of royal government. Distances were not sufficient to isolate the villein, or cut off the smaller tenants from redress. Flight to neighbouring towns was available to the poor, and the processes of the king's courts for the rich. Feudal oppression was not, there-fore, a marked characteristic of the time, although later writers, such as Thomas Starkey or Sir Henry Spelman, thought differently. Feudalism provided a reasonably firm organisation of government and estate to aid the development of the economy. Great lords, such as Henry de Lacy or Edmund of Lancaster, began in the thirteenth century a long tradition of progressive economic development within a traditional framework. Although custom played a major role in determining feudal values, it was not sufficient to prevent feudalism from changing very considerably, so that by the fifteenth century it was no longer the basis of landholding or the plexus of the social organism.

CHAPTER 5

THE MEDIEVAL ECONOMY IN COUNTRY AND TOWN

AGRICULTURE: MANOR AND VILLAGE

Very few ordinary medieval village dwellings have survived but larger buildings still remain. Aerial photography reveals the survival of the original village street plan, and provides evidence of the methods of cultivation in use at this time. At Laxton in Nottinghamshire, the three fields (West, Mill, South) have survived, although the old narrow strips have been consolidated into rectangular holdings. Oakley Reynes in Bedfordshire has its West, Road and Church Fields. Elsewhere, as for example at Soulbury in Buckinghamshire, the ridge and furrow made common by the method of medieval ploughing may still be seen. Very few houses such as that at Dalderby in Lincolnshire have survived, although the foundations of many medieval buildings still exist. Each region built as far as possible from local materials, and this gave rise to a wide variety of buildings. Timber was used in all houses and timber combined with wattle and daub, plaster or stone was common. In the eastern counties, where clay was available, bricks were in use by the end of the thirteenth century. With sandstone and flint, bricks were also used in the south, and Little Wenham Hall in Sussex is one of the earliest brick buildings. The Midlands and south were the region for timbered and thatched houses with whitewashed bricks, or further west, walls of cob made from alternate layers of mud and straw. From Dorset across the Cotswolds towards Northamptonshire and Lincoln stretched a belt of limestone-built houses. In the north and west stone was the usual material.

Buildings which have survived are very often ecclesiastical. Churches were the dominant buildings in all villages, used for communal activities as well as church services, for purposes of defence, and for holding the village school in the porch. Tithe barns for the reception of the tenth due to the Church have survived at such places as Bradford-on-Avon in Wiltshire. Manor courts were held in the manor house, or sometimes in the village. At Slaidburn in Yorkshire the courtroom still exists in the village inn. Very few of the great number of mills have survived, but there is an abbey

103

mill at Whalley in Lancashire. Stone crosses, maypoles like that at Kettlewell in Yorkshire, village stocks such as those at Ottery St Mary, and many other features of medieval rural life are still preserved. There were 10,000 to 15,000 villages in medieval England, and 90 per cent of the people lived in them at the time of *Domesday Book*. It has been estimated that there were 14,000 manors. Any attempt to describe the typical manor or village is likely therefore to fail to do justice to the considerable varieties that existed. It is important to realise that an estate consisted of several manors scattered quite widely. Villages and manors did not coincide and in one sample of 650 sites, 336 were not co-extensive. By concentrating solely on legal aspects, to the neglect of environmental factors such as topography, soil and climate, it is easily forgotten that types of village, methods of landholding, and systems of farming varied as much as the local building materials.

What used to be described as the typical manor was one farmed on the three-field system, where the great majority of the villagers rendered services in labour and kind in return for their land, lived in a largely self-sufficient, but curiously almost entirely agricultural community, and owed suit to a manor court and service to a village church which conveniently coincided. Some romantics even embellished their village plans with an elaborate manor house of the kind which few mesne tenants could ever have afforded. There may well have been a few villages where this ideal pattern prevailed, but since the feudalisation of the village was most intensive in the part of the country where villages were the least isolated, the likelihood is small. At the moment, Kosminsky's figures are still used to explain the extent of manoralisation. He claimed that 69 per cent of all villages were typical manors, and that 39 per cent of those had a relatively complete manorial organisation. Such villages were most likely to be found in an area within a triangle with its bases on the Devon border and the east of Sussex and its apex in south Yorkshire. Yet it seems likely that this estimate is too high because, although some areas outside this region such as Pembrokeshire or Durham were similarly organised, a very considerable number of villages within the region farmed, for example, on a two-field system rather than a three-field one. Moreover, the situation where all tenancies were directed to serving the lord of the demesne and all village production went to the demesne was very rare. A wide variety of tenancy of a socage nature always existed. Even *Domesday Book* with its limited definition admitted 12 per cent to be *liberi homines*. Many villeins owned sufficient land or stock by the thirteenth century to make a profit for themselves.

Even a small village such as South Domerton in Wiltshire had 4,000 sheep owned by the villeins.

Consideration of the manor should, therefore, begin with an assessment of the varieties of medieval farming and land tenure that prevented the typical manor from being typical of more than half our agricultural system at the most. Variety was produced by a number of factors. Pastoral farming tended to produce a larger unit than the manor or the village. It is not easy to estimate the total number of sheep but estimates of flocks belonging to the great owners and the villein breeders are both high. Around Winchester, the Bishop's estates had 29,000 and, a little later, the Priory of St Swithun's had 20,000. The Cistercian monks were famous for their sheep and the best wool in England was said to come from Tintern, Stansfield, and Abbey Dore on the Welsh border. Their extensive granges in the Yorkshire valleys are well known. Besides sheep-rearing, cattle-farming was also widespread. Vaccaries for cattle were to be found in the Fens, Devonshire, the Peak District and on de Lacy lands in Derbyshire and north-west Staffordshire. It is sometimes forgotten that the Cistercian monks also reared cattle at places as far apart as Valle Crucis in Wales, Nidderdale, Sawtre in the Fens and Jervaulx and Kirkstall abbeys in Yorkshire. The method of farming arable land varied from place to place. One-field systems survived in parts of Norfolk and Suffolk. Two-field systems continued to prevail in many places in spite of the advantages of the three-field system. Although the line of Watling Street might conveniently divide two- and three-field areas within the region of typical manors, it is more likely that two-field systems operated where assarting had first taken place on both sides of such a line. The breck system close to the forests, was typical in the Midlands. The fully developed two-field system of infield and outfield, combined with the division of the tenement among all the children, was prevalent in the north and along the Welsh border called run-rig or Welshry according to the area. Kentish fields were smaller being very often a rectangular plot which was also the basis of the tenure. Here also, equal heritable right called gavelkind prevailed. In East Anglia the fertility of the soil enabled a one-field system to operate. Even the nature of the strips themselves would vary in size and distribution according to the topography.

The third set of circumstances that altered the structure of the typical manor was tenurial. Kosminsky produced important evidence to illustrate the prevalence of money rents in the thirteenth century, and it is now clear that these were widespread from the first. According, for example, to Pollard and Crossley, "in the twelfth century commutation of labour services for money rents was fairly common." If evidence of this nature continues to increase the view of a manor as an economic unit relying basically on an exchange of services, rents in kind and self-sufficient farming will have been greatly altered. If the amount of money involved in paying villeins' dues and earned by the villeins from the sale of their croft produce and livestock was considerable, it is clear that the cash nexus was a constant dissolvant of the typical manor. It altered the demesne from a series of scattered strips to a consolidated and sometimes enclosed compact profit-making unit. It transformed the small villein virgate into the basis of a group of holdings which earned the villein a profit. In the north, on the other hand, food rents remained typical. In areas which had once been part of the Danelaw, particularly south Yorkshire and East Anglia, compact smallholdings were already common, and villages without a lord's demesne were not unknown in an area of dense settlement. Manors are by no means frequently mentioned in twelfth-century charters dealing with the eastern part of England. Widespread though villein tenure was, it was unknown in Kent.

Accepting that varieties of manor and village were produced by farming and tenurial differences, it is still possible to discuss the large number of manors where villein holdings and the lords demesne worked together to provide both subsistence and profit, and where arable and livestock activities created a varied agricultural pattern within a fairly rigid and customary organisation of manorial duties enforced in the court leet. The main activity of such a village was the cultivation of the three fields, where at first the lords' and the villeins' strips were intermingled. It is important to realise that these fields contributed to the pastoral, as well as the arable, farming on the manor. After harvest, the stubble in the fields was grazed until the time for ploughing came again. This right of shack was in addition to rights of pasture elsewhere, and it allowed manuring to take place, although this was not adequate enough to keep up grain yields per acre over a long period. There was considerable variety in the rotation used, as a survey of the Ramsey Abbey estate in the 1400s shows, but there was also a fairly common pattern. The fallow field was ploughed in October for the winter wheat sowing. This wheat was harvested in August. Barley was sown in March and harvested in August. The third field was left fallow and ploughed in June, preparatory to the October ploughing and sowing. The advantage of using the three-field system in terms of yield in relation to the amount of necessary ploughing was clearly shown by Walter of Henley (Table 2).

Table 2—Crop Yields of the Two- and Three-field Systems

Two-field system (each of 80 acres)	Three-field system (each of 80 acres)
40 to plough — wheat	60 to plough — wheat
40 for barley	60 for barley
80 for stubble	60 for stubble
$40 + 40 + (80 \times 2) = 240$	$60 + 60 + (60 \times 2) = 240$

In spite of this arithmetical truth, there was no hasty adoption of the three-field method, although some efforts were made to improve the efficiency of the rotation. On the lands of the Canterbury monks, liming and marling were used and on one manor this increased the yield by a third. In other parts of the country, shell and sand were used to improve the quality of the soil. However, as the proportion of meadow to arable land was low, manure was not available in sufficient quantities. Henley advocated experimenting with seed and such experiments as producing mixed crops at Crowland in 1283, or large oats at Tavistock in 1332, showed that such advice did not go entirely unheeded. It was a curiosity of agricultural progress that, while the soil was badly treated, its more intensive use in a three-field system might well have retarded the yield levels. Lipson went too far, however, when he suggested that the method of farming was "wasteful unsystematic and in every way bad economy." Its endurance for a thousand years would in itself suggest that it had certain advantages as well as disadvantages.

These disadvantages are well known. The intermingling of strips made ploughing difficult, and sizeable parts of the field called gores or headlands avoided the plough. Distinguishing one holding from another by rough stone boundaries (mere-stones), or in some cases by a doubly ploughed baulk of raised earth made for constant day to day disputes and legal arguments. Time was wasted in moving from one strip to another. Improvement was difficult when weeds could easily spread, or animal infection could rapidly be carried from place to place. Communal agriculture prevented experimentation. The whole system left a third of the land fallow and did not sufficiently replenish the soil. On the other hand, the method of farming had advantages. It prevented total negligence and to that extent made good use of the land. Decisons to plough or reap were made collectively, with the wisdom of the whole community being used to determine a matter of life or death. A basic rhythm of activity related to the seasons was developed. In a time of poverty, joint ploughing made the use of an expensive item available to all. In a time of prosperity, a villein already owning his virgate had a guaranteed base for further economic activities, and although the tenure was often harsh and restrictive, the possession of a croft as well as a virgate was a position much envied by later landless labourers.

The lord's desmesne constituted the largest holding in the manor. At first it was almost entirely scattered, but later came to consist of an integrated holding and some scattered strips. This demesne was farmed for the benefit of the lord and his household and was soon turned to profitable advantage. When a lord held several manors he appointed a steward whose duties were outlined in a *Seneschaucie* of the thirteenth century which has survived. On the individual manor, the chief officials were the bailiff, who was the farm manager, and the reeve, who was often chosen by the villagers, and carried out the day to day execution of the bailiff's orders. These officials were required to keep up yields and make sure of profits, and if they failed they were forced to make up the losses themselves. Lipson's statement that "the tillage of the Middle Ages was not primarily conducted with a view to profit" is the reverse of the truth. Indeed, having said the demand for corn was limited, he went on to discuss the rapid growth of a class of dealers in corn and the export of corn and "ministerial accounts showing frequent and extensive sales of surplus produce in markets." The increase of wool exports by 10,000 sacks between 1280 and 1310 would, by itself, indicate a sharp rise in pastoral farming for a profit. Some recent studies of estate incomes show that they rose steadily in the twelfth and thirteenth centuries on Church and lay estates. One estimate is that incomes from land rose 60 per cent between 1086 and 1220 and 50 per cent between 1220 and 1250, levelling off to rise by 30 per cent from 1250 to 1350. Even allowing for a price rise in the same period, this is a substantial increase, and it will later be shown that better management and accounting were features of agricultural improvement during this period. Thus, it is clear that the system had its advantages, and although influenced by custom, was capable of responding satisfactorily to market demands.

Day-to-day operation of the manor was regulated by manorial custom. Although older historians regarded this as a guarantee against the lord's tyranny, it is now fairly clear that "though the manor court probably achieved about the same proportion of abstract justice as the other court of those days, yet it must be obvious that the lord was able to load the dice." The court was presided over by the bailiff or steward, and the reeve was scarcely likely to take the villein's part. There were three types of manorial court. Courts Customary met on every manor to discuss day to day working. Courts Baron were held for freeholders every three weeks and determined all land disputes. Finally, there were the Courts Leet which were held once a year, and resembled the proceedings of the court leet of the hundred dealing with simple cases. From the court rolls the most intimate glimpses of the ordinary villeins are obtained, for they were themselves almost entirely illiterate. In the court a variety of cases was heard. The court was a source of revenue because it collected the personal fines due from the villeins and imposed the petty judicial fines. Also, it adjudicated on matters of ownership and farming particularly fencing, intercommunal grazing and collective ploughing. In 1280 William Dergate, a tenant of the Abbot of Hales, was fined for using a mill other than the lord's. In 1443 Robert Ludlow of Stepney was fined for his part in an affray. The majority of cases were concerned with enforcing the law or the lord's rights, and there were a few cases where a villein challenged a lord in his own court.

Theoretically, the demesne land was farmed by the villeins on the estate, although there were specialised workers and paid hands as well. A villein was required to render week works and boon works; and, in addition, special services such as carting. Week work was the ordinary day to day labour on the lord's demesne and was often heavy. At Great Chesterford in 1270, each villein owed 714 quarter days. Boon works (*precariae*) could vary immensely and were often complicated. Frequently they fell at times of the year when the villein was anxious to work his own lands. At Great Chesterford they had, for example, to plough $16\frac{1}{4}$ acres at ploughing time which was nearly three days' extra work. Firm measures were taken to ensure that the full quota of week and boon works were carried out. On some of the Ramsey Abbey manors "if any holy-day come upon the day when the serfs should work . . . it shall not be allowed to them, but they shall work on another day instead." Bad weather was not permitted to reduce the lord's requirements, and even (absences) because of illness had to be made up later. On the Ramsey estates, "if he [the serf] be so ill as to take the Holy Communion, then he shall be quit of all work for the next fortnight following." Such a method of exacting work was never popular. Inducements in the form of gifts were sometimes given, such as some sheaves of corn to the harvesters. Henley commented on the need to watch very carefully the performance of villein labour, and lords early found it more convenient to commute the services for a money rent and pay hired labour. It is wrong to associate commutation directly with either the rise of a money economy or the growing wealth of individual villeins. It was a constant practice and may be found, for instance, at Harmondsworth in 1110. Henley's comment that "customary servants neglect their work and it is necessary to guard against their fraud" indicated the main reason for lords wishing to free themselves from older obligations. This was particularly so when a smaller labour force was needed for sheep-rearing. Moreover, although the lord could usually have his own way, it was not always possible as long as agreement had to be obtained from the whole community of the manor. Thus, at Alsiston in Sussex, although tenants were required to carry out unlimited cartage, in fact, if they could not return in a day, the expense of the journey was borne by the lord. At Weston, a Ramsey Abbey manor, the tenants prevented the bailiff from delaying the ploughing on customary grounds. From a practical point of view, commutation was bound to spread.

Most villages were engaged in mixed farming, and too little attention is often paid to the other main divisions of land besides the three-fields and the demesne, consolidated or scattered. It has been stressed recently that the amount of specific pasture land (meadows) was small in relation to the arable, or to the number of animals. In one sample of villages in Leicestershire, only twenty had a ratio of arable to pasture of 20:1. The meadows were treated in the same way as the three fields being divided communally into strips called doles instead of selions. Hay was always scarce and the value of meadow pasture was double that per acre of arable land. Not until the decline in population, decreasing yields per acre and the rise in the profitability of sheep and cattle farming were combined in the fourteenth century did the amount of pasture sizeably increase. Lipson cited the example of Dorset, which had only 7,000 acres of meadow in 1086 compared with 95,000 in 1915. After the hay was mown, the fields were used for pasture and, as this was from February to August, the fields concerned were known as Lammas meadows. They should not be confused with Michaelmas land, which was the open fields used for pasture between harvest and seed times.

To meet the deficiencies of grazing, the villeins had the right of using the commonland of the village. Some commons were waste marsh, brushwood or heath—but more often they were cleared areas. The villeins had certain valuable rights. Estover allowed them to take timber; pannage allowed them to pasture pigs on acorns and beech-mast, and as pork was the staple meat of the villeins it was a greatly valued right. Turbary was the right to cut peat and turf in more marshy regions. The right to pasture cattle or sheep on one's "stint" of the common was jealously guarded and was of immense importance because the villein would sell his animals, and could not rear them on his croft where he usually grew vegetables. There were three basic pasture rights: "appendant" pasturing was a general permission for commonable beasts, "appurtenant" was for animals other than those used in tillage such as pigs, goats or geese, and "in gross" was when all (including non-virgate holders) might take advantage of the commons. Such rights were carefully guarded and attempts to curtail them had resulted in the Statute of Merton (1236). Where the lord required a particular area he would often grant a new common in exchange.

Villeins themselves had their own lands besides their virgate, and it will later be shown that during the thirteenth century they added to these in such a way as to make themselves copyholders and leaseholders. Villeins formed 108,000 of the 238,000 tenants recorded in *Domesday Book*—approximately 38 per cent of the population. The percentage varied from place to place. In Kent there was no villein tenure, in East Anglia about 15 per cent were villeins, while in fully manorialised counties the figure could be nearer 60 per cent. Villein land consisted of a virgate which could vary from 15 to 80 acres although 30 is taken to be a rough average. The villein possessed his own house and a surrounding toft or croft. Usually the holding was indivisible, although this did not apply in Kent, the north or the west. Lesser villeins—the bordars and cottars—accounted for a further 32 per cent of the population at the time of *Domesday*. There was no important legal difference between villeins and cottars; rather it was economic. The average cottar's holding was from 2 to 10 acres, but usually about 5. As they were poorer, they had less labour services to perform and did not, for example, take part in carting. They formed the pool for hired labour, and menial tasks such as hedge-cutting. It has been said that if he was not a substantial farmer, the villein was a good deal more than a landless peasant. Many villeins were indeed free ceorls before the Conquest and they were depressed into being villeins by legal definition and economic weakness. At Cambridge, the number of socmen fell from 900 in 1066 to 213 in 1086. This process can be seen at work considerably later. Thus, when the manor of Martham was given by the Bishop of Norwich in 1101 to the monks of the cathedral, the thirty-six freemen became villeins outright and the twenty-seven socmen lost their position and became customary tenants.

Villeins rendered heavy services and owed a considerable number of dues to the lord. These duties distinguished them from free tenants who had fixed services. Although custom may well have dictated the general amount of services which might be demanded, the lord kept the right to vary them, or, as the jurist Henry de Bracton wrote, a villein should not know today what he may be asked to do tomorrow. On taking up his holding, the villein paid a fine for entry, and gave the best beast to his lord (heriot). He had to give the second-best beast to the parish clergyman. The villein was *adscriptus glebae* (bound to the soil) so that he had no right to leave the manor. If he did he had to pay a fine called chevage, which was still being paid at Gimingham in Norfolk in the reign of Henry VIII. Lords had the right to pursue villeins who had left the manor, and a writ in Common Law, *de nativo habendo*, could be invoked. Even the right of the villein to leave the manor to join holy orders was restricted by the Constitutions of Clarendon in 1164 and a licence was required. Similarly, the education or apprenticeship of a son required the lord's permission. Villein marriages were carefully controlled, and daughters and even sons could not marry without the payment of a fine (merchet). Villeins could have their children married off against their will. It was significant that medieval lawyers referred to a villein's offspring as *sequela* (litter) not *familia* (family). On the death of a villein, the lord took a beast or some important item, and the Church the next-best item for a mortuary fee. Enforced marriage was the most disliked of villein burdens. At Halesowen in 1274 we find: "Thomas Robins of Oldbury came on summons, and was commanded to take Agatha Halesowen to wife; he said he would rather be fined; . . . it was ordered that he should be distrained." Fines were also extracted if a villein was found to have an illegitimate daughter. Thus, personal status was clearly degraded, and, on the manors of the monks of Durham, fines had to be levied on those who taunted others with being villeins.

Beyond these personal obligations, there were also financial penalties involved in being a villein. Indirectly, by the levying of demands in kind for eggs or poultry, the villein suffered. He had to provide ploughs and carts for those particular services if necessary. The villein had to have his corn ground at the lord's mill, and paid a duty (multure) of something in the range of a sixteenth for the privilege. The right to tallage or to tax the villein at will was the lord's prerogative, but this was clearly limited by the customary nature of the requirements. Moreover, amercements or fines were limited so that if, for example, the lord took all a man's chattels so that he could not perform future services, then the lord could be sued in the Common Law courts. Magna Carta re-enforced this, and specifically referred to wainage or the duty of carting. In theory also, villeins ought not sell their own produce, or even be engaged in industry, without the lord's consent. In one case, an abbot of St Alban's finding tenants had made their own millstones, ordered them to be turned into paving-stones.

Status for the villein was a complicated matter. Although there was a distinction drawn beween villeins by birth (*nativi*) and villeins by tenure (*villani*) this tended to disappear. Since many *nativi* had been slaves previously, the status of villeins was depressed by lawyers, so that villein and servile rank were indistinguishable. Azo of Bologna formulated the status of villiens on the Continent and depressed them to the level of slaves. Bracton repeated the view that there were only two classes: "aut liberi aut servi." The misfortune of English villeins was that whereas in the French and German regions *chartes-lois* and *Weistümer* had limited villein services, this was not the case in England. To that extent, English villeins were worse off than their continental contemporaries. But the villein was not a slave. He was free against everyone except his lord. He had the right to bear arms. He could serve on juries in the Common Law courts. Even the lord's rights were restricted, according to Bracton, "by civil right, so that life and limb are under the protection of the king." What seems almost certain is that the villein's right often corresponded to the degree of manorialisation. In places such as Durham, in Lancashire on the de Lacy estates, Gloucestershire and Worcestershire, villein and servile status were equated. In other places where tenants took in their own lands by assarting, as in Nottinghamshire and Northamptonshire, where free tenants had survived as in East Anglia, or where production for a market increased villein wealth as in Essex or Hertfordshire, villeins were less restricted. It is clear, however, that villein tenure was more strictly and adversely defined from the villein's point of view as the Middle Ages passed. That this should happen, when, for a number of reasons, the proportion of villeins to freemen was declining, was an important reason for later villein discontent, particularly when lords tried to enforce legal rights over villeins who had become economically and tenurially more independent. Villein status long remained alive after villeins by tenure had largely ceased to exist. Parliament refused to abolish it in 1536 and, before the last villein status case concerning one Pigg had been brought in the reign of James I, even so important a person as the Mayor of Bristol might find himself legally a villein in 1586.

Villein holdings underwent a series of changes in size and

organisation in the period before the thirteenth century, when en-
largement or consolidation coupled with the spread of rents and
payment for labour were the main characteristics. Fragmentation was
a feature of villein holding in contradistinction to freeholdings which
were compact. One manor at Martham in Norfolk shows that
between *Domesday* and 1293 the number of tenants had risen
from 63 to 107, and that the sub-division of holdings was to the
extent of 935 holdings in more than 2,000 separate strips. This was
brought about by pressure on the available land. At Taunton the
average size of holding for each tenant fell from 3·3 acres to 2·5
acres between 1248 and 1311 and this tendency was widespread.
Since estimates of the amount of land necessary to maintain a
proper standard of living vary considerably, it is not easy to claim
that those divisions indicated increasing poverty. Villeins supplemented their incomes by production for the market, and wage
labour; and although villein lands were divided, a villein often
acquired other lands by purchase or on leasehold. Pollard and
Crossley state that "only about one per cent of villeins and eight
per cent of free tenants in Midland England were farming holdings
of more than one virgate in 1274." However, taking other less-
manorialised areas into consideration, and assessing all a villein's
possessions, his position had improved considerably during this
period. Thus, Hilton argues that the *Extenta Manerii* for 1279–80
show a considerable increase in the number of free tenants. Whereas, in 1086 4 per cent was the highest percentage of freemen,
in 1279–80 somewhere between 55 and 70 per cent "of the total
recorded peasant households were holding in free tenure." This
growth of free tenure was likely to occur on the fringes of large
estates, when assarting or intaking was common, or where the full
range of manorial obligations had never been established. It depended also on the extent to which the demesne itself was leased
out, because, in order to consolidate his demesne, a lord might
well lease outlying strips or even sell off parts he did not require.
The movement towards the fragmentation of original villein lands
accompanied by the acquisition of new ones reached its height
in the thirteenth century.

Paradoxically, while villein status was more strictly defined, the
economic power and tenurial independence of the individual villein
grew. For example, the Randall family of Wigston Magna accumulated land for a hundred years to become substantial farmers. In
some cases, farmers combined to buy holdings, as they did in
the fens on the Ramsey Abbey estates. It was only when the lords
insisted that commutations were temporary and sought to regain
labour services, or when a well-off villein owning his land was

required to do carting or pay multure, that friction arose. It was in the areas where manorial burdens were pressed most heavily, or in places where villein tenure had not been common, that trouble arose in the fourteenth century. This problem was particularly acute in places where an increasing number of villeins had in practice abandoned their old status while the remainder were forced to perform an ever-increasing burden of services. At St Albans Abbey, which was notorious for disputes, free newcomers from London were the problem. In Essex and Suffolk, craftsmen in the new cloth industry were the exemplars to villeins oppressed on the estates of Bury St Edmunds. The Bishop of Winchester, who was forced to follow fleeing villeins to the gates of London, had only 5 per cent of free tenants. Economic changes eventually replaced villein tenure by the smallholding or copyhold, and later the leasehold.

Villein status could only be removed by manumission and, in the fourteenth and fifteenth centuries, this became increasingly common. As Barbour said:

"Ah, freedom is a noble thing,
Who freedom hath, hath great liking."

It was this wish to be freed from any trace of servile status that lay behind the demands of Essex and Kent rebels in the Peasants' Revolt of 1381. The same demand was still made during Ket's Rebellion in 1549, although only about 1 per cent of the population were involved. Manumissions were a source of income for lords, so that it cost about £10 to be freed from villein status. The Church, influenced by Roman law, and also by the Canon Law that forbade the sale of chattels, required a dispensation from the Pope before villeins were freed. Thus, the Bishop of Chichester freed bondmen in 1522. Crown lands had bondmen, as those who were still villeins came to be known. Henry VII freed some and Elizabeth seems to have freed 300 through the agency of Sir Henry Lee in the 1570s in the Duchy of Lancaster. Under the Tudors, the numbers of villeins fell rapidly. At Forncett in Norfolk they declined from eight in 1500 to three in 1550 and disappeared by 1575. By the end, manumission cost as much as £120 in one case at Forncett. By 1577, however, William Harrison's contention that "as for slaves and bondmen we have none" was reasonably accurate.

In the same way as the villein turned his attention from serving the lord to making a profit and becoming a free landowner, the lords were consolidating demesnes, substituting rents for complicated customary services and money wages for boon works, introducing techniques of estate management, and seeking for a profit. Only when the price of labour rose did they prefer services, particularly since rents and wages were not always influenced to the same extent by custom. Incomes from manors seem to have increased considerably in the early medieval period. Thus, the revenues of the Bishop of Winchester (82 per cent of whose grain was marketed) recorded a rise from between £2,000 and £3,000 in the early thirteenth century to £5,350 by the third quarter of the century. This was true for most of the larger landowners. Fifty-four barons in the late twelfth century had an average income of £202. At the end of the next century, of twenty-seven so far examined, the average income was £668. In some cases, as much as 5 per cent of income was ploughed back in investments. Allowing for the increasing range of expenditure relative to the amount of imported goods consumed and to the rising prices at home, there is little doubt that manorial incomes rose fairly steadily, if not dramatically, during the period up to the beginning of the fourteenth century.

Manors were not isolated and static communities uninfluenced by economic considerations. Tradition and custom played a large part in the administration and farming methods. Self-sufficiency was the first consideration as of necessity it had to be. But rents and incomes, profits and losses were the concern of landlords, stewards and bailiffs from the earliest times. Demand from the local population and the more widespread attractions of a local market in corn or wool led landlords and villeins to assart and to enclose, to approve the commons, to engross the demesnes, to buy subsidiary holdings, to lease manors, to let villages decay, or to substitute one form of production for another. Such was the pattern particularly on church estates, and although evidence is heavily weighted towards consideration of these estates, the trend on lay manors would scarcely have been very different. Villeins were oppressed, but they were not slaves. They had servile status, but sufficient economic power and political rights to gradually eliminate the status after they had removed the obligations. These burdens were removed by commutation and manumission in response to the lord's financial needs and the increasing ability of villeins to pay for both. Opinions on the life of the villager have varied. Even Coulton was moved to write "that the life of the medieval village had a true dignity at its best, and even a true glory in the highest sense of that word, no man can doubt who reads Chaucer's brief description of the ploughman." Yet, for so many, it was a life of poverty, low living standards, constant demands for services in body, cash and kind, and an annual routine which changed but little in its fundamentals over hundreds of years.

THE EVIDENCE OF *DOMESDAY BOOK* AND THE
CHARACTER OF THE TWELFTH-CENTURY ECONOMY

From the Norman Conquest in the 1060s to the beginning of the thirteenth century stretches a period with certain common characteristics. It is not an easy period to analyse. Evidence is still "necessarily impressionistic and resists any exact measurement." Lady Stenton remarks that "to trace the ups and downs of economic life during this period is impossible, but certain facts and tendencies seem to appear from the thinning mists of the past." However, with *Domesday Book* as an initial guide, and an increasing weight of official and local records available in printed form as the years pass, we are not entirely without evidence. The period concerned was the feudal epoch in English history. At the beginning, the revenues of the state were almost entirely feudal. By the end, the revenue from customary sources (£8,000 a year) was inadequate for the expenditure of a government that had increased enormously in size and required £17,000 a year. From this dilemma developed the complicated series of extraordinary taxes which were to multiply in the succeeding centuries. The Royal Council (Curia Regis) was the centre-piece of administration at the beginning of the period, but by the end the Exchequer had developed into a large and complicated government department, and a network of courts (King's Bench and Common Pleas in particular) had developed to strengthen royal power. Magna Carta marked the determination of the upper estates of the realm to have a say in the running of finance and administration, and the concept of inviting other *communitas*, such as the merchant, to participate in those matters had already started.

Politically, the period was one in which England was closely linked to the Continent from 1066 until the loss of Normandy in 1204. The impact of this on economic development was great. Landowners held land on both sides of the Channel. Feudal methods spread here. Various monastic groups established sister houses in England, and spread their important influence in certain parts of the economy. It has been said that "the commerce of the Twelfth Century was municipal rather than national" so that close links between towns on each side of the Channel were important. Thus, "many of the citizens of Rouen and Caen passed over thither, preferring to be dwelling in this city [London] in as much as it was fitter for their trading." Rouen and Saint Omer under Henry II and Calais under Richard I traded in this country free from tolls. It was no coincidence that Richard I first formulated a code of conduct for seamen in 1190 and that, by 1266, these laws of Oléron had been applied on both sides of the Channel. Although it is difficult, it has to be realised that no English king spoke English in this period, and that most of them spent many years abroad. Richard I was only in England for six months of his reign.

This cross-Channel unity can be easily illustrated by some brief consideration of the important religious figures of the time. The reform of the English Church under the Normans, which set on foot a massive building revolution and a great monastic revival, was the work of Lanfranc and Anselm of Le Bec in Normandy. At Le Bec, Theodore, future Archbishop of Canterbury, was trained together with John of Salisbury. Under Anselm studied another Anselm who went to Laôn. There, the second Anselm educated William de Corbeuil, rebuilder of Rochester Castle and another Archbishop of Canterbury, and Alexander and Nigel FitzNeal, Bishops of Lincoln and Salisbury. The latter's son was the author of the famous *Dialogus de Seccario*. Thomas à Becket, the English martyr, went to Le Bec. He was the son of Gilbert Becket, Port Reeve of London under Stephen and ex-burgher of Rouen. Becket was commemorated not only at Canterbury, but also at Lille, Lyons, Verona, Florence, Palermo and Monreale in Sicily.

From this close interconnection arose many new features in our economic life and alterations in the pattern of our industry and trade. Along the Welsh border, towns received charters modelled on the customs of Breteuil. Frenchmen settled in London and Norwich, Flemings in Pembrokeshire, Jews in Norwich, Lincoln and York. Feudalism was introduced. Feudal law reduced the number of freemen, but it abolished slavery, so that by the *Extenta Manerii* of 1279 the status had vanished. Lanfranc and Wulfstan had done their work, as the continuance of the trade at Narbonne and Marseilles in the thirteenth century showed that it was necessary for them to do. The Church was reformed and brought more closely under Papal control. England became involved in financing the Crusades. The gathering of 164 ships at Dartmouth in 1147 for the Second Crusade prepared the way for the rise of the western ports, whose prosperity was increased by fleets of pilgrim ships bound for St James of Compostella's shrine in Spain. Aquitaine was acquired by Henry II in 1152 and the foundation laid for the medieval wine trade as that area of France gave up corn for the vine. By 1272, Southampton imported 3,147 tuns and London 3,799.

Destruction and economic decline were, however, the immediate effects of the Conquest. There was loss of life and destruction of property on a wide scale. The movement of armies and castle building were largely, but not entirely, responsible. Towns in the wake of the campaigns in the south-east, Midlands and north suffered from destruction. At Canterbury the building of a moat cost eleven burgesses their property. At Lincoln 240 properties were "waste" including 166 for the building of the castle, and 74 by "misfortune, poverty, and ravage by fire." The number of burgesses at Chester fell by 205 between 1066 and 1086. Destruction was recorded at Barnstaple, Wareham, Dorchester and many other places. Some towns not directly involved in either campaigns or castle building were also affected. Ipswich burgesses fell in numbers from 538 to 210, and those at Derby from 243 to 140 between 1066 and 1086, although those falls were no doubt partly the result of stricter tenurial definitions.

Decline in valuations in rural areas was most noticeable in Yorkshire, Derbyshire and Cheshire which William laid waste in 1069 to 1070, and this is clearly revealed in *Domesday Book*. From a sum of £3,479 in 1066, the valuations for Yorkshire had fallen in twenty years to £1,168. So savage was the attack that, of the 1,900 villages dealt with, 850 were depopulated, 300 laid waste, and 400 underpopulated. A complete change had come about fairly quickly as a result. People had moved from the wolds and moors into the vales of Derwent and Pickering, unable to sustain themselves any longer on the higher ground. Fifty villages in the lowlands recorded large increases in population. The population had been brought within the strictest feudal control of men such as the Count of Mortain or the Count of Brittany in the honour of Richmond only 6 per cent of the population were free tenants in an area which had been previously settled by the Danes and would have been likely to have contained a higher proportion. To this destruction must be added that in Hampshire for the New Forest.

As the land was handed over to the new tenants-in-chief and feudal law began to operate, there was a shift in the total numbers of the main classes. The number of slaves fell at once, but this was because Norman lawyers tended to class them as bordars and cottars and to equate the two groups. What was, from one point of view, gain was, from another, a setback. The number of freemen fell considerably. It has been shown that encroachments of the Norman lords led to the widespread depression of the social classes in East Anglia. But this development should not be too strongly emphasised. The percentages for eastern counties (Lincolnshire 45 per cent, Norfolk 32 per cent and Suffolk 40 per cent) remained high in 1086 even if the national percentage was only 12 per cent. What had happened, however, at the same time, was that predial services had been extended to places, such as Leicester, where they had not been in force before and they had been increased in other

E

places, such as the estates of Ramsey and Ely Abbeys. *Domesday* was in some ways the record of a war-weary economy. By its limitations in excluding London and Winchester, and paying little attention to industry or areas of non-demesne farming such as Lancashire, the work added to an impression of a low-powered economy. But it has to be remembered that it was not primarily an economic document. If anything, it will underestimate the amount of economic activity, and it should be taken into consideration with other evidence, such as a slow inflation, rising population, growing trade, and massive investment in building, which indicate a more buoyant economy. The ability of the Norman kings and the long peaces under Henry I and Henry II enabled the economy to progress. Even Stephen's reign with a civil war or Richard I's reckless expenditure and careless government did not halt the trend upwards. The foundation of 109 new towns between 1100 and 1300, or 228 new monasteries between 1135 and 1189, rising wool exports, and tin production, the granting of charters for boroughs and fairs—all were indications that the initial disadvantages of the Norman Conquest were soon outweighed by gains.

Clearly, at first, many people suffered. There were exiled and debased Saxon ceorls. Geburs and geneats found they had heavier week and boon works to perform. In certain towns, tallages fell only on the English burgesses while foreigners were exempted in such places as Shrewsbury. New lords, particularly the Church, were anxious to reap a quick profit from their new boroughs. Castle building implied subjugation, necessitated destruction and involved the use of forced labour. The great mounds at Dover and York, for example, were each built in eight days. Severe penalties, particularly mutilation, were increased in the tracts of the royal forests, and also for other offences. There was no significant alteration in the design of coins in Norman times, but a systematic attempt was made to reduce the large number of mints. Twelve mints ceased to operate under Henry I and when Henry II came to the throne there were only thirty mints. In 1125, those who produced badly minted money were subjected to the loss of their right hands, and one contemporary said no less than ninety-four moneyers were so treated. Other disabilities such as the curfew or presentment of Englishry are well known.

Nevertheless, the systematic creation of a new landowning class, the spread of feudal organisation, and the reform of the Church lay at the basis of twelfth-century growth. The new landowners, of which a third were great churchmen, not only brought new ideas but also new ambitions. Farming for a profit and the development of a corn market, and the sale of borough and market rights in return for a fixed levy were two indications of the Norman barons' concern with financial matters. English feudalism was less disruptive of royal authority than its continental counterpart. Estates were scattered, honours were few, mesne tenants still owed direct allegiance to the Crown. Moreover, William kept the Saxon forms of taxation (geld was levied in 1084) and military organisation (the fyrd was used in 1088 and 1106) to ensure that the Crown was not completely dependent on feudal sources. In particular, the old hundred and shire courts remained. Twice yearly, the sheriff collected the royal revenue from the shires, and during Henry I's reign the Exchequer was organised by Roger le Poer, Bishop of Salisbury. Church reform brought clerical celibacy, the expulsion of secular clergy from the monasteries, a new system of Church courts under archdeacons and increased Papal control, emphasised by appeals to Rome and the presence of legates in the country in 1070. The change was accompanied by violence. One Bishop actually had Saxon clergy shot down with arrows at the altar of Glastonbury in 1083 for refusing to adopt new services.

Yet the overall effect was an immense gain in administrative efficiency, scholastic prowess and new ventures for the Church. Canterbury's supremacy over York was decided. The *Use of Salisbury* was adopted as a common service book from 1085 onwards. Diocesan structure was reformed so that cathedrals were no longer situated in dwindling villages, but became the flourishing centres for population. Sherborne and Ramsbury were moved to Old Salisbury and from there in 1220 to the newly planned present town of Salisbury. Selsey, largely cut off by the sea, was moved to Chichester. Dorchester became the See of Lincoln. Elmham moved temporarily to Thetford, and then in 1096 together with Dunwich was moved to Norwich. Where complete removal was not possible, sees such as Bath and Wells and Coventry and Lichfield were created. Later, in Henry I's reign, new sees such as Carlisle and Ely were created. In these sees a generation of Norman bishops launched a building revolution which in its extent was the greatest single economic event in medieval history. It involved the construction of new cathedrals and churches on so wide a scale that today only 300 ecclesiastical buildings have any trace of Saxon work. Gundulf of Rochester, Remigius of Fécamp, Herbert de Losinga, Ranulf Flambard, William de Corbeuil, William de St Calais and William Walkelin were bishops who understood architectural principles, introduced new techniques and provided the finance for what one writer has called a "proto-industrial revolution."

Nor were the monastic clergy any the less energetic in this period. In 1066 there were only thirty-five monasteries and nine nunneries in the country. During the twelfth century, new monastic and military Church orders spread into the country, and the numbers of regular clergy rose steadily. At Gloucester, under Abbot Serlo, numbers rose from ten to one hundred monks between 1072 and 1104. This change was part of a European revival of monasticism which had begun at Cluny with the reform of the Benedictines, or "black monks." Then came attempts to make monastic life more vigorous—the Grandimontans (1074) or the Carthusians (1084) and the less well-known Praemonstratensians (1119). These foundations had little effect in England where there were only nine Carthusian houses, but the Cistercian order, founded by Robert of Molesme at Cîteaux near Chartreuse in 1098, was to have a massive impact on England. The second prior of the order was an Englishman, Stephen Harding, and in 1119 he drew up the *Carta Caritas* outlining the need for a more active vocational monasticism. Monks were to work for themselves, and thus the Cistercians in the early generations went out into the wilder parts of the country to settle. They arrived in England in 1128 at Waverley in Surrey, but their key foundations occurred in the 1130s. Tintern (1131), Rievaulx and Fountains (1132) were among the first, and by 1216 there were 68 Cistercian monasteries in England. In all Europe, there were nearly 500. Cistercian agricultural activities will claim much attention later. England's own orders, the Austin Canons and the Gilbertians, also developed at this time. One indication of monastic influence on the economy was their power over boroughs, twenty of which were in Benedictine hands. Abbot Baldwin developed Bury St Edmunds, the Abbots of Burton founded Burton-on-Trent and Abbot's Bromley. The Bishops of Norwich encouraged the development of Bishop's Lynn (now King's), and Robert of Bath and Wells that of the town of Wells between 1136 and 1166. Such improvements need to be set against later efforts by the Church to restrict the rights of boroughs, and the long period when the Church resisted agricultural change as far as improving the lot of its tenants was concerned.

Military church orders may at first seem to have little to do with economic development. Yet their mere existence helped to bring new ideas from the Near East including possibly the earliest windmills and fulling-mills. The Knights Hospitaller who were founded in 1092 provided for the sustenence of pilgrims, and were often known as the Knights of St John of Jerusalem. They were established in Clerkenwell, London, in 1144. More important were the Knights Templar, founded by Hugh de Payens in 1118. They were formed to protect pilgrims, but soon became a residential order. They were in England by the late 1120s, but their headquarters in the New Temple, London, was founded in 1161. Places such as Temple Combe and Cloud in Somerset, Temple Newsam in Yorkshire and Temple Cressing in Essex are indications of their influence. An examination of their estates at Temple Bruer in Lincolnshire will indicate their economic importance. In 1185 rents in money were well established on this manor, which by 1316 was held almost entirely by rent-paying villeins. Between 1328 and 1332, the manor produced an annual surplus averaging 200 bushels of grain and between 2,700 and 4,500 sheep.

Domesday Book was so important a record of the late-eleventh-century economy that its defects have often been overlooked. Why William I wanted such a work produced is still not clear, and until further light is thrown on this aspect, it will be impossible to describe accurately the purposes of *Domesday Book*. It may have been a "geld book" but the geld was levied in 1084 and an Inquisitatio Geldi had been held. It may have been a feodary, that is, a feudal document. For this, different motives have been ascribed. Some have suggested that having apportioned England among his tenants-in-chief, William wanted to assess their power. Yet this could have been done more simply. Others have suggested that Odo's revolt (1082) combined with the threat of Danish invasion and French war to force William to take hasty action. If this was so, and the aim was a quick realisation of military potential, then it is difficult to see why trivial manorial details should have been included. Moreover, information was collected from the hundreds and not from the tenants-in-chief and the mesne tenants directly. This created language problems, for the villeins spoke Anglo-Saxon, the lords Norman-French and the lawyers and clerks Latin. The process was too complicated to indicate a work done under pressure. Breves were prepared on the manors. Regional and detailed books such as those known as *Exon Domesday* and *Inquisitatio Elienis*, were prepared, and then a final abbreviated form was produced in London, which it is unlikely William himself lived to see. The information required was for the period before the Conquest, for 1066, and for 1086. Such information would have been hard to come by or to check, and it must be assumed that some at least of the *Domesday* figures are inaccurate. Inelastic legal terminology hid the varieties of agricultural life. Since it was not an economic record, *Domesday* does not provide us even with basic figures such as the population. Evidence of economic activity has to be drawn from between the lines. Tolls indicate the existence of trade; water-mills, the presence of industry; rents, the circulation of money. Perhaps the biggest defects, however, were that *Domesday Book* did not deal with industrial activity such as the cloth industry or mining, and that since London and Winchester, the largest towns, were not included, it devoted a disproportionate amount of attention to agriculture. The negative inference that neither industry nor towns were of much account and that the level of trade was low has often been drawn, whereas it has already been shown that in all these spheres of activity the period after *Domesday Book* witnessed important developments. The number of town guilds, charters, markets and fairs, the rise in revenues, the attention paid to a national coinage and weights and measures, the rise of the Cinque Ports, and the growth of the cloth industry would all indicate the presence of a more complex economy than the one illustrated in *Domesday Book*. Lady Stenton described the twelfth century in its middle years as one of "stimulus, activity, an incitement to effort. New markets, arising everywhere, vied with the ancient centres for local economic leadership." Even if the economy remained localised, "the beginnings of a national economy" are to be seen, according to Lipson, in "the national regulation of the assize of bread, of weights and measures, of currency, and of the customs system." Magna Carta itself, with numerous clauses concerning weights and measures, navigation of rivers, or borough privileges, was an indication of the previous developments. The groundwork for thirteenth-century expansion was laid in the earlier period.

Which features of economic development are the best indicators of these changes? The growth in the urban sector of the economy involving the development of merchant guilds and the beginning of the great international fairs is one indication. The rise of the cloth industry, the revolution in building, the increases in mining output of metals and stone are also important. Financial organisation and the rise of what may be loosely called a taxation system, together with the attempts at national regulation mentioned above, indicate the part played by the government. New ports, the spread of traders from England throughout Europe, the rising customs revenue, and the increased dispersal of a wide range of luxury imports illustrate the growth of trade. Regulation of the currency, the exploitation of the Jews, the use of the Easterlings and Italians for financial purposes, the evolution of a credit system are evidence for the growth of commerce. The spread of economic activities, agricultural and urban, to remoter parts of the island, and the presence of foreign traders, particularly Flemings and Hanseatic merchants, show the existence of considerable surplus wealth. Castles, monasteries, cathedrals and less well-known halls, bridges and roads are tangible evidence of a century of slow but decisive growth, limited by the size of the population, the shortage of money and great technological restrictions in power and machinery. Once these factors were to some extent combatted, the thirteenth century was to be a period of more rapid expansion.

The distribution of the English population in *Domesday* is shown in Table 3.

Table 3—Population Distribution in the Early Middle Ages

Villeins	108,456
Bordars and cottars	88,952
Free tenants	35,513
Slaves	26,362
Manorial lords	9,271
Burgesses	7,968
Labourers, etc.	5,296

The low percentage of townsmen is attributable in the first place to the absence of London and Winchester, whose populations would have easily doubled the *Domesday* figure. Yet even after making every allowance for the rest of the town population, a figure of some 10 per cent of the people as town-dwellers may seem low. But the distribution of the towns and the concentration of privileges helping trade to develop within their walls made them far more significant than the smallness of their population suggests. Towns were catalysts of demand for the surrounding countryside. Their industries only accounted for part of the nation's industrial activity and a figure of 20 per cent involved in industry has been suggested. The character of the medieval town is assessed later. Here, we are concerned with the reasons for, and the way in which, growth occurred. Fundamentally, towns arose where environment dictated that they should. York, for example, was an administrative centre, and a centre for food and drink manufacture. In addition, wool from the Pennines served the cloth industry, and iron and skins from the same region provided the bases for other industries. For building, York drew lead from the Dales, limestone from east Yorkshire and wood from the forest of Galtres. Other towns, such as those developed by the Benedictines, a local landlord or even royal planning, had some artificial encouragement. Thus, William Briwerre, one of John's ministers, helped Chesterfield in Derbyshire and Bridgwater in Somerset to develop. Sometimes local geographical advantages were combined with a specific historical advantage. St Ives in Huntingdonshire was one such town. Originally, the neighbouring village of Slepe was more important, but in 1107 the building of a new bridge near the Abbey focused attention elsewhere. The Abbey itself, having its share of pilgrims to the shrine, was able to secure the grant of a market in 1110 and the town arose at that point. The Norman Conquest contributed to town development because it was followed by foreign settlements. At first there was a measure of political significance in these settlements. The French communities in towns such as Shrewsbury, Nottingham and York were kept separate and acted as a counterbalance to the activities of the English burgesses. However, it was not long before sizeable settlements of merchants took place, such as the one in London already mentioned. Thus, sixty-five Frenchmen were settled at Southampton and forty-one in Norwich.

In the period up to the death of John in 1216, there was a steady rise in the number of incorporated towns with a guild merchant and in the number of towns with the right to hold a market. If Tait's figure of seventy-one boroughs in 1066 is accepted, the number had risen by over a hundred to between 170 and 200 in the 1200s, including no less than seventy in Wales and Ireland. *Domesday Book* listed forty-two markets, but by the early 1200s about 200 places had the right to hold markets. With the caution that borough and market status were easily undermined, so that of the twenty-three boroughs of Lancashire in 1372 only four were there in 1485, these two figures indicate a considerable increase in urban wealth and population. Estimates of the actual size of the towns are difficult to make. *Domesday* estimates have to be guesses. London may have reached 20,000 by the beginning of the thirteenth century, but no other town was so large, and towns such as Bury and Ipswich had about 3,000 inhabitants. The only large towns were York (8,000), Norwich and Lincoln (6,000) and Bristol (5,000). Moreover, markets were sometimes established in smaller villages, so that, for example, in Suffolk there were seven towns and five other places with markets. Assessments of total trade based solely on borough records will therefore underestimate the amount. It is not until 1204, that the relative yields of *firma burgi* (the commuted dues) to the Crown can be assessed and the relative importance of towns can be considered. Then London and Boston were the chief ports of the country. Lincoln (£556), Hull (£344) and York (£175); all paid less than London's £836 and Boston's £780. On the south coast, Southampton already paid £712 compared with the Cinque Ports of Dover (£32) and Winchelsea (£62).

London and Winchester were, perhaps, the two most important towns. Quickly recovering from being overawed by Gundulf's Tower of London (1078) and Baynard's Castle by the Fleet, and from the whirlwind, fire and famine of 1091–2, London developed under a series of vigorous Port Reeves. It soon boasted thirteen conventual and one hundred parochial churches and such important adjuncts as Rahere's St Bartholomew or the headquarters of the Templars. London's organisation of a folkmoot, aldermen and wards meant that it was more independent than most towns and needed no guild merchant. In 1130 Londoners urged that they might be free to levy their own dues and to appoint their own officials, and these demands were granted in 1131. Only five boroughs (one of which was Winchester) had such privileges in 1189. London profited from the demands of Richard I and John to establish their first mayor (Henry FitzAylwin) in 1193, who by a charter of 1215 was to be elected annually. Slowly the concept of an elected mayor, a body of aldermen and a voting community of burgesses spread to other towns. Winchester had grown in importance after the building of a bridge by St Swithun. Although it ceased to be a royal residence and was sacked in the civil war of Stephen's reign, Winchester remained an important city and in 1216 was one of the six minting centres left. The others were London, Canterbury, Durham, Bury St Edmunds and York. The new cathedral, the priory of St Swithun's and the Hospital of St Cross meant that Winchester was an important religious centre, and it was the starting place for many pilgrims to Becket's shrine at Canterbury. It was the centre of a thriving agricultural region and the estates of the Bishop and Prior have provided much information on the functioning of large estates. It was a centre for collecting wool and making cloth. Above all, it was the site of St Giles's Fair, a grant for which was obtained by William Walkelin in 1096. This was the first of England's great fairs and, helped by this and privileges similar to those of London merchants, Winchester grew rapidly. The fair which lasted for three days was extended until it lasted for three weeks, and with the growth of Southampton, Winchester's position was strengthened as an entrepôt for London. The Bishops of Winchester even planned to build new towns as centres for their produce, but their plans came to nothing.

Merchant guilds were associations of townsmen, usually burgesses, for the purposes of protecting trade and developing the organisation and independence of that particular *communitas*. Their functions had been anticipated in Saxon times, but the first organised merchant guilds were at Burford in 1087 and Canterbury in 1093. Towns were jealous of any rights and privileges they might obtain, and they regarded even neighbouring towns as foreign. Thus, guild merchants not only regulated the trade of the town, but also regulated its relations with other towns. On the Continent, the cities of northern Italy or northern Germany attained sovereign

E*

independence. No English town claimed this, although London was powerful enough to be dealt with in its own right, and towards the end of the Middle Ages some towns achieved the status of a county. Towns achieved their independence by means of a charter which granted them certain privileges such as the *firma burgi*, the right to elect their own officials, the right to collect port duties, or the right to have a guild merchant. The relationship of the guild merchant to the government of the town was complex. The town moot had already acquired several privileges in Saxon times and those were extended by the activities of the guild merchant or of the burgesses as individuals. As both guild and moot became more restricted, the two mingled so that the burgesses of the town and the brethren of the guild merchant became very largely the same people. In some towns, Saxon frith guilds, which had regulated economic matters, had already combined the functions of municipal administration and economic regulation. It is clear from the records of the Leicester guild merchants that, although the two organisations were seen as distinct legal entities, for all practical purposes they were united. The earliest seals in use in the town of Gloucester in the thirteenth century bore the Latin inscription: "seal of the burgesses of the guild merchant."

The primary aim was to maintain the town's monopoly by making sure that only guildsmen profited from transactions and that losses were spread evenly in the community. On the one hand, the individual merchant had a protected market, but on the other, he had to pay entrance fees and accept overall regulations concerning such matters as the quality of goods or the wages to be paid. In some towns the right of "lot" prevailed, whereby merchants could claim part of the benefits of their colleagues' transactions. At Grimsby, for example, this was laid down in the town charter. Guild merchants intervened to prevent the commercial practices like regrating or forestalling which were not approved of by medieval merchants. At Bristol all cargoes were subject to a general meeting of the traders "for the weal of the said fellowship." A typical clash over regrating occurred in 1221, when Worcester complained that Droitwich was cornering the market to raise the price of food. In the matter of debt collecting, the right of "withernam" spread widely, whereby one townsman could be distrained for the debts of another, and this was permitted at Leicester. Gradually, however, they found this onerous and early charters such as those of Bristol (1188) or Winchester (1215) restricted this right which was later replaced by laws on the subject of debts in 1283 and 1285. Merchant guilds also regulated weights and measures through the Assize of Bread and Ale or where individual craft guilds did not exercise that function. Attempts such as that of 1197 or 1340 to create a uniform system throughout the kingdom failed, and this important matter remained in the hands of the guilds.

The intensity of borough rivalry led to the signing of treaties between towns, such as that between Winchester and Southampton in 1265 or that between Nottingham and Derby in 1279. Very often these treaties involved the right of citizens of one borough to trade in another. Sometimes, as in the cases of London and Winchester, the right had been secured by charter, in other cases, it was guaranteed by treaty. Moreover, this measure of liberalisation in town relations also affected foreign towns. The citizens of Amiens, for example, had certain privileges in London and Norwich. The distinctions between the various boroughs were blurred in another way. When town charters were requested and granted, it was usual to model them on other town charters. Thus, when Chesterfield obtained a charter it was based on that of Nottingham. The customs of London were widespread and the example of Winchester and Bristol was also followed. By far the most interesting group of towns were those affected by the customs of Breteuil in the Welsh and Irish marches. The example was first set by William FitzOsbern at Hereford, and it was followed elsewhere. Although some of the boroughs planned in this region, such as New Radnor, did not flourish others, such as Ludlow with its gridiron of streets, were effective foundations.

Prospects for obtaining a charter varied with the landlord of the borough. The Crown was by far the most generous granter of charters. At first William had refused to recognise the demands of Saxon boroughs that claimed ancient rights. This attitude was paralleled by Henry II's activities in 1180 when boroughs such as Barnstaple and Totnes were fined. Henry II's attack extended to "adulterine" craft guilds which had grown up. In London nineteen guilds were fined a sum of £120. To suggest that the Crown was an easy master is by no means true, for tallages were exacted from all towns except London, increasing in severity under Henry II. At certain periods, however, the Crown found itself short of money or eager to conciliate the merchants, and at such times charters were freely granted. They conferred four main privileges. The payment of a fixed feorm to the Exchequer instead of being subject to the sheriff was the most important, but it was not always granted irrevocably. Bristol obtained its grant in 1227, but not in perpetuity until 1462. Second in importance came the right to have a borough court which was often the town moot and became the town council. Then the town obtained the right to appoint their own officials.

Nottingham in 1189 was allowed to "make whom they will of their people to be their reeve at the end of the year." Lastly, the right to confer free status on inhabitants was conceded, although the period of residence necessary to free a villein from his lord varied from town to town. The right to hold a guild merchant conferred considerable economic privileges, as we have seen. The worsening financial situation in John's reign and in the later years of Henry III meant that these were the two periods when the most borough charters were granted.

Mention has been made of craft guilds. The heyday of those guilds was the fourteenth century, but in the cloth industry at least they have very much earlier origins. Cloth manufacture had been widespread in Saxon times, and during the twelfth century a large number of towns were involved in cloth production. Higher grade cloth was located at Stamford, Beverley, Lincoln, Louth and Northampton, while cheaper cloth came from London, Colchester and Oxford. Winchester, St Ives, Boston, Huntingdon and York were other centres of manufacture. Moreover, although these thirteen towns were the most important, cloth was produced elsewhere. The *Boldon Book* referred to dyers at Darlington in 1183. One writer in 1174 described the inhabitants of Norwich as "for the most part . . . weavers." Until the early years of the thirteenth century, cloth manufacture flourished in the towns, encouraged by Crown demands and an export trade. Flemish craftsmen helped the industry to develop, and the increasing output of wool was absorbed as well as a considerable import. Guilds of the various groups in this industry were the earliest to evolve. Under Henry I, weavers' guilds were established at London, Winchester, Oxford, Lincoln and Huntingdon by 1130 and among fullers at Winchester and cordwainers at Oxford. By Henry II's time, York and Nottingham had guilds of weavers, and Stamford a dyer's guild.

Cloth was exported to a variety of places including Aragon, Ireland, the north of Germany and even as far away as Venice, to which Stamfords found their way by 1265. Crown purchases, such as those made by Henry II in Lincolnshire in 1182 and 1184, were of considerable advantage to the industry. Some kind of regulation was necessary to control the industry in the interests of purchasers, and thus, in 1197, an Assize of Cloth was issued by Richard I, requiring each borough to appoint cloth surveyors to regulate the size. However, many towns, such as Stamford and Lincoln, purchased immunity from this regulation and a further attempt was made in 1215 when clause 35 of Magna Carta tried to resolve the difficulty. Cloth was measured in ells (lengths of 45 inches) and were either broad or narrow cloths. There were already many different varieties, as variations in price indicated. Thus, in 1184 scarlet cost 6s. 8d. an ell, but green only 3s. Although England was a cloth exporter it should, however, be remembered that during this period, the export of wool to feed the industries of Flanders and the north Italian towns, and the import of fine cloths were in all probability of more importance.

Trade in the period underwent a considerable expansion in several directions. Northwards, our trading pattern was affected by the arrival of the Hanseatic merchants. The Hanseatic towns developed in the middle of the twelfth century (Lübeck was founded in 1143) and when, in 1241, Hamburg and Lübeck combined, the basis was laid for the suppression of piracy and the defeat of Danish power which was completed by the Treaty of Stralsund in 1370. The Hansa headquarters in London was the Steelyard (now the site of Cannon Street Station) and there were settlements at east coast ports such as Boston and King's Lynn. Trade with Flanders increased, so that the Easterlings were among the providers of credit for the economy. Settlements of Flemings were made at Tenby in South Wales in 1106 and in Tweeddale in the 1130s. It is possible they also contributed to the development of the cloth trade by settling in Yorkshire. By far the most important extension of trade was, however, into the Mediterranean region caused by the Norman links with Sicily and later with Constantinople and by the impact of the first three Crusades of 1096, 1147 and 1189. English travellers and merchants were well known in the Mediterranean. Saewulf, a monk of Malmesbury, reached Jaffa. St Godric of Finchdale had visited Jerusalem and St James of Compostella's shrine in Spain. In Henry I's reign, Wulfric, a Lincoln man, was to be found at Constantinople.

The impact of the Crusades was enormous. At home the demand for money helped to free many boroughs and to develop the national taxation system. Methods of navigation, particularly the use of the rudder and compass, and laws for conduct at sea, were both developed. Venice, Genoa and other towns grew rich supplying the Crusaders and industries such as cloth and iron were stimulated to meet the demands of the largest medieval armies. Guilds and military orders provided for hospitality, and in hospices and hotels, such as the "Maison Dieu" at Calais, laid the foundations of the catering trade. Some of the earliest inns are called the "Saracen's Head" such as the one at Dunnow, and there is an inn called "Trip to Jerusalem" at Nottingham. From the East, new building developments aided by the use of mathematics spread including the ogee arch. Mechanical knowledge, particularly of new kinds of mills, was widely diffused. The southern countries became bright with orange, mulberry and rose trees from Palestine. The rich wore Arab damask from Damascus, muslin and velvet. Craftsmen learnt new techniques of wall-painting, of using glass (which was found in windows in 1177 for the first time) and of writing on paper. Such inventions as gunpowder, together with other Chinese products, particularly silk, spread from the great entrepôts of the Middle East that tapped the caravan routes from Cathay. New products such as sugar or cauliflowers began to diversify the ordinary diet. The Crusaders' contacts were those of warriors filled with contempt for barbarians and clearly all the effects were not intentional. They did not produce a genuine admiration for the skills of Arab or Levantine. Yet, on the other hand, the inpouring of wealth to Europe, the great wave of commercial enterprise which spread out, when in 1101 to 1102 Genoa and Venice staked out their claims, had their effects on the level of activity in many northern towns. The seizure of Mediterranean islands such as Cyprus paved the way for commerce. Thus, it is no coincidence that the period of the Crusades saw the rise of Southampton, Portsmouth and ports further west. The amount of luxuries imported increased, and also their variety, and in return our exports of corn, cloth and other products rose. The first customs duty to be levied was prisage on the import of wine, which amounted to one cask out of every ten casks in a ship, at the rate of 20*s.* a cask. Of the thirty-two ports, excluding Bristol, for which figures are available in 1202 to 1203 a sum of £4,958 was raised in customs duties over a period of twenty-nine months. There also seem to have been some smaller duties on exports, called lastage, which may have been paid on the export of such commodities as lead leaving Boston for France and the Rhineland or salt for the Low Countries and Norway.

Trade expansion cannot be directly measured, although sufficient indication has been given to show that it was considerable. However, the spread of trading facilities, the growth of numbers in those involved in credit activities, the rising scale of capital enterprises and the increasing variety of taxation all point towards an expansion which the growth of towns substantiates. Since trade was first localised and eventually between urban centres, it passed along dangerous and inadequate routes. It is not true that the roads of this time were extremely poor. A number of causeways were constructed in the region of the Wash. Henry I took an active interest in communications, re-opening the Fossedyke between Lincoln and Torksey and constructing roads in Wales. Magna Carta referred to the need for free navigation of the rivers. However, trade was made easier by the existence of fairs and markets protected by definite systems of laws, opened for specific periods of time, and encouraging the provision of credit facilities. Humbert de Romans defined the important difference between a fair and a market: "Fairs deal with the larger things . . . and to them come men from afar. . . . Markets are for lesser things, the daily necessities of life . . . and only people from near at hand come." Markets thus arose in all the main towns and in other places as well, for retail and wholesale purposes. Fairs arose in response to the demands of foreign trade and were related to port facilities. Fairs often owed something to the gathering of people for religious purposes at such places as St Cuthbert's Fair in Durham or St Ives's in Huntingdonshire. The first major English fair, St Giles's at Winchester, established in 1096, was founded by a churchman for economic purposes. Earlier legislation concerning trading before witnesses was supplemented by regulations to protect or to tax alien merchants. Thus, Henry II required all foreign merchants in the county to trade at Lincoln. Finally, as with the granting of town charters, the granting of the right to hold a fair was a further source of revenue, although a borough such as Cambridge paid for the right to have a fair when the neighbouring Stourbridge Fair already tapped the trade of the region.

Fairs were both small and large. As early as Norman times, places such as Chester and Arundel, and later small towns like Hereford and Preston had fairs. The great fairs were limited in number. Apart from Winchester, London was the only other southern town to have fairs. Bartholomew Fair was founded in 1133 by a monk called Rahere who was said to have been Henry I's jester. Like St Giles's, this was a cloth fair. Close by was Smithfield, first mentioned in 1253, and Billingsgate, first referred to in 1297. Henry III founded a rival fair at Westminster, modelled on St Giles's Fairs were also to be found at Northampton, Bristol, Stamford and Boston but the most important was Stourbridge, founded in John's reign, upon which north European trade with England was focused. Mention should also be made of certain specialised fairs such as Weyhill (cheese) or Yarmouth and Scarborough (fish). On the continent, the cities of Flanders and the Rhine Valley contained great fairs such as Bruges, Ghent, Leipzig, Frankfurt, Nuremberg or Augsburg, but the main fairs were those of Champagne in France. At Troyes, Lagny, Bar and Provins, exchange occurred between southern and northern Europe. It was not until their decline in the fourteenth century that Flanders became the great entrêpot for cloth and Mediterranean traders went by sea in preference to crossing Europe to the Champagne fairs.

MONEY, CREDIT AND TAXATION

Traditionally the period discussed in the last section has been regarded as a time when money and its use as credit was of little account. This traditional view may be stated as follows:

"Down to the middle of the fourteenth century money played a very minor role in the medieval economy, especially in agriculture. Some money payments were made, but they were almost entirely restricted to trade and industry, then in the infant stage and to the king's taxes. The manorial economy was not based on a monetary foundation; rents were usually paid in services, or in kind . . . In any case money payments could not be general before the second half of the fourteenth century on account of the shortage of silver. The supply of silver in Western Europe was insufficient to meet the demand until the mines of the new world were opened up in the early sixteenth century. Valuable deposits were discovered at Freiburg in the twelfth, and Saxony, Bohemia and Hungary in the fourteenth and fifteenth centuries, but additions to the supply were largely offset by a steady drain of silver to the East."

Thus, according to this view, it was possible in the second half of the fourteenth century for "a money economy . . . to develop although progress was limited until after the discovery of America." Although almost every part of this statement can be questioned and it can be shown, for example, that farming for a profit, money rents, wages, rising taxes paid in money, credit dealings, credit organisations, and the yield of customs, feudal financial dues, and manorial financial obligations all increased steadily throughout the eleventh and twelfth centuries and even more so in the thirteenth, this view still persists in many quarters. Professor M. M. Postan has adequately refuted the thinking behind the concept of a money economy as distinct from any other kind of economy, and has shown how, in spite of church theories, and limitations in the supply and velocity of circulation of money, credit was the basis of medieval trading enterprise. During the twelfth and thirteenth centuries, the amount of silver in England in fact increased to meet the demands of increased trade. Silver was being mined in several areas where lead was found. In Somerset the miners around Alston Moor were active by 1133 and they had organised a code of conduct by 1235. By 1196 silver was being produced in Weardale in mines previously royal but by then transferred to the Bishop. Derbyshire and Shropshire produced small amounts which tended to move eastwards to lubricate trade in the Stamford region. By the end of the thirteenth century, Devon had joined the producing areas and from 1290 to 1340 was a flourishing centre of production.

Thus, the yield of the mines between 1292 and 1297 was £4,046 of silver and £360 of lead. Although there was a decline, so that the figures for 1305 were £1,773 and £180 respectively, Cumberland and Westmorland were added to the producing regions in the 1320s.

Medieval currency, like that of Saxon England, was largely made from silver. In the Early Middle Ages, the Saxon concept of widely scattered mints to provide local supplies of coin was slowly replaced by the concept of a national currency. The Crown found that the evils attendant on these many mints, together with the possibility of profit, favoured the steady concentration of production. The old connection between borough rights and the number of moneyers gradually became irrelevant. Silver pennies were the basis of the currency. They were in use for a long period, subject to clipping and, for a time after the Conquest, in the hands of poor craftsmen. Even the dies of the London goldsmiths were poorly made. Recoinages took place in 1158, 1180 and 1205 to try and reduce the amount of bad money in circulation, but no real change occurred in the design. In spite of orders in 1205 and 1215 concerning uniform coinage, this was not achieved. However, the number of mints fell erratically but surely from the thirty places from which the 1158 issue was made to six at the beginning of Henry III's reign. However, temporary minting in places such as Corfe brought the number at times to twenty-one. It was the recoinage of 1247 that was decisive. Only three mints (London, Canterbury, Bury St Edmunds) were then functioning and sixteen temporary mints were founded to cope with the new coinage. Long-cross replaced the short-cross pennies in an effort to reduce clipping. Soon after England developed a bimetallic system, although the ratio was too low in relation to gold. Gold coinage in imitation of the Florentine was introduced in 1257, fell out of use and was revived in the 1330s. Edward I completed the process of creating a national coinage by appointing a Master of the Mint and introducing new low-value coins such as the groat (4*d*.), halfpenny and farthing. Apart from such exceptions as the Bishop of Durham's private mint or temporary ones created by the exigencies of war, production was concentrated in London where there were no less than thirty furnaces. Although he in fact depreciated the coinage, Edward I took severe measures against coin clipping and issued the statute De Falsa Moneta to keep out depreciated coins.

Thus, while, according to some historians, England had scarcely a trace of a money economy, Lady Stenton has claimed boldly that: "the volume of money current at once in this period was very large and it is quite impossible to make any estimates of the amount that was turned out from the mints year by year. . . . It was in sacks and barrels that they [coins] were sent about England in the early thirteenth century."

One important indication of the amount of money available was the size of both feudal and non-feudal taxation demands by the Crown and the creation of a large government department to deal with their collection. The total expenditure of the government has been estimated at £17,000 a year by the end of Henry II's reign, and the amount raised from customary sources to have come to £8,000. From the time of Henry I, when scutage had developed and the coiners had been attacked, the shortages of Crown income became more apparent and were made worse by the slow rise in prices. The sale of charters for towns and markets was a further indication of this shortage, together with Henry II's vigorous attempt to increase royal revenues from judicial fines. The creation of the Exchequer by Henry I and of the Exchequer of the Jews under Richard I were attempts to systematise the collection of the feorm from the counties and the irregular sources of income. In Saxon times, the Treasury had, it will be recalled, been the central financial department, but under Ranulf Flambard and Roger, Bishop of Salisbury, the Exchequer evolved into the more important organisation. A parallel body was established in Normandy by 1130. From that year, Pipe Rolls or Exchequer records became available and from 1155–6 there was a regular series lasting until 1830–1. The Exchequer was centralised at Westminster, and by the early 1170s had evolved its traditional procedure of a twice-yearly collection of the feorm at Easter and Michaelmas. At first, the Exchequer was a court for financial pleas as well as an administrative body, but by 1215 the two functions had been separated. The system of Receipt in the Lower Exchequer and Audit in the Upper Exchequer was organised by three great Treasurers. Roger Le Poer, Chancellor in 1100 and later Treasurer; his nephew, Nigel, Bishop of Ely; and his son Richard FitzNigel, Treasurer from 1160 to 1198, and Bishop of London. The Lower Exchequer dealt with the currency and there was a silverer responsible for calling in the coins for inspection. Its main purpose was to receive the sheriffs' feorm twice yearly "at the Tallies." Recording was by means of a set of tallies, 8 inches long and bored for filing. The size of the cut made indicated the sum received, each party retaining one half. When the audit was held in the Upper Exchequer, sheriffs and stewards of honours rendered "proffers" of their accounts, and handed in their tallies. The system was complicated and cumbersome and broke down between 1214 and 1217, for example, but the procedure continued until the 1830s. The Exchequer of the Jews was started in 1194 as a court for Jewish cases and more particularly financial matters. One Jew, a layman called the Arch-Presbyter, was appointed to act with his fellow justices. A system of enrolling transactions was evolved.

The early Angevins attempted to increase their customary revenues. Increments to the county farms occurred and were forbidden in Magna Carta. Forest fines were exacted. Tallages were imposed. Special custodians were appointed to the honours and abused the royal rights of wardship and marriage. Aids were constantly demanded and reliefs rose steadily in assessment. Scutage was doubled, made into a regular tax and collected for non-military purposes. Geld was levied occasionally until 1162 at 2s. a hide, but its yield was so low that it was virtually abolished. Nevertheless, in 1198 a carucage of 5s. on every hundred acres was charged, instead of on the customary hide. Opposition came from St Hugh, Bishop of Lincoln, and from William FitzOsbert in London. The main additional form of taxation developed, which in itself reflected the growing wealth of the country, was the tax on moveables first used in 1166, repeated in 1184 and levied as the Saladin Tithe of 1188. This tax was levied to provide for the Third Crusade and asked for a tenth of the value of all moveables, which was to be assessed by a local jury. Richard I and John exploited this new source of revenue. In 1194 a quarter was asked for; in 1203 a seventh; in 1207 a thirteenth. These were assessed by justices appointed by the king, and were likely to be heavier. Taxes on moveables tended to become either tenths or fifteenths and by 1290 the yield from those was about £116,000. After that date, they were restricted gradually until in 1334 a customary assessment amounting to £38,000 was established. Increases in customs duties and actual seizures of goods were resorted to as well. Apart from the normal prise or butlerage on wine there was, for example, the levying of a fifteenth on all exports and imports between 1202 and 1207. The main increase in customs came in 1275 with the Magna Custuma et Antiqua which added duties of 6s. 8d. on each woolsack and on every 300 woolfells (fleeces), a duty of 13s. 4d. on every last (120 hides) of leather. In 1303 the Nova Custuma added 3s. 4d. and 6s. 8d. respectively to those two rates of duties when aliens were involved in the trade.

One other way by which the Crown could finance its activities was to incur debts by acquiring loans, and this proceeding was made possible by the existence of a wide range of possible sources. Throughout western Europe, a number of different agencies met the financial needs of the throne. The Church, which in theory opposed money and excessive profit-making, provided for itself by means of *arra* or *collecta*, which were forms of forward payment. Chevisances were used to avoid a distinction between the capital sum and the interest since both were regarded as part of the trans- action. In addition to borrowing short, long-term loans could also be contracted from a wide variety of sources. There were English financiers, such as William Cade in the twelfth century. There were the Flemings or Easterlings, like John Van. After the needs of the Crown had been met, there were the Jews. The Knights Templar were wealthy enough to contribute specially to the Saladin Tithe of 1188 and, until they were bankrupted and dissolved by Edward II in 1312, provided a source for loans. Lastly, there were the Italian financiers, whose role has often been underestimated. The Arta della Lana, or cloth guild, of Florence was one wealthy organisa- tion which brought the cities of northern Italy and the early capita- lists of England into contact. The links created by the export of wool and the import of cloth were strengthened by the growth of trade at the time of the Crusades. Florence had 300,000 inhabitants and Milan and Venice each nearly 200,000. Richard I began with borrowings from Piacenza and soon a host of Italian financial groups were involved in meeting the Crown's needs and financing the operation of the wine and wool trades. The Riccardi, Peruzzi, Bardi, Frescobaldi, Pulci, Acciaiuoli and Bonsignori were among the most important. Demand was insatiable and financial integrity limited. Gradually the Italians were bankrupted, the Riccardi and Bonsignori perishing in 1301–2, the Bardi and Peruzzi in 1345. By then, however, the inflow of money and the knowledge of tech- nique was sufficient to enable an English financial network to emerge in the middle of the fourteenth century.

Supply of credit remained largely in foreign hands until then, but the use of the money is the significant matter. It is clear that, in spite of all the restrictions of law and circumstance, twelfth- and thirteenth-century merchants understood the nature of credit deal- ings. The evidence for this state of affairs has now been well charted. In trades which have been studied, the existence of power- ful middlemen in wine and cloth dealing has been shown. William Barnache, Simon de Farnham and Alan of Suffolk in the wine trade, or John Ludlow in wool, were thirteenth century precursors of the *nouveaux riches* of the fourteenth century, such as Gregory de Rokesley, William of Doncaster, Reginald and William de Conduit and William de la Pole. Industries such as tin and lead mining, and the building trade show sizeable capital expenditure, which must be have been raised in part on credit. Attempts by towns to escape mutual responsibility for debts, and the steadily rising number of debt cases indicate in part at least an increase in credit dealings. The charter granted to Dunwich in 1205, which stated that burgesses were not to be distrained for the debts of a fellow burgess unless the town had failed to do justice, served as the model for future charters. In those granted between 1255 and 1263 to places such as Norwich, York, Hereford and Worcester, a similar clause was inserted. The same policy was soon applied to alien merchants from such places as Saint-Omer (1255), Lübeck (1266) and Abbeville (1269). It was made a general legislative provision in 1275, and was followed in 1283 by the Statute of Acton Burnell. This law passed at the residence of Robert Burnell, the Chancellor, pointed out that those lending money had suffered and required that debts should be enrolled at London, York or Bristol. If payment was not made, distraint and imprisonment were prescribed. In 1285 this was followed by the Statute of Merchants which allowed enrolment to take place in any town, and provided for the seizure and transfer of real estate if the debt was not paid. These severe laws were not widely enforced, and the process of borough reprisals went on, because, as one Sandwich enactment remarked, "new statutes do not alter the free customs of the said town." This was particularly true in Wales and the west where, following Richard II's refusal to extend the law in 1391, Hereford and Shrewsbury in 1394 and 1396 secured a right they had previously been reluctant to possess.

In considering the impact of trading and financial activities, the overall smallness of the national product and population have to be borne in mind. In assessing the slow rate of growth, the large number of factors which militated against growth should be remembered. In exceptional cases, considerable rises in profits were achieved. For example, incomes from town rents or fair revenue and even direct yield from estates could all show substantial rises. Money was in good supply but ill-distributed and lacking in proper security. It was restrained a little by the prevalent economic theories on usury and just price. In trade sale credits formed the basis of transactions since the low profits of the time meant that deferred payments were essential. Money was least used in the agricultural section of the economy, but there rents and profits were commonplace by the beginning of the thirteenth century.

THE INFLUENCE OF THE CHURCH AND THE BUILDING REVOLUTION

It was once suggested that, because the Church was the largest landowner of the Middle Ages, "the needs of the bourgeoisie . . . ran counter to all the interests and ideas of a society dominated by the owners of large landed property, and spiritually by the Church.

whose aversion to trade was unconquerable." This suggestion has two faults. The first is the creation of an antithesis between agriculture and trade which was not then in existence, because the connection between wool production, our chief industry, and our major export was all too obvious. Secondly, because the Church was a landowner, it developed the economy partly out of its own volition but also because it was the organisation most fitted for large-scale capital operations and because its size affected the economy by creating new sources of demand and supply.

Various kinds of monastic estate lay at the basis of medieval agricultural progress, and this impression is not gained merely because more church than lay estate records have survived. The evidence is varied. For example, the possessions of the Templars were surveyed in 1185 and showed the pace of innovation in techniques and methods of tenure to be considerable. Commenting on the quality of English wool in the 1300s, Pegolotti pointed out that the best came from the Cistercian abbeys of Tintern and Abbey Dore. Estates were efficiently managed in order to obtain a profit. The twenty-one manors of St Augustine, Canterbury, yielded a profit of £3,000 a year for sixty monks in the mid thirteenth century. Among the most progressive landlords of the period were Sampson of Bury, Henry of Eastry at Christ Church, Canterbury, Marlborough of Evesham, Roger of St Albans and the more famous Michael Ambresbury and Roger Ford of Glastonbury. Such landlords experimented with reorganisation of field systems, new crops, attempts to improve crop yields and fertilising techniques, as investigations of Ramsey Abbey estates or those of the Bishop of Winchester at the end of the fourteenth century have shown. Any method whereby estate profits could be raised was used. This might mean the construction of fulling-mills (the Bishops of Winchester had eight) in the thirteenth century or pressure to keep villein obligations in the fourteenth, but the underlying aim was the same. From one point of view, the trial of the Abbot of Tintern in 1346 for exacting heavy labour services or the efforts of the Bishop of Winchester to recapture runaway villeins in London in 1351 were attempts to hold back progress. On the other hand, they reflected an active response to market forces since labour services were then cheaper than renting out and commuting. Accounting methods were stricter on church estates. The first full set of estate accounts come from Winchester in 1208–9, and during the next century the form of the accounts developed, so that, by the 1280s, Norwich Cathedral estates had accounts giving them the profit from various parts of the holdings.

In 1337 it was estimated that a third of the nation's property was in the hands of the Church and in certain counties, such as Kent and Worcestershire, we have already seen that this was the case. Some of the Abbeys held large numbers of manors: Bury St Edmunds had 170 and Fountains 150. Moreover, these estates were scattered, allowing for an exchange of produce, and permanently held by the Church, thus encouraging long-term development. The Church could be a harsh landlord, because it was jealous of its privileges, influenced by continental feudal law and the most powerful corporation in the country. It held two great monopoly positions: at least until the fourteenth century, all government offices were in the hands of churchmen, and at least until the same time, the belief was held that the Church alone had the power to save a man from Hell. The Church was in a position to exercise an active moral influence and to defy its own teachings. It was thus always guilty of double-thinking: banning usury, denouncing profit, and calling businessmen evil, while promoting building and agricultural production. The Church opposed the growth of urban independence when it threatened their income, and yet stimulated the growth of towns such as Bishop's Lynn or Salisbury. They hastened to commute services and establish a rentier class, and then equally vigorously opposed the trend when it became uneconomic from the landlord's point of view.

The various orders of regular clergy should be noticed for their different contributions to agriculture. The Benedictine houses of eastern and southern England were the strongholds of the typical manor, and exacted full manorial services. Nevertheless, they aimed at making a profit and the estates of the Bishops of Winchester produced both corn and sheep for that purpose. Cistercian houses, in their earlier days, were famed for their work. Harding in the *Carta Caritas* urged the need for self-sacrifice and self-sufficiency and for those reasons the Cistercians went to Yorkshire and the Welsh border. Their granges for sheep and vaccaries for cattle were famous and they tended towards the creation of larger holdings. The Templars placed most emphasis on the cash nexus and their estates rapidly developed into a series of leased and rented properties. Sheep-farming became a vital activity. It led to the drainage operations in the south and east, and to the intakes of the moors in the north. There was a degree of ruthlessness in the elimination of villages such as Old Byland and Kirkstall in Yorkshire. Flocks were vast: Ely had 13,400 sheep; Winchester had 29,000 and the total *Domesday* reckoning of sheep (300,000 on the demesne) must have sizeably increased in the next hundred years. At Minchinhampton, even nuns had a flock of sheep.

If the monastery is visualised as a community containing a

religious element, it may be seen in a better perspective. Only about a third of the inmates of monasteries were directly bound up with religious duties. Besides the monks there were the lay brothers and *conversi* or ordinary workers and the obedientiaries who performed all manner of duties. Rievaulx had 140 monks and 500 lay brothers, Bury 80 and 120, and Gloucester 50 and 200 respectively. Even the largest monasteries, such as St Albans, rarely had more than 100 monks. Such a community created a number of demands. Ramsey Abbey required 2,000 loaves, 12 quarters of flour, 10 fat pigs, 14 lambs, 120 hens, 2,000 eggs, malt, honey, lard, cheese, butter, beans and horse fodder. More widely required were iron, wax, wine, stone, glass, timber, parchment, special cloth and luxury items which were the products of various crafts. Monasteries stimulated the building industry and a host of subsidiary crafts and skills. For example, they were sometimes progressive enough to install water supplies and heating systems. Monastic requirements were refined and supplemented by continental influence. Taking Chambertin as the example, the cultivation of the grape was reintroduced, and the Bishop of Hereford had a particularly good vine at Ledbury in 1289. Cheeses were developed, such as Wensleydale. Fruit trees were grown, particularly cherries and plums, and the earliest horticultural works were, it will be recalled, by churchmen. In sheep breeding, the Ryelands of Herefordshire, the Lions of the Cotswolds, and the Lincolns of the east were developed on church estates and represented the best in both short and long wools.

Industrial affairs were very much the concern of the Church. The Bishop of Durham's lead and coal mines or the lead mines of the Bishop of Bath and Wells were evidence of this, as also was the part played by the Church in introducing and spreading the fulling-mill. By far their most spectacular contribution was to the growth of the building industry. This was not of course exclusively developed by the Church. Castle building was nearly as important as abbey or cathedral construction. However, the number of medieval castles has been exaggerated. In the period down to the reign of Henry II, some thirty to thirty-five English castles and a further thirty in the Welsh region were constructed. Apart from the piecemeal construction of twenty-three cathedrals, the Church was responsible for hundreds of monasteries, priories, abbeys, nunneries, friaries, hospitals, almshouses and for thousands of parish churches. The English vernacular building style later evolved from the achievements of medieval Gothic architecture so pervasive was its influence. As late as 1530, there were 825 religious houses with 9,300 inmates and with a collective income of about £200,000.

Norman architecture prevailed as a style from the middle of the eleventh to the end of the twelfth century and, during that time, major reconstructions or rebuildings of all the Saxon cathedrals, the building of new cathedrals, and the rebuilding or construction of parish churches occurred. In Scotland and Ireland the style survived much longer. This great development has been described as a "proto-industrial revolution" in which the "characteristics of modern industry make their appearance." It is always difficult to decide if the word revolution is applicable to any economic development, and a similar problem of definition will have to be faced when dealing with the "industrial revolution" of the thirteenth century caused by the introduction of the fulling-mill. Quantitatively, the scope of the change was enormous. London alone had over a hundred churches by the reign of Henry II. Between 1135 and 1189, 228 monasteries were built. The amount of capital and the amount of labour involved were the vehicles for capitalist organisation of funds, and for the appearance of a large and well-organised body of wage labourers, the masons, with their craft guild.

Technical innovation was a feature of the revolution. Freeman spoke of "several changes" in the Norman style but these changes in ornamentation, or more fundamentally in building design, were the consequence of technical changes. Lacking any accurate mathematical knowledge, without detailed plans, and with wooden scaffolding and poor tools, the early builders made many mistakes. The most spectacular was probably the building of Winchester over a marsh, which was only discovered in 1908. The consequence was that the early central tower collapsed in 1107 and on two subsequent occasions. Other towers also fell. Thus, that at Worcester collapsed in 1175 and the towers of Evesham, Chichester and Bury St Edmunds did likewise. At Ely the central tower collapsed, to be replaced by the present Octagon. The roof of St Albans Abbey collapsed due to badly built columns, and at Wells the threat of collapse, resulting from the insufficient support given to the central tower, led to massive interior reinforcement. An examination of the crooked nave of Gloucester Cathedral, or the serious threat of the collapse of York Minster, indicate that unqualified praise is out of place. A number of important changes were made, partly as a result of native experience and partly as a result of foreign example. Stone largely replaced wood. From the beginning with Church buildings and from the 1100s in the case of castles, granite, sandstone, chalk and flint were used, later followed by Caen and Portland stone. When Winchester was constructed by William Walkelin, stone was brought from quarries at Beer in Devon and

Quarr Abbey on the Isle of Wight and floated down the Itchen on barges. The walls of the cathedral were filled with local flints and rubble. The earliest stone castles were built in 1078 in London and soon afterwards at Colchester. It is likely from the similarity of style that Gundulf, Bishop of Rochester, had a hand in building both. One of the earliest and most impressive stone keeps was at Rochester, built by William de Corbeuil, Archbishop of Canterbury, with walls 12 feet thick and 113 feet high. Stone was soon applied to other buildings. The most spectacular of those was the original Westminster Hall, which was the largest stone building in Europe—240 feet by 67½ feet started in 1097 and never completed. In 1176 a start was made on the construction of a stone bridge for London, and about this time stone seems to have been in use for domestic buildings like the castle hall at Oakham or the houses at Lincoln and Bury St Edmunds, built in all probability by the Jews and spoken of as "palaces" at the time.

At first the size of the building was determined by the need to stretch a timber roof from one side of it to another. To support this, massive columns were used and not placed very far apart. Examples of this style are Winchester, Norwich, Gloucester, and Tewkesbury. However, it was not long before modification occurred and the vault was introduced. This major innovation, which dominated the size of buildings until the introduction of pre-stressed concrete in the 1930s, is an undocumented one, and has been the subject of much argument. It had been suggested that the work of William de St Calais and his successors at Durham followed soon after by the works of Roger of Salisbury, Remigius of Lincoln, and his successor, Alexander, Roger's nephew, and of Walkelin's brother, Simon, at Ely from 1109 were indications of the period when vaulting was introduced. It has also been argued that the vaulting at Durham was very much later, but it now seems to be accepted that it was done in the 1130s. Lady Stenton mentions a very early example at a church in Blyth built in the 1090s, and the vaults of Durham, completed in 1133, and Lincoln, started in 1141. Vaulting is considered to have developed when it was realised that, if the rounded arch were bisected, a greater space could be covered and that a number of vaults could then be supported from one pillar and reinforced by buttresses built to resist the downward thrust. It was possible to have as much as a sexpartite vault. At first vaults were simply ribbed along the groins or joints, but before long lierne vaults appeared in which ribs not directly related to the groins were used and eventually these expanded into great fans or formed the points for hanging pendants and roof bosses. If Durham was indeed the first cathedral to include this development, it stands as the finest and most significant example of Norman architecture.

Massive masonry characterised Norman work for the technical reason of the need for roof support and for defensive motives in the case of castle building. Thus, windows heavily splayed internally and externally, together with doors having deeply inset porches, are characteristic. Moulding and ornament is rare and at first fairly primitive. Heavy cushion capitals and serried dog's tooth or chevron carving is typical, although, with the combination of colour and dimness, an air of Byzantine effulgence may well have clung to buildings now more grimly austere. At the beginning of the twelfth century, a great technical improvement was effected by the use of finely chiselled masonry instead of more rough-hewn axe-cut blocks. The works of Roger of Salisbury, said one contemporary, looked as if they were all of one stone. More skilful quarrying, the use of the chisel, and the later pre-fabrication of certain parts all helped effect an immense improvement, seen most clearly perhaps in the contrasts on the west front of Lincoln. Lipson underestimated the widespread nature of the masons, saying that regulations for their guild were only found in London, when we now have *Mason's Ordinances* for York in 1370. Labour was supplied very often on an indentured basis and the masons moving from place to place provided the skilled nucleus of this labour force. Thus, continental examples, such as Rouen or Cîteaux influenced English work, and such English development as Perpendicular design were spread by these men. Canterbury Cathedral was built by a Frenchman, William of Sens, and London Bridge was finished by a Frenchman called Isembert.

By the end of the twelfth century, the English economy was ready for a period of rapid expansion. Steady progression in agriculture, industry and trade had paved the way for the rising population of the thirteenth century to exploit a wide variety of resources. The overall lack of financial expertise and technical skill was to limit this expansion and produce the impression that resources were under considerable strain. Already "the woollen and worsted manufacturer and the building industry covered too large a range of economic activity to be treated as exceptions to the general rule; nor do they stand alone in the evidence which they afford of the existence of capitalism." Feudal, manorial and ecclesiastical organisation was already involved with the profit motive, the payment of money wages and the rentier and bourgeois type of society. All those developments had received nourishment from the Norman Conquest after the initial shock, and they had gathered momentum under the strong rule of the two Henrys.

Urban wealth and power and ever-widening trade contacts made England part of a European economy, internationally financed from the gates of the Jewish ghetto at York to the bustling Hansard wharves of the City of London. In view of the enormous limitations present in any underdeveloped economy, the achievements had been considerable and although the rising standard of living most closely affected the landowning classes, there was evidence in the size of villeins' houses and in their acquisition of freehold property that some at least of the increasing wealth was being shared by the poorer people.

CHAPTER 6

THE EVOLUTION AND MODIFICATION OF THE MEDIEVAL ECONOMY

THE THIRTEENTH-CENTURY BOOM

In many ways the thirteenth century represented the period in which the Middle Ages developed its most characteristic features. The power of the Roman Church never stood higher than under Innocent III. Frederick II may well be taken as the most significant of the Holy Roman Emperors. St Louis IX of France and Edward I of England represented the quintessence of chivalry and law-giving feudal monarchy. It was an age of great scholarship, in which Oxford and Cambridge came into prominence and the Franciscan friars encouraged a scholastic revival which carried further the achievement of the twelfth century with the work of St Thomas Aquinas of Naples. In England the work of Duns Scotus, Roger Bacon of Oxford and William of Occam were the results of this intellectual renaissance. In Italy, Dante, Boccaccio, Petrarch, Cimabue and Giotto prepared the way for a revival of national letters and painting. It was the century of the craft guild foundations, the last five Crusades, the Latin kingdom of Constantinople, the travels of Marco Polo in China, and the rise of the sea princes of the Hanseatic and Venetian coasts. The Church was revitalised by the friars—followers of either St Dominic or St Francis of Assisi. Medieval government in Castile, France and England made a decisive step towards a parliament representing all the communities of the realm. National spirit developed in England after the separation from Normandy and was marked by Edward I's attempt to unite the whole island. It was the age in which many regard Gothic architecture as reaching the summit of its development at Chartres and Rheims, Wells and Salisbury.

Expansion, even if on a somewhat uneven scale, was the keynote of the period in agriculture and industry. The underlying cause was the rapid acceleration in population growth which meant that in all probability the population had doubled by the end of the century as compared with early twelfth-century figures. Pressure on resources was bound to follow in an economy where expansion of the cultivable area was limited by technical factors, and the possible increase in yield per acre failed to meet demand. A price inflation was the result. Land prices rose, particularly for pastoral purposes. Arable land was worth about 2*s*. 6*d*. an acre compared with anything up to 4*s*. an acre for pastoral land. Enclosure and the consolidation of the demesne was the consequence. Prices of all agricultural products underwent an increase. Wheat prices rose sharply by 50 per cent and then levelled out, but the price of wool, salt and oxen all rose steadily throughout the period. Wages, on the other hand, remained fairly constant and there was a tendency to move towards wage labour instead of villein services. Manorial lords commuted services for rents and employed wage labour so that, by the end of the period, Kosminsky estimated that 40 per cent of tenants were paying money rents and this figure is now regarded as a low one. Where it can be measured, it is clear that the amount of trade increased in wine and wool. By the end of the century, there were some 3,300 markets in existence. During the next century, only 1,560 were added to this total. Evidence for the prosperity of the home market is to be found in the increase of cloth imports from about 1250, in spite of a widespread development of the home cloth industry. The expansion was limited in several ways. The rise of cloth production in the western counties was accompanied by a decline in the traditional cloth-producing towns. Bad harvests affected agricultural expansion at the end of the period. English trade remained in the hands of aliens. However, in comparison with the slow development since the Conquest and the vicissitudes of the fourteenth century, the thirteenth may be regarded as being an important period of expansion comparable to the tenth or the sixteenth centuries.

However, two misconceptions, one about agriculture, and the other about industry, have given the thirteenth century a false importance. It was not the period when the feudal economy began to disintegrate because of the rise of a money economy. Nor was it the time when credit first played any important part in the development of the economy. Enough has been said already to indicate that the trends towards wage labour and a rentier class had more to do with economic pressures on particular landlords than with any deliberate move from one economic stage to another, and that such trends were advancing steadily before the reign of Henry III. In the same way it has been stressed that the Middle Ages always had a money economy and that the existence of new bankers and larger sums of capital in the thirteenth century merely reflected an increasing volume of industry and trade and the need to provide for it. On the manor, there were a number of develop-

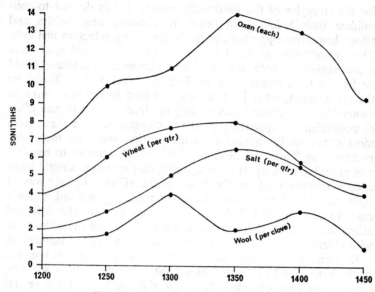

Fig. 1. Some medieval prices, 1200–1450.

ments common to the larger and more prosperous estates in the thirteenth century, and they were the products not of a conscious rejection of feudal and manorial concepts, but of the need to make a profit. The fourteenth century was to demonstrate that neither ideal had lost its effective power. Improvements in estate management involved the limited use of the treatises produced by men such as Walter of Henley, enforcement of stricter administrative standards on stewards and reeves who were made responsible for estate losses, the tightening of villein status and the enforcement of services, and the adoption of various methods of accounting. Experiments with crops yields, fertilising, and more varied farming, and the spread of sheep-rearing on enclosed pastures were the practical signs of an attempt to raise yields. With wages low, feudal burdens relaxed (only 1,200 knights were forthcoming by the middle of the century) and uneconomic services replaced by rents, landlords managed to increase their profits, but it seems likely that yield per acre fell due to intensive non-scientific use, and that there was insufficient wheat and barley to meet the nation's needs. Similarly, the wool produced was inadequate to meet the demand for cloth from a buoyant home market.

The basic field pattern was not altered in the thirteenth century, but there were a number of related changes that paved the way for the struggles of the fourteenth century. Lords desired to consolidate their holdings, in order to eliminate irregularities and allow themselves opportunities to change their production methods. The consolidation of the demesne to provide a central estate was accompanied by both enclosure and alienation. Enclosure could be by the little assart, or extending the existing three fields; or the great assart, whereby new areas of land under new terms of ownership were created. Engrossing the lord's demesne was often accompanied by approving of the commons, because these were most conveniently situated for consolidation and were useful for pasture. The Statute of Merton (1236) was an attempt to regulate this procedure but, apart from agreeing that enclosure should leave enough commonland for the needs of the village, the Act was of little value. Enclosure was carried out ruthlessly and led in some cases to depopulation. This process of consolidation also involved alienation of the outlying parts of the demesne and these, together with villein assarts, provided the basis for a new type of landowner.

Kosminsky argued that, whereas large estates such as the honours of the barons and the Benedictine abbeys retained labour services, there came into existence "side by side with the large feudal estate . . . many others, small and medium sized properties in which . . . money rents decidedly predominate in the obligations of the villeins." This change was not, however, a concerted and final one. Commutation of villein services occurred either where lords found it profitable or where tenants could afford it. The lord gained a steady income and the villein was able to devote himself to his own lands. Such villeins were not, as Lipson argued, "a class of molmen." but a varied group of small landowners. The change was not regarded as permanent, and it did not affect villein status. Increasing numbers of flights by villeins, and the determined effort in the fourteenth century to restore labour services, showed that the change was confined to places where the economic circumstances justified it. The researches of such historians as Page and Gray have shown that labour services had by no means disappeared before the middle of the fourteeenth century, as Thorold Rogers had once argued. Nevertheless, a considerable number of villeins managed not only to commute services, but also to acquire landholdings other than their traditional virgate and toft. In cases examined in Yorkshire, one finds such examples as a holding at Ingelby Greenhow consisting of 2 carucutes and 28 acres of intake, and one at Hulton Rudby consisting of 12 bovates and appurtenant enclosed clearings. The word close was sometimes synonymous with assart or intake. Villeins inherited land which was in free tenure as well as villein land, and although the average holding remained small, there were many in the region of fifty acres in some parts of the country.

As a result of these changes, a number of different kinds of manor were created. The largest number retained the outline of a typical manor. Thus, a survey of eighty-one manors spread over twenty counties shows that on forty-four of them labour services were general and on twenty-two of them a large amount of the work was done by labour services in the 1340s. In other manors there was a "complex of free tenants standing in feudal relation to the lord." By and large, they would be rent payers or wage earners. In some parts of the country there were manors which consisted entirely of demesne, such as those in the smallholding region of East Anglia. In other places where the lord had consolidated or sold out, there was no demesne and only a free village, although this was likely to be rare except in places such as Kent. It seems most likely that typical manors were retained in the parts of the country where feudalisation and manorialisation had been most obviously influential. Yet those areas, such as Essex, Hertfordshire or Hampshire, were the most liable to economic changes spreading from the towns. It is possible to suggest also that it is less likely that the manor was retained in its traditional framework south of a line from Boston to the mouth of the Severn, than that, within that area, the position varied from place to place. Thus, it seems likely that, on the Bishop of Winchester's estates, outlying areas turned into regions of smallholdings, whereas the central parts of the estates remained fully manorialised.

The most important economic development of the thirteenth century was a change in the character of the English cloth industry. This change has been described by Carus-Wilson as an industrial revolution, and in so far as clothmaking was the main industry, any change in it might be said to constitute a revolution. By the end of the twelfth century, the distribution of production was widespread, so that there were few large towns that did not produce some cloth, but the quality was poor and Flemish cloth imports began to make inroads on English cloth production. Although the export of wool fell during the thirteenth century, it was thought that too much was exported to be made up into cloth abroad, and in 1258 the export of wool was forbidden. This ban was imposed again in 1271 and accompanied by a declaration that "all workers of woollen cloths, male and female, as well of Flanders as of other lands" were welcome in this country. Technically, the industry needed to improve by cutting costs for low-quality products or by developing superior cloths. Management was also defective. The various guilds of weavers and fullers restricted apprenticeships, and

F

closely regulated wages and standards. As a result, some enterprising cloth manufacturers had moved into the countryside and rural production in the West Riding and Kent already indicated a cheaper way of production. In the early years of the thirteenth century, guilds at York and Winchester were running into trouble, and by the end of the century, many had disappeared altogether. At Lincoln, which was a flourishing cloth-producer in John's reign, there was no guild by 1321. In London, the number of looms fell from 380 to 80 during the century, and an attempt to keep up production by offering piece-work rates failed. Apart from York, all the major sources of twelfth-century production experienced a decline and only recovered when some towns specialised in high quality cloth such as Lincoln greens or Oxford scarlets.

Cloth was produced by three main processes, after it had been carded or combed with wire brushes. Spinning was done on a distaff until the fourteenth century when the spinning-wheel was introduced. The spun thread was woven on a foot-operated loom, the warp (length) being carried over the weft (width) by a shuttle. Finally, the cloth was fulled by being soaked in water with fuller's earth to produce a thickened surface due to shrinkage, and to clean the oil or grease from the cloth by the combined action of earth and water. Fulling had been practised since Roman times, when it was done in shallow troughs and hand- or foot-fulling was retained in use, as it tended to be best for superior cloths. In 1404 the Hatters' Guild in London protested against innovation and maintained that foot-fulling was best. However, by the middle of the twelfth century, a fulling-mill had been developed in Europe. This was operated by means of water power revolving a drum to which hammers were attached to perform the task normally done manually. The use of mills for various purposes is a matter of great importance in considering the growth of medieval technology. There is evidence of a paper mill at Bermondsey Abbey as early as 1082, and mills for tanning (1267), paint-making (1361) and sawing (1376) have been located. The fulling-mill, however, made a far greater impact.

It is not clear precisely when the first fulling-mill was introduced, but it seems likely that it was in the late 1180s, either at Temple Guiting near Barton in the Cotswolds or at Temple Newsam near Leeds. By 1197, there was a mill at Minster Lovell in Oxfordshire, and by 1206 there was one owned by the Abbot of Evesham at Bourton-on-the-Water in the Cotswolds. Mills are found most frequently on the estates of the Templars, the Church and the Crown. Carus-Wilson estimated that there were about 160 fulling-mills and, since that estimate was made, about 30 more have come to light. In comparison with 3,000 corn-mills, there were not many. They were costly and came under the control of the lord of the manor. At St Albans the mill cost £100 and the Abbot ordered all cloth to be fulled in his mill to recoup his losses. On one occasion, women workers surrounded Queen Eleanor, wife of Edward I, begging for redress, but it was not granted. By being dependent on swift-flowing streams, the fulling-mills moved the industry away from the eastern ports and fairs, and caused poverty in several towns. The westwards move may have increased costs and this may explain why the introduction of the fulling-mill was not followed by the sudden "take-off" in production with which a revolutionary industrial change is usually associated.

However, two important changes followed the introduction of the fulling-mill. With the exception of York and a few towns such as Carlisle, Monmouth and Winchester, the fulling-mills were located in the country and, by and large, in the western half of England. The Lake District, the western and eastern slopes of the Cotswolds, the Kennett and Avon valleys, Wiltshire and Somerset were the most important cloth-producing regions, although they were soon joined by the West Riding of Yorkshire and Suffolk. The consequences were that collecting centres grew up in smaller towns, such as Kendal, Bradford, Taunton, Witney, Kersey or Worstead, and that semi-urban villages, such as Stroudwater made their appearance with a ring of spinners and weavers gathered around a fulling-mill. The second important result was the organisation of what is called the domestic or putting-out system of production due to the scattered nature of the industry. This system was operated until well into the nineteenth century and is, therefore, of considerable importance. Wool was collected from the scattered farms or granges by a wool dealer or brogger who then sold it to the country clothier or manufacturer. He put out the work to spinners and weavers and collected it for the fulling-mill. The cloth was then taken to the market or a cloth fair for distribution by merchants.

Evidence for the existence of fulling-mills is often only readily apparent to the experienced eye, but the evidence for the achievement of the thirteenth century building industry is more obvious. Gothic architecture was an international idiom. Thus, stained glass was a development of the Byzantine glass mosaic, with the pieces bound together by a framework of lead, found possibly for the first time at Le Mans in France, and imported into this country until native stained glass was produced in the fifteenth century. Gothic architecture was based upon the uniting of the pointed arch, developed after Saracen example, to a concept of an heroic and saintly aspiration in which the medieval mind found a release from scholasticism and penury. Gothic architecture was not esoteric, but the everyday expression of one aspect of religious life. It is not easy to classify the styles although, in England, Rickman's early nineteenth-century division into Early English, Decorated and Perpendicular is generally accepted, with the introduction of a transitional period from Norman to Early English. On the continent the styles varied from those here, so that a Flamboyant style has been introduced to match English Perpendicular. Amiens and Rheims rose at the same time as Lincoln or Salisbury, but they were rather different in concept. Only in places such as the east end of Westminster Abbey or one of the transepts of Hereford can it be said that continental influence was deep.

The thirteenth century was the period of Transitional and Early English construction, and it marked in several ways the vernacular differences from continental Gothic. Large churches tended to be longer than those on the Continent. The continental apse, with a cluster of chapels, was replaced by a squared east end which had a lower Lady Chapel beyond it. Apses such as those at Peterborough and Norwich remained exceptions largely confined to Norman work. Whereas French architects emphasised the west front with its towers, the English emphasised the central tower and thus obtained a more impressive sky-line. The overall effect was partially spoilt by the prevalence of narrow lancet windows, as distinct from the extensive and immediate use of glass on the Continent which made their interiors superior to some in England. English west fronts were either of little relevance, as at Lincoln, or incomplete, as at Wells. The great constructions of the Early English style are Wells and Salisbury. At Wells, the rebuilding was started under Bishop Reginald, with the nave, and completed under Bishop Jocelin by 1239. Wells was built of stone from local quarries at Shepton Mallet, with insets of lias for shafts and abaci used until marble became more usual. Salisbury was started in 1220 by Bishop Richard le Poer and completed (apart from the tower and spire) within forty years. Besides those two outstanding examples, the east end of Ely (1229–54), the nave and west front of Lincoln completed under Bishop Hugh (1209–35) and Robert Grosseteste (1235–53), and the choir at Worcester (1224–60) may be considered as surpassing Wells or Salisbury in proportion and detail.

Early English developed the height of cathedrals to include a clerestory and a triforium, and in addition to the tower, the spire was developed purely as an extension of the tower by four broachs at the corner. Windows which were originally long and narrow with one or two lights were gradually extended to reach fulfilment in the Five Sisters window at York. Occasionally, Saracen influence may be seen in three- or five-pointed designs within the general pattern of pointed arches. After the Transitional stage, columns became slender with a cluster of shafts and with round instead of square abaci, sometimes ornamented with foliage. Vaulting was still largely confined to the bigger churches and wooden roofs were retained. Roofs were high-pitched with a simple tie beam and very few survive. In order to carry out the delicate new work and to graft it on to existing Norman structures, considerable advances were necessary in the building industry itself. Much of the labour involved in non-ecclesiastical building was compulsory, particularly in the building of castles, but the masons grew increasingly prominent. When Caernavon Castle was built, 2,000 unskilled labourers and 400 masons were employed. Names of masons themselves now become fairly common and indicate their rising status. In Henry III's reign, Elias of Oxford and John of Gloucester are mentioned. Edward I's castles were constructed by Walter of Hereford or James of St George, a Savoyard. Families such as the Hotons of York became renowned for their craft. The stone the masons used was in many cases prefabricated, that is to say, worked up in standard parts at the quarry and transported by water. Caen stone was three times as expensive as English stone and was largely replaced by native stone. The most important were the quarries at Beer in Devon, which Winchester, Rochester, Chichester and Westminster used, and those on the Isle of Purbeck and around Corfe, used at Exeter. Stone for York Minster was brought from the Pennines down the Wharfe and Aire. The most spectacular quarries were at Barnack on the Welland. Stone from here was used at Bury St Edmunds, Norwich, Crowland, Ramsey, Barnwell, Peterborough and for Cambridge colleges. Sawtre Abbey actually had a canal constructed to move the stone. In addition to the expansion of the quarrying industry, the production of marble also increased. From the 1190s there is evidence of production at Purbeck. Marble was used instead of lias in columns and also for mass-produced effigies. By the end of the thirteenth century, William and Robert Marbler of Corfe were famous and the latter helped to construct the fourteen Eleanor Crosses. In London, there is mention of Adam the Marbler by the 1320s. Later, England was to take the lead in the development of alabaster, quarried around Tutbury and Nottingham, and to establish a flourishing export trade by the beginning of the fifteenth century.

Apart from the cathedrals, the great group of Welsh castles represent the other summit of thirteenth-century building achievement. In 1278, Rhuddlan, Flint, Aberystwyth and Builth were started; in 1283, Conway Caernarvon and Harlech; and in 1295, Beaumaris. Caerphilly was a later addition. Those fortresses represented a triumph for the concentric principle in castle-building, which had started in the time of the Crusades with castles in the Near East such as Krak des Chevaliers and had seen its first European fruition in Richard I's Château Gaillard. Round towers replaced square keeps, the gateway was given more attention, and a series of baileys with containing curtain walls were erected. Edward's interest in town planning extended to his Welsh operations and castle-building was linked to the granting of borough status and the establishment of fairs in order to stimulate trade. Towns were given the customs of Hereford. Few of the new boroughs were successful, but they were a further indication of the increased emphasis on urban development, which the foundation of boroughs in the later years of Henry III showed to be an important part of the economy. Thus, charters were given to Norwich, Nottingham, Northampton, Lincoln and Lynn in 1255, York, Scarborough, Hereford, Shrewsbury, Southampton, Cambridge, Canterbury and Bridgnorth in 1256, Oxford, Stamford and Guildford in 1257 and Berwick in 1260.

Pressure from the towns for charters and the extension of their existing rights began to run into opposition during the thirteenth century from the Church, which, although it had been anxious to gain a quick return by the sale of simple rights, had no desire to lose the profits from the ownership of market and toll. This also applied to lay landlords, so that Manchester which had been acknowledged as a borough in 1301 had lost its privileges by 1359 and remained, until the middle of the nineteenth century, under manorial jurisdiction. In 1229, according to the Prior of Dunstable, the burgesses, unmoved by a threat of excommunication, refused to give way and "to descend into Hell altogether." This state of affairs was to become part of the medieval and Early Tudor scene and, at times of national crisis, opportunity was not lost to attack the Church which oppressed various towns. This is evident for the first time in the De Montfort troubles when, in 1264, the people of Bury St Edmunds opposed the Abbot. In 1327 there were widespread disturbances in the year of Edward II's deposition which served as a prelude for the more violent outbreak of 1381. Besides episcopal profits, the rights of ecclesiastics to jurisdiction over burgesses and to collect taxes were the cause of trouble. At Gloucester the servants and tenants of the monastery were excluded from the operation of borough administration. At Canterbury, in 1227, the town bailiffs ordered the conventual Christ Church to contribute men-at-arms. In 1329 the Prior refused to pay any town taxes, and there was a sharp conflict in which pilgrims were prevented from contributing to St Thomas's shrine. At Norwich there was a full-scale riot in 1272 and the cathedral and surrounding buildings went up in flames. No settlement was reached until 1306. Assertions of manorial rights were the subject of frequent clashes at St Alban's in 1274, 1327 and 1381. Finally, the Church alienated the merchant community by its extensive rights of sanctuary. At Hereford, fraudulent traders plied their trade on ecclesiastical territory. In London false coins were issued from one sanctuary, and debtors were protected at Westminster and Durham. In later years, the conflicts were to become more severe, but already sufficient indication was being given that the new community of merchants would not allow itself to be dominated by the old corporation of the Church.

During the thirteenth century, the merchant *communitas* emerged to play a full and separate part in the nation's life. With the periodic collapse of Italian financiers and the steady exhaustion of Jewish resources, the Crown turned increasingly to English merchants. They in turn were anxious to secure uniform weights and measures, a stable currency, redress for debt and the greatest possible freedom for individual guilds and towns to exercise their privileges. The Crown's need was expressed in the sale of privileges to the merchant community and taxes levied on imports and exports during the reign of Edward I. As Crown demands grew, the need for a widening basis of consent was obvious, and at first this involved the summoning of the knights of the shires to larger meetings of the Council. The first distinct summons to the county representative was in 1254, but long before then knights had been summoned, as in 1226, for general consultations on Magna Carta or the sheriffs. The earliest examples of these practices as regards the boroughs were in 1204 and 1207, when representatives of the Cinque Ports, and then of some boroughs, were summoned to discuss matters including a recoinage. De Montfort summoned borough representatives in 1265 and they were present in the Parliament of 1275 which introduced the customs on wool and leather. At the time of the Statute of Acton Burnell, an assembly with four knights from each shire and two representatives of each city, borough and market town was summoned, and in 1295 two representatives for each county and two for each borough attended the Model Parliament. Between 1294 and 1297, the Crown tried no less than fourteen different ways of raising money and under these circumstances it is not surprising that an increasing measure of consent was needed. From this involvement of the merchants in government, it is possible to see a slow but ultimately decisive trend towards policies designed to protect English merchants, control alien merchants and even attempt a measure of national organisation through the staple of our main export. This never amounted to a considered economic policy, but it meant that economic matters were to become of increasing importance in Parliamentary legislation during the fourteenth century.

Under the stimulus of a rising population, the national economy developed more rapidly than it was to do perhaps until the third quarter of the fifteenth century. Many of the advances were later limited by population decline and the impact of the Hundred Years War, but they should not be underestimated. By the end of the thirteenth century, the manorial economy was being rapidly transformed by money and the profit motive. Both villeins and lords were consolidating holdings, attempting to rationalise existing procedures and to produce for the market. Pastoral farming was growing in importance and arable farming was showing a tendency towards diversification. Wool exports had declined and cloth imports increased, but at the same time the cloth industry had changed its location, developed a new organisation and mechanised one of its processes. Other industries such as coal, lead, iron and tin mining all showed increased production. The building industry continued to advance its technical skills and to develop wage earning and credit financing and to bring an ever-increasing demand on stone and marble quarrying activities. With the rapid granting of borough status, towns developed quickly, helped by the expansion of trade in the western ports, town planning activities in Wales and elsewhere by Edward I, and the increasing power of their burgesses united in guilds merchant and, in some cases, in craft guilds. Yet there were also signs of reaction. Monasteries began to resent the increasing freedom of towns on their demesne. Lords found that villeins were defying labour services or leaving the manor and started to re-enforce their position by strictly defining villein status and making it plain that commutation was temporary. A succession of bad harvests in the 1290s preceded a period of famine and pestilence in the first quarter of the fourteenth century and this led to far less consistent economic development in the next fifty years.

THE FOURTEENTH-CENTURY DEPRESSION

The fourteenth century was the age of chivalry, but in the same way as the ostentatious splendours of the later Roman Empire were indications of decay and the decline of older ideals, so also the growth of chivalry was accompanied by an artificial retention of principles that parted company with the substance of everyday life. Whatever warfare may have been when Edward I fought in a tournament in 1274 or the Black Prince won his spurs in 1346, the horrors of Limoges in 1370 or Winchelsea in 1377 were the ultimate results of a society which elevated the prosecution of war to a noble ideal. Whatever the saintly virtues of courtly love and holy benediction upon new knights, the dissolution of the Templars for corruption in 1312, the attack by John Wycliffe on the upper clergy, the spread of anti-clericalism among the poor and the literate, and the expulsion of the alien priorities in 1410, marked the drift of sentiment away from the ideal of the thirteenth century. International Christendom ceased to be. The Holy Roman Empire fell into decay and the Papacy, after undergoing fifty years' captivity at Avignon, produced two divine heads of the Church. The power of both institutions had been weakened by the Crusades and the struggles of Guelfs and Ghibellines, Hohenstuffens and Holy Fathers. Heresy appeared in England and Bohemia as it had not done before, except possibly in the days of the Albigensians. In the cities of Europe there was revolt. The towns of Bury and St Albans rose in 1381, the Arteveldts raised the Flemish towns until they were defeated in 1382, Rienzi appeared at Rome, Ciompi at Florence in the 1380s. In the countryside also, the spirit of revolution was abroad. In Spain, every state except Castile experienced uprisings. In France, there was a Jacquerie in 1358; in England, the revolts of 1381 were preceded by many smaller ones. Revolt spread into Bohemia in 1419 and Transylvania in 1437.

Yet chivalry deserves some attention from the economic historian for it did more than conceal latent economic discontents and gild the stresses of a changing society. Perhaps unwittingly, it helped to bring feudal society to an end and replace it with one where hereditary position, guaranteed by birth and insured by force, maintained the interest of the landed class. Chivalry evolved originally in the feudal atmosphere of late-twelfth-century Provence, flourished in the thirteenth century and was recognised as the supreme ideal in the age of Froissart. It was, together with the friars and universities, the last of the great international medieval ideals. But by the end of the fourteenth century, the "nation-state" concept was alive, precipitated in all probability by the constant series of wars from 1275 for nearly 150 years. Edward I was in many ways a chivalrous king, but his attempts to subdue the whole of the British Isles provoked national sentiments. The Welsh, defeated in 1283–4, rose in 1294 and 1403. The Irish, forced to submit to a Parliament in 1297, revolted and, by the late 1360s, had contained the English within the Pale. The Scottish revolt, which followed the exercise of Edward's feudal right as overlord of Scotland and ended with their victory at Bannockburn in 1314, is well known. Edward I contributed to the growth of nationalism more by the opposition he aroused than by the unity he fostered. Edward III, who built the Round Tower of Windsor for the Round Table of Arthur, founded the Order of the Garter, and maintained a glittering Court, represented the climax of expansion, chivalry and expenditure. Edward I and Edward III cost the country, and more particularly the whole nobility, so much that they caused great changes to occur in taxation, money supply and credit facilities on the one hand and in the position and wealth of the landed classes on the other.

Superficially, chivalry had little to do with money, although Froissart's estimate of ransoms is interesting. Chaucer's *Troilus and Criseyde* and his more famous *Knight's Tale* and Malory's *Morte Darthur* represented and stylised a world of courtly love, individual honour and *noblesse oblige*. In reality, the world of chivalry was involved in ever-increasing overheads, the continuous competition for rank and office, and the miserable consequences of long-term warfare and absenteeism. During the fourteenth century, the landed class most probably suffered loss of real income to a greater extent than any other sector of the community. For this the reasons were many and it is wise to remember "not to credit to the war what was due to the hundred years." Nevertheless, it seems clear that the war had a very serious effect on baronial, as well as royal, financial stability. It used to be thought that the war, by bringing in ransoms, helped baronial incomes, but allowance must be made both ways. To make any net gain, it would be necessary to have English demands for ransoms equivalent to three times the amount of the French. There was some gain to be had from plunder and France suffered more than us in this respect, although Scottish raids on the north and French attacks on the declining Cinque Ports need to be taken into account. Offices and fiefs added to the gains, but against this must be set the costs of equipment and transport, the hiring of mercenaries or the employment of retinues, and the consequences of absentee ownership. Cases such as that of Sir John Fastolf, who raised the value of his estates from £46 to £1,061 a year, seem so far to be exceptional.

The decline in the lord's economic viability was at bottom a combination of high expenditure, outdated sources of income, rising prices and falling rents. Expenditure seems to have remained high and to have increased in certain cases. By Edward IV's time, household costs were running at £500 a year, and the Northumberland *Household Book* gives some indications of the difficulties nobility faced. Although some of those in the middle income group, such as the Stonors and Pastons, were able to do well, others such as the Plumptons in Yorkshire did far less well. Perhaps the most startling example of the decay was that of the Berkeley inheritance in Gloucestershire. Thomas, Lord Berkeley, began to sell and lease lands in the 1380s and by 1449 Lady Berkeley had to ask her husband to raise money to stop her horse going into pawn, and he was forced to raise £15 by selling furnishings from the family chapel. The landed class paid little attention to the laws of livery and maintenance and were unaffected by the sumptuary laws, both of which might have reduced their overheads. Yet, in the face of declining revenue from their lands, they maintained a level of expenditure which Froissart regarded as excessively high. On their lands, some attempts were made to recoup losses, but the overall decline in landed incomes in the period 1340 to 1440 was in the region of 25 per cent. Pressure mounted from the beginning of the fourteenth century, when wages started to rise from the 1320s, and was accelerated when they doubled temporarily after the Black Death. Lords were increasingly dependent on wage labour and, for a variety of reasons, found it difficult to revert to labour services for the sake of economy. The fall in population added to their problems because it became more difficult to find new tenants and the lords were forced to make leases favourable to the tenant. By the 1380s, Ramsey had leased their best manors and in some cases, such as Durham Cathedral Priory, nearly all their lands were leased. After the Black Death the alienation of demesne continued apace. Leasing of the demesne lands *en bloc* became common; some of the earliest examples being Cuxham in 1359 and Tamworth in 1381. At Battle Abbey, the twenty-two manors were leased out, nineteen as single units, one by two farmers, one by three farmers and only one was left as a home farm. Traditional recipients, such as bailiffs or reeves, were supplemented by the wealthier villeins. Stock and land leases proved useful to aspiring farmers. The terms granted were generous and, although the leases were limited for a term of years, the rent tended to be customary and fixed and to benefit the smaller farmers.

However, it is important not to exaggerate this decline. There were many estates where the trend continued to be profitable, and the shedding of lands, either marginal or surplus to needs in a period of declining population, was of immediate even if not of long-term advantage. Sheep farming used labour less intensively and was more prosperous. The revival of the cloth industry and the organisation of the staple provided an excellent basis for the change. Canterbury Cathedral Priory, Dorchester and Winchcombe Abbeys were examples of the new trend towards enclosure for sheep in order to combat rising wages and, later, falling arable prices. The Cotswold region was largely converted from arable to sheep farming after 1350, and by the early fifteenth century enclosure had become an agricultural problem. The conversion of land of marginal arable utility and the economic use of depopulated land helped to re-establish rural prosperity and enclosure was only resented when the pressure of population started to mount again in the middle of the next century. Enclosure raised the value of lands from ten to sixteen years equivalent of the purchase price. In some cases, manorial lords reacted by a determined effort to maintain traditional demesne farming which met with some success. Thus, Leicester Abbey increased grain production between 1388 and 1408. New investment in improvements was to be found and 10 per cent of some manorial incomes was being ploughed back on, for example, the Bishops of Winchester's estates. It has been suggested that evidence for such revival indicates that the overall loss incurred by the landed class was not great, and that the fifteenth-century tenant farmers did not gain exclusively from a straight transfer of power, but also from the existence of vacant tenancies.

Falls in the rents of the Percy estates from a quarter to a half, a 20 per cent decline in the rents of the Duchy of Lancaster, and the prevalence on previously well-organised estates, such as Ramsey or Durham, of the symptoms of agricultural decay were all indications of a state of affairs the nobility were anxious to rectify. Marriage was one method resorted to by families such as Lancaster or Warwick. Intermarriage with the commercial classes was another method. The fourteenth century saw the creation of peerages based on commercial achievement, such as that given to Michael de la Pole. City magnates such as Walworth and, in the next century, the Boleyns, were admitted to the ranks of knighthood. The *nouveaux riches* aroused strong resentment when, as Piers Plowman said, "soap-sellers and their sons for silver are made knights," but they contributed to the wealth of the landed class as a whole. New orders of peers were created to accommodate the aspiring nobility with titles such as marquess or viscount. Peers obtained retinues of followers paid by themselves to match the feudal dignities of the older honorial barons. Competition for office and particularly for the highest office of all, the Crown, became endemic. By encouraging marriages between the royal family and the nobility, Edward III initiated what is known as the appanage policy. The consequence was that various families, such as the Hollands, Cambridges, Beauforts and others, came to have a close interest in the settlement of the succession. There was a breakdown in the concept of a nobility of service on the land, and it was replaced by a nobility of caste, based upon inheritance and titles. Only in places such as the far north did a territorially based nobility retain its interests and its following. The new relationship was based often on money and introduced, therefore, a new concept known as "bastard feudalism." In the fifteenth century this was to have serious consequences.

This breakdown in the upper echelons of the feudal structure was accompanied by far-reaching changes among the villeins and small landowners. Together, these changes altered the whole organisation of the manor. In the early 1300s demesne farming was common; by the 1400s it was exceptional. During the same period, labour services declined in importance almost to vanishing point, a wage-earning rural proletariat grew in inverse proportion to that change, and villein holdings increased greatly. Thus, by the early 1400s, the tendency towards smaller estates was well established and there had been a downwards distribution of income to benefit copyhold and leasehold tenants. The fall in population had opened a market for land which the lord's necessity and the villein's wealth was able to adjust. Low rents and high wages favoured the smaller farmers working their own lands and also the day labourers. They did not favour the larger landlord and the villein bound to him by labour services. The growth of industry widened employment opportunities and the demands for soldiers and retainers widened the labour market. Villeins were able to secure high wages and reject labour services and lords were forced to increase wages, end labour services, lease lands and try to cut costs. Changes such as these were part of a long-term process which had developed in the thirteenth century and was largely completed by Henry VII's time. But the sudden acceleration of the process was due to the influences at work in the fourteenth century, among which the Black Death and subsequent plagues are the most notorious.

Discontent with the pace of agrarian change showed itself by the end of the thirteenth century in increasing flights of villeins and the developing mobility of the rural population. Rejection of customary services and attempts to increase wages soon followed. The flight of villeins was illegal and attempts were made to return them, so that often they took to the forests and wastes and formed bands of sturdy beggars or *traîlbatons*. Thus, in 1376 during the Good Parliament, complaint was made that "if their masters reprove them for bad service, or offer to pay them for the said service according to the form of the said statute [of labourers] they fly and suddenly run away . . . and many of them become staff strikers and live also wicked lives." The Black Death, by severely reducing the population of some villages, either tended to off-load the remaining villein duties on to the remainder who there-upon left or demanded wages, or forced the lords to accept labour from other manors. At Woodeaton, for example, the remaining tenants threatened to go, until the owner was forced to grant more liberal terms. Variations in wage rates added to the incentive to move and the Statute of Labourers forbade lords to raise wages as a bribe, but in places such as Essex the contrast with the wages of clothworkers was too obvious to be missed by the villeins. The Black Death accelerated these movements by encouraging the taking of new holdings and the desertion of marginal land for more suitable centres of settlement. Take-overs were rapid on the better lands, particularly where there had been a surplus of villeins willing to acquire land. Thus, in Glastonbury manors, even a heavy death-rate would have left enough villeins to provide new owners, and on the estates of Durham Cathedral Priory, new lands were almost immediately occupied. It was not until the end of the century that real difficulty was experienced in finding new tenants. New tenants were available so that, at Cuxham, nine holdings were all occupied by outsiders by 1355. Between 1281 and 1424, the number of tenancies at Hulton in Essex fell from forty to twenty-seven and only one was the same in the last year as the first. Resistance to attempts to return villeins was so strong that the Steward of the Prior of Ely, having secured villeins who had fled, was forced to release them by a mob in 1349. Although the Statute of Labourers forbade labourers to withdraw services and leave the manor, it was not successful. It is clear that there was a real change in the social composition of many villages and the substitution of a smaller number of holdings for the large number of previous villein tenancies. At Chippenham, for example, the number of holdings over 30 acres rose from a fifth to a third between 1400 and 1480. There is some evidence that dilapidated and uneconomic holdings either went out of cultivation or reverted to the demesne.

Week works and boon works were the most serious cause of contention. Lords faced with rising costs and social expenditure wished to economise by reversing the trend of the thirteenth cen-tury, and they were encouraged in this by the stricter legal definition of villein status which had emerged. The inconvenience, humiliation and cost per man-hour led to strong villein opposition. If a com-parison is made between rents demanded and the value of the services, it is clear that it was to the villein's advantage to become a rentier. At Forncett in Norfolk, in 1378, land was rented at 10d. an acre whereas villein services amounted to 3s. 9d. an acre.

Heavy services had not always been exacted, but the shortage of labour forced lords to exact full services. Lords tried to prevent villeins from giving up their services and between 1279 and 1311 there were 146 cases involving this matter on the estates of the Abbots of Ramsey. By the 1320s there were serious clashes between lords and tenants at such places as the great Cistercian Abbey of Vale Royal in Cheshire. As Wycliffe said: "Strifes, contests and debates ben used in our land, for lords striven with their tenants to bring them in thraldom more than they should by reason and charity." On royal estates villeins used the writ *monstraverunt*; elsewhere, the issue was also tried in the courts. In 1346 the tenants of Acle summoned the Abbot of Tintern on the grounds that they were on "ancient demesne," although they failed in the attempt. Events at St Albans illustrate the crisis. In 1327 and 1336, there were clashes over jurisdiction at the Abbey mills, but the real issue at stake was an attempt by the Abbot to keep villeins liable to customary dues and to forbid them to engage in land market operations. The struggle swayed back and forward, the Abbot winning in 1345, the villeins in 1381.

How far did the villeins succeeed in freeing themselves from labour services? It is clear that, until the Black Death, lords had been moderately successful in retaining a residue of services. Although commutation had been widespread, services were retained and could be invoked. At a manor such as Wilburton in Cambridgeshire in 1393 a large number of works (*opera*) were commuted, whereas in 1397 only seven were so treated. It was not until the lease of the demesne for an annual rental of £8 in the fifteenth century that the labour services disappeared. According to Page, a comparison of a selection of 126 manors in 1380 with a selection of 81 manors in 1350, showed that in thirty years the percentage of total commutation rose from 18 per cent to 62 per cent. Nevertheless, this change must be modified by the considerations that the change varied from year to year, and that on some specific estates, such as those at Winchester, it is clear that the lords could afford a rise in the wage bill when it was only a small proportion of expenditure and that they paid this and concentrated on raising feudal revenues. For example, new tenants meant a handsome yield of heriots and on one manor the fines rose from £34 in 1348 to £191 in 1349. One of the most spectacular examples of the continued assertion of rights to services occurred at Cirencester. The Abbot secured a statement of the custumal in 1371, and in 1400 he joined battle with recalcitrant tenants. Over thirty years, thirty-one villeins were prosecuted for withdrawing services, and seventy-four for aiding and abetting them. Fines totalling

£6,000 were imposed and the authority of the lord of the manor re-established. Leases elsewhere as late as 1417 contained references to termination if a newcomer should take on the holding on the old terms. Villein services continued to be exacted on many manors in the fifteenth century in all parts of the country. Lipson referred to examples at Gimingham in Norfolk, Harmondsworth in Middlesex, and the Ramsey estates, as late as 1466.

In spite of the continuation of labour services and the successful rearguard action of some landlords, the main trend was for their abandonment. Witney in Oxfordshire might be taken as a typical example of what was most probably an often repeated pattern. Two-thirds of the tenants died, the cost of labour rose six times, and the lord consequently commuted his services and introduced stock and land leases. Evidence for the widespread and willing commutation of services is considerable. The time scale varied, so that Ramsey reduced works in the 1350s and Crowland in the 1390s, but even ecclesiastical landlords had come to realise that Tresilian's remark in 1381—"villeins ye are and villeins ye shall remain"—was not in accordance with the facts. Thus, when the tenants of the Bishop of Bath and Wells, at Wellington in Somerset, refused to do carting services in 1398, the Bishop soon dropped his case against them. Even in a county such as Essex, where a determined effort was made to enforce the Statute of Labourers involving fines on over 800 people, it was impossible to stop the operation of market forces which ensured that scarce labour should command its price or, as Lipson said, "the system of villein tenures died out, in reality, as the result of economic changes which were already at work before 1381, and continued in operation long after the insurrection had run its course."

These economic forces had centred around the decline in population and the fall in prices before the Black Death. There were a series of bad harvests in 1292, 1311, 1315–19 and 1332. In the 1320s, a series of epidemics affected cattle and sheep. Low corn yields raised prices and this led to famine. From this period there is considerable evidence of declining population. With the fall in demand came a decline in prices in the 1320s. Thus, on the Ely manor of Shelford, income from manorial surplus fell by half between 1325 and 1333, although this is partly accounted for by the leasing of the demesne. Declining productivity and population affected the existing lords disadvantageously, and made land available for new tenants, or, in some cases, caused it to go out of cultivation. Wages showed a tendency to rise because workers were unwilling to perform services. Falling prices meant that real incomes increased and the villeins became more independent. Thus, whereas assarting and intaking still continued and were even found more at the end of the century, there was considerable evidence of a declining cultivable area. The *Nonarum Inquisitiones* of 1342 reveal this trend in some of the eastern counties. Agriculture as a whole suffered from a decline in the level of investment. In the late 1340s and early 1350s, three factors accelerated these unfavourable conditions into a period of depression: the Hundred Years War, the debasement of the coinage, and the Black Death; and the seriousness of the situation by that time was revealed in a government attempt to control the problem by economic legislation.

The Black Death and subsequent plague cycle have already been considered in relation to population growth and public health. It remains to give an account of its course through the country from August 1348 to September 1349, and to consider the effects. Spread by rat-borne fleas and carried on board ship and up the waterways, the plague reached England in August 1348 at Melcombe Regis in Dorset. That month, the Bishop of Bath and Wells ordered processions in his diocese. The Bishop himself remained in retreat at Wiveliscombe, although this was his usual practice and did not necessarily imply cowardice. In September, the plague was at Bristol, and during the autumn it spread across Dorset and Gloucestershire. By November, the plague had penetrated Hampshire and Surrey and finally reached London. Norfolk was suffering by the spring of 1349, and during the remainder of that year the plague spread to Wales and Scotland; and finally in 1350 to Ireland. The impact it made was tremendous. It was not only that it struck down two Archbishops of Canterbury, killed the rich financier Sir Thomas Pulteney, or devastated whole chapters of monks. The plague upset religious faith and brought to an end the enthusiasm of earlier years. Episcopal negligence was easily compared with the devotion of parish priests. All the chroniclers agree that a bad example was set by many clergy: "the pope, shut up in his own chamber, wherein great fires were constantly burning, gave access to no man." Not so had Christ dealt with the sick. The bishops should not be condemned wholesale in the manner adopted by Coulton, when he compared their mortality rate of 18 per cent with that of the clergy running at 40 per cent. Some bishops such as Gynwell of Lincoln, or Grandisson of Exeter made efforts to move among their flocks. Considerable attention has always been focused on the consequences of the plague as far as the clergy were concerned. Monasteries were closed communities and plague spread rapidly—two abbots of St Nicholas, Exeter, perished in quick succession; at Meaux in east Yorkshire all but ten members of the community perished.

Parish priests were exposed to the danger of infection while giving the last rites and it seems hard to reconcile the chronicler's censure that "even the priests and doctors fled in fear from the sick and dead" with the high death-rate among the clergy. The average figure usually given is 40 per cent of the parish clergy. It is important to realise that figures of total deaths and plague deaths are not similar. Thus, although 44 per cent of vacancies in the dioceses of Lincoln and York were caused by death, those from plague are considerably lower. York, in fact, had the lowest percentage of deaths (38·97 per cent). Exeter, Winchester, Norwich and Ely recorded the highest numbers of deaths, approaching 50 per cent in each case. It is significant that they were all dioceses with large towns and seaports; Winchester included Southampton and Southwark. It has been suggested that respect for the clergy should be limited by at least two considerations: impoverishment led to clergy seeking to acquire pluralities, and fear and economic want led to a considerable outburst of resignations. Those clergy who stayed, however, did well because their stipends shared in the general rise of wages sometimes doubling from £5 to £10 a year.

It is far more difficult to decide what effects the plague had on the total population. The statement of Thomas of Walsingham, that half the population was destroyed, may be regarded as an exaggeration. Nevertheless, the impact of the plague on certain specific areas was devastating. At Old Hunstanton in Norfolk, 172 tenants died. In three manors of Crowland Abbey, eighty-eight out of a hundred tenants died. Death-rates of 50 per cent are quite frequently met with, and in towns the number of deaths was also large. Poole was devastated so severely that it remained in decline for nearly a hundred years. At Leicester, three parishes lost 1,480 people according to the local chronicler. In assessing the national total, it is suggested that a figure of a third of the population is appropriate and, if the normally high death-rate and the over-populated nature of many villages are both taken into account, this number may seem less horrifying and even of some value to those that remained. In particular villages, a higher figure can be given and there is evidence of both immediate and long-term depopulation as a result. Thus, Tilgarsley in Oxfordshire and Middle Carlton and Ambion in Leicestershire disappeared almost immediately. Seacourt in Berkshire, Standelf in Oxfordshire and Wyville in Lincolnshire declined slowly. By the time such villages disappeared, it becomes difficult to distinguish depopulation due to a decline in natural increase resulting from the pressures of enclosure for sheep from that caused by the plague.

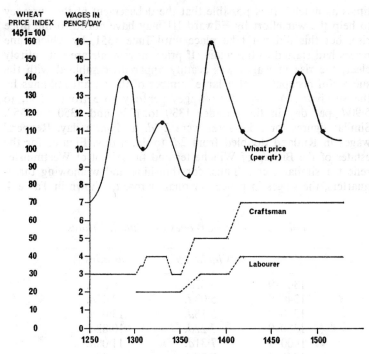

Fig. 2. Some medieval wages, 1250–1500 (Phelps-Brown-Hopkins generalised
prices of labour).

The immediate effects of the Black Death were serious. The
harvest of 1348 was not collected and markets could not function.
The decline in population was followed by a fall in price for agricultural products. On the other hand there was a serious shortage of
villeins to perform services or hired labourers to replace them.
Land went out of cultivation. Tenants at first refused to take on
new lands in case they died as well, and lands reverted to the
demesne for want of tenants. On the Winchester estate whole
families were sometimes swept away; tenements were left vacant
on the lord's land; and on the account rolls appears again and
again the entry: "Nothing, because he was dead." Before long,
however, the price situation changed. The revival of demand led
to a sharp rise in prices in 1349. The comment of Henry Knighton,
the Leicester chronicler, that "everything was low in price because
of the fear of death, for few took care of riches or property of
any kind," was soon overtaken by a fresh statement that "what
in former time was worth a penny now was worth four or five

times as much." It is possible that the debasement of the currency to help the war effort by Edward III may have added to the price rise, but this did not take place until June 1351, by which time prices had started to fall again. If price movements are not entirely clear, the rise in wages was readily apparent, combined with the successful occupation of a large number of the vacant holdings by the survivors. A carpenter's wages per day rose from 4·56d. to 5·90d. per day in the decades 1330 to 1339 and 1350 to 1359. Similar figures for a labourer were 2·8d. to 4·0d. a day. Reapers' wages in Rutland doubled from 2d. to 4d. a day. Figures for the estates of the Bishop of Winchester and the Abbot of Westminster reflect a similar trend. Thus, for threshing and winnowing three-quarters, the wages in pence per quarter rose as shown in Table 4.

Table 4—Selected Wages on Church Estates

Years	Winchester	Westminster
1300–9	3·83d.	6·51d.
1340–9	5·03d.	7·41d.
1350–9	5·18d.	13·02d.
1380–9	7·22d.	10·82d.
1400–9	7·31d.	11·00d.
1440–9	7·25d.	13·00d.

A more generalised set of figures, based on the exchange rate of silver, for the estates of the Bishop of Winchester, gives the results in Table 5.

Table 5—Corn Prices and Real Wages

Years	Corn price index	Wages index
1300–19	100	100
1320–39	90	124
1340–59	79	133
1360–79	89	169
1380–99	65	188
1420–39	64	189
1460–79	47	188

Low prices for agricultural produce, high prices for victuals and imported commodities, low rents and high wages all adversely affected the landowners, and a note of near panic enters their pronouncements. Nothing less than direct government intervention was urged to stabilise prices and wages. Similar legislation was introduced in France.

Although wages had risen since the 1320s, the decision to act was precipitated by the Black Death. In June 1349, the first emergency Ordinance of Labourers was issued and this was supplemented in November. These proved inadequate, and in February the Commons petitioned for further powers. A Statute of Labourers was devised, in all probability by Sir William Shareshull, Chief Justice of the King's Bench and himself an Oxfordshire landowner. This Act was followed by others in 1357, 1361, 1388, 1390, 1427, 1445, 1495, and 1515, and attempts were made to enforce these statutes with justices of labourers, whose duties were taken over by the justices of the peace and also by special commissions to inquire into their effectiveness. The Ordinances were sweeping in their scope, and the Statute even more so, although it must be remembered that in some respects enunciation and practice were quite often different matters. Villeins were to receive wages equivalent to the average wage obtaining between 1325 and 1331. They were forbidden to withdraw from ordinary services, and lords were forbidden to raise wages in order to induce labourers to their manors. Wage scales were laid down including 1d. a day for hay-making, 3d. for reaping and 5d. for mowing. In order that these wage reductions (which is what they amounted to) should be effective, prices were also to be controlled. Those who performed public services, such as boatmen or carters, were to keep to their old charges and food salesmen such as fishmongers, butchers and bakers were "to sell such victuals for a reasonable price" obtaining a "moderate profit and not excessive." Finally, the Act attempted to deal with the able-bodied who had no work. Alms were not to be granted and severe measures, including the use of the stocks, were to be applied "so they may be compelled to labour for the necessaries of life." In order to relate labour supply and demand, hiring fairs were to be held in certain towns, and there is evidence for them at Worcester as late as 1497. They were known as statute sessions and labourers were required "that they with their tools in their hands daily stand at the Grass-Cross on the workdays within the said city, and be there ready to all such persons that will hire them."

The defects in these measures soon became obvious, and they were the cause of much popular discontent. Local conditions made it impossible to enforce the laws, so that in some counties such as Northamptonshire and Lincolnshire the justices' sessions were broken up by labourers. Knighton declared that the people turned a deaf ear to the laws, but it seems that, in some counties such as Berkshire, Middlesex and Essex, an attempt was made to enforce the statutes. This did not have more than a temporary effect, and it is clear that real wages doubled during the century in spite of the operation and re-enforcement of the Acts. Opposition to the justices was very marked in the later peasant uprisings, particularly in Essex. Yet the government seems to have pursued the policy, and added to its unpopularity by increasing taxation under Richard II. The Good Parliament of 1376 renewed the criticism that vagabondage and villein defiance were widespread and should be controlled and between 1377 and 1381 there was a definite attempt to enforce the statutes. By this time, however, the scales of wages were unrelated to earnings, for whereas labourers were ordered to work for 1d. or 2d., they could earn 6d. to 8d. Some employers paid the higher wages and in 1390 the Master of Oxford Hospital was charged with breaking the law. In spite of strong opposition the statute was re-enacted in 1388, when all who had worked on the land for twelve years were ordered to remain there, and stern measures against "sturdy beggars" were announced. Continued disturbances combined with the findings of a commission to persuade the government to change its mind. In 1390, a new Statute of Labourers introduced a sliding scale, whereby wages and prices were to be fixed locally by the justices of the peace. In spite of this relaxation, the labour laws continued to be severe. In 1408, for example, no family earning less than eighty shillings a year was allowed to have any child made an apprentice.

It is not surprising that the statutes failed and added to the discontent of the population. They covered wages and prices and therefore intruded into a wide field of social activities. Problems concerning vagabondage and unemployment were dealt with haphazardly in Acts which were mainly concerned with able-bodied workers. The germs of the justice of the peace's power in labour matters and the long attempt to restrict the mobility of labour by enforcing residence had begun, and was to continue until the early nineteenth century. The laws tried to control economic changes which had been coming long before the Black Death, and as population started to grow slowly, wages and prices increased, and there was nothing that the government could usefully do. An examination of the situation in Essex makes this very plain. Villeins were determined to discard their obligations and work for wages. They were liable for 308 days' work a year, but it seems that a figure of some 120 days was being worked at the end of the fourteenth century. Shorter working hours and the widespread adoption of casual labour increased real wages. The growth of manufacturing compelled employers to adjust their payments. Thus, at Thaxsted in Essex, local cutlery manufacture raised neighbouring agricultural wages. Demand from a better-off peasantry led to pressure on resources and there were price rises. In Essex, ale was selling at Chelmsford at 4d. instead of 1d. a gallon. At Ongar, shoe-makers were making 50 per cent profit. Under these conditions, villeins could only be induced to return by higher wages and the leasing of lands for rents, which by reducing villein costs again raised consumer demand. There was something of an inflationary spiral at work and prosecutions under the Statute of Labourers could not arrest it.

RADICALISM, SOCIAL CHANGE AND REVOLUTION

The state of the poor in the Middle Ages has received little attention, and it has been too often assumed that they were few in number in a well-organised hierarchical society and that they were adequately cared for by church organisations and guilds of many kinds. Widespread disturbance in town and country in the fourteenth century focuses attention on this matter, particularly since the well-known revolt of 1381 was clearly much more than a revolt of discontented villeins. To describe the Peasants' Revolt as "a passing episode" is to minimise its importance as an illustration of many aspects of social affairs. It may have been of little importance in hastening the end of villeinage, for this was a continuous process, but it revealed a wide variety of articulate opposition to the social structures of the Middle Ages and coincided with a period of intellectual ferment among high and low. From this period, social criticism and a radical tradition start to influence economic development, even if only marginally.

The basis of medieval relief was the concept of charity and this was administered mainly by religious houses or religious fraternities and guilds. Monastic charity was widely distributed, because there were at least 800 religious houses of one kind or another, but the amount given varied from place to place. Alms were either the casual gift of "broken meats" or the donation of the benefits allocated to the poor in wills. The average proportion of monastic income devoted to charity was $2\frac{1}{2}$ per cent, although, since this calculation does not include irregular gifts, the actual amount may have been higher. In the north, according to the leader of a later Tudor rebellion, "much of the relief of the commons was by succour of abbeys." The percentage set aside for alms varied widely, so that at Fountains it was only 1·7 per cent, whereas at Whalley in Lancashire it was 22·1 per cent. Some monasteries such as St Peter's, Gloucester, which disbursed 6·6 per cent of its income, clearly made a reasonable contribution to the relief of the poor. Benedictine monasteries had an almoner to deal with the poor, and, in addition to direct almsgiving, a number of monasteries had annuities and corrodies. The annuity was a grant of money to a monastery in return for which an annual pension was received. A corrodian might make a payment in cash or kind and receive back either money, or food and shelter. In some counties there were quite heavy concentrations. In Hampshire there were nine corrodians in seven monasteries. Elsewhere, as in Yorkshire or Norfolk, there were fewer. Monastic charity could only cope with a small percentage of the population, but it could provide individual places with adequate coverage. For example, at Winchester, Henry of Blois founded the Hospital of St Cross as a home for "the poor in Christ." The original foundation provided for thirteen residents and a daily meal for a hundred poor. Later, Cardinal Beaufort, in contrition for his part in the death of Joan of Arc, added the Almshouse of Noble Poverty, providing for thirty-five brethren, a project so ambitious that his successor William of Waynflete was forced to reduce its size.

The Hospital of St Cross also provided a wayfarer's dole for travellers, and many monasteries had a hosteller to deal with another of their charitable functions: the sustenance of travellers. Adjoining the Priory of St Swithun at Winchester, for example, there was a Pilgrims' Hall where pilgrims from Southampton to Canterbury might rest. At Netley further south, "the King's subjects and strangers travelling the seas" received "great relief and comfort." Monasteries and the military orders were both concerned with providing for travellers, particularly pilgrims. On the continent, there were large Maisons Dieu at Calais, Boulogne and Amiens for English pilgrims travelling overseas. Although some historians have maintained that this particular aspect of monastic charity was successfully carried out and that "there is no evidence of any general falling off in the standards of monastic hospitality in the early sixteenth century" before that time, some claimed that the monasteries tended only to treat well-off guests to the full benefits of the *hospitium*. Edward I issued an order that said "the king intendeth not that the grace of hospitality should be withdrawn from the destitute." However, this had little effect, for during the fourteenth century, secular innkeepers began to take over from monasteries and charge for their services. At places such as Abingdon, Gloucester and Glastonbury, the new hostelry was leased out by the monastery. At St Albans, ideally situated for travellers on the Great North Road, the "George Inn" was established with stabling for 300 horses, where the monastery had formerly done service for travellers.

It has already been suggested that the Church was more opposed to the practice of medicine than to providing hospital treatment even of a rudimentary kind. It was St Bernard who once remarked: "you are a monk, not a physician." The infirmary of the monastery was for the monks, not for lay people, and if the Church chose to establish hospitals, these were separate institutions. Outdoor relief was more frequent, so that the Austin canons were exhorted to "often visit and suitably supply" old men "who are decrepit, lame and blind or bedridden." On the other hand, infectious diseases attracted some attention from the Church. St Anthony's Fire, caused by eating too much rye-bread, and leprosy, caused by the consumption of dried fish, were their particular concern, and a number of lepers' hospitals were set up, such as that at Sherborne in Dorset with accommodation for sixty-five patients. In 1311, Pope Clement V denounced those who had allowed leper houses or hospitals to be deprived of their funds. Some of the famous London hospitals were established during the Middle Ages, but did not fulfil their proper function until Tudor times. Bedlam, or Bethlehem Priory, was founded in 1247 and was the second oldest lunatic asylum in Europe. It was incorporated in 1547. St Bartholomew's was established by Rahere in 1123 and refounded in 1544. St Thomas's started as almshouses in Southwark in 1213 and was incorporated in 1553. No other town in the country was so well provided with hospitals.

As for the monastic contribution to the education of the poor, this is still a matter of dispute. Monasteries had schools, but it seems likely that the masters of grammar taught only those in the service of the Church and that the schools were largely for choristers. Schools such as King's, Canterbury, or York developed in this way. Some monasteries, such as Evesham, provided for a schoolmaster in a local grammar school, or, as at Sherborne, provided financial assistance for boys wishing to attend grammar school. Leach argued that King's, Canterbury, was the oldest English school, although it was refounded in 1541. St Peter's, York, has a very well-documented history and seems to have had separate headmasters (including Alcuin) from the eighth century. The school was rebuilt in 1289 and again in 1557. Stephen Harding, the Cistercian leader, was educated at Sherborne and the school was rebuilt in 1437. Ely educated Edward the Confessor, and in 1448

there is a record of the appointment of a master to teach grammar
to five poor boys in the monastery. At St Alban's, the monastery
maintained a famous school, which educated Alexander Neckham.
It was rebuilt in 1286 and the master was to "take no fees from
the sixteen poorest scholars of the said school." Winchester was
founded by William of Wykeham in 1382, the buildings started in
1387 and the statutes drawn up in 1400. Wykeham included sixteen choristers, but the main bulk of the school was to be seventy
poor scholars. Eton was founded in 1440 for "twenty-five poor and
needy scholars to learn grammar there" and villeins, *nativi* and
illegitimate children were excluded. There were many other
medieval grammar schools, such as King's, Rochester, Beverley,
Durham, Worcester Royal Grammar School, Hereford Cathedral
School, Norwich Royal Grammar School, Lancaster, Reading,
Abingdon, and Carlisle, which were partly religious and partly
secular foundations. It is one of the paradoxes of English life
that the public schools "which were intended to be charitable
institutions for the poor" gradually came to be almost exclusively
for the rich.

Lay charity functioned through religious and craft guilds and
by means of private benefactions. Religious guilds, such as the
Guild of the Virgin at Hull (1357) and the Guild of the Resurrec-
tion at Lincoln (1374), provided for travellers. The Guild of Corpus
Christi founded a college. Craft guilds were both fraternities for
religious and social work and misteries in relation to economic
activities. It should not be forgotten that prayer was an important
social duty in the Middle Ages and the monasteries, chantry
chapels, and guilds all performed this function. In addition the
religious function of the guilds gave rise to the cycles of mystery
plays of which four (Coventry, Chester, Towneley and York) still
survive. The guilds acted as friendly societies to their members.
The Mercers' Guild developed in 1357, when thirteen brethren (who
were also merchants) came together in the guild and fraternity
at the Holy Trinity. In 1333, the London Carpenters decreed that
"if any brother or sister fall into poverty by God's hand or in
sickness" a payment of 14*d.* a week was to be made. The Drapers
and Barber Surgeons provided 10½*d.* a week. Almshouses were
founded by guilds "for the brethren of the livery or clothing falling
into poverty." Typical of those were the London foundations of
the Goldsmiths (1341) and the Merchant Taylors (1406). The guilds
supplemented the work of the Church by providing hospitals, such
as that of the Mercers of York in 1371, and schools, such as that
maintained by the Drapers at Shrewsbury in 1492. They provided
educational grants and legal expenses for members, and tried to

deal with unemployment among their members. Thus, the Carpenters of York had an employment officer in 1482. Private charity led to the establishment of almshouses, such as those built by Richard Whittington or William of Elsing, and to the making of charitable bequests, like that of a draper of York who provided a hundred beds for the poor, or the weaver of Gloucester who gave £40 a year to be distributed among the poor. The guilds were exclusive, but they made some attempt to curb urban poverty.

What was the effect of those many different forms of poor relief? As Leonard has pointed out, it was indiscriminate and therefore may have led to an increase in pauperism at the expense of more-deserving poor. A provision in Bishop Drokensford's will in 1313 to feed 200 poor people might well have led to unnecessarily lavish distribution. On the other hand, fixed annuities or gifts bore little relation to economic circumstances and in bad years would have been quite inadequate. Charity was found where people were disposed to be charitable, rather than where it was needed, although the two coincided on occasion. The basis of charitable work was often income from land or the profits of a particular trade and was subject to decline at the time when it was most needed. Although St Swithun's, Winchester, set aside a manor to provide revenue for charity, the administration proved costly. St Peter's, Gloucester, set aside Stanedisch Manor in a similar way in 1301. It is unlikely that all the provisions for charitable relief by Church and secular bodies were able to cope with the demands made on them.

Poverty was, therefore, a principal cause of the lawlessness and criminality of the Middle Ages which provided the raw material for revolution, and, when added to by the agricultural troubles of the fourteenth century, presented the government with a problem of law and order. Justice and police were administered in the hundreds and the shires which had developed in Saxon times. Every township had one or two constables. Thus, at Norwich, there were 160 tithings and one constable to every hundred able-bodied men. In the country, the police coverage was considerably less. The enforcement of law and order was connected with measures for defence, and the main regulations before the fourteenth century were the Assizes of Arms in 1181 and 1252, and the Statute of Winchester in 1285. All men, except Jews and villeins, were to arm themselves appropriately for defence in 1181; in 1252 villeins were also allowed to bear arms. The two constables were to hold "a view of arms" to see that this was carried out. Edward I appreciated the value of archery, so that by the fourteenth century men were turning out with a club or knife, a sword, an axe, a bow or even fully armed. This system may have helped when it was necessary to increase the army, but it also left many with rudimentary military knowledge. In the cities from 1181 the duty of hue and cry was supplemented by watch and ward, whereby "no stranger abide in the township except by day, and that he depart while it is yet day light." City gates were locked at night. By the statute of 1285, brushwood and trees (except oaks) were to be cleared 200 feet back from roads to try and combat highway robbery.

The fourteenth century accordingly saw a rapid increase in legislation dealing with crime and referring to the serious danger of large bands of armed robbers. Conservators of the peace had supplemented the view of frankpledge in 1289, and in 1327 *custodes pacis* were to be appointed in every county, taking the title justices of the peace in 1360. They gradually took over duties from the shire courts and were, according to a statute of 1389, paid for their work. A writ called *traîlbaton* was started in 1305 to empower judges to take severe measures against ruffians armed with clubs. But the problem grew rather than diminished as the fourteenth century went by. The number of unemployed was swelled by outlaws and weyves (female outlaws), by soldiers who had deserted or learnt to live only by plunder, by runaway villeins about whom complaints were loud in 1350 and 1354, and by the ordinary criminals. Thus, Parliament complained about gangs who "do ride in great routs in divers parts of England . . . do ravish women and damsels . . . do beat and maim, murder and slay the people."

Medieval life was violent. One instance will illustrate this. The Northumberland records for 1279 detail seventy-two murders and forty-three accidental deaths. Of the eighty-three indicted murderers, only three were hanged. Six took sanctuary, one pleaded benefit of clergy, and sixty-nine escaped altogether. One reason at least for this state of affairs was the widespread use of sanctuary. Debtors took refuge from creditors at Westminster and, after the sanctuary was violated in 1377, Richard tried to alter the law in 1379. He failed and complaints were renewed in 1399. In the sanctuary of St Martin's in the City of London, a forger set up in business in 1447 to the great annoyance of London merchants. The sanctuary at Durham protected 195 murderers between 1464 and 1524. Those who sought sanctuary were supposed to abjure the realm and leave the country within forty days. They dressed in a pilgrim's habit and left from a port assigned by the coroner. More often than not, the criminal would break parole and join the bands of outlaws in the forests. From the ranks of these dispossessed, the lords were able to recruit retainers and the later part of the fourteenth century saw a threefold attempt to reduce their numbers. The Statutes of Labourers enforced residence and forbade movement. The Statutes of Livery and Maintenance (1377, 1389, 1393, 1397, 1399) tried to restrict the granting of livery and the practice of using groups to "maintain" support in law courts and overawe judges. Statutes dealing with rogues and vagabonds, of which there were a large number between 1377 and 1388, tried to enforce severe penalties on "sturdy beggars" who were sharply distinguished from the impotent poor. But the circumstances of the period meant that, to the traditionally large number of criminals and unemployed, there were added an increasing number of villeins and demobilised soldiers, referred to in *Piers Plowman* as one of the great social evils.

There had always been popular folk heroes associated with the bands of dwellers in the woods, such as Wilikin of the Weald in Henry III's time, but in the fourteenth century there developed a host of songs, ballads and legends, concerning such men as Adam Bell, Clym of the Clough and William of Cloudesley who were the heroes of the North Country. By far the most famous was Robin Hood, the subject of the *Lytell Geste of Robin*. The tale of Robin Hood is an allegory and the characters epitomise the state of affairs at this time. Friar Tuck represents the better type of clergyman and corresponds with Chaucer's poor priest. Hood, Scarlet, Alan O'Dale were not villeins, but of good birth, and they represent the sufferers from injustice who outwit the forces of evil and live well. Thus:

> "brede and wyne they had ynough
> and noombles of the deer;
> Swannes and fesauntes they had full good,
> And foules of the revere."

The forests were the natural places of refuge, and it seems that Hood lived in Barnsdale and Sherwood, and was known from Robin Hood's chair in Derbyshire to Robin Hood's Bay in Yorkshire. The existence of these outlaw bands was a key factor in the revolts of the fourteenth century, for they were always available to add strength of numbers to a cause.

One result of the accumulation of distress, poverty and crime was to prepare men's minds for the attack made on society in the fourteenth century by the first radicals. In the revolts of 1381 and those before and after, England participated in a widespread upsurge of popular discontent. The revolts were not peasants' revolts, although agrarian discontent played the major role. They involved townsmen. They were directed against government and Church.

They spread from one end of the country to the other. Economic circumstances conditioned the revolts but they did not cause them. The outbreak was due to immediate political frustrations with the government of John of Gaunt, and the mood in which they occurred had developed in the middle decades of the century. 1381 was in many ways similar to 1789 in France. It may be seen as a single revolt unrelated to European developments, or as part of a more widespread movement. It can be considered as an economic uprising precipitated by poverty and starvation and feudal pressures in the countryside, and the discontent of workers with masters and citizens with landlords in the towns. Or it may be regarded as an expression of certain ideas which became current through word of mouth, ballad and change of mood. What influence ideas have on men's activity cannot be precisely defined, but that does not mean that narrow materialism need colour judgment and the revolts of 1381 be looked on solely as economic phenomena. Radicalism, involving the ideal of the Great Society, of equality, an end to serfdom and personal liberty, was spreading. At the same time the abuses of the Church were exposed and ideas of expropriation were discussed. Froissart blamed the revolt on agitators, which is to give them too much influence, but that they had some impact is clear from contemporary sources. The mood of the period between the Black Death and the Peasants' Revolt is most brilliantly displayed in Langland's work *Piers Plowman* which was first written in 1362 and added to twice in the years before 1377 and before 1399.

Langland was the son of Eustace de Rokayle, a tenant of Hugh Despenser, and he was born at Ledbury about 1332. It seems that he was illegitimate, and took holy orders to free himself from villein status. Moreover, he tells us: "I am too weak to work with sickle or with scythe." It seems that he performed clerical services wherever they were needed and eventually drifted to London where he lived, regretting the past. In dreams and melancholic depressions, he began to recall the Malvern Hills. Langland's work is strikingly similar to Chaucer's *Canterbury Tales* in that it is a pilgrimage but by one man. Peterkin sets out to travel through society in search of justice for the common man, thwarted by Lady Mead or corruption at every turn and coming across all manner of people including weavers, labourers, townsmen and priests:

> "By Christ, said Conscience then, I will
>   become a pilgrim
> And walk on, as wide as the world lasts
> To seek Piers the Ploughman, that Pride may
>   be destroyed."

Langland, like Wycliffe, looked back to the example of Christ as a poor man, and he tried to relate that aspect of Him to the circumstances of the time. He was not a Lollard, because he accepted the teachings of the Church, but he wanted to broaden the concept beyond the formalism of the Catholic Church, and to condemn evils in the Church. Thus:

> "Counsel I you that be rich on this earth,
> Upon trust of your treasure pardons to have
> Be you never the bolder to break the Ten
> > Commands.
> And especially you masters, mayors and Judges
> That have the wealth of this world, and
> > for wise men are taken . . .
> At the dreadful doom, when the dead shall arise
> And comen all before Christ, their accounts
> > for to yield
> How then leddest they life here and His laws
> > keptest
> And how thou didst day by day, the doom will
> > rehearse."

Langland's poem has been described as "an alliterative rendering of the complaints of the House of Commons preserved in the Rolls of Parliament," and to an extent this is true because Langland's denunciation, although allegorical and in general terms, was also specific. Thus, Langland attacked the Statute of Labourers:

> "He grieves against God and murmers against reason
> And then curses he the King, and all his counsel
> > after
> For making such laws, labourers to grieve."

He denounced "maintainders" and the bands of sturdy beggars, but he also sympathised with the lot of the people:

> "But I warn you, workmen, win money while you may,
> For hunger hitherward hasteth him fast
> He shall awake with the waterfloods to
> > chastise the wasteful."

He talked about the misery of the cottage women who:

> "Also themselves suffer much hunger
> And woe in winter-time, with waking at nights . . .
> Both to card and to comb, to clouten and to wash . . .
> The woe of these women that wonyeth in cotes."

Langland's attack is impressive because it is based on personal experience, and his deep anguish and biting sarcasm are bound together by a note of hope. The tone of his criticism is socialist. It aims at redressing the balance between the rich and the poor and highlights the differences:

> "I have heard high men eating at table,
> Carping, as they clerks were, of Christ and of His mights . . .
> Why should we, that now live, for the works of Adam
> Rot or suffer torment? reason would it never."

Langland was not alone in his denunciation of the evils of a Christian society in decay, in his demand for peace with France, and in his defence of the poor. Chaucer's thirty pilgrims in the *Canterbury Tales* uphold the ideals of medieval society and also act as a commentary on its defects. The earthy vigour and humour of Chaucer was in common with much medieval poetry, but the attacks on the Church indicated a change in emphasis. The parish priest, although a good enough character, is addressed by the shipman who is "a good fellow":

> "Here he shall not preach
> He shall no gospel gloss here or teach."

The shipman then tells a story at the expense of the monk. John Gower, a Norfolk man who died in 1408, was a friend of Chaucer's and also wrote against the evils of the age in *Vox Clamantis* (1381) and *Mirour de l'Omme* describing the Peasants' Revolt. John Lydgate, a monk at Bury St Edmunds, who was born in 1370 and became a priest by 1397, joined the ranks of the social protest writers with *London Lickpenny*, describing the misadventures of a countryman in London. There is a little of the same mood in Occleve, who had an office in the Privy Seal in 1387, and was thus like Chaucer, a government servant. Gower denounced the war and Occleve joined his voice to this demand:

> "If but of you might be read or sung
> That you were one in heart, there is no tongue
> That might express how profitable and good
> Unto all people it were of Christian blood."

The writings of this group of authors were not of immediate influence, but they illustrate a number of important points. They show that articulate criticism was abroad among members of the establishment and among the poor. They indicate matters on which the depth of feeling was sufficient to produce written and literate opposition. Most likely, they were read in official circles and exerted influence in the literate classes, acting as a possible stimulus to the clerical opponents of the existing state of affairs. In a way the writing of Langland, Chaucer, Gower, Lydgate and Occleve was "the Enlightenment" of the fourteenth century. It differed from its eighteenth century counterpart in that religion was central to the critic's solution as well as their attack.

Chaucer referred to "a Lollard" when the parish priest wanted to stop the host swearing. John Wycliffe and his followers, "the poor priests," provided the means whereby social discontent was articulated among the lower classes. Contemporary opponents of the people's demands, such as Froissart and Thomas of Walsingham, attacked the Lollards, thereby indicating how important they believed their influence to be. Defects in the late-fourteenth-century Church were many and nearly all Chaucer's church characters reveal the Church in a bad light. After the Papal captivity at Avignon, there were two and sometimes three rival Popes between 1378 and 1414 and 63 per cent of Papal revenue went on war. Throughout most of the century, vigorous efforts were made to restrict Papal claims in England and the Statute of Provisors and Praemunire indicate this trend. A demand for the arrears in John's tribute was rejected in 1315. By filling sees with minors and foreigners, the Church reduced the effective authority of the episcopate, which had not distinguished itself at the time of the Black Death. The wealth of the "Caesarean" clergy in contrast to the poverty of ordinary clergy was all too evident, in spite of the fact that clergymen's wages had doubled from £5 to £10 a year during the century. Wycliffe's theory of dominion urged the Church to adopt a sense of trust for its wealth and do its duty by the people, and this was misinterpreted to mean expropriation. His own views on the social ills of the time were also clear: "And thus lords devour poor men's goods in gluttony and waste and pride, and they perish for mischief and hunger and thirst and cold, and their children also. . . . And so in a manner they eat and drink poor men's flesh and blood." It is too extreme to suggest that Wycliffe's advocacy of a social conscience for the rich was "giving his blessing to the theory of communism." Rather, the extremes of criticisms reflected the profound pessimism created by the Black Death, and are the social counterpart of the introverted self-criticism of the mystics.

The Church may have added to the grievances of the time by its wealth and pride. By developing the doctrine of the treasury and starting the system of indulgences, it certainly helped to provide criticism of itself so that Chaucer could condemn the Pardoner—

G

"Bret ful of pardoun come from Rome al hoot." Benefit of clergy and sanctuary helped to stimulate the criminal element in the community, and the harsh attitude of monastic lords to villeins and townsmen alike was one of the main targets of the revolt. Yet this was the age in Europe of Ruysbroek, Tauler and Thomas à Kempis. Walter Hilton, an Austin canon of Thurgarton in Nottinghamshire, Richard Rolle of Hampole in Richmond Palatine and two famous women, Margery Kempe and Juliana of Norwich, contributed to a pattern of self-denigration and self-criticism which centred upon the need to put one's own soul or conscience right before doing battle with the sins of the world or, as Rolle said: "force thyself in all that thou mayest, that thou mayest be no worse than thou seemest." This was partly defeatist, for if individual perfection is impossible the problems of the world will not be easily solved. Yet the mood was influential. William of Rymington, Prior of Sawley, asked how a priest "given over to filthy lucre . . . and engrossed in vain or illicit pursuits" could correct a layman. Walsingham's quotation of one of John Ball's sermons—"he also taught that tithes and oblations should be withheld if the parishioner was known to be a better man than the priest"—echoed with some exaggeration the same viewpoint.

Langland referred to the prevalence of reforming ideas, although he attributed them to the friars rather than the priests:

"They preach men of Plato and prove it by Seneca
That all things under Heaven ought to be in common."

The doctrine of universal equality, popularised in the famous couplet

"When Adam delved and Eve span
Who was then the gentleman,"

combined with the theory of dominion and the view that property should be justly distributed to create an impression that the whole framework of society was to be overthrown. In the disturbed conditions of the 1370s and 1380s, strong reaction to this was inevitable. A number of poor priests, including John Wrawe and John Battisford, were involved in the risings in the same way as the poorer curés were in France in 1789. The most famous was John Ball. Walsingham said that he preached "those things which he knew would be pleasing to the common people, speaking evil both of ecclesiastical and temporal lords, and won the goodwill of the common people." Froissart claimed to have quoted from his sermons, in which he said "matters cannot go well in England until all things be held in common," and denounced lords and the poor conditions of the people who "must brave the wind and rain in our labours in the field; and it is by our labours that they have wherewith to support their pomp." Even if Ball did not preach those exact words, Froissart was hardly likely to have invented the point of view for himself. It reflected contemporary opinion. As for Ball himself, he was constantly harried by Sudbury as Bishop of London and Archbishop and he was in prison when the revolt started in Kent.

The consequence of these new ideas was the creation of a feeling of unrest and social malaise which added to the already widespread economic confusion and distress and produced an atmosphere closely resembling "Le Grand Peur" before the French Revolution. It is found in the texts of numerous politically orientated rhymes of the period, and in the cryptic semi-allegorical messages passed by word of mouth among the poorer people. Aware of what some priests and some laity were saying, but unable to comprehend it, the people vaguely felt that revolt was near. This crystallised into what Trevelyan called "the Great Society." He attributed to it an unnecessary degree of organisation, but there can be no doubt about the views held by those concerned. Thus, one message found on a rioter read : "John Schep, some time Saint Mary's priest of York, and now of Colchester, greeteth well John Nameless and John the Miller and John Carter and biddeth them that they beware of guile in borough and stand together in God's name, and biddeth Piers Ploughman go to his work, and chastize well Hob the Robber." Another referred to : "John Ball, St Mary's priest greeteth well all manner of men and biddeth them in the name of the Trinity, Father, Son and Holy Ghost, stand manlike together in truth, and help truth, and truth shall help you." These show all too clearly the temper of the times and the way in which ordinary people had been affected. The Parliamentary rolls for some years before 1381 echoed with complaints about the situation. In 1376, it was said that "if their masters reprove them for bad service, or offer to pay them for their services according to the form of the said statutes," villeins left the manor to become rogues and vagabonds. The next year, the same theme was renewed that the villeins "will not suffer any distress or other justice to be made upon them; but do menace the ministers of their lords of life and member and, which more is, gather themselves together in great routs and agree by such confederacy that everyone shall aid other to resist their lords with strong hand." In 1377, the conclusion Parliament reached was that "if due remedy be not the rather provided upon the same rebels, great mischief, which God forbid, may thereof spring through the Realm."

It is likely that the misfortunes of the ordinary Englishmen were less affected by the course of the Hundred Years War than his French counterpart. The French chronicler Thomas Basin lamented the constant passage of war across the fertile land of Normandy, and the French evidence is of a widespread decay culminating in the collapse of the Champagne fairs in the fourteenth century. This was not the case in England, but the war still had serious effects. England lost control of the sea in the 1370s, and it had to be regained by a fleet fitted out by Philpott, a wealthy London merchant. Expeditions by John of Gaunt in 1373 and 1377 failed to achieve any result. English possessions, which had been considerable in 1360, had shrunk by 1376 to a coastal strip around Bordeaux and Bayonne. Economic gain was hazarded by the cost of garrisons, particularly Calais, and Cherbourg and Brest from 1378. Activities of mercenaries and free companies produced plunder, but no new provinces. In 1380, 1381 and 1382, three expeditions under Woodstock, Cambridge, and York met with no success. England had a Flemish alliance with the Arteveldts but this was a further drain on resources and did not prevent their defeat in 1382 and 1385. John of Gaunt sidetracked our interests for the Portuguese alliance, and a claim to the throne of Castile. The French had a Scottish alliance and the north of England was frequently raided. Gaunt was in Scotland at the time of the uprising. It was the time of border raids in the north such as the famous raid in 1388. In 1385, a French fleet attacked the Northumberland coast. Before that, many towns in southern England had suffered, including Hastings, Dover, Rye, and Gravesend. Twenty-five ships of the fleet were lost in a gale in 1379, and command of the sea was not re-established until 1387. Opposition to the government was widespread and Gaunt, who had set aside the Council and made himself Regent, was the particular enemy of the people.

His government had, however, made some attempt to grapple with the problems of the day and thereby increased its unpopularity. A serious attempt was made from 1378 to enforce the Statute of Labourers, but this only led to further opposition and to the murder during the rebellion of Sir John Cavendish, Chief Justice of the King's Bench, who had enforced the law in Suffolk and Essex. The government tried to finance the war effort by a poll tax. The tax was imposed every year from 1377 to 1381, and the burden became increasingly severe. The tax had been graduated in 1379 from £6 13s. 4d. to a groat (4d.) per head, and in 1380 this was levied again. Then, in November, a flat rate of 3 groats, equivalent to the monthly wage of a working man, was levied. Evasion was resorted to on a widespread scale, so that a third of those who paid in 1377 did not pay in 1381. Again, the government took action which had some effect. In Suffolk, 58,610 had been assessed in 1377 and in the first poll tax of 1380, only 31,734 were assessed. After the commission, the number rose to 44,635. The commissioners were empowered to fine up to £10 for defaults and they aroused opposition from yeomen as well as villeins:

> "Tax has troubled us all,
> Probat hoc mors tot validorum.
> The king thereof had small,
> Fuit in manibus cupidorum."

Even the commissioners were not above a little peculation, and new ones were appointed in March 1381. This caused the revolt in Essex. In May 1381, John Bampton, a commissioner, was forced to flee from Brentwood. Chief Justice Belknap went down to Essex to punish the villagers, but the jurors and three clerks were seized and executed and Belknap forced to return to London. In June 1381, the villeins of Essex were in revolt.

Parliamentary complaints and the preambles of statutes were the record of a prejudiced minority. An analysis of the 1,636 knights of the shire in Edward III's Parliament showed that 125 were escheators, 371 collectors of taxes, 381 sheriffs and 641 justices of the peace. They suffered as landowners and administrators. Chroniclers such as Knighton, Walsingham, or the *Anominalle Chronicalle* of St Mary's at York, were limited observers of the social scene. Yet it seems that both sources reflected a genuine change in attitude and that they did not exaggerate the degree to which a wide section of the people rejected society and were prepared to use force. Mob violence was a tradition of medieval England as it was of eighteenth-century France. The London mob rose to protect Wycliffe and to break sanctuary at Westminster in 1378. In part, it was opposition to the wealthy group led by John Philpott, William Walworth and Nicholas Brembre, and it was led by John of Northampton and John Horn. Oxford had experienced riots in 1355, directed against the university by townsmen and villagers, which was paralleled by the attack in 1381 at Cambridge on Corpus Christi College, and the burning of records. Alien merchants had to receive protection in 1336, 1352 and 1354 "in order to replenish the said realm and lands . . . with merchandise of other lands," but in 1381 the Flemings were attacked and thirty-four burnt alive in St Martin Vintry. It was the only event of 1381 that attracted Chaucer's attention:

> "Certes Jack Straw and his meines
> Ne maden never shoutes half so shrill
> When than they wolden any Fleming kille."

Such riots were to recur on Evil May Day, 1517. Clashes outside the monasteries of St Albans and Bury had their counterparts in 1327. 1381 was a focus for a wide range of economic and social grievances in town and country, but it is also possible to discern the involvement of wider issues.

Before 1377, only sixteen cases of English heresy were known and England had a reputation for being a loyal province of the Church. Yet, in 1382, an Act was passed for the punishment of preachers, and there was a strong clerical reaction to the Lollards. Anti-clericalism, manifest at the trials of Wycliffe, was created and was to flourish for the rest of the Middle Ages. At the same time a new spirit had developed inside the Church, conscious of failure and eager for change. Awareness of failure developed into the gloomy cadavers of fifteenth-century tombs and the reiterated "timor mortis conturbet me." The willingness to change led to the view that the Church was socially involved, which showed itself most remarkably in wall-paintings of Christ of the trades, in which Christ was crowned with a halo of tools. Examples may still be seen at Ampney St Mary in the Cotswolds or Hessett in Suffolk. Lollardry continued in spite of persecution and retained its hold in the Cotswolds and East Anglia during the next century. In a sense, the revolt changed nothing because the trends it revealed continued in spite of the reaction that followed and the severe legislation. Villeins withdrew their services in spite of the Act of 1382. Examples occur at Leighton in Huntingdonshire (1385), Haugh in Suffolk (1385-9), and Balsall (1394). Lords continued freely to commute services. Evidence for combination and the continuance of rioting showed that peace was not to be obtained until the changes were completed. There were combinations in Somerset, Lincolnshire, Shropshire and Suffolk. From 1383 to 1385, the villeins of Littlehaw near Bury, with the help of their clergyman opposed the return of services. In 1398 there was a revolt of villeins in Oxfordshire. The factors that caused the revolt of 1381 were more deep-seated than the fusion of grievances under the stress of bad government. They sprang from the economic changes accelerated since the Black Death, and from the alteration of attitude which accompanied them.

The actual events of 1381 have been dealt with by Trevelyan in *England in the Age of Wycliffe*, and in Powell's work on the rising in East Anglia. Events in London were the most dramatic, but it must not be forgotten that there were nationwide disturbances. The capture of the capital by the combined forces of the Essex rebels under Jack Straw and the Kentish rebels under Wat Tyler took place when John Horn, a fishmonger, and another alderman, lowered the drawbridge on London Bridge and opened Aldgate on 13th June 1381. Before that, Rochester Castle had fallen, Canterbury pillaged, and John Ball released from Maidstone gaol. For three days, London was in the hands of the rebels and the fall of the Tower was as symbolic as the capture of the Bastille in July 1789. John Legge, Sir Robert Hales and Simon of Sudbury, the Archbishop, were held responsible for the poll tax and executed. Gaunt's physician was murdered and the Regent's palace of the Savoy went up in flames. The Temple, the Priory of St John at Clerkenwell, Lambeth Palace, and the property of alien merchants were attacked. The rebellion was fused so that the villeins were in part used by city men, such as Horn, or enemies of the government, such as Thomas Frandon, to obtain their own ends. Lacking military force and with Gaunt absent, the government temporised. Richard II met the rebels three times—in a boat off Rotherhithe, at Mile End, and at Smithfield. Promises of pardon and manumission were drawn up and thirty clerks set to work on them. Meanwhile, the King's party withdrew to Baynard's Castle, Sir Robert Knolles rallied the citizens against Sybyle and Horn, and after Lord Mayor Walworth had killed Tyler, the rebellion collapsed.

Meanwhile, revolution was widespread in the country. It eventually affected twenty-eight counties. In Suffolk, the Prior of Bury was executed. There, the revolt was led by John Wrawe and John Battisford. To the north of London, William Grindcobbe led an attack on St Alban's Abbey. The Abbot's prison was opened, grain reserves seized, fishponds decimated, and records burnt. Rioting spread to Dunstable, Huntingdon, Ely, Ramsey, Thorney, Peterborough and Barnwell. Opposition to the Church was widespread. In the Wirral, there were riots against the Abbey of Chester. At Bridgwater in Somerset, a clergyman called Frampton led an attack on the Priory of St John. North Leicestershire villages, such as Rothley and Wartnaby, rose against manorial monkish jurisdictions. In the south, there were risings at Croydon, Kingston, Guildford, Harrow and Barnet in June and July, and later risings at Salisbury in September and Maidstone in October. Private wars, such as that between Grimsby and Yarmouth, broke out. There were risings in many towns: William Napton at Northampton, or John Gisborne and Simon Quixley at Beverley and York are examples. At Scarborough the Flemish example of a hooded fraternity was followed by the rebels. In East Anglia, Geoffrey Lister, a dyer of Felmingham, initiated the revolt with a massacre of Flemings at Yarmouth. He was joined by Sir Roger Bacon, Sir William Morley, Sir Stephen Hales, Sir John Brewes and Sir Roger Scales. Although these men may have been compelled to join by fear—Gower was in hiding—it is significant that, in only 2 of the 153 villages where revolt occurred, were landlords attacked. On 21st June envoys were sent south, but by then the tide was turning.

That it did so was largely due to the initiative of Henry Despenser, Bishop of Norwich. Arriving at Peterborough just as rebels were about to sack the Abbey, Despenser attacked them, and in the words of Walsingham, "deigned to give them absolution with the sword that so the words of Holy Writ might be fulfilled, 'thou shalt break them in pieces like a potter's vessel'." When he had raised an army, Despenser rode on to Ramsey and defeated local insurgents. A day later, he entered Cambridge where severe riots had taken place at St Mary's and Corpus Christi. As Despenser entered Norfolk, he met Lister's emissaries in the charge of Lord Morley. On his own initiative, Despenser executed them and marched on Norwich. Lister was defeated soon after at North Walsham and executed after Despenser had heard his confession. The Earl of Suffolk pacified his own county, and in December, Bury was fined 2,000 marks. Canterbury and Cambridge also paid heavy fines. In Essex, the lead in suppression was taken by the Earl of Buckingham and Sir Robert Tresilian, the new Lord Chief Justice. Richard himself advanced to Waltham Abbey and sent on Thomas of Woodstock, his uncle, and Sir Thomas Percy who dispersed the rebels at Billericay and entered Colchester. Early in July, Richard moved to Chelmsford and from there to St Albans, Berkhamsted and Reading where he was joined by Gaunt. Knollys and the sheriff of Kent crushed resistance in the Home Counties and the Earl of Salisbury did the same in the West Country. Straw and John Starling (murderer of the Archbishop) were executed in Cheapside, Ball was captured at Coventry and executed at St Albans, together with Grindcobbe and Wrawe. As usual, exaggerated estimates were made of the executions, but a figure of about 120 seems likely. As late as 1830, the government transported 457 labourers in the last of the rural revolts of which the 1381 uprising was the most famous. The example of the "hurling time" could not be forgotten easily by either side.

After vengeance came reaction. The participation of Wycliffite priests had proved their sympathy for the revolt. Those who go "from county to county and from town to town in certain habits under pretence of great holiness, preaching not only in churches and graveyards, but in markets, fairs and other public places . . . cause discord and dissention between divers estates of the said realm" were no longer to be countenanced. In 1382 a law to punish itinerant preachers was passed. Oxford expelled the Lollards. A

Council at Blackfriars condemned Wycliffe's teachings. Villeins at Chelmsford and St Albans tried to plead that they had received pardons and manumissions, but Richard rejected these claims. A statute was passed in 1382 which declared "all manner manumissions, obligations, releases and other bonds made by compulsion . . . shall be wholly annulled and holden for void." In 1383 a further Act declared that if manorial rolls recording customs had been destroyed they were to be re-imposed the same as before. A further attempt was made to enforce the Statute of Labourers in 1388, and a commission was appointed to punish defaulters. It was only in 1390 that the statute was modified, more as a result of the revelations of this commission than as a consequence of the 1381 revolt. The law continued to bear harshly on the villeins, and in 1389 the first game law was passed forbidding laymen with less than 40s. and clerks with less than £10 a year from taking game. In 1388 the Statute of Labourers covered a wide range of topics. It referred to able-bodied poor and distinguished them from genuine paupers. Attempts were made to fix wages on an anuual basis. Shepherds and carters were not to receive more than 10s. and ploughmen more than 7s. a week. A firm attempt was made to control the movement of villeins. The Act stated that "no servant or labourer, either man or woman, at the end of his term shall move out of the hundred . . . where he is dwelling to serve or to live elsewhere, or even to go on pilgrimage, unless he carries under the King's seal letters patent stating the reason for his journey." Anyone found "in any city, borough or elsewhere" who had no such letter was to be put in the stocks and to find a surety that he would return to his place of origin. The same Act required all people leaving the country to bring their letters patent to eleven specified ports, and in 1389 this was cut to two. It is significant that during a depression in the 1630s, the Stuart government resorted to similar restrictions at the time of the great emigration.

The government was stirred, therefore, to considerable activity by the revolt, but the Acts were not sufficiently related to reality to have much effect. Riots and disturbances continued and the government itself weakened under pressure from the nobles in 1386–7, and 1399. After renewed disturbances at Maidstone and Salisbury, the government exempted 6 towns and 287 persons from the general pardon, but juries acquitted the few who were captured. Parliament, guided by Sir Hugh Segrave, the new Treasurer, might declare the concessions invalid, but they were allowed to remain and voluntarily imitated by other lords. Although some abbeys such as Ramsey took advantage of the situation to enforce villein services, the process of commutation went ahead in other places,

G*

such as Crowland. Even where villein duties were exacted, the fines were much lower. The number of wage labourers in some counties was as high as 30 per cent. Moreover, the leasing of land, including the whole demesne, continued apace accompanied by an increase in the size of villein holdings so that yeomen families were emerging. Early in the new century, families such as the Stonors and Pastons were starting to acquire a new status. Yeomen were sometimes the old freemen; more often, they were the new leaseholders.

Statutes did not succeed either in curbing the Lollards, or in suppressing the literature of popular discontent. Wycliffite influence remained strong in Oxford, London, Leicester and Bristol. A whole host of Lollard preachers, such as Peter Pateshul, William de Swinderby, John Aston, John Purvey, Walter Brute, and Nicholas of Hereford, kept up a constant wave of criticism, and in 1395 they even petitioned Parliament. Eventually, in 1401, a statute for the burning of heretics had to be passed, but Lollardry spread from the seven counties it was found in under Richard to another eleven counties in the early fifteenth century and possibly to a further thirteen. These "hedge priests" were critics of the social order. They helped the villeins. They served as an inspiration to popular poets. Brute is mentioned, for example, in *Piers Plowman* and another poem *Complaint of the Ploughman* is Lollard in tone. Poets such as Gower continued to lament the condition of the country and clerical involvement in war. The complaints of the latter part of the fourteenth century were generalised and inclined to be concentrated on the view that personal suffering was the result of corruption in the service of God. These critics, however, prepared the way for the more economically orientated critics of society who were to emerge in the next forty years. The manor remained the unit of production, but to the large estate had been added a sizeable number of yeomen and a larger number of wage labourers. These classes gained from the availability of land and the rise of wages. During the next century, while the landlords suffered increasing losses, yeomen and labourers were to assert their legal rights. New forms of leasehold and copyhold were to be recognised in the courts of law, and labourers were to be manumitted from their servile status. The drift to the age of the small farmer was well under way as a result of the economic changes since the 1320s. The revolution of 1381 had indicated the magnitude of the changes in medieval society, and had been a manifestation of social distress and economic burdens, alleviated by gleams of light from poor priests and a folk law of secular social justice. The revolt occurred because the villeins by 1381 were no longer willing to accept so subordinate a role as earlier economic weakness and manorial custom had required of them. It was the counterpart of the breakdown of feudalism in the higher ranks of society and the civil wars which this encouraged from the 1380s onwards until they culminated in the Wars of the Roses.

INDUSTRIAL GROWTH AND ORGANISATION

Throughout the Middle Ages the building trade was representative of the state of the economy, and in many respects it set precedents for other industries in organising capital and labour. During the later part of the thirteenth century and during the fourteenth century, a definite limitation appeared on the amount of medieval building. No more cathedrals were constructed, and very few other religious buildings. The only abbey built in the new Decorated style was Milton, because the previous one had been destroyed by fire. The Black Death temporarily suspended building operations and the decline in population limited the demand for new large buildings. Castles became more compact and domestic in structure, and although this seems to have been attributed in the past to the use of gunpowder from the 1320s, it seems more likely that the rise in the standard of living accounted for a preference for quadrilateral castles of which Sir Edward Dalgngrage's, built at Bodiam in Sussex in 1386, was one of the earliest examples. Medieval castles such as Pontefract and Scarborough were strong enough to resist the cannon of the Civil War period. Rebuilding was the keynote of the Decorated period in cathedral architecture, but it is noticeable that little attempt was made to imitate earlier styles. At Lichfield, for example, where the choir deflected to the north, the east half was rebuilt from 1325 and the junction of styles is apparent. Rebuilding occurred at Carlisle where the Early English structure of 1245 was burnt down in 1292 and a new choir completed by 1377. Parts of the choir at Norwich were rebuilt after the riots of the 1270s. Structural problems also produced additions. At Wells in 1338, three great double arches were inserted to prevent the collapse of the new tower. At Ely, after a collapse had occurred, John of Ramsey and Peter Quadraterius created the Octagon.

The Decorated style was a rejection of foreign influence such as that which had characterised Henry III's rebuilding of Westminster Abbey. The earlier or Geometrical period gave way to the later or Curvilinear period, neither of which resembled the prevalent Flamboyant style in France. The differences between the two epochs were considerable, as a comparison of the Geometrical east window of Lincoln with the Curvilinear east window of Carlisle or west window of York will indicate. At the east end of Selby Abbey, the two are juxtaposed. The style has been much criticised as a "more worldly phase of art," which was only capable of the meticulous copying of natural forms. On the other hand, it has been said that it was "more skilful from a purely constructive point of view." The style emphasised the characteristics of English Gothic. Cathedrals remained long in the nave and St Paul's (700 feet) was the longest in Europe. Breadth rather than overall height was emphasised, and this is particularly true at Exeter, which was the outstanding example of the style. Vaults developed through lierne and tiercene so that they became extremely intricate. Windows were made larger and developed fresh structures, such as the rose windows at Lincoln. Arches became wider and more intricate with frequent use of the ogee. Roofs, still of wood, became lighter, and buttresses more slender. Increased window space was obtained by raising the clerestory and reducing the triforium. Towers were built at Salisbury, Hereford and Wells and soon spread to smaller churches such as Ludlow, Ledbury and Leominster. Spires were developed in their own right and both Lincoln and Lichfield had three. The slender individual spire, such as that at St Mary's, Oxford, was characteristic. The outlines of the building were broken by finials, crockets and pinnacles. Roofs were adorned with bosses. At Exeter there were 500 and at St Mary Redcliffe, Bristol, over 1,110. Carving became intricate and detailed, laying stress on natural features such as flora and fauna and the masons themselves. A host of auxiliary crafts helped to decorate these products, which were the Church's counterpart of lay excesses in the age of chivalry. The Church was rich. St Hugh's shrine at Lincoln helped to finance the Angel Choir between 1258 and 1280. St Thomas's shrine, built by Walter of Colchester, helped to finance the later rebuilding of Canterbury. St Swithun at Winchester or St Edward at Westminster fulfilled a similar function. So necessary was it considered to have a ghostly patron, that Gloucester monks obtained the body of Edward II from Bristol monks and enshrined him for the economic benefit of the cathedral.

Chester, which was then a monastery, rebuilt the choir in Geometrical Decorated style between 1280 and 1300. Lichfield west front was started at about the same time and was adorned with 113 statues. The choir was rebuilt in 1325 and the nave by 1370. Carlisle and Bristol were both rebuilt, but the most famous rebuilding was that of Exeter. Freeman pointed out that the symmetry of this cathedral was something comparatively rare up until that date. Some monasteries such as Rievaulx and Byland were completely rebuilt, and, in the monastic cathedrals, polygonal chapter houses were constructed. Of the twenty-five known to have been built, few remain, but Wells, Salisbury, York and Southwell are good examples. Even the friars erected new houses for themselves. Many parish churches were reconstructed during the period and it is significant of the economic development of the time that seaports such as Hull, Beverley, Boston, Yarmouth and Rye contain some of the most impressive examples. Nor should domestic architecture be ignored, for the period saw the development of the hall into a manor house. The ruins of the Great Hall at Wells (1274–92) indicate the proportions. John of Gaunt had Kenilworth Hall built, and it is another indication of economic trends that the hall of Penshurst Place was built for Sir John Pulteney, one of the new financiers of the City.

Architectural construction was becoming more expert and making greater use of technical aids. The French architect, Villard de Honnecourt, had been among the first to use plans, and by the fifteenth century architects' drawings were in use in this country. No distinction was drawn between masons and architects until 1563, but in 1308 a Carpenters' Guild recognised their independent contribution to construction. During the fourteenth century, a hoisting machine referred to variously as a gin, crane, and verne was in general use. Forced labour was still used for the basic jobs and 720 workmen were employed on the building of the Round Tower at Windsor Castle in 1344. The masons themselves became highly organised and masonic guilds were established at Coventry, London (by 1356) and York (by 1370). Some of the masons, such as William de Hoton of York, who was guaranteed a salary of £10 a year for life, were well known. Two of the most important were William of Ramsey and Henry Yevele, who were leading exponents of the Perpendicular style towards the middle of the fourteenth century. Masons were in high demand and seem to have been guilty of restrictive practices and defiance of the Statute of Labourers. Thus, Wycliffe said masons "conspired together that no man of their craft shall take less on a day than they agree . . . and that none of them shall do anything but only hew stone, though he might profit his master twenty pounds by a day's work by laying stones on a wall." As late as 1518, the masons of Coventry were forbidden to form a guild and ordered to take the wages prescribed in law.

In the period affected by the economic disasters from the 1320s, it was inevitable that all new architecture could not be as opulent as Decorated, and in the 1330s a new style, Perpendicular, began to develop. The style was easier to undertake and therefore encouraged prefabricated structures. It was simpler to construct and therefore reduced costs at a time when the masons sought advanced contracts. The Perpendicular style was characterised by the use of vertical lines in tracery, rectilinear wall-panelling, broader mouldings and a wide four-centred arch. Willis argued in 1860 that Perpendicular originated at Gloucester under Abbot Wigmore, but Harvey has since argued that the earliest evidence for its appearance was in St Paul's chapterhouse in the 1330s. Whatever its origins, the new style gained ground after the Black Death had held up building, and was revealed in the choir of Gloucester with the largest window in Europe commemorating Crécy (1346) and Calais (1347). At Worcester, the rebuilding of the nave had started in the Decorated style, six bays were completed, and there was a gap of forty years before the work was resumed. Under Henry Wakefield, a new enclosed cloister was built and the nave vaulted in stone. This became possible since the vaults could be standardised and required less buttressing. At Winchester, the work of Bishop Edington was brought to a halt by the Black Death, and it was left to William of Wykeham to complete the nave in Perpendicular style. Wykeham used the same style for Winchester College and New College, Oxford, and thus contributed to the adoption of Gothic as the English vernacular style. Henry Yevele rebuilt Canterbury between 1380 and 1410 and was also responsible for the new Westminster Hall. The choir at York was another prominent example of Early Perpendicular. The style flourished extensively in the next century and it is sufficient here to indicate the change taking place.

Church building was the basis of a large number of craft industries and provided shelter for the arts of the illuminator and tapestry-worker. According to Saltzman, "church decoration was . . . a highly organised business by the fifteenth century." Quarrying has already been considered, and this industry continued to develop in the fourteenth century when free stone was increasingly used, as it was easier to cut. Wood-carving became a specialised craft, not only for men like Hugh Herland who constructed the roof of Westminster Hall, but also in the provision of choir stalls and misericords, of which the forty-eight at Chester and the sixty-two at Lincoln are perhaps the most famous. Lime was required and kilns were in existence by 1236 and using coal instead of charcoal by 1278, when 1,166 quarters of coal were ordered for London lime-kilns. Marblework was important and by the sixteenth century marblers and stone-cutters had their own company. Alabaster-work became famous in this period with Nottingham as the centre. In 1414, the Abbey of Fécamp received English alabaster-work and distinguished alabastermen, such as Nicholas Hill of Nottingham, Richard Cowper of Coventry, and Gilbert Twist of Burton-on-Trent were in business in the late fifteenth century. Bell-founding was established at such places as Gloucester and York, where a window commemorates their work. English white glass at 4*d*. to 5*d*. a square foot was cheaper than continental stained glass at 2*s*. a square foot. English glass manufacture was centred on the Surrey-Sussex borders of the Weald, where the Shorter, Ropley and Peyter families became famous. Stained glass was imported from the Île de France, Normandy, Hesse and Lorraine. By the 1380s, an English craftsman, Thomas the Glazier, is referred to at work at Windsor and Winchester. Glaziers' guilds existed at London and York. Iron-work of distinction was carried on in churches, and one of the most famous craftsmen was Thomas of Leighton, whose work is found at Chester, Lichfield and Leighton Buzzard. On other occasions, work was less skilled. At Tewkesbury, the monks lined the door of the strong room with iron seized on the field of battle in 1471. Lead was increasingly used for roofs and for guttering. Pottery tiles also came into use and by 1468 a guild of tilers had emerged. Parliament passed an Act to regulate the manufacture of tiles in 1477. Production rose quite sharply and the kilns of the Abbot of Battle at Wye in Kent increased their output from 1355, when there were 10 kilns producing 98,500 tiles, to 1370, when 13 kilns produced 169,000 tiles. Bricks were introduced from Flanders in the fourteenth century, and were in general use by the 1440s. However, the heavy Flemish bricks were soon replaced by smaller English-produced ones.

Highly specialised crafts contributed to the splendour of cathedrals and provided work for smaller groups. Wall-painting was widespread, either in simple colours in parish churches or in the richer hues of royal churches. They were made possible by the use of tempera composed of wood, linen and plaster of paris. Ordinary paint was made with dyes, the white of eggs and honey, and, by Richard II's reign, had produced such masterpieces as the Wilton Diptych (*c*. 1395). Nearly all medieval churches had a large number of wall-paintings. Stained glass was made by putting a wash on the glass and scratching the design in with ground copper. Details of its production occur in Theophilus Rogerus's *Diversis Artibus*. Sculpture in free stone and occasionally in other materials occurred. William Torel produced a number of bronze effigies for Westminster Abbey. The metal-working industries in gold, silver, brass and copper all contributed some of their products to the Church. In many churches tapestries were hung, usually in the gold and yellow-green preferred by English craftsmen. Although Edward III played the part of Louis XIV in encouraging tapestry work with a King's Tapestry Maker, and English work spread from Sweden to Spain, this particular craft was in decline before the superior products of Burgundy. Finally, the contribution of the churches to the book trade should be noticed. English illuminated manuscripts reached their greatest height in the fourteenth century, providing work for skinners, parchment-makers, scribes and illuminators. Such work as that of the East Anglian school (Gorleston and Ormesby Psalters) and the Luttrell Psalter of about 1340 represent this development—all revealing the characteristic preoccupation with natural ornamentation, grotesque humour and rich colour which characterise medieval art.

Rich variety was the characteristic of the medieval mining industries which flourished in the fourteenth century. They were nearly all highly capitalised, capable of technical innovation, and relied on highly organised and semi-skilled wage labourers. In nearly every case, the miners were organised in a fraternity which was in many ways a guild for their particular occupation. By the fourteenth century, coal-mining was an important medieval industry relying on domestic consumption—the first London laws against smoke were passed in 1307—industrial use and a flourishing export trade. At first, narrow shafts hollowed out into shallow pits (bell pits) had been used, but by the fourteenth century, drainage methods by means of an adit or horizontal shaft cut in the hillside had enabled deeper pits to be sunk and the coal brought up in a corve or basket attached to a windlass. Monks in Durham were using adits by 1354 and they were in general use in the 1360s. At Finchdale in 1486, horse-powered pumps were being used to help drainage. The miners themselves were divided into a number of groups. Heavers cut the coal under the supervision of a viewer and bearers carted it under the direction of an overman. Mining was not a popular occupation due to the danger, and there is little evidence of organisation, except in the Forest of Dean where they were associated with the iron workers. In 1349 and 1366 forced labour was used in the mines of the north-east. The lord of the manor had control over the mines and let them out. Thus, in 1356 Bishop Hatfield of Durham let mines out to Sir Thomas Gray for 500 marks. Apart from transport costs, the mines were fairly profitable and made the fortune of Richard Whittington, who organised the transporting of sea-coal in "cats" from Newcastle. Complaint was made of "the stench of burning sea coal." There are no accurate production figures and the measurement of coal by cauldron and corf tended to be variable. However, in 1377 to 1378, Newcastle mines produced 7,388 cauldrons (one cauldron equalled 10 tons) at 2*s*. a cauldron. Of this, it seems that 1,000 cauldrons were exported to Flushing and Dunkirk.

Iron production developed steadily in the Middle Ages, and was to be found over a wide area of the North Country. As early as 1161, there were four forges at Kirkstall Abbey near Leeds, and in 1180 there was a dispute between Rievaulx and Byland Abbeys over the ownership of an iron-mine. Cleveland iron ore was in use by 1271, and in Lancashire, Furness Abbey was an important centre of production with over forty forges using peat from the Fylde peninsula as well as charcoal for a fuel. In 1366 the profits from sheep-farming yielded £3 11*s*. 3*d*. a year and from the forges £6 13*s*. 4*d*. Northern production was on a much smaller scale than in the south. At first, the Forest of Dean area in Herefordshire and Gloucestershire was the main region of production. As early as 1086, six smiths at Hereford produced 120 horseshoes and by the 1190s, Gloucester was producing 50,000 for the Crusade of that year. The region produced hammers, nails, spades, horseshoes, arrowheads and bells, and in the fourteenth century, cross-bow manufacture developed under the Malemort family. At the end of the thirteenth century, there were at least sixty forges in the Forest of Dean. The industry gave rise to a considerable number of employment opportunities for miners, workers in the furnace, craftsmen in the forges and suppliers of wood for charcoal as the main fuel. The miners were associated in a fraternity called the Free Miners of Dean and had privileges in return for a levy of a halfpenny on every load of iron which was paid to the king. They had a court at St Briavels, with their own constable and officials. A brass in Newland Church shows a miner in his costume of the time. In the early fourteenth century, however, production in the Forest of Dean began to fall as an examination of the fall in the yield of the King's halfpenny shows: in 1280, it yielded £23, equal to 10,000 loads; in 1340, £3 10*s*., or 1,700 loads.

As Dean declined, the Weald grew as the centre for iron production. Export had been possible from Gloucestershire because iron goods had been taken to the fair at Winchester and exported to Flushing, but it was much easier from the Cinque Ports. London was a large and growing market for iron. The extent of the forest was greater, and when it is realised that, according to Norden, each of the 140 forges in the Weald used three to four loads of charcoal a day, this was clearly of the utmost importance. Already the Weald was an industrial area well provided with tracks. Glass manufacture in Surrey and Sussex was made possible by the existence of sand and potash, together with clay for crucibles and trees for furnaces. As early as 1254, the sheriff of Sussex provided

30,000 horseshoes and 60,000 nails for Henry III, and by the fourteenth century, the Weald was well established, although there are no production figures available.

The manufacture of iron was a complicated process in which slow technical innovation was present. The difficulty was that higher-grade ores were found, for example, in Spain, and accounts for the construction of siege machines in 1278–9 show that 65 per cent of the iron was imported. Spain, Normandy and Sweden were the main sources of imported iron and, as this was used for superior weapons and even in building, there was a deterrent to technical innovation. The iron ore was smelted on an open-hearth furnace, where it was placed between layers of charcoal. Around this was a layer of clay and then of stone in a conical shape. This method of production, however, failed to remove impurities and a blast furnace operated by hand- or foot-bellows was in use by the 1350s. It is suggested that a rise in demand produced by the war coupled with a rise in the price of labour after the Black Death to effect this change. The ore was washed, and subjected to a preliminary burning, before being placed in the large sandstone conical furnace which could be as much as 30 feet high. The iron was then heated and emerged in a large bloom (or sow) which was divided into smaller portions (pigs). By the beginning of the fifteenth century, water-power had been applied and this had led to an increase in production from 2–3 tons to 25–30 tons a year, and had cut costs by a sixth. The advance can be illustrated by comparing the works at Tudeley in Kent in the 1350s with those in Weardale in Durham in the 1400s. Finally the iron had to be forged, and this was done by hand-beating. Towards the end of the fifteenth century, at Ashdown there is evidence that a simple mechanical tilt-hammer was being used, although not at all widely.

Perhaps the most famous of the medieval miners' organisations was that of the Stannaries in Devon and Cornwall. Tin was an export industry of the thirteenth century, with much going to Bruges, and production increased steadily during this period. However, in the fourteenth century, Devon production fell off, although output was helped by a growth in Cornish supplies. The Black Death created havoc and output fell between 1337 and 1355 by three-fifths. The position did not improve until the 1390s, but there was little permanent increase from the thirteenth to the seventeenth century. At first tin was open-cast, but then a shamell, or platform which could be lowered into deeper shafts, was devised, production then being hampered by drainage problems. In the 1320s, an avidod or simple water pump was introduced by a German called Tidemann, but this had very little effect.

The Stannaries were organised in 1198 when William de Wrotham was made Warden, and attempts were made to eliminate sharp practices made possible by the varying size of a lode of tin (100 lb in Devon, 200 lb in Cornwall). Tin staples were set up at Bodmin, Liskeard, Helston, Truro and Lostwithiel in Cornwall and Chagford, Tavistock, Plympton and Ashburton in Devonshire. These staples were confirmed in 1353. In 1201 a charter was given to the workers which was amplified in 1305 and 1377. A complicated system of apprenticeship from entry as a sapper was developed, together with wage-fixing. The miners could only be sued or sue (except in cases of land, life and member) in the Stannaries Courts, of which there were four for Devon and five for Cornwall. Delegates from these attended a stannary parliament. However, the independence of the tin-workers was limited in two ways. The Earldom of Cornwall passed to the Crown, and in 1337 the title was given to the Prince of Wales. Secondly, mention of Abraham the Tinner with 300 workers in 1342 showed the growth of capitalist employers who reduced wages with "the result that the tinners have all left their mines." Despite earlier promise, medieval tin-mining was not particularly successful.

Table 6—Medieval Tin Production

Year	Tons	Thousand Weight	Number of tinners
1156	70	—	—
1160	—	133	—
1171	350	640	—
1198	—	900	—
1200	450	—	—
1212	—	1,000	—
1214	600	—	—
1243	—	—	149
1295	—	—	453
1300	—	—	436
1337	700	1,328	—

Reference has already been made to the expansion of lead-mining with particular reference to the increased production of silver in the thirteenth century. During that period, there was a considerable export of lead through east coast ports such as Boston, but by the fourteenth century there was some decline in the amount produced.

The three main areas of production were Derbyshire and Shropshire, Somerset and Devon, and Cumberland and Westmorland. Lead was found in rakes, and a claim or meer was staked out which allowed the claimant to take timber and build roads. The owner of the land took a tenth, and in Derbyshire, the king had a thirteenth. The Church was entitled to tithes because it was claimed that lead "grew" in the ground but, in spite of these overheads, large-scale employers had appeared by the 1390s, and in 1475 three of the largest mines in the north were owned by the Earl of Northumberland and the Duke of Gloucester. The miners were organised in groups as with tin- and iron-workers: the Alston miners' code of 1235 is one example of their organisation. In the Mendips, there was a lead reeve and a barmote court to decide matters. Conditions were sometimes severe, so that in Devon in 1302, miners who stole silver were to be dropped into specially dug pits. The miners were on a piecework system and in Devon in 1297, men were paid 5s. for loads of nine dishes (a dish was the amount one man could carry). Attempts by stronger employers to import foreign labour and to reduce wages, led to a considerable decline; between 1300 and 1350 the number of pieceworkers in Devon fell from 700 to 60. As with tin-mining, drainage was the main problem and the Somerset mines were closed in winter. In the 1220s, a system of buckets was in use. In 1297 under William Peppercorn, horizontal adits were introduced. Lead was hammered, washed in shallow troughs (buddles) and sieved before it was smelted. The furnaces, known as boles, were conically shaped with hand-operated bellows, but by 1295 water-powered bellows were in use and in 1302 there were smaller more efficient mobile furnaces. Lead production, like tin, was of less importance towards the end of the Middle Ages than at the beginning and was to be revived in Tudor times.

Salt was a key commodity in the medieval economy, due to its use as a preservative for meat in the "hungry gap" when cattle were killed off, and later for the growing fish trade, in spite of the serious medical effects. Salt-works were found in Cheshire and Worcestershire and salt-panning was well established in the southern counties. Salt was exported to Norway and the Low Countries, and sent to the fairs for purchase by the bailiff of the manor. Profits from salt-mining went to the lord, as the lord of Salford kept this right when he granted a charter. However, salt-panning became less economically effective and by the fourteenth century, England had started to import salt from Normandy and from La Rochelle where bay salt was obtained in large quantities.

Fishing was an important medieval industry. Inland, there was river fishing, of which salmon in the Wye, Dee and Severn was the most important. In 1285, a close season for salmon between 8th September and 11th November was introduced. The lord of the manor controlled fishing rights and an example would be that at Stokenham in Devon in 1310. Netting with a kiddle was permitted, but the construction of fish weirs was banned in Magna Carta and subsequent enactments. Salmon were exported. Inland also were the fishponds, particularly those of the monasteries. Sea fisheries were of considerable variety. The east and south-east coasts were the centre of herring fisheries, whiting and plaice were landed at the Cinque Ports, pilchards caught off Cornwall, and cod off the north-east coast. A cod fair was established at Blakeney by 1258, and Stourbridge and Yarmouth were the leading fish fairs of eastern England. Temporarily, England broke into the Iceland cod fisheries in the middle of the fifteenth century but was driven out by the Danes. Herrings were easily cured and suitable for internal trade (Coventry was an internal fish centre) and also for export. Fishermen had the right of dennage, or dene and strand, whereby they might use the foreshore for curing and net-repairing. It was only when ships ventured further afield that curing was done on board. The great herring fair at Yarmouth in October soon developed the town in its own right and the inhabitants began to resent the presence of Cinque Port fishers on the foreshore. Some of them, such as Hastings, had charter rights and there were sharp disputes, including rioting in the town and piracy on the high seas. A settlement was reached in 1277, but the steady decline of the Cinque Ports redoubled their efforts and in 1297 Yarmouth and Cinque Ports ships gathered for a royal fleet fell to battle at Winchelsea and Yarmouth lost seventeen craft. Clashes continued up to the reign of Elizabeth and the final eclipse of the Cinque Ports. The demand for fish was not met completely by those home fleets. Herrings were imported from the Netherlands and by the 1370s English merchants were venturing into the Hanseatic League's preserves in the Baltic.

The east and south coasts were the centres of the medieval shipbuilding industry, which underwent a process of slow technical change during the period. In the York pageant, the Shipwrights performed the building of Noah's Ark as the counterpart to the Fishers' portrayal of the Flood. Ships were constructed of wood from English forests, together with iron, timber, pitch and tar brought by the Hansards; and during the Middle Ages, underwent systematic improvement. The thirteenth century saw the establishment of the single-masted sailing-ship, and this had developed into a two- or three-masted ship by 1400. In the early fifteenth century, a revolution in construction occurred when clinker-built ships familiar since Saxon times were replaced by carvel-built ships, in which the planks were caulked together instead of overlapping. A third important change was the development of the rudder in the thirteenth century which replaced the steering oar (starboard) and differentiated the stern from the bow of the ship. Fleets were organised by the Cinque Ports and London merchants such as Philpott, and the fleet of Newcastle colliers was famous. Sir Richard Whittington's connection with this trade helped him to be Lord Mayor of London four times and to leave £4,000 to charity. William Canynges of Bristol had an even more impressive shipping interest. He is said to have had 800 shipmen and 100 ship-workers under him and to have had 10 ships, 4 under 200 tons, 3 between 200 and 250 tons, 1 of 400 tons, 1 of 500 tons, and 1 of 900 tons. Increasing evidence of long medieval sea voyages suggests that those figures may not be an exaggeration. The fifteenth century was a period of complaint about the decline of English shipping, but technically the industry developed rapidly. This was considerably helped by the decision to create a Royal Navy, which led to the development of dockyards and victualling facilities in the southern ports. Henry V and his Surveyor of the King's Ships, a Southampton merchant and draper, William Soper, organised the building of a fleet where 14 ships were over 300 tons and one, the *Grace Dieu*, was said to be 1,400 tons. This fleet declined, but Henry VII revived it with Robert Brigandyne. Southampton was supplemented by Portsmouth, where a dry-dock was built in 1495, and Greenwich and Woolwich were made centres for naval supplies. However, it has been suggested that naval revival began under Edward IV and that ship construction slackened under Henry VII. In spite of this, Portsmouth dry-dock was engaged in refitting the ships of Edward IV's navy.

Apart from the cloth industry, medieval manufacturing industries have received little attention. Shipbuilding was clearly, in Lipson's words, a large employer of labour and "working under the direction of capitalist employers." The leather industry was of great importance because it supplied clothes and shoes, harness and a multitude of lesser items such as buckets or book covers. Tanning from the hides of ox, cow and calf or tawing from deer, sheep and horses were recognised as separate crafts in 1351, and both are likely to have been widespread. Leather was an export in the form of raw hides or as a finished product and St Ives was one of the main export centres. Superior leather goods came from Spain, and we exported leather shoes, bottles and bellows. Hides were among the commodities taxed by the customs in 1275 and 1303 and included in the staple regulations of 1326 and 1353. The staple for hides was fixed at Calais in 1370. Attempts to keep up the quality of leather goods were made by the Leathersellers Guild in London, who had the right to search for false wares as had the Embroiderers, Goldsmiths, Pewterers and other guilds concerned with manufacture. Tanners' guilds were located at Coventry, Gloucester and York. Newcastle, Norwich and Worcester were well known for leather goods. Bristol, and various Irish towns such as Dublin, Waterford and Drogheda, issued regulations concerning the selling of leather, and all the indications are that tanning hides and leather goods manufacture were widespread and, in all probability, were our second most-important export.

A better-known group of manufacturing industries were those concerned with metalworking in precious metals or producing specialised products. A little gold was mined in England, but the majority of supplies came from the East or from southern Germany. Gold was used mainly as a form of investment, made up into plate, candlesticks or ornaments, and the goldsmiths became the earliest English bankers. Otto the German founded the FitzOtto family, who became Masters of the Mint for nearly 200 years from 1100 to 1300 and organised the Goldsmiths' Guild, which was in being by 1180. In 1327 their privileges were extended to allow the right of search for faulty products and they developed the system of hall-marks, beginning with a leopard to indicate the genuineness of an article. They became a liveried company in 1394. Deposits of gold meant that the goldsmiths assumed a simple banking function, although there is little evidence that they extended their operations to loans. During the fourteenth century, the number of goldsmiths rose rapidly from 25 in 1340 to 60 in 1360 and 135 in 1368. London was their main centre and in 1500 there were 52 goldsmiths' shops in Cheapside alone. Silver was the medium of exchange and was thus less usually made-up but cups and salt cellars were produced. England was more famous for brassware and for by-products of brass such as pewter and latten, which were amalgams of tin and lead, and of brass and tin. Pewterers Companies were established in London (1348) and York (1416). Bronzework was produced in small amounts, particularly for tombs, by William Torel and John Orchard in the reigns of Edward I and Edward III. The by-products of iron were very numerous, including all kinds of implement, weapons, door-fittings and domestic objects. Two important branches of iron manufacture were bells and armaments. Bells were produced by forming a core of clay, covering this with a cope and then pouring metal between the two layers. Aldgate in London, Gloucester,

Leicester, and York were all bell-making centres. John of Gloucester produced bells for Ely in the 1340s. John de Stafford,
bell-maker or bellyter of Leicester, became mayor in 1366–70.
Richard Tunnoc of York produced bells for Canterbury and Bury.
Ordnance of various types appeared in the 1320s, and was first
used at the siege of Cambrai in 1338. At first small culverines were
in use, but by the 1380s, cannon were being made weighing between
70 and 300 lb. Carlisle was an early centre for their manufacture
and London and Bristol works were established in the early years
of the fifteenth century. The barrel and chamber were made
separately and the cannon-balls were of bronze and later of iron.

Leather and cloth were both consumer as well as export industries. Fish and bread were the main food industries. Something
should be said about the primary drink industries. Wine was a
drink for the rich and homegrown wines were few. Our French
possessions were the centres of the wine trade concentrated on
London and Southampton. Cider and perry were produced in
Worcestershire, Kent and Sussex. At Pagham in west Sussex, an
apple-mill was in existence in the 1340s. Eighty Sussex parishes
paid cider tithes. Ale was the main drink—made up of malt, water
and barley. A fee (totsester) was paid to the lord of the manor for
the right to manufacture ale; and this was widespread. In 1327
Faversham in Kent had 232 traders and 84 ale-wives. Alehouses
were so frequent that a law had to be passed in 1375 to limit the
length of their poles. In *Piers Plowman* there is a reference to
the whores to be found in alehouses and Chaucer has the hated
Pardoner remark:

> "But first quod he her at this ale-stake
> I wil bothe drynke and byten a cake."

The view of frankpledge tried to reduce the violence in alehouses.
The Assize of Bread and Ale—regulated in 1283—punished false
measures. An Act in 1354 complained about exorbitant prices.
Beer made its appearance from Flanders in the 1400s, made of
malt, water and hops. These new plants were soon in cultivation
near Rye and Winchelsea, and in spite of opposition, an order of
1436 allowed the "Hollanders" to continue production. In 1418
supplies for the army included 300 tuns of beer and 200 tuns of
ale. Regulations were soon introduced and in 1441, Richard
Lounde and William Veysey were appointed to inspect beer. The
Brewers' Guild was formed in 1493.

When the overall significance of the cloth industry in the fourteenth century is remembered, this survey of the more important
medieval industries indicates that industry was widespread and,

although involving small amounts of capital and labour, was by no means devoid of sizeable works or considerable employers of wage labour. Organisation of manufacturers in guilds and of workers in fraternities, such as the masons or free miners, was widespread. Technical innovation was marginal in effect, piecemeal in application and slow in development, but in the mining industries in particular it was evident. Many industries such as iron and leather had to be supplemented by superior imports, but they produced themselves for the export market. The organisation of some industries, such as leather and shipping, has been neglected by historians, and it is likely that medieval industrial activity will be shown in future to exceed the level suggested here. The growth of better communications, the organisation of an English financial class, the development of taxation and royal intervention, the increase of trade, the rise of the craft guilds and the growth of many towns, which will be illustrated subsequently, were all part of a framework of an economy in which industrial and commercial matters were of rapidly increasing importance.

TRADE AND FINANCE: THE ORIGINS OF A NATIONAL ECONOMIC POLICY

The fourteenth century was neither the period when capitalism evolved nor when the state decided to intervene actively in economic affairs for the first time. The views of earlier writers ignored the evidence for capitalism before this period and underestimated the previous amount of government intervention. Edward III's vigorous but contradictory and *ad hoc* methods of raising money or protecting shipping and industry, in order to raise yet more money, were not a coherent economic policy. Bearing these limitations in mind, however, it is clear that the industrial, commercial and trading aspects of the economy became for a time a matter of national concern, and that a definite increase in the wealth and numbers of the English mercantile classes occurred. The impact of the Hundred Years War with the decline of continental financial stability and the rising demands of the Crown was one important reason for the change in the focus of interest. The decline in agriculture and the rise of alternative sources of income and employment was another, particularly when these were upset by prevailing tendencies for high wages and low prices. The development of the cloth industry with the change in trading and taxation patterns, the organisation of the wool and cloth trades, the spread of the domestic system and the rise of the clothier were the most important, single, economic factors in producing the economic changes of the fourteenth century. What was possible in the cloth trade was copied elsewhere and the building, mining and shipping industries "were more or less capitalist undertakings." Craft industries, in the narrowest sense, probably employed a smaller proportion of labourers than these larger undertakings.

England's medieval trading pattern in the fourteenth and early fifteenth centuries was one in which volume and value, although adversely affected by the Black Death and the war, continued to rise. By this period, it is no longer true to say that "almost all European trade with the East was conducted to supply the luxuries of castle and manor house." With the 50 per cent wage increase which took place during the century, and the considerable redistribution of landed wealth in favour of a greater number of small but by no means poor leaseholders or yeomen, domestic demand for a greater variety of goods developed and by the fifteenth century ordinary families, such as the Stonors, Pastons and Celys, had a greatly improved standard of living. Evidence of this buoyant domestic market may be obtained from the aulnage accounts of the number of cloths sealed in varying areas. Although it has been demonstrated that these contain inaccuracies for the purposes of calculating total cloth production, Bridbury has more recently suggested that the late-fourteenth-century accounts provide a reasonably accurate guide to home production. Home consumption rose from 5,000 to 10,000 cloths between 1356–8 and 1392–5. Moreover, this figure excludes cloth produced at home for the family. Industrial growth required an increasing range of imports as well as the growth of the consumer market. For the building industry, bricks from Flanders and, to a lesser extent, stones from France were needed. Shipbuilding required timber, pitch and tar from the Baltic. Iron was imported from Spain and Sweden. Salt was imported from France. The cloth industry created a great demand for dyes: red-dye from Portugal, woad from Picardy, madder from southern Europe, "brazil" from the East Indies. Alum was imported from the Black Sea area until home supplies were located in the Isle of Wight. Potash used as a mordaunt or fixer came from the Baltic. Only in fuller's earth, which was found in Surrey and south of Northampton, was the cloth industry self-sufficient in materials for finishing cloth. Wine was the most important import; the greater part coming from Gascony. This commodity was clearly not reserved for the rich alone: it was needed in every village for communion, and it seems that the rich provided a market for luxury wines from the Mediterranean. The wine trade was important to London, it raised Southampton to a port of nearly equal importance, and it developed western ports such as Dartmouth, which became a borough in 1341. By 1372, over 200 ships a year were trading with Bordeaux, and in spite of scores of interruptions caused by the war, the trade flourished until the 1440s when there was a serious decline, Gascony was lost, and Flemings and Hansa temporarily controlled the trade.

Food products were among our imports. Fish came from Brabant and later from Iceland, from the 1420s. Fruits came from the Mediterranean. More important were the spices such as pepper, cloves, nutmeg, cinnamon and rhubarb which were not luxuries but common preservatives to supplement salt. In spite of attempts to control the domestic market for luxury cloths by passing sumptuary laws and demands that the poor should only wear English woven cloths, the amount of luxury cloths imported diversified, even if there was a fall in the ordinary Flemish cloths to a mere 2,000 a year by 1350. Fustian from Germany, cambric from Cambrai, and arras from Arras were the main northern European cloth imports. From the Mediterranean came sarcenet or muslin, damask, silk, velvet, cloth of gold, bawdkin, carpets and tapestries. Critics maintained by the 1430s that the Italians were doing us a disservice by importing these commodities, but it is hard to see how this was so. Although they were costly, they were exchanged for heavy goods in bulk and in spite of the critics it seems likely that a favourable balance of trade amounting to £15,000 a year was achieved. This rose to £37,000 by 1446–8 and in part was due to re-exports of such commodities to Ireland or the Baltic. Armaments constituted another important import. Swords and long-bows came from Spain; armour and cross-bows from north Italy, and later gunpowder and cannon from the same region. As for minor items found among imports, there were jewels (rubies), perfumes (frankincense), ivory, mirrors, clocks, spectacles, playing cards, curtains, beds, books and writing paper, or as one writer described them:

> "Apes and japes and marmusettes tailed,
> Nifles, trifles, that have little availed,
> And things with which they fetely blear our eye,
> With things not enduring that we buy."

Alien merchants controlled a considerable proportion of our trade, although during the fourteenth century this share was reduced. Thus, in 1273 only 35 per cent of the wool trade was in our hands; by 1336, some 75 per cent; and by 1448, some 80 per cent. In cloth, which was the rising trade, however, there was a decline so that 80 per cent control in 1360 had fallen to 59 per cent in 1482, much of this being in the hands of the Hansards. Attempts to restrict the wine trade to English ships failed, and the Navigation Act of 1381 was largely ineffective. By the fifteenth century, the control of the carrying trade by aliens was a source of bitter reproach. Aliens were disliked because it was claimed they drained the country of coin and that this reduced the amount of trade. An Act in 1335 forbidding travellers and pilgrims to take out bullion was followed by further measures in 1343, 1364 and 1382, which were directed against aliens. Similarly, the government discouraged the bill of exchange and urged that deals with aliens abroad should lead to the return of gold and silver to this country. However, an attempt to legislate on this matter (Partition Ordinance, 1429) collapsed in fourteen years.

There was no consistency in the treatment of aliens, the attitude reflecting a change from the town-based economy to one where national groups of merchants demanded protection against others. Edward III protected alien merchants, as Edward I had, in order to encourage trade; or, as the Act of 1354 said: "in order to replenish the said realm and lands . . . with merchandise of other lands." An Act of 1335, renewed in 1351, urged that all merchants should be able to trade freely. Flemings were encouraged "in view of the decay of the art of weaving" in 1331 and 1337, but this policy was largely due to the fiscal needs of the Crown, and the value of an alliance with the Arteveldts against the pro-French Counts of Flanders. Aliens remained unpopular. There were disturbances in Norwich early in the fourteenth century, anti-Lombard riots in London in 1359, riots against the Flemings in London and Yarmouth in 1381, and in 1456–7 riots so serious in London that Italian merchants were forced to withdraw to Southampton. Parliament continued to receive constant complaints and the boroughs took their own measures to restrict aliens by means of the hosting system. Foreigners were forbidden to open shops, or to keep inns. They were compelled to live with English hosts and to pay a residence tax of 6d. from 1439. The system was general by the beginning of the fifteenth century, and in 1406, William Overary was made responsible for controlling the alien community in Southampton. Differentials were operated against aliens in the customs and taxes. In the case of wool, the 6s. 8d. paid by denizens was 10s. for aliens and the denizen's home subsidy of 33s. 4d. was 43s. 4d. for an alien. The cloth duty of 1347 for denizens was from 1d. to 3s. 4d., and for aliens from 1½d. to 3s. 6d. The staple system discussed later was also aimed to some extent at aliens. Thus, it is clear that there was a growing awareness of the value of securing the carrying and commercial facilities of trade in national hands, and of ensuring a rising export trend to pay for imports. The theory of a balance of trade was enunciated by Richard of Aylesbury (Master of the Mint) in the 1380s. Together with the bullionist theory, that a surplus of coin should be retained, developed simultaneously by Oresme, these ideas formed the basis for the fifteenth-century criticisms of aliens and the subsequent growth of mercantilism.

The two most important groups of aliens concerned with trade were the Hansa and the Italians from Genoa and Venice. Each controlled a vital area. The Hansa controlled naval supplies and iron and one of our biggest cloth markets. The Italian cities were the entrepôt for southern European trade and the principal link with vital dyes and spices. The Hansa privileges steadily grew during the thirteenth century in 1213, 1235, 1257, 1260 and 1266. In London, they settled in the Steelyard as early as 1320, although they were not owners until 1475. For a time (1282 to 1461) they were even responsible for the upkeep of Bishopsgate, and Hansa merchants shared in the government of London. Although they paid tunnage on wine they were exempt from poundage (a duty of 1s. in the £ on all exports apart from those covered by the customs), and they were given preferential treatment in the export of cloth. In 1446 they were responsible for the export of 21 per cent of broadcloths, and during the fifteenth century, as a result of royal weakness, the powers of the Hansa were to expand.

Our relations with the Mediterranean towns changed. The Italian wool-merchants, like Pegolotti, buying for the cloth manufacturers of Florence, and the numerous Italian bankers were of little importance by the end of the fourteenth century. The English woolman and financier had replaced them. Genoa with her carracks and Venice with her galleys were threats to English shipping and at the same time a necessary part of our trading pattern. The most important development was the arrival of the Flanders galleys in 1317. Disruption of overland trade routes combined with the improvement of the galley as a sea-going vessel to make sea voyages more profitable. Venice organised galleys varying between 150 and 250 tons in a state shipping line, each fleet being commanded by a captain from the Venetian nobility and armed with twenty bowmen. These fleets anchored in the Downs and despatched ships to Sluys or London and increasingly to Southampton. The early arrival of the fleet in 1319 and 1323 was followed by riots, but by the end of the fourteenth century they were coming regularly, Sandwich was abandoned, due to silting, and London, due to the serious riots of 1456 to 1457, and Southampton became the centre for the three or five vessels that came each year. From Winchester Fair and the manufacturing centre of Salisbury, they took wool and cloth. Southampton contributed 21 ships with 576 men to a fleet in 1345.

England's exports were more diverse than some have suggested. Wool, woolfells, and woollen cloth were the main exports in varying degrees in the fourteenth and fifteenth centuries. Leather was also considered important enough to be the subject of a specific customs duty. There was an export trade in minerals such as coal, iron and lead, and during the early fifteenth century a sharp rise in the export of alabaster. There was a considerable export of corn to France which underwent an increase in the late 1420s, although some restrictions were imposed. English meat, cheese, butter, honey, herrings and salmon were exported to the Low Countries. Among manufactured articles exported were embroidery and cutlery. Knife-making had become a specialised craft by the early fifteenth century, blade, handle and sheath all being separately made.

Wool was the main export in the first half of the fourteenth century, or as Sir Arthur Bryant has put it:

> "One sees the traces of this rural industry everywhere—the open downlands nibbled close by immense flocks of tiny sheep with their shepherds tinkling bells, sheepcotes and dewponds; the fells and fleeces stacked in great barns of stone and timber; the up-country towns and the market places of York and Lincoln, Grantham, Louth, Ludlow and Shrewsbury, Winchester and Andover crowded with dealers and factors: the trains of pack horses and barges moving towards the sea; the London merchants in their furred robes doing business with the king's officers: the English cogs and tall Italian carracks beating out from the Thames estuary and southern ports towards the hungry mills of Flanders and distant Tuscany."

Wool was said to account for half the wealth of England by 1300. Baled in sacks of 364 lb worth £8 each, at the end of the century English wool was the best in Europe. There were fifty-one types of wool, but Pegolotti in 1317 stressed the superiority of the Welsh border breeds and behind them came the Cotswolds and the Downs breeds. Wool exports rose to a climax in this period because Spanish competition was restricted by the Mesta formed in 1273, and England was able to supply Flanders as well as north Italy as a result of government policy. By the 1350s, an annual figure of 37,691 sacks was reached, but from then on, the rise of home demand meant a steady, if slow, fall in exports, which by the 1390s were down to 19,357 sacks. They fell away sharply in the fifteenth century to as little as 8,000 sacks by the 1440s. There was a recovery to nearer 9,000 in the 1460s, but this fell away to 8,000 sacks again by the 1500s. English wool was expensive because it was the subject of heavy duties, which eventually amounted to between 28 and 33 per cent. Besides, taxes in wool were also taken. Wool customs yielded £68,000 in the late fourteenth century, but

this had fallen to £12,000 by 1449. Cloth carried a light duty of some 2·5 per cent and was more favourably placed. Wool became the subject of extensive regulation by means of a staple. There was considerable wool smuggling. Financial gain, control of alien merchants, and the use of a valuable political weapon induced the Crown to adopt the staple policy. Wool staples had developed of their own accord at Antwerp and Bruges, and an Ordinance of 1313 seems to indicate that the Merchant Staplers were a private company to which the Crown was prepared to give a monopoly in return for efficient supervision. A further Ordinance in 1326 established eight English, three Welsh and three Irish towns as wool staples in this country, but this policy was abandoned in 1328. The staple remained abroad and moved between Antwerp, Bruges and Saint Omer. By 1343, owing to royal pressure, it was fixed at Bruges, but English merchants complained that the Flemings bought up wool and would not allow them to sell direct to European markets. In 1353 the Statute of the Staple marked the triumph of the English merchants, in that the staples for wool, woolfells, leather, tin and lead were to be located in England. The wool staples were Bristol, Canterbury, Chichester, Exeter, Lincoln, Newcastle, Norwich, Westminster, Winchester and York. The staple was to have a mayor, two denizen and two alien assessors and to operate the Law Merchant rather than borough or Common Law. Wool was to be weighed and sealed, and, if it had to be conveyed to a port, had to have this done twice. Foreign merchants were only to trade in those towns named. But the staple did not work.

Calais had been captured in 1347, and made the staple for cloth the following year. In 1363 the wool staple was also moved there, apart from the Italian merchants who continued to trade directly in England. By 1391 the wool staple had finally settled at Calais, although interloping was not infrequent. Thus, Calais became the centre of our wool and cloth trades. It was expensive to maintain, for the garrison cost £9,000 a year, but its obvious advantage as a continental town under English control was undeniable. The Merchant Staplers, who had developed in the early part of the century, became a large and powerful body of some 400 merchants by the end of the century. Eventually, in 1466, by the Act of Retainer, they were given the right to farm the customs of Calais in order to pay for its upkeep. Wool sold in Calais was either paid for by bills of exchange, or directly in gold or silver, or replaced by goods to be sold in England. By this means, bills of exchange, developed in Florence as early as the eleventh century, had become common here by the fifteenth century.

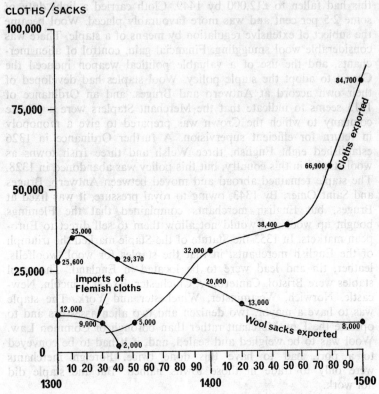

Fig. 3. Cloth and wool exports, 1300–1500. *N.B.* 4¼ cloths = 1 sack of wool (approx.).

The export of wool declined as the export of cloth grew. After the dramatic changes of the thirteenth century, the time was ripe for the growth of the cloth industry. Embargoes were placed on imported cloth in 1332 and 1337 and on exported wool in 1337. The heavy duties on wool were paralleled by the light duty on cloth imposed in 1347. Exports of cloth rose dramatically, ninefold in the second half of the fourteenth century, sixteenfold between 1354 and 1509. Cloths were of three main types: broadcloths (24 yards by 1¾ yards) narrow cloths (12 yards by 1 yard) and worsteds, which varied so much it is impossible to be definite as to their size. In the 1350s, some 5,000 broadcloths were being exported, and by the 1480s, this had risen to 66,900. Growth was rapid until the 1420s, when it levelled until the 1460s. After that, cloth production rose until 1551. Fifty per cent of production was centred on the western counties although East Anglia and the West

Riding were important. London was the main centre of export, but southern ports, from Rye to Bridport, gained from the new trade. As in the case of wool, there was government regulation, but this was to ensure that the Assize of Wool and Cloth should be enforced. Acts were passed to this effect in 1351, 1373 and 1411. and government aulnagers appointed to supervise their carrying out. It became the practice for cloth to concentrate at certain markets. In London, Blackwell Hall became the centre in 1396, and other towns such as Southampton, Beverley and Winchester had cloth halls. Those concerned in cloth export at Brabant and Antwerp seem to have been members of the Staplers, but their conflicting interests soon led to a change, and by 1360 John Walewayn was referred to as "governor of our merchants in Flanders." There seem to have been a number of groups of merchant adventurers. Thus, in 1391 John Bebys was referred to in connection with Merchant Adventurers in Germany. Their privileges were confirmed in 1404. Merchants in Flanders had their privileges confirmed in 1407 and the following year a third group trading to the Northern Kingdom created in 1389 were also given privileges. Bristol had its Merchant Venturers, whose privileges were confirmed in 1467. Nevertheless, the most important group were those trading in Flanders largely composed of members of the Mercers Company of London, who acted as a regulated company and came to hold a virtual monopoly over cloth export by the time of Henry VII.

The manufacture of cloth was something which had been developed in the thirteenth century. The replacement of the horizontal by the upright loom in the eleventh century, the fulling-mill in the thirteenth century, and the spinning-wheel gradually replacing the distaff at the end of the fourteenth century—these were the main technical improvements. England could produce good-quality cloths in small numbers, but constant complaints were made that English cloths were not well finished. The fourteenth century saw the development of worsteds as well as woollens. Woollens are made from short carded wool and worsteds from long combed wool. They are referred to as early as 1301, and by 1315 attempts were being made to regulate worsted quality. John Pecock and Robert de Poleye failed to do this, and although aulnagers continued to operate at Norwich, it seems that worsted manufacture at Worstead and Aylsham was exempt. These changes are far more important than the advent of Flemish weavers in the country. John Kempe in 1331, John Belle and Nicholas Appelman in 1337, and John de Bruyn in 1343 led numbers of settlers. Flemings settled in London, Winchester, Norwich, Bristol, Yarmouth and York. They

H

were also to be found in smaller country towns, such as Cranbrook in Kent or Abingdon in Berkshire, and even scattered in the clothing villages of west Yorkshire. There is no evidence that this influx brought new methods to the existing industry and it may have been the result of the dissension and warfare in Flanders.

It was in the fifteenth century that the wealth created by the cloth trade was to be seen in the tombs and chantrys of merchant princes in Essex and Oxfordshire. Then began the flow of money to almshouses and grammar schools, for which Tudor merchants were to be so famous, along with patronage of the arts and a new civilisation in town and country. The West Country was the main centre of the medieval cloth industry. Broadcloth production was found in the counties on either flank of the Cotswolds from Stroud through Northleach to Chipping Norton and Chipping Campden. Production spread east to Oxfordshire and Wiltshire, to centres such as Cirencester, Malmesbury, Calne, Bradford-on-Avon and Salisbury. Southwards, Dorset and Devonshire were production regions. In eastern England, broadcloths came from Essex and Lavenham, Coggeshall, Hadleigh, Kersey and Colchester were important centres. In Norfolk, Norwich, Thetford and Diss produced woollens and Aylsham and Worstead, worsteds. In the West Riding, Bradford and Leeds were coming into importance as clothmaking villages. Collected at the main fairs of Stourbridge, London and Winchester, the cloths were exported from Hull, London and Southampton to the Low Countries or southern Europe.

The development of trade in the fourteenth century owed little to royal assistance. It may be argued that war, taxation and the treatment of aliens were barriers to more effective trade. There was no royal economic policy of protection discernible in relations with Flanders, which were based more on political considerations. Sporadic attempts at a navigation policy or bullion control failed. Government attempts to regulate cloth quality through aulnagers did not succeed. In the organisation of both wool and cloth, the government, for the purposes of helping its own revenues, had to concede monopolies on a national scale to Staplers and Adventurers. Yet, in these activities, may be discerned an awareness of national trading considerations, of pressure by merchants on the government and of an increasing complexity in the organisation of trade. Commercial treaties between nations were still rare, although one was signed with Norway in 1216 and another with Prussia in 1388, but in the fifteenth century, there was a rapid rise in their number from the 1460s. A national had replaced a municipal trading policy. The roots of this mercantilism were derived from the piecemeal efforts of the fourteenth-century governments. They were given substance by the *nouveaux riches* who gained from the expansion of trade in the period. It was on these grounds that Postan might well describe the period as "the great breeding season of English capitalism."

During the fourteenth century, "a new race of war financiers and commercial speculators, army purveyors and wool monopolists" emerged to replace alien control of the financial resources for capital. In the fifteenth century "the business man was coming into his own." This was evident in industries such as the building, shipping and mining trades which had always been to some extent capitalist. The raising of credit by a class concerned with profit, the employment of considerable numbers by a single employer, the rise of wage labourers, and the divisions in guilds between masters and men were all indications that, "in the fourteenth century, if England was suffering from a spiritual decline, she was wide awake to the main chance and busily laying the foundations of her industrial and commercial prosperity." This was followed by the fifteenth century when society benefited from a rise and redistribution in the national income. Thus, "if the capitalist as financier and public creditor was found chiefly in the wool trade, the beginning of the capitalist as organiser of industry was found during the same period in the cloth manufacture."

Who were the creators of English capitalism, the men of enterprise and capacity for business who stimulated economic growth in the century after the Black Death? In shipping, some of the early large private owners appeared in the 1370s. In London, Sir John Philpott, a member of the Grocers' Company fitted out a fleet in 1378 to defeat French Channel pirates. At Dartmouth, John Hawley, a seaman and shipowner, was prominent in the town between 1372 and 1408 and was ten times mayor. Shipowning reached its climax a hundred years later in the career of William Canynge of Bristol and other contemporary Bristol merchants, such as Shipward and Frampton. In the wool trade, the woolmen who acted as go-betweens among wool producers and wool merchants and the financiers of credits between woolmen and merchants rose to power in their own right and as the leaders of syndicates formed to finance the Crown after 1345. Laurence of Ludlow, the Shropshire woolman drowned in an overloaded ship, was one of the earliest, together with his son, Nicholas, Gilbert of Chesterton and Thomas Duraunt of Dunstable. Other important financiers were Henry de Waleys and Bartholomew de Castell. John Kempe of Norwich, Thomas Blanket of Bristol and William Grevel of Chipping Campden were good examples of men made wealthy by the wool trade. The wine trade produced early examples of partnerships, such as that between William de Flete and John de Chigwell. By 1422, John Bourton of Bristol and John Tamworth of Winchelsea, who were wine merchants, were in Parliament. Foreigners continued to be frequent in the lists of early financial rings such as Bocointes, Buckerell, and Araxes, but the English share soon rose. The first outstanding example was the financial circle—formed by the Pepperers and Grocers under Thomas de Swanland, Walter de Cheriton and Gilbert of Wendlingborough—to finance Edward III, by taking over a royal debt of £120,000, and who were granted the farm of the customs in 1348.

London merchants were the most prominent in the new developments. Sir John Pulteney was a member of the Drapers' Company and four times mayor. William and Reginald de Conduit were able to lend the Crown £18,000 in 1338. Henry Picard was owed £23,000. In the 1370s and 1380s, struggles between the rich London companies became a matter of national politics. William Walworth of the Fishmongers and Sir Nicholas Brembre of the Grocers clashed with John of Northampton and the Mercers. John was imprisoned in Tintagel by Richard II in 1382, but Brembre was executed in 1388 for replacing him, after fraudulent and violent elections. Early in the fifteenth century, Richard Whittington, William Eastfield of the Mercers and Simon Eyre began the great tradition of London merchant munificence with the Guildhall, the rebuilding of Newgate, street lighting, a water supply and a grain store in Leadenhall in case of famine. Nor were provincial towns without their famous merchants and financiers. The Russells founded their wealth at Weymouth with the wine trade. William de la Pole of Hull and his brother Richard farmed the customs for £50,000 in 1343. William became a baron of the Exchequer, like Conduit, and his son became an earl. At King's Lynn, John de Wesenham and Thomas de Melchbourn were famous. With this new enterprise, there were accusations of corruption and there were financial crashes. Conduit was imprisoned in 1340. The Cheriton group collapsed in 1349–50. Richard Lyons, the royal favourite, was ruined and impeached. Yet many noble families, including the Bedfords, Suffolks and Baths, take their origin from this time. Merchants entered Parliament, and between 1445 and 1491 there were twenty-six merchant M.P.s. Stokesay Castle in Shropshire, the rich houses in the Strand, and the church of Chipping Campden were early examples of a fifteenth-century trend that would enrich culture from the products of trade and facilitate the arrival of the Renaissance. The great merchants of the fifteenth century were clothiers and shipowners. Their position and traditions had been secured by the woolmen, wine merchants, shipmen and wealthy guildsmen of the fourteenth century. They were a numerous and widespread class who prepared the way for the advances of the next hundred years and whose importance has often been underestimated. Chaucer's Merchant and Shipman were important characters, soon to outweigh the economic power of the Church.

This change was part of a European movement, marked by struggles in the Flemish and Italian towns, where disparities of wealth became obvious. On the Continent, towns like Bruges or Antwerp, Hamburg or Lübeck, Venice or Florence contained merchant princes who were virtually independent of local authority. London exercised a similarly powerful influence. Some towns such as Coventry or Bristol attained the status of counties; one, Berwick, seems to have been recognised as independent. The English merchant princes, however, were loyal servants of the Crown who lent money, provided fleets, served in government office and received rewards as peers or with the hand of an heiress. Spring of Lavenham's daughter married a De Vere. The fourteenth and fifteenth centuries thus saw the emergence of a trend of co-operation between the remains of feudalism and the growing capitalist class, which materially influenced the Tudor and Stuart periods. In the same way that many landowners had taken to farming for a profit, they now intervened in financial dealings. Cardinal Beaufort, with his gigantic loans to the Crown and his munificence to the Church at Winchester, stands at the cross roads. By Tudor times, great financial undertakings were lay matters. Government was increasingly in secular hands. Yet the new capitalists did not desert the land. The Springs of Lavenham returned to farm after three generations. John Tame of Cirencester, clothier, had a son, Edmund, knighted by Henry VII and he became Lord of the manor of Fairford. Thus was established that unique link between traditional landed power and new industrial power, which determined the growth of industrial wealth in a predominantly agricultural community. Even more important from a consideration of economic evolution is this emergence of a capitalist class long before the Reformation. It had been a long process and even in the twelfth century there had been a financier like William Cade and a building enterprise such as Durham Cathedral. Capitalism was the product of supply and demand and did not need Protestantism to help its growth. The late Professor R. H. Tawney's contention that capitalism and the Protestant religion developed together is factually inaccurate, since capitalism antedated Protestantism by at least 200 years. This makes the Reformation, as an economic event, much clearer. If it had any effect, it was to further a process of secular control of wealth in land and industry, and to provide an excuse for expropriation. It has already been shown that Church theories had little effect, and that the coincidence of economic organisations, such as guilds, with religious aims was a product of the time and not a necessary relationship. Wealth, to put it in an oversimplified manner, provided the patronage for the Renaissance before the Reformation. Beaufort's contemporary, John, Duke of Gloucester, was one of its early supporters. The fifteenth, rather than the sixteenth, century was the age of the rise of capitalism.

Variety and increase in foreign trade and the rise of industry, together with the spreading interests of woolmen, clothiers and financiers, all suggest that the facilities for travel and transport had undergone some improvements since Norman times and the road-building activities of Henry I. The roads from Chester to Caernarvon and Hereford to Brecon constructed then were part of the military penetration of Wales and there were similar road-building activities under Edward I. Apart from these instances, it is true that there is scarcely any evidence of medieval road construction, but, to draw from this the inference that there was very little would seem to be inaccurate, because the fourteenth-century Gough Map shows a considerable network of roads based on the four major Roman roads. Roads were maintained locally with some statutory assistance, such as that in the Statute of Winchester. The poor conditions of the road were such that even Parliament could be delayed by travelling difficulties, as it was in 1339, and these conditions were made worse by the lawless state of the country. The Abbot of Gloucester in 1281 referred to wolves and outlaws in neighbouring woods, and the outlaws at least increased considerably in numbers during the fourteenth century.

Bridges were much better provided for in the Middle Ages; indeed, in France the Pontife Brothers were an order of monks concerned with the construction of bridges such as that at Avignon. Bridge maintenance was carried out in the first place by the Church directly or by religious guilds of the bridge, who regarded it as a suitable social duty, or punishment in remission of sins, to repair bridges. Thus, in Durham diocese between 1311 and 1316, various religious penalties in the Church courts were commuted in return for bridge repairwork. The Guild of the Holy Cross at Birmingham was responsible for bridge construction there, and a similar guild at Abingdon diverted traffic from Wallingford between 1416 and 1437 by constructing a bridge. At Arundel in Sussex, the Priory of St Bartholomew of the Causeway collected tolls for the bridge, and in other places chapels were to be found on bridges such as that to St Thomas on London Bridge. Bridge repair remained part of the *trimoda necessitas*, but where roads were heavily used, it became necessary to maintain bridges by means of a levy. Such levies were charged and known as pontage. In 1356 the City of London introduced a tax on goods crossing London Bridge for the upkeep of the road because merchants were "often times in peril of losing what they bring." Bridges, like cathedrals, suffered from the lack of geometrical knowledge and there were collapses at Berwick and Chester on more than one occasion. All early bridges were of wood and among the first to be built in stone was London Bridge, started in 1176 by Peter Colechurch and finished in 1209 by Isembert the Frenchman. Perhaps the earliest surviving stone bridges are those at Huntingdon and Norwich Castle. In the later Middle Ages, wooden bridges were replaced by stone ones, like that at Bideford in 1460, and it was calculated in the 1930s that 150 bridges contained a considerable amount of medieval work. Those at Wakefield and Rotherham had chapels, and others, such as those at Monmouth and Newcastle, had defences.

Carting services in large, square, box-like carts were by no means unknown (as the *Cely Papers* indicate) and they were regular between London and such towns as Oxford and Winchester. A rudimentary postal service for the Crown was initiated with twelve royal messengers, but this was not available to the general public. Travel was slow and it took four days for a traveller to reach London from Exeter. It took ten days for a letter to travel from York to Laôn in 1316. Facilities for refreshment were, therefore, vital and at first were provided almost entirely by the Church. However, the fourteenth century saw the establishment of the catering trade, and there are numerous examples of medieval inns in existence today such as "The New Inn" at Gloucester, "The George" at Glastonbury, and the hostel of Godbegot at Winchester. These inns were criticised by Langland in the fourteenth, and Deloney in the fifteenth, century for their corrupt practice with customers. Acts such as those of 1350 and 1354 endeavoured to control prices, but it was more difficult to protect passengers from other difficulties on the way. According to Deloney, a group of clothiers calling at an inn were sure of a welcome and one Cuthbert of Kendal "was of another mind, for no meat pleased him so well as mutton such as was laced in a red petticoat." Some of our earliest inn signs date from coats of arms of importance at this time, including the White Hart (Richard II), the Bear and Ragged Staff (Warwick the King Maker), the Red Lion (John of Gaunt), the Black Lion (Philippa, wife of Edward III) and the Blue Boar (Earls of Oxford).

There were many travellers on medieval roads and few villages would have been as isolated as older historians used to claim. The division of English estates encouraged lords to travel, so that Froissart remarked that "the lands and revenues of the English barons are here and there and much scattered." The Court moved frequently. In one year (1299–1300), the Court of Edward I moved seventy-five times. Bishops were constantly on visitation or confirmation journeys. Internal trade flourished with chapmen and pedlars, woolmen and broggers, clothiers and merchants. Undoubtedly, the largest number of travellers were likely to be on some religious errand, because travelling for pleasure was not in vogue; although by the fourteenth century, cumbrous carriages and horse-litters were available. Religious officials, such as pardoners, and religious people, such as palmers, would be met with frequently, pilgrims most of all.

Pilgrimage contributed to the development of the medieval economy because such large numbers were involved. The trade in relics and the donations to the shrines were by-products by no means to be sneered at, and in the 1530s the monasteries alone yielded £75,000 in value of the weight of gold, silver and jewels. Shrines ransacked in 1538 must have brought in considerably more, since the loot from Thomas à Becket's shrine was said to have filled twenty-six large carts. The most famous pilgrimage was from Southampton to St Swithun at Winchester and then across the Downs by the Pilgrims' Way to Canterbury. Yet although this was in part the route taken by the most important band of pilgrims in history, it was by no means the only one. The transfer of Edward II's body to Gloucester, followed by his sanctification, was also succeeded by the rebuilding of the Abbey on the proceeds. Popular leaders' tombs, such as those of Simon de Montfort and Thomas of Lancaster, were frequented as well as the shrines of Saxon churchmen and kings. Glastonbury, site of the Holy Thorn and supposed resting-place of the Holy Grail, had little West Country competition, but there were other equally famous places of pilgrimage, such as Walsingham in Norfolk or Boxley in Kent. Pilgrimage encouraged overseas travel and helped to develop certain ports, particularly Dartmouth. Apart from the journey to Jerusalem, the most famous overseas shrine was that of St James of Compostella in Spain, and it is clear that the ships returned with European pilgrims visiting Canterbury. The church at Kingswear is dedicated to St Thomas. The lengthy voyage across the Bay of Biscay helped to develop ships in the fourteenth century. It is likely that such developments as the compass (from the 1260s) and the astrolabe (1480) were introduced into England by contact with Portugal and Spain. The finest representations of medieval ships are to be found in the aisle built by John Greenway at Tiverton Church in 1517.

By the beginning of the fifteenth century, based upon a not inadequate road and sea transport system, and a satisfactory financial basis of credit dealings, English trade was complex and growing rapidly. The country was less of a primary producer, and its main exports were manufactures. Its national income and its distribution were sufficient to create demands for a wide range of imports. But there must not be too strong a contrast drawn between imports and exports. Both contained luxury manufactures and simple food products. Many imports such as dye-stuffs, salt and iron were necessities. England had obtained, in all probability, a favourable balance of trade, and had greatly increased her share in the carrying trade, although the Hansa and the Italian cities blocked her mercantile expansion in two directions. The effects of the Black Death on industry such as building or tin-mining were not long-term enough to be serious, and the rise in wages in the later part of the century points to a fair degree of recovery in industry, paralleled by that already mentioned in agriculture. The checks which were imposed on this growth in the fifteenth century were to be the basis of much of the criticism of that time—that we were losing a strong international trading position. Government policies for bullion, shipping and general industrial protection may have done a little to forward economic growth, but it is not enough to argue that failure to carry out these measures was the root cause of the trade depression of the 1440s onwards. For this, the causes lay very much deeper: decay of "good governance" was only part of the problem.

TOWNS DURING THE CRAFT GUILD PERIOD

During the fourteenth and fifteenth centuries, the medieval towns continued to enjoy a very great measure of independence. Treaties such as those already noted in the thirteenth century between towns were still quite common, and one was signed by Cambridge and King's Lynn as late as 1549. London was of such importance that, as late as 1442, a commercial treaty was signed with Bayonne. Some towns, such as Bristol (1373) and Coventry (1451), were given the status of counties. The struggle of certain towns to free themselves from manorial jurisdiction continued, and was particularly noticeable in the riots of 1327 and 1381. They were not successful in every case and even an important clothmaking centre such as Salisbury had to concede obedience to the Church in 1495. At Bury and St Albans, the Church retained much of its power until the 1550s, and in Peterborough for much longer. The erection of town walls was perhaps the last dramatic assertion of the burgesses' sense of corporate responsibility. The walls of Norwich were completed in 1342 and it seems that, in those cities where medieval walls survive to any great extent such as Chester, York and Southampton, they were built in the fourteenth century. By 1377 all but three of the fourteen main English towns had extensive

H*

fortifications. Yet it should also be noticed that the increasing intervention of the state in matters of law and order, regulation of industry, and attempts to control prices and wages, indicated that the position of the towns as the independent centres of local economies was in decline. The rise in population developed demand, and in the case of London, this was already giving rise to a wide-spread food market. Moreover there was an increasing tendency for business to become a national rather than a local matter. The London merchants were increasingly to include in their numbers men such as Robert Chichele from Northampton, Stephen Browne of Newcastle, and Thomas Cooke from Lavenham. The interests of city merchants tended to become nationwide so that, for example, Stephen Browne, a London corn factor, in 1439 had a licence to buy wheat from York to Sussex. Geoffrey Boleyn, Lord Mayor in 1457, had business contacts from Essex to Dorset. In 1453 Godfrey Feilding, a London merchant, traded in Derbyshire and Lancashire. The system of middlemen and credit dealing reduced the impor-tance of the fairs and gave trade a national character. To the older similarities in their charters were added new ones, such as those in apprenticeship regulations. The towns were less independent than they seemed and at no point claimed or exercised the great urban jurisdictions of Flemish or Italian towns.

In some respects, this was a matter of size. Forty towns had more than 1,000 inhabitants in the fourteenth century. London, described by Dunbar as the "flower of cities all," was exceptional in having a population as large as 50,000. The expansion of London's population was shown by the division of the ward of Farringdon into two in 1394. This raised the number of aldermen to twenty, a figure unchanged until 1550. York, Bristol, Plymouth and Coventry seem to have had as many as 12,000; Norwich, Gloucester, Newcastle, Salisbury and Winchester as many as 5,000. In other towns, there was evidence of fourteenth-century expan-sion. At Chester, for example, when the walls were rebuilt, one was moved a considerable distance to accommodate new popula-tion. Guild complaints that certain crafts were being practised close to cities by large numbers outside their jurisdiction were a further indication of such growth. Yet with very few exceptions, such as London, the commonalty was not large enough to form the seedbed for urban disturbance or strong enough to resist severe urban and guild regulation. In turn, the towns were not powerful enough to defy the Crown.

Medieval towns may in the majority of cases have shaken off the legal restrictions of their previous agricultural position, but they remained closely linked to the countryside. Thus, Leicester had its West Field, South Field or St Mary's Field, and St Margaret's Field. Townsmen were required to work in the fields and, as late as 1388, London guildsmen were warned of their obligation. Half the inhabitants of Colchester worked in the open fields. Burgesses also possessed manorial rights such as the use of common pastures at Oxford and Norwich, and as late as 1549, there was a dispute at Bristol over such rights. Medieval London was densely populated in parts, with streets, sometimes no more than 20 feet across, darkened by the overhanging houses. One parish in Farringdon Without in 1426 had 2,000 inhabitants. On the other hand, it should be remembered that sizeable Church properties and the townhouses of many merchants were found within the City and that houses such as Crosby Place had a 60-foot square courtyard, with a garden and even a vinery. From Temple Bar to Charing Cross, there stretched a row of palaces and large country mansions. London was still a part of the rural economy. Its cloth market at Blackwell was of only slightly greater importance than the meat market at Smithfield. Nor was the house of Sir John Crosby exceptional, for Stephen Browne's house in Thames Street was equally impressive; in other medieval towns, such as Bristol where William Canynge had a large house in Redcliffe Street, town residence was normal.

Municipal independence had been the great issue of the twelfth and thirteenth centuries, but the main consideration in the later Middle Ages was the relationship of the town authorities to the craft guilds. Of almost equal importance were the relations between the guilds and the gradual emergence of new and more restrictive bodies—liveried companies for the rich merchants, and journeymen's guilds for the poorer workers. There were many different kinds of guild. Merchant guilds were governing bodies as much as trading organisations and claimed to represent the whole town. There were craft guilds which sought to include all those in a particular craft operating in the town. This led to disputes between one craft and another over demarcation, and to difficulties with craftsmen who claimed to be outside the jurisdiction of the guild. The authority for setting up a craft guild was in dispute, the towns at first claiming that their spontaneous creation was illegal and being supported by the Crown in their attacks on "adulterine" guilds. Later, the guilds became almost co-extensive with the governing oligarchy of the town. This was particularly true in London where, for example, of the eighty-eight Lord Mayors in the fifteenth century, sixty-one were either mercers, grocers or drapers. Guilds at first embraced journey or day workers and craftsmen, but increasing wealth and the rise in the scale of industry led to the appearance of rich employers and less well-off workers, and it became impossible for all workers to rise to the position of crafts-men. The craftsmen imposed burdens, such as extremely high apprenticeship entrance fees, in order to reduce the prospects of journeymen becoming full guild members. Fraternity was replaced by oligarchy. Moreover, although there were many guilds, so that London had at least 100 or Norwich 130, there was a distinction between large guilds which absorbed others and smaller guilds associated with declining or, alternatively, with new crafts. Thus, the number of effective guilds was much smaller and at Norwich numbered sixteen, Winchester twenty, Coventry twenty-three and York forty-one. The richer incorporated guilds and the Adventurers of London or Bristol were powerful employers' associations. In London in the fifteenth century, only 1 alderman out of 173 alder-men elected was from any guild other than the twelve largest incorporated guilds or liveried companies. Journeymen, deprived of full guild membership and increasing in numbers, founded their own organisations. Thus, at York the masters complained of "con-federacies" in the guilds in the 1430s, and it is clear that this trend was strengthened by the rise in wages and resistance to it. The earlier example of the masons was followed, so that in London in 1396, the Saddlers complained that journeymen, who could have been hired for 5 marks now cost 10 marks. The struggles of masters and journeymen were complicated from the 1350s by the Statute of Labourers and from 1495 by an Act regulating hours of work. This trend was to culminate in the Statute of Artificers in 1563, which marked the transfer of these matters from guild control to that of the justice of the peace.

Guilds were monopolistic and showed an increasing, rather than a decreasing, trend in this direction. Yet it must be remembered that their main function was to regulate industrial organisation at a time when this was rudimentary. If they were small-minded oligarchies, they were not at least impersonal large monopolies. They sought as much to protect the consumer as their own interests. They emphasised training through the system of apprenticeship and later by "the master-piece" practice. They maintained high standards in the production of their goods, punishing defaulting workers, carrying out rigorous searches (which in some cases became national), forbidding night work and Sunday labour, and regulating prices, quality and wages. Guilds also had important social functions as friendly societies, to provide for those in need, to help the poor to educate their children (some guilds founding schools), to seek to mitigate the difficulties of unemployment, and even to determine disputes by arbitration. These functions were in no sense a deliberate anticipation of later trade unions. The securing of living standards was part of the medieval concept of a charitable group helping each other as fellow Christians. The religious functions of guilds, in holding pageants, performing miracle plays, endowing charities such as almshouses, providing bridges, burning candles, and maintaining chapels, were of great importance.

Guild practice differed from town to town, but there were aspects of similarity. There was no national guild system, but there was a guild system of organisation for many crafts. Guilds were for crafts and they also existed in larger industries, such as building and mining in its various branches. Later, the guilds tended to become manufacturers' or merchants' organisations, so that the Mercers became co-extensive with the main groups of Merchant Adventurers and were more concerned with general trade than with a particular commodity or the regulation of a particular process. Apprenticeship was the foundation of the guild, and was so popular that, from 1164, laws were constantly passed against those of humble origin taking it up. There was no national scheme of apprenticeship, but by the time the earliest indentures of service appear (London 1291, Lincoln 1328, Bristol 1344) it is clear that the seven-year example of London was general, although between 1309 and 1312 a quarter of the apprentices served longer than this. In Tudor times, laws of 1495 and 1552 accepted the seven-year period, and it was included in the famous Act of 1563. Apprentices may seem, superficially, to have been rather like slaves. Many guilds referred to the need for apprentices to be strong and "whole of limbs," and indentured work was to acquire unpleasant overtones in the colonies in the seventeenth century. Apprentice riots, such as those in 1400, have been taken as signs of oppression. It seems likely, however, that the craftsman stood *in loco parentis* for his boys, and that his obligations to them were enforced.

On completion of his apprenticeship, the boy became a day labourer or journeyman. During this time he would try and collect sufficient capital to produce a worthy master-piece in order to be elected a craftsman. Increasing competition and high entry fines made this difficult, although it was also possible to become a full guild member by gift, purchase, birth or marriage—even if these were rare. One cause of the unpopularity of aliens was the belief that they contributed to this problem and the clashes of 1457 in London revealed this ugly mood. The journeymen's guilds were much disliked by the craftsmen and subjected to attempts to crush them which seem to have largely succeeded. Eventually, the government intervened in this matter as well, and in 1548 a statute declared that journeymen had "made confederacies and promises and have sworn mutual oaths" and forbade them to organise themselves. Fines of £10, £20, and the additional threat of imprisonment, the pillory and the loss of an ear were imposed. In the next year, Coventry suppressed the yeomen guilds which had developed into a regular organisation as early as 1424.

In theory, guilds were supposed to include all local workers, but where there was no local guild, or where the workers were too widespread, this was impossible. Moreover, the later trend was to fragment, rather than consolidate, the various groups of workers. Guilds were run by wardens numbering two or four appointed or elected in various places. Originally, election had been by the commonalty of the guild, but this was increasingly restricted. Guild authority was considerable because craft industry was on a small scale, and it was significant that complaints about standards were most often heard in connection with cloth production, where guild supervision became increasingly difficult, and government aulnagers did not prove effective. The craft guild assembled at certain times in the year and, in some places, there was a common council selected for the purposes of day to day administration. At Bristol, the Fullers had a common council of twelve approved "by the commons of the same mystery." In order to enforce their requirements, the guilds had courts but it proved difficult to enforce guild regulations in this way and there were cases of guildsmen being handed over to secular, and even ecclesiastical, courts for disobedience or perjury as a result of breaking their contract.

Guild politics give the impression of being acrimonious because the greater part of their work went unrecorded. Nevertheless, there were a number of causes of friction. Within guilds, the employment of women aroused resentment and although a quarter of Yorkshire cloth was produced by women at the end of the fourteenth century, weavers at Bristol in 1461 complained about their employment. There were interguild disputes over rival jurisdictions, such as those between the Tanners and Cordwainers of York concerning the view of tanned leather. At first, there was considerable opposition from merchant guilds to craft guilds and in the later part of the thirteenth century, complaints of the poorer guildsmen at York (1272), Carlisle (1281) and Bishop's Lynn (1304) were the forerunners of contests between the oligarchic governing body, and a wider section of citizens representing the guilds. Thus, in 1272 Walter Hervey was the centre of disturbances in London; in 1366, Adam de Bury; in 1381, Horne and Sybyle; in 1383, John of Northampton; and in 1450, Thomas Coke and Laurence Stokewode. However, in London as elsewhere, as the guilds became more exclusive, the link of burgess, alderman and guildman became more unitary and the threat of the journeymen guilds turned the groups towards each other for support. Thus, attempts by guilds to break free from town government, or to widen its basis, made in the fourteenth century had failed to make any impact. As Lipson said, "the fourteenth century thus marks a period of transition in the history of the London guilds." It opened with the submission of the Weavers and it ended with the submission of the Fishmongers and all the other crafts who had offered resistance to the mayor's jurisdiction. Lipson illustrated the ultimate control of the urban authorities over the guilds with reference to Norwich and Bristol, where municipal control was asserted in 1286 and 1346. The Tailors of Exeter failed in their struggle with the mayoralty between 1466 and 1482.

The guilds were constantly changing their structure so that it is difficult to assess the numbers involved or to generalise about the kind of government to be found in them at any particular period. Those who have suggested a decline in guild power in the early fifteenth century have claimed that their numbers were reduced. This was so, but it often reflected the amalgamation of crafts. Thus, the Leathersellers absorbed the White Tawyers in 1479 and the Pouchmakers in 1517. They combined in 1502 with the Pursers and Glovers, who had previously amalgamated in 1498. New crafts also continued to emerge, such as the Salters, who supplied three mayors towards the end of the fifteenth century. There was also a decline in guild pageantry and resistance to taking part in it, at Worcester in 1467 or Canterbury in 1490, for example. However, this did not necessarily reflect a decline in income, but a change in its use. Guildhalls, hospitals, almshouses and schools tended to receive the profits of guildsmen and to benefit the guild at the same time.

At the time when some forms of guild pageantry were in decline, others were appearing, and it is significant that in one of the many statutes dealing with livery and maintenance, in 1411 liveries were permitted for craft guilds, although forbidden to great households. The rise of the liveried company has been the cause of some confusion. They were not new organisations but a result of the split between craftwork at the workshop level and the growth of mercantile capital involved in trade. In some ways the development represented an advance because it reflected changing economic circumstances. On the other hand, the wealth and exclusiveness of these organisations led to bitter complaint, and in 1437 and 1504, reference was made to guilds who "for their singular profit and common damage to the people" had created price rings, and excluded those with legal rights. The most notorious example was the Merchant Adventurers, and this growing exclusiveness was to be a serious Tudor economic problem. Most of the livery companies were founded as guilds in the fourteenth century and obtained their charter of incorporation some time later. There were groups of incorporated merchants in many towns, but the most important were the twelve great livery companies of London (*see* Table 7) who came to control City politics. After the great clash of the 1370s to 1390s, between the victualling guilds, led by the Fishmongers and Grocers, and the cloth companies, led by the Drapers, Taylors and Mercers, the latter held a disproportionate amount of power even within this group, and the monopolistic position of the Mercers in the cloth trade was very great.

Table 7—The Twelve Great Livery Companies of London

Company (1516 precedence)	Founded	Incorporated	1400–1500 Mayors	Aldermen
Mercers	1357	1393	25	41
Grocers	1345	1428	18	31
Drapers	1364	1438	18	33
Fishmongers	1272	—	10*	14
Goldsmiths	1327	1394	6	16
Skinners	1327	—	5	13
Merchant Taylors	1326	1407	1	8
Haberdashers	—	1448	1	3
Salters	—	1558	3	3
Ironmongers	—	1464	1	7
Vintners	1364	—	—	2
Clothworkers	1528	1528	—	—

* One of whom was also a Salter.

These regulated companies, with their trading interests and steady acquisition of wealth and power, were the link between the more broadly based guilds, and the more profit-conscious regulated companies of Tudor England. They mark a decisive step forward in business influence in the country and they were to determine the growth of London as a source of inspiration to business enterprise—"the mirror and exemplar of the whole realm." Through the agency of these liveried companies, the fifteenth century saw the development of a class of prosperous and related London merchants. In the Drapers' charter of 1438, reference was made to "the business as well of the mistery as of the guild and fraternity." The leader of the Court party in the 1440s was Philip Malpas, who had two sons-in-law, Thomas Cooke and Sir Ralph Josselyn, both prominent City men. William Gregory, Mayor in 1451-2, had a daughter who married an alderman and a grand-daughter who was wife of the Mayor in 1471-2. Men such as Richard Whittington, Robert Chichele, William Sevenoke, Stephen Browne, William Gregory, and Thomas Cooke made sizeable fortunes. Others such as Nicholas Wotton (Mayor 1415), Geoffrey Boleyn (Mayor 1457), Thomas Knolles (Mayor 1410), and Ralph Josselyn (Mayor 1466) were to be the founders of great landed families. Already the trends which were to grow in Tudor times were apparent, and all the indications were that London was a place of mercantile growth and prosperity in the fifteenth century, although this may not necessarily reflect the position in regard to the whole economy.

CHAPTER 7

THE DEVELOPMENT OF MERCANTILISM

GROWTH AND DECAY IN THE FIFTEENTH CENTURY

Many attempts have been made to isolate various economic phenomena of the fifteenth century in order to prove that it was either a period of growth or a time of stagnation. The results have varied from the conclusion that it was a time in which the rural poor shared in rising prosperity and the towns in the profits of increasing trade and expanding industry to the view that baronial strife and government incompetence in a time of feudal and ecclesiastical decline led to a period of severe economic depression. Historians differ as to the length of the depression and about the time that it ended. Some argue that it was a long-term trend marked by the plateau in cloth exports, the decay of towns, the depopulation of many villages and the loss of large parts of our foreign trade to the Hansa and the Italians. Others claim that the depression was shorter and essentially confined to trade as a result of international difficulties in the 1440s and 1450s. The end of the depression is placed either in the reign of Edward IV or Henry VII, or it is suggested that there was a steady recovery due to overall circumstances rather than to the adoption of any new policy by either king.

The earlier economic historians adopted an optimistic viewpoint. They suggested that the Wars of the Roses had little effect on the economy, and that the fifteenth century was a period of "solid, substantial, unbroken prosperity." On the other hand, Denton, and to a lesser extent Lipson and Trevelyan, argued that it was a period of decline, particularly in agriculture. In the late 1930s and early 1940s, Postan and Saltmarsh, while conceding some agricultural progress and discounting the more extreme views concerning soil exhaustion and the impact of periodic plagues, still claimed that there was considerably less economic activity than in the preceding or succeeding centuries. In order to explain the paradox of a nearly stationary national income reflected in cloth export or wine import figures and the evidence of prosperity among a sizeable section of paid labourers, husbandmen and yeomen, the

232

concept of redistribution of the national product was developed. Thus, "the effects of a falling population and depressed prices on the condition of the peasant is easily imagined. It meant a greater supply of land and lower rents. The improvement in the position of the landowner was accompanied by an improvement in the position of the hired labourer." More recently there has been a slow shift back to the views held by the earlier generation of historians. Bridbury, in an analysis of the fifteenth century as a growth problem, suggests that the decline of the towns had been exaggerated and that neither agriculture nor industry were badly hit by prolonged depression. Only the trade depression is left relatively untouched, although the growth of London, Southampton and Bristol would tend to weaken the case for this phenomenon. Similar views were put forward by Green in *Town Life in the Fifteenth Century* (1894) and by Kingsford in the Ford Lectures for 1923. Kingsford pointed out that 1459 to 1461 was the only period when warfare was in any sense continuous. In London it was "a time of abiding prosperity on which the political turmoil had no lasting effect." On the other hand, Kingsford provided considerable evidence to indicate that lawlessness in the Channel was rife. Myers has spoken of "a time of prosperity for the peasantry" and "a time of agricultural depression." According to his view, the 1450s were "the blackest decade for English commerce in the fifteenth century," no recovery being discernible until the 1470s. As a result, "nearly all towns" were adversely affected and the great fairs declined.

This dispute among historians is somewhat unnecessary. In the first place, detailed figures for exports have been collected and accurately chart the trade depression. A century is far too long a time to be either a depression or a boom and clearly England in 1500 had advanced economically on the position in 1400. However, the rate of growth had been slower than one might have expected after the recovery from the Black Death, and much of the growth was concentrated into the last quarter of the century. Economic growth is the rise of income. National income did not increase, as far as we can tell, but it was distributed more widely by the demise of feudalism as the basis of land-holding as well as by ordinary economic forces. The decline in wool production was not, perhaps, matched by the rise in cloth exports, but the size of the domestic market is not certain. Enclosure clearly increased sharply in the second half of the century. Some towns declined, such as Chester and Sandwich on the coast, and Norwich, Northampton, and Leicester inland. On the other hand, Carus-Wilson has pointed out, population was spread in industrial villages over wide areas which are not easily measurable. Other towns grew steadily during the period. Fairs declined, but merchant capitalism developed. Sea transport was menaced by war and piracy, but the type of ship improved enormously. The rise of carriers services and the building of bridges indicated the continued flow of internal trade. If the Hundred Years War damaged trade in the 1420s and 1430s, its cessation was an immense benefit not shared by the fourteenth century. The Wars of the Roses led to a demand for a stronger monarchy, and this in turn to government concern, which involved the re-enactment of economic laws and the conclusion of a network of commercial treaties to restore our European position. On this basis a rapid expansion of the cloth industry followed.

The period of time and the diversity of factors both suggest that the fifteenth century needs very careful analysis. Contemporary evidence too is by no means lacking, because, as Kingsford said, official documents, borough and company records, deeds, inventories and wills and above all letters and accounts "far excel those of any previous age." It is at last possible to supplement literary sources such as political poems or monastic chronicles. Add to this a considerable literature with a specific economic content and the work of such valuable writers as Fortescue and Commines. Much of the contemporary evidence supports the claims of those that argue for the fifteenth century as a period of economic decay, but when some allowance is made for the way in which medieval writers phrased their arguments, this evidence is much less convincing. Moreover, it is important to remember the context in which those criticisms were made. From 1414 to 1453, England was almost continuously at war with France and the war ended in defeat and the loss of valuable territories. From 1455 to 1497, there was no period of more than five years without rebellion or civil war, except between 1471 and 1483. Although the impact of both wars was geographically limited, the constant reverses abroad and disorder at home produced defeatist writing. This accurately reflects opinion, if not facts, in the same way as the Tudor outcry against enclosures revealed the feelings of many people, but is not substantiated by enclosure statistics. Evidence for disorder and the decay of "good governance" is often founded on quotations from the *Paston Letters*, where such incidents as the dispute over Gresham Manor between the Pastons and Moleyns (1448), the private siege of Caistor Castle by an army of 3,000 (1469), and the kidnapping of people from the beach by pirates give the impression of a deep social malaise. On the other hand, the *Stonor Letters*, which relate to south Oxfordshire, Gloucestershire, Hampshire, Kent and Devon, have little evidence of a breakdown in social relations. The major clash between Thomas Stonor and Richard Fortescue at Ermington was settled at law, and the only serious riot mentioned seems to have occurred in 1491. When the lawless state of medieval society and the obvious bias of bills of complaint in court cases are borne in mind, these incidents do not in themselves indicate sufficient disturbance to cause economic disruption. In the *Paston Letters* there were seven cases of robbery, but they were in periods of severe disturbance. The *Stonor Letters* and the *Cely Papers* have many references to unmolested travel in the countryside.

During the fifteenth century, the two most important relationships in medieval society—of man with the Church, and of man with his lord—both underwent severe modification. It is not necessary to say that the Church declined in economic or even political prominence or that the nobility suffered crushing decimation from acts of attainder and death in battle. It was sufficient that "the relations of persons became less important than the exchange of commodities" as the manor and guild were influenced by the rise of capitalism, and that the Church was no longer either admired from afar or the only instrument of social reform and spiritual guidance. Strong anti-clericalism, the spread of the Renaissance and the use of commercial wealth to build churches and endow almshouses and schools all combined to weaken the Church's exclusive position. However, consideration of the careers of Cardinal Beaufort in the 1440s and Cardinal Wolsey in the 1520s is a sufficient warning against taking the case for Church decline too far.

Nevertheless, it is clear that there was a continuous anti-clerical following and an increasing sense of insecurity in the Church. Thus, in the period 1414–24 of the twenty-five heretics, eleven were priests, and in 1457 Bishop Pecock only managed to escape the fire by a public recantation at St Paul's Cross. His solitary imprisonment and death on Thorney Abbey Island by no means reduced the volume of complaint against the Church. The age of Aquinas had been replaced by that of Marsiglio. This spirit of doubt and criticism showed itself in many ways. The spread of mysticism, the appearance of "timor mortis conturbat me" on tombs, the cadavers, like those at Winchester and Tewkesbury, and the decline of the monastic ideal were some reflections. At Wymondham in Norfolk, a visitation in 1492 reported the monks reciting the service "morosely." The *élan vital* was leaving the Church, even if it was not accompanied by such widespread corruption as was once thought. The higher clergy remained open to criticism. Many foreigners, such as Giovanni di Gigli and Sylvester de Gigli, Bishops

of Worcester, were appointed to English sees. Young members of
the nobility were raised to the episcopate, including a Bishop of
Ely at twenty-one and a Bishop of Exeter at twenty-two. Poor
clergy continued to suffer. In the diocese of Chichester in 1440,
eighty-four livings received no more than an annual income of
twelve marks. Lollardry, consecrated by martyrs such as Sawtree
and Badby and influenced by the existence of the Lollard Bible,
continued to flourish. In the west, criticisms of pilgrimage led to
threats of excommunication from the Bishop of Bath and Wells
in 1431, but in 1447, when parishioners at Langport chased out
their priest and attacked the Bishop's officers, they were backed
by the Earl of Somerset. Disendowment was mooted as a solution
and in 1410 it was proposed to disendow the Church and establish
among other things a hundred almshouses. Alien priories were
dissolved in 1411 and Wolsey put an end to monasteries with less
than seven inmates in 1524. The idea of disendowment was revived
in 1431 and there were Lollard disturbances in East Anglia. In
the Midland counties, Lollardry remained strong and in the 1490s
revived in Berkshire and Buckinghamshire, where many were
executed. In 1521 what was virtually a crusade against Lollards
was initiated by the Bishops of Lincoln and London. By then it
was too late. Contact had been made with the forces of the
Reformation, and as Tunstall of London said "it is no new question
of some pernicious novelty; it is only that new arms are being
added to the great band of Wycliffite heretics." The decline in the
monasteries with scarcely any new foundations, little rebuilding,
the decline of monastic chronicles and the increasing evidence of
poverty or opulence, ill-directed to religious purposes, was only
part of a wider picture.

Fifteenth-century Church decline should not be exaggerated.
There were several features of ecclesiastical life that gave evidence
that the Church was by no means a spent force. Monastic estates
passed into the hands of leaseholders who were very often laymen,
so that one historian could claim that the actual transfer of land
at the time of the Dissolution was the completion of a process. Thus,
at Great Coxwell in Berkshire, Beaulieu had a sheep grange where
a fourteenth-century barn was built. This was leased early in the
sixteenth century. Monasteries were by no means always successful
in attempts to recoup losses, although they achieved the reputation
of being harsh landlords. For example, Ingarsby in Leicestershire
was enclosed in 1469 in order to increase profits for Leicester
Abbey, although it seems that it was in considerable debt in the
1530s. Monastic debts were considerable, so that at St Albans "the
house is in such debt we think no man will take the office of abbot

upon him." However, in other abbeys there was evidence of efficient estate management. The Priors of St Augustine, Canterbury, continued their drainage schemes. Thomas Golston (1449–68) spent £1,200 on Appledore Marsh and William Petham (1471–2) £300 on reclaiming 600 acres (240 ha). Monastic rebuilding was not unknown and included the naves of Westminster and Crowland and the cloisters of Durham and Hereford. Abbot Huby (1494–1526) had the tower of Fountains Abbey constructed. At Bath a completely new abbey was started in 1499. Chantries and collegiate foundations, together with religious fraternities, showed an increase in number during the century. The Hospital of St Cross at Winchester was rebuilt in 1445. Lord Cromwell founded a religious college at Tattershall soon after 1434 and the Duke of Suffolk did likewise at Ewelme in 1436. Some of the chantries, such as that of Henry V at Westminster Abbey which took twenty-five years to build, were particularly fine and the chantries at Wells and Salisbury provide considerable evidence that these buildings were not solely costly additions, and even as such indicate a considerable degree of wealth. Church art reached new heights of development. The alabaster industry flourished. Woodcarving of rood screens, such as those at Shoreham (Kent) and Cullompton (Devonshire), or choir stalls like those at Lincoln, Chester, Carlisle, Ripon or Beverley, can scarcely be described as "shallow." Painting made considerable headway with such frescoes as those by William Baker at Eton College Chapel. Stained glass was installed, if not manufactured as yet, by English craftsmen and the century opened with John Thornton of Coventry executing the contract for the east window of York Minster. Church music, which manifested itself early in gymels and carols, was crowned by the achievements of John Dunstable. He died in 1453 and was buried at St Stephen's Walbrook, and is acknowledged as the first composer aware of harmonic sequences. The Church even patronised new arts, for the first printing press in the West Country was set up in Taunton Abbey.

It is surprising that some historians have claimed that the Perpendicular architecture, which characterised Church building until it ceased at the time of the Reformation, was evidence for the decline of the greatest medieval crafts and one of its greatest industries. It is true that, apart from Bath Abbey, no new large church was constructed in the fifteenth century, but this was equally true of the fourteenth. However, it is clear that a larger number of sizeable parish churches were created during this period than at any other. In the Midlands, there were few new churches, although Fotheringhay built by William Horwode of Stamford after 1404 was a notable exception. Yet at Coventry, St Michael's and Holy

Trinity were built in a period when the population of the town was falling. In other parts of the country, Perpendicular architecture produced magnificent churches. They were widely dispersed, including the Collegiate Church at Manchester, Christ Church Priory, Hampshire, St Mary Redcliffe, Bristol, Sherborne Minster, Barton and Newark churches. In two areas in particular, there was a great rise in church building. In the West Country clothing region, Northleach, Thornbury, Winchcombe, Chipping Campden, Fairford, Long Melford and Cirencester might be mentioned. In the East Anglian clothing region, Lowestoft, Saffron Walden, Lavenham, Chelmsford, Coggeshall, two churches at Bungay and Beccles, and three (All Saints, St Peter's, St Gregory's) at Sudbury might be added to the already imposing list. Even in London there was evidence of some rebuilding and of new churches. Over 50 London churches were either rebuilt or enlarged and over 160 fraternities were associated with the 100 churches of the City. In the cathedrals, after the achievements at Winchester, Westminster and Gloucester, there was less to show, although central towers were raised such as that at Gloucester, and in some cases, like Beverley, considerable rebuilding was effected. The great achievements of church architecture in this period were the four chapels at Windsor, Westminster, King's College, Cambridge and Eton College. In the last case the simple ground plan was a culmination rather than a modification of Gothic practice, because English cathedrals had tended towards a rectangular shape in the past.

Perpendicular architecture was more regular and repetitive and it made use of mass production methods. Some of the details were coarser and there was little inventiveness in ornamentation. In certain cases, such as the peculiar shape of Bath Abbey, errors of proportion were committed. Yet none of these criticisms really weaken the case against Perpendicular architecture as a progression of Gothic. The exterior of churches was distinguished by massive central or detached towers, flying buttresses and the elaboration of the porch into a kind of ecclesiastical barbican. Interiors were light and the elimination of the triforium enabled walls to become curtains of glass, separated by thin screens of stone. Such in essence was the east window of Gloucester. The four-centred arch, fan vaulting and stone panelling were all typical of the style. If the developments of linenfold panelling and hammer-beam roofs are added, it is clear that Perpendicular represented a style at variance with the gloom of many critics. It reflected wealth, a rising population which it was necessary to accommodate, and a continuing religious spirit which had the backing of the foremost industrialists of East Anglia and the Cotswolds. This "lovely and harmonious compromise" in architecture is difficult to explain away in a time which it has been claimed was a depression. Its influence on domestic building was of even more importance as the masons extended their activities to include the development of a vernacular style based on Perpendicular, Gothic harmonised with the Renaissance and provided the settings for tombs like that by John Massingham for Richard Beauchamp, Earl of Warwick, begun in 1443, or for Henry VII at Westminster, but it never developed a new and distinctive style after the fifteenth century. Tudor and Jacobean architecture was the true Gothic compromise.

Similar caution to the considerations for and against church decline as a factor in fifteenth-century decay needs to be extended to the second of the three main underlying "causes" of decay. This was the demise of feudalism accompanied by the creation of "bastard feudalism" and the decline of the medieval baronage. The underlying economic situation was that the landowners were worse off than their tenants, because high wages and low prices were the prevailing trend. Yet, at the same time, the demands of an ostentatious chivalry and the cost of upkeep for large households and retainers rose during the period. Bastard feudalism was a term used in 1885 to describe the situation where there was less connection between lordship and land and more between lordship and money. Leasing, sale, the decline in the cultivable area, and Acts of Attainder all helped to weaken the territorial nobility. This led to counter-measures. The nobility competed for office, particularly at Court, and eventually for the Crown. They were concerned to build up affinities by marriage. They tried to overawe districts by force. Falling rent-rolls led to rapacity and the evils of livery and maintenance to violence. Thus, it was argued, the Crown was unable to control "overmighty subjects" and Acts against livery and maintenance, such as those in 1411 and 1468, were of little use. In order to explain the decline of the nobles' power, it was suggested that the strife led to the extinction of many noble families and that this process was completed by Acts of Attainder. Then the Tudors, it was argued, suppressed livery and maintenance and a more ordered society emerged by the end of the century.

However, this picture needs considerable modification. The decline of the territorial nobility was a long process; in some parts of the country, such as Norfolk and Northumberland it was not completed until late in the sixteenth century. There was a new nobility, in as much as thirty leading families were destroyed, but the new nobility were by no means new men except in a few cases.

As yet the concept of a nobility of service created from the lower ranks of society had scarcely emerged. The nobles kept their dominant position in the Council. Militarily, the situation of a feudal host being replaced by a paid army had developed since the days of Edward I. Licences to build castles declined from 181 under Edward III to 5 under Henry VI and 3 under Edward IV. The new castles were much more like fortified houses than great defensive structures. Sir John Falstolf's Caistor Castle (1450), Suffolk's Tattershall (1434 onwards) or Sir Roger Fiennes's Hurstmonceaux (1460s) were no longer in the tradition of late fourteenth century castles such as Bolton or Raby. Retainers were costly and many of the baronage were poor so that these were by no means large armies. The Earl of Warwick had a payroll of £490 (ten per cent of his income) and fifty-three retainers, and this was less than the army of domestic servants employed by some Victorian noblemen. It was possible to raise a larger army by indenture but it would be untrained and disloyal and it is significant that the only sustained period of warfare (1459–61) occurred when soldiers experienced in the French wars were available. There were notorious cases of open violence and intimidation by the nobility, as there always had been, but Henry VII dealt with few cases in spite of the Acts of 1487 and 1504. Retinues were a normal part of a noble's household until the end of the sixteenth century. The Earl of Leicester and the Earl of Essex, favourites of Elizabeth, had private armies and, even in the Civil War, territorial affinity was at the basis of Newcastle's "Whitecoats." Henry VII executed more rivals to the throne than any member of Lancaster or York and his 138 Acts of Attainder, together with resumptions of crown lands with heavy alienation fines, are the likely causes of any decline that there was in the nobles' power. Early Tudor England was still, in spite of the Wars of the Roses, an aristocratically ruled country. In Henry VII's Council, only Empson, whose father was a leading citizen of Towcester, came from a non-landed background. Noblemen were in nominal command of the main campaigns throughout the Tudor period. Any exaggeration of the nobility's decline in the late fifteenth century encounters the problem of explaining how they recovered under Henry VIII only to decline again at the end of the Tudor period. It is more likely that the nobles as a class lost their feudal power, but retained sufficient political and even economic influence to remain a dominating force.

Therefore, it can be asserted that the rise of the yeomen and freeholders, in many cases, to the status of gentry in the fifteenth century may well have been in some cases the result of obtaining favourable leases, but it was as often due to the making of a fortune in trade and commerce or the creation of an affinity with the nobility. As a class, the new medium-sized landowners lacked any real power at this time, and they were subject to intimidation by the nobility. However, their work as justices, sheriffs and escheators gave them considerable influence and during the fifteenth century they secured their position as Members of Parliament. Two knights were elected from each of the thirty-seven shires by freeholders who held land to the value of 40s. and the 222 borough members were very often influenced by the surrounding landowners, who offered to pay their expenses. Enclosure of smaller farms, the lack of heavy overheads, the long and favourable leases, and the steady expansion of markets such as that supplying London, all enabled the smaller landowners to gain immensely during the fifteenth century. They were rarely involved in the wars and, even if these caused disturbances, the conflict for the throne only involved thirteen weeks' active campaigning between 1455 and 1487. The new House of Commons "of gentry, prosperous freeholders, richer merchants and lawyers" was more in contact with the economic development of the time—enclosure, "stops" of trade, the pressure of taxation. Moreover, the rise of the gentry was, in the end, the revival of the nobility, because the one has always aspired to the ranks of the other. The creation of peerages, the claiming of knighthoods as rewards for services and the pressure among smaller landowners for coats of arms were all to be marked features of the new nobility of Tudor times.

Examples of this new class and its successful fifteenth-century development were widely spread in the country, and they indicate the underlying health of the economy as the population rose from the 1450s. They prove that there was a redistribution of income and, in all probability, an increase as well, because they were affected by the revival of the cloth trade and the need to produce more wool. This developed from the 1450s, so that, throughout the Wars of the Roses and the struggles of Henry VII's reign, enclosure was rapidly increasing and cloth production expanding. Cloth exports rose from 38,400 cloths in 1450 to 66,900 in 1480 and to 84,700 in 1500. Wool exports which had declined rapidly from 20,000 sacks in 1390 to 13,000 sacks in 1420, continued to decline until the 1480s. Then they levelled off at about 8,000 sacks and even rose slightly. Some of this increased export may have been caused by a decline in the home market, but the rise of the East Anglian, Yorkshire and Cotswold cloth industry suggests that it was not. During the century, enclosure for arable was replaced by enclosure for pastoral purposes until this reached serious proportions. Thus, of the 1,600 acres of Northamptonshire, Warwickshire, Oxfordshire, Buckinghamshire and Berkshire enclosed between

1485 and 1500, 1,300 were for pasture. The diffusion of wealth and a higher standard of living among the smaller landowners as a result can be shown in many ways.

Perhaps the most interesting of these is the development of the courtyarded manor house, which indicated a more settled state of affairs in the country than some have thought possible. In towns, the equivalent was the great merchant's house, such as Paycocke's at Coggeshall in Essex. Manor houses were castellated and very often moated, but they were now composed of suites of rooms indicating widening domestic comforts and the means to pay for them. Privacy in sleeping quarters was accompanied, as wills and inventories show, by the provision of beds, sheets and blankets. Chimneys indicated the widespread use of fires, still mainly wood-burning. Tiled floors, panelled walls, tapestries and carpets were common. Even toilets of a kind were in existence as a kind of cell built out over the moat. By the end of the sixteenth century, Sir John Harington had invented a water-closet, but it was not widely adopted. Examples of the fifteenth century manor house are numerous, although rebuilding in Tudor times altered many of them. Within a few miles of Bradford-on-Avon in Wiltshire, lie South Wraxall, Great Chalfield and Farleigh Castle. Minster Lovell, Oxfordshire, represents the smaller type whereas Coughton Court, Warwickshire, Ashby de la Zouche (1475–80) and Kirby Muxloe (1480–4), Leicestershire represent the more impressive forms. Such houses required considerable labour and materials. Kirby Muxloe needed stone, lime for mortar, wood for carving, clay for filling-in walls, lead and tiles, and it employed masons, carpenters and ditchers. Bricks became an important building material during the fifteenth century. Hull had brickyards by 1303 and those flourished in the fifteenth century. The municipal brickyard had an output at one stage of 100,000 bricks a year. Turf was used as a fuel and each firing of bricks took four days. The cost of moving bricks was expensive, so that when Tattershall Castle was built the bricks were brought by water transport along the Lincolnshire dykes. Bricks were used in large quantities and Eton College used 2·5 million between 1442 and 1451. By the same decade, bricks were being used for Hurstmonceaux Castle. Hull also produced tiles, although Beverley was their main centre of production. Thatch was replaced by tiles in towns by ordinance (such as that for Norwich in 1509) and tiles were widely used in manor houses. Their manufacture was regulated in 1477. Stone remained the main building material and the masons' powers increased so much that in 1424 a national union of masons had to be forbidden by Parliament.

The fifteenth century cannot be said to have seen a decline either in the Church or the nobility as the two most powerful estates of the realm. Both ceased to occupy their exclusive roles. The Church had to acknowledge increasing lay control of its lands and lay charitable activity. The nobility had to concede that the wealth which had been almost exclusively theirs was now shared with an increasing group of gentry and wealthy yeomen. The Church was threatened by disendowment and the nobility by Acts of Attainder. Both suffered because they were in receipt of traditional revenues and could not easily adapt to the new sources of wealth. It is difficult, however, to see Lollardy and pushing gentry as evidence for decline and neither the Perpendicular churches nor manor houses reflect other than a prosperous society. This growth was achieved in spite of the lack of good governance which is the third underlying factor said to account for fifteenth century decay. Institutionally, English medieval government continued to develop in this period. The Privy Council emerged as the key administrative body and it was to remain so until the 1640s. The Exchequer proved to be too antiquated as a financial department and Edward IV and Henry VII with their Treasurers of the Chamber, Sir Thomas Vaughan, Thomas Lovell and John Heron created a new department to deal with the finances of the realm. The Duchy of Lancaster, which yielded £3,500 was regarded as a model for financial administration. Under Sir Reginald Bray, Henry VII improved the administration considerably, helped by Sir Robert Southwell. Feudal rights were carefully maintained and in 1503 Sir John Hussey was made Master of Wards. Revenue from this source rose from £350 in 1487 to £6,000 in 1507. Edward IV, under the influence of John Harrington, allowed the Council to take into account "bills, requests and supplications of poor persons." Richard III set up a Court of Requests which lapsed under Henry VII and revived under Cardinal Wolsey. Edward IV had made his brother, Richard, Lieutenant of the North in 1482 and this Council of the North developed under Thomas, Earl of Surrey and William Sever (later Bishop of Carlisle). Finally, since the Chancery Court had been separated from the Council, its judicial function was strengthened by creating smaller judicial bodies instead of the whole Council of forty or so members. These judicial bodies included the Council Learned, and the Council in Star Chamber, and tended to deal with the richer and more powerful of the King's subjects.

Henry VII may justly be accepted as the key figure, therefore, in a period of government expansion and reorganisation at the end of the fifteenth century. This was a necessary prelude to the growth of government supervision implicit in mercantilist and paternalist rule and marked by the 120 Public Acts of Parliament in Henry VII's reign. Similarly, the position of the justices of the peace was strengthened and their functions expanded. In 1487 they were allowed to take bail and in 1495 to act upon information without waiting for a grand jury. A statute in 1489 provided a procedure for the poor to use if the justices failed to act, for "by the negligence and misdemeaning, favour and other inordinate causes of the Justices of the Peace in every shire . . . the laws and ordinances made for the politic weal . . . be not duly executed." In 1495 the poor were even given free writs and counsel. Justices were made responsible for hours and wages and in 1495 became licensers of alehouses.

These changes reflected a change in government attitude and they do not necessarily prove that the fifteenth century was a time of thoroughly incompetent administration. Sir John Fortescue's *Governance of England* (written about 1469) was the work of the Chief Justice of the King's Bench. At no time in the fifteenth century did the law courts or Parliament cease to operate. Fortescue praised the state of government and approved the fact that the "king may not rule his people by other laws than such as they assent to." His other main work, *The Commodities of the Realm*, was very much an enthusiastic account of England's wealth and advantages. These two works cannot be dismissed as mere Lancastrian propaganda and they serve as useful counter-balances to the more often quoted *Libel of English Policy* by Adam de Moleyns, Bishop of Chichester, who perished at the hands of discontented sailors in 1450. Bad government in medieval times was co-extensive with weakened royal authority. Henry IV, Henry V, Edward IV, Richard III and Henry VII were all competent monarchs and even in the long minority of Henry VI there were adequate Regents. The period of disruption was that of Henry VI's majority, during which time there is ample evidence of disorder by land and sea. The Wars of the Roses were preceded by Jack Cade's revolt in 1450, which had a number of similarities with the risings of 1381. Allegations in the Parliamentary rolls of widespread disorder need to be treated with care, and it is unlikely that isolated incidents succeeded in restricting internal trade, although they may have affected sea transport.

Lawlessness at sea was one indication of weak government and repeated Acts were passed against it such as that of 1414. But pressures from those who found piracy profitable led to the repeal of the Acts between 1435 and 1451. The government issued letters of marque, and condoned acts of piracy by those whom it instructed

to curb the evil. Thus, Robert Wennington, who received orders
to clear the Channel of pirates, proceeded to capture a Hanseatic
and Flemish salt fleet off Portland and forced the government to
pay compensation (1449). Warwick had some success in clearing
the Narrow Seas in the late 1450s, but it was not until 1474 that
Edward IV, apparently under pressure from the King of Castile,
issued a general commission to suppress Channel piracy. Henry
VII put a stop to Scottish piracy in the North Sea in 1489. The
pirates originated in a "tip and run" wargame with the French
and centred on the western ports. Stung by the activities of Frenchmen such as Sieur de Chastel, the West Country sailors took the
law into their own hands. John Hawley of Dartmouth, Mark and
John Mixton of Fowey, Richard Spicer of Plymouth, Thomas
Norton of Bristol and Harry Pay of Poole were among the most
famous. It is difficult to assess the economic consequence of their
activities, but Kingsford's optimistic claim that it was "the school
of English seamen" is open to question. It is true that West Country
ports flourished. Plymouth had a population of 6,000 and a charter
by 1439–40. Southampton, Fowey, Poole and Bristol were all flourishing. Yet this was due in many ways to the development of the
Iceland fisheries in the 1420s and of southern European trade.
Piracy damaged legitimate trade. Thus in 1433 Mixtow seized a
Genoese carrack. In 1449 Francesce Jungent of Barcelona took
refuge in Plymouth harbour and was captured by Fowey pirates
led by John Trevelyan, Sir Hugh Courtenay and Thomas Tre-
garthen. Since local justice was often closely linked with piracy,
redress was difficult to obtain. Richard Penpons, justice of the peace
in 1451, was also the owner of the pirate ship, *Catherine* of St Ives.
It seems likely that, as in Tudor times, piracy was not a paying
proposition economically for the country, even if individually it
yielded a seaman's experience and a pirate's reward. Fowey had
twenty ships in its harbour and was a prosperous town in spite of
interruptions to the wine trade. New Cornish towns made their
appearance at this time, such as Mevagissey, first mentioned in 1410.

    On land, the disruption of trade by violence seems to have been
less prevalent. On the other hand, the London riots of 1456–7,
which led to the withdrawal of the Florentines from England and
the movement of the Venetians to Southampton, could not have
helped trade. Tudor government was unable to check these attacks
on foreign merchants. In 1493 the Steelyard in London was raided
and Henry paid little compensation, and in 1517 the apprentices
of London rioted against the Flemings. Robbery of travellers was
common, but it did not deter traders. The Stonors and Pastons both
refer to local carriers' services which had developed. One took

four days from Norwich to London. There were regular barge services on the Thames to places such as Henley, and travel by the dykes of eastern England was also common. The fifteenth century was a bridge-building age. Thus, Bishop Fox still regarded it as a Christian duty to build the Elvet Bridge at Durham. In the West Country, in the area between the flourishing ports and the clothmaking region, a large number of bridges were built. The Tamar was bridged three times in 1437, 1439 and 1530. Looe Bridge (1411–36), Bideford (from 1460) and Wadebridge (1468–70) were other examples. The increasing trade of the times is indicated by the width of London merchants' activities and by imports of coal at ports around the country. A network of salter's ways and drover's ways in the hilly districts of northern England were evidence of the demands of the lowland markets. A national market had all but been created by Tudor times and Henry's pressure for uniform weights and measures in 1491 and 1495 was an indication of this trend. Fairs declined because seaborne trade and local manufacture reduced the need for them, rather than because it was impossible to trade. Thus, by 1416 St Botolph's Fair had not been held for some years, but Boston also suffered from the withdrawal of the Hansards and was burnt in the wars. St Ives was said to have collapsed in 1363 and again in 1442. Complaints were made that Pie Powder Courts were being badly managed and Edward IV legislated against this. During the years 1476–85, ten new fairs were created and in some places the markets indicated their flourishing nature by erecting market crosses, such as those at Chichester and Winchester.

Urban development in the fifteenth century provides further evidence for the contention that the period was one of economic growth rather than decline. It used to be argued that town life underwent a decline in this period and falling population and capacity to meet tax assessments were brought forward as evidence. Some towns undoubtedly suffered from the war; Peterborough, Cambridge, and Boston were all burnt. Traditional clothmaking centres continued to decline, particularly York (where the population fell from 14,000 to 8,000), Colchester and Norwich. Yet it is important not to see declining population as evidence for decay. Coventry fell from 10,000 to 7,000, but the Coventry miracle plays started in 1416 and two fine Perpendicular churches were built in the period. The mobility and wide dispersal of population needs to be considered, and it should also be remembered that there were areas outside the city's jurisdiction which could experience a rise in population. Thus, if York declined, Halifax and Bradford appear in the aulnage accounts and the Wakefield mystery cycle began in

1425. If Colchester declined, Lavenham and Hadleigh were heavily populated industrial villages. At Coventry, the Guild Hall (1394–1414) contained a great tapestry produced about 1450. The York guildhall was built in 1446. Taxation assessments were notoriously fickle and it was pointed out long ago that towns tried to pretend poverty in order to get assessments reduced. Thus, Great Yarmouth and Lincoln complained in 1433 and were relieved altogether of taxes in 1453. Cheltenham, Scarborough (1442) and Cambridge (1472) were other examples.

In view of the ten fifteenth-century plagues mainly concentrated in urban areas, the decline of some towns was to be expected, but it was not as great as an examination of the figures for population and tax assessment alone suggest. Many towns flourished in spite of the mid-century depression in trade. On the south coast, Plymouth grew during the fifteenth century until it was claimed that it was the fourth town of the realm and there is considerable evidence of building development at this time in the Barbican area of that city. Other ports, such as Fowey, with twenty vessels based there in 1450, or Dartmouth, still profiting from Spanish contacts, were in a flourishing state and the most spectacular port of all was Southampton which was the centre for Florentine (1425–77) as well as Venetian fleets and gained immensely after the London riots of 1457. The population of the town was comparatively small, but its customs receipts made it the second port of the realm. As late as 1504–9, they averaged £10,341 a year, and Southampton's decline came under the Tudors. Bristol was a flourishing port in the fifteenth century, influenced by the Iceland, Irish and Spanish trades and by an increasing share of French trade when this revived in the 1460s. Backed by the cloth-producing Cotswolds and the lead and tin mines of Somerset and Devon, the town became the chief west coast port, a position it retained until it was overtaken by Liverpool in the eighteenth century. Bath declined in spite of its fair, as Bristol became more important.

Bristol's fifteenth-century significance was illustrated in two ways: by the enterprise of her merchants in seeking new trade routes, and by the magnificent remains of former merchant splendour which managed to survive until World War II. English merchants were anxious in the fifteenth century to trade in the Mediterranean and, as early as 1411, merchants had petitioned Parliament on this matter. However, the naval strength of the Venetians combined with the depredations of Channel pirates, and actions such as the government's attempted seizure of the Venetian fleet in 1460, to keep Englishmen out of the area. In 1446 Richard Sturmy of Bristol sailed to Jaffa, but he was wrecked

I

on the return voyage. In 1457 he tried again and was destroyed off Malta by the Genoese. Restricted by the Italian monopoly, the Bristoleans tried other routes. In 1497 John and Sebastian Cabot sailed in the *Mathew* from Bristol, sighted Labrador, and claimed Newfoundland, returning after four months to receive £10 for their pains from Henry VII. Next year, Sebastian sailed with five ships and explored the coastline of Labrador. Within a few years (the 1520s), a fleet of fifty fishing vessels were off the Grand Banks. William Canynges was a fourteenth-century Bristol merchant, and it was his son, William Canynges II who was most justly famous. He was not the founder of St Mary Redcliffe (as A. R. Myers has stated) but he established two chantries and gave the Church £340. His shipping interests have already been examined, and his city interests, including the mayoralty on five occasions, were those of Member of Parliament and sheriff. In St Mary Redcliffe, memorial brasses to John Jay and John Brook are evidence for other notable figures of the time. Bristol city churches provide further evidence of those expansionist times. St Stephen's is a fine Perpendicular church built by a merchant called Shipward; another merchant Frampton, lies in St John's. The tower of the cathedral is a Perpendicular addition, built between 1450 and 1470 when it was still a monastery.

London's growth and the significance of her mercantile interests have already been discussed, and as those three towns handled the greater share of England's fifteenth-century trade, they form a powerful indication of that trade's underlying growth. Towns of smaller size also provide evidence of considerable fifteenth-century growth. Cloth towns such as Wilton, Devizes, Castlecombe, Mere and Stroudwater in the west or Lavenham, Hadleigh or Colchester in the east were all growing. Merchant's houses, such as Paycocke's at Coggeshall, or a Wool-stapler's Hall like that at Salisbury provide scattered but not irrelevant evidence for growth. Even towns some distance from industrial development showed by the rebuilding of important streets that they were by no means poor. Friar Street, Worcester and Streets in Shrewsbury and Chester are early indictations of the substantial building revolution of later Tudor times.

Disputes about the decline or otherwise of fifteenth-century towns will not of themselves resolve the overall problem of economic growth or decline since they account for a small proportion of the market and occupy at most twelve to fifteen per cent of the people. Agricultural change needs to be considered in order to assess the national situation, and yet less work has been done on fifteenth-century agriculture than on that of the preceding two centuries. It was not a period of agricultural innovation comparable with either the thirteenth or sixteenth centuries, but there were a number of decisive changes. Arable farming underwent a measure of contraction, but pastoral farming underwent a period of expansion. Large estates found it harder to make ends meet, but smaller estates became increasingly prosperous. Among agricultural labourers, there was a period of high wages and low prices, although it should not be forgotten that this was also a period of declining employment opportunities and depopulation on a widespread scale. Even if yields per acre do not indicate a fall in fertility, the utilisation of less fertile land proved to be a short-term measure, and there was a contraction in the total cultivable area. On one sample of 450 manors, 400 showed a contraction in the area, but it should not be forgotten that, although this meant an overall fall in rent, the remaining land was more valuable and thus yielded greater profits per acre. The fifteenth century was the period in which the transition to a profit-concerned, small and medium-sized farming community was largely effected, even if this was often done within the legal and tenurial framework of the manorial system. By the end of the century, typical manors had ceased to exist as a result of the alienation of demesne, the purchase of consolidated smallholdings and the engrossing of the existing strips into more compact holdings. This change suggests a response to increasing demand and possible profit, and it was also made feasible, to some extent by the weakening of manorial custom in a situation where land often changed hands. As in the sixteenth century, changing ownership caused instability and occasional riots, and it was left to Tudor Common Law to work out an increasingly strict legal framework for landownership to replace feudal law except in the case of the great estates.

Enclosure has for too long been regarded as a Tudor phenomenon. Whatever type of enclosure—of strips, of waste of common, of arable for pastoral—is included in the definition of enclosure, it was a continuous movement in English agriculture, and there is no period when it was not in progress. Beresford and others have traced at least 1,300 deserted English villages and many of these desertions were caused by enclosure. Bosworth was fought over the empty site of Ambion in west Leicestershire. Writing in Tudor times, John Hales, a leading opponent of indiscriminate enclosure, said "the chief destruction of towns [i.e. townships or villages] and decay of houses was before the beginning of the reign of King Henry VII." Hoskins cited an early and interesting example at Crowndale Farm, near Tavistock, the possible birthplace of Sir Francis Drake. In 1336 there was a hamlet at Crowndale. By 1396, there was one holding and a deserted cornmill.

The early years of the fifteenth century saw the first complaints to Parliament about enclosure from Cambridgeshire and Nottinghamshire in 1414, and throughout the rest of the fifteenth century enclosure for sheep continued to gain over enclosure for arable, bringing depopulation, unemployment, and eventually arable land shortage with rising prices and a danger of famine. It was this movement which aroused the Early Tudor propagandists against enclosure, and it was the continued increase in enclosure for both arable and pastoral under the Early Tudors that made agricultural improvement and profit a matter of national concern. Ultimately, enclosure increased agricultural prosperity, as the investment of Sir John Falstolf's profits or the fortunes of the Howards, Stonors and Hungerfords showed. Fortescue in *Commodities of the Realm* praised sheep as the producers of national wealth, and enclosure enabled the cloth industry to develop after the 1470s. Deserted villages were often the product of economic reorganisation rather than decay. Thus, the twenty-eight deserted village sites on Norfolk breckland, or the decayed churches on the Wolds of Lincolnshire, reflected a retreat from less usable areas and the adoption of more profitable farming. In a way, the sense of outrage among the poor was therefore misplaced, although understandable. During the fifteenth century, there was an undercurrent of agricultural discontent which showed itself, as Lipson suggested, in "a new offence, the destruction of hedges [which] began repeatedly to recur in the court rolls in spite of heavy fines." The uprisings of 1450 have not been fully studied but the disturbances in Wiltshire, Hampshire, Suffolk and Kent that year have all the indications of a possible agrarian revolt. Adam de Moleyns, Bishop of Chichester, who was murdered in 1450 had "emparked" 12,000 acres (4,800 ha). William Ayscough, Bishop of Salisbury, was accused of never having "kept open house, so let him die." In spite of the possible suffering, it is important to realise that enclosure, like the introduction of machinery in later times, meant unemployment and caused riots, but also indicated economic growth. By Tudor times, wheat and wool prices were both rising together with the population, and a new period of land hunger emerged to add to discontents. However, industrial growth was to provide some at least with alternative sources of employment.

A rapid rise in demands for manumission from serfdom combined with pressure for a guaranteed legal status for the small farmers to show that they were economically prosperous and growing in numbers. By the end of the century there were a variety of agricultural holdings: freehold (either freemen or demesne farms under their lord), leasehold (let out from the demesne by the lord) and copyhold (which in theory had neither permanent nor temporary legal security). Leadham maintained that "the legal rights of the copyholders were such as to enable them to weather the storm," and Maitland argued that in 1457, 1467 and 1481–2, "the manorial custom thus becomes a recognised part of the law of the land," when copyholders secured the right to sue the lord for violation of manorial custom. This was made clear in Brian's Decision of 1482, although such tenants were to require additional help from the Tudor Court of Requests. The life of the Pastons and Stonors reflected the rise of a group of well-off "gentry" or yeomen, who varied in status from freeman to copyholder, but shared in rising prosperity. John Paston went to Cambridge and Walter to Oxford in 1474, while another Paston, William, arrived at Eton in 1477. The foundation of grammar schools in country and town for the education of a new class, who had some concern with bookwork and some acquaintance with culture, is only one indication of a new prosperity. This was widespread from the Royal Grammar School at Lancaster (1472) to Ipswich Grammar School (1482), endowed by John Gardyner and Richard Felaw respectively, and Leach and others have shown how thickly these schools were distributed. Increasing literacy, with the spread of English as a conmmon language in the first half of the century, adds to this picture of an increasing share of the population removed from the subsistence level. The first letters in English occurred in 1392–3, and from 1424 the *Paston Letters* were in their native tongue. William Caxton introduced the printing press in 1476–7 and within a few years the invention had spread, new editions were being produced (Caxton's *Chronicles* went through thirty editions in fifty years) and in 1482, Henry Franckenburg and Bernard van Stonds were in business in London selling books. Expansion in the universities and the patronage of the nobility, such as Cardinal Beaufort and John Tiptoft, Earl of Worcester, paved the way for the English Renaissance in the bloodiest days of the strife for the Crown.

It was in trade that the clearest evidence for depression was provided and even this decline was temporary, covering at most twenty years. Although constantly interrupted over a hundred years, the wine trade never wholly ceased and, indeed, revived to include Bristol as well as the south coast ports after the treaty of 1478 with France. Trade with Burgundy (which had acquired Flanders) was interrupted by the disputes of the 1430s and the Franco-Burgundian Alliance, but this also recovered after the treaty of 1467. Trade with Castile seems to have increased in spite of piracy and English agents such as John Chirche or John Davell were to be found at San Lucar and Seville. This trade was further extended by the treaty of 1489. Elsewhere, England was less successful. An attempt to break into the Iceland trade started in the 1420s had collapsed by the 1450s. After piracy and what amounted to direct war, Denmark reasserted her control in 1476. The long-drawn-out dispute with the Hanseatic League ended in Yorkist recognition of the Hansa privileges at Utrecht in 1474. Attempts to enter the Mediterranean to trade directly failed and the Italian trade was subjected to severe stresses and gradually passed out of our hands, although Richard III established our first trade consul, Lorenzo Strozzi, at Pisa in 1485. Calais proved costly to run and the government had to concede power to the Merchant Staplers to farm the taxes in the Act of Retainer in 1466. The Merchant Adventurers monopoly grew and in spite of repeated government aulnager Acts (1465, 1467, 1474, 1484) the quality of our exports did not improve. Cloth exports hardly grew at all between 1420 and 1470, although with the network of Yorkist commercial settlements, there was a rapid development thereafter. England's recovery owed much to the unification of Burgundy, the recovery of France under Louis XI, and the unification of Castile and Aragon under Ferdinand and Isabella.

The laments of the *Libel of English Policy* were to a considerable extent justified, although they took little account of unfavourable international conditions and exaggerated the gains of the fourteenth century. The navy declined, the carrying trade was lost, the Narrow Seas were infested with pirates. What the *Libel* omitted to say was that the reckless war in France and anti-alien disturbances had helped to disrupt trade. The *Libel* and a later work *On England's Commercial Policy* both advocated the control of the Channel by a strong fleet and the taking of the carrying trade into English hands, although they did not advocate navigation laws. To some extent their criticisms were as much moral as economic, complaining about the uselessness of much that was traded. Behind this was concealed one of the basic fears of mercantilism—that by trading, other countries could weaken us by removing gold and taking less than they sold. Commercial retaliation was urged on the grounds that England's wool "sustaineth the commons" of Flanders and was a useful bargaining counter. Out of adversity the watchwords of mercantilism had emerged—national protected trade and a favourable balance of payments. Edward IV and Henry VII, and even Richard III, were all to some extent responsible for accepting that the government should act along these lines and during the last thirty years of the century mercantilism became the basis of government economic activity. By then, trade had undoubtedly recovered and Henry VII's rising revenue was a further indication of the nation's wealth.

Viewed as a whole, the fifteenth century was not a period of prolonged or widespread depression. Industry developed its organisation and scale, under men such as Tame of Fairford and Spring of Lavenham, Paycocke of Coggeshall and Winchcombe of Newbury. In certain industries, such as iron, with the development of the blast furnace, or shipbuilding, with a wide range of technical changes in building and navigational aids, it was a period of considerable improvement. It was a time in which the beer, brick, glass, alabaster and printing industries all became important. The country's main industry suffered a period of stagnation and then recovered. In agriculture, although landlord's rents were depressed, the profits were spread more evenly. Landless labourers and small farmers gained from changes in the law, good wages and the almost complete elimination of manorial burdens. Depopulation and unemployment accompanied the necessary expansion of sheep-farming. Arable farming suffered and, with the recovery of the population in spite of war and plague, it was necessary to improve yield from a reduced cultivable area. A prosperous gentry or yeomanry was created and together with a sizeable merchant class who made their mark in Parliament and the land market provided the impetus for lavish church and chantry building and the widespread endowment of guilds, almshouses and grammar schools. War and government incompetence and a measure of social disturbance, caused by the decline of the manorial and guild framework as far as day labourers were concerned, slowed the rate of progress. They halted the recovery apparent in the 1380s and 1390s and led to the stagnation of trade for nearly twenty years before the upward trend from the 1460s and 1470s. It was an era of redeployment of the population, so that the decline of some towns was accompanied by a far more widespread growth of other towns, exemplified by Bristol, Southampton and London, and also apparent in towns such as Coventry, which appeared superficially to be declining. It was an age of promise deferred and disaster averted and, in view of the many obstacles to economic growth, this says much for the underlying structure of the economy by this time. The Tudors reaped the benefit of the economic growth which had been initiated, slowly and inadequately, during the earlier years of the fifteenth century.

MERCANTILISM AND THE NEW FRONTIERS IN THE TUDOR ECONOMY

By the end of the fifteenth century and the beginning of the sixteenth, England's geographical position had been altered by a series of discoveries that were to revolutionise the economy. The voyages of discovery transferred the country from the edge of the known world to the hub of an Atlantic-based economy with markets in Europe and North America; and further south, in the West Indies. By the end of the sixteenth century, England's involvement in the East Indies and mainland Asian trade was also about to start. These changes were initiated by Portugal under Prince Henry the Navigator and his successor, John II, and came about as a result of a series of important technical improvements. The size of ships increased after the appearance of the first known three-masted vessel in 1436 and by 1618 ships three times their breadth in length were normal. A further impetus to the increase of size was given by the development of longer voyages particularly to the East Indies. Technical improvements helped the navigation of these larger ships. Compasses were in use by 1411 and the magnetic variation was understood by the 1490s. Chaucer's *Of the Astrolabie* (1391) was in advance of its time and no really efficient astrolabe was developed until 1480. Prince Henry established a school of seamanship at Sagres, where Jewish astronomers and Arab map-makers laboured to improve and make scientific the art of exploration. Map-making advanced considerably from Toscanelli's map of the world in the early fifteenth century to Mercator's in 1564, and was soon applied to many other purposes. In England, a series of county maps were made by men such as Saxton and in 1593 the Privy Council appointed John Norden to produce a series of county maps. On individual estates, map-making became important and the estate maps of men such as Ralph Aggas or Robert Adams reflected the keen struggle for land in their delimitation of boundaries.

Scientific improvements made longer voyages possible but the main motive remained a curious mixture of medieval religion, hearsay and economic sense, or as Henry put it "for the glory of God and the profit of Portugal." Prince Henry's main aims seem to have been to overthrow the Moors and penetrate Africa, and it was his successor, John II, who took up the cause of African circumnavigation. Even he refused to countenance Christopher Columbus, who consequently had to wait ten years to add the Spanish contribution to the age of discovery. Sailing from the Portuguese town of Lagos, the ships sent by Henry discovered Madeira and the Azores and reached the Gulf of Guinea by the 1460s. Diniz Dios reached Cape Verde, for example, in 1445, and Diego Gomez sighted the Rio Grande in 1458. Henry started the importation of slaves from Guinea to Lagos and thus gave a hint that African trade itself might not be unprofitable. In 1487 John II sent out three expeditions. One, under Pedro Covilham, reached Abyssinia (the land of Prester John) by land and the other under Bartholomew Dias reached the Cape of Good Hope. Finally, in the reign of Manuel I, Vasco da Gama rounded the Cape and reached India in May 1498.

The voyage of Christopher Columbus in 1492 which reached Watling Island, in the Bahamas, and Cuba introduced an element of competition. It has been suggested that North America had already been discovered by the Portuguese in 1448. Thus, John II in urging Pope Alexander VI to move the division of territory between the two powers 270 leagues (710 miles) further to the west, secured, in the Treaty of Tordesillas, a right to Brazil. This was formalised by Cabral in 1500 and Vespucci in 1501. Now that Turkish power had closed the Mediterranean and carried forward the decline of Venice and Genoa, the Portuguese hastened to establish a world-wide empire. Brazil, the Guinea Coast, the Persian Gulf, Ceylon, the Straits, and most of the East Indies came into their grasp by the 1520s, particularly as a result of the work of Almeida and Albuquerque. From 1505 trading fleets from Goa to Lisbon were established which by-passed the Mediterranean. By 1517 China had been reached by sea. Spices, silks, wines, precious stones flowed in, accompanied by more exotic items, "the wealth of Ormuz and of Ind" as Milton described it. Portugal's empire succumbed to Spain in 1580.

By then the Spanish had established themselves as the other great imperial power. Cuba (known as Hispaniola) and the West Indies were conquered, and the natives killed by disease and slaughter. The slave trade spread across the Atlantic. Then the Spaniards set about the conquest of the new continent. Del Soto in Florida and California, Cortés in Mexico, and Pizarro in Peru typified the era of the *conquistadores*. Whole civilisations were wiped out and the Old World looted the New. Balboa sighted the Pacific in 1513, and in 1519 Ferdinand Magellan was sent by Charles V to assert Spanish sovereignty in their part of the East Indies. In doing so, he circumnavigated the globe between 1519 and 1522, dying on the way, so that Sebastian Del Cano may justly claim to have been the first to complete such a voyage. The tiny fleet was reduced to one ship and eighteen men but the expedition brought back enough to pay for itself. Spain had obtained the Philippines. Seville became as great a port as Lisbon and dwarfed Venice and Genoa. The first evidence of wealth from the Spanish Empire came in 1503. By the 1530s, the riches of Peru were being exploited. In 1545 the Potosi silver mines in Peru started work and maintained a high yield until about 1630. West Africa also

I*

proved a source of gold, from the civilisations of Ghana and the Arab kingdoms. The yield of treasure from the Spanish Empire rose from £52,000 in 1521 to £630,000 in 1545. After that it fell to £440,000 by 1575 and £280,000 by 1600.

As far as England was concerned, these world-wide discoveries at first concerned her little. It is important to realise that there was no permanent colony established in Tudor times nor was there any significant shift of English trade away from Europe. England's share in the early discoveries was comparatively small, although economically just as important. Isolated voyages, such as that in 1480 of Thomas Lloyd of Bristol ("the most scientific mariner in all England"), were held back by storms. It seems possible that a Frenchman, Cousin of Dieppe, may well have reached Brazil as early as 1488 before either the Spanish or English. If Henry VII had not temporised, Columbus might well have sailed under his patronage. As it was, 1497 was the first date when an authenticated English landing was made after "the people of Bristol have for the last seven years every year sent out two, three or four light ships in search of the island of Brazil." In order to prevent too open a clash with Spain, with whom England had good trading relations, Henry VII required the expedition not to sail south. The result of the first voyage was, as has already been detailed, the discovery of Newfoundland. The first fishing fleets left by 1501 and in the 1520s a fleet of at least fifty vessels was involved. Bristol was the leading port, and later western ports, such as Plymouth, Dartmouth, Bideford and Fowey, participated. A new school of seamen were trained. Immense profits were made, so that by 1615 the catch was worth £200,000, £700,000 by 1640, and £800,000 by 1670. Fish was as important to sixteenth-century Europe as gold, and Spain and Portugal came to depend on this supply.

Other voyages followed, but failed to produce any spectacular developments. Sir Thomas More's *Utopia* (1516) was set in the new Americas and in 1517 his brother-in-law, John Rastell, tried to sail to Newfoundland although mutineers prevented him from going beyond Cork. In 1517 also, Sebastian Cabot and Sir Thomas Perte were concerned in a voyage to discover a way round the new continent. The search for the North-west Passage had started, but the expedition which may have reached 67°N was not followed up. Elyot and Thorne (1501–2) had reached Labrador and returned with three eskimos, but Bristol's interest seemed to lapse. Plymouth provided Robert Thorne, who sailed in 1536, and the same year a group of London lawyers under a Master Hore also set out, ran out of supplies, turned to cannibalism and returned in a captured

French ship. Thus, Newfoundland's early promise was not followed by any dramatic move towards the north-west.

On the other hand, the Portuguese-Spanish monopoly of trade further south quickly attracted attention and efforts were made to join in the trade. Good trading relations with Spain encouraged the English to attempt direct commerce with Spanish colonies in the 1520s when English factors reached Hispaniola and even Mexico. However, in 1527 an English ship seeking to trade at San Domingo was fired on. By 1545 there was open conflict between the two nations on the sea. William Hawkins I (d. 1554)—several times Mayor of Plymouth, Member of Parliament, and father of William and John Hawkins—was the man responsible for starting the interloping in Portuguese trade. In 1528, as Hakluyt put it, "not contented with the short voyages commonly made then only to the known coast of Europe," he sailed on the first of three to Brazil. In 1530 he sailed to Sestos on the Guinea Coast and thence to Brazil. One customs record of a voyage in 1540 showed that the cargo brought back was worth twenty times that taken out. Southampton followed Plymouth's example and Robert Renegar took the lead in establishing a fort in Brazil near Bahia by 1542, although little is known of this project. The significance of these events was to appear later. England had been ousted from the wealth of the West Indies and South America, not to mention the East Indies, and in her struggle to beat this monopoly, created a new network of trading interests in Elizabeth's reign. They, in turn, were the prelude to the establishment of a maritime and commercial empire.

Tudor expansion was due to less spectacular but more important trends, which developed in the last quarter of the fifteenth century. Of these, the most fundamental was the rise in population which started in the 1470s and continued steadily for at least 200 years. The Tudors regarded themselves as over-populated and Hakluyt saw maritime and colonial enterprise as a solution for those "which do now live idly at home and are burthensome, chargeable and unprofitable to this realm." In James I's time, it was a commonplace that "there is an overplus of people." This burden of criticism only diminished in the 1660s. In part, the complaint was due to the inadequacy of resources rather than the real increase in population, but there was a substantial increase, even if it was small enough compared with that in France or Holland. Estimates of population vary considerably but it seems fairly certain that the population of 2·5 million in 1500 rose to 3·5 million in the 1540s, 4 million by 1600 and 4·5 million by 1660; in other words, the population doubled in 150 years. These figures are open to question, as an examination of one of the key features in the growth pattern indicates. This was the increasingly disproportionate share of the nation living in London, which continued to widen from the already established medieval discrepancy. Four-fifths of the population lay east of a line from the Wash to the Bristol Channel. Twenty per cent concentrated in the Thames Valley. A quarter of the population lived in towns which in 1600 were categorised by Thomas Wilson as 25 episcopal cities and 441 great market towns. London's share of the nation's population rose from 5·6 per cent in 1605 to 7·6 per cent in 1634 and 9·2 per cent in 1661. As a result, nearly the whole country became to an extent part of a great market to feed the capital, while London merchants competed in the provinces to the annoyance of everyone from Newcastle to Bristol. One by one the great ports declined, Southampton, the Cinque Ports, the East Anglian ports. It was not until the rise of colonial trade developed Bristol, Liverpool and Glasgow that the trend was reversed. Yet there is considerable uncertainty about the total population of London at any given time, as Table 8 indicates.

Table 8—London's Population (selected figures), 1500–1700

Date	Estimate	Source
1500	75,000	Bindoff
1557	185,000	Lipson
1600	200,000	Elton
1603	232,000	Lipson
1605	224,275	Bridenbaugh
1625	285,000	Lipson
1634	339,824	Bridenbaugh
1640	350,000	Bridenbaugh
1687	696,000	Petty
1688	530,000	King
1700	674,000	Rickman

Before considering the reasons for this overall rise, it is important to bear in mind other alterations in the population structure. During the period, population became considerably more mobile and movement from Wales and Scotland into England was one feature of the period. Another was the movement of English settlers to Ireland in a series of plantations from the reign of Mary I to that of Charles II. The Irish had also begun to emigrate to England by the 1600s and in 1628 assisted passages encouraged them. By far the largest influx of population came from the Continent and consisted in large part of religious refugees, such as the Huguenots of France or the Calvinists of Holland. By 1570 it was estimated there were 300,000 foreign migrants in the country. This had risen by 1588 to 360,300 and continued to rise during the Thirty Years War. The last influx was of French Huguenots after the revocation of the Edict of Nantes (1685). As early as 1551, a deputation called on the Lord Mayor of London to say that "by reason of the great dearth they cannot live for these strangers." Elizabeth encouraged foreign immigration on political and economic grounds and the contribution of aliens to the economy. According to one writer, they

> "introduced the new draperies: they revived the decaying fortunes of the silk industry: they started the making of fine linen: they established the copper and brass industries: they practically created the glass making industry: they helped to build up the steel and cutlery trades: they developed the manufacture of china, paper and cordage: they provided the engineering skill to drain the Fens and make harbours: they improved the art of dyeing: they were prominent as book-sellers and stationers."

In addition, their services to the development of mining, the spread of agricultural techniques and their involvement with the development of financial institutions need to be taken into account. These skilful minority groups contributed greatly to the economy but they also aroused resentment, and in 1621 Commissioners for Aliens were established. Archbishop Laud contributed to the miseries of the foreign communities by religious persecution in Kent, Essex, Suffolk and Norfolk in the 1630s, but by then many of the alien groups were declining in importance. Second-generation foreigners tended to conform to the Church.

Perhaps even more important to the population structure was the amount of emigration from the country. This emigration was to three main areas: Ireland, the Low Countries and the colonies. In the Ulster plantation of 1611, when Londonderry was founded, 20,000 went to Ireland. The Low Countries attracted English communities because of the degree of religious toleration and the Pilgrim Fathers, for example, had first emigrated to the United Provinces in 1605. One writer estimated that a quarter of the inhabitants of Rotterdam, Middelburg and Flushing were English. The presence of one of the Merchant Adventurers' staples, the recruiting of English for continental armies and the relative prosperity of Dutch industry induced much of this emigration. As one observer said, "the chiefest cause of their departure was the small wages which were given to the poor workmen." Religious persecution was an additional factor, which in 1635–8 coincided with trade depression when emigration reached its peak. In February 1635, one witness spoke of two ships full of people "discontented with the government of the church" waiting to leave and others to follow. Government alarm led to stringent controls on emigrants at the ports which were extremely unpopular, because in 1636 a serious plague added to the difficulties of the situation. Passenger lists at Great Yarmouth and other ports show that in the period March to September 1637 the ratio of emigrants to the United Provinces and New England was 4:1. The Civil War may have led to a decline in religious persecution but it increased the desire for emigration. In 1643 an observer at The Hague wrote: "artisans and substantial persons are daily seeking refuge in those parts from England, bringing population, skill and wealth to the country," and in 1650 it was still reported that emigration was "the issue of the sad distractions."

More well known was the emigration to New England and to a much lesser degree to the West Indies. This important development will be examined in the context of the depressions of Early Stuart industry; here, it is important to emphasise that the emigration has been underestimated. The figure of 20,000 between 1630 and 1640, given by Davies in the 1930s, has now been revised by Bridenbaugh. He calculates that between 1620 and 1642, 80,000 people emigrated, including 58,000 who went to the New England colonies. This amounted to some two per cent of the population, but the effects were not widely distributed in the country, even if only two counties—Monmouthshire and Westmorland—sent no migrants. One Laudian bishop, when he was accused of being responsible for causing this emigration, said that men went from "dioceses where they could have no pretence of vigorous persecutions." He pointed out that the chief towns in New England were called Boston and Plymouth because people "went so plentifully" from those places. The percentages varied: 10 per cent of the migrants came from the north, 18 per cent from the Midlands and 66 per cent from the southern and western counties. Emigration to New England grew rapidly after the Restoration, when "many of the military saints at his majesty's restoration (flying thither richly laden with the plunder of old England) carried over great riches."

One reason for this emigration was the great poverty of many people. Half the population, according to one authority, lived below subsistence level and periods of bad harvests (such as the 1530s, 1590s or 1630s) or of industrial depression (the 1550s, 1620s and late 1630s) added considerably to this number. Although the demand for food products rose from the second half of the sixteenth century and included an increasing proportion of meat, there was little change in the basic diet. It was not until the second half of the seventeenth century that the decline of salt meat, brought about by the introduction of turnips and clover, began to reduce the incidence of scurvy and to provide a more balanced diet. Wages are not a particularly reliable guide to any possible rise in the standard of living because many families supplemented these by their use of common rights or by the wages of those engaged in the domestic industries. Yet the price rise of the Tudor and Early Stuart periods was continuous and often steep and wages lagged behind in real terms. By the late 1620s, there were endemic agricultural disturbances in the most prosperous southern counties and the difficulties of Tudor agriculture had been even greater. Birth-rates and death-rates remained high, life expectancy was little more than thirty-five years and frequent marriages, accompanied by high infant mortality, were common. There was therefore a high proportion of child-bearing people to the total population. This was supplemented to some extent by the ending of clerical celibacy. It may have been helped by the creation and development of the Poor Law; still more, by the growth of private charity. On the other hand, enclosure, depopulation and the movement of people into the insanitary towns combined with the continued prevalence of disease to counteract these beneficial influences to some extent. In one village, the population doubled between 1525 and 1625 and this Leicestershire example reflects the national trend.

A possible explanation for the growth of population is the decline of serious epidemics of which there had been ten in the fifteenth century. It is true that nationwide outbreaks were no longer in evidence, because they were concentrated in cities, particularly London from where traders spread the disease of bubonic plague. Figures for plague deaths were by no means small, particularly when coronation years encouraged an outbreak. It seems that bubonic, pneumonic and typhus plagues all played their part and the figures for some of the major outbreaks are given in Table 9.

Table 9—London Plague Deaths

1592	11,505
1603	34,000
1625	35,428
1636–7	14,978
1665	100,000

Outbreaks spread to other parts of the country: to Devon in 1625 and to Norfolk and Suffolk in 1636. Moreover, plague was found in other years or in remoter parts of the country. The impact of returning armies led to plague in the West Country in the late 1620s and it recurred in 1630–1. Plague often came from the Far East or the Mediterranean and the outbreak in Norfolk and Suffolk, although fed from London, started in the port of Yarmouth a year before the London outbreak, and a plague house was set aside in the town in May 1636. In one parish of King's Lynn (St Margaret's), seventy-eight people died between August 1636 and April 1637. Little was done to stop the spread of the plague apart from the holding of national fast days, and it was not until the 1660s that a scientific interest in death and its causes was stimulated by Sir William Petty and John Graunt's *Observations upon the Bills of Mortality* (1662) and Dr Nathaniel Hodges's *Loimologia, an Historical Account of the Plague* stimulated by the outbreak of 1665. The reasons for the decline of the plague are no less clear, for the 1666 fire did not touch parts of London such as St Giles or Whitechapel. It seems that the development of immunity, a decline in the violence of the bacillus and the ecological substitution of brown for black rats finally led to the disappearance of the plague in the 1720s. The last threat came in 1721 when, passing through Marseilles, the plague ravaged Provence. The government took swift action. Doctors were called in to give advice, a Quarantine Act was passed, and such distinguished men as Edmund Gibson and Daniel Defoe were called on by the government to deploy their pens in aid of public health. The threat was averted.

The expansion of the world geographically combined with a rise in European trading activity and the influx of precious metals to create a buoyant economic situation until the 1550s, when it was seriously deflected by the religious wars. By the 1600s, both France and Holland were recovering, although Spain and later Austria sank under the burden of preserving Roman Catholicism by brute force. It was a period of international inflation caused, it used to be argued, by the influx of precious metals from the New World. Although this clearly contributed, since Antwerp, the key to Western trade, lay in Spanish hands as much as Seville and Lisbon (after 1580), the price rise started earlier and finished later than this influx. To some extent, Europe increased her own supplies of precious metals. Gold was worked near Salzburg and, from 1574, in the Ural Mountains. Silver was exploited in Bohemia, Saxony and the Tyrol and from 1571 a new extractive method produced higher yields. The expansion of the population also played its part, because the pressure on resources was very great and a land shortage led to agrarian disturbance in England and the Rhineland among other places. Rents rose steeply and the price of land increased. Food prices rose due to scarcity, and manufacturing prices were affected. Thus, the Tudor Age witnessed an intensive and acute interest in money. The cash nexus became all-important to many and the characteristic features of the age were self-advancement, capital formation, company flotation, mineral exploitation and the formation of monopolies and price rings. It was a good period for profit-making farmers and industrialists or "new-men." The reverse of this coin was the social disruption and distress caused by re-deployment of resources in a boom period, particularly when wages did not keep pace with prices. In our time we have witnessed a fourfold price increase in forty years (1924–64); the Tudors witnessed a fourfold price increase in ninety years (1510–1600), but this should be set against the slower rate of medieval growth and the definite slackening of prices in the second half of the seventeenth century. This price rise lay at the basis of Tudor economic develop-ment, and it was caused by economic factors. The business enterprise and the emphasis on profit were not new phenomena produced, for example, by a breakdown of medieval restraints on usury and banking, but the result of economic recovery. Mercan-tilism was the result of government reaction to the social and political dangers of the changed growth rate and the increasing pace of international competition as prices soared and internal order was threatened.

No definite answer can be given to the question: which, of all the factors causing the price rise, was the most significant? It is no longer possible to say that the expansion of European trade alone was responsible. The amount of silver in Europe may have quadrupled in a hundred years and, in a period where output could not match this rise, the price of goods would rise in relation to the total amount of money. Extra-European discoveries and the heightened pace of commercial enterprise caused by the shift of commerce to the Atlantic seaboard produced an era of speculators, investment and expansion. This was stimulated still further when the Mediterranean was reopened to trade in the 1570s. The new nation states with increasingly powerful monarchs demanded increasing taxation and urged the protection of economic activity for strategic reasons and, consequently, economic expansion followed. When the Church was attacked, lands and other forms of wealth were added to the market. There is little need of any hypothesis about the connection between the Reformation and capitalism to explain the expansion of European trade. Industry centred as much on Catholic Seville and Antwerp in the first half

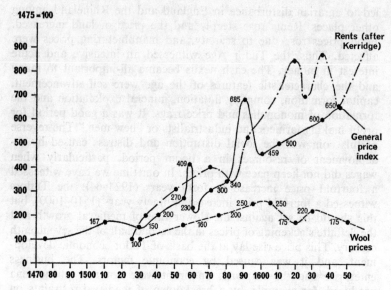

Fig. 4. The great inflation of Tudor and Early Stuart England.

of the century as it did on Protestant Amsterdam and London later. For a combination of political and economic reasons there was a development in European trade and because England traded direct with Spain and was closely connected with Antwerp, the European situation was bound to have an effect in this country.

In an age of expansionist fever, England was not excepted. Far from contemporary explanations of the price rise, which included the export of bullion and the hoarding of money, being correct, it was the increased velocity of circulation consequent upon demand that caused the price rise to have so serious an effect. There is no need to speculate about the rise of capitalism; that already flourished. Nor is there any need to explain the movement by suggesting that a new middle class was "the glory of the Tudor Age." Hexter has adequately shown that the concept of the middle class is misleading, since it varies from generation to generation. Merchant princes, industrial capitalists and financial intermediaries already existed. Rising population led to rising demand; in the case of food prices those rose even more steeply because demand exceeded supply. Thus, wheat selling at 5s. per quarter in 1510 sold for 34s. 10¼d. in 1590 and between 1550 and 1610 there was a 75 per cent increase in wheat prices. Protected by favourable political conditions and combined in a powerful monopoly bearing

down all opposition, England's main industry, cloth, kept up with
an insatiable demand until the 1550s when the market collapsed.
Yet there also, between 1550 and 1610 there was a 50 per cent price
increase. Because agricultural improvement was limited, the cultivable area showed little tendency to expand and the price of land
rose. Bitter dispute over landownership reached fever pitch with
the speculation involved in the sale of the monastic lands and the
dispersal of Crown lands over a longer period. Faced with rising
prices and costs, the Tudor landlord rack-rented and there was a
steady rise in rents until the mid 1630s. Industry and trade were
restrained as well as encouraged by government control, and were
often subject to monopoly control, which in turn led to price
increases. Tudor England was a period in which the power of the
producer was much greater than that of the worker or the consumer. While wages did not rise in step with the estimated cost
of living, prices were able to continue rising unabated, although
the government tried to mitigate the effects.

Trade expansion as a result of the opening of new markets, the
increased level of economic activity related to an increased flow
of money, and the pressure of demand in circumstances of restricted
supply underlay the Tudor price rise. But inflation is almost
inevitable in economic development, and static or falling prices
are not usually taken as useful signs in an economy. The Tudor
price rise was traceable to economic laws and in 1574, Jean Bodin
developed the view that the quantity of money is the cause of
inflation or deflation. However, the price rise was spectacular; both
in comparison with developments before and after the Tudor
period, and in the way prices varied enormously from year to year.
Medieval price changes seem to have been replaced, almost within
a few decades, by a modern situation of boom and slump. In
comparison with later growth rates, however, the overall increase
in production was very low, the population rise spread over 150
years, and the shifts in the economy did not amount to a decisive
reallocation of resources. Boom and slump was less of a cyclical
than a spasmodic phenomenon of Tudor times, and for this a
number of reasons have been put forward. Perhaps the most
important is debasement or, as it would now be called, devaluation.
Rising prices affected those with fixed incomes, particularly the
Crown. Henry VIII, faced with increasing expenditure, and having
failed to reap more than a temporary gain from the sale of monastic
property in the 1530s, resorted to debasement in the 1540s. Wolsey
set a precedent by a debasement in 1526 which was the first since
the days of Edward III. This had as its aim the reduction in the
weight of silver to a parity with foreign coinage, but Henry VIII's

devaluation went much further. Between 1542 and 1547, Henry altered both the weight and the proportion of pure silver to alloy. The amount of silver was reduced to one half of what it had been and the Crown pocketed £237,000 profit on this operation. Further debasement followed in 1549 and 1551, so that the amount of silver was reduced to one sixth, and a further £273,000 accrued to the Crown. The sums obtained did little to recoup financial insolvency and the harmful effects were very great.

Face value and intrinsic value correspond at this time and, therefore, there was a rise in prices, since new coins were seen as being worth less than old ones. Gresham's Law then operated. Those with good coin were reluctant to part with it, and "bad money drives out good." Moreover, the volume of money being circulated had increased, but productive capacity had not thereby automatically been expanded. Thus, prices rose as a result of a shortage of good coin and the increased circulation of money which, according to Latimer, had been reduced in value by a third. Prices rose rapidly (by a quarter) in the 1540s, and even more rapidly in the early 1550s, when they doubled, reaching their peak in the late 1550s. Yet rises in domestic prices were offset by the cheapening of exports, and the late 1540s and early 1550s saw the all-time record for cloth exports established. On the other hand, the value of sterling depreciated so that, whereas internal prices were doubled, exchange value was more than halved. This is shown by a consideration of the exchange rate between the English and the Flemish pound during the period which varied as follows:

Table 10—English and Flemish Exchange Rates

1522	£1 = 32s. Fl.
1542	£1 = 27s. Fl.
1547	£1 = 21s. Fl.
1551	£1 = 15s. Fl.

The situation was not remedied until 1551, when the government saw that a recoinage was necessary, but unfortunately announced it four months in advance, thereby precipitating a final price rise before government measures took effect. Only in 1560, under the guidance of Sir Thomas Gresham, was the coinage adequately restored.

Three factors, therefore, account for the buoyancy and disturbance of the Tudor economy in comparison with earlier times. New markets, which were increasingly favourable to an England at the centre of world trade, provided the stimulus for exploration and company foundation. Changes in old markets, particularly for cloth, encouraged this move still further. Population increase leading to a sharp rise in demand, in prices and in output had to be met by new agricultural methods, new sources of supply for food and consumer products and an increasing demand for imports from a wide variety of places. The price rise, by making possible quick profits in a speculator's market and investment more likely to yield returns, enabled the economy to expand part of the way to meet this demand. All three factors—new markets, population increase and inflation—were European phenomena, but England was particularly suited to gain from this period of economic boom. Tudor governments helped to provide a political and economic stimulus by their policies, especially in their assumption of an economic role for the state, implicit in the economic policy known subsequently as mercantilism.

England had been the largest free trade area in medieval Europe, but the country had not been strongly administered at the centre. It was the achievement of the Tudors that such a centralised government machine emerged—foreshadowed by the work of Henry VII, quickened by Thomas Cromwell, and brought to a fine art by William Cecil, Lord Burleigh, Secretary of State from 1560 to 1598. In some ways, the new government was the result of the disappearance of feudalism as a governing force and its replacement by the concept of a nation state in which the sovereign was supreme. Local feudal loyalties died hard particularly in the north, where the Duke of Newcastle could still raise his own troops in the 1640s, but the decline of a territorial nobility inevitably accompanied the growth of a territorial monarchy. Treason was strictly defined as a crime against the Crown; no longer was it the feudal concept of broken allegiance to any lord. The decline of the Earls of Norfolk, Suffolk, Northumberland and Westmorland brought about a need for fresh government bodies to control the remoter regions. When James I confined Northumberland to the south of England in 1605, he was completing a process which the defeat of rebellion in 1536 and 1569 had begun. The monarchy gained from the concept of the nation and Church as one, with a royal supremacy and a politically enforced uniformity. With the disappearance of the abbots from the Lords and the appointment of bishops in reality by the Crown, the territorial power of the Church was also reduced. Divinity began to hedge the monarch who became the embodiment of the nation. Sovereignty was the key to the new role of the government: "This realm of England is an empire, and so hath been accepted in the world, governed by one Supreme Head and King having the dignity and royal estate of the imperial crown of the same, unto whom a body politic, compact of all sorts and degrees of people . . . be bounden and owe to bear next to God a natural and humble obedience." Political unity was not fully established until 1601, but it was the work of the Tudor period. The Council of the North was reorganised in 1536–7 and the liberties of Tynedale (1504), Richmond and Durham (1536) were brought to an end. On the Welsh border, with possibly 4,000 executions to his credit, Rowland Lee, Bishop of Coventry and Lichfield, began the organisation of Wales; 200 Marcher lords lost their jurisdiction and in 1536 and 1543 two statutes incorporated Wales and England, creating five new counties and appointing twenty-four Welsh members of Parliament. The Council of the Marches met at Ludlow to control the region. Calais (1536–1558) and Chester (given two members in 1543) lost their independence and only Durham did not return members until 1675. Ireland was conquered, the Irish parliament subordinated and the Court of Castle Chamber established. Henry VIII took the title of King of Ireland in 1540, and the conquest was completed in 1601.

This new and united kingdom carried with it an exclusive claim to its citizens' loyalty. The local bonds of guild or lord were held to be subordinate to the welfare of the realm and the realm so precariously established could not permit much liberty. Tudor government was never despotic but it was absolutist. It controlled and manipulated Parliament even if it was allowed to exist. It enforced changes in religion to suit the will and pleasure of the sovereign. Government interfered with every aspect of supply and demand and therefore with every aspect of day-to-day existence. For the sake of its own safety, the government elaborated a paternalism which was as harsh as it was beneficent. Rebellion caused by economic and religious discontent was frequent in Tudor times and was fiercely denounced as destructive of the whole social order. These views were elaborated politically and economically to bind men to the state by a theory of obligation, if not by the force of arms. Tudor paternalism or the ideal of a well-regulated "commonwealth" was the social counterpart of political change. Edmund Dudley in his *Tree of Commonwealth* (1509) was among the first to elaborate these views. Thomas Cromwell can be given the credit for turning them to the use of the state. Richard Morrison in his *Lamentation* (1536) stressed the danger to the social fabric of rebellion, and Thomas Starkey, Richard Taverner, William Marshall, Thomas Gibson and Robert Barnes all wrote in similar vein. Later, their views became part of the accepted norms of society. Sir John Cheke in *Hurt of Sedition*, Thomas Cranmer and Hugh Latimer in their sermons and others like William Gouge or

Nicholas Udall elaborated the viewpoint in the 1540s and 1550s. There were three distinct groups: economic writers with practical experience such as John Rastell, the shipowner, or Clement Armstrong, a London merchant; political advocates of government policy; and social reformers. This latter group polarised later into two. Some advocated unfaltering obedience to the state and concentrated on the need for a hierarchical and well-organised state. Sir Thomas Elyot said: "where there is any lack of order needs must be perpetual conflict," and this state of affairs, argued Morrison, would lead to economic collapse *(A Remedy for Sedition)*. These views of man needing strong government and society, because of the "carnal liberty, enormity, sin and babylonical confusion" its disruption would produce, led eventually to Hobbes's *Leviathan* in 1651.

Others, however, gravitated towards a more liberal view and tended to be concerned more with social justice than political sense. More's *Utopia* was an early and impracticable work in the tradition of social reform which created the "Common-wealth" movement. This was the equivalent of the radicalism of the fourteenth century and was produced by the economic and social distress caused by the great inflation. By James I's reign, the term "leveller" was in use for social reformers and their work culminated in the Leveller Movement of the 1640s and Harrington's *Oceana* (1656). It was significant that among the earlier followers of the movement, such as Henry Brinkelow, was Robert Crowley who reprinted *Piers Plowman*. Laymen, such as the authors of the *Dialogue between Pole and Lupset* (definitely not written by Starkey) and *A Discourse of the Common Weal* (possibly by John Hales), contributed to the movement, and in its early days churchmen such as Hugh Latimer, Bishop of Worcester, also assisted the movement. Gradually with the establishment of the Church as a pillar of the Elizabethan state, Church interest declined, and the cause of social reform was espoused more frequently by Puritans. By Stuart times, it was argued by some, that it was possible to improve society by "the perfection of the social order." Socialism had its origins in the seventeenth century, when radicals gave up the idea of a Christian order and replaced it with the social order. In this sense, the political view of the well-balanced state was complemented by the economic view of an harmonious economy as the solution to the problem of society. Tudor and Stuarts gave little scope to the latter view and a great deal to the former. Economic and social policy was dictated by government decree.

The centre of Tudor government was the Privy Council which influenced the decisions of Parliament, ruled large parts of the country through conciliar courts and, in theory, directed local administration through the well-established justices of the peace and the newly created (1557) Lords Lieutenant of the counties. The Tudor Privy Council was a powerful and increasingly professional body of administrators, which usually numbered about ten to twenty. By 1540 the judicial functions of the Council had been largely delegated to prerogative courts—Requests for the poor, Star Chamber for more powerful subjects. The Council was an executive and administrative body which issued proclamations or drafted Bills, kept an eye on local government by means of local commissions or the services of paid informers, and tried through instructions to local officials to bridge the gap between the law and its enforcement. Ministers as such were not part of Tudor government structure but the period saw the creation of two Secretaryships of State. The first of these, Thomas Wriothesley and Ralph Sadler, were appointed in 1540, following from the increased importance given to the post by Thomas Cromwell's tenure from 1534 to 1540. In August 1540, the Privy Council appointed a clerk and started a register so that it was a more formalised central body than the eighteenth-century Cabinet. Strong central government enabled mercantilist economics and paternalist social policies to be formulated, but weak local administration prevented the Council from being as effective in practice as it claimed to be on paper. Justices of the peace were the key to Tudor administration and their powers were increased considerably from the time of Henry VII. But their responsibilities increased as well and William Lambarde spoke of "stacks of statutes" which they had to enforce, unpaid, and lacking any administrative staff. Communications were poor and the problems of enforcement enormous. Information was difficult to obtain. The justices themselves, as landlords, were often opposed to the laws they were required to enforce and the flight of the justices from Norfolk during the 1549 rebellion was the action of guilty men. The commission of justice was a valuable social acquisition and there were many justices of known probity; Justice Shallow was not, however, without his real-life counterparts.

Thus, although Tudor government marked an advance in national and administrative unity, it was by no means highly efficient. Its economic policies were dictated much more by a fear of rebellion and a consequent hatred of the common people or by danger from abroad and the loss of national prestige than by economic or social motives. At times, however, economic pressure groups obtained the ear of the government. Gresham and others influenced the government's fiscal measures. John Hales, Clerk of the Hanaper, obtained influence through Sir Thomas Smyth, Secretary of State to

Somerset. However, it cannot be said that Tudor governments deliberately pursued a coherent policy of mercantilism or paternalism. Archbishop Whitgift once said "the people are commonly bent to novelties and to factions," and Smyth himself said in 1565 "the poorer and meaner people . . . have no interest in the commonwealth." It was to preserve the chain of social precedence when "they that are superiors to some are inferiors to others," and to preserve the prosperity of the realm for reasons of security, that the government acted. As Nicholas Udall told the rebels of 1549: "what other fruit or end may hereof ensue unto you but devouring one another and an universal desolation of your own selves" as a result of social and economic disorder?

At the root of mercantilism lay fears concerning the loss of bullion to the benefit of other nations and the depleting of our war chest, and from this developed the view of the balance of trade, whereby England had to export more than she imported and it was best that England relied as little as possible upon imports. The aims of mercantilism were not essentially different from those of the guilds, only in this case the nation had replaced the guilds' self-sufficiency through regulation. This concept of national self-sufficiency arose from an exaggerated calculation of the nation's capacity to provide for itself and the still wilder view that foreign trade was a malevolent influence designed to ruin the nation. Thus, all countries, claimed a writer in 1713 "concur in this maxim that the less they consume of foreign commodities the better it is for them." This view did not extend to all commodities, because the import of raw materials helped home industries, but luxuries were held to drain the realm of currency, a charge frequently levelled at the East India Company. The need for a surplus of bullion was further augmented by the view that wealth was money or, as Sir Thomas Roe said in 1641, "if money increase the kingdom doth gain by trade; if it be scarce it loseth." Early evidence for mercantilist thought is not widespread, although the *Discourse of the Common Weal* stated that "we must always take heed that we buy no more of strangers than we sell them, for so we should impoverish ourselves and enrich others." It was only in the early seventeenth century, with the rise in interest in the nature of trade, that the government called on writers to explain matters. These included Gerard Malynes, Edward Misselden and Thomas Mun. Misselden wrote *The Circle of Commerce* in 1623 but Mun's work *England's Treasure by Foreign Trade* was not published until 1664. Mun stated as early as 1623 the views he expressed later: "the ordinary means therefore to increase our wealth and treasure is by foreign trade wherein ye must ever observe this rule; to sell more to strangers yearly than we consume of theirs in value." In a sense, mercantilism restricted trade, because it failed to grasp the essential connection between buying imports and selling exports and the resources of the realm lay untapped.

Mercantilism was operated by forbidding the export of bullion and trying to prevent trade in commodities that took coin out of the realm. Imports were discouraged by duties and exports encouraged by bounties. Home industries, particularly corn, were protected by duties. New industries were developed and encouraged by government-granted monopolies and overseas trade expanded by means of government-chartered companies. The fishing industry was protected to encourage seamen, and navigation laws encouraged the development of shipping and the retention of the carrying trade in our hands. Our main industry, cloth, was controlled by one company and that condemned "interlopers." Free trade was held to enhance difficulties and to provide wasteful competition, whereas regulated trade was held to be advisable for protection and profit. Industries at home were minutely supervised, particularly the cloth, leather and iron industries which were the main exporters. Mining and the manufacture of armaments was carefully controlled; two government companies had a monopoly of the production side and government finance closely controlled mining itself. The export of timber, iron and horses were all controlled as being a danger to the security of the realm. When the great number of enactments on enclosure, the regulation of hours and wages in industry and measures concerned with the relief of the poor are added, the amount of legislation that mercantilism produced is self-evident. There were forty-nine Acts affecting the cloth trade, for example, during the Tudor period.

Yet all this legislation would have been of little effect if the economy had not been responding to new opportunities. By itself, mercantilism did not create favourable economic conditions; it merely regulated and organised and not always for the benefit of the country. Towards the end of Elizabeth's reign and during that of James, the first works which attempt to give economic details as such made their appearance. In the earlier years of the sixteenth century, John Leland, chaplain and librarian to Henry VIII, had toured the country between 1534 and 1543 (and had given incidentally a good deal of economic information). Others followed him, including William Lambarde with his *Perambulation* and William Camden whose *Britannia* was published in 1586. Sir Thomas Smith and William Harrison attempted to produce accounts of the structure of society in the 1570s. Harrison produced his *Description of England* in 1577, and it contains much valuable information on class structure and living standards. Within thirty years, it was followed by Thomas Wilson's *The State of England* in 1600. Wilson was a consul abroad and then took the post of government archivist. Foreign trade and exploration was dealt with by Richard Hakluyt, a cartographer and adviser to the East India Company, who produced *The Principal Navigations, Voyages and Discoveries of the English Nation* in 1589 and reissued it in three volumes in 1599. The seventeenth century opened with a great debate in Parliament in 1604 on the nature of trade, and economic matters had definitely become part of everyday Parliamentary as well as government concern. Therein lay the roots of the great change, by which mercantilism was to become the merchant's policy urged on the government rather than the government's policy enforced on the merchants. These works reflected a growth in national pride concerning our natural resources. Fortescue's *Commodities of the Realm* found its echo in the Parliamentary debates of 1621: "No kingdom so happy as ours by situation, by seas, rivers, staple commodities." Even the fisheries of the coast were worth more "than the King of Spain's West Indies." Parliament voiced complaints against our rivals, particularly the Dutch whose ability "eat us out in our navigation," while they were but "a handful of the world" and possessed "neither wool nor cloth, nor few other commodities." The war with Spain had been under the banner of religion, but the wars with the Dutch were under the flag that follows trade.

Provided with maps and descriptions of the country, and indeed of the New World, economic historians have tended to make the Tudor changes too dramatic. When the sixteenth century passed, England was still a small power in terms of population and wealth. Agriculture was the pursuit of the great majority of the people. Society was held together, not by feudal nobility, but by a more diverse landed gentry. English trade still lay in her traditional commodities, with the notable exception of coal. Her main markets were still in Europe, and 88 per cent of the cloth trade was in the hands of the Merchant Adventurers. Yet there were also striking changes. Hansards, Italians, foreign bankers had gone and English financial and maritime interests were firmly established. The latter was evidenced by her fleet, second only to Holland. English traders were to be found from Newfoundland and Muscovy to Japan and the Moluccas. The Mediterranean was reopened and the centre of a flourishing trade. Industry was growing rapidly, technical innovation was widespread, even if ineffective in application, and many new industries were growing. On the land, very often on ex-monastic or ex-Crown lands, a prosperous middle group of landowners farmed profitably and, by their lights, progressively. Soon they were to be joined by a reviving nobility, although not by the impoverished Crown. England had a Poor Law; the first in history, and, in spite of lowered living standards for the poor, had weathered numerous rebellions and invasions without serious dislocation. Relative peace was one of the keys to Tudor popularity and prosperity. From 1560 onwards, Europe's religious wars found little echo here, until the policy of Charles I and Laud precipitated conflict. If the Crown lacked power, it lacked the means to be oppressive, and if the nobility had declined, it was military power which they had lost. Commerce was now to be organised to protect it in national rather than local disputes. A national economy was the product of the expansion towards new frontiers brought about by the population and price rises, the expansion of markets and the intervention of the government in the organisation of the economy. This favourable picture must, however, be redressed by remembering the serious consequences of rapid economic change which was ill-understood. Nowhere were the consequences fought out with more bitterness, prompting violent pamphlet warfare and hopeless revolt year after year, than in the rural parts of the kingdom. Fortunately for the Tudors, paternalism and the moderate use of force prevented any greater calamity, although the results were serious enough to produce the lengthy series of measures against enclosure and when these had failed the lengthy series of Poor Law measures to redress grievances. As Burleigh said, "there is nothing will sooner lead men into sedition than dearth of victual." For many, "dearth of victual" was common in the sixteenth century.

ENCLOSURE, THE TUDOR AGRICULTURAL LABOURER AND REVOLT

During the fifteenth century the amount of available land had been more than sufficient to meet the needs of a slowly growing population, but the sixty per cent increase in the sixteenth century outstripped the needs of the people both in supply of food and demand for land to own. Rising prices of land encouraged land grabbing, as Thomas Starkey observed in 1538 when he spoke of "the enhancing of rents of late days induced." Rising prices of food encouraged the development of farming for the market and the demand of London was so great by the end of the period that the presence of London merchants to buy food automatically increased prices. At times of dearth, producers preferred to meet the demand of London rather than the local market and famine was common in periods of bad harvest such as the 1530s or 1590s. Food prices, it has been estimated, rose five times during the Tudor period and it is clear that "the enclosure of arable was a movement contemporary with that of conversion to pasture." Pasture met two needs

One was the growing demand for meat and dairy produce. Thus, Kent, the West Midlands, Cheshire, Dorset and the borders of Scotland and Wales saw an increase in cattle-rearing and the Home Counties, north-west Wiltshire, Cheshire and Staffordshire produced dairy produce for the London market. The other was for sheep and the demand for wool grew steadily from the 1460s and reaching its peak in the 1540s, then declined.

Enclosure was one symptom among many illustrating the basic drive towards more efficient and profitable farming. Landlords responded by seeking to increase profits from their leases and copyholds and this process started long before the middle of the century. There was some justification for their action since prices had risen and they were under pressure. Moreover, there was no lack of new tenants who were prepared to pay heavy entry fines and increased rents. In many parts of the country customary rents had been fixed for a long time and in parts of Leicestershire these had been fixed at 6d. per acre in the fourteenth century. In one survey, carried out for Sir Nicholas Bacon on his Suffolk lands in 1562, it was found that the rents were little more than half their economic level. The restrictions imposed by customary tenure were a continuing problem, for in the 1630s Bishop Wren of Ely complained to Archbishop Laud that leases of his lands would bear "much more than a double rent." Long leases which had been reasonable in a period of slow-moving prices now became antiquated. On the estates of Leicester Abbey, for example, some leases were fixed for more than forty years. Landlords tried to recoup their losses by "onering the gressoms" or increasing entry fines, and by rack-renting, which usually meant forcing leaseholders to take shorter leases at higher rates. In the north, Henry Clifford, first Earl of Cumberland, served as a good example of these changes. Entry fines amounting to seven or eight years' rent equivalent were charged on intakes at Stainmore and Mallerstang in Yorkshire, and in 1537 it was reported to Thomas Cromwell that Cumberland "must be brought to change his conditions and not be so greedy to get money of his tenants." Monastic landlords had been particularly lax in the matter of leasing or, as Brinklow said in 1542, "they never enhanced their rents nor took so cruel fines." When monastic lands came into lay ownership, enclosure was rapid and so was the increase of rents. Families with ready capital and considerable business experience moved into the land market, or as Thomas Lever said "their riches must abroad in the country to buy farms out of the hands of . . . honest yeomen and poor labouring husbandmen." Thus, Newstead in Nottinghamshire went to three London aldermen.

Rises in rents and entry fines led to a bitter outcry and featured among the complaints in the major rebellions of 1536 and 1549. Crowley in *The Way to Wealth* claimed that rents had doubled or quadrupled in just over a decade, and evidence from the Herbert estates between 1540 and 1620 showed that such rises were feasible. Crowley included a verse to make his point:

> "A man that had lands
> Of ten pounds a year,
> Surveyed the same,
> And let it out dear.
> So that of ten pound
> He made well a score
> More pounds by the year
> Than other did before."

Rack-renting was brought about by sharp practice and constant resort to courts, particularly where copyholders were concerned. They were also affected by entry fine increases, for it seems that in most manors these were not fixed, although it was customary to make them equivalent to two years' rents. Protest from such men as Lever and Crowley and the passion of Latimer's sermons ("you rent-raisers, I may say you step-lords, you unnatural lords") have their sober counterpart in government pronouncements. Reporting on the Lakeland counties in 1537, the Duke of Norfolk told Cromwell "what the gressing of them so marvellously sore in time past and with increasing of lords rents by inclosing" had contributed to discontent. Of course, not all landlords were extortionate and in 1540 Sir John Gostwick of Bedfordshire pointed out the advantage of prosperous tenants being able to invest as well as pay rents. However, it seems that those who desired to take advantage of the situation were well in evidence. The northern rebels in 1536 demanded that "the lands in Westmorland, Cumberland, Kendal . . . and the abbays lands in Mashamshire, Kirkbyshire, Nitherdale may be by tenant right, and the lord to have at every charge two years rent for gressom and rismore." In 1549 the Norfolk rebels demanded that "copyhold land that is unreasonably rented may go as it did in the first year of King Henry VII and that at the death of a tenant or of the sale of the same lands to be charged with an easy fine as a capon or a reasonable sum of money."

Landlords cast their eyes over their neighbours' possessions. They were anxious to engross lands and buy up holdings and to get as much of the commonland into their hands as possible. Enclosure by means of consolidating strips won the approval of agricultural improvers such as Tusser and Fitzherbert and even in *A Discourse of the Common Weal* it was stated that "tenants in common be no so good husbands as when every man hath his part in several." It is significant that enclosure of this kind was not resisted, particularly if it was for arable, and it is clear that the value of land so enclosed rose to at least double what it had been. On the other hand, consolidation of smaller farms into medium-sized holdings was brought about by sharp practice against the copyholders, who obtained little redress from the Court of Requests, although Cardinal Wolsey, for example, sought to activate it. Thus Lever criticised farmers who "to get your neighbour's farm . . . will offer and desire them to take bribes, fines and rents, more than they look for or than you yourselves be well able to pay." Moreover, even enclosure for arable could arouse opposition, although it is difficult to justify this in view of the need for increased yield. Leland commented that the Duke of Buckingham was "cursed" for his enclosed lands. Where lords were unable to increase yield by consolidating strips or enlarging holdings, they tried to take advantage of common rights. For example, in the north arable farmers in the valleys had to supplement their income by grazing on moor commons and when these were enclosed, there was great opposition. Before the Pilgrimage of Grace focused attention on this matter there had been at least sixteen enclosure riots in the period 1528–47 besides the more spectacular rebellion itself. In 1536 the *Pontefract Articles* asked that the "statute for enclosures and intakes . . . be put into execution, and that all intakes, enclosures since Henry VII . . . be pulled down except mountains, forests and parks." In other words, new enclosures were acceptable and old were not, since these often involved the loss of the commons.

Opposition to the enclosure of commons was more specific during Ket's Rebellion. In East Anglia, the use of sheep for manure on the light soils by arable farmers made common rights vital to arable as well as to pastoral farmers. Thus, the stronger farmers tried to reduce stints and to fold their sheep on their tenants' land. In one case, that of Sir Roger Townsend, it seems that the use of the fold course system was a prelude to weakening freeholders in an area where copyholders were fewer. Thus, the rebels demanded that "no lord of no manor shall common upon the commons" and that "all freeholders and copyholders may take the profits of all commons, and there to common, and the lords not to common nor take profits of the same." The rebels urged Somerset "to take all liberty of late into your own hands whereby all men may quietly enjoy their commons with all profits." All the critics of the landlords agreed that this was a serious matter. Hales pointed out that "there may be a thousand cottagers" who depended upon the commons. This was because their wages were low and their employment haphazard. Clearly the ranks of the unemployed were thus swelled, for "if the sturdy fall to stealing and robbing, then are you the causers thereof, for you dig in, enclose and withold from the earth." Lever said "the greatest grief that hath been into the people of this realm, hath been the enclosing of commons," and another writer drew attention to the "forage and feeding" obtained there for the cattle of the poor.

The activities of the landlords produced a variety of results. It is clear that they profited. Rents on the Herbert estates rose five-fold and those "may be taken as generally applicable to lowland England." With the additional wealth, agricultural improvement was possible, the gentry emerged as a powerful social class and the richer yeomen benefited considerably. Higher rents and higher selling prices for agricultural produce, together with low wages (and a reduced labour bill in enclosure for sheep), have to be balanced against higher prices for consumer goods, the demands made by a rising standard of living in such matters as education and the legal costs involved in frequent litigation. Yet the balance was clearly favourable to the landlord. The Tudor period was one for the rising gentry, and the land was a profitable investment so that "every gentleman flieth into the country." Moreover, the gentry gained from the Crown, Church and nobles, as well as from the smaller farmers, although this trend was reversed in the seventeenth century. Norden estimated that enclosed land was worth fifty per cent more than open fields and this was due partly to rising prices and partly to improvements. The yeomanry who came between about £30 and £500 a year experienced "a general improvement in wealth and living standards" and the more successful were able to rehouse themselves in "a style little different from many gentry."

For "the commons" of Tudor England, the ordinary wage labourers, however, the land war had largely bad effects, and the bitter opposition of the people like the women of Enfield in 1589, "armed with swords, daggers . . . and other weapons," was widespread. Poverty was commented upon both by those who feared it and those who disapproved of it. Few had a solution apart from the simple expedient of all-out opposition to enclosures which were a symptom of the real difficulties. The poor suffered from loss of their lands, particularly the commons. Rising prices hit them. Thus, the troubles of the 1590s, like the endemic bread riots of eighteenth-century France, were closely related to wheat prices and the riots of 1596 coincided with a famine.

Table 11—Wheat Prices, 1592–9

1592–3	per qtr	20s. 10d.
1593–4		24s. 9d.
1596–7		56s. 6d.
1598–9		31s. 2d.

But these were national averages. In some places, matters were much worse. At Newcastle the price of rye reached 96s. a quarter and only the arrival of three Dutch grain ships in 1597 averted disaster. The poor suffered from low wages, although these varied so much from place to place and were supplemented in so many different ways that it is difficult to arrive at an accurate assessment. Thorold Rogers calculated that wages rose from 7d. a week in the 1560s, to 8d. in the 1570s, 9d. in the 1590s, $9\frac{1}{2}d$. in the 1630s and 11d. in 1640. Government or establishment comment confirmed the impression. Sometimes this showed itself in blind hatred. In 1497 Cornish rebel leaders were from "the dregs of the people." In 1569 Sir Ralph Sadler described the common people as "ignorant, superstitious and altogether blinded with the old popish doctrine." Writing to Somerset about his lenient policies, one adviser spoke of "the King's subjects out of all discipline, out of obedience, caring neither for Protector nor King." Government pronouncements confirmed that matters were amiss. Thus, the Council of the North in 1574 was instructed to investigate "decay of husbandry and oppression of the poor." In the *Discourse* it was argued that enclosure was the main cause of social distress and "these wild and unhappy uproars amongst us. . . . Hunger is a bitter thing to bear. Wherefore, when they talk, they must murmur . . . and so stir up these tumults." Legislation, like that of July 1549, requiring justices to fix food prices and force hoarded supplies on to the market, showed that the government realised that hunger was the cause of sedition. Government legislation against enclosure was due less to acceptance of current propaganda and more to Burleigh's view that "I think whosoever doth not maintain the plough destroys this kingdom." Between 1547 and 1553, according to Tawney, half the agricultural counties experienced disturbances.

Enclosure was one of the most significant features of Tudor England, brought about by what William Cholmeley called in 1553 "the insatiable desire of pasture for sheep and cattle." In spite of a large amount of work by historians, the extent of enclosure has not been accurately determined, mainly because the term is so

K

elastic and the process continuous, so that it is difficult to decide whether "old enclosed" should be included or not. Moreover, contemporary evidence is conflicting. In 1597 the Dean of Durham claimed that enclosure in the Palatinate had cut 8,000 acres of tillage to 160 acres and that the towns were full of unemployed. Yet both Johnson and Hoskins have argued that "the common fields of township were for the most part enclosed soon after the Restoration in that region." Figures for displacement of population as a result of all kinds of enclosure vary between a contemporary estimate of 300,000 and a modern one of 50,000. An estimate by one historian that 500,000 acres or 2·76 per cent of the total area of England was enclosed is of little value, because what matters is the total cultivable area and of this we have no contemporary estimate. Before examining the consequences of enclosure, however, it is necessary to try and assess the extent of the movement. It was not uniform either in point of time or place of occurrence, and it is highly significant that the central period of Tudor England was the period of least enclosure. Thus, of the total of enclosure taking place between 1450 and 1607, 33 per cent was between 1450 and 1510, 18 per cent between 1510 and 1580 and 48 per cent between 1580 and 1607. The highest percentage of enclosed land was to be found in the Midlands (13 per cent of the total area in Huntingdonshire and Northamptonshire) and the lowest in Cornwall (1·5 per cent). On the other hand, Kent has always been enclosed and Leland commented that "most part of all Somersetshire is in hedgerows enclosed," so it is clear that the figures are not particularly reliable. Nevertheless, they serve to illustrate the smallness of a problem which seemed vast to contemporaries.

Enclosure was of many kinds, but the chief opposition was to enclosure for sheep. Sheep-farming was profitable and, during the first half of the century at least, wool prices encouraged farmers to turn to sheep-rearing on account of the smaller costs of labour. More said that "the price of wool is so risen that poor folks which were wont to work it, and make cloth thereof, be now able to buy none at all" and it seems that sheep enclosures were mainly concentrated in the first half of the century. Authorities such as Hales or Bacon agreed that it was in this earlier period that "the chief destruction of towns and decay of houses was." Later, there was an increasing demand for cattle and this had similar effects to sheep enclosures, thus ensuring that although England was becoming a wool-importing country and the number of sheep was about 8 million, enclosure for pasture continued. The effects of sheep enclosure were attacked by propagandists, particularly those in the

Table 12—Some Percentage Figures to Illustrate the Area of Selected Counties Affected by Enclosure Between 1450 and 1607 (after Gay)

24 Counties in 1517 up to 1607		6 Counties in 1607		
Leicestershire	⎫ 8·94	Warwickshire	0·93	⎫
Northamptonshire		Leicestershire	2·32	
Rutland		Northamptonshire	4·30	average 2·53
S.E. Warwickshire	⎭	Buckinghamshire	1·48	
Bedfordshire	⎫ 8·45	Bedfordshire	3·32	
Berkshire		Huntingdonshire	3·29	⎭
Buckinghamshire				
Middlesex		Cornwall, Devon,		
Oxfordshire	⎭	S.W. Dorset, W. Som.,		
Cambridgeshire	⎫ 5·25	Essex, Herts., Kent,		
Huntingdonshire	⎭	E. Norfolk, Weald of		
Derbyshire	⎫ 1·0	Surrey and Sussex,		
N.W. Essex		N.W. Warwickshire,		
Gloucs., Hereford, E.	⎭	E. Worcs. were		
Lincs., W. Norf.,	⎫ 2·0	"old enclosed."		
Notts., Shrops., Staffs.	⎭			
Cheshire	⎫			
Hants.				
Somerset	⎬ 1			
Yorkshire				
I. of Wight	⎭			

Commonwealth group, and these attacks were not baseless. Government reports tended to confirm them and the enclosure commissions of 1517 and 1548 were evidence of government concern. For this there were varied reasons. Depopulation was among the main dangers because it reduced the security of the realm. Movement of population was dangerous as it increased the danger of sedition, particularly in towns. Unemployment produced discontent. Thus, the government acted because it feared revolt, not because it opposed enclosure. Popular opposition to enclosure was widespread. It was not only on such occasions as the Pilgrimage of Grace in 1536 or Ket's Rebellion in 1549 that this was made clear. Anti-enclosure disturbances were endemic in the 1540s and increased during Elizabeth's reign. Thus, in 1549 not only were Norfolk and Suffolk disturbed, but there were riots in Hertfordshire, Hampshire and Worcestershire and troops sent to crush a Cornish uprising in July that year were sent to deal with a "stir here in Buckinghamshire and Oxfordshire." In 1550 there were murmurs in Kent; in 1552, in Buckinghamshire once more. During Elizabeth's reign, disturbances continued and Elizabeth herself was personally involved when Sir Thomas Gresham's enclosures were attacked while she was staying with him and in 1576 when the people protested to the Queen at Woodstock. In 1596 there were serious disturbances in Oxfordshire concerning enclosures at Banbury, and in May 1607 Northamptonshire, Warwickshire and Leicestershire experienced riots. During these, the term "leveller" was first used and this illustrates the connection between the agricultural distress of the poor and their later interest in leveller and "clubmen" activities. These disturbances took place in an age of almost constantly flickering rebellion and, although they were by no means the only cause, enclosure riots were a major factor.

Riots and the extent of government concern are forceful supports for the arguments of the Tudor anti-enclosure propagandists. Depopulation was not as widespread as contemporaries thought, but it was significant. Thus, in Leicestershire between 1450 and 1600, sixty settlements amounting to one in six were wiped out. In Warwickshire between 1501 and 1506, Wolfhamcote, Braunstonberry and Wormleighton disappeared. In the last case, the conversion of 240 acres cost sixty men their jobs. Nor should it be forgotten that some of these enclosures were "emparking" and had little direct economic value. As late as 1598, the Parliamentary statute referred to "sundry towns parishes and houses of husbandry . . . been destroyed and become desolate." In order to control the movements of population thus produced, the government passed a number of Acts. Poor Law measures contained an element of settlement in the parish of origin. In order to prevent dispossessed people from becoming squatters, a law was passed forbidding the erection of cottages with less than 4 acres of ground appurtenant (1589) and laws were passed to restrict the building of houses in London. Laws were passed for England (1589) and London (1593) known as the Statutes of Inmates to forbid more than one family to live in a house.

Such measures were, however, an admission of the government's failure to secure compliance with enclosure statutes. This failure was due to a number of factors but perhaps the two main ones were the confused and vacillating policy of the government, and the failure of the justices of the peace to enforce the laws. As Burnet said, "no man that is in fault himself, can punish another for the same offence." Hence the demand in 1536 for the enforce-

ment of Acts concerning enclosure and that in 1549 for the Duke
of Somerset "to give licence and authority . . . to such commissioners as your poor commons hath chosen . . . to redress and
reform all such good laws, statutes, proclamations . . . which hath
been bidden by your justices of your peace . . . since the first
year of the reign of . . . King Henry VII." The rebels of 1549
specifically complained not only about enclosure of commons for
sheep, but also about enclosure for saffron and grazing of bullocks
and sheep. Pious exhortation was not enough where profit was
concerned. The *Second Prayer Book* (1552) contained a prayer that
landlords "remembering themselves to be Thy tenants, may not
rack and stretch out the rents of their houses and lands, nor yet
take unreasonable fines and measures after the manner of covetous
worldlings." Convocation in 1569 criticised the conversion of arable
to pasture. Yet as long as the government measures were inadequate, little could be done.

The first general Act against enclosure was passed in 1489
criticising the evils of sheep enclosure. It was preceded by an Act
dealing with the Isle of Wight, for "if hasty remedy be not provided that Isle cannot be long kept and defended." The Act had
no specific recommendations and enclosure continued. In 1496,
for example, the common fields of Coventry were enclosed by the
burgesses in spite of strong protest. Wormleighton was enclosed
by William Cope, Cofferer of the Household. In order to curb
public disturbance caused by heavy taxation, Wolsey intervened
in the enclosure problem. He encouraged the Court of Requests to
hear cases. An Act in 1515 required the reconversion of pastoral
to arable, and this was followed by a commission to enquire into
all enclosure since 1488. The 1517–18 commission covered twenty-
four counties and it was followed by another in 1526. Some proceedings against offending landlords were taken in Chancery in
1518–19 and in Exchequer Court at a later date (1539–42). In the
mid 1530s taxation troubles, the enforcement of cloth statutes and
the Dissolution of the Monasteries produced a fresh outbreak of
trouble. The Lincolnshire revolt of Captain Cobbler (Nicholas
Melton) was followed by the Yorkshire rising of Robert Aske, and
the Cumberland revolt under a poor clergyman, Robert Thompson
of Brough. Cromwell contemplated a law to control landlords,
passed a fresh Enclosure Act and required the Council of the
North to enquire into enclosure and other matters. His gloomy
reports were not followed up, although in 1555 a Tillage Act, by
abolishing tanistry (equal heritable jurisdiction) and feudal burdens
such as "neat geld" and "serjeant corn," tried to improve matters
in the north. Acts of 1534 and 1536 required the reconversion to

arable and limited the size of flocks to 2,000 sheep. Attempts were made to relate the number of sheep to the number of cattle and there were proclamations in 1526, 1528, 1529 and 1548.

These measures failed. As Latimer said, "let the preacher preach till his tongue be worn to the stump, nothing is amended." Somerset said "private-profit, self-love, money and such like the devil's instruments" had encouraged enclosure. John Hales, a Coventry man and Clerk of the Hanaper, possible author of the *Discourse*, and under the patronage of Somerset, was appointed to a new commission in 1548. At Court, Latimer and Lever denounced the evils of enclosure and in the country at large, Starkey and Crowley did their work. Hales's Commission was to enquire into all breaches of previous laws and to see if owners of new monastic property had retained it as arable. A fresh government proclamation denounced enclosure and Hales prepared three Bills which were introduced into Parliament and defeated in 1547. Somerset had told the Council he supported the distressed cry of the poor and a proclamation of July 1549 showed his sincerity, as also did a tax on sheep and cloth imposed earlier in March. But although Hales's Commission began work and authorised the destruction of many enclosures, including those of the Earl of Warwick, it did not succeed. An accumulation of grievances, of which enclosure was clearly one, as is evidenced by events at Hingham and Great Dunham in the 1540s, led to Ket's Rebellion. The mood of the landowners was ugly and William Paget told Somerset in July 1549 that "your softness" was "an occasion of so great an evil as has now chanced in England by these rebels." Warwick sided with the landlords and helped to suppress the revolt. Hales continued to sit in Parliament to see the Statute of Merton re-enacted, but he was not able to exert any more influence. Yet the writings of men such as Crowley, who produced *Way to Wealth* (1550) defending the Norfolk rebels, formed the links in a chain which led eventually to the early leveller literature.

Moreover, it became clear that, if the Acts of 1489, 1534, and 1536 were to be enforced, there was need of further enforcement machinery. Bodies of enclosure commissioners sat at various dates after 1550 with powers to rebuild depeopled settlements and to order the ploughing-up of pasture. Legal chicanery, such as the ploughing of a single furrow across a field, weakened the impact of the commissioners and local juries were still packed by landlords' servants. Redress usually had to be sought from the central courts. Troubles in Essex in 1563 quickly brought a re-enactment of previous Acts and in 1565 the commissioners were instructed to be vigilant. In 1574 the Council of the North and for Wales were required to enquire into matters. Sheep-farming interests managed to secure the repeal of the Enclosure Acts in 1593, but the subsequent rise in wheat prices forced the government to re-enact the laws against depopulation and pasture land. Parliamentary complaint continued into Stuart times, as did the riots. As late as 1613 to 1614, there were disturbances in Surrey and Wiltshire.

Enclosure was by no means the only major cause of revolt and it is likely that the land war was a more widespread phenomenon. High taxation was another cause of discontent as the Early Tudors developed the subsidy as the main form of tax. The yield from Parliamentary taxes rose sharply: 1485–1509, £282,000; 1509–40, £520,463; 1540–47, £656,245. The principle that the King should live off his own died hard and Parliamentary taxation was regarded as exceptional. It was not until 1534 that a subsidy was demanded as normal peacetime taxation. Early Tudor rebellions, as Anthony Fletcher has shown, often revolved around taxation questions, and these were not negligible in later outbreaks. In 1497 "two men out of the dregs of the people, to wit Thomas Flammock, a lawyer and Michael Joseph, a blacksmith" led a Cornish revolt over taxation for the Scottish war of the time. There were taxation disturbances in Yorkshire in 1489, 1513–15, and 1525. The troubles of the last year, taking place at the same time as the great peasants' risings in the Rhineland, were significant. In Suffolk, for example, wage earners contributed over half the taxable population, but only owned 3 per cent of the property. In the Pilgrimage of Grace, the Yorkshire rising was to some extent encouraged by the incidence of taxation in the West Riding, although only 1·4 per cent of the taxable population had been assessed. Thus, Nicholas Leche, a priest from Belchford in Lincolnshire, urged that "the King should remit the subsidy," and the Pontefract Articles asked "to be discharged of the . . . taxes now granted by act of parliament." Economic motives were supplemented by religious grievances and influenced by political ideals or individually ambitious men. Yet as far as the commons were concerned, poverty was brought about by the activity of the landlords and the inertia of the government and most urgently demonstrated in the rise of unemployment, the loss of security afforded by the commonlands and the consequences of enclosure, particularly for sheep.

This somewhat forbidding picture of wage labourers, less well-off in real money terms and oppressed by the consequences of inflation, needs to be modified by recalling, as Harrison did in 1577, that servile status was largely unknown. In 1549 the rebels in

Norfolk asked "that all bondmen may be made free for God made all free with his precious blood shedding." It has been suggested that this reference, which is similar to demands in German peasant articles, indicates foreign influence and it may well be that continental social ideas entered England through the same ports as Protestant Bibles. Yet Norfolk was an area where there was no servile status, and in 1552 tenants at Gimingham successfully maintained that labour services were servile and therefore illegal. It is more likely that this article derives from the native Lollard tradition of social protest. Even a conservative such as Sir Thomas Smith could remark in 1565 in *De Republica Anglorum* that there were "so few there be that it is not almost worth the speaking." By 1600 Wilson made no mention of villeinage or bondage. Legal protection slowly extended to tenants. In 1529 leaseholders gained a little protection, and copyholders gained ground also so that in 1630, Coke could declare in the *Complete Copyholder*: "now copyholders stand upon a sure ground, now they weigh not their lord's displeasure . . . for if the lord's anger grow to expulsion, the law hath provided several weapons of remedy. . . Time hath dealt very favourably with copyholders in divers respects." Copyholders by inheritance were protected by custom, if it could be proved in the Court of Chancery. Copyholders for leases had a more difficult time, but it should be remembered that copyhold leases were for long periods. On one Cambridgeshire manor in 1609, the rents had been fixed in the reign of Henry VI. When lords reaped a profit from an entry fine and a limited lease, they also gave the tenant the added protection afforded by leasehold. Fitzherbert strongly recommended that leases should not be for more than three lives—that is the possession of three living persons, not for three generations. Thus, on one manor, whereas in the 1560s tenancies in copyhold were small and many, by 1636 this had changed.

Table 13—Changes in Tenure on a Selected Manor, 1560–1636

	Total of holdings	Leasehold	Copyhold Freehold
1560	1,225	126	1,099
1636	1,275	702	523

Some argued that, in spite of the poverty, the standards of the poor showed an increase in creature comforts, and the rise in population suggests that this was likely. Tusser pointed out that enclosure meant more and better mutton, beef, corn, butter and cheese. New food products in vegetables and fruit were used widely and many writers spoke of the well-off nature of the ordinary people. Harrison said "the bread throughout our land is made of such grain as the soil yieldeth . . . poor neighbours in some shires are forced to content themselves with rye or barley, yea and in time of dearth many with bread made out of beans . . . and some acorns among." Fynes Morrison agreed that the husbandmen ate rye brown bread, but he also claimed that meat played a substantial part in the diet. He referred to geese, hares, rabbits, deer, and fowls and fish. English beef and mutton, he declared, were superior to any in Europe and our pork to everywhere except Westphalia. A comparison between food prices, which trebled between 1500 and 1560, and building wages, which hardly doubled, does not indicate sufficiently the wealth of the peasantry from other sources. Piecework was paid higher than day labour. Many families were involved in the domestic production of cloth. Wages were supplemented by food and boarding allowances. Moreover, considerable variations between regions meant that wages could be increased by moving closer to London. Peasants who were able to secure smallholdings were able to hold their own, and even day labourers seem to have owned land. One labourer, John Winter, cited by Pollard and Crossley, had property worth £17, a cow and fifteen sheep, and lived in a two-roomed cottage with out-buildings.

Agrarian disturbance in Tudor times was caused by rising prices, increased taxation and the consequence of a land war for a limited amount of increasingly profitable acreage. It was accentuated by political and religious factors. Enclosure was a symptom more than a cause, but the "Commonwealth" propagandists needed a scapegoat in the "great multitude of sheep." Government policy was ineffective, because the pressure for more wool and more food could not be set aside nor supplied by imports. As it was, England became both a wool- and corn-importing country and there was dearth and famine. The intervention of the state may have acted as a brake, but no more, and by supporting the rapid expansion of the cloth industry and removing restrictions on corn export, the government also provided accelerators. As Birnie has said, "once again in a contest between a government and an economic tendency, the government was beaten." On the other hand, there was no widespread peasants' revolt and the rebellions were crushed by a Tudor government which relied more on popular support than force of arms.

K *

THE DECLINE OF THE CHURCH, PATERNALISM AND THE POOR LAW

Unemployment with little hope of redress, unless it was from a guild or charity, sickness with no proper medical care and an early death, childbirth accompanied by pain and, in all likelihood, followed by infant mortality, and an old age with no certain comfort or protection were the lot of many in Tudor England. It is difficult to prove that there was a rise in the standard of living and yet it seems that contemporaries were under the impression that one had occurred. That the middle and lower middle class experienced an improvement may be shown by referring to two known sets of facts. The first was the building revolution, which between the 1540s and the 1640s seems to have transformed living conditions, so that those in the country at least equalled their counterparts in the towns, where there had been extensive house-building in the fifteenth century and "waste places in the boroughs were covered with buildings and formed into new wards." The size of houses increased so that those of the yeomen were indistinguish-able from the gentry. Brick was increasingly available and used to provide fireplaces and chimneys, as wood shortage started a rapid increase in coal consumption for domestic purposes. Contemporaries such as Richard Carew and, later, Robert Loder, referred to these changes and there can be little doubt that they were widespread. Harrison (1577) spoke of "the village where I remain" in which chimneys had appeared in small cottages. Evidence from counties as far apart as Essex, Yorkshire and Monmouthshire justifies Hoskins's use of the word revolution to illustrate the change.

The second group of facts may be obtained from an examination of household inventories. Harrison made a number of observations concerning improvements since the time of Henry VIII, "not among the nobility and gentry only but likewise of the lowest sort in most places of our south country." He maintained that, whereas straw and a log had been normal for the bedding of the poor, sheets and pillows were becoming common. He noticed that wooden plates were being replaced by pewter and wooden spoons by tin ones. These changes are confirmed by the inventories where as much as 15 per cent of the poor smallholder's inventory and between a quarter and a half of a yeoman's was devoted to household effects. Glazed windows, carpets instead of rushes, linen, furniture and tableware became common among all classes except the day labourer, and the trend in Oxfordshire inventories is for this to increase. In Leicestershire, the value of farmers' inventories (averaged out) rose from over £14 in 1500–31 to about £67 in

1603, which was a rise greater than that necessary to counter the price rise.

Improvements were offset by the increasing number of destitute people and the rise of town population. In towns it was necessary that public health provisions should keep pace with internal living standards, but this was clearly not the case. Moreover, medical improvement was appallingly slow. Plagues continued to affect towns and these factors, together with the demographic features already noticed, explain why the population rise was slow, even if sustained. In early Tudor times, the sweating sickness was prevalent and occurred in 1485, 1487, 1499 and 1504. Ordinary bubonic plague continued and was liable to occur without warning. In 1563, over 1,000 people a week were dying in London and Elizabeth fled to Windsor. A gallows was erected to execute anyone following her example. London was the centre of these plagues, which culminated in that of 1665, when 100,000 died in seven months. They continued until 1679. London was badly overcrowded and Howes complained in 1587 that landlords were "pestering three or four inmates into one room." In 1582 the Recorder of the City complained that vagrants seized in the town came from Essex and Berkshire and, further afield, from Shropshire and Cheshire. For these reasons, the Statute of Inmates of 1593 was passed, but it did not stop overcrowding. London in Stuart times was described as full of "foul streams like the Fleet, defiled from every overhanging house. . . . Laystalls of rotting town refuse, the sweepings of the streets, houses and middens, were piled high . . . low over-hanging wooden houses ill-kept, dark and congested, covered the ground in seemingly impenetrable rookeries of filthy courts and blind alleys." Such conditions bred rats and fleas and thus illness spread frequently and rapidly. When Wolsey's physician received a letter from Erasmus in 1524, it was full of criticism of public health standards. It pointed out that rush-covered or clay floors harboured "spittle and vomit and urine of dogs and men, beer that hath been cast forth and remnants of fishes and other filth unnamable." Erasmus proposed a number of domestic remedies and also some public ones. It would help "if public opinion required of the officials that the streets should be less defiled with filth and urine and that the roads in the neighbourhood should be cared for. You will laugh, I know, at my idleness which allows me to trouble myself about such things."

This ugly picture of public health was not without a few shafts of light, although they did little to disperse what Sir John Simon called "streams of uncleanliness, and . . . an infinity of ancestral frowsiness and infection." Some fifteenth-century towns had been paved or provided with a rudimentary water supply and there is some evidence that these were considered of importance in the sixteenth and seventeenth centuries. In 1532 an Act for improving and paving the City was passed, because the roads were "very foul and full of pits and sloughs, very perilous and noxious as well for all the king's subjects on horseback as on foot." Water was obtained either from water-carriers or from conduits, which were still being erected in 1655. Attempts were made, however, to provide a public water supply. In 1582 Peter Morris, a Dutchman, developed a water-pump and in 1584 the experiment was extended, although the water only reached Gracechurch Street. Sir Bevis Bulmer developed a chain-pump and in 1594 new waterworks to supply the Fleet Street area were built. Early in James I's reign, Sir Hugh Middleton (proceeding under an Act passed in Elizabeth's reign) between 1609 and 1613 brought water from Chadwell and Amwell in Hertfordshire. In return for a share in the profits, James I agreed to assist him. Although the earliest dividend was only some £11, it later rose to as much as £14,000. In 1619 the New River Company was founded to develop the scheme, but it remained an isolated achievement. "I question," said one contemporary, "if the celebrated aqueducts in ancient Rome equalled in magnitude . . . the beneficial effects of this undertaking." London remained a foetid slum and no attempt was made to carry out Sir Christopher Wren's plans for a great rebuilding after the fire of 1666. So appalling was the stench of the streets that, when the windows of the Old Bailey were opened in 1750, forty-four people were killed as a result. In spite of Erasmus's plea for wide glass windows, the government imposed a window tax in 1695 which was increased regularly until 1825 and not abolished until 1851.

Medical practice improved little and what there was scarcely affected the bulk of the population. The Church continued to retain some hold over the practice of medicine and the right of bishops to license was confirmed in 1511. This right included midwives. Three incorporated bodies were responsible for the organisation of medical practice. The Royal College of Surgeon-Barbers was incorporated in 1540, the two functions not being separated until 1745. The right to examine was granted in 1629. The Royal College of Physicians was set up in 1518, and had its powers extended in 1540 and 1553. Examination rights were granted in 1522. For Scotland, similar groups were founded in 1505 and 1681. Lastly, there were the Apothecaries who separated from the Grocers to form a society in 1617 and were responsible for dispensing medicines. Some towns appointed a town physician, such as the one at Newcastle, and bone-setters were also appointed. After prolonged dispute, free treatment was permitted in 1687 by the College of Physicians, but the Apothecaries opposed the development of free medicine for the poor and this was not to come until the eighteenth century. Hospitals were few and far between except in London, where St Bartholomew's (1544) and St Thomas's (1551) were reorganised under the influence of Henry VIII. The population of Tudor and Stuart England was, by any standards, unhealthy.

Neglect of this important aspect of welfare is sufficient indication that Tudor paternalism was not motivated by new-found consideration or understanding of the poor. It was true that a "social conscience," similar to that in the fourteenth century, was in evidence as a result of the manifest economic difficulties of the population. This concept was European in extent, and developed at a time when the price rise was causing severe disconent. The ethic was a social one rather than a religious one, deriving from Marsiglio of Padua, who had argued that charity lay at the basis of society for practical rather than moral reasons. A Spaniard, Vives, who visited Henry VIII, wrote De Subventione Pauperum in which he advocated co-operation between private charity and municipal organisation. Ypres put this idea into practice in 1525. Ten years later, William Marshall, a protégé of Anne Boleyn, published a Latin account of the work at Ypres. Reginald Pole at Padua was the centre of similar influence and both Thomas Starkey and Richard Morrison were resident there. One of the most important works, the Dialogue between Pole and Lupset, was closely influenced by the need for reform. Thus, to the older ideal of charity was added that of "Commonwealth" so well united in the oath taken by the rebels of 1536: "Ye shall not enter into this our Pilgrimage of Grace for the Commonwealth. . ." The Commonwealth writers and preachers were a powerful group who at certain times, such as the mid 1530s or late 1540s, exercised some direct influence on the government's policy. William Marshall in 1535 drew up a complete scheme of poor relief for Cromwell, involving a scheme of public works and a hierarchy of officials. This influenced the Act of 1536. Somerset was clearly moved by the plight of the poor.

More likely to influence the government was the magnitude of the problem, upon which all were agreed. Clearly the pamphleteers exaggerated, but the economic conditions of the time indicate that there must have been a serious problem. The term "poor" covered at least three classes: the impotent poor, ranging from foundlings to the sick and aged; sturdy beggars, willing but unable to obtain work; and rogues and vagabonds, who were often indistinguishable from the criminal under-world of Alsatia. The decline of the retainer system, the Dissolution of the Monasteries, depopulation in rural areas, seasonal unemployment in industrial towns, unemployed sailors and soldiers, and a vast number of "wandering men" made up the numbers, which are likely to have been between about 30,000 and 50,000 of the population. London was regarded as particularly vulnerable and it is no coincidence, therefore, that municipal activity was first prominent in that city. Brinkelow commented in 1545 that vast numbers begged in the streets and "many not able to do for other but lie in their houses in most grievous pains and die for lack of aid of the rich." In 1587 he referred to a "great concourse of people of all sorts," that flooded into the city. Yet it was a national problem. Bernard Gilpin declared that "thousands in England beg now from door to door." In the *Dialogue*, it was stated that in "no country of Christendom, for the number of people, you shall find so many beggars as be here in England."

The growth of the problem to such an extent forced the government to act, out of fear of rebellion. The contemporary events in Europe, including peasant war and Anabaptist urban revolt, were influential in forcing the government's hand. It is not at all clear whether or not the attack on the Church was a major cause of poverty, as was once thought likely when it was assumed that large numbers of dispossessed religious swelled the ranks of the poor, the closure of the monasteries left the poor as a whole destitute and the attack on the guilds brought to an end the dispersal of charity in the cities. Such an event as the Dissolution, together with the attack on a large number of religious institutions, was bound to have some effect, if only in contributing to general insecurity. Yet, paradoxically, the attack on the Church was supported by the Protestant Commonwealth men who lamented its consequences. In the Pilgrimage of Grace, it is clear that religious and economic discontents were inextricably mixed. Captain Cobbler in Lincolnshire and Captain Poverty in Cumberland were in the tradition of rural revolt from the days of Tyler to those of Captain Swing. The rebels' song reflected the connection:

> "In trouble and care,
> Where that we were
> In manner all bare
> Of our substance
> We found good bait
> At Churchmen gate,
> Without checkmate
> Or variance."

Among their demands was one that the abbeys which had been suppressed should be restored (clause 4 of the *Pontefract Articles*) and sixteen out of fifty-five suppressed religious houses were to some extent reoccupied. Aske argued that "the abbeys in the north parts gave great alms to poor men" and because "divers and many of the said abbeys were in the mountains and desert places" they helped travellers, particularly merchants, so that the decay of the Commonwealth threatened. They were "maintainers of sea walls and dykes, maintainers and builders of bridges and highways." Their contribution to agriculture and industry is well known.

Therefore, social distress may have been increased and the western rebels of 1549 were to advance strong arguments for the Church, including one that "the half part of the abbey lands and church lands" should be restored (clause 14). Yet it must be pointed out that the monasteries' contribution to the relief of the poor had been small and that the Dissolution added little directly to the problem of unemployment, although the new landlords tended to be rack-renters and sheep-farmers. Nearly all the monks and nuns were pensioned and in 1552, 1554 and 1562 investigations were held to see how effective these were. The last pensioned religious died in 1604. Pensions varied and could be as high as £100 a year (Fountains) while the ordinary monk obtained about £5. It was one example of Tudor paternalism which is often neglected.

Government action over the poor may have been stimulated by the Reformation because of the social upheaval rather than from any wish to replace Church by state charity. Poor Law administration had been continuous since medieval times, and Henry VII had taken action in line with the fourteenth-century measures concerning vagrancy. In 1495 provision was made for their treatment in the stocks and in 1504 this Act was strengthened to require justices to seek out vagabonds. However, those enactments had little effect, for the preamble to the next statute stated that "whereas in all places throughout this realm of England vagabonds and beggars have of long time increased and daily do increase in great and excessive numbers" the law should be stricter. An Act of 1531 ordered vagrants to be whipped, returned to their place of birth and put to work. A clear distinction was drawn between those licensed to beg (the aged and impotent poor) and rogues and the able-bodied who were forbidden to ask for alms. However, even this did not seem to be sufficiently severe and in 1547 another Act ordered vagabonds to be branded with a "V" and compelled to serve as a slave for two years. If he absconded, the vagabond was to be branded with an "S" and to be executed if a second attempt was made to escape. This Act was repealed in 1549 and the 1531 Act revived. The Act of 1572 provided for prison and the Act of 1598 continued that of 1531. Later, branding was reintroduced (1604) and transportation added to the list of punishments (1662). The magnitude of the problem induced the authorities to embark upon a scheme to reduce the number of vagrants by imitating the London example of the Bridewell. This had been established in 1552 for vagrants and discharged prisoners and in 1576 an Act provided for the erection of "houses of correction" in every county, where a store of materials were provided to set the poor at work, but these were not widely established and a further Act was passed in 1610. As penal establishments, they were "odious in the ears of the people," although some of them, such as that at Winchester, provided a rudimentary form of industrial training.

In dealing with the children, the aged and the sick, the Tudor Poor Law was, perhaps, a little less harsh. The example was set by municipalities and private charities and it is important to realise that these operated a far larger proportion of available relief than the state. London, because of its acute problem, was the first to organise. In 1533 officials were appointed to collect voluntary alms and in 1547 these were made into a compulsory poor rate. London established a series of institutions to deal with the poor: Christ's Hospital (1552) for the children; the Bridewell (1552) for vagrants; and St Thomas's and St Bartholomew's for the aged and the sick. In Bristol, Queen Elizabeth's Hospital (1596) for the poor children of the town was established and much later (1698) John Cary opened St Peter's Hospital for the poor. At Norwich a compulsory rate in 1549 was followed in 1570 by a Book of Orders establishing a bridewell, St Giles's Hospital for children and even family care units for young girls. Coventry ordered an enquiry into the poor in 1547 and at York, St George's House for the poor was established in 1569. In 1587 relief in the city was reorganised. In the later seventeenth century, municipal enterprise was regulated by creating corporations for the poor and these, following the example of Bristol (1696), were widespread.

National legislation began in 1536 which laid down many of the key principles which were to be built up into the code of practice known as the Old Poor Law, mistakenly attributed solely to the Act of 1601. Begging was forbidden except under licence and parishes were to organise the collection and distribution of alms. This fund was voluntary and in charge was the local clergyman. Able-bodied poor were divided into those willing to work (unemployed) and those unwilling (vagrants). Both were to be set to work and the parish was to help find work for them. Children between the ages of five and fourteen were to be apprenticed, particularly on farms. Although it has been claimed that this Act was revolutionary, it was essentially voluntary and religious, rather than secular, in orientation. Attempts were made to keep up this system, but they failed. In 1547 the clergy were to give "a godly and brief exhortation to their parishioners moving and exciting them to remember the poor people and the duty of Christian charity." In 1552 recalcitrant parishioners were to be reported to the Bishop, and some attempt to tighten administration was made by appointing two collectors to help the churchwardens. Elizabeth strengthened provisions again in 1563 by continuing the alms collectors and requiring justices to take over when the parish clergy had failed and levy a suitable rate. Licensed begging was to be allowed when the burden was too great for the parish.

Compulsion made its appearance in the Act of 1572, whereby a poor rate was introduced to be paid by the parish, assessed by the justices of the peace and collected by overseers of the poor. They were to hold office for one year and were compelled to serve as it was likely to be an unpopular post. Begging was forbidden, but seems to have been allowed to continue; perforce, when the rate was not collected it had to be allowed. Finally, the aged and impotent were to be registered and placed in fixed habitations. In 1576, when the houses of correction were established, the problem of the industrious poor was tackled. The aged and impotent were to be left in "abiding places." Vagabonds and those refusing work were placed in houses of correction and workhouses, "for setting the poor on work and for avoiding of idleness," were to be established. A stock of material, entrusted to the collectors or overseers, was to be made available for outdoor and indoor relief. The stock was raised by assessment, the use of legacies and the leasing of town property. Work was done in workhouses, by letting-out to clothiers, by the "roundsman" system of requiring householders directly to provide work, or by compulsory labour on the roads. Following the recrudescence of troubles in the famine and enclosure period of the 1590s, the government decided to codify the existing law, since sixteen statutes concerning the poor had been passed. The Act of 1598 was part of a policy which included Acts against overcrowding, enclosure, and for the encouragement of corn distribution. It was re-enacted in 1601 and strengthened by Acts in 1607 for the provision of a stock of materials and 1610 for houses of correction. These acts together formed the famous "spirit and intention of the 43rd of Elizabeth." They recur in the Poor Law Act of 1930 and were not finally abolished until 1948.

No new principle was introduced, apart from an administrative change whereby the duty of assessment was passed from the justices to the overseers. The justice of the peace now had enormous control over the everyday life of people. In 1555 the Highways Act had given him power to appoint Surveyors of Highways and to enforce labour on the roads. These measures were re-enforced in 1562 and 1586. An Act of 1495 and others of the 1550s had given the justice considerable power over wages and conditions of work and these were codified in the Statute of Apprentices of 1563. Thus, Poor Law provisions for setting men on work and putting children out as apprentices were already part of a justice's powers. The justice was liable to be inefficient, or, as an Act of 1489 had said, "by the negligence and misdemeaning, favour and other inordinate causes of the justices of the peace . . . the laws and ordinances made for the politic weal . . . be not duly executed." Thus, in 1621 Dekker complained that there had been no collection for the poor in many parishes for some years. The officials were local, untrained and incompetent, and although the Act allowed the assessment of rates over a hundred or county, this was scarcely ever applied. It is not difficult to criticise the administrative machinery but it needs to be judged in relation to other government measures and the provision of charity. Moreover, it is by no means certain that the administration was always ineffective as long as the Privy Council kept up pressure on the justices. Thus, in the north, commissions in 1542 and 1550 on the state of the border estimated there were 1,500 armed and able-bodied men in Redesdale and Tynedale. In 1557 the Council of the North issued Articles requiring the strict enforcement of the Poor Law including the appointment of overseers, and the provision of stock for work. Again, in 1574 the Council of the North was required to investigate the "oppression of the poor." In these activities, there were precedents for the activity of the Privy Council under the Stuarts.

The provisions of the Act summarised previous enactments. Children were to be apprenticed. A stock of materials and a workhouse were to be provided for the industrious poor. A poor rate was to be levied for the lame, impotent, blind and sick, who were to be accommodated if necessary in abiding places. Sturdy beggars were to be sent to houses of correction. In practice, the system provided for more outdoor than indoor relief, since only in the larger towns were provisions made for three separate institutions. Although the poor rate was levied, the amount of the national income which it took was small in a time of rising prices and population. Down to the Civil War, something like 7 per cent of national income went on the organised Poor Law. Private charity, as both Leonard and Jordan have stressed, played the key role.

The Poor Law Acts had all contained provisions for protecting charities and in 1601 the basis of the modern Charity Acts was laid. It was an age in which the flood of bequests and legacies which had formerly gone to the Church were channelled into direct gifts, almshouses, hospitals, apprenticeships and schools for the poor. Professor W. K. Jordan has shown that, in an area of one-third of England between 1500 and 1640, some £3 million was left for charitable institutions, one-third of which (with a capital of £750,000) have survived to the 1970s. It is easy to forget that much of this money still went directly for religious purposes, so that between 1580 and 1660 £70,267 was donated to lectureships for the preaching of God's Word. Estimates of the amount directly used for the poor vary, but the proportions involved may be seen by comparing the £12,000 given by the government and the £174,000 by private charity between 1560 and 1600.

Tudor paternalism was by no means lacking in education. The foundation of colleges at Oxford and Cambridge, the refounding of famous monastic schools, such as King's, Canterbury (1541), and the establishment under the Act of 1547 "of grammar schools to the education of youth in virtue and godliness" were part of the same royal concern which Henry VIII showed for London hospitals in the 1540s. Ridley persuaded Edward VI to found Christ's Hospital, which opened with 380 children in 1552. But the main educational developments of the time were based on acts of private charity, made possible by the growth of wealth—Peter Blundell of Tiverton left £40,000—and the existence of monastic buildings, such as those used for Repton when it was founded in 1557. The establishment of these schools, where both rich and poor were educated and where a high proportion of the middle and upper classes obtained an education, had a considerable influence on England's position in the sixteenth and seventeenth centuries. The spread of education coincided with the renaissance of English letters. It also was co-extensive with the rise of an inventive and rational spirit, which placed England in the forefront of scientific development by the 1660s. Latimer's "supplication that ye would bestow so much to the finding of scholars of good wits, of poor men's sons . . . in relieving scholars" was granted. Very often, the school was associated with another charitable institution, such as the "hospital and free grammar school" founded by a successful coal merchant, Thomas Sutton, in the London Charterhouse in 1611. Although it was true that these grammar schools based their curriculum on Latin grammar, English was taught at Oldham in 1611, for example, and Richard Mulcaster, the first headmaster of Merchant Taylors (1561–86) advocated the teaching of English grammar. Mulcaster was, however, in advance of his times in suggesting that dancing, football, wrestling and amateur dramatics should be included in the curriculum. The number of grammar schools has never been accurately determined, but, if a remote and mainly agricultural county such as Lancashire is taken as an example, the numbers increased as follows:

Table 14—Lancashire Grammar Schools

pre-1500	6
1500–58	12
1558–1603	12
1603–60	14

The number of schools in this county suggests a total of some 1,600 for the whole country, if one estimates 40 per county. Clearly some counties had less, although others, like Norfolk, had many more and the total excludes at least 20 schools in the City of London. A yeoman, John Lyon, founded Harrow in 1571. Rugby was founded by a member of the Grocers' Company, Laurence Sheriff, in 1567. Another member of the same company, Sir William Laxton, founded Oundle in 1566. Sutton Valence was founded by William Lambe, a cloth-worker. Peter Blundell established his school at Tiverton in 1604. It is difficult to date accurately the foundation of those schools, since they were planned in wills and not immediately created, or followed in places where a school-master had previously taken pupils. Thus, Manchester Grammar School was originally planned by a clothier, founded in 1515 by Hugh Oldham, Bishop of Exeter, and re-endowed in 1525.

Provision for the poor by means of private charity and public action extended in Tudor times to the diet of the people concerned. Tudor government showed an interest in both fish and wheat. Fishing was essential to national security, and the government took a close interest in the industry. Navigation laws, regulation of hours and wages, and measures to control the Newfoundland fleets were all part of a policy designed to keep a steady supply of trained sailors available for the navy. Before the Reformation, there had been days of abstinence from meat and in 1549 Edward VI's Pro-testant government continued the observance for Fridays, Saturdays and Lent. These provisions, it was hoped, might also reduce the demand for cattle meat. This law was enforced and in 1563 a London woman was pilloried for meat-eating in Lent. 1564 saw the re-enactment of the law, whereby every Wednesday, Friday,

Saturday and Lent day was to be observed as a fish day—Cecil's Fast, as it became known. The Privy Council took an active part in enforcing this law and in 1571 there was something like a series of national returns concerning its observance. However, the Act was impracticable. Wednesday was abandoned in 1585 and the penalities reduced in 1593. During the seventeenth century, a number of proclamations ordered their observance but by the 1670s contemporaries argued that fish days were no longer observed.

Control of wheat was more important and in this, as in other matters, municipal enterprise set the example, because London, it will be recalled, had established granaries early in the fifteenth century. From 1578 to 1665, when the granaries were destroyed, many of the City companies maintained them. James I put forward a proposal for a series of national granaries. Philanthropic individuals gave gifts of corn, although this was haphazard and subject to market forces. The government was forced to intervene in times of dearth, high prices and agricultural disturbances. There arose gradually a number of corn laws designed to encourage import and discourage export, although these had to be modified. In 1544 and 1549, the Privy Council required corn-hoarders to bring their crops to market. Export was placed under licence in 1534 and local commissions, under the Commission for Restraint of Grain, controlled export from 1571 until 1670 when the policy was reversed. Import was unpopular with growers and popular with the people and in the 1590s, for example, Burleigh permitted import, pointing out that "contrary to former times the realm is driven to be furnished with foreign corn." The government acted also to try and control the corn-dealers. Corn Dealers' Acts were passed in 1552 and 1563. In January 1587, the Privy Council issued a Book of Orders, whereby the justices were to intervene in the market for corn attending in the very market-place to see it sold at "convenient and charitable prices." The Book of Orders was reissued in 1594, 1605, 1608, 1622 and finally in 1630 (Orders for the Preventing and Remedying of the Dearth of Grain). It is difficult to assess the effect. Corn prices rose steadily, but it is likely that the Orders prevented even sharper rises in famine years such as the mid 1590s or late 1620s. They served to reassure the public. On the other hand, the regulations tended to drive corn off the market. Export was restrained from 1555 to 1663 by price regulations, and was not allowed again until the price was sufficiently low. As a result, dealers sold a little at a cheap price in order to obtain licence to export.

Regulation of the people extended to a network of industrial legislation on the production and labour sides. Sufficient has been said to indicate the general nature of paternalism. It rested on the twin powers of the justices and the Privy Council. It relied for enforcement on a host of laws, proclamations and court cases in the prerogative courts. Motives for this series of Acts were mixed. Some ministers, such as Wolsey, who "favoured the people exceedingly and especially the poor," were to some extent altruistic. Others, such as Cromwell and Burleigh, had the safety of the realm uppermost in their minds. There is evidence that Henry VIII, Edward VI and Elizabeth were genuinely and personally concerned with certain aspects of social policy, even if they did not understand the underlying economic factors. The Council of the North, told to hear "the petition of the poorest man against the richest," the work of the Court of Requests, the cases of the poorest brought before the Privy Council—all show that, in spite of administrative inefficiency and the inexorable operation of economic laws, Tudor paternalism was real and widespread. It was one of the misfortunes of the Stuarts that they let the policy decay and then revived it so forcefully that they drove the governing class into opposition. Yet the existence of paternalism helps to explain the adulation of a Henry VIII or a Charles I by humble people. Abandoned by the government after 1660, paternalism was taken up by the landed aristocracy. Until recently, it was a central part of English economic and social life. Yet it must not be forgotten that government charity under the Tudors and Stuarts never exceeded private efforts. Indeed, when compared with the eighteenth century, the amount of government concern seems to have dwindled gradually. It was only revived by the fresh possibilities of revolution produced by industrial change in the nineteenth century.

CHAPTER 8

THE MERCANTILIST PERIOD OF TUDOR AND EARLY STUART ENGLAND

AGRICULTURE: THE AGE OF THE GENTRY AND THE IMPROVING SMALL FARMER

Agricultural disturbance and the plight of many agricultural labourers reflected only one aspect of the rural scene. They were circumstances brought about by land hunger and its consequences—enclosure and expropriation of tenants by force and law. A 40 per cent increase in population before 1600 and a 30 per cent increase down to 1640 kept demand high. Prices rose; some more steadily than others. Wool prices fluctuated with the demands of industry and the availability of foreign imports. After a sharp rise in Early Tudor times, a fall and then a steady rise down to the end of Elizabeth's reign, they tended to fall by about half under the Early Stuarts. By the 1620s, there was evidence of reconversion to arable, and enclosure disturbances became rarer after the troubles of 1629 to 1631. By the 1640s, farmers in Herefordshire were complaining about the way in which Spanish wool imports had ruined them. Corn prices, helped by rises in population and government pressure to keep up supplies, increased steadily throughout the Tudor period, and this rise continued under the Stuarts, subject to setbacks, until they began to fall in the late 1630s. The average rose from 34s. 9½d. a quarter (1600 to 1610) to 43s. 0¾d. (1620 to 1630). Stimulated by the growth, particularly of the London market, and the increased propensity of consumers to buy food, cattle and dairy products, fruit, vegetables and hops together with industrial crops, such as flax and saffron, were all increasingly profitable. Rents could rise as much as sixfold in the first forty years of the century.

Attempts were made to extend the amount of cultivable land by enclosure of moor and forest and even more significantly by draining large areas of eastern England. The decline of the forests was brought about as much by demands for charcoal, ship- and house-building materials as by direct agricultural demand. As late as the 1690s, Gregory King estimated that 3 million acres of woodland remained and Charles Davenant commented that there had been more in 1600 than this. An example of the limitations were those imposed on the royal forests, which the Long Parliament ordered to be kept as they had been in 1621 after attempts to enforce the forest laws, where encroachment had taken place between 1634 and 1638. However, not all forests passed to agricultural use. King also estimated that there were 3 million acres of "forests, parks and commons" and emparking for deer-hunting was quite common. Pressure from the London food market initiated drainage developments. In the 1560s, Jacobus Acontius was responsible for the draining of the Lea Valley and during the 1620s, Canvey Island was reclaimed by Dutch engineers. The most spectacular development, however, was the addition of 380,000 acres out of a projected 400,000 acres of the great medieval fens to the agricultural land of the country. This project had been discussed in Elizabeth's reign and an Act passed in 1600 to facilitate it. A combination of circumstances led to the start of the project. A survey of Crown lands in 1607 suggested it might be profitable if the traditional drains were cleared to increase agricultural land. In 1618 the Commissioners for Sewers were instructed to proceed. Speculators such as Alderman Cockayne became interested when rents on the west Fen (Crown land) rose from £18 to £600 a year. James I called in Cornelius Vermuyden and Hatfield Chase was reclaimed with an increase of £1,200 in annual rents. Riots by commoners and marshmen in the Isle of Ely showed that agricultural improvement intruded upon common rights. Francis, Earl of Bedford and his son William, Duke of Bedford, decided that local landlords stood to gain by joining in these projects. In 1630 a Company of Adventurers was founded in which the Bedfords eventually invested at least £100,000. The plan was to drain the area around Ely. Bedford and his fellow Adventurers, such as the Earl of Lindsey, Sir Anthony Thomas and Sir John Monson, began to reap profits and in 1634 fourteen Adventurers constituted a company for the purpose of encouraging greater works. Vermuyden built the Old Bedford River from Earith to Denver Sluice, which was a canal 70 ft wide and 21 miles long. Twenty years later, the New Bedford Level was added to improve Ouse drainage.

Reaction to this activity was mixed. In the first place, it was resented by the local inhabitants. In 1638 the Bishop of Ely wrote to Laud about "a great grievance which concerns . . . all your Majesty's liege people inhabiting within the Isle of Ely," and about the Adventurers' "exaction." In 1637, 1638 and 1640, there were riots in the Ely and Wisbech areas and in 1638 Oliver Cromwell objected to the violation of commoners' rights. The strange life of the "Upland men" described by Camden in the *Britannia* had little to commend it, but turf, reed, withy and willow-cutting, fishing, eeling and netting of geese and duck provided a livelihood. The feudal rights of the commoners remained strongly entrenched and popular opposition was to be expected The local landowners found it difficult to keep the project in their own hands. After Cockayne, of the Skinners' Company of London, had put in an appearance, he was followed by others, such as Cornelius Drebbel and Sir Robert Killigrew. The latter was a Cornish courtier and aroused resentment from local owners such as Lord Lincoln and the Dymokes. The Bishop of Ely who retained feudal rights in the Palatinate of Ely and was anxious to increase the yield of his fisheries opposed the Adventurers. Charles gave in to pressure and in 1638 the Adventurers were replaced by the Undertakers, the chief of which was the King. However, this helped little, for financial troubles followed and with the outbreak of the Civil War, the fenmen retaliated with the backing of some of the local gentry. In power, Cromwell was less willing to see authority set aside. In 1649, with the help of Dutch and Scottish prisoners, the scheme went forward. The New Cut helped to change the course of the Welland, but it was not until the eighteenth century that the northern followed the southern Fens into extinction. By 1660 the Russell estates of the Bedfords no longer had a mortgage.

The consequences of this great change were many. An area 80 miles long and 30 miles broad was added to England for the purposes of agriculture. However, the marshland economy did not perish and during the Civil War former owners regained their land. Thus, in 1710, some 3,400 acres near Spalding were still in the hands of commoners. The drainage of the land lowered the peat level, thus exposing the area to dangerous flooding. Primitive bucket-and-chain methods of draining were of little use, and interest in hydraulics was stimulated. The earliest patent for a suction-pump was taken out in 1618, but this was to be developed in the mines rather than in agriculture. Manuals on the subject appeared, such as John Bates's *Mysteries of Art and Nature* (1634), which had reached its third edition in 1654, and Richard D'Acres's *Elements of Water Drawing* (1659). It was not until the 1660s that windmills began to make their appearance, together with improved drainage-wheels. The earliest use to which the land was put was for cattle. Later, however, it was used for arable as well. Coleseed was grown for the first time in England to make oil for lamps and to feed sheep. Oil-mills were to be found using water power at such places as Santoft in north Lincolnshire. Oats were grown in increasing quantities, so that the proportion of farmers growing them had risen from 1 in 11 (1630s) to 1 in 2 (1690s). Hemp for naval supplies and flax for rough garments and sailcloth were also grown. Changes in Lincolnshire, it has been suggested, acted as a model for other parts of the country.

Since these new lands did not add substantially to output before the Restoration, the increased yield of crops and stock came from the improvement of agricultural technique. The pressures of the market and the smallness of many holdings compelled farmers to take a more active interest in improvements. Measured and surveyed, their lands became a matter of profit for the yeoman and gentleman, driven by rising prices and standards of living to increase his profit. Limited though enclosure and the consequent improvements were, the period 1500 to 1640 was "profoundly disturbed by the conflict between those who wished to preserve, and those who sought to destroy the traditional methods of common-field cultivation." Enclosure for arable and consolidation of holdings were seen as fundamental to this change, both by improvers and owners of strips and common land who opposed change. Thus, Tusser wrote

"The country enclosed I praise
The other delighteth not me."

He argued that improved methods would result and, in this, he was supported by Sir Thomas Fitzherbert, who argued that land which was enclosed would double its value. Gervase Markham in *The English Husbandman* (1613) claimed that rents rose more rapidly on enclosed properties, and the plea that enclosure was of benefit was kept up by later writers. Thus, John Blith wrote *A Vindication of the Considerations concerning Common Felds and Enclosures* (1656). Even the opponents of enclosure had to agree that it had beneficial effects and the *Discourse of the Common Weal* said that farmers "in several were better than those in common." John Norden also claimed that enclosed land was worth twice as much and, on one Somerset manor at Porlock, this was so. Needless to say, those who enclosed made exaggerated claims for their improvements. Claims that yield increased from 6 to 16 bushels per acre have now been reduced to a rise from $8\frac{1}{4}$ to 11 bushels an acre. Fleece-weights of sheep improved from an average of about 1·4 lb per sheep in medieval times to about 2 lb by the middle of the seventeenth century. In some cases the yield was as high as 7 lb and this compares very favourably with the average of 3–5 lb in the middle of the eighteenth century. Carcase weights of meat also improved. The enclosed farm encouraged the farmer to diversify, to experiment and even to revolutionise. It freed him from the three-field system where, according to Mantoux, "landlords and tenants were equally ignorant and sunken in routine." By giving greater security of tenure, it encouraged investment, and by en-couraging mixed farming, it helped to improve production for the market.

Thus, in spite of the rebellions of Tudor times and vehement opposition in 1607 and 1629–31, enclosure continued in Stuart England. In spite of protests about the fate of commons in the Parliament of 1621, that of 1624 repealed the enclosure statutes and attempts in 1656 and 1664 to reintroduce them failed. Blith pointed out that commoners' opposition could be met by providing for their needs by regulated stints, but this was rarely done. Protest continued such as Powell's *Depopulation Arraigned* (1636), the pamphlets of the early 1640s, like *London and the Country Car-bonadoed*, or Moore's *The Crying Sin of England* (1653). Govern-ment policy was not at all clear. The reforming party wanted to curb enclosures as part of their social activities and in November 1630 new enclosures were to be levelled, unless they did not involve the decay of farms, and the justices were to report on changes over the previous two years. In Warwickshire alone, 2,000 acres had been enclosed. In 1632, 1635 and 1636, there were commissions on depopulation, but the policy was not effective. Courtiers such as Christopher Villiers (Buckingham's brother), who enclosed land round Melksham and Chippenham, had no wish to surrender their gains. Thus, wrote Clarendon, "the revenues of too many of the Court consisted principally in enclosures and improvements of that nature which he [*Laud*] still opposed passionately except they were founded upon law . . . and so he did a little too much coun-tenance the commission for depopulation." In fact this was a biased landowner's viewpoint. Government policy was unpopular because it was ineffective. It annoyed the gentry and it drove the people to desperation. One writer has gone so far as to suggest that extreme discontent, fostered by the failure of Stuart benevolence, ushered in the Civil War. At least it was responsible for continuing agrarian troubles, exemplified by Levellers and Diggers.

In order that those who were able to should profit from the enclosure of their lands, knowledge of agricultural techniques was necessary and although the enthusiastic John Norden complained that many farmers "only shape their courses as their father did," the impact of new farming literature in an age of increasing literacy and printing should not be underestimated. Farming literature re-veals the topics as well as the level of interest among farmers. It shows the possibilities, even if it does not always illustrate the conditions. In the 1520s began a series of some eighty or ninety books dealing with agriculture which swept away the medieval tracts and went through numerous editions. Sir Anthony (or Alexander)

FitzHerbert, a Derbyshire horse-breeder, was the first in this new school of writers with his *Book of Husbandry* (1523) and his *Book of Surveying* (1539). These two branches of agricultural science were developed by the other two most well-known writers on the subject. Thomas Tusser, a courtier who retired to his estates at Brantham in Suffolk, wrote *Hundred Points of Husbandry* in 1557, and although this was in verse and thus found it difficult to be practical, it was reissued as *Five Hundred Points* in 1573. By 1600 the book had reached its thirteenth edition. John Norden, the Crown Surveyor and an important map-maker, produced *The Surveyor's Dialogue* in 1608 These books were general in theme and did little beyond advocate the advantages of enclosure and existing practices, such as the use of different varieties of seed. Other writers became more specialised. Sir Hugh Plat's *A New and Admirable Art of Setting of Corn* (1600) and Edward Maxey's *New Instructions of Ploughing and Setting of Corn* (1601) dealt with the most profitable aspect of farming, but less significant branches of the industry were not ignored. Reginald Scot wrote *A Perfect Platform of a Hop Garden* (1574). He lived at Bethersden in Kent where hops had been grown since the 1530s, and he was also the author of a notable book on witchcraft. In the neighbouring county of Sussex, Leonard Mascall of Lewes wrote the first work on the scientific breeding of cattle (1587) which soon went through six editions. Thomas Hill wrote on gardening and bee-keeping: Lord Cobham on viticulture.

The Early Stuart period saw no slackening in the number of works produced. There was, however, a tendency to revert to more general works. Gervase Markham's *The English Husbandman* (1613) and *A Way to Get Wealth* (1625) set the trend which was followed, although much more brilliantly, by Walter Blith, author of *The English Improver* (1649) and *The English Improver Improved* (1652), and by Samuel Hartlib, a famous religious writer and associate of Cromwell, who wrote *The Legacy of Husbandry* (1665), and *The Complete Husbandman* (1659). These works prepared the way for the more scientific works of the post-Restoration epoch, such as those of Worlidge, Houghton, Fortrey and Yarranton. By far the most significant writers, however, were Barnaby Goodge and Sir Richard Weston. Goodge, a Lincolnshire farmer, translated the works of a Dutch writer on agricultural matters and, although confused, this work contained the details of the more intensive methods of farming in the Low Countries. North Holland was perhaps one of the few truly industrial regions of Europe. Flanders was still a great trading and manufacturing centre. Population far exceeded demand, so that production of cash crops and intensive methods had long been in use. It was Sir Richard Weston's *Discourse on the Husbandry used in Brabant and Flanders* (1645) that first made these methods more clearly known, together with the influx of immigrants, particularly those connected with Vermuyden's schemes in eastern England. The improvers tended to be discontented with their influence. Blith complained about "the scandalous prejudice among many of you against new projections" and a farmer who "will toil all his days . . . rather than he will cast how he may improve." Yet other contemporaries saw matters differently. One remarked how the Civil War period saw farmers fall "to such an industry and caused such an improvement as England never knew before . . . pushed on by the industry and indefatigable pains of Mr Hartlib and some others."

Improvements influenced the whole range of farming activities and although it is convenient to divide these into arable and pastoral, it should be remembered that between the two there was the important connection that sheep manure improved wheat yield. Convertible husbandry, that is alternating wheat growing and pasture for sheep and cattle over periods of three to six years was an extension of the fold-course system sometimes used in East Anglia. Fodder crops enabled the ground to be replenished by the operation of the nitrogen cycle, so that wheat yield improved as well as the quality of meat. Thus, although agricultural improvement was based on corn-growing, each improvement in that branch stimulated a further move from starch to protein in the diet of the people. Fynes Morrison compared English diets most favourably with those of other countries and foreign observers, such as the Duke of Stettin, noticed how the English rejected inferior parts of the meat, such as the feet or entrails. Although rye and barley were the normal bread grains here as in Europe, "citizens and gentlemen eat most pure white bread." Travelling abroad, the English were surprised to find that people lived on "grass herbs and roots." Improvement to provide this diet was so widespread that even the traditional three-field areas were affected. It was possible to carry out folding with temporary fences and to grow a root crop and this was done in counties as far apart as Leicestershire and Sussex.

Arable improvements involved three changes designed to improve yield per acre. Attempts were made to distinguish the various types of seeds, and Harrison claimed that this was common. At least twelve varieties of seed were known to Fitzherbert and there is evidence of experimentation. The need to improve the yield of corn was very great indeed; London's demand rose fivefold between 1570 and 1638, and the grain ships came from King's Lynn and even as far away as Scotland. It was estimated later in the seventeenth century that 8 million acres of arable land yielded 70 million bushels a year, and the yield per acre was increased. Improvements in rotation were a second way of improving yield. At first, Goodge merely advocated ploughing up, but before long the idea of ley grasses, clover, coleseed, flax or saffron being grown began to spread and then the use of root crops, such as turnips. Water meadows helped to improve the yield by providing early grass in mid March. These were developed in Herefordshire as early as 1604 and were common in Wiltshire by the late 1630s. Thirdly, by deep ploughing and the use of various fertilisers, yield could be as much as doubled. Manure was obtained by folding sheep, which required 1,000 sheep to manure an acre in one night and was therefore by no means easy to obtain. Various substitutes were tried. In Devon, there was denshiring or spreading the ashes of burnt turf. Sedge from rivers was used in the Thames Valley, seaweed in Cornwall, and ash, marl and lime over a wide area, including Wiltshire, Berkshire and Shropshire. It is not at all clear whether these arable improvements had much effect, for, in spite of the rising wheat prices, pasture remained more valuable per acre than arable. In the 1650s, the difference between them was put at 14s. 6d. and 4s. 6d. an acre respectively. Some farmers adopted the new methods. Robert Loder of Harwell in Berkshire, whose accounts for the period of 1610–20 have been published, Henry Best of Yorkshire, and Sir Richard Weston of Sutton Place, Surrey, were enthusiastic improvers, but the ready acceptance of root crops and fertilisers was still awaited by the agricultural writers of the 1660s.

Pastoral changes were more spectacular, although in this sphere there has been a tendency to emphasise sheep rather than cattle as the mainstay of pastoral improvement. Sheep-farming was profitable for about a hundred years and new landlords who took monastic properties in the sales of the 1540s hastened into sheep-rearing. By the 1580s, a trend which had been dicernible even earlier on the Bacon and FitzWilliam estates to reduce flocks was gathering speed, and with the seventeenth-century fall in prices, sheep-farming was badly hit. In 1623–4 Sir Thomas Temple of Stowe sold his flocks and returned to arable farming. Yet the number of sheep seems to have risen from about 5 million in the 1480s to about 11 million in the 1680s, and allowing for the rise of population, this is a sizeable increase, part of which is explained by the increasing popularity of mutton for which flocks on the newly drained fenlands were reared. There were some examples of attempts to deliberately improve sheep breeds, such as those by John Spencer of Althorp, and Richard Carew maintained that

Cornish sheep had been greatly improved during the sixteenth century. However, English wool began to decline in quality, because richer pastures produced coarser wool, at a time when the market was becoming more specialised. English wools were short, but the worsted and new draperies needed long wool and resorted to imports. Traditional enclosure areas, where wool-yields per sheep had been highest, experienced a decline and new areas such as Hampshire and Sussex became more prominent.

Cattle were, however, the most significant gainers from agricultural improvement. Their importance was twofold. They provided the basis of our second largest industry by value—leather-making. Regulated in 1563 to 1664, this large industry was concentrated on the Midland towns, where a fifth of Leicester workers was involved in its manufacture. Birmingham rose in its importance during the seventeenth century and Sheffield and London were other centres. In Bermondsey and Southwark, there were eighty tanneries. Cattle also provided food products. Dairy cattle were important in Wiltshire, Somerset and Gloucestershire. Cheese-making was widespread in Cheshire, where Camden mentioned Uttoxeter cheese market, and in Somerset, Oxfordshire and Suffolk. Meat was produced in Northamptonshire, Leicestershire and closer to London. Cattle moved towards London at 8 miles a day to be bought at Smithfield and fattened by local graziers according to Norden. Gregory King estimated there were 4·5 million cattle in the kingdom and the consumption of meat at the expense of other agricultural products was the burden of Cooke's criticism in *Unum Necessarium* (1648). There is little evidence of cattle-breeding in spite of Mascall's book, and lactations of 200 gallons do not show any startling improvement. It has recently been estimated that cattle accounted for 30 per cent of total farm incomes and the great fairs of the Midlands, such as Rugby and Birmingham, became famous. It might also be noticed in this connection that pork remained popular, with 2 million pigs in the country and that this meat was supplemented by deer, hares and rabbits. Horse-breeding had started under the aegis of the first two Stuarts with the work of Sir John Fenwick of Wallington. The Verney family bred horses and used shire horses instead of oxen, although that particular change had scarcely started.

Hops, vegetables, fruits and herbs varied diet and established local centres of production. Market gardening and the ordinary garden were co-extensive in their growth and techniques applied by the gardeners of the nobility could be used in humbler walks of life. Thus, Charles I's gardener, John Tradescant, introduced the willow and through the gardens of Osborne at Oxford or Ingram at York, new fruits such as damsons were introduced. Transplanting was discussed in Norden's *The Art of Gardening* in 1640. Some counties, such as Gloucestershire "that rich and fruitful gardenshire," were renowned for their fruit and one authority claimed there were over 500 different varieties of apple available. John Shermenden of Surrey was producing a wide variety of fruits, including raspberries and gooseberries, by 1637. Market gardening, first introduced by the Huguenots, spread rapidly and the Society of Market Gardeners was incorporated in 1605. Although the Thames Valley was pre-eminent, vegetable cultivation spread to Kent and Suffolk, where, from Aldeburgh and Sandwich respectively, onions, leeks, lettuces, cauliflowers, carrots, and turnips were brought to London. In 10-acre gardens, at such places as Fulham, artichokes were growing by the 1620s. The potato had been brought from America in the 1580s but was not widely in use. Although mead had been replaced by beer, honey was still the chief sweetener and Durham and Hampshire both claimed to produce the best. Beer made with hops was now brewed in Suffolk, Essex, Kent, Sussex and Herefordshire and by 1701, 3·4 million gallons were being produced yearly.

Changes in landownership, consequent upon the Dissolution of the Monasteries and the spread of enclosure, together with the shifts in agriculture produced by the rising demand for food, particularly from London, and for increasing variety, combined with the results of price changes for such products as wool, mutton, beef, hides, wheat, barley and oats and the demands of industry for coleseed, hops, flax, hemp or saffron to produce a profit-conscious yeomanry and gentry. The effects of these changes on the workers and consumers have been examined and it remains to examine their effect on the producers. Sociology was one by-product of the changes in agriculture. Observations on the varieties of status and the changing social composition of the nation became more frequent. Attempts were made to quantify these changes and even to evaluate them by reference to factors such as social mobility. William Harrison and Thomas Wilson were the earliest in a group of writers which culminated in the work of Edward Waterhouse. Moreover, the changes were so obvious and widespread that the earliest English biographers, such as Aubrey, North and Clarendon, had something to say about the changing composition of the landed classes. Others even more remotely removed from an understanding of economics, such as Richard Baxter, felt they had to comment, for it was a status-ridden age. All the estimates of these writers are statistically inadequate, but they have some bearing on the post-Restoration calculations of men such as King, Petty and Davenport. It is important, however, to realise that the finality so often desired by modern analysts of social change, particularly Marxist theorists, cannot obtain sufficient substantiation from the available evidence. Too much has already been said about these important changes which is little more than the building of theories on ideas, and a number of historians have been involved for years in the greatest dispute in modern history. This is the issue concerning the relationship of capitalism and the Reformation, which in this country has been concentrated more and more closely on the matter of the relative position of nobility and gentry in the social hierarchy as a result of the economic changes. This has considerable bearing on the political events of the time and the question will be discussed later when considering the causes of the Civil War, in so far as they were economic. At this point we are concerned with establishing what the major social changes were.

It was the golden age of the small landowner, particularly if he was a yeoman and also if he was a freeman, leaseholder, or copyholder with sufficient legal protection. Yeomen, such as Adam Martindale and Adam Eyre in the 1640s, covered a wide range of the community—between the poorest labourers and cottagers and those with pretensions to gentility. They varied considerably in income, so that "a yeoman of Kent with one year's rent could buy out the gentleman of Wales . . . and a lord of the North Country." In theory, a man had to have a £2 freehold to be considered a yeoman, but the term was applied to anyone with between £40 and £500 a year. The Cumberland "statesman," with an income of £50, was considered a yeoman as much as the famous Kentish yeoman, who could have between £400 and £1,200 a year. King calculated in the 1680s that there were 180,000 yeomen, Davenant that there were 160,000, so that there does seem to have been general agreement at the time as to who constituted the yeomanry. They were held in high regard, for it "is an estate of people almost peculiar to England," and they were regarded as the backbone of the nation's defences. Between the yeoman and the gentry stretched a difficult boundary to define. Throughout the Tudor and Early Stuart period, the demands of yeomen for higher status were reinforced by the pressure to buy land by successful London merchants or lawyers, and by the struggle to obtain local or national office which would give added prestige and increased income. "Gentility is nothing but ancient riches," said Burleigh, and this was to some extent true.

Wilson estimated in 1600 that there were 16,000 gentry and 500 knights whose incomes ranged between £500 and £2,000. Gentry incomes, he maintained, were between £500 and £1,000, and one writer has pointed out that, if the average income is put as low as £300 and it is estimated that half of them held office bringing in an additional £500,000, the total wealth of the gentry was £5·3 million. The remark made in 1628, that the House of Commons might buy out the Lords three times over, was an indication that the gentry were considered to be the wealthy section of the landed classes. An analysis of the members of the Long Parliament of 1640 gives the result that 60 per cent had incomes over £1,000 and some of the leading gentry, such as Hampden, reached an annual income of £3,000. Court gentry managed to supplement their income by holding office at Whitehall, but the country gentry had ample opportunity to exert influence at a local level. Thus, among the members of the Long Parliament, there were 70 Deputy-Lieutenants, 122 sheriffs, 219 justices of the peace, and 250 members of local commissions of one kind or another. As a class, the gentry rose into fame and prominence and the numbers of them who were able to become peers, with the lavish creations of James I and Charles I, was considerable. The Russells, Seymours, Bacons, Dudleys, Cecils, Herberts and Cavendishes were examples of a class that took advantage of the sale of monastic lands, served under the Crown, became gentry and then peers. Cromwell, Wriothesley, Paulet, Petrie, Paget, Carew and many others repeated the pattern. The gentry were recruited from many different places, or, as Ben Jonson said, "many great men were rocked in mean cradles." The purchase of land became the sign of respectability. Administrators such as Cranfield, projectors like Middleton, merchants like Sir Baptist Hickes, Sir Arthur Ingram or Sir William Cockayne, or lawyers such as Bacon and Coke sought to be numbered among the gentry. The Royal College of Heralds founded in 1485, started its visitations in 1566, and the right to bear arms was anxiously sought. Yet, in spite of this evidence for a rising gentry, it is important not to allow the gentry to be "transfigured into a bourgeoise." In order to be gentry, a man had to be recognised as such in his local community. Mere landownership does not qualify a man to be regarded as gentry, and Professor R. H. Tawney made a mistake in the 1940s, when he classed yeomen merchants and lawyers thrusting upwards as the gentry, merely because they held land.

The impact of this new class on the community was considerable. In order to accommodate the wants of the new group, there was a rise in the numbers of the professional classes. Between 1590 and 1640, the number of lawyers increased by two-thirds. For example, the number of attorneys at Common Pleas rose from 313 in 1578 to 1,383 in 1633. There was a rise in demand for education, and schools to provide for the gentry, akin to that in mid-Victorian times generated by the new industrialists. 185 schools were founded between 1501 and 1601, and 186 more between 1601 and 1651. These schools contained both gentry and the sons of the yeomen, for, as Cranmer said in 1541 when an attempt was made to restrict entry to King's, Canterbury, "if the gentleman's son be apt for learning, let him be admitted; if not apt, let the poor man's child that is apt enter in his room." As a result, there was a rise in the teaching profession, and famous headmasters, such as Nicholas Udall and William Mulcaster, made their appearance. There was pressure on the universities to found new colleges and provide for the gentry and poor by means of scholarships As Harrison said, "gentlemen or rich men's sons often bring the Universities into much slander for standing upon their reputation . . . they ruffle and roist it out." New statutes for Oxford and Cambridge were drawn up and college authority strengthened. Cambridge had 1,500 students by 1586. Merchant Taylors' School provided the Watts scholarship, which sent 83 boys to university between 1571 and 1636 and these included future bishops who rose from the ranks of tradesmen. In 1644–5 the school register shows six sons of yeomen at the school. The social composition of the university is shown by an examination of Gonville and Caius register for 1600–9. 116 entrants were sons of the nobility and gentry, 65 sons of merchants and 62 sons of those of smaller means. There was an increasing demand for household chaplains and by the 1620s the universities were turning out a hundred ordinands surplus to the Church's requirements, who found work as tutors, chaplains or lecturers in the houses of gentlemen These developments were once taken to indicate a rise of a specific middle class when taken together with an increase in the numbers of merchants and financiers. However, in an age when land and birth were of importance, the main aim of the new class was to serve the nobility and gentry or to enter their ranks. The wealth of the gentry supported the new professional class and intermarriage was common. Sons of the gentry returned to trade and entered the professions, so that there was more social fluidity than irreconcilable rivalry.

Creation of a new professional class to serve the landed gentry and not the Church was one important consequence of the rise of the gentry. Another was the building revolution of the period 1540 to 1640 and the rise in social comforts which accompanied it. Harrison referred to the change, saying "the ancient manors and houses of our gentlemen are yet and for the most part of strong timber . . . howbeit such as be lately builded are commonly either of brick or of hard stone . . . their rooms large and comely." Tudor and Jacobean architecture, with some notable exceptions, continued the use of Gothic but adapted it to domestic use, for it was not an age of church building. In the vernacular of hundreds of town and country houses, it became the national style as masons and others turned from the service of the Church to the new landed classes. Although the names of a number of architects, such as John Shute, John Thorpe and John Smithson, together with drawings and evidence of visits to Italy to study the new "renaissance" influences, indicate the rise of the architects' profession, this had still not fully developed at the end of the seventeenth century Most of the smaller buildings were the anonymous work of masons skilled in Gothic and with little knowledge of the Classical orders. By James I's reign, the ideas of Vitruvius and Palladio were becoming known, but apart from the largest houses, there was little departure from the forms of Perpendicular. Interior design made considerable advances with the development of a set of rooms and the creation of a staircase instead of a central hall.

Tudor and Jacobean architecture retained in outline a number of medieval features, so that although castles were no longer fashionable and Thornbury (1511–21) was never completed, crenellation and moats were favoured in some manor houses Larger manor houses had three basic patterns: a simple hall with additions to one side or the other; a court with wings, sometimes in the shape of an H or an E; and a quadrangle. Windows were small and mullioned in stone, although by Jacobean times wooden frames were in use. Diamond-paned glass was used until plate glass was developed in Elizabeth's reign The largest and most "renaissance"-featured houses then had large windows. Externally, the roofs were marked by crenellations, corbel patterns (steps), curved Dutch gables, dormer windows and profusions of chimneys, both external and springing from the roof. Ornamentation varied and included elaborate woodwork and plaster interiors and, externally, the use of bricks and beams in various patterns. Stone was used in the stone belts, so that Gloucestershire, Northamptonshire and Yorkshire are profuse in these. Brick became universally popular, worked in herring-bone patterns, while half-timbered houses were built, particularly in Cheshire and Lancashire with their "black-and-white" designs. The larger houses were inclined to include a profusion of Classical ornaments, including pilasters, pediments and evidence of the three "orders," but these did not conceal the basic Gothic concept of an irregular outline, and even if the Gothic arch was flattened out of existence, the windows retained a Perpendicular look. Even the ordinary farmers were able to afford to rebuild. In the north, bleak peel towers gave way to stone mansions surrounded by sycamores. In the West Midlands, numerous timbered farmhouses were built and in the southern counties, tile-hung Kentish farmhouses were popular. Town houses followed the same patterns.

The great rebuilding was a sign of landed wealth, but it is significant that it affected nearly all income groups. Castles declined, so that Robert Reyce the antiquary could remark "here is in Suffolk no castle fully standing, or at least none fortified and defensible." Royal palaces, such as Nonesuch and Hampton Court, St James's and Whitehall, replaced residence in the Tower or Windsor. But the nobility were quite capable of finding the capital to erect the Elizabethan and Jacobean houses whose size and magnificence indicate either sufficient wealth or too much indebtedness. Three main periods of development may be distinguished. There was a period of predominantly Gothic building, where castles such as Thornbury were started and houses still had a medieval great hall such as that at Hampton Court, completed in 1526. Manor houses such as Compton Wyngates (1528) or Hengrave Hall (1538) exhibited more complicated features. Elizabethan buildings were a compromise between Gothic and Renaissance features. Thus, Penshurst (1570–85) and Knole (1570) in Kent were predominantly Gothic. Charlecote (1558), Longleat (1567), Wollaton (1580–8) and Hardwick Hall (1590–7) exhibit more Renaissance features. By Jacobean times, these had come to predominate in such buildings as Audley End (1603–16), Ingestre (1601) and Hatfield (1611). If the gentry were able to create large numbers of country residences, the nobility were able to build London residences along the Strand.

The rise of the gentry was reflected in other ways. Numerous books on how to be a gentleman made their appearance, of which Henry Peacham's *The Complete Gentleman* (1622) was perhaps the most famous, but there were others such as Richard Braithwaite's *The English Gentleman*. Although the gentry were prepared to apprentice their sons in trade, and in Gloucestershire there were "gentlemen clothiers," attempts were made to maintain social distinctions. The gentry took up the pursuits of duelling, hunting and foreign travel in order to equate themselves with the nobility. On the one hand, the right to hunt over others' lands was asserted; on the other, estates were emparked and laws passed to control the rights of inferiors. Clark was wrong to suggest that the infamous game laws developed under Charles II. They began in the reign of James I. Pride was taken in possessions, such as the miniatures of Nicholas Hilliard, or a new garden laid out in the Dutch manner with clipped yew hedges. Camden referred to Buxton as a resort for "great numbers of nobility and gentry" in the 1580s and Shrewsbury's development of that town was followed by that of Tunbridge

Wells by Lord North after 1605. Office under the Crown, a seat in Parliament, marriage with the nobility—all were much sought after. Inevitably, not all the gentry could gain from these changes. The limited nature of agricultural production and restricted number of official posts led to fierce local disputes. Perhaps it does not do justice to divide the gentry into Court and county, for nearly all Court gentry resided, and were forced by the early Stuarts, to do so, in the country and the holding of office under the Crown in the country was an equal cause of local friction. With the recovery of the nobility under the Early Stuarts and the slackening pace of economic change, combined with heavy taxation and government policies of interfering with local politics through the Privy Council, a number of the gentry became disgruntled. Such men might be described as country-house radicals. Few of them reached Parliament, so that of the 233 Independents in the Long Parliament, only 63 were lesser gentry. In some counties very few held office, so that in Yorkshire, out of 679 gentry only 22 held salaried posts. Yet far from living in the poorest counties the less well-off gentry were resident in the richer counties, where competition was fierce and the status of gentleman more difficult to acquire. The poorer gentry of the west and Wales (where "you can sooner find fifty gentlemen of £100 a year than five of £500") were for the king. The more money-conscious gentry of Yorkshire and the eastern counties were divided.

In the rise of the gentry, most stood to gain from "those roaring days" when "the annual rental on some estates climbed to a third of what those estates had sold for a few decades earlier." There was also a sizeable minority who did not gain. Whether the rise in landholding and real income was the cause of a redistribution of income, or merely a symptom of an overall growth in the national product, is a more complicated question. If there was little conscious antagonism to the nobility or by the nobility for the gentry, was there, nevertheless, a shift of economic power? This broader question will be discussed in connection with the Civil War. Here it is noticed that the locality mattered most. Whether a man was gentry or not depended on this factor and the means of advancement. Impoverished gentry in the west fought for the king because by western standards they were not poor. Oliver Cromwell and John Hampden, both wealthy men, fought for "grievances against the property of our goods" because the pressures on them were greater and in the struggle to maintain their social position, actions on the king's part could have serious repercussions. In part at least, the Civil War was fought to preserve the social dignity and "degree" of the gentry, who had profited from agricultural change, suffered economic hardships in the late 1630s, and had no wish to loose a penny either to Charles's tax gatherers or to Laud's tithe collectors.

THE DEVELOPMENT OF OVERSEAS TRADE

The early part of the Tudor period saw the restoration and expansion of England's trade with Europe and, until the commercial collapse of 1551, the main trading interest lies in Europe and more particularly with the cloth trade. Protected by the monopoly of the Merchant Adventurers and helped by international agreements, cloth exports rose spectacularly.

Table 15—Cloth Exports, 1460–1550

1460	38,000
1480	66,900
1509	84,700
1530	102,000
1538	118,000
1542	99,000
1550	133,000

Although there were small depressions during this period (in 1527 to 1528, 1542 and 1547, for example), the trend was upward. Our main European market was the Low Countries but trade with France and Spain also developed. Most of the cloth trade was concentrated not only in the hands of the Merchant Adventurers but also in the port of London. Over 90 per cent of cloth exports were sent from there and this led to strong provincial opposition from towns as far away as Exeter, and to heated attacks on the Merchant Adventurers' monopoly. Concentration on one product and dependence on one market was a dangerous situation and in 1551 there was a serious collapse of the cloth trade, so that exports fell from 85,000 cloths in 1552 to 61,000 in 1562.

The consequences of the collapse were very great. A search for new markets began and various companies, such as the Muscovy and Eastland Companies, were established in part at least to break the Adventurers' monopoly. Due to a series of political and other difficulties the Adventurers were forced to move from Antwerp and settle in various German and Dutch towns. Their position was constantly under attack by "interlopers" and they ceased to have an absolute monopoly, particularly in areas further afield, such as the Mediterranean. Renewed attention was given to the problem of the finishing of cloth, but the industry never made a sufficient adjustment. The rise of the Dutch finishing industry, which took the profits from producing the best finished cloths, became a serious menace and neither the breaking of the Hanseatic League's power in the Baltic by 1598, nor the expansion of cloth exports to the Mediterranean and the colonies, was able to save the trade from a slow decline.

Yet there is a danger that interest in Tudor and Early Stuart trade may be diverted away from the European markets and the cloth trade and this would distort the picture. There was a decline in the wool trade, which had ceased to be of much importance by the time that the staple at Calais was lost in 1558. England became a wool-importer in the seventeenth century, producing the so-called Spanish cloths as a result. The cloth trade recovered, in spite of stops of trade in 1564, 1569 and 1576, and this recovery was mainly in European markets, not in the new markets which Trevelyan once maintained stood "in place of that commerce with the Netherlands and France." The foundation of the Merchant Adventurers of Exeter in 1558 to strengthen trade with France might be cited as one example; the European companies were another. By 1606 exports had risen to 120,000 cloths from London, which then controlled 93 per cent of the trade. Calculations made in 1600 show that, of the 105,000 cloths exported that year, 75,000 went to the Merchant Adventurers' staples in Germany and the Low Countries, 12,000 to the Baltic and 6,500 to the Levant.

Cloth exports rose to a new peak of 127,000 cloths in 1614 but thereafter began a long and serious decline. The attempt of James I to follow progressive opinion and break the monopoly of the Merchant Adventurers by creating a new one for Alderman Cockayne was the starting point of the difficulties, but the real causes were the technical deficiencies of the English industry in the face of Dutch competition, the collapse of the Merchant Adventurers, the great European wars and accompanying currency upheaval, and the closing of various markets by the Baltic powers. By 1640, exports had fallen to 45,000 cloths. By the 1630s, depression, which had occurred in 1614 and 1621–3, was regarded as chronic and after 1636, with the outbreak of plague and the emigration of skilled workers for higher wages or safer places of Puritan worship, internal difficulties were added to external pressures. The commission enquiring into the cloth trade in 1638 produced a very gloomy picture. Yet this should not be exaggerated. For example, the better-quality Spanish cloths rose as a proportion of exports from 3,000 in 1628 to 14,000 in 1640 and thus the fall in value of cloth exports may have been less than that of its volume. Moreover, the proportion of the cloth trade in English hands increased. It was estimated that 60,000 cloths were exported by foreigners in the 1540s and only 5,000 by 1610, although this continued to arouse the keenest antipathy against the Dutch as the main carriers.

The period of Henry VII's reign, and to some extent his policies, forwarded the revival in trade which had been discernible from the late 1460s and during his reign the yield from the customs rose from £33,000 to £40,000 and the cloth trade experienced a 60 per cent increase in exports. The most important parts of Henry's policy concerned the Antwerp market and his dealings with the Merchant Adventurers. After a three-year trade war, the Magnus Intercursus of 1496 granted the English very favourable rights and these were confirmed in 1499. Following further disputes and the shipwreck of the ruler of the Netherlands in England, an even more favourable agreement (Malus Intercursus) was signed in 1506, but this led to a glut and in 1507 it was rescinded in favour of the earlier treaty. The Merchant Adventurers took advantage of their prosperous position to increase fees and to restrict the rights of entry. Fines were raised to £20 in 1496, but Henry opposed the move and they were restrained by statute in 1504; the renewed Charter of 1505 fixed the entry fine at £5. Although heavy entrance fees, including some of a hundred marks, were charged, it seems that they remained generally low and there were 120,000 members in the 1540s. The company was accused of making excessive profits, but although this was true, the ordinary profits were not often more than 15 per cent. The criticisms of the Adventurers which bear more weight are allowing the market to be glutted, charging high prices for a low-quality commodity, and concentrating trade on one town to the detriment of the outposts

It was necessary to try and regain England's lost European markets and in this task Henry VII was partly successful. Although there had been Navigation Acts in the past, that passed by Henry in 1485 (amplified in 1489) was the first to have any practical effect. The aim was to recover the carrying trade with France, particularly the Bordeaux wine trade, and to stop the "great minishing and decay that hath been now of late time of the navy . . . and idleness of the mariners." All wines were to be brought in English ships and those that were not were to be forfeited. Henry combined this with a policy of naval building which left a fleet of seven ships in 1509 and swept Scottish pirates, such as Sir Andrew Barton, from the North Sea in 1511. A commercial agreement was signed with France in 1486 and after it had lapsed due to political

L   *

difficulties, it was renewed in 1497. The navigation policy was not particularly successful under the Tudors and with the decline of shipping in the 1540s, the carrying trade again came into foreign hands. Under the Early Stuarts, Dutch competition and the serious difficulties that shipping encountered from Dunkirk and Barbary pirates forced renewed attention to be paid to the preservation of a mercantile marine.

A treaty with Portugal in 1489 and another with Spain in the same year (Medina del Campo) were probably the most significant of Henry's new measures. The Spanish trade of the 1450s was now revitalised by a lowering of duties and the granting of reciprocal trading rights. Cloth, linen, hides, lead and tin were exchanged for wine, oil, soap, salt, sword blades and iron. Portugal obtained wheat, butter, cheese, and the same commodities in exchange for spices, salt, citrus fruits and, later, calicoes. Trade with Spain centred on the northern ports for iron and with Seville where England was able to share in the fruits of colonial trade. In 1517 Robert Thorne of Bristol obtained privileges for English merchants at San Lucar and in 1530 the Andalusian Company was set up to regulate matters. Three factors, however, combined to weaken the Spanish trade. Pirates such as Robert Reneger of Southampton and William Hawkins of Plymouth attacked Spanish ships and in 1545 a large Spanish galleon was taken. The English tried to trade directly with Portuguese and Spanish colonies and to develop the slave trade. Finally, the Inquisition became a menace to English traders, so that in 1562, for example, twenty-six English sailors were executed in the Canary Islands. Ordinary merchants tried to keep legitimate trade going and in 1577 the Spanish Company was reconstituted but this ran into trouble with other western ports like Chester and was soon overtaken by direct war between England and Spain. Moreover, as William Harborne stated in 1588, the Spanish tried to "surcease" our trade, and English merchants trading in the Mediterranean were liable to be killed. James I restored peace with Spain and in 1606 the Spanish trade was thrown open and the company dissolved. The Exeter Company lost its privileges in 1606 and this, together with the fact that Portuguese trade was not organised by a company, makes an important exception to the new mercantilist trade universally conducted by companies.

Henry also made attempts to develop English Mediterranean trade and to take advantage of friendship with Spain, the conflict of the Turks and Moors, and the decline of Venice. A trading consul had already been established at Pisa and in 1490 the town was made a staple. Venice attempted to retaliate and from 1488 there was a tariff war which culminated in a duty of 18s. a butt on Malmsey wines from the Greek possessions of Venice (1491). The Venetians gave way and English trading consuls were established at Scios (1513) and Candia (1530). Haklyut referred to direct trade with Sicily, Crete, Chios and Cyprus in the early part of the sixteenth century and this was to pave the way for the great expansion of English Mediterranean trade in Elizabeth's reign. The other great European commercial monopoly, the Hanseatic League, was more powerful. Henry was forced to confirm their privileges in 1486. Opposition showed itself in an attack on the Steelyard in 1493, but in 1504 Hanseatic privileges were again confirmed. Henry endeavoured to infiltrate the northern European markets. A treaty with Denmark was made in 1489, and extended in 1490, by which England regained a place in the Iceland fishing trade. In 1499 a staple was established at Bergen but this failed to develop. Treaties with Riga (1498), the Emperor (1502) and Friesland (1505) did not succeed in raising English trade in the Baltic.

Portuguese and Spanish enterprise was the spur that induced the English to take a more active role in Atlantic trade from the 1530s and her efforts were mainly concentrated on West Africa and Brazil, in the hope that she might participate directly in American trade. When this attempt collapsed in the 1560s, an added impetus was given to voyages of exploration. Hanseatic power in the Baltic, Spanish power in the Mediterranean and West Indies, and Portuguese dominance of Brazil and the East Indies were all blockages to English expansion. Thus, whereas England played only a small part in the earlier voyages of discovery, her later efforts to find a north-east passage or a north-west passage were to be spectacular, but the practical results were to be small. Throughout the Tudor period, the Newfoundland fish trade was our most important American trade and proved a more valuable maritime asset than privateering, piracy and daring voyages. It was also the cause of much West Country prosperity. Bideford, Fowey, Dartmouth, Plymouth, Weymouth and Poole were all involved. Early fleets sailed in 1501 and 1522 and they soon became annual. By the 1590s, a fleet of a hundred vessels was involved and the catch sold for £200,000 in 1615. The government intervened to regulate the trade in 1541 and 1548 and in 1634 the whole trade was carefully reorganised. The fleet sailed out in March and back in July, after the fish had been cured on the beaches, and by 1637 there were some 500 ships and 18,000 men involved. The trade not only served as a school of seamanship, but helped to develop shipping. In the 1540s, the average ship was of 50 tons and carried 20 men, but by the 1630s, those figures had risen to 100 tons and a crew of 40. The building of Dartmouth Butterwalk in 1640 indicates that this was one part of the fishing industry that did not decline. That year the catch was estimated at £700,000. Newfoundland was annexed in 1583 and a proposal for colonisation was put forward by John Gay of Bristol in 1610, but it was not decided to retain the island until a Governor was appointed as late as 1680.

The other focus of interest for the southern and western ports was Africa and the West Indies, and the most important aspect was the slave trade. The Hawkins family played the major part in stimulating the development of trade in these areas William Hawkins, in a ship of 250 tons sailed to the coast of Liberia (Sestos) in 1530, collected ivory and pepper and sold them in Brazil, there taking on wood to bring to England. It is believed that he made two more voyages. His son William started his career as a privateer, but in 1562, with his brother John, they embarked on a fresh voyage taking slaves to Hispaniola and bringing back gold, sugar and hides. Strong Spanish protests were ignored by Elizabeth who invested £2,000 in the next voyage (1564–5). The famous triangular trade was established. Hawkins's third voyage (1567–8) ran into trouble at San Juan d'Ulloa and from that time onwards there was an unofficial war "beyond the line" between Spain and England. In spite of the seizure of Portugal by Spain in 1580, which made it even more difficult to trade on the West African coast, William sent out an expedition in 1582–3 which reached Brazil and is believed to have captured a treasure ship. On this voyage, William Hawkins III and Richard Hawkins (John's son) were both present. John became Treasurer of the Navy in 1577 and was responsible for important shipping reforms. Richard was tried for piracy by James I in 1608 but survived to take part in an expedition against the Barbary Corsairs in 1621. The efforts of the Hawkins family stimulated sufficient interest for Exeter merchants to take out a patent in 1588 for trade in the region and this was renewed in 1598. Direct trade with Spain resumed in 1606 and by 1610 was running at the 1550 level. Spanish sherry was well established as a Bristol import by 1634, but the lure of gold and slaves induced merchants to concentrate on the African trade and in 1618 a company for trading in the Gulf of Guinea, south of the Barbary merchants, was formed. It was opposed because it caused a sharp rise in the price of imported dye-stuffs at a time of crisis in the cloth trade. In 1631, under pressure from Nicholas Crisp, the company was re-formed and managed to last the thirty-one years prescribed in the patent, although Dutch influence soon became paramount on the West African coast.

Morocco was the scene of the other Tudor African enterprises.

In 1551 Thomas Wyndham, a privateer, visited Morocco and from 1552 regular trade was established. We exported fine cloths, and armour and received sugar, saltpetre, dates, molasses, carpets and cotton. By 1600, some 2,000 cloths (about the same as those sent to Italy or Russia) were being exported. The trade of the area was helped considerably by Portuguese Jews and the English took out Hebrew Bibles for them. The Barbary Coast was infested with pirates and the risks involved were great. In 1585 a Barbary Company was established, in which the Earl of Leicester and the Earl of Warwick were prominent members, but the company did not prosper. Interlopers continued to trade and the profits of the company were eaten away by demands for tribute from the Sultan. As a result, the Moroccan trade declined and it was not revived by further attempts made to establish a company in the 1630s. By then, the area had joined the non-regulated section of English commerce.

Barbary Corsairs were perhaps the most dangerous of the pirates which shipping in European waters had to contend with early in the seventeenth century. Scottish pirates remained a menace and in 1577 and 1584 the Mayor of Poole was requested to fit out a ship to deal with them On the east coast, the Dunkirk rovers were the main menace, and in 1628 French pirates from Le Havre were operating in the Severn. The Barbary Corsairs were regarded with the greatest fear because they kidnapped people for the galleys and forced them to apostatise to Mohammedism In 1637 Hall, the Bishop of Exeter, asked Archbishop Laud to consider a service to be used for the large numbers or returned captives and one was later drawn up. Walter Yonge, a Jacobean diarist of a small town near Lyme Regis, recorded in 1627 that a neighbour, Sir William Courtenay, had been robbed of his pewter by pirates. Between 1609 and 1616, no less than 466 vessels were seized and in 1625 27 ships were taken in ten days. It became necessary to extinguish coastal lights as they served as guides for the raiders. A number of expeditions, such as that of 1621, were sent to punish the pirates and one of the main purposes of levying ship money in the late 1630s was an effort to subdue them, but to little avail. In 1645, twenty-six children were kidnapped from the shores of Cornwall and it was not until Blake bombarded Tunis and extracted submission from the Dey of Algiers in 1654 that the menace diminished.

Trade clearly depended upon the effective protection of a navy and the navy depended upon the growth of oceanic commerce to develop a large merchant marine and a sizeable body of seamen ready for the defence of the realm. Navigational improvements were made on both the civil and naval sides and they tended to influence each other. The navy was established by Henry VIII who increased the fleet from nineteen in 1512 to about forty in 1545 and created the Navy Board by 1546. Although his larger ships reached 1,000 tons, they were not successful and the English confined themselves to smaller vessels of between 400 and 450 tons. John Hawkins improved their design immensely, but there were no advances comparable to those in the fifteenth century. The main advance was in size and this is reflected in the growing number of vessels which exceeded 100 tons.

Table 16—Vessels over 100 tons

1540s	92
1560s	76
1577	135
1588	183
1624	350
1635	499

Shipbuilding and shipping services created a large industry, consumed vast quantities of timber and brought about the rise of several towns. Henry VIII favoured Portsmouth but later inclined to Woolwich and Deptford. By the end of the Tudor period, Chatham had replaced Portsmouth as the leading shipping centre. Shipbuilding concentrated on the Thames and Medway and towns such as Southampton lost their importance—the castle there was sold in 1618 as no longer being of use. Naval demand, the Newfoundland trade, the increase in coastal shipping and the demand for larger ships, particularly by the East India Company which favoured ships between 600 and 1,000 tons, all helped to stimulate growth.

After the collapse of 1551, the Merchant Adventurers made shift to reorganise but they found it extremely difficult. Politics intervened because both Elizabeth and Philip found that stops of trade were diplomatically useful. Moreover, the movement of the cloth staple to Germany involved disputes with the Hansa and the movement to the United Provinces brought the problems of war after 1572. The staple was settled at Emden in 1564 where 500 English traders were to be found, but it proved to be unsuitable. In 1567 they settled at Hamburg and concluded a ten-year agreement. The next year, the seizure of the pay for Alva's soldiers and the embargo placed by the Spanish led to the end of trade with Antwerp and, although the dispute ended with a treaty (Bristol 1573), the sack of Antwerp in 1576 brought its long period of commercial dominance to an end. The way was open for the economic growth of the United Provinces, and the Merchant Adventurers could not return. When the ten years expired, Hamburg tried to impose conditions on the English and the English removed again to Emden (1579). The Hansa persuaded the Imperial Diet to expel the English but no action was taken. Emden was dangerously close to the advance of Parma and in 1587 they moved on to Stade and Middelburg. Thus, the Dutch staple was established. The Hansa then tried to get the Adventurers removed from Stade and an Imperial edict to that effect was passed in 1597. By this time, however, the Hansa was weakening. Its economic strength had been weakened by the loss of Russian trade, and constant war with Poland and Denmark. Moreover, according to Camden, "those herrings which in the times of our grandfathers swarmed only about Norway now in our times by the bounty of Providence swim in great shoals round our coasts every year." Elizabeth brought the Hansards' privileges in England to an end in 1598 and the merchants remained at Stade, damaged by interlopers to some extent, although the proportion of exports was 60 to 5 in favour of the Merchant Adventurers.

James I endeavoured to improve the situation in 1610 by asking for the edict to be lifted, and in 1611 a reconciliation was effected. The Steelyard was reopened and Hamburg became the German staple of the company. There it remained until it was finally abolished in 1807. Trouble still beset the company in the United Provinces where the staple was moved from Middleburg to Delft and Rotterdam before settling at Dordrecht in 1655. These difficulties did not prevent the growth of cloth exports, but they encouraged the view that free trade was better than a regulated one and in 1604 the Commons debated this issue. The Charter of 1564 was the legal basis of the company's troubled history in these years and the whole organisation of the company was open to criticism. It was claimed that the seat of government was abroad, that membership fees were too high (fixed at £100 in 1634), that it encouraged high prices and reduced production by stints and that it concentrated trade on London. Criticism of the Adventurers was probably based less on a consistent wish to add the cloth trade to the "free trade area" than to opposition to London. Since London embraced a tenth of the population and four-fifths of the trade of the country, the concentration of three-quarters of our cloth exports in the city was not surprising. However, outports declining for more than one reason could easily blame their poverty on

London. In 1602 London paid £69,803 and the outports £17,726 in customs. In 1621 the Commons complained that "London engross-eth all trades and places." Merchants from such towns as Exeter took a leading part in opposing the company and even the con-stituent branches of the Adventurers voiced their indignation at the state of affairs. York in the sixteenth and Newcastle in the seven-teenth century led the opposition and it is clear that dislike of London was an important factor in rallying opposition to the Stuarts who after a period of confusion, confirmed the company's privileges in 1634. The Long Parliament was bought over with a loan of £30,000 in 1643 and the Charter confirmed by Cromwell in 1656. York, Hull and Newcastle protested in 1651, in vain, that "in equity and reason the benefit of trade should be equally disposed into all the veins of the commonwealth." In spite of prolonged economic crisis and political vicissitudes, the Merchant Adventurers retained much of their power.

The challenge to them came from two companys, the Muscovy and the Eastland, which were concerned in theory to forward trade by a north-east passage, but in reality to avoid the monopolies of the Hansa and the Merchant Adventurers. In 1553 a number of London merchants subscribed £6,000 for a voyage to the north-east. The expedition was led by Sir Hugh Willoughby and Richard Chancellor, and consisted of three ships between 90 and 160 tons. Willoughby perished but Chancellor reached Moscow and returned in 1554 with letters asking for the opening of trade. In spite of protests from the Hansa at Novgorod, permission was granted, and in 1555 the Muscovy Company was established with Sebastian Cabot as the first governor. The Tsar, Ivan the Terrible, gave the English merchants special privileges and in 1566 an Act of Parlia-ment confirmed the company's rights including a "navigation" clause on the use of English ships and another allowing merchants from outports such as York and Boston to take part in the trade. The next year, the Tsar confirmed the privileges and "factories" (or trading posts) were established at Moscow and Novgorod. The first voyage occurred in 1555 and was significant for the use of log-books and lead sheathing on the ships, but it ended in shipwreck off Scotland. Chancellor was kept prisoner by pirates until 1557. It was not until 1558 that a successful voyage was made.

Chancellor had been much impressed with the possibilities for trade, referring to 800 sleds of corn on their way to Moscow. Furs, wax, oil, timber, pitch, tar, tallow, hemp and cordage, together with wheat, were imported by the company and cloth, wine and salt exported. The English company continued to seek for a north-east passage—John Dee moved east in 1580—but although the

English had reached Spitzbergen by 1613, they were supplanted by the Dutch. The latter appeared in the Russian trade in 1583 and it was a Dutchman, Barents, who pushed the furthest east in 1594. The company also opened an overland route to Persia, Anthony Jenkinson in 1561 was the leader of the first of six expeditions and the company's agent, Michael Lock, claimed that this would save the company. However, the trade of Persia was already being disputed by the Levant and East India Companies and the efforts proved fruitless. In the early 1580s, the Russian trade still flourished with ten ships a year involved, but after Ivan IV's death in 1584 civil wars and Dutch intervention combined with our uncompetitive prices to destroy the trade. Even the advantages of joint-stock organisation could not compensate for the serious risks involved and, after a slow decline, the Tsar put an end to trade between 1646 and 1649 when he claimed the English merchants were "unfit to live in any Christian state" because of the execution of Charles I.

The Eastland Company was chartered in 1579. There had been a separate group of Merchant Adventurers in the Baltic and in 1579 English merchants trading in the area asked for incorporation. Strained relations with the Hansa led to doubts about naval supplies from the area. The main group of merchants came from London, but a number of other towns, such as Hull and Newcastle, were involved and, under James I, London's share in the Baltic cloth trade was less than half. A keen rivalry was established with the Merchant Adventurers and the Eastland Company tended to gain popular support as being less formidable than its rival. It was a regulated company and was completely oligarchic, all power being vested in the governing body. Cloth and naval stores were the main commodities exchanged and the company prospered, so that by 1590 over 11 per cent of English exports were in its hands. Their staple was fixed at Elbing but later moved to Danzig. Because the company was less open to criticism having its headquarters in England, for example, and because it brought coin into the realm, it was highly favoured. In 1600, 12,000 cloths were going to the Baltic and in 1659 this had risen to 14,000.

Alderman Cockayne was an Eastland merchant and he persuaded James to forbid the export of undyed "whites" in favour of the finished cloths which the Eastland Company exported. In many ways, Cockayne's scheme of 1614 was a sensible one because it would increase the value of exports and add to the customs charged on dye-stuffs imported for the finishing processes. By 1616 the project was in serious difficulties since the Dutch retaliated by closing the staple for unfinished cloth and there was a serious depression. Only after exports had fallen by one third was James convinced of the mistake and in 1617 the patent was revoked. The English cloth industry remained technically inferior to that of Holland and the way was paved for the crisis of the 1630s. The Merchant Adventurers, as we have seen, regained much of their former position. Thus, the value of cloth exports fell from £200,000 to £80,000 per annum while Dutch competitors took over. Denmark added to our difficulties by raising tolls in the Sound from £20 to £100 a ship. The Eastland Company became one of the earliest protagonists of a navigation policy and in 1622 a proclamation required all Eastland commodities to be imported in English ships. The Navigation Act of 1651 extended this to all European trade and the company recovered a little. Their Charter was renewed in 1661 but by then foreign competition and interlopers had seriously weakened their position.

The Tudors also attempted to find a north-west passage in order to open the trade to Asia. In this aim they were to be disappointed but their activities prepared the way for the struggle between France and England for the wealth of Canada, and focused attention on the New England region of the American continent. Martin Frobisher, Humphrey Gilbert and John Davis edged their way further north-west from 1576 onwards and in the early 1600s, the East India Company gave fresh impetus to these voyages. Bartholomew Gosnold and Martin Pring explored the coast of New England. John Knight (1606) and James Hall (1612) were killed by Eskimos in voyages along the west of Greenland. Henry Hudson was the most significant of the explorers. In 1609 he explored the New England coast to the Hudson River and in 1610 he sailed into Hudson's Bay in an expedition financed by Dudley Digges. The crew mutinied and Hudson was set adrift in a boat. A Company of Merchants Trading in the North-West Passage (1612) was founded. William Baffin made a number of voyages and reached Baffin Island (1616). As late as 1631, Luke Foxe and William James of Hull were exploring in Hudson's Bay, but for many years the French continued to control the fur trade of the region.

No colony was successfully established in Elizabeth's reign, although Raleigh made several attempts to do so in Virginia. It was under the first two Stuarts that the first British Empire was founded and settlement of the New England Colonies undertaken. Colonisation was big business and involved London merchants, western adventurers and many of the wealthy of Court and country in its promotion. Sir Thomas Smyth, Governor of the East India and Muscovy Companies and Treasurer of the Virginia Company,

Commissioner for the Navy and patron of Arctic exploration was typical of a new class of merchants intimately connected with Atlantic trade. Sir Edwin Sandys, Dudley Digges, Lord Rich, the Earl of Warwick, Samuel Purchas, Sir Paul Pindar and many others were involved. Courtiers such as Sir William Courteen or Sir George Calvert (Lord Baltimore) were closely connected with the new enterprises. A new class of merchants concerned with the government's economic policies and a new interest in economic theories were the products of this change. The period of company promotion helped to destabilise the Early Stuart economy and led to a major upheaval with the encouragement of emigration. Lord Baltimore set up an office at the upper end of Bloomsbury to encourage emigrants to Maryland. Commercial interest and religious sympathies became closely allied and the Providence Island Company, which included Lord Say and Sele, Lord Brook, John Pym and Robert Rich, Earl of Warwick, was one of the centres for a Parliamentary opposition to whom colonial grants to courtiers were matters of grievance. A merchant such as Samuel Vassall was typical of the Caroline entrepreneurs. A Puritan member of the Levant Company, he pioneered the sale of cloth at Ragusa, then turned to tobacco in 1630. He was a member of the Massachusetts Bay Company and in the Long Parliament was one of the City members. Government interest was reflected in the creation of a number of organisations to control the colonies. A Council for New England under Sir Ferdinando Gorges was set up in 1622 and in that year and in 1625-6 and 1630 there were Committees of Trade. In 1634 a Committee for Trade and Plantations was created. It was scrapped in 1640 and another under the Earl of Warwick (1643-9) fared no better. A Board of Trade set up in 1650 was under the Council of State and the Trade Committee of 1655 was short-lived. The government was quite prepared to listen to the advice of economists, such as Mun and others in 1621 or Noell and Povey in the 1650s, but there was no settled colonial or mercantile policy. The Crown was anxious to secure quick returns from promoting companies with royal charters or patents and the outcry against these came from interested parties in many cases.

These new men and organisations were indications of a coming commercial revolution which was helped by the continuing serious decline of the cloth trade and the persistent opposition of the Dutch in our well-established trading areas. In 1621-4, a fresh depression affected the cloth industry for which the government was less to blame, since it arose in part from overseas devaluations and from the wars in Poland and Germany. The government did what it could, sending out commissioners requiring the putting of people to work, but unemployment was rife. Walter Yonge reported 300 unemployed at Exeter and the justices of Wiltshire and Devon were warned that the people were "ready to mutiny for want of work." In 1625 there was a plague there; this was followed in the West Country by imprisonment and forced billeting of soldiers. From the mid-1630s, "depression was generally regarded as chronic," and the main reason for this was a fall in overseas demand. This was because the rapidly growing Dutch industry obtained an almost complete monopoly of the finishing process and had access to superior Brazil dye-stuffs. Although the number of finished cloths exported was rising, Holland and Poland banned them in 1635. A commission appointed in 1635 did no more than ban the export of fuller's earth. The commission of 1638 had no proposals to offer. Skilled workers were attracted to Holland by higher wages and unemployed weavers emigrated to New England. In 1636 a serious plague "stopped the weekly intercourse of stuffs and other commodities" from Norwich to London and added to the difficulties. The effects of these economic disasters on the ordinary people will be considered later but their effect on the economy as a whole was far less serious than one might expect. Peter Mundy writing about England's advantages in economic development spoke of "so many incorporated companies of merchants for foreign trade." Bacon said that "trading in companies is most agreeable to the English nature." In 1618 the Venetian ambassador reported "the English trade in all parts of the world with large capital." The merchant class increased rapidly so that many had "risen out of poor men's sons." Many merchants were "gentlemen's sons or men's children of good means or quality" and the rise of successful merchants into Court positions and the ownership of land is well known. London alone was calculated to have 3,000 merchants by the 1660s.

Three areas of settlement can be discerned: Virginia and Maryland; the New England colonies; and the West Indies. Colonisation originated in the group surrounding Raleigh, his half-brother, Gilbert, and their friend, Richard Hakluyt, who recommended "the deducting of some colonies of our superfluous people into those temperate and fertile parts of America." Raleigh's interest was more in the possible discovery of gold than settlement, and the Roanoke colonies of the 1580s failed. Raleigh turned his attention to Guiana and eventually met his death in 1618 for intervening in the area. A Guiana Company founded in 1627 came to nothing. Interest in Virginia was renewed by Bartholomew Gosnold of Plymouth in 1602 and two groups formed the London Company in which Cecil, Smith, Rich and Somers were involved. Plymouth was to occupy the northern region and London the south. In 1607 a settlement was made on the James river. After initial difficulties, the settlement prospered and tobacco-growing started. Two more Charters were granted, but the company fell into considerable difficulties. Smith attacked it in *The Unmasking of Virginia* and in 1624 the company surrendered its rights to the Crown. Tobacco was known in England in 1597 and James attacked it in his *Counterblast to Tobacco* (1604), but it soon proved to be a popular crop. In 1619 slaves were introduced into Virginia and the plantation system started. Sir George Calvert, secretary to Cecil, Secretary of State and a Roman Catholic, obtained a patent to settle Maryland in 1632. The expedition was led by his brother Leonard and sailed in 1634. Corn and tobacco were the chief crops of the new colony.

In New England, matters were more complicated. The Plymouth Company had little success, although one of its founder members, Sir Ferdinando Gorges, obtained Maine and another proprietor, Mason, the area that was to become New Hampshire. The first settlement in the region occurred in 1620 when emigrants arrived at Plymouth. This was followed by other settlements and the Massachusetts Bay Company was established in 1629. By 1633 settlements were being made on the Connecticut river. The colony became associated with the rich Puritan peers, and the stricter Puritans under the influence of John Winthrop founded Rhode Island and New Providence. At first, the colonists were mainly agricultural and their dislike of enclosure was reflected in an attempt at open-field farming. Later, skilled craftsmen established the cloth industry and New England, besides providing furs and fish, began to export manufactures.

The West Indies rose more rapidly into prominence, although the pattern of settlement was complex. Sir George Somers was wrecked in Bermuda on his way to Virginia and established a settlement there in 1612. Bermuda became a colony in 1684. France, Spain and England competed for the various colonies. In 1623 Thomas Warner obtained St Kitts; Nevis (1628), Montserrat and Antigua (1632) were all settled. In 1627 proprietary rights over the Leeward Islands were granted to the Earl of Carlisle. Barbados had been annexed in theory in 1605, but not until 1625 was settlement made. Sir William Courteen controlled the colony and early in the 1640s it was decided to change from tobacco to sugar production. Crushing-mills and boiling-plants were installed and slaves imported in large numbers for the plantations. Bristol was refining sugar in 1637 and Liverpool by 1667. The Providence Company founded by the Puritans Warwick and Brook did less well, since it was expelled by the Spanish in 1635. Jamaica was seized in 1655, the Spanish fought on until 1660 and the island was definitely ceded in 1670. In 1615, 50,000 lb of sugar were imported by England and this had risen to 14·8 million lb by the 1660s.

A new trading pattern was starting to emerge. By 1640 re-exports of goods brought from the colonies equalled in value all our other exports apart from cloth. Western ports such as Liverpool and Bristol were showing the benefits of colonial trade and the lengthy dominance of London was being slowly weakened. New commodities of all kinds appeared. In 1628 England was trading in the Persian Gulf, where Mohca was the centre for coffee. Evelyn referred to coffee in 1637 and it was later to be an extremely important import. In 1642 the Portuguese signed an agreement about the Persian Gulf. Silk imports from the Levant Company trebled between 1621 and 1669. Mediterranean trade was, by Stuart times, a flourishing affair and the Levant Company, fighting off the Muscovy and East India Companies, one of the most enterprising of the companies. The defeat of the Turks at Lepanto in 1571 and the elimination of Venice as a trading power left a vacuum in the eastern Mediterranean which Anthony Jenkinson was the first to see. In 1575 Sir Edward Osborne and Richard Staper went to Constantinople to procure a safe-conduct for William Harborne. He went out in 1578 and 1580 and obtained thirty-five capitulations from the Turks to develop trade in the empire. A joint-stock Turkey Company was established in 1581. Meanwhile, the Earl of Leicester had obtained a patent to control Levantine imports and this was given to a group of merchants in 1583. The Venice Company had the right to import currants, wine and oil. Both Charters lapsed and it was decided to create a new company.

Thus, in 1592 the Levant Company was established as a joint-stock company containing fifty-three members. Harborne had urged the creation of a joint stock, but by the early years of the century, this seems to have broken down and in the 1604 debate on trade it was claimed it was non-regulated. By 1605 the company had reverted to a regulated instead of a joint-stock basis. The company regulated the trade mainly through the ambassador who was a representative of the Crown and a company agent, and through trading consuls. Merchants were established at Alexandria, Aleppo, Smyrna and Candia and by 1598, eighty-seven merchants were engaged in the trade of the area. Cloth (6,500 pieces in 1600), lead, tin, hides and herrings were exported in return for a wide variety of products. Silk, cotton, currants, alum, dye-stuffs, oil and spices were imported. Mun claimed that this company added to our favourable balance of trade, although this seems to have changed by the end of the century. In spite of French competition created by the rise of a woollen industry in the 1650s, exports had risen to 18,000 pieces by 1665 and by 1706 had reached twenty thousand pieces. There were clashes with the Muscovy and East India Companies, but the Levant Company kept its footing and the charter was re-enforced in 1605 and 1644. The value of Mediterranean trade was so great that in 1606 James I issued a new Book of Rates to replace that of 1560 and secure customs duties on the imports. Thomas Bate, a Turkey merchant, opposed the new rates but they were enforced after a decision in the Exchequer Court in 1608.

New markets for cloth and a new route to the Spice Islands to avoid the Portuguese monopoly had been the main motives of the numerous companies of explorers and traders. The Tudors also tried a direct approach to the East Indies by land and sea and the interest aroused by these voyages led to the foundation of the largest and most controversial organisation of all, the East India Company. Drake was the first English navigator to pass through the East Indies (1577–80) but he was followed in circumnavigation by John Cavendish (1586–8) and James Lancaster (1595–6). Drake signed an agreement with the Sultan of Ternate and for many years the English struggled to obtain a direct foothold in the East Indies. However, in 1595 the Dutch despatched their first fleet to the East Indies and in 1602 the Dutch East India Company was founded. The Portuguese were expelled from Amboyna (1605), the Moluccas (1607) and Bantaam (1609). The Dutch encouraged the natives to attack the English stations and from 1611 there was constant skirmishing. James sent a fleet under Sir Thomas Dale in 1617 and arranged a treaty with the Dutch in 1619, which they broke. In 1621 our settlement at Bantaam was destroyed and in the next few years our agent Nathaniel Courthope was murdered, our settlement at Polaroon expelled and ten English merchants executed at Amboyna in 1623. Although Cromwell secured compensation from the Dutch in 1654, it proved impossible to maintain settlement and in 1684 all Far Eastern factories, except Bencoolen, were abandoned. English merchants reached Japan and William Adams helped to build ships, but they were expelled by 1620. Rivalry between the British and the Dutch was intense, so that in 1651 the British occupation of St Helena was followed in 1652 by a Dutch settlement at the Cape to protect the Indian route and it was not until 1674 that the Dutch recognised St Helena as British.

Failure in the East Indies necessitated a new move and the activities of the Levant Company had paved the way to India. Osborne and Staper sent out Fitch and Newbury in the 1580s to travel overland to India. Newbury perished but Fitch reached Burma. Dutch control of the East Indies and the rise in the price of pepper forced the London merchants to act, and £30,000 was subscribed. In December 1600, the joint-stock East India Company was established. The trade was more complicated and dangerous than any other. Cloth was not much use as an export so the company was empowered to take out £30,000 in defiance of mercantilist ideals. The voyage was long and necessitated large ships. By the 1620s, thirty ships over 600 tons were involved and "filled the nation with great ships and expert mariners." Others argued that losses at sea were so great that, of every three seamen that went out, only two returned. The 218 merchants involved came from the Muscovy and Levant Companies, but the stock was not permanent. From 1600 to 1613, capital was subscribed at the beginning of each voyage; after that for a number of voyages, including four joint stocks, three Persian stocks and two general voyage stocks. This meant that various stocks were co-extensive so that in 1657 a permanent single joint stock was created.

James Lancaster returned from the first voyage in 1603 with 1 million lb of pepper and this voyage was followed by twelve separate voyages which were extremely profitable. Sir Hugh Middleton and Sir Edward Mitchelborne were among the most successful commanders and 234 per cent dividends were declared. The Charter was renewed in 1609 and, although the Dutch expelled them from the East Indies, they moved northwards. In 1612 Thomas Best and Thomas Aldworth established a factory at Surat. A Portuguese attempt to expel them was defeated in 1615 and Sir Thomas Roe sent to Agra by James I to obtain concessions. Madras on the east coast was established by Francis Day in 1639. Roe visited the Shah of Persia in 1616 and the company captured Ormuz in 1622. Bombay was ceded by Portugal in 1662. Madras was the first presidency in 1654; Bombay took over from Surat in 1685, and Bengal followed in 1681. Exports of cloth and coin were exchanged for saltpetre, silk, spices, coffee, porcelain and, after 1660, tea. Because the imports were of rare commodities, the trade soon came in for strong criticism.

In 1615 Robert Kayll attacked the East India Company in *The Trades Increase* and the depression of the 1620s was blamed on the export of bullion. No one seemed clear as to the exact amount. Mun said that between 1601 and 1620 £548,090 out of a permitted £720,000 had been exported. The company, defended by Digges in *The Defence of Trade* (1615) and Mun in *A Discourse of Trade* (1622) maintained that coin was secured by re-exports. Thus, in 1621, although £100,000 had been exported, £380,000 had been sold abroad and this argument was always supported by later economists. Most of the imports were for luxuries but in two respects this was not so. Cottons came in and were used in Lancashire. Calicoes were imported from 1604, but later these also came under fire when they displaced pepper as the main import by the 1670s and were said to threaten the cloth industry. Yet, in spite of the criticisms, attempts to create rival companies failed because the strength of the company's fleets and forts was necessary to the trade menaced by pirates, Dutch and Portuguese. "The wealth of Ormuz and of Ind" (as Milton referred to it) became one of the main sources of rising prosperity.

What were the effects of the developments in trade under the Tudors and Early Stuarts? In many ways, they were curiously contradictory. Trade did not alter fundamentally during the period and in 1640 three-quarters of it was still in the hands of the Merchant Adventurers. Our main exports remained the same with cloth accounting for nine-tenths of our exports in 1621. Imports had shown increasing diversity, but the cost was considerable and total figures for trade suggest that an unfavourable balance was the result in spite of increased emphasis on bullionist and balance of trade theories. Companies developed apace but considerable sections of trade were outside their operation. Joint-stock companies did not always succeed better than regulated ones and all the companies experienced difficulty from interlopers. Trade revival under the Early Tudors had been followed by the crash of 1551 and revival in the early years of Elizabeth was followed by depression in the 1590s. Early Stuart progress was followed by the short-lived crises of 1614–17 and 1621–4 and then by the collapse of the 1630s. The Civil War disrupted trade and it was only for a brief period in the 1650s that recovery was noticeable. Figures for total trade given by Misselden and Davenant are defective, but they reflect the virtual stabilisation of exports and the steady rise of imports which was to justify the introduction of the Navigation Acts.

Table 17—Estimates of Total Trade (by value) under the Early Stuarts

	Exports	Imports
1613	£2,487,435	£2,141,151
1622	£2,320,436	£2,619,315
1663	£2,022,812	£4,016,019*

* Add 27 per cent for outports, as this figure is for London only.

Yields from customs revenue continued to show the increasing value of foreign trade. Thus, between 1603 and 1621, customs revenue more than doubled. Customs farming from 1604 helped to reduce the yield, but Parliamentary stringency from 1643 meant that the yield rose three and a half times by 1659. Shipping showed a considerable increase in the size of individual ships, and the total tonnage. Thus, Table 18 shows a real increase.

Table 18—Shipping Tonnage, 1615–60

	Total (tonnage)	Colliers (tonnage)
1615	102,000	28,000
1660	162,000	71,000

Note: These figures are from Harper, but Davis gives a tonnage of 115,000 in 1629 and 200,000 in 1660.

Mercantile wealth was a feature of Late Tudor and Early Stuart social structure. London merchants were well-off compared with their provincial brethren, although some, like Henry Tooley of Ipswich or Christopher Spicer of Exeter, could equal them. City men such as Sir Baptist Hickes or Lionel Cranfield in James's reign were followed in Charles's reign by men such as Sir Paul Pindar and Sir John Jacob.

It is clear that this was above all a period of underlying re-adjustment which was ill-understood and that, therefore, complaints were made about decline and threats to the balance of trade which were greatly exaggerated. On the other hand, the adjustment from Europe to a world-wide economy could not take place in a vacuum and England was affected by wars and continental price changes, as trade became a steadily increasing share of the national income. Unaware of the changes, contemporaries either reacted by seeking quick profits through monopolies or failed to take advantage at all. The result was that the economy was frequently undermined by commercial crisis. Security for investment was weak and reaction accordingly panic-stricken. In times of dearth or high prices, speculators quickly became public enemies and the manipulations of patentees and monopolists added to the uncertainty. Price rises indicated a period of expansion, but there was always the danger of losing the market to more effective and cheaper competitors. The Dutch proved in the fisheries, the cloth trade, the carrying trade and colonial enterprise to be a barrier to development, but England's financial resources were not yet equal to the task of outbidding the Dutch with technological invention, naval supremacy and heavy investment. Yet the period was decisive, in that it saw the swing towards a colonial economy and a recognition that England's interests needed the protection of a navigation system. The framework of the old colonial system was in being; it needed only to be secured.

TUDOR AND EARLY STUART INDUSTRIAL GROWTH

During the sixteenth and early seventeenth centuries, nearly all the medieval industries with the exception of tin-mining underwent expansion, increased the size of their capital units and embarked on cautious and piecemeal innovation. Cloth remained the main industry in both volume and value of trade throughout the period, but production inadequacies and commercial restrictions prevented any large expansion. What occurred was a threefold process: an attempt to open new markets; an attempt to diversify production; and a series of changes in the location of what Defoe called "the richest and most valuable manufacture in the world." In many respects, these alterations were sizeable, but they were not able to create an industry which could effectively compete with the Dutch. The building industry deprived of its ecclesiastical patronage, turned to secular work and the building "revolution" occurred in the hundred years preceding the Civil War, in which large amounts of middle- and lower-class housing was rebuilt or constructed in a more spacious and slightly more hygienic style. During the sixteenth century, the leather industry returned to its position as our second largest export industry and, in value at least, it was still in that position at the end of the seventeenth century. Shipbuilding increased so greatly that a serious timber shortage was apparent by the middle of the sixteenth century and this coincided with the increasing use of coal for domestic and then industrial purposes. Coal production underwent a spectacular increase in the hundred years after 1540. The iron industry, restricted by technical and fuel deficiencies, did not expand as much as might be expected, but tended to shift its location slowly from the Weald towards the Forest of Dean and new supplies of timber.

However, these traditional industries were joined during the period by a number of new ones. Iron production was followed by iron manufacture and although a sizeable proportion of the iron used was imported, this does not affect the importance of the rise of the Midland iron industries. Influenced by mercantilist ideas, a native armaments industry was established by the middle of the sixteenth century, and this in turn stimulated other mining industries such as copper. Textile industries diversified so that the Lancashire cotton industries were developing by Elizabeth's reign. Cottons were originally poor-quality woollen cloths, but during this period they were a mixture of Irish linen and cotton imported from the Levant or later from the American colonies. From the 1590s, the hosiery industry developed in Derbyshire, Leicestershire and Nottinghamshire. Flax growing was encouraged and linen manufacture stimulated for a time by measures in 1533, 1563 and 1622. Silk manufacture based on imports from the Levant developed more slowly until it was stimulated by French weavers in the second half of the seventeenth century. Other new industries were the result of increased consumption of a wider variety of goods, such as paper or glass, or the necessity of dealing with colonial imports, such as sugar.

The background to the growth of industry was the price rise and the development of machinery and attitudes designed to facilitate economic growth. It was an age of projects and "adventurers" and these were the predecessors of the innovation and entrepreneurship which England developed in competition and co-operation with the Dutch. The rate of interest was fixed in 1545 at 10 per cent and although for a short time this legislation was repealed (1552–71), it was re-established and the average rate charged fell to 8 per cent in 1625 and 6 per cent in 1651. John Selden remarked: " 'tis a vain thing to say money begets not money, for that no doubt it does." Although the Bourse at Amsterdam replaced Antwerp as the financial centre of Europe, and English financial practice followed Dutch precedent, there was a definite financial sector of the City of London dealing with such matters as insurance and banking. In many ways this development was linked with the career of Sir Thomas Gresham of Holt in Norfolk, the financial agent of the government at Antwerp in 1551. In co-operation with the Marquess of Winchester and Sir Robert Cecil, he carried out a reform of the currency in 1560 which rescued it from the long series of debasements and no further reform was attempted until the 1690s. During the 1560s and 1570s, there is evidence that the goldsmiths and scriveners (financial agents for the landed estates) had started to lend some of their wealth and thus perform a rudimentary banking function akin to that of foreign firms such as the Medici or Fuggers. Lombard Street was the centre of these early bankers, who included such men as Hagenbuck, Pallavicino, Perrot and Pindar. The Royal Exchange was opened in 1570 and in 1573 the Chamber of Assurance settled there to provide the earliest shipping insurance policies. In 1571 Parliament was faced with a Bill against private banks but the phase for preventing such developments was over. During the seventeenth century, helped by the increasing concentration of trade in London, the farming of the customs from 1604 to 1671, and the needs of the Crown, the City as a financial institution emerged as a powerful force. Deposits with the goldsmiths, made in the Civil Wars, stimulated growth even more, and by the second half of the century the City was ready to play its role in the commercial revolution.

Capitalism expanded and came into its own during the period, throwing off the guild system in the most advanced part of the economy and scarcely restrained by the flood of economic legislation. To earlier historians, this would seem something of a contradiction, but it must be emphasised that capital formation and profit-making experienced their first major period of success, not in a period of *laissez-faire*, but in one of mercantilism. Two trends of organisation were plain: the persistent but sure decline of the guilds and the continuous increase of government regulation. Guild decline can easily be exaggerated because although there was a decline in the first fifty years of the sixteenth century, this was by no means a constant trend. Guilds suffered from outdated restrictions and from the rise of new areas of production or new products which did not require them. Thus, the movement of the cloth industry from its older centres caused Beverley to be in "great ruin and decay" in 1535 and guilds were less powerful in Leeds or Bradford. Similarly the new cotton-linen manufactures were found in towns, such as Bolton, with little guild organisation. Large parts of the cloth industry remained outside guild towns. Thus, Rochdale had a large woollen market in the seventeenth century, but manufacture was carried on in the area surrounding the town. New industries were rarely controlled by guilds to the same extent even if they formed a guild, and the government, by legislating on guild matters in 1504, 1531 and 1536, weakened their authority to such a degree that the Statute of Apprentices of 1563 transferred some old guild functions to the justices of the peace. In some trades, attempts to create guilds ran into opposition and were defeated as an attempt to create a linen guild in Lancashire and its failure in 1622 illustrate.

Yet the decline of the guilds is too easily exaggerated. The view that the Act of 1547 was a disaster has now been shown to be false because the Act dealt with "religious" guilds, such as those looking after travellers or bridges, and its bad effects were felt in those aspects of economic activity, rather than in industry as a whole. On the contrary, the period was one of guild growth. The Weavers' Company of York was founded in 1548. New guilds such as the Stationers and Blacksmiths were established in Elizabeth's reign.

It was true that there was a fall in the number of guilds. London's guilds declined from ninety to forty-five. At Northampton, seven guilds united into one by 1574 and at Maidstone in 1605, there were four guilds, one of which included both goldsmiths and mercers. The contraction in the number of guilds in the old guild cities, so that by 1607 Gloucester had only eight or Norwich only twelve in 1622, was a process of readjustment. Once their overall functions of charitable and economic regulation had gone, the guilds became producers' associations and gatherings of the leading merchants. As such, they continued to develop even in towns where a traditional guild had not existed. The Leeds Clothing Corporation was founded in 1626.

Mercantile economics made the whole nation a guild regulated by the government. Sixteenth- and seventeenth-century England saw the creation of a vast bulk of legislation on economic matters. Thus, during the Tudor period there were 250 statutes, including 44 concerning the cloth and 15 the leather industry and these were augmented by proclamations and by instructions from the Privy Council. Spurred on by fear of unrest caused by industrial change, by the mercantilist theories of a balance of payments and a favourable trade surplus, and by a desire to protect and preserve rather than stimulate industry, the government interfered in the most trivial of matters, such as the manufacture of wax candles in 1581. Government policy was soon a mass of contradictions, particularly since it undermined industries it tried to preserve by granting monopolies for the financial benefit of the Crown. Mercantilism (or Colbertism, as it was known in France) was only an adjunct to the economic circumstances of an inflationary period, and there is little evidence to show that it stimulated growth in the seventeenth century, except in isolated and short-term ways such as the effect of the Mines Royal and Batterys Royal Companies which as government monopolies stimulated armament manufacture, saltpetre imports and the mining of copper and lead. Elaborate regulation of the cloth industry could do little to influence foreign buyers. One example will suffice to show the importance and at the same time the irrelevance of mercantile regulation to the growth of industry.

Perhaps the most serious economic problem, apart from the cloth depression, was the increasing shortage of wood. Tree growth was essential to shipbuilding and as the tonnage doubled between 1540 and 1660, this produced a serious strain. On the other hand, building continued to make its demand and the iron industry used charcoal smelting. Moreover, other manufactures of southern England, such as glass and paper, constantly increased the demand for fuel for heating as well as charcoal for glass-making itself. The respective use to which trees might be put is represented as follows: 3 loads of wood = 2 trees = 1 load of charcoal. To some extent, the needs were complementary for, as Defoe pointed out, ships took trunks and charcoal took branches, but the fact remains that the price of timber per ton is estimated to have risen from £2 to £6 between 1603 and 1660. Camden referred to the decline of the forests in Worcestershire: "as the woods about here decay so the glass houses remove and follow the woods." In the early seventeenth century, Arden Forest disappeared and the decline of the Midland forests went on throughout the century, due to agricultural and industrial pressures. The survey of Crown lands in 1608 and Standish's *New Directions for Planting Timber* (1602) were indications of deep national concern, and John Evelyn's *Sylva* about tree cultivation was a famous work. This serious problem was solved, however, by the substitution where possible of coal in domestic and industrial use and much later by the creation of coke smelting. Government legislation concerned itself with a series of restrictions on the use of timber and did little to encourage numerous patentees of coke smelting who came forward from 1589. Thus, in 1559 no oaks, beeches or ashes within fourteen miles of rivers or coasts were to be cut except in the Weald. Complaints from the Cinque Ports and the pressures resulting from London's growth led to an Act in 1581 forbidding cutting within twenty-two miles of London. In 1581, 1584 and 1597, those engaged in Wealden industry were made responsible for road upkeep by spreading cinders and in 1585 ironmills were forbidden in Kent, Sussex and Surrey. Later, Charles I appointed a Surveyor of the Iron Works and required the enforcement of these laws, but the continued fear of timber shortage indicated that they had little effect.

Therefore, individual merchants and industrialists were of great importance in forwarding production. Both classes increased in numbers during the period and the scale of some of their gains reflects the unfettered activities of entrepreneurs in a period of rising prices. Criticised for buying themselves into the landed classes, the Tudor businessmen won recognition, so that Mun could declare "the merchant is worthily called the steward of the kingdom's stock." Only in London was the merchant class large; in other cities it was much smaller, so that Bristol had some hundred merchants early in the seventeenth century. In Exeter, the merchant community was particularly active in the Tudor period, leading the outport's attack on London, seeking to divert trade from Topsham with a canal, and establishing a trading company. Seven per cent of the population of Exeter owned two-thirds of the city's wealth. In other towns, the proportion was less restricted, so that at Nottingham 12·5 per cent owned 67 per cent of the wealth. Ordinary merchants in the provinces were worth little more than £500 per annum, although in London the figure was doubled. Yet if merchants and industrialists were prepared to speculate, wealth was theirs for the taking. As yet, specialisation was largely confined to cloth production, so the most wealthy industrialists and financiers had a variety of interests. Lord Willoughby was a landowner who obtained £600 a year from his ironworks and glass manufacture and is credited with the development of the first working steam-engine in 1603. Men such as Sir Arthur Ingram, Sir Baptist Hickes and Sir William Cockayne were involved in a number of projects. In the cloth industry, rich owners had appeared in the fifteenth century and increased during the period. Cuthbert of Kendal, Hodgkin of Halifax, Brian of Manchester, Dolman of Newbury and Tucker of Abingdon, were the successors of Spring and Lavenham and Tame of Cirencester. John Winchcombe of Newbury was famous for the large numbers he employed. Stumpe of Malmesbury obtained Malmesbury (1536) and Osney (1546) Abbeys and employed 2,000 workers. Tucker planned to buy Abingdon Abbey in 1538. Peter Blundell of Tiverton died worth £40,000.

It is clear that wealth was available to the merchant and industrialist, although they were inclined to invest this wealth in land rather than in industry itself. Much of the capital was produced by speculation in a period of price rises and the monopolistic nature of much trade tended to keep prices high. Successful traders were often the target for bitter opposition and in the 1640s the Levellers were to attack the merchant class for their privileges, particularly the Merchant Adventurers. By 1559 it has been estimated £10,000 was invested in joint stock and by 1695 this was £4 million. Little of this money came from an investment market, although companies tended to finance one another, so that Levant profits helped to found the East India Company. Even less came from the almost non-existent banking system and the transfer of credit was still difficult. Although there are glimpses of the use of bills of exchange and they were frequently used in Holland, Malynes said in 1622 that they were unknown. They did not become legal until 1698, and it was maintained that this limited trade.

At the time, the new available wealth was attributed to a number of factors. The increase in the amount of money was held to be a cause, and inasmuch as this situation created inflation, contemporaries were right. They were less correct in their estimation of the effects of privateering, which was held to account for an import of £12 million during Elizabeth's reign by a Member of Parliament in 1621. To some extent, privateering had increased the wealth of the kingdom, as West Country town growth and manor construction showed. Courtiers and the Queen herself found investment profitable. A writer declared in 1598 that "the war with Spain hath been profitable." Now this view has been considerably modified. Some voyages were prosperous, but the English never captured the main treasure fleet, which was an honour left to our Dutch competitors. Thus, a ship called the *Bond* made £5,000 on a voyage in 1589 and Drake produced a handsome haul from his world voyage, estimated at £600,000. Individual captures were also profitable, so that Cecil, for an outlay of £700, received £7,000 in a privateering venture of 1601. Against these gains, the disruption of normal trade by war and piracy, the cost of the expeditions and the losses we incurred have to be balanced.

To a certain extent, England was a successful magnet for foreign investment, although the Dutch for long controlled the money market of Europe. This was partly due to the high level of interest which was only slowly reduced. German money was invested in mining. The Dutch invested in land drainage and even in trading companies. Yet the main source of capital remained trade and industry itself. It is clear that capital flowed to the land rather than from it, so that agricultural prosperity was not the root of industrial growth, except where landowners were directly concerned in, for example, mining. During the Tudor period, the joint-stock company and the regulated company emerged as the main form of business enterprise. They were not revolutionary because they were in many respects like guild organisations, being groups of interested merchants or adventurers anxious to create a monopoly. Yet, in a period when English industry competed seriously for the first time in Europe, such monopolistic protection was a gain. Whatever the financial and political disadvantages of patents and royal charters, they fulfilled a necessary protective role. It is significant that Sir Thomas Gresham, who lodged with a famous German monopolist, Jaspar Schutz, is credited with introducing monopolies with the issue of a glass patent to Henry Smyth in 1552.

The possibility of profit tempted the Merchant Adventurers, the clothiers and the sheepmen into a pattern of accelerated output and rising prices which led to the collapse of 1551. After that time, although more attention was paid to the cloth industry than any other, it was remarkable for its failure to adapt in spite of new commodities at home and fierce Dutch competition. At the beginning of the sixteenth century, England produced broadcloths, kerseys and worsteds, which were exported in an unfinished state.

M

The main production areas were East Anglia and the West Country, although specialised higher quality cloths were still produced in towns scattered throughout the country. In order to stimulate production, the government tried to maintain the urban cloth industry. In 1555 the Weavers Act limited the number of looms to two per house outside the towns. In 1557 the sale of cloth outside towns was restricted, although this Act was repealed in 1624. Concern over the decline of corporation towns led to an Act of 1554, forbidding drapers and haberdashers from selling in towns where they did not live. Government policy also aimed at a closer regulation of the industry and in 1552 and 1566 attempts to regulate sizes and weights were made in accordance with the ulnager policy of earlier times. In 1563 came a comprehensive statute to re-enforce guild restrictions. The Statute of Apprentices laid down the terms of engagement, hours of labour, and means of giving notice. Wages were to be assessed yearly by justices of the peace and higher wages were to be penalised. Apprenticeship rules, based on those of London, were extended to the whole country. Provision was made for the justices to make orders to compel craftsmen to work in the fields at harvest time. The Act was modified in 1593 and 1603 to include a minimum wage. But all this legislation had little effect. The Weavers Act contained a number of exempted counties, such as Yorkshire and later Suffolk, Essex, Somerset and Wiltshire, were added. The Artificers Statute depended upon local enforcement, and its operation was sporadic. In Yorkshire in 1640 there was "not one clothier in the county but is guilty of the penalties of the said statute."

The 1551 crisis produced surprisingly little immediate change, apart from government legislation, and by the 1560s at a much reduced level, the Merchant Adventurers were restored to their power and this meant that the pattern of demand for cloth also returned to its traditional balance. In 1566, for every nine unfinished cloths, only one finished cloth was exported. Pressure for change came from two main sources: overseas markets increasingly demanded better-quality and lighter cloths, and immigrants from the more advanced continental cloth industry found their way to this country under the stress of religious persecution. The earliest arrivals were French Huguenots who arrived in Kent in the 1550s and Norfolk in the 1560s. They were followed by Walloons and Dutch Calvinists from the 1570s. Thus, in 1565 Norwich welcomed aliens to manufacture "bays, arras, says, tapestry, staments, kersey and such other outlandish commodities" and Colchester in 1570 referred to Dutchmen making bays and serges "trades not commonly known." By 1588 there were about 360,000 aliens settled in the country. In Kent, Canterbury and Sandwich, in Essex, Colchester and Halstead, and in Norfolk, Norwich were the main centres. Similar in religious persuasion to the natives and adept in skills, the immigrants found a ready welcome.

Thus, East Anglia came to produce two main types of cloth. In the rural areas, the coarser types of woollens such as the worsteds continued, but the main emphasis lay on the "New Draperies." Says were a hardwearing fabric used for monks' habits in Italy and Spain. Bays were used as linings for uniforms, and there were numerous other types such as bombazines for ladies' dresses. By the end of the sixteenth century, the new draperies had brought a revival to East Anglia, and early in the seventeenth century, they began to spread to the west. Clothiers in that region were more conservative and an attempt was made to revive broadcloths by concentrating on dyed and better-quality cloths, such as the scarlets of Stroudwater in Gloucestershire. Exports rose from 3,000 cloths in 1628 to 14,000 in 1640 and the Spanish cloths, as they were known, were well established. However, this development was not quick enough to prevent the cloth crisis of the 1620s in the west. After this the new draperies began to gain influence, gradually ousting the kerseys with serges. Serges had a wollen weft and a worsted warp, utilising short Spanish wool and long Irish wool, and their manufacture was established at Exeter and Taunton. By the 1660s, the change-over was rapid in such towns as Tiverton and the later part of the seventeenth century saw a great rise in their production. Although serges were a heavier form of new drapery, the West Country also began to develop specialised cloths, such as the medleys of Kingswood in Gloucestershire.

With the increased variety of cloth, the industry was structured so that a number of specialist areas were to some extent competing against each other. The west continued woollens as Spanish cloths, developed serges and produced some specialist cloths. East Anglia produced worsteds and "stuffs," as the new draperies came to be known. In the 1630s this part of the industry ran into difficulties and by 1636, with the flight of the Protestant congregations, the emigration of skilled weavers and the increasing fierceness of Dutch competition, the region suffered considerably. Moreover, Yorkshire had entered the field as an important area of production. The independent clothiers of the region, exempt from guild controls or legislative interference, and close to his wool supply, developed the industry mainly for the home market in the sixteenth century. At first, production was more often than not a supplement to hill-farming, but by the 1630s some improvements were being made. However, the severity of the Civil War in the West Riding and a plague outbreak in 1644–5 restricted growth in the area, and this helped the recovery of East Anglia. By the 1650s, "lower wages, lower taxes and cheaper more abundant supplies of the coarser wools" had helped to restore confidence. The Hansa and even the Dutch had been challenged for markets, and in 1662 the Royal Society turned its attention to the dyeing of cloth. Although the volume of cloth production was thus scarcely kept up, its value became increasingly greater and by the middle of the seventeenth century, cloth was ready for a new period of expansion.

The continued importance of the traditional cloth industry should be remembered when considering the impact of other industries on the economy. By far the most important change was the growth of the coal industry, because this not only represented a shift away from wood as a fuel and thus prepared the way for England to overtake Dutch and French wood-based industries, but also because it prepared the way for the use of coke as a substitute for charcoal, thus guaranteeing the rise of an iron industry. These developments were in the future and coal did not produce a significant alteration in either respect in this period. However, it was utilised in a large number of industries as a fuel and may thus be regarded as the cause of a technological change of significance involving a greater capitalisation and higher productivity. Moreover, the coal trade was "the especial nursery" of seamen and stimulated the shipbuilding industry. Harrison said, in 1577, "of coalmines we have . . . plenty in the north and western parts of our island as may suffice for all the realm." Medieval production had been widespread but small in total output. During the Tudor and Early Stuart period, production increased in spite of difficulties of extraction, the resistance of the iron industry to its use, and the monopolistic situation prevailing in the main producing region. Production figures do not always take into account small scattered individual producers and, because of the wide variety of tonnages used, must necessarily be limited in their accuracy. A remarkable increase in production is clearly indicated by them for the period 1550 to 1660 (*see* Table 19).

These figures represent a fourteenfold increase during a period of a hundred years, and can scarcely be said to indicate a revolutionary change, but after this period, there was a slowing down in output due to transport, drainage and ventilation problems, so that the period represents a dramatic peak of development. This is also reflected in figures for the coastal trade in coal. Shipments from the Tyne and Wear increased from 250,909 tons in 1609 to 537,000 tons in 1660. The number of ships involved in the coastal trade increased from 400 to 1,000 during the century. Coal for

Table 19—Coal Production

Coalfield	1551–1560	1681–1690
	tons	tons
Northumberland/Durham	65,000	1,225,000
Scotland	40,000	475,000
Wales	20,000	200,000
Midlands	65,000	850,000
Cumberland	6,000	100,000
West Country	10,000	100,000
Forest of Dean	3,000	25,000
Devon and Ireland	1,000	7,000
Estimated annual production	210,000	2,982,000

domestic and industrial use became so important that the Scottish occupations of Newcastle in 1640 and 1644 produced near panic. The price of coal remained high and rose even more rapidly in the 1640s, and the reasons for this were variously estimated. The host-men of Newcastle, taking advantage of an Act of 1529, obtained a charter in 1600 and began to operate a stint of coal. Movement of coal from the pits to the staithes for shipping was in the hands of the keelmen whose privileges were confirmed in 1637 and who also exercised a monopoly. Shipowners, particularly those like lightermen involved in inshore movements (Defoe estimated there were 10,000), were also accused of raising prices. By the 1660s, some individuals, such as Sir Edmund Godfrey, were making specu-lative gains from the high price of coal and there was strong public opposition. These monopolies may have contributed to high prices, but it is more likely that high prices were caused by high costs. Transport was a serious problem for a bulk commodity and long sea voyages were necessary to avoid expensive land journeys. Land-sale coal was disposed of close to the pit head and sea-coal was dispersed over a wider region. Packhorse provision for places such as Coventry and Leicester must have raised prices, since it was calculated in 1675 that 15 miles land transport cost as much as 300 sea miles.

There were also technical difficulties in mining. Drainage con-tinued to be by means of adits and this tended to limit the type of seams that could be exploited. To sink deep shafts, as Wil-loughby did in Nottinghamshire, was shown to be courting risks. Chain-pumps were used, and as late as 1667, one writer complained that this was a major limitation. As early as 1618, a patent was taken out for a suction-pump, and in 1663 the Marquess of Worcester in *A Century of Inventions* referred to a steam-pump, but this was not developed practicably until the 1680s, and Sir Bevis Bulmer's 1590s chain-pump remained in use. In strong contrast, the iron industry, while resisting any attempt to change from charcoal to coke smelting so that although the first patent was taken out in 1589, and Dud Dudley effected it in 1621, the change was not adopted widely until after 1709, was, nevertheless, the field for important technical change. Iron supply was plentiful and in 1601 a member of the Commons referred to it as "a particular blessing of God given only to England." The main centre in Tudor England of the iron industry was the Weald where as Camden said in 1601, the area "is full of iron mines" and "abundance of wood is yearly spent" in the furnaces and forges. The changes in forging, such as the introduction of tilt-hammers in the 1490s, were followed by the introduction of the blast furnace from Europe in 1496. Development was slow and early in the 1540s there were still only three operating. By 1578 there were 67 blast furnaces in the Weald. They appeared in the Welsh region in the 1560s, in Staffordshire by 1583, and by the beginning of the seventeenth century, the Forest of Dean had a small number.

Larger working units were the result of this innovation and furnaces and forges tended to draw together in complex ironworks. About £300 was needed to construct a works, including furnaces, forges, millponds, and dams, ironworkers' homes and suitable roadways, but by the later part of the sixteenth century, such works were numerous and the Weald alone contained 115. This area was particularly suited for development, because the high quality castings produced were of value for the armaments industry. In 1543 Ralphe Hogge and Peter Bawd cast cannon at Buxted in Sussex and there and at Worth and Cowden cannon works were established. The new blast furnaces also produced a greater proportion of iron from the ore and it is estimated that a furnace could produce five to ten times as much as the bloomery equivalent. Prosperous iron producers began to appear in the 1560s, such as Sir William Sidney with his Robertsbridge Works which produced 200 tons and made £400 profit by 1562. By the seventeenth century, however, timber shortage and a decline in demand from London weakened the Wealden industry, while new demands were made from Midland manufacturers which stimulated growth elsewhere. As late as 1623, a bloomery was built at Eskdale in Cumberland but after that the blast furnace gained ground and the way was opened for Midland ironmasters such as Foley and their

northern counterparts such as Crowley. It is difficult to estimate
the growth in output, since individual bloomeries will often be left
out of account, but S. Pollard and D. W. Crossley have suggested
that, if an annual output of 140 tons of bar iron equivalent is
assumed, an increase of furnace production may be calculated as in
Table 20.

Table 20—Iron Production

1500	140
1540	1,400
1570	7,000
1600	10,000

Iron was needed for domestic purposes, particularly for the provision of fire-backs, but much of the demand came from a growing
number of simple manufactures concentrated in the Midlands and,
from an early stage, tending towards specialisation. The development of cutting- and slitting-mills such as Sir Bevis Bulmer's at
Dartford in 1588 and the Tintern Abbey wire works were indications of an increasing variety of applications for iron. Birmingham
and Coventry specialised in scythes and nails. Sheffield developed
cutlery and the Cutlers' Company was founded in 1624. However,
the new manufactures required higher quality iron, in other words,
a steel equivalent, and although Sir Henry Sidney started this in
the 1560s, it was not successful because Swedish and Russian
imports were cheaper. In 1615 Ellyot and Meysey produced a
new furnace and a small amount of high-grade iron or steel was
produced. Two-thirds of the iron used was imported, so that
although total home iron production may have risen to 20,000 tons
by 1660, 12,000 tons were imported mainly from Sweden and this
rose to 20,000 by 1714.

Glass-making was another industry which benefited from the
increasing use of coal instead of charcoal, culminating in Mansell's
patent of 1615 by which the industry came to depend entirely on
coal. In the fifteenth century, England had been a glass-importer,
but the Tudor period witnessed the establishment of a native industry based on increased domestic and container use. It was one
example of an industry where the granting of monopolies was of
advantage in deterring imports and thus establishing a nascent
industry. Both in the west Midlands and the Weald, glass-making
became a major industry. Patents were granted to Verselini for
drinking vessels and to Becku and Carré for window glass in 1574
and 1567 respectively. Workmen were obtained from France and

three "glass-houses" were built. Huguenot *émigrés* contributed to its growth in the 1580s, but the use of timber (one glass works used 2,000 loads a year) forced the industry to move to the Forest of Dean and Worcestershire. Mansell's patent of 1615 attempted to solve the fuel problem and it also forbade the import of foreign glass. Mansell claimed to have spent £30,000 on his three furnaces near Newcastle. His patent was ended in 1642 and the works destroyed in the Civil War.

The glass industry was to some extent typical of a group of industries which Nef rather unjustly claimed as "new," including alum and salt production and brewing. These industries already existed in the Middle Ages but developed rapidly in the Late Tudor period, together with the new manufacture of paper. The use of coal, the operation of patents and the sizeable capitalisation of some of their undertakings makes them significant. In 1566 a patent for the production of salt by an evaporation process was granted to the Earls of Pembroke and Leicester. Installations were to be found at the mouth of the Tyne and Wear and one was estimated to be capitalised at £4,000 and to employ 300 men. The procedure was costly and four loads of wood were needed to produce a ton of salt. The salt patents proved unpopular and the price was high. They were abolished in 1642. Alum was a mordaunt, or fixing agent, imported from abroad, and in order to help the cloth industry, patents were granted in 1564 and 1566. Development was slow but early in James's reign, alum was detected in Yorkshire and in 1609 the Crown farmed out its rights and forbade the import of alum. Whitby became a centre of production, with as many as twelve alum houses some capitalised at over £1,000 and employing 60 workers. Paper manufacture proved difficult to establish in this country. John Tate was perhaps the first to do so at Hertford in 1495–6. Thomas Thirlby, Bishop of Ely, tried at Fen Ditton. It was not until Elizabeth granted her Court Jeweller, John Spilman, a monopoly that production began. He established a mill at Dartford in 1589. It was said that the mill employed 600, and there were ten or more paper mills by the 1630s. However, France continued to supply our needs and paper production only developed after the arrival of the Huguenots in the 1680s. Brewing was carried out with coal, in spite of complaints that the beer was tainted. London became a brewing centre using the barley from East Anglia, where malting-houses were established at Royston and Ware. Round the Tower and in Southwark, the ancestors of the late-seventeenth-century brewers were well established. Soap-making from olive oil and tallow developed with the use of coal and in 1631 was made the subject of one of the most notorious patents.

Mining underwent considerable expansion during the period, due to the demands of the Crown, the granting of patents, the import of foreign workers, and the utilisation of foreign skills. Tin-mining was more difficult and it became necessary to deepen mines, and although Cornish families such as the Godolphins called in German experts, little was done and production was stabilised around 500 tons a year. Pewter gradually lost ground to glass and pottery and demand for tin accordingly declined. Lead-mining was more profitable and the three producing regions of Somerset, Derbyshire and Alston all developed. In 1566 Christopher Schutz was called in to help with technical problems in Somerset and mines at Priddy, Harptree and Chewton Mendip were developed, particularly since it was hoped that silver might be located. A new form of furnace was developed by William Humphrey and Sir Bevis Bulmer's chain-pumps were put to work. By Charles I's reign, annual output had reached 12,000 tons where it remained for over a hundred years. One indication of the profitability of lead was the increase in the net value of the mines belonging to the Bishops of Bath and Wells: from £33 in 1583 to £152 in 1637; it fell to £70 in 1640. Lead was used for roofing and sheathing ships.

Bronze replaced brass during the period in a wide range of manufactures, such as bells and cannon, thus reducing the demand for tin and increasing that for copper and zinc. Attempts to mine copper had been made from the 1470s, in England, and from the 1520s in Scotland, but it was not until the 1560s that active development came about, due partly to the mistaken hope that calamine with zinc and copper had silver deposits and partly to the government's wish to establish a home-based armament industry. In 1564 Daniel Höchstetter, a Tyrolean miner, was given patent rights in the Lake District and work began in 1568. Two groups were incorporated—the Mines Royal for mining copper and the Mineral and Battery Works for making brass and producing wire. For twenty years, there was no return on the capital, the Germans withdrew and the English ran the company with German labour at Keswick. The Mineral and Battery Works set up a wireworks at Tintern to produce wool-combing cards, but this was mainly iron and not brass. The company succeeded in locating zinc in Somerset and in 1582 Martyn established brass works at Isleworth. By the late 1590s, production was at last started on a commercial scale, but never developed to any extent. Swedish copper and German brass sheet and wire were imported and, after an attack on the Germans at Keswick in 1642, production declined. It was not until the repeal of the two companies' monopolies in 1689 that any fresh advance was made.

M *

The effect of increased industrial activity may be seen in the continued rise of urban communities during the period. In Early Tudor times, a number of towns, such as Lincoln, Beverley and Stamford, declined when the cloth industry was not replaced by any new occupation. Specialising in some branch of the supply or consumer industries rescued many towns, particularly those influenced by the growth of London, such as Hertford or Maidstone. Towns with a more varied group of industries, such as York and Norwich, continued to grow and Bristol continued its recovery. West Country ports, such as Exeter, Plymouth and Fowey, expanded and no less than 32 new boroughs were created in the south-west of England during the Tudor period. Newcastle grew into a flourishing port and the east coast ports, like Hull and King's Lynn, flourished with the coal and agricultural coastal trades. Some towns whose growth is often placed at a later date also developed during this period. Birmingham was described by Camden as "swarming with inhabitants and echoing with the noise of anvils." Manchester had attracted the attention of Leland as the "fairest, best builded, quickest and most populous town of all Lancashire." Camden noticed its industry and merchants such as John Lacy, Nicholas Mosley and Humphrey Chetham increased its prestige. Although Chester made vigorous attempts to preserve her position, building a new port at Neston at the cost of £6,000 and founding the Merchant Venturers of Chester in 1553, Liverpool began to gain in prestige. Camden noticed the Mersey as the most-frequented river. Neston was abandoned in 1608, and Queensferry failed. By the 1660s, Liverpool was a flourishing port. Halifax and Leeds, Bolton, Bury and Rochdale reflected the growth of textile industries on both sides of the Pennines. By 1600 one writer could claim that there were 700 market towns in the country. Yet they remained small. If London had 300,000 inhabitants, Bristol had only 12,000. Moreover, industry still tended to be scattered and not concentrated in particular towns.

Table 21—Major Occupations in Towns, 1570

Trade	Gloucester		Northampton
Cloth	50	*per cent of population*	15
Retailers and dealers	19		21
Labourers	15		—
Leather	—		23
Building	—		7½

It has been claimed that the kind of changes discussed in this section amount to an industrial revolution. This claim was put forward by J. U. Nef in 1954 and strongly criticised by D. C. Coleman in 1956. Although specialisation had started, it was not yet well established and if the urban-industrial sector of the economy was growing, it was still comparatively small. Cloth was the main industry and remained so. Leather remained the second largest export industry, although coal was rapidly overtaking it. Coal was used in a number of industries such as salt, alum, brewing, saltpetre and sugar production, but it was not used in the iron industry. There was expansion in iron production, armaments and hardware, but the best iron was imported. A number of consumer industries such as hosiery, cotton goods, paper and glass grew rapidly with the rise in the standard of living. The tonnage of shipping doubled and most of it was built here. The building industry underwent a revolution in accepting its role as a consumer industry for ordinary lay people rather than a specialised craft. Technical innovations were apparent and monopolies were used to stimulate them and preserve newly started industries. The size of plant, the number of workers per unit and the possible profits all showed an increase. Sometimes both technical changes and enterpreneurial changes were highly significant but they were limited in extent. Although it is possible to point out inventions, such as the first steam-engine or the discovery of electricity, these had little impact. In spite of Bacon, it was not a scientific age. Nef's case was that new industries, new methods in old industries and new technical approaches constituted a change so radical that a revolution might be said to have occurred, but it seems that the argument against this point of view is more acceptable.

This suggests that industrialisation, which can proceed at various speeds, is a different phenomenon from an industrial revolution. There can be a revolution in a particular industry connected with a dramatic increase in output as a result of a technical innovation or a change in organisation. Thus, it has been claimed there was a revolution in the thirteenth-century cloth industry and others in the building industry in the twelfth and sixteenth centuries. There was such a revolution in coal production during the period 1550 to 1660. A revolution must, however, be seen in perspective. What may appear as a revolution in a short-term context may not prove to be in the long term. Taking the paper industry as his example, Coleman claimed that the revolution was not the introduction of papermills, but an important change in production methods at the end of the eighteenth century. There may be more than one revolution in an industry but the term cannot be applied with any validity unless the percentage growth on different occasions is roughly similar. The coal industry still qualifies as having experienced a revolution because the rate of growth was not to be equalled until after 1780.

Revolution has acquired, however, a wider and, at the same time, more specific meaning. An industrial revolution implies a significant shift towards or growth in industrial resources over a wide range of activities. The portion of the national income devoted to industry must rise. The structure of society must be altered towards the complex of relations we understand as industrial. Although economic change is slow, such a revolution will be marked by managerial changes, technical innovations, changes in scale and an increase of volume of production. According to Rostow, such changes need to be preceded by a period of rising demand, income and standards of living, together with the growth of adequate capital and the means to distribute it. Such conditions prevailed by the third quarter of the seventeenth century, but they were not apparent in the Tudor and early Stuart periods. The term industrial revolution has been applied to the eighteenth-century changes and cannot therefore be applied as well to earlier ones. Moreover, it has been emphasised by some historians that, although economic change is gradual, a "take-off" period can be distinguished in which there is a unique rise due to a comparative advantage. Coleman charted this in the paper industry and it is apparent in trades as widely varying as brewing, cotton and iron in the period 1782 to 1801.

These conditions were not fulfilled in the early seventeenth century. Industrially, England lagged behind Holland in this period. France with a rapid growth of population and a flourishing transport system seemed more likely to accomplish an industrial revolution. On all sides, industry was restricted by technical difficulties of production and distribution. A capital market could scarcely be said to exist. The number of large concerns in any one industry, let alone in the country as a whole, remains to be calculated, but as yet, apart from the coal industry, claims for tens of thousands of industrial workers and hundreds of new factories remain as unsubstantiated as when they were made. The pattern of production and of trade only indicated the likelihood of impending change and marked accelerating industrialisation and this was limited by monopolies and government restrictions and by depressions in 1594–7, 1614–17, 1621–4, 1629–31, and 1636–40. The Civil War disrupted progress still further and there were slumps in 1646–9, 1652–4, and 1656–60. Far from being a period of rapidly expanding trade and industry, it was a period in which the initial gains of a long period of inflation were scarcely sustained. The diversification of industry by the rise of challenges to the monopoly position of cloth and the increase in consumer industries laid the basis for thought on industrial innovation and fiscal operations, and it was the successful task of the second half of the seventeenth century to answer these difficulties. It was closer to 1700 than 1640 when the trend towards industrialisation became decisive and apparent to observers.

THE ECONOMIC CAUSES AND SIGNIFICANCE OF THE CIVIL WAR AND REVOLUTION

In 1642 the first of three Civil Wars started, which were to last with intervals until 1651, and in Ireland and the colonies for an even longer period. The destruction of effective royal control from 1642 and the abolition of monarchy in 1649 created a revolutionary state of affairs. A series of illegal governments followed one another as Cromwell tried to obtain consent, failed, tried military dictatorship, resorted to an imitation of monarchy and bequeathed so unstable a situation to his son that in two years the monarchy was restored. This period of warfare and governmental confusion was the most sustained period of political disturbance in our history and considerably affected the economic development of the country. Some 10 per cent of the male population was killed. Towns such as Birmingham (1643), Bolton (1644) and Leicester (1645) were sacked. Outbreaks of plague, poor harvests and the disruption of trade created severe hardships. One historian said that the Civil War was humane in comparison with the Thirty Years War. This was so, but it was a good deal more violent than is often represented. The castles and houses of the gentry and nobility were sacked (such as Sherborne and Basing), and "slighted" to prevent their use in future campaigns or because they were no longer of service. Thus, Queenborough in Kent was demolished because "the whole was much out of repair and no ways defensive of the Commonwealth." The Rump Parliament debated in February 1651, July 1652 and January 1653 the destruction of all English cathedrals and in 1656 block and tackle were affixed to the tower of Gloucester Cathedral to demolish it and turn it into a school. A transfer of lands equivalent to the other great land settlements of the Conquest and the Reformation occurred, although it was later largely reversed. £3½ million of Crown lands, and £1 million of Royalist lands changed hands by sale or confiscation. Bishops' lands were sold in 1646 and dean and chapters' lands in 1649, amounting altogether to £2½ million.

Under these circumstances, radicalism flourished, stimulated by religious Independency, and influenced by political and economic grievances. Although it is true that "it fared in those counties as in all others of the kingdom that the number of those who desired to sit still was greater than of those who desired to engage in either party," it is less clear whether large numbers of people were not in some way influenced by the changes of the previous ten years and were actively concerned. Sir Edmund Verney commented that poorer people took advantage of the war, saying gentry "have been our masters a long time and now we may chance to master them." There had been an undercurrent of discontent among the poor in town and country before 1642. Trevelyan's claim, that "the only other stirring of peasant revolt throughout the Stuart period" was in 1607, was wide of the mark. Uprisings in Wiltshire in 1629–31 and the Fenland riots of 1637 and 1640 were two of many other examples, and the emigration during those years was an important indication of discontent. Thus, the Clubmen developed in the west in 1643. The Leveller Movement was based on the towns and the Independent army and never succeeded in rallying wider discontents. Yet the insistence on the abolition of tithes was interpreted as a threat to rents and the attempt to secure elected ministers had serious implications for the landed classes, because as Sir John Strangeways had said, "if we make a parity in the Church we must come to a parity in the Commonwealth." The Fifth Monarchy Men and the Diggers represented the extremes to which the times conduced and although it is true "they had much more in common with William Langland than with Thomas Paine or Karl Marx," such movements were indications of important trends in society.

The revolutionary events and ideas of the period have readily lent themselves to interpretations of the Civil War and the Revolution as being events similar to other revolts particularly the French Revolution. One theory links the events of 1642–60 to a general European crisis, similar to that detectable at the time of the Peasants' Revolt in 1381 and the French Revolution in 1789. Another theory is based on the views of Weber and R. H. Tawney. Their argument was that capitalism emerged at the Reformation, found its religion in Puritanism and its expression in the opposition of a rising bourgeoisie to feudalism; and that the struggles of the period represent an early triumph of the middle classes over the feudal powers of Crown, Church and landlord. This theory is full of difficulties. Lipson once said "the progress of capitalism before the Reformation forbids us to regard the capitalist spirit as a product of the Puritan movement." Although feudal elements remained in society and continued to long after 1660, the feudal structure had been in decline from the middle of the fourteenth century. Seventeenth-century writers who spoke of "the Norman yoke" were arguing about a myth because the power of the nobility had already been weakened, not by a bourgeoisie but by the gentry. Bourgeoise is a term capable of many definitions, but it is difficult to see how it can include Lords Manchester, Essex, Fairfax and Brook and wealthy landowners, such as Hampden or Cromwell. The Long Parliament was scarcely a bourgeois institution and the War was started by a rift in the nobility and gentry of that Parliament. Loyalty to the Crown or religious faith were stronger motives than economic gain in the seventeenth century. Clarendon said "religion was made a cloak to cover the most impious designs," but it was also often the substance of the quarrel.

An interpretation of the Civil War that claimed it was fundamentally a class struggle would have to prove the existence of classes and their relative homogeneity. It would have to show that people took sides in 1642 with acute awareness of class as well as mere economic grievances which they would have as individuals. Moreover, since contemporaries clearly maintained they fought for political and religious issues, it would be necessary to prove the Marxist claim that "the mode of production in material life determines the general character of the social, political and spiritual processes of life." It is never easy to interpret men's motives, but to ask us to make this assumption, that environment is more important than the individual, is to start with an unproven case. To state, as Brailsford has, that "if we are asking what went on in the daylight of men's conscious emotions, the answer is . . . that their differences over religion raised the temperature to battle point" is quite as specious, but it corresponds to a greater degree with seventeenth-century opinion. Those such as Richard Baxter, who could discern economic and social motives in the two sides, maintained that it was "principally the differences about religious matters that filled up the Parliament's armies and put the resolution and valour into their soldiers."

Alfred Marshall once said that "the two great forming agencies of the world's history have been the religious and the economic" and if this statement had been acceptable to some English historians, the somewhat unnecessary dispute about the essential nature of the Civil War might have been avoided. Lipson argued that "the causes of the Civil War were primarily religious and constitutional, but the economic factor was not absent." This was an echo of the greatest authority on the period, S. R. Gardiner, who said that "no such conflict could be successfully waged without reliance on spiritual forces as well as on the craving for the material advantages." If it can be accepted that what Professor Aylmer has called "the old-fashioned Marxist view" is now regarded as no more than an interesting interpretation based on the views of one nineteenth-century economist, three important matters concern the economic historian. To what extent was the situation in 1640–2 the result of economic events? How far can the division into two sides in 1642 and the subsequent rallying of supporters be interpreted along economic and social lines? Was there in any sense what Christopher Hill has called an "economic and political revolution" during these years? Trevelyan reiterated his belief in 1942, which he had first expressed in 1904, that "it was not, like the French Revolution, a war of classes," when he stated that "the Civil War was not therefore a social war, but a struggle in which parties divided on political and religious issues, along a line of cleavage that answered roughly and with many personal exceptions, to certain divisions of social type." He suggested that it could not be a class war, since the classes who fought were divided and had all reached a wealthy enough position to take decisions, and in doing this underestimated the participation of ordinary people in the War. On this matter, Trevelyan did not clarify his position. In 1904 he stated it was a war "waged by two small minorities," but in 1942 he stated "in 1642 town and country alike rushed to arms." If, as Trevelyan said, "the hired labourer in the field remained neutral to the end," the New Model Army is a difficult phenomenon to explain. Cromwell described the Parliamentary army as consisting of "old decayed serving men and tapsters" and wished to add the "plain russet-coated Captain" rather "than that which you call a Gentleman and is nothing else."

Our understanding of economic change has grown since Marx wrote. The theory of the business cycle involving depression and inflation seems a more likely explanation of economic discontent, in view of the prolonged price rise followed by the depression from 1636. Moreover, it is now clear that economic and social growth is evolutionary and not revolutionary, and a society as wedded to stability and hierarchy as seventeenth-century England was unlikely to experience a revolution. Professor C. Wilson has rightly observed that "dramatic politically, the Civil War was not in any economic or social sense revolutionary." Consideration of the economic causes of the Civil War may well start, therefore, with an examination of three important economic developments which clearly had an influence on events in 1640–2. These were the effects of the depression in agriculture and industry, the financial crisis of the Early Stuarts and the impact of economic change upon the landed nobility and gentry.

It used to be considered that, after the social stresses caused by the Tudor inflation, the Early Stuart period was one of comparative calm. Clarendon was in many ways an acute observer of economic conditions; yet he maintained that England in the 1630s "enjoyed the greatest calm and the fullest measure of felicity." Thus, Trevelyan once wrote that, in economic affairs, the Early Stuart period was "an uneventful and prosperous prolongation of the Elizabethan era." In fact, the period was marked by a series of economic crises. For the landlord, there was a period in which prices only just managed to keep their 1600 level, and then fell during the 1630s. The later 1630s saw the steady fall of wool prices followed by barley and then by wheat prices from 1638. It is clear that the poor and the less economically viable gentry suffered considerably from falling rents in the same period. The people's opposition was shown in revolts such as that of 1629–31. The gentry had to wait until the Long Parliament voiced their grievances. They were affected by additional royal taxes and by increasing demands for tithes and church rates from clergy influenced by Laud's reforms. Thus, Sir Simonds D'Ewes, Member for Sudbury in the Long Parliament, spoke of the "poor inhabitants whose souls already groaned under the burden of ship money" being forced to pay for clerical maintenance and church repairs. In Cambridgeshire, a petition signed by a third of gentry complained in 1640 that ecclesiastical burdens "exceeded the burden of ship money" and that as a result of pressure from a Laudian bishop "divers farmers left the country and sold their lands and stock with great loss." Demands for nationwide contributions to the rebuilding of St. Paul's ran into opposition in 1638, when petitions from counties as far apart as Suffolk and Hereford protested both their loyalty and their inability to pay the necessary sums.

Industrial depression was widespread, and added to the poverty and frequent unemployment of a large proportion of urban populations. One writer has suggested that "grinding poverty was the lot of more than half the population" of Exeter in this period. Another authority has spoken of half the population of Coventry and a third of that of Leicester and Exeter being "close to subsistence." As a result of the cloth crises of 1614–17, 1621–4, and after 1636 this situation was greatly aggravated and it is significant that the Levellers found more support among the poorer town-dwellers than in the country. The depression of the 1620s was estimated by a Parliamentary committee in 1624 to have thrown 12,000 out of work. In 1636 the clothiers of Norwich, unable to find a market for their produce, "forbore a great while to set so many on work." This particular depression was made more acute by a plague which added the disruption of the home market to the problems of exporters. The "weekly intercourse of stuffs and other commodities from Norwich" was held up, and it seems that the cloth industry did not recover from this depression before the war. In 1638 a royal commission reported on the cloth trade and a year later, "great parts of the estates of sundry persons of this country do now lie dead in London in woollen manufactures." One commentator spoke of trade both at home and abroad which "declineth very fast," and in 1641 the Long Parliament was being petitioned about this decline of trade.

In some ways this situation produced a retreat from reality, because although government commissions in 1622 and 1638 explained some at least of the reasons for this decline, there was an increasing tendency to blame the decay of trade and the subsequent emigration to Holland and New England on ecclesiastical policies. The government accepted, in a proclamation in April 1637, that people left the country "that they might be out of reach of ecclesiastical authority." Henry Dade, one of Laud's officials, commented in 1635 on two ships waiting to leave east coast ports full of people "discontented with the government of the church" and that "about 600 more will shortly go over." He said that if this went on, "trade will be overthrown." It is true that a vigorous Laudian bishop would be likely to increase the flow of emigration because he would offend Puritan consciences and require an increased outlay from Puritan pockets. Emigration from Norfolk and Suffolk reached a peak in the period April to September 1637. Later, Bishop Wren of Norwich was impeached by the Long Parliament and one of the charges was that he caused at least 3,000 people, "many of which used trades, spinning, weaving, knitting and making of cloth and stuff," to leave the realm. Clarendon claimed that Laudian bishops had caused the decline of cloth manufacture, particularly kerseys and narrow cloths.

Stuart government showed concern about the rate of emigration in 1635, when it tightened the regulations for leaving the country. The lists of passengers compiled at the ports help to reveal the type of emigrant and the areas from which they came. Emigrants to Holland included a large number said to be visiting relatives and others taking service with the Dutch army. Emigrants to New England were poor clothiers and farmers, together with a number of skilled craftsmen and fishermen. Those leaving from one port (Yarmouth) came from no less than twenty counties. Over a hundred places in Norfolk provided emigrants. Thus, although religion was an important element in causing emigration, widespread economic discontent and grinding poverty were equally strong motives. A figure of some 2 per cent of the population emigrating between 1620 and 1642 has been given by Bridenbaugh. Ulster received another 20,000 including, for example, unemployed Kentish spinners.

Particular areas had other problems besides those common to the rest of the country. A wide area of eastern England was disturbed by the attempts to drain the Fens. Thus, in June 1638, Edward Powell led a revolt at Wisbech which claimed that the "losing of the fens would be the losing of their livelihood." In East Anglia, coastal defences erected in Elizabeth's reign had been neglected and there was the possibility of flooding. Ports such as King's Lynn, Yarmouth and Ipswich were silting up. The fishing industry was suffering from three problems. There was increasing competition from the Dutch, who had developed curing processes. Dunkirk pirates preyed on shipping. Impressment was frequently used by the navy in sea ports. In Herefordshire, farmers complained about the imports of Spanish wool, which were causing poverty. Stuart England was a nation beset by numerous economic problems and these were exacerbated by royal action. Monopolies and patents produced easy popular scapegoats as "unjust projects of all kinds, many ridiculous, many scandalous, all very grievous." Poor gentry were annoyed by Court gentry, particularly if they were wealthier. Government financial demands aggravated the gentry and brought in little enough after 1636. Ship money became a general burden of increasing uselessness and danger to the Crown. Thus, the yields for three seaport towns in East Anglia, which were most likely to benefit from a revived fleet, fell sharply and although a Laudian clergyman might preach at the Temple Church in Ipswich that "they were traitors and rebels that did not pay ship money," it proved impossible to collect what the country could scarcely afford. On issues such as these, the Long Parliament was united; the abolition of ship money was a unanimous move on their part.

Table 22—The Decline in Ship Money Yields, 1635–9

Boroughs	1635–6	1637–8	1638–9
Norwich	£740	£400	£150
Yarmouth	£220	£220	£80
King's Lynn	£300	£200	£72

In the depression periods of the Early Stuart epoch, the government continued the paternalism of its predecessors out of the mixed motives of fear and moral virtue. Yet it was paradoxical that, in Christopher Hill's words, "the poor law . . . was administered best before 1640 in the areas where the opposition was strongest and which supported Parliament in the Civil War." This was due to resentment at interference by the government in local affairs, the cost of carrying out government requests and, in the case of the Puritan gentry, to a growing belief that to continue paternalism only encouraged unemployment. If the "meaner sort" fought for Parliament, they fought on the wrong side, since the Puritan gentry had no wish to protect them and in the 1640s the Poor Law largely ceased to exist, with obvious consequences as the rise of Clubmen or Levellers showed.

For many people, the grimness of life was relieved by Stuart paternalism at a time when attitudes towards the poor were hardening. The tradition of charity by great households was dying, although Thomas Sackville, first Earl of Dorset, fed 200 daily for 20 years. In 1597, one Parliamentarian suggested that with a decline in hospitality by the nobility, the gentry were forced to take up the duty. Puritan gentry maintained, under the influence of writers like William Perkins, that such idleness was wrong and that people should be put to work or apprenticed rather than receive alms. The great number of vagrants and poor, estimated at a quarter of the people by a pamphlet in 1641 and still a quarter in 1696, were held to be evidence enough for the justice of this view. Unemployment was a serious problem, due to the increase of paupers in larger towns and to the substitution of seasonal unemployment for underemployment in agriculture. Moreover, in spite of the large amount of charitable giving for almshouses, the indigenous poor could not be dealt with by putting them to work. In 1619 pauper children were said to be dying in the streets of London. Stuart government brought to an end the last vestige of medieval charity in 1624, when the hospitality statutes imposing fines on those who did not keep up monastic charities were abolished. Henceforward, the government's policy was based firmly on the Act of 1597. Attempts to regulate the price of corn for the benefit of the public, by reissuing the Book of Orders, were made in 1622 and 1630, but the justices of Hertfordshire reported that "their strict looking to the markets is an occasion that the markets are the smaller" because it was unlikely that wheat farmers would lower their prices still further. Influenced by Wentworth's work in the north and by Laud, Charles I embarked upon a policy of enforcing the Poor Law in 1629 when letters were sent out by the Privy Council stating that there was "more than ordinary occasion to use all diligence and industry at this time." The Orders and

Directions of 1631 sought to infuse fresh life into the Elizabethan laws and some justices responded to demands that they should meet periodically and instruct parish officials in their duties. The Directions included demands for houses of correction to be built and for landowners to see that their tenants and workers were relieved and "not suffered to straggle and beg up and down in their parishes."

It is not clear how far this policy was effective; inasmuch as the Civil War was not a mass popular uprising, it had some effect, but to depend upon overworked and often financially impecunious justices was to court disaster. Isolated examples indicate that there was a response in parts of the country as far apart as London and Monmouthshire. When Gloucester was in difficulties in 1638, the justices were required to levy a weekly contribution. Yet the attempt to enforce the Poor Law and the attempt to restrict the enclosure movement, aroused the anger of the gentry at the same time as it failed to have a decisive result for the people it tried to help. The continued flow of emigration and the presence of a popular element in the events of 1640–2 indicate that the Stuarts failed to win peace by their social policies. The London mob was one example. In Lancashire on the outbreak of war, "men of no name and contemned interest by the mere credit of parliament and frenzy of the people on a sudden snatched that large and populous county from their devotion to the great Earl of Derby." Endemic popular discontent may be seen as a root cause of the Civil War, because it provided the material for the armies that fought the cause of others.

Popular feeling was of little consequence to the Long Parliament, even if Pym declared at one point: "God forbid that the Commons should do anything to dishearten the people to obtain their just desires in such a way." In November 1640, the Commons were united in representing the grievances of the landed gentry against the government. Although these may seem at first sight to be national issues, and the gentry a class united in expressing them, it is more likely that local disagreement and difficulties provoked the temporary alienation of the landed classes from the Crown. For this alienation, there were a host of reasons, political, economic and religious, often little separated one from the other. In a society which placed more emphasis on rank than class and on the locality than on any national policies, local factionalism was likely to be a key issue in deciding the way the political nation would divide. Strafford's rule as President of the Council of the North (1628–32) alienated the local gentry and elsewhere this process was repeated. In Somerset, a clash between Laud and the local justices over the enforcement of a ban on church wakes in 1633 increased tension. In the eastern counties, the impact of the Court drainage projects and of the most active of Laud's bishops, Wren, aggravated the gentry. The petition of the gentry of Cambridgeshire in 1640 enumerated their grievances and in the two years before this, a number of them had been alienated from their loyalty by Wren. The Bishop had complained of Sir John Monson and Sir Edward Ayscough to the King. Sir John Cutts and Sir Francis Hynd were in trouble over such matters as keeping private chaplains or failing to keep up impropriations. The list of local gentry offended by Wren was lengthy. Sir Henry Mallory of Graveley, Sir Anthony Cage of Swaffham Bulbeck, and Sir Robert Huddleston of Wilbraham Magna were fined for not paying church rates. At Meldreth, "John Ayloff, Kt." was presented for failing to attend church at all. The gentry regarded themselves as a caste entitled to deference, even from bishops and when the Laudian clergy began to remove family pews or newly erected tombs, which belonged to the gentry and blocked up parish churches, they ran into opposition. Lady Hynd at Huxton and Lady Hatton at Whittlesy St Mary were prosecuted by the same bishop for their indiscriminate erection of pews.

Disputes between Laudian clergy and the gentry may have been based on a genuine religious conflict, but it was also a social struggle for local dignity and prestige and an economic battle to force the landed classes to pay for a Church they had long neglected. Clarendon observed this situation in his usual shrewd manner. Many Laudian bishops were of low social standing and the clergy were often so poor that their stipends in "divers parts of Wales and of Norfolk" were less than "an ordinary ploughman's wages." Lord Brook described the Laudian bishops as *de faece populi*; D'Ewes spoke of "prelates raised from the dust," Prynne sarcastically observed that such men "thought no nobleman in the realm worthy to be their equal." Clarendon said that Wren in Norwich (1636–8) and Pierce in Bath and Wells (from 1633) had "provoked all the gentry and in truth most of the inhabitants within their dioceses." The gentry and nobility objected to being punished by threats or prosecutions from High Commission; "the shame . . . was never forgotten," said Clarendon. Moreover, "by want of temper or want of breeding," Clarendon said the bishops had not behaved "with that decency in their debates towards the greatest . . . as in discretion they ought to have done." John Hampden was one of the richest of the Buckinghamshire gentry and his grievances were not only about ship money, but because he had been prosecuted for holding musters in the local churchyard.

The social incubus of the bishops made it difficult for them to fight the local community in country or town. In the counties, holders of impropriations formed a property interest established at the time of the Reformation which had damaged the Church, but which the gentry were not likely to abandon. An impropriation was a benefice under the appointment of a lay patron, who either appointed a poor vicar or kept a Puritan chaplain for family use, while neglecting the interest of the parish. Sometimes the gentry just kept the tithes and paid nothing for the upkeep of the church and rectory, which then decayed. In Suffolk, according to the figures of a 1603 survey, 32·3 per cent of the impropriated livings were in the hands of the gentry and the Suffolk gentry were a closely knit group revolving round the Barnardiston family. As early as 1618, Robert Reyce had commented on them: "the gentry of Suffolk meet often, conversing most familiarly together." When Wren was impeached in July 1641, one clause condemned his interference with the rights of patrons. In Scotland (1625) and Germany (1629), attempts had been made to resume Church lands lost at the Reformation, and the English landed classes had some fear of a similar policy. Their expropriation of the Church in the 1640s, and their zealous defence of tithes in the 1650s, showed the importance of the financial stake.

Laudian changes caused constant friction. The Corporation of Norwich was involved in a dispute with two bishops over their rights to enter and leave cathedral services when they wished. A royal letter sent in March 1636 to settle the dispute was not accepted until December 1637. There were similar disputes in such towns as Winchester and Bristol. The right of the gentry to keep chaplains was a status symbol as well as an indication of Puritan household religion and Laudian attempts to suppress them led to bitter clashes. Thus, in April 1637, Wren wrote to his diocesan chancellor "to send Mr Harper from Sir Thomas Gawdy, and so all other household chaplains." In February 1638, Gawdy was also required to reduce the height of his pew. Wren was involved in a dispute with Lord Brook over his household chaplain, in a clash with the relatives of Sir William Withipool over the positioning of a tomb, and in altercations with Lord Maltravers over the storing of his gunpowder in a church. Wedgwood has rightly observed that the Puritan gentry were more concerned with "social distinctions . . . than reverence towards God." One member of the Suffolk gentry even stabled his horse in the church when he came to hear the sermon. Elizabeth had used ecclesiastical commissioners to overawe the gentry in Gloucestershire in 1574. Under Laud, the central authority again asserted itself and ran into opposition. The Root and Branch Petition of December 1640 spoke of ministers encouraged "to despise the temporal magistracy, the nobles and gentry of the land."

Moreover, Laudian changes were costly in several ways. Impropriators were required to repair chancels and pay vicars proper stipends. The local "grandees," as one Buckinghamshire clergyman called them, were ordered to pay their rates, tithes and other ecclesiastical obligations. With some exaggeration, the gentry said the church fees exceeded the burden of ship money. Wren tried to get the clergy of Norwich and Ipswich paid stipends and was condemned for levying a rate of 2*s.* in the £ in the City. When a clergyman such as Randolph Gilpin of Barningham in Suffolk complained that the parishioners, supported "by the richer sort," had refused his dues, Wren secured redress for him. The vicar of Wymondham complained that the impropriator had seized "besides the benefits of his house glebe . . . all the lesser oblations, all churchings, marriage and burial fees." Wren compelled the impropriator to pay a £17 annual stipend and all the correct fees. In addition, Laudian ceremonial changes cost money and in Wren's impeachment, article fourteen stated:

> "that during the time he was bishop of the said see of Norwich he did unlawfully compel the inhabitants of the several parishes within that diocese . . . to rail in their communion tables, to remove pews . . . and to make other alterations in the respectives churches; in the doing of which the said inhabitants were put to great, excessive and unnecessary charges and expenses amounting in the whole to the sum of five thousand pounds."

Difficulties between the landed classes and the clergy were one important indication of a breakdown of the relationship between central and local authority, but this had many other causes. The attempt of the Stuarts to stress paternal concern for the poor led to the opposition of the gentry, so that Sir John Oglander, Governor of the Isle of Wight, when he was faced with requests to enforce corn protective measures, complained that "whereas you think to help, you may undo the poor." One Essex farmer stated that he had defied the statutes because the local justices had not enforced them. The gentry were already aggravated by a constant stream of tax abuses and expedients, which ever since the forced loan of 1626 had aroused resentment and brought little return. The Grand Remonstrance referred to the loan and "divers gentlemen and others imprisoned for not yielding to pay that loan." Charles' government displayed a lack of sympathy to the unpaid, overworked justices and local officials, exemplified by a sharp criticism of a report by the sheriff of Lincoln in 1640, which said it was "frivolous." By 1640 it was becoming difficult to secure a local magistracy and those who had served turned against the Crown. In Somerset all nine Parliament members had held office in the county and all but one voted for the attainder of Strafford, the advocate of "thorough" as a solution to government weakness at a local level. Half of the revenue collected went to support the Court. Nobility and gentry connected with the Court replaced the mean profits of local office with the perquisites of monopolies, charters, patents and sinecures and aroused still further the dislike of the gentry on the spot, who regarded London and the Popish court with increasing disfavour. Henry Oxinden of Kent wrote from London to his wife: "I will make all the haste I can to thee, taking no more pleasure in being at London than in being amongst my enemies."

This intensive regionalism helps to explain the divisions of the landed classes at the time of the Civil War. It was the events of the previous ten years rather than any long-term class interest or movement that determined the division; even more so, in some cases, the events of the last twelve months of peace. Sir Edward Nicholas said that "popery hath and doth more than anything prejudice your Majesty in the esteem and affection of the people." When Charles's dedication to the Anglican cause became clearer, with the issuing of statements possibly drafted by Hyde during 1641 and 1642, areas which had suffered economically and produced a vigorous opposition in 1640 changed sides. Herefordshire, which had returned the Puritan Sir Robert Harley and contained the formidable Lady Brilliana Harley and such important Puritan preachers as Gower and Toombes, came out for the king. This was in spite of poverty caused by imports of Spanish wool, "great fears" about the strong Papist minority in the county, and the presence of a fiercely Laudian bishop, Coke, whose brother had been a Caroline Secretary of State.

Clarendon reflected the varied discontents of the gentry. Taxation had led to the imprisonment of "very many gentlemen of prime quality." Moreover, these new projects for money "served only to offend and incense the people and brought little supply to the King's occasions." Prosecutions in High Commission were "an insolent triumph upon their degree and quality, and levelling them with the common people." By supporting reforms of the Poor Law, and attempts to control enclosures, the Crown had "brought much charge and trouble upon the people." Clarendon spoke of "the excess of the court in the greatest want" and of "projects of all kinds" which added to discontent. Forest fines, distraints on knighthoods, the Adventurers' gains at the expense of the local gentry, the doubling of revenues from the Court of Wards, compositions for defying ancient statutes extracted under *quo warranto* writs, forced loans and ship money were among the "grievances against the property of our goods" that the Commons attacked. Cottington at the Court of Wards had, in Clarendon's view, incensed "all the rich families of England."

In 1642 the governing class of England was split. Nobility and gentry fought on both sides, and forty-eight Members of the Commons were relatives of the Lords. It was not a division between nobility and gentry but according to a host of personal considerations and local matters. Contemporaries agreed that the greater part of the landed class remained loyal to the Crown. Clarendon said "most of the gentry" were Royalists in counties as far apart as Somerset and Sussex. The gentry of Kent rose for the King as a county community as late as 1648. Oldmixon said "it is very true a major part of the nobility and perhaps the gentry did side with the King." Oglander said "the King's side were almost all gentlemen." Nevertheless, there was a division among the gentry. In Parliament, the split came over religion and was intensified by the Irish Rebellion during 1641. Gardiner described this as "the event which precipitated the division." A contemporary, Ludlow, put the split later and said the Nineteen Propositions were "the principal foundation of the ensuing war." Clarendon agreed that there was no need to "look far back as believing the design to be so long since formed." In spite of the likelihood that a conservative and loyal Commons in 1640, not intending to fight a war, was forced to take sides by events after that date, many historians have tried to argue that there is a discernible pattern of economic and social changes that account for that division. Although, in the end, the landed class remained loyal to the Crown and, in Baxter's words, "the smaller part (as some thought) of the gentry" were on Parliament's side, the rebellion has been seen as a revolt by the gentry of one kind or another, and attempts have been made to trace a pattern of change for a period of a hundred years before 1640 which accounts for this phenomenon of class warfare.

This aspect of economic history, known as "the controversy over the gentry," is in reality linked to much larger questions involving the other owners of land, such as the Crown and the nobility, and underlying economic changes, such as prices and incomes, rents and taxation. On an even wider canvas, the controversy is linked to the issue of feudalism and its conflict with capitalism, which Marxist writers believe to have occurred at this time and which has been discussed at the beginning of this section. The matters involved were first raised in their modern context by Tawney in 1941. Two changes were said to have constituted a radical altera- tion in the balance of power and wealth among the landed interest: the fall of the nobility and the rise of the gentry, one taking place at the expense of the other. The nobility were to some extent equated with feudal power and thus allied to the Crown, whose revenues were feudal, and opposed to the gentry, who were equated with a wide range of merchants, lawyers and ex-yeomen who had acquired land and a coat of arms. By a sleight of hand, the gentry were "transfigured into a bourgeoisie" and the Civil War became a conflict between feudal collectivism and capitalist individualism. Tawney's arguments were supported, in so far as they affected the nobility, by Stone in 1948, although more recently (1965) he has modified this measure of support.

Aristocratic decline was a feature of the later Tudor period and for this there were a number of reasons. The peerage remained small and grew smaller in proportion to the rise of numbers in other sectors of the landowning classes, particularly the gentry, who were well-established in counties like Kent and rose rapidly in others, such as Northampton. There were 55 peers in 1485 and still 55 in 1603. Elizabeth created hardly any and by 1572 there were no dukes. Under the Stuarts, a reversal took place. Numbers grew to 81 in 1615, 126 in 1628 and amounted to 121 in 1641. Dukedoms were revived for Buckingham. Baronets were created as a new order in 1611. In the Early Tudor period, new nobles had been Court officials or administrators rewarded for services, so that of the 39 creations between 1485 and 1547, 25 had such ante- cedents. This new nobility had to establish themselves in a land market where conditions were unfavourable and they did not profit greatly from the distribution of monastic lands or the sale of Crown lands. It was on these lands, rather than on the breakdown of the older landed estates, that the mid-Tudor gentry rose to power, although there were some examples of utter collapse among the old nobility, such as the Earls of Sussex.

The reasons why the nobility, rather than the gentry, suffered from the great inflation were because their revenues were more rigid and their expenses greater. The Earl of Derby employed 120 retainers and their upkeep, together with lavish hospitality, public charity and the dignity of what amounted to a small Court, was very great. Nevertheless, the nobility could dismiss retainers. The Berkeley family cut theirs from 150 in 1572 to 70 in 1580 and this was not, therefore, an indefinite burden. Overheads could be reduced, but fixed capital could only be liquidated, mortgaged or sold if it could not be made to produce a direct profit. The nobility incurred heavy debts and were forced to sell many of their lands. Yet this change has been misinterpreted by Tawney. Debts implied credit-worthiness. Sales suggested a rationalisation policy, and they were accompanied by a number of other adjustments. Some of the nobility became agricultural progressives, such as Lord Spencer. They profited from enclosure, like Lord Brudenell or Lord Saye and Sell. The Bedfords gained from Fenland drainage; the Willoughbys were involved in mining; others were involved in trading enterprises, like the Earl of Warwick. Some of the nobility intermarried with the City, like the Compton and Holdernesse families. The nobility received new and rich additions from the gentry and from the rising merchant class. The rise in the population of London created opportunities for noble land speculators such as Cleveland, Northampton, Salisbury and Clare. Studies of individual families show that, after a serious decline, the nobility recovered in a manner exemplified by that of the Herberts between 1590 and 1610 and the Percys between 1611 and 1615.

Militarily, the nobility was less important, although it remained customary for them to command armies and in the Civil War, they commanded on both sides. Their castles were of less significance but some of their houses were able to resist for the King. Personal service declined, so that Leicester and Essex were really the last feudal nobles with large armed retinues. Yet the territorial nobility remained firmly entrenched. A medieval Magnum Concilium was summoned in 1640 to York. In spite of the actions of Charles I, three-quarters of the Lords supported him, and where a lord was unable to secure a personal following in his district, this was considered remarkable as when, for example, Lancashire did not follow "their devotion to the great Earl of Derby." If the nobility had declined under the Early Stuarts, they would hardly have fought for the government, whose taxation was supposed to have helped the decline. Unlike the French nobility, the English remained loyal to the Crown. There was no Fronde. This indicates loyalty and common interest and suggests that as a class they had recovered. Stone has spoken of a period of "rigorous re-organisation and exploitation." A calculation of the total income of the peerage from land suggests a rise from £170,000 in 1600 to £700,000 in 1641. This was as great, in real terms, as in 1558 and much greater than in 1602. Moreover, the incomes of the peerage included non-landed sources, so that Lord Goring, for example, drew £3,300 from land and £26,000 from office. If ownership of Irish lands is also taken into account, it is likely that the peerage were even richer than the estimate given above. One example will suffice to show the limitation of Tawney's general case of a decline in the nobility's economic power. Among the heaviest debtors he instanced as an indication of decline was the Earl of Cleveland, but he was also one of the most successful property speculators of the Stuart period, and he was able later to recoup his losses.

It is safe to state that Tawney's argument concerning the nobility does not hold true for the whole period 1540 to 1640. There was a decline under the Tudors and a recovery under the Stuarts and little connection, therefore, between the distress of feudal magnates under Elizabeth and the outbreak of war in 1642. As to the rise of the gentry discerned by Tawney, this has been criticised in two different ways. Professor H. R. Trevor-Roper has challenged the concept of a rising group of gentry with one of a falling collection of "radicals" in poorer country houses. In 1958, Hexter criticised the basis of the limited statistics Tawney produced and also rebutted the argument in favour of a falling gentry produced by Trevor-Roper without the comforting prop of statistics of any kind. Tawney's statistics were based on two samples of manors and may be summarised as follows: (a) 2,500 manors, of which one in three changed hands between 1560 and 1640; (b) 3,300 manors, in which the peers' share fell from one-eighth to a sixteenth and the gentry's rose from two-thirds to four-fifths.

Unless statistics for all the counties are to be provided, such a selection will of itself indicate possibilities, rather than prove a case. Moreover, its limitations are considerable. Manors are not homogenous units for the purpose of counting. They may well be sold for the sake of efficiency or bought by someone who is non-resident. The sale of land in one county may be compensated for by purchases in another. Land sales, in a period when from the 1580s the annual rental on some estates climbed to a third of what they had been in the 1550s, indicate a determination to recoup losses. Crown lands are included in the statistics and, if they are removed, Hexter claims that the percentage shift of landownership indicated by the statistics is no more than $\frac{1}{2}$ per cent. Monastic lands in the earlier period, and Crown lands in the later, enabled the gentry who wished to rise to do so in company with a better organised peerage who retained their lands. Stone's contention, that "the rise of the gentry is to some extent . . . an optical illusion," is true, if by this it is meant that the rise was at the expense of the nobility. But there was a very definite rise in the total wealth of the gentry and the wealth of the Long Parliament reflected this. Those who disputed royal exactions were wealthy enough to afford the journey to London and there was no significant difference in the wealth of Court and country gentry in that Parliament. Of the four-fifths of the Parliament investigated by one authority, 60 per cent had incomes over £1,000 and there were scarcely 50 merchants in the House.

Trevor-Roper claimed that Tawney had misinterpreted the role of the gentry by including in his definition of that class those who were not strictly speaking gentry. The contention was, that if those who drew their income principally from the land were considered in a period of falling rents and prices and increased royal demands, the gentry as a class would be seen to be falling. Such men espoused Puritanism in opposition to the Court Anglicanism, stood against instead of for Spain and for the country against the Court men. There were such men, and in the mid 1640s they took over the County Committees to the disgust of the better-off gentry, so that Oglander on the Isle of Wight might lament that "we had here a thing called a committee, which over-ruled Deputy Lieutenants and also Justices of the Peace." In Kent, the triumph of those poorer factions led to the pro-Royalist revolt of 1648. Baxter referred to "freeholders and the middle sort of men" who supported Parliament. Clarendon referred to yeomen on the side of Parliament in the Forest of Dean and Gloucestershire and "some gleanings of the gentry." Oldmixon referred to "Middling Yeomanry" on Parliament's side. The defect in the argument that this group caused the war is that they were politically ineffective in 1640–2. Their rise in 1644–5 was a result of the weakening of their wealthier brethren and the growth of deeper social changes produced by the War. Moreover, the falling gentry are of two different social groupings. Although the poorer gentry of the east, excluded by sheer numbers from office at Court or elsewhere, supported Parliament, those of Devon and Wales supported the King. In Somerset, "the gentlemen of ancient families and estates in that county were for the most part well affected to the King." Thus, the down-at-heels ancient gentry supported the Crown. The other group were the inferior gentry, not in wealth but in position. In Somerset, those "by degrees getting themselves into the gentlemen's estates, were angry that they found not themselves in the same esteem" and became "fast friends to the Parliament." By this argument, the successful risen gentry initiated the War and the rising radical and wealthy gentry carried it further. The poor gentry presumably had not even the means to take part in the War and to leave a precarious estate to fight or even to attend Parliament would have been unlikely expedients.

The Civil War was not caused by either a rising gentry trying to set aside the aristocracy or by a falling gentry resorting to arms to destroy their better-off relations and fellow gentry. The gentry and the nobility were both affected by the same economic forces and both were endeavouring to preserve their incomes in a period of economic decline and governmental pressures. Some won through and others lost out but the use of "rising" and "falling" indicates a social change which does not correspond to reality. It was status, not wealth, that determined which side the nobility or gentry took in as far as economic and social considerations had weight with them. Court connections, relationships by marriage, county politics, religious affiliations, particular acts of royal folly and clemency, determined the divisions of family and county rather than a clash between conservative and radical elements. The radicalism was far more inclined to be religious or political than economic even in Parliament and the rise of stronger radicalism in the 1640s soon brought the governing classes to their senses.

The Civil War was not a war of town against country but in discussing the gentry question it is often forgotten that the townspeople were also involved in the War and that Stuart taxation demands, financial expedients and bankruptcy had affected the mercantile community as well as the county landowners. 60 per cent of the bishops' lands sold in 1646–50 went to London merchants. Fifty merchants sat in the Long Parliament. Baxter and others saw "correspondency with London" as a reason for taking sides. Trevelyan mentioned that the towns were divided, but some of them declared outright for Parliament. Manchester "had from the beginning (out of that factious humour which possessed most corporations, and the pride of their wealth) opposed the King." Others were as strong for the King, so that in Bristol, Royalist members were returned and expelled from the Commons, and that City was besieged for the King. The Leveller Movement drew much of its strength from discontented townsmen and the London corporation, train bands and mob all exercised a significant influence over events.

London's discontent with Charles, and provincial opposition to the stranglehold of London on commerce were influential factors in the pre-Civil War tensions, and it has been pointed out that mercantile interests were not ignored by the Long Parliament. Laudian bishops like Wren were charged with wrecking the cloth trade. Monopolies were again (as in 1621 and 1624) the subject of attack. Many members had suffered from Charles's policies, such as the Puritan members of the New Providence Company who had been expelled from the West Indies by the Spanish in 1635. The Grand Remonstrance referred to a number of grievances which fell mainly on the merchant community. A new Book of Rates had been issued in 1608 and it had been proposed to raise customs duties (or impositions, as they were known) still further in 1610.

Lionel Cranfield, as Surveyor-General of Customs, had helped to develop this form of royal revenue, which had increased considerably. However, the impositions met with opposition and there were two celebrated cases of resistance. Thomas Bate, who traded in currants, opposed the new rates and the Exchequer in a high-handed manner and declared that all matters of commerce were matters affecting foreign nations and therefore came within the sphere of foreign policy. The second case arose from the decision in 1604 to farm the customs, but as royal credit declined, the City or individual merchants became less willing to lend, and syndicates were created. The Court syndicate eventually beat the City syndicate of Sir Paul Pindar. In 1629 John Rolle refused to pay the customs and was supported by Richard Chambers, John Fowkes and Bartholomew Gilman. The House summoned the customs farmers, but they refused to plead saying Charles had forbidden them to do so. In March 1629, the King supported the farmers and condemned the Commons for "sundry other strange and exorbitant encroachments and usurpations."

This dispute had been made worse by a quarrel over tonnage and poundage, which had been granted for life to every sovereign from the reign of Richard III, but had been granted on an annual basis in 1625. Charles claimed that he had the right to collect the customs because of the "necessity for the receiving of the ordinary duties in the Customs House." He admitted, however, that "a few merchants (being at first but one or two) fomented" against the decision. His action in supporting the customs officers was backed by precedent and the opinion of the judges, but it ran into strong opposition in the Commons and two of the Three Resolutions of March 1629 concerned tonnage and poundage, which was declared illegal and any merchant paying them called "a betrayer of the liberty of England." Charles had the offending merchants persecuted in Star Chamber and carried on collecting the duties. The Grand Remonstrance referred to tonnage and poundage, "received without colour or pretence of law; many other heavy impositions continued against law, and some so unreasonable that the sum of the charge exceeds the value of the goods." It criticised the Book of Rates, "lately enhanced to a high proportion." The Act Against Tonnage and Poundage passed in June 1641 fixed them on an annual basis and declared Parliament's right to alter the duties "as shall be thought fit." The customs farmers were charged with having taken "divers great sums of money" and were forced to compound their sequestration for £150,000.

Ship money was a particular target for the merchant community, although it is clear that it became generally resented as a form of permanent land-tax and bore heavily on the poor as well as on gentry and merchants. The Remonstrance said it was "a new unheard of tax," although it had been levied in 1588 and on other occasions. It was levied on the seaports in 1634 but, as no ports could supply ships of sufficient tonnage, it was agreed they should provide a composition and Charles would build the ships. The necessity of such a tax was obvious in view of the Channel pirates, the Dutch threat and the need to have a force in being with Spanish-Dutch hostilities in the Narrow Seas. However, Charles carried the measure to extremes by extending the levy to the whole country in 1635 and this was met by protests from people such as Lord Danby and the Earl of Warwick. Ten out of twelve judges declared Charles to be in the right and in 1636, a third writ was issued. In 1637 a fourth writ was issued and a *cause célèbre* made of the trial of John Hampden. The twelve Exchequer barons decided seven to five against him and of the five, two were influenced by a technical point. Lord Keeper Finch declared that "Acts of Parliament to take away his royal power in the defence of his Kingdom are void."

Although Charles was legally entitled to decide defence matters, and it is clear that he used the money to re-equip the fleet, the possibility of taxation without the consent of Parliament was now apparent and the example of France not unknown. Moreover, in spite of Rainborough's Algerian expedition, little was done. The Remonstrance declared that "yet the merchants have been left so naked to the violence of the Turkey pirates, that many great ships of value and thousands of His Majesty's subjects have been taken by them." Although the yield fell steadily, Charles persisted in levying the tax which the Remonstrance estimated to cost between £200,000 (clause 113) and £700,000 (clause 20) in some years. In August 1641, the Hampden judgment was reversed and ship money declared illegal. Ship money had fallen, it will be recalled, on ports already suffering from economic depression. Resistance to the tax has not been adequately studied, but there are indications that it was intensely unpopular. Pym's later assessments, which were based on the machinery used for collecting ship money, were to arouse strong opposition.

Merchants were also oppressed by what they called "the restraints of the liberties of the subjects in their habitation, trades and other interests." The London merchants, incensed by royal debts and the customs farm, were aggravated by a series of fines for various offences amounting to £100,000 (1630), £33,000 (1632), and £70,000 (1635). The most infuriating of royal activities was the continued use of monopolies. The Grand Remonstrance referred to "soap,

N

salt, wine, leather, sea-coal and in a manner of all things of most common and necessary use." It was estimated that the monopolies "did prejudice the subject, above £1,000,000 yearly." The soap patent was estimated at £100,000, the wine at £300,000, "the leather must needs exceed both, and salt could be no less than that." The Act of 1624 had been meant to stop monopolies but Charles replaced patents by Charters of Incorporation. Soap was said to be controlled by Popish lords. The wine project of Alderman Abel and Richard Kilvert was particularly unpopular, and Pym, in the *Kingdom's Manifestation* (1641), claimed they had made a profit of £60,000, while consumers had to pay an extra £360,000. In the background of the Long Parliament's attack were memories of Cockayne, Mompesson and Bartlett. Culpepper denounced these "frogs of Egypt." Pym condemned "the great inundation of monopolies . . . very chargeable to the kingdom and bringing very little treasure into His Majesty's coffers." Although the Long Parliament condemned monopolies, it was unable to bring them to an end, and the Levellers were to continue the attack on this particular abuse.

At the time, it was claimed that the majority of the merchant community opposed the King. One contemporary said that "for the sea-coasts of the west, the great trading towns of Bristol, Lyme, Falmouth, Plymouth and Exeter" were for Parliament, whereas "the inland towns and cities in the west were most for the king." One modern historian has taken this further and claimed that the ports were "all for Parliament." Yet this was by no means true. Bristol, Falmouth and Exeter were Royalist. On the east coast, Newcastle was Royalist if Hull was not; even a port such as King's Lynn, which had suffered considerably, rose for Charles. On the west coast, Liverpool was Roundhead, but Chester was Royalist. London had often been claimed as the very backbone of resistance to Charles, but this conflicts with the view that royal policy favoured London at the expense of the outports by, for example, confirming the Charter of the Merchant Adventurers. Until 1638, London continued to lend to Charles. It was not until 1642 that the City government became hostile to the King, under the influence of men such as Thomas Soames, brother-in-law to Sir Nathaniel Barnardiston of Suffolk. The new Mayor, Alderman Pennington, was vigorously attacked in January by Alderman Garraway, who said: "Mr Pym told me there was no proof that my Lord Mayor and the other persons named were countenancers of Brownists. . . . Did not my Lord Mayor first enter upon his office with a speech against the Book of Common Prayer . . . the greatest jewel and treasure of our religion." In the same speech, Garraway threw some light

on the views of the fleet, which has been described as Puritan.
It is true that Warwick secured it for Parliament, but the sailors,
it was claimed by Garraway, "then despised all the world but the
King and the Common Prayer Book." Later, part of the fleet returned to Charles I in 1648.

Writing of the towns, Trevelyan said they were "the strength of
the Roundheads, although in every town there was a Cavalier
party." In the same way as the gentry decided on a wide range
of local issues and personal sympathies, so did the merchants, for,
as Supple has said, "the word merchant covered a multitude of
activities." Clarendon's contention that townsmen had a "natural
malignity" was by no means always true, although it was often
the case. The West Riding towns of Leeds, Halifax and Bradford
"which depended wholly upon clothiers, naturally maligned the
gentry." Lancashire revealed a clear distinction between the west of
the county, strong for the King and Roman Catholic, and the
manufacturing towns in the Pennine foothills. At the beginning
of the War, towns such as Manchester and Wigan rose for Parliament and the Earl of Derby was executed, in "a town of his
own," at Bolton in 1651. Salford, on the other hand, was mainly
Royalist. Eight Roundheads and six Royalists represented the division of opinion in that county.

It is a little too sweeping to say "that the mass of the people
were indifferent to the great issues at stake." They were not involved
in the decisions of the governing class and they were reluctant to
join in 1642, but this did not mean that they were without a point
of view. For many of them, religion was a matter on which they
felt deeply. In Herefordshire, Puritan reformers found that "the
common people" condemned them. Lady Brilliana told her husband that "many in this country say within six weeks all the
Puritans shall be rid out of the country." When Charles issued a
proclamation supporting the Book of Common Prayer, a traveller
commented that the people of Dover called out: "God Bless His
Majesty, we shall have our old religion settled again." Poverty and
unemployment were reasons enough to fight for others and Clarendon commented that "the common people . . . were in all places
grown to that barbarity and rage against the nobility and gentry."
In the clothing towns of Norfolk and Somerset, "the common
people" were for Parliament. Yet this section of the community was
largely inarticulate and only rose to prominence later in the 1640s.
The War was a split in the ruling classes and its causes are to be
sought in their motives, although the reasons for individuals taking
sides were their own as well as their leaders. There was no clear-
cut distinction, of town against country, of north and west against

south and east, or of one class against another. There was no over-riding economic motive and the concept of class warfare was apparently not known to the participants. Clarendon's comments were mere asides to an analysis which claimed that the main cause of the War was constitutional—failure on Charles' part to stay within the law after making concessions. Religion was the deepest motive present. Violent hatred of Roman Catholicism, opposition to Laudianism, loyalty to the Reformed Churches and a revival of Anglican support from the middle of 1641—all were important factors. Popish soap, opposition to Laudian finance, and anger at a pro-Spanish foreign policy had their economic aspect, but they were still religious matters.

A combination of economic circumstances helped to produce a situation which politicians and religious leaders used for their respective causes. Prolonged depression and financial exactions were thus of importance in causing the Civil War. The struggle in individual counties between those who had won through this period (loosely called the Court gentry) and those who had not (the Country) helped to determine local groupings. These were influenced by considerations such as religion and family loyalties. The nobility had managed to recover their economic position and inclined to the King. The gentry were influenced in the same direction, because they were closely connected with the nobility in interest and outlook. In towns, those groups of merchants or corporations that had suffered from royal interference were opposed by bodies of loyalists. The poor, particularly in clothing towns, sided with Parliament. In the countryside, the poor were divided. Cornwall, Lancashire and Kent produced Royalists from the ranks of the poor, while in Sussex, "the common people of the county" sided with Parliament against the Royalist town of Chichester. Some towns were seized for one side or the other by minorities; possession decided the matter.

Various occupational groups and ranks of Stuart society were involved in the Civil War and their economic interests were all to some extent at stake. There was no revolutionary intent on either side and no determination to set class against class. Cromwell's rule was as arbitrary as that of Charles. It was no people's revolution and it achieved no alteration in the balance of society. The significant change was the loss of royal power and that was a political change. Landed power was regained in 1660. Whatever radicalism there was derived from Independency rather than Communism and in many ways resembled the Great Society of the fourteenth and the Commonwealth of the sixteenth century as idealised Christian solutions to the problems of society. Radicals had no mass following and the only motive which can clearly be seen to have influenced ordinary people was conservatism rather than radicalism. When John Yates, a Puritan, tried to preach at Hereford in January 1643, the bells were rung to drown his voice and the congregation shouted "Roundhead" at him. This was an epitome of the kind of society from which the armies of the Civil War were raised.

Under these circumstances, government failure was great and to have alienated people so inclined to loyalty and ingrained with habit required gross mismanagement. James I and Charles I helped to create a wide range of grievances which politicians like John Pym were able to exploit. These grievances were partly of their own making, and they had constitutional, legal and religious significance. Economic conditions made the situation of the government desperate and the crisis of Early Stuart government was, at its basis, a financial one. The economic slump of the late 1630s made the government's policies an unacceptable burden to landowners, industrialists and merchants. Social policies failed to win popular support and aggravated the governing classes still more, although the issue of cost and the issue of local dignity were inextricably mixed in the minds of Oxindens and Oglanders. Religion was an issue of conscience and it also affected Puritan pockets. In the eyes of a D'Ewes or a Barnardiston, Laudian ceremonial and the cost of their Popish changes were indivisible. It was an issue of caste; royal policies caused not only economic distress but social umbrage. To many in the Long Parliament of 1640, matters of faith and matters of honour were of equal importance to matters of economics. It is likely that the Civil War is best interpreted by regarding it as a phenomenon of its own times rather than as the victim for the theories of the materialist historians of our own day and age. It was a national event fought over local issues. It was a struggle, with economic implications, concerning political and religious points of view.

CHAPTER 9

THE DEVELOPMENT OF THE OLD
COLONIAL ECONOMY

AGRICULTURE: THE AGE OF THE SQUIRE
AND IMPROVING HUSBANDRY

The Civil War involved both town and country, but the dislocation
it caused affected the landed classes to such an extent that they
overcame their differences and combined together, Anglican or
Presbyterians, to provide a political basis for the Restoration of
1660. Division in the ranks of the landed classes had allowed the
discontent of poorer people to come to the surface, and in the period
of bad harvests from 1646 to 1650, the Leveller Movement had
attracted a widespread support from the poorer classes in towns
and even in the country. It was the weakness of the movement
that it did not rally sufficient support from the countryside, where
discontent was great. In Cumberland, many "died in the highways
for lack of bread," and disturbances such as those of the Clubmen
or enclosure rioters were symptoms of the discontent. Leveller
propaganda sometimes reflected these feelings, but it was not a
sustained element in their thinking, even if William Walwyn was
the son of a Worcestershire landowner.

In the *Case of the Army Truly Stated*, the Levellers demanded
restrictions on enclosures and that it should be made easy for copyholders to become freeholders. Later demands for minimum wages
and for the abolition of tithes were included. The Earnest Petition
contained a demand for the election of justices of the peace.
Influenced by prevailing radicalism, another group, the Diggers,
led by Gerrard Winstanley, a cloth merchant of Wigan, tried to
practise communal farming on St George's Hill near Walton-on-
Thames. These indications of popular demands forced the gentry
to consider their position. Enclosure was profitable and copyholders were easy to dispossess. Tithes were often paid to laymen
in impropriations. The extremists melted away with the end of
the War and the return of prosperity leading to the boom of 1654–6,
but the warning was not forgotten.

It has been said that the 1660 Restoration was a landlord's
restoration. It was much more than this and trading interests were

of almost equal importance in deciding Parliamentary policies in
the 1660s and 1670s. However, the next hundred years were an
age of squires and landowners governing in their own interest and
keeping political power. With the decline of the Privy Council, a
new era of local *laissez-faire* was brought about, in which the justice
was the man that counted. Enclosure now proceeded without
government opposition. The independence of copyholders was
weakened by legal decisions, particularly one in 1677, and co-
extensively the law of entail was strengthened to prevent the
sub-division of estates. Landlords, alarmed possibly by rural disturbances, obtained the first major Game Law in 1671 and this was
re-enacted in Anne's reign. The Poor Law was strengthened by
Acts, such as those of 1662 and 1697 which increased their deterrent
aspect. In 1668 Parliament agreed to devote fines on nonconformists to the relief of the poor; an ironical gesture in view
of the unemployed Puritan soldiers and clergymen then in existence.
In 1663 the majority of laws forbidding practices such as forestalling
in selling corn were repealed and the Restoration Corn Laws were
for the benefit of the producer not the consumer. The powers of
the justice of the peace were increased, although there were few
attempts to see that he enforced the many existing paternalistic
statutes.

What kind of man was the average Late Stuart squire? Macaulay
had a low opinion of the squire, whose "chief serious employment
was the care of his property," and there was more than a little
bias in his view that "the gross, uneducated, untravelled country
gentleman was commonly a Tory." Pepys said that "our gentry are
grown ignorant in everything of good husbandry," and Defoe
commented similarly at a later date. Yet such descriptions hardly
fit such men as Sir John Reresby and Addison's Sir Roger de
Coverley had some basis in fact. As usual, it is probably unwise to
generalise about a whole class. It is clear that agricultural improvement was advocated with increasing vigour during the period, in a
way which was not to be seen again until the 1760s. Fortrey commented in the 1660s that "the profit of a great part of the land
and stock in this kingdom as now employed is wholly lost." There
was an awareness that some response to a situation of static rents
and a slowly rising population required more efficient production
if profits were to be raised.

It must be admitted that the landed classes took refuge in protection. They secured the abolition of the onerous feudal dues on
land and their replacement with a tax on commerce. The land-tax
was kept low and the Tory squires opposed the extension of commercial wars to the colonies, because it would mean an increase.

The Corn Laws were the outstanding example of protection, and the Revolution of 1688 served only to strengthen them. The Act of 1660 imposed a restriction of 2s. a quarter on imports when the price of home-grown wheat was under 44s. a quarter and reduced this to 4d. when that point was reached. The 1670 Act imposed a tax of 16s. when the price was under 53s. 4d.; 8s. when it was between 53s. 4d. and 80s.; and 4d. when it exceeded that price. In spite of this, the imports of wheat rose and between 1697 and 1731 averaged 770,680 quarters a year from the Baltic and Russia. Coupled to restrictions on imports was an encouragement of export, which was allowed in 1670 "for the raising land rents." Restrictions were still imposed in bad years such as 1709, 1741 and 1757–9, but the prevalence of bread riots, like those of 1738, indicated the consequences of the policy. Freed, exports led to a sharp rise in the corn trade. Between 1675 and 1677, 303,925 quarters a year were exported to the United Provinces alone and an observer at Bridlington commented that wheat was "already a considerable price for the encouragement of husbandry." Bounties were offered to encourage exports and these were renewed in 1689. In 1699 all remaining duties on exports of wheat were removed. Exports to such places as the American colonies became more prevalent with the collapse of European grain markets in the 1720s. Between 1697 and 1731, 12,367,357 quarters of wheat, flour, barley, malt, rye, ryemeal, oats and oatmeal were exported and between 1697 and 1705, £289,670 was paid in bounties.

A trend towards acceptance of enclosures was discernible from the 1650s when, in 1656 and again in 1664, Parliament rejected Bills to stop them. In 1656 Blith produced his *Vindication of the Considerations concerning Common Fields and Enclosures* and this reflected a new attitude to enclosure. This was either for arable farming, in the more progressive counties such as Norfolk or Wiltshire, or, for pasture, in the Weald and Midlands. Fortrey's *England's Interest and Improvement* (1663), Yarranton's *England's Improvement* (1677) and Houghton's *England's Great Happiness: or a Dialogue between Content and Complaint* (1677) were among the works advocating enclosure. In the Midlands at least, enclosure went steadily forward, most often by agreement made at Common Law. Between 1633 and 1700, there were at least twenty-eight enclosure agreements in the Palatinate of Durham. King's College, Cambridge, carried out such enclosures on its Norfolk estates. Only towards the end of the period was an Act of Parliament used to facilitate the process, although the numbers remained small: four for the reign of Charles II, two for that of William III, three for that of Anne and sixteen for that of George I. By the turn of the

Bounties [margin annotation]

eighteenth century, somewhere about 30 per cent of the total cultivable area was enclosed. Some 1,439 acres were enclosed in Anne's reign and 17,960 in George I's.

Agricultural improvements to existing land, rather than any increase in enclosure or in the cultivable area, were the main reason for the recovery of agriculture in spite of the depression of the 1690s. Three causes for this situation can be discerned: the spread of Dutch ideas in eastern and southern England; the lengthy list of agricultural writers, some of them being specialised and systematic in their work; and the activity of the Royal Society. Two of these influences had long been at work stimulating agricultural change but the Royal Society, created in 1660, was a new one. It reflected the interest in science which characterised a wide range of society in the post-Restoration period. The Society established an agricultural or Georgical Committee; from 1665 this produced what may be classed as the first farming statistics. However, it should be remembered that they were unsystematic and that they would most likely have been read only by the more progressive farmers. The thirty-two members of the committee concerned themselves with such matters as the size of cartwheels and the design of scythes and harrows. John Houghton, a leading agricultural writer and a Fellow of the Society, claimed that "since His Majesty's most happy Restoration the whole land hath been fermented and stirred up by the profitable hints it hath received from the Royal Society." This was something of an exaggeration, even if the closely knit landed community acted as a sounding-board for new ideas. On the other hand, it seems likely that the use of the potato, which the Society recommended for cultivation as an insurance against famine in 1662, developed as a result. Lancashire became the centre for potatoes and Wigan had an important potato market. The Royal Society's interest extended to the diseases of trees and to the different types of grass seed. Moreover, the link with science gave rise to the earliest indications of two important ways of improving agriculture—mechanisation and agronomy.

John Worlidge, a Hampshire farmer and author of *Systema Agriculturae* (1669), may perhaps be described as the first agricultural inventor to be specifically known to us. He invented a seed-drill, but it was not adopted, and it was left to Jethro Tull to exploit the invention. Tull was regarded by earlier writers, such as Lord Ernle, as one of those who liberated agriculture from a long period of atrophy. This can no longer be accepted, partly because it is clear that agriculture developed considerably before the eighteenth century and partly because Tull was by no means as original or as progressive as he claimed to be. Tull was a farmer at Crowmarsh

N *

Gifford in Oxfordshire and later at Prosperous Farm, Shalbourne, Wiltshire. In 1693-9, he visited the United Provinces where the new husbandry was practised. This had already been practised in England in individual cases; Goodge had used turnips in 1577 and Robert Loder at Harwell in Berkshire had used root crops and clover. Sir Richard Weston in 1645 and Samuel Hartlib in 1655 were among the earliest advocates of the system. Tull's fame rested on his seed-drill, invented in 1701, which aimed to stop seed wastage and to sow evenly. This would facilitate the use of a plough with the mould-board removed and used as a hoe. In 1731 he produced his *New Horse-Hoeing Husbandry*, but his ideas were not readily followed by others.

Soil chemistry and agricultural biology played an equally small part in farming progress in this period. Nevertheless, improvements which had started in Tudor times now became more general. Manure was regularly used. Chalk, marl, sand, seaweed, ashes, salt and many other commodities were used on the soil to improve its yield. Professor Wilson has referred to "barges . . . loaded with metropolitan dung that helped to establish for Hertfordshire farming a very high reputation." The Royal Society's interests in fruit trees was followed by such writers as Richard Bradley who produced twenty-four books on pollination between 1714 and 1730. Others such as Nehemiah Grew concerned themselves with the relative value of the various soil treatments and helped to elucidate the nitrate group of fertilisers in saltpetre used for gunpowder. The impact of these activities was not as narrow as might at first be thought. John Houghton produced his *Collection of Letters for the Improvement of Husbandry and Trade* which were published in nearly weekly issues between 1681 and 1683 and between 1691 and 1703. Edward Lisle's *Observations in Husbandry* (1757) were made in 1713 to 1722 and indicated that a number of developments had proceeded some way at least in certain areas.

Turnips were well suited to the light soils of Norfolk and Suffolk and soon spread to other regions. Worlidge referred in 1669 to their use "in some parts of England" and by the end of the century, both Hampshire and the Vale of Pewsey were growing them. One writer in 1726 said that there is "nothing which of late years has turned to greater profit to the farmer than sowing of turnips in his fields." Clover was the other requisite of a four-course rotation and as early as the 1690s, the Commissioners for Trade and Plantations referred to the fact that "the land in England hath been very much improved since the year 1670 by clover and other grass seeds." Calculations have been made that suggest that 15,000–16,000 acres or 1 acre in 580 was operating a four-course system, but it was clearly established in East Anglia and Wiltshire and was known as far north as Worksop in 1692. Other crops such as barley, for malting, coleseed, hops and flax all increased in acreage during the period. On the other hand, in order to protect colonial imports, the home tobacco-growing industry in Gloucestershire and Worcestershire was finally banned in 1694.

Grasses such as lucerne and vetch and clover increased soil fertility and added to hay as fodder. Together with the various types of turnip, these crops enabled continuous cultivation to occur, went a long way towards ending the "hungry gap" with its salted meat, and led to the joint development of arable and animal farming. There was a shift away from pastoral farming for sheep, because whereas grain prices were relatively stable and export encouraged, wool prices were lower each year and the export of wool was strictly forbidden. The government tried in every way to encourage the cloth industry and thus wool production. Colonial woollens were forbidden and the Irish industry destroyed in 1699. Calicoes were restricted in 1700 and banned in 1721. In 1667 the dead were to be buried in woollen shrouds. In 1678, in a belated revival of the sumptuary laws, woollen garments were prescribed for certain months of the year. Undergraduates were required to wear gowns of wool in 1698. These pressures failed. In East Anglia, pasture was turned into arable, particularly for barley. In Wiltshire, it was wheat that ousted sheep. In the home counties, Hertfordshire and Leicestershire, cattle became more important than sheep. Even if England failed to produce enough meat for her needs and Scotland sent 30,000 cattle to England a year, regional breeds were appearing, including Lincolnshire shorthorns.

Change and scientific attitudes were at last beginning to influence the agricultural way of life in quite wide areas of the country and to be part of the ordinary squire's life as well as the pursuit of isolated rural experimenters. Yet these changes continued to be limited in extent by the prevalence of unenclosed fields, three-course rotation and the diversity of ownership. The Norfolk gentry have received perhaps more attention than other groups and they reflect a widespread attention to new methods. Sir Edward Coke had bought Holkham in 1610 and this was to be, perhaps, the most important of the estates. Ten miles south lay Raynham, to which Lord Townshend retired in 1730. Close by were Houghton and Dersingham, which were the Walpole estates. The reputations of Lord Townshend and Thomas Coke were built on many years of solid progress because "it is in those two Counties beyond all others in England that some fine improvements in husbandry may be seen, to the infinite profit of both landlords and tenants." In the Midlands, another group of squires—the Ishams and Treshams, Drydens and Osbornes—were also effecting improvements. Yet, although the period was one in which the squire is often regarded as the typical figure, the trend was towards the creation of larger estates.

As in every period of agricultural history, the nature of those ownership changes has become a matter of dispute, but the overall trend seems to be clear. From the 1690s, burdens on the yeomen (copyholders and freeholders) and the tenant farmers became more severe with a steep rise in the land-tax and an increase in the cost of the poor rate. Moreover, in a market which was not renowned for buoyant prices and experienced notable depressions in the 1690s and more spectacularly in the 1730s and 1740s, the need to invest to improve income was essential. Unless alternative sources of income were available, this was difficult because there was no system of credit for small farmers. Larger estate owners had income from office, trade, mining rights and property development with which to supplement their purely agricultural gains. Land conveyed "social prestige and political power" and was acquired by those with sufficient income to build and to invest. Thus, from about 1680, historians have detected a trend away from the golden age of the small farmer towards an epoch of larger estates. Entail had been in existence since 1472, but it was now used increasingly to give a stability to the pattern of development and thus of invest-ment. An oligarchy was brought into being, so that all the major landed families of 1640 remained in possession in 1740 and many of them belonged to a closely interwoven network of Whig aristo-crats whose political power and rural wealth were opposed by no comparable interest.

Such a change took many years. In 1696 Gregory King estimated that there were between 160,000 and 180,000 yeomen, 140,000 to 150,000 tenant farmers and 16,000 landowners. Gradually, the smaller farmers were eliminated. The earliest complaint about this trend was made in 1732, but thereafter it became common. In 1775 one writer referred to "the destructive practice which has prevailed for near half a century back of demolishing small farms." One writer has estimated that from 1740 to 1788 between 40,000 and 50,000 farms disappeared. Landowners either tried to improve the conditions of tenant farms, by prescribing in detail the agri-cultural methods to be used, or to introduce long leases for high rents. If tenants would not respond they were driven out. The land agent or steward whose importance was stressed when dealing with medieval estates made his reappearance and in one *Advice to the Stewards of Estates* (1731) stewards were urged to buy freehold land and convert copyhold to leasehold. A trend which used to be associated more specifically with later enclosure was brought about considerably earlier by the demands which higher taxes, and higher investment requirements forced landlords to make on their tenants. Landed wealth reached its ostentatious peak in the eighteenth century when the level of conspicuous consumption on artistic and sensual pleasures was to affect the amount available for agricultural investment. The later part of the seventeenth century saw a more modest response, reflected in particular in the development of horse-breeding and hunting, the creation of spas and holiday resorts for the landed classes and, as usual, by a change in building design and architectural style.

Horse-breeding had developed under the Tudors and Early Stuarts and during this period the use of the horse for racing, hunting, coaching and to a lesser extent for ploughing became common. Although Macaulay claimed that the famous shire horses came from Flanders at a later date, it is now accepted that Suffolk punches were developed at this time. It is likely that they came from the Flanders mares commonly used for the heavy coaches of the time. Game laws restricted hunting to richer people (that of 1671 required an income of £100) and thus following on foot was replaced by mounted hunting, more particularly of foxes, since deer herds had been seriously depleted in the Civil War. James I had patronised horse-racing at Newmarket and the later Stuarts showed equal interest, particularly Charles II and Anne. A stand was erected at Newmarket in 1667 and Anne gave plates to be raced for at Newcastle and Datchet. From 1709 records were kept of racing performances and soon various famous meetings came into being; Ascot in 1727 was one of the earliest. Efforts were made to improve breeds by developing a rival to the Spanish jennets. A new breed was introduced from the Barbary coast which had possibly originated in Arabia. It used to be claimed that Charles II was directly responsible for this, but it seems more likely that it was either the Duke of Newcastle or Sir John Fenwick who made the initial moves and Godolphin who increased the numbers in the 1700s. All three men were noted breeders and Newcastle wrote *Horsemanship* in 1686.

Taking the waters, or retiring to a watering place for a holiday, became increasingly fashionable to such an extent that we find Pepys at both Epsom and Bath in 1668. Tunbridge Wells became fashionable in the second half of the century, after visits by Charles II and Anne. Its growth was marked by the opening of a church built by public subscription and dedicated to King Charles the Martyr in 1685. The fame of Bath was established by Richard

"Beau" Nash, a man who had failed at a number of activities, but eventually found his metier as the organiser of social life in the town from 1705. Buxton had been the resort of several of the landed classes in the time of Elizabeth and a number of lodging houses were built around the medicinal spring. Malvern developed after 1654 and among other fashionable resorts were Leamington, Cheltenham, Matlock and Ilkley.

Architecture in the last forty years of the century reflected both the wealth of the gentry and the power of the aristocracy. Various influences from abroad, particularly the work of Palladio, and features from Dutch architecture such as sash windows, were noticeable in the new vernacular style which replaced Jacobean architecture. Smaller houses were built in what is called Queen Anne style. This involved elegant proportioning, high-pitched roofs, rows of identical sashed windows and a central porticoed doorway. Internally, increasingly elaborate furniture, panelling and plaster-work was to be found and the plan of the house was now system-atically divided into rooms. The larger houses were influenced much more by classical designs and in this development Sir Christopher Wren was the most famous exponent. After the Great Fire, he was appointed Surveyor-General of London. St Paul's Cathedral and nearly forty London churches were built by him, although Wren was never allowed to carry out his plan for radiating roads and piazzas in the City. John Vanbrugh, born possibly in 1666, was a playwright and architect, best remembered for Blenheim and Castle Howard. Nicholas Hawksmoor was a pupil of both Wren and Vanbrugh. Wren also trained William Talman, who built Chatsworth. This house and other famous houses, such as Petworth in Sussex and Belton House in Lincolnshire, tended to be unneces-sarily rigid in plan and over-large for their purposes. Later works by such architects as William Kent, who built Holkham Hall in Norfolk, or James Gibbs, who was responsible for St Martins-in-the-Fields, tended to refine the treatment of classical style more successfully. The earlier buildings were often built for prestige and tended to weaken the financial position of their owners. Some such as Mereworth Castle built by Colin Campbell in 1723 were hardly worth constructing. Thus, one of the great scriveners of the age, Sir Robert Clayton, acquired his large house at Bletchingly from an insolvent Lord Peterborough.

The countryside reflected the wealth of the greater landlords, but the ostentation and elegance should not blind us to the reality of an unswerving and narrow power, which yielded little to con-tinental counterparts in firm enforcement of its position. In a hundred years from 1680, the number of offences for which the death penalty could be prescribed rose from 50 to 300. In 1718 justices of the peace acquired the right to transport on their own authority. They controlled the right of assembly (Riot Act, 1715) and the military (Militia Act, 1661). The landowning class took care that its position in government should not be challenged. From 1710 there was a property qualification for entering Parliament, so that country members had to own £600 of property and town members £300. This was not modified until 1838 or abolished until 1858. From 1732 until 1906, there was a £100 property quali- fication for being a justice. Thus, Parliament passed turnpike, enclosure, game and corn laws to suit the landowners, while at a local level, their powers to control wages, regulate the Poor Law and appoint officials such as Surveyors of the Roads ensured that their wishes would be obeyed by the humblest.

The justices tended to maintain those paternalistic laws which suited their interest. The Assize of Bread which maintained the quality of the article was re-enacted in 1710 and elaborated in 1758. It was not completely abolished until 1836, and the substi- tution of wheat for barley bread proceeded steadily in the eighteenth century. The Acts restricting the building of cottages were kept until 1775 and, combined with a decline in new cottage building, led to overcrowding, so that sometimes as many as four families lived in one cottage. On the other hand, hearth tax returns such as those of 1685 indicated that most cottages retained their crofts. Perhaps the most important survival was in the matter of wage regulation. Agricultural wages are notoriously difficult to assess because of the regional variations, the seasonal nature of their payment, the allowances given in kind and income available from other sources, such as cottage industries. Wages, like prices, tended to be stable, although the indications are that purchasing power among the poor for items such as tea increased in the eighteenth century. In part, this was due to the low prices for wheat, which enabled a greater diversification of diet to take place. Thus, Defoe commented in 1709 that the labouring man was consuming more bread, beer, beef and bacon. In some parts of the country, agricul- tural wages rose in response to an urban challenge. Arthur Young claimed that there was a direct relationship between wages and distance from London, and "it is likely that rural wages in the vicinity of industrial centres rose faster than any others in this century, and cottage building there improved after about 1750." It is true, however, that wage rates in Yorkshire (West Riding) were the same as those of Essex fifty years earlier. Roger North commented that wages in Norfolk, Suffolk and Essex were 12d. a day, in Oxfordshire 8d., and in the north 6d. or less. Defoe estimated the average wage at $8d.-12d.$ a day in 1728 and in 1767 to 1770 Arthur Young calculated that it was still the same.

Wage regulation under the Acts of 1495 and 1563 was used less and less in industry from the reign of Charles II, but in country districts the assessments were continued. Petty calculated that a labourer needed $4d.$ a day with food and $8d.$ a day without it in the 1680s; that is $4s.$ $8d.$ a week. Assessments had continued during the Interregnum in counties such as Devonshire (1654) and Wiltshire (1655). During the period of the later Stuarts, assessments started in 1661. That year a Worcestershire Grand Jury asked that servants' wages should be regulated and in 1663 there were wage assessments in the county. In 1674 the enforcement of the statutes was recommended and wage assessments from Hertfordshire (1678) indicate that some effort was made. During the 1680s, there are numerous examples cited by Lipson from Lincolnshire (1680), Suffolk (1682), Warwickshire (1684), Wiltshire and Somerset (1685) and Buckinghamshire (1687). The Warwickshire scale was for $4s.$ a week from March to September and $3s.$ $6d.$ in the winter months. Richard Dunning claimed that wages in Devonshire in 1685 were $5s.$ a week. Closer to London assessments of $6s.$ and $7s.$ were made, but it is likely that these were lower than the wages received. In 1704 the judges pronounced that the Statute of Apprentices "extends only to servants in husbandry, not to gentlemen's servants, nor to journeymen with their masters." Assessments continued in counties such as Warwickshire (1710), Devonshire (1713), Kent (1724), Lancashire (1725), and Gloucestershire (1728). A Parliamentary committee tried to establish more effective means of enforcement in 1724 but no action was taken.

It is impossible to generalise about the state of the rural poor. Gregory King estimated that the poor people numbered 364,000 "labouring people and not servants," 400,000 "cottagers and paupers," and 30,000 vagrants. 440,000 families ate meat twice a week and the rest did not. Yet if meat was restricted as an element in diets and made more difficult to obtain by game laws, the supply of non-salted meat increased with pastoral prosperity. With low wheat prices, the poor had a wider variety of vegetables such as carrots and cabbages to eat. Instances of arbitrary enclosure, such as that of the Marquess of Powys in Northamptonshire in 1712, were still rare at this time, although they were to increase at least until the regulations of 1773. Rural discontent was, however, hidden. Perhaps the passing of the first laws against rick-burning and cattle-maiming in 1671 are an indication of the mood of some labourers. The trouble was that cottagers with a small amount of common and most probably little more than squatter's rights, copyholders with dubious titles to possession and the poorer yeomen and free-holders were unable to find capital for improvements. Since it was an age of low prices, returns could only be increased by more efficient production. Where this occurred among the squires and great landowners, it was possible to prosper, even in the agricultural depression of the 1730s and 1740s, because the export market for wheat remained buoyant and reached its peak in 1749–51, and there was an ever-rising demand from the towns, where wages of labourers increased by a third between 1676 and 1730.

Agriculture under the later Stuarts was at the beginning of its slow decline as the most important producer of national wealth and it was already regarded as less significant than commerce as a creator of economic prosperity, with the notable exception of the corn trade. There were disputes on such matters as the relative value of high and low corn prices to the community, but economic writers concentrated increasingly on trade and industry as spheres of activity where new ideas were needed, profits made, and national wealth and honour sustained. The period was one of slow progress towards more efficient farming but this was limited by the pre-valence of the three-field system, small increasingly uneconomic farms and failure to apply known techniques of improvement. Among the nobility and gentry there were numerous examples of rising rent rolls, but these were not based on agricultural profits alone, coming as they did from town properties and mines. Invest-ment often involved indebtedness, and the increasing expenditure on houses, furnishing, travel and other pleasures meant that some landlords suffered during the period of the depression in the 1730s and 1740s. Agricultural production shifted considerably towards wheat rather than other bread crops, diversified with vegetable, grass and root crops and improved the quality of meat. These changes to some extent compensated for the decline in wool pro-duction but they involved more complicated techniques and the use of greater knowledge than many possessed. Farm stewards such as John Spedding, agent to the Lowthers of Whitehaven, often provided the necessary expertise for the landowners themselves. Steady and then falling prices did not mark a confident agricultural section of the economy.

On the other hand, with certain limitations, such as the famine years 1708–9, agriculture provided for the increasing population and responded more effectively than French agriculture, as Arthur Young was to observe. The wheatlands which Defoe praised accounted for a 15 per cent increase in corn production, and it was not until the 1750s that this trend was reversed. Scientific agriculture was now more than the prerogative of the occasional experimenter. Small estate offices in the squires' houses testified to a change in attitude. From 1732 statistics of cattle and sheep at Smithfield were kept. Four-course rotation was established in a number of counties and mixed farming and a wider variety of crops testified to a deeper understanding of agronomic principles. From 1685 there was internal peace in spite of the alarms of 1688 and 1745. Transport and postal services, pamphlet and newspaper all improved steadily, if slowly, the means of spreading information. In some ways the assured position of the landed classes helped agriculture, because it ensured favourable legislative treatment but it helped also to foster Augustan complacency and Georgian sloth. The amount of land under cultivation was not greatly increased. Enclosure did not proceed rapidly. Machinery was not introduced. Moreover, it has recently been suggested that the oligarchy of the early eighteenth century spent more than was wise on non-agricultural commodities. Others merely bought land for social prestige and did little to improve it. Agriculture needed the stimulus of a new factor before it could take advantage of existing techniques, and this was found in the rise of population in the middle of the eighteenth century.

THE COMMERCIAL REVOLUTION AND COLONIAL TRADE

From the 1650s, trade and related matters such as shipping were the increasing preoccupation of economic writers and of politicians. It came to be accepted that trade was important in developing the wealth of the country. Earlier mercantilists had stressed the bullionist argument for the accumulation of specie as the main purpose of trade, but writers such as Gregory King and Charles Davenant were aware that wealth could be measured in other ways. Davenant said that wealth was the "national stock" and consisted in manufactures, building, shipping, bullion and money. Writers such as Thomas and North advocated the creation of a free exchange and from 1663 the free export of bullion was allowed. This was followed by a period in which large amounts of capital were able to flow into the country. The activity of Jewish financiers from Portugal and the United Provinces, the Huguenot immigrants and the tapping of Brazil's trade through Portugal after the signing of a treaty in 1703 have been said to account for this inflationary situation. Brazil was particularly important, because gold was discovered in the Minas Gerais in the 1690s and diamonds in 1723. Silver smuggling from Spanish possessions also increased after 1713. In 1711 the Lisbon factory referred to "the Brazils and the great quantity of gold that is brought from thence." Money still remained a matter of grave concern because it provided the sinews of war and because it was the basis of trade credits or, as Davenant said, credit requires "sufficient quantity of the species." As a result there was a great controversy in the 1690s over the state of the currency and in one year, 1695–6, over 250 pamphlets appeared on this matter. A new currency was produced by Sir Isaac Newton, Master of the Mint, and this facilitated circulation still more. Government concern with trading matters started with members of the royal family. Prince Rupert was closely involved with a company to obtain furs from Canada. James, Duke of York, was involved with a fishery company. Both princes and the Duke of Monmouth (illegitimate son of Charles II) fought in naval battles with the Dutch, our main mid-century commercial foe. Charles and James were involved with the Royal Adventurers Trading Into Africa (1662) for gold bullion and the profits of slavery. At a lower level, there were many members of government departments who showed an understanding of trade matters and came to influence government decisions. Merchants such as Povey, Noell and Vyner had been consulted by Cromwell. Now they initiated policies and the influence of William and Henry Coventry, Sir George Downing, Sir Leoline Jenkins and Sir William Blathwayt was considerable. This influence is shown by the continuous attempt to set up a government department to regulate trade. The Committee of Trade had been a temporary expedient until 1630. The permanent committee lapsed and was replaced by a Board of Trade under the Council of State in 1650. This in turn was replaced by a Trade Committee (1655). After the Restoration, a Council of Trade was created which was unable to make headway against the companies and ceased to meet in 1667. In 1670 a Council for the Colonies was established and this became the Council for Trade and Plantations in 1672. After a short existence with John Locke as secretary it lapsed in 1675. Merchant pressure led to the creation of the permanent Board of Trade in 1696 which included among its members Wren, Newton, Locke, Davenant and such important merchant figures as Sir Josiah Child. The connection between government and trade was not purely in the national interest. The Duke of Leeds (Danby) received 5,500 guineas in order to forward the renewal of the East India Company's Charter. However, in collecting statistics and investigating ways of improving trade, the Board of Trade became an important pressure group and was by no means always subordinated to the merchants.

In the 1660s, writers complained that our trade was in a state of decay. Gloomy estimates were made of an unfavourable visible balance and works such as Samuel Fortrey's *England's Interest and*

Improvement (1663) advocated urgent measures to change the situation. By the 1700s, the state of trade was a matter of delight and pride to all and in this sense the period clearly witnessed an overall increase in trade. In the official statistics there was a tendency to overvalue exports by including re-exports, but since invisible exports were not calculated, the overall balance was almost certainly moving from unfavourable to favourable between 1668 and 1696. However, this was by no means a steady movement and it is possible to discern a trade cycle with a series of short-term booms and slumps often related to the wars of the period. There was a depression in the years 1664–7 brought about by the Second Dutch War and made more serious by the effects of the plague and fire. A second depression occurred between 1671 and 1674, influenced to some extent by the repudiation of government debts to the bankers in 1672. One critic at least saw another reason for the depressions of the 1660s in the disturbance of nonconformists by the Clarendon Code which deterred skilled foreign artisans from entering the country and affected clothing towns such as Norwich and Taunton. Thus, Fortrey opposed Acts against nonconformists and another critic wrote in 1664: "trade has decayed greatly since the Act of Restraint [Conventicle Act] came out."

With the Parliamentary skill of Shaftesbury to help them, the merchants obtained their trade war with Holland in 1672, and there was a period of prosperity, broken temporarily by the upheaval of the Popish Plot in 1678, which lasted until 1681. This was followed by a depression in 1682–90, ended by a series of measures designed to free trade in the 1690s. Prosperity in the 1690s was affected by the war and in 1696–8 there was a severe depression which has been compared with that of 1636 or 1621. Recovery was rapid and continued until the War of the Spanish Succession affected trade and there was a depression from 1704 to 1708. Recovery then continued, in spite of slight falls in 1715–18, until the crash of 1720 caused by the South Sea Bubble. It is significant that the growth period of the 1690s coincided with bad harvests. England's wealth was clearly less dependent on agriculture, and more on the free passage of colonial trade.

It was a period in which "armed aggression was the heart of commerce" and trade followed the flag. The seventeenth century was a period of continuous struggle with the Dutch, marked by the wars of 1652–4, 1665–7 and 1672–4. Dutch decline was more the consequence of endless continental war than direct defeat by Britain. Moreover, the government continued to see the Dutch as our main enemy, when in reality France was becoming the main commercial adversary. Trade wars with France in 1648–57 and

1678–85 were followed by armed conflict in 1689–97 and 1702–13; the Methuen Treaty with Portugal damaged French trade seriously after 1703. Sir Josiah Child said that "profit and power ought jointly to be considered" and governments were convinced that the two were closely linked, particularly those influenced by Whig financial interests. It was a period in which the Atlantic seaboard powers "were like cardsharpers in a Western saloon." Political considerations determined ultimately whether or not there was to be a war, so that the Third Dutch War, for example, was in part the result of a secret treaty between Charles II and Louis XIV of France. The English succession was at stake in both the later wars with France. Yet it remained true that English commercial interests found themselves menaced by rivals willing to use force. Our trading stations in the East Indies were eliminated by the Dutch and our last one at Bantaam was given up in 1682. The French threatened Newfoundland in 1680 and forced the government to decide to make it a permanent colony. The Hudson's Bay Company was attacked by the French in 1682 and again in 1686. A remark made to Pepys about the Dutch in February 1664 might well have been applied to the French at a later date: "To the coffee-house with Captain Cocke, who discoursed well of the good effects in some kind of a Dutch war and conquest . . . that is, that the trade of the world is too little for us two, therefore one must down." This was popular opinion, rather than government policy, at that time, because even a financial expert like Downing had opposed the war. Yet it was significant that one of the main causes of the war was the seizure of New Amsterdam in 1664 before war was declared. Over considerable periods of time, such as the 1680s, there were "wars beyond the line," that is, outside Europe, which governments recognised as necessary and allowed to continue even if there was officially peace between them. Halifax's comment, that "we are to consider that we are a very little spot in the map of the world and make a great figure only by trade," reflected a view taken increasingly by Whig governments.

A protective policy was adopted to support the growth of trade under these circumstances and, although older historians concentrated on criticising its obvious anomalies and dangers, it has now been accepted that what is loosely called the Old Colonial System worked with prevailing trends and successfully combated the protective policies of France and Spain. Whatever the original reasons for mercantilism advanced by the early theorists, the twin systems of navigation laws and trade laws were advocated in this period by the traders and economists. In view of the fact that the ideal conditions for developing trade—such as peace, a complicated credit system, good harvests and a buoyant domestic market and open foreign markets—were not available to Late Stuart traders, the record of growth achieved with protection was impressive. Navigation laws had long been in force, but had lapsed under the Early Stuarts. Efforts to promote a new navigation law had failed in the Parliament of 1621 and in 1622 a proclamation said the Acts "of latter years have been much neglected." Protection was extended first of all to the valuable tobacco imports, which were to be brought in English ships (1621), not exported to other countries except in English ships (1624), and to be shipped directly to this country for re-export (1633). Dislocation caused by the war years, increasing Dutch and French competition, the weakening of the great trading companies and the wish to stimulate shipbuilding were all arguments used by advocates of this policy, such as Lewis Roberts and Benjamin Worsley. The latter was Secretary of the Council of Trade and, with merchants such as Thomas Povey, was responsible for the proclamation of 1650 and the Act of 1651. All extra-European imports were to be carried in English ships. No fish was to be imported except in English craft. In European waters, imports were to come directly from their country of origin. The Act was aimed at the Dutch but it cannot be blamed for the outbreak of war in 1652, which arose from a variety of causes. The Dutch had made an agreement with the Danes in 1648 over the use of the Sound and it was necessary to modify the Act in 1653 to exclude naval stores from the Baltic. It is possible that the Dutch, whose rates were cheaper and whose craft were more effective, lost very little by the first Act.

However, mercantile interests were sufficiently in its favour to demand its re-enactment with stricter clauses. The Navigation Act of 1660 required the master and three-quarters of the crew of a ship claiming to be English to be natives of this country. All imports and exports of the colonies were to be in English ships. Certain commodities (sugar, tobacco, cotton, indigo, ginger and wood dyes) were "enumerated" and were only to be exported to other colonies or to England. Their re-export was to be a lucrative part of our trade. In Europe, timber and naval stores, fruits, oils, wines, spirits and salt were "enumerated." A register of foreign craft in English ownership was established. The Act of Frauds (1662) enforced this provision. English-built ships were not, however, registered until the 1690s. The Staple Act of 1663 required all colonial imports to come from England. In 1673 duties were imposed on goods moved from one colony to another and in 1696 all foreign-built or owned ships were excluded from our trade. The list of enumerated commodities grew steadily to include rice, molasses (1705), beaver skins (1722), copper-ore (1722), iron, coffee, coconuts, and silk (1764). Modifications occurred, so that the Treaty of Breda in 1667 recognised that goods from the staple at Dordrecht might be imported in Dutch ships, but the three Acts constituted the basis of the navigation system which was not swept away until 1849.

Contemporaries were divided over the effects of the policy. Coke in 1675 claimed that it damaged the Baltic trade, but Brewster argued the opposite viewpoint in 1695. It is true that the costs of shipping rose, since our craft were "near double as dear built and sailed with near double the charge of the Dutch," but part of this increase in costs was explained by the increasing cost of timber. The Baltic trade was damaged, so that one commentator in 1675 said that of the 1,500 ships entering the Baltic only 9 were English. On the other hand, the Dutch were injured by the laws, and the Acts had the advantage of increasing invisible exports (shipping services) and creating a re-export trade which increased revenue and industry. Between 1660 and 1688, the tonnage of English shipping increased from 200,000 tons to 340,000 tons, although the increase in volume of trade needs to be taken into account. By 1750, it had risen to 421,000 tons. The figures for the total entries and clearances at English ports were 827,000 tons in 1686, and 1,451,000 tons in 1765. Naval tonnage underwent an equally spectacular increase to protect the new colonies and trades. From 100,000 tons in 1660, the Navy rose to 200,000 in 1702 and 330,000 in 1760. Naval dockyards expanded and introduced new ideas such as lead-sheathing, started by Sir Philip Howard and Francis Watson (1670), caulking with pitch, developed by Mr Lee of Portsmouth, and eventually copper-plating in 1759–61 which eliminated the need for careening. By the 1700s, commercial craft were following the Navy in such matters and English "pinks" were able to oust the famous Dutch flyboats. Defoe claimed that 2,000 boats and ships used the Port of London in Anne's reign. Shipping was protected by the creation of signal codes from 1673, the charting and buoying of estuaries, and the erection of lighthouses. Henry Winstanley built the first Eddystone Lighthouse (1691–8), which was destroyed in the great storm of 1703 and replaced by one constructed in 1708 by John Rudyerd.

Governments hoped to gain from the import and export duties involved in the system of trade regulation. Customs farming was resorted to in the early years of Charles II but it was brought to an end in 1671, when the government began to collect them directly. The excise raised by Pym in 1643 had been strongly resented and there were riots against it in 1647. However, it had contributed to the greatly increased revenues of the 1650s and it was therefore retained in 1660 and granted to Charles II in exchange for his remaining feudal privileges. The customs were estimated to yield £400,000 but were scarcely up to £300,000 in the 1660s. Thereafter, they rose and passed £500,000 by 1674. The excise raised £268,000 in the 1660s but they also rose to about £400,000 by 1674. Excise farming went on until 1683. Excise was never popular because it was a tax on consumption, applying to tobacco, wines, spirits, beer, grocery, soap and pepper. An attempt to make it general, in order to replace the inefficient customs revenues, was defeated by public outcry in 1733. The revenue from the customs and excise was never sufficient to prevent resort to direct taxation, such as the hearth-tax (1662–88) and the window-tax (1698–1851) and increases in land-tax when it was re-assessed in 1692. Moreover, their collection encouraged smuggling, which became more than a widespread abuse, particularly when the enumerated commodities subject to excise were increased. Cocoa, malt, hops, salt, candles leather and paper were added to the original list of goods, as were tea and coffee. Smuggling also involved exports, particularly wool, so that William Carter could claim: "First is, Romney Marsh in Kent where the greatest part of rough wool is exported from England" and where were well-organised gangs involved in owling. Some places, such as Lymington in Hampshire, were said to live by smuggling. Estimates of the amount involved are likely to be inaccurate, but the official import of brandy fell from 42,000 lots a year between 1676 and 1696 to 5,000 a year between 1696 and 1712 and the difference was likely to have been made up in smuggled spirits. In 1743 it was calculated that the smuggled trade in tea was greater than the official imports and one estimate has put the volume of smuggled goods at 2 million lb increasing to 4 million by the 1780s. Moreover, it should be remembered that the direct smuggling of imports was accompanied by the secret return of re-exports and fraudulent entries in the port books. The increase of domestic consumption and the low retail prices of goods like tea and sugar suggest a widespread smuggling import.

Measures were first taken against smuggling in 1660. In 1669 cruising vessels were established near the coast and in 1689, 1692 and 1698 a series of Acts provided the basis of smuggling legislation. Seventeen surveyors, with 299 officers, were appointed at a cost of £20,000 a year to curb the smugglers, although the coastguards had little success. In 1721 laws restricting boats in coastal waters were tried and in 1745–6 loitering within 5 miles of the coast was forbidden. An Act of 1736 provided rewards for informers, but the close involvement of whole communities prevented the suppression of smuggling and in 1746, for example, there was a Parliamentary enquiry into tea-smuggling. Seaborne smuggling brought the goods from France, and land smugglers moved the goods on packhorses to inland centres, such as Hawkhurst. In 1747 the customs house at Poole was raided by smugglers It was not until 1817 that a coastal blockade was established and in 1831–3 there was a war with the smugglers, involving clashes at Worthing, Eastbourne and Pevensey, before this particular consequence of the Old Colonial System was destroyed.

Charles II ruled Scotland and Ireland as well as England and Wales and the problem of their inclusion or exclusion from the trade laws was one that was only solved with a good deal of bitterness being created. In 1668 a commission was established to consider the inclusion of Scotland, but this had lapsed by 1675. Thereafter, there was fierce commercial rivalry until the Act of Union in 1707. Animosities were aroused in the reign of William III by the failure of the Darien Scheme. William Paterson, a West Indian merchant, secured an act to establish a Company of Scotland trading to Africa and the Indies (1698). The site chosen was on the Isthmus of Darien, which offended the Spanish. William would not support the scheme and it collapsed in 1700. Ships belonging to the Scottish company were impounded as late as 1704. Scottish counter-measures included a Wine Act in 1703 to permit trade with France, with whom England was at war. Relations were embittered still further by the seizure of the *Worcester* and the execution of her master in 1705. However, the chief fact as far as Scotland was concerned was that the country was well behind England. The population of Glasgow was only 12,500, although after the Union of 1707 it rose to 40,000 on the strength of colonial trade. The number of ships increased from fifteen to sixty-seven between 1707 and 1740. The Act of Union included Scotland within the Old Colonial System with immense benefits to the country, particularly in developing Glasgow's share of the tobacco trade and the export of Scottish linens.

Ireland suffered from the opposite policy, because whereas she was included in 1660 the country was gradually subordinated to English interests, so that it was effectively treated as a colony. In order to encourage English cattle-breeders, the Irish were forbidden to export cattle in 1667 and this prohibition remained until 1776. However, this had the opposite effect from the desired one, because ships called at Irish ports to victual and English farmers were deprived of good breeding stock. In 1681 exports of Irish butter and cheese were stopped and in 1699 Irish woollen exports were forbidden. However, again in mitigation, it should be noticed that from 1696 Irish linen exports were allowed duty free, although this concession was weakened by the growth of the Scottish linen industry after 1707. Together, the two countries replaced European linen imports by the 1740s. Ireland in the eighteenth century was increasingly impoverished. Famines in 1726–9 and 1739–41 carried off 400,000 people and by 1750, 750,000 had emigrated. But this decline was mainly in agriculture. Irish linen was revived by Louis Crommelin at Lisburn, 10 miles south-west of Belfast. Output rose steeply from 1·7 million yards (1710) to 4·1 million yards (1730) and 11·2 million yards (1750).

The later Stuart period was one of colonial consolidation, rather than of expansion, and in contrast to previous periods, concern was expressed about emigration to the colonies depleting this country of skilled workers and necessary labour. Evelyn, the diarist, spoke of "the ruinous numbers of our men daily flocking to the American Plantations." However, the colonial population rose to approximately 350,000 in the North American colonies by Anne's reign, and this rise provided a new market for our exports. In 1700–5, the average value of American trade (exports) was £259,000. By 1766–70, this had risen to a peak of £1·8 million. Slavery developed rapidly during this period and spread from the West Indies to the southern colonies, where there were approximately 38,850 negroes by the turn of the century. Since emigration was not popular, the colonies obtained some of their population by less willing methods. Cromwell started the practice of sending rebels into slavery in 1649 and this continued until 1685. The Law of Settlement allowed justices to sentence vagabonds to seven years' transportation and in 1671 transportation was adopted in the Criminal Law. Indentured labour, whereby people contracted to serve a number of years, was another practice for obtaining colonial labour and this also led to spiriting or luring people to the colonies with false promises, against which Acts were passed.

These three examples indicate that forced labour was considered to be normal practice at the time and it is in the light of this that the development of slavery should be considered. Started by the Portuguese and Spanish, slavery had been mainly developed as a profitable trade by these powers and the Dutch, who established forts at such places as Elmina on the Gold Coast. England had participated in the trade sporadically in the days of Hawkins and by the 1620s slavery was established in Virginia. It was particularly appropriate for the cash crop economies of the southern states and the West Indies, which had insufficient attraction for immigrants or a sufficiently large indigenous population. England's concern to develop the slave trade led to peace with Spain, which was secured by a commercial treaty in 1667 and political treaties in 1670 and 1680. Eventually, in 1713, the Asiento or right to transport about 5,000 slaves a year to the Spanish West Indies was obtained. An English company was formed in 1660 and reconstituted in 1663 known as The Company of Royal Adventurers of England trading into Africa. However, conflict with the Dutch and the granting of licences to interlopers, weakened this organisation and it was replaced by the Royal African Company in 1672.

This company had the exclusive right to trade in Africa and it was concerned with selling gold, ivory, dye-woods, hides and wax in England. These were purchased by barter on the African coast with fire-arms, beads, shells, brassware, silks, knives and rum. However, it soon became clear that this part of the trade was less profitable than slaving. Tribes on the coast were willing to supply slaves from inland and where they were not, force was used. Forts were established by the company, such as Fort James on the Gambia and Cape Coast Castle on the Gold Coast. Sherbo, Whydah, Lagos, Bonny and Old Calabar were other centres of the trade. Although it cost money to transport slaves, they could be sold for five times their transport costs and as early as 1675 Barbados merchants complained that the company had raised the price of slaves from £16 to as much as £22 each. On the other hand, the company was faced with the upkeep of eight forts costing £20,000. The government appointed a committee in 1690 to investigate matters but it was not until 1730 that the forts were granted £10,000 a year for maintenance by the government. Closely associated with the fallen Stuarts, the company was suspect in the 1690s and, under combined criticism from shareholders and merchants, an Act was passed in 1698 which ended the company's monopoly. Trade was freed but those engaged in it were to pay a duty of 10 per cent on all goods, except gold and negroes, for the upkeep of the company's forts. The Royal African Company lingered on and was not finally dissolved until 1821. In 1750 it was expressly forbidden to trade in a joint-stock capacity.

In spite of the failure of the Royal African Company as a joint-stock venture, the slave trade was rapidly developed by private traders. The company itself despatched 500 ships to Africa, imported 100,000 slaves to the plantations and coined half a million guineas. By 1710 the regulated company sent only 3 ships while private traders sent 44—25 from London, 18 from Bristol and 1 from Liverpool. In twenty years (1680–1700), the number of slaves imported rose five times to 25,000–30,000 a year by the 1700s. In the eighteenth century, the annual total grew to 100,000. As far

as England was concerned, the two main economic consequences
of slavery were the establishment of the plantation economies and
the rise of the western ports to bring to an end London's unchal-
lenged position as the controller of the greater part of England's
trade. The West Indies were the main centre for sugar production
and, apart from Jamaica which was recognised as English by Spain
in 1670, no further possessions were acquired in that region. The
only major change was that the Leeward Islands were made a
separate colony in 1672. The value of trade with the West Indies
rose as follows: imports, from £609,000 in 1701–5 to £3,110,000
in 1771–5; exports, from £305,000 to £1,400,000. It was in the
southern states of America that the main expansion occurred. In
1663 eight proprietors, including Clarendon and Shaftesbury,
received a grant of the territory between Virginia and Florida.
North Carolina developed from Albemarle (1663) and South
Carolina from Charlestown (1670). Settlers came from the West
Indies, and the area became strongly Anglican and Royalist, in
contrast to the earlier New England colonies. John Locke drew
up an astonishingly reactionary constitution in 1668 but this lapsed
and, together with Virginia and Maryland, the Carolinas remained
proprietary.

Outport development was due to the overall rise in foreign trade
and to an increasing trend away from European to colonial trade.
In 1700 it has been calculated that the tonnage owned in various
ports was 140,000 (London), 17,300 (Bristol), 11,200 (Ipswich–
Harwich), 11,000 (Newcastle), 9,900 (Yarmouth), and 8,600 (Liverpool). When Pepys visited Bristol in 1668, he commented that it
was "in every respect another London." By 1700 the population
had risen to 30,000 and it was the second city of the kingdom.
Bristol's position was founded on tobacco and sugar and the revival
of Iberian trade in the 1660s. It took the manufactures of the
Midlands industries brought down the Severn in trows and exported
these to New England and West Africa. With the growth of the
slave trade, population rose even more rapidly. By 1714 it was
48,000 and by 1750 it was 100,000. Liverpool's growth was caused
by a more complicated series of factors, particularly the decline
of Chester. Liverpool obtained its Charter in 1677. The population
rose rapidly from 1,800 in 1660 to 6,000 in 1708 and 34,407 in
1773. Sugar-refining started in Dale Street in 1667. Thomas Patten
widened the Mersey and in 1710–15 Thomas Steers opened the
first dock built for 100-ton ships. In 1738 Henry Berny and Steers
constructed Salthouse Dock for 300-ton ships. Two generations of
Liverpool merchants built the port's greatness, so that by the
1750s it had overtaken Bristol as the chief slave port. In Late Stuart

times, the Mores, Claytons, Clevelands and Houghtons and in Georgian times, the Aspinalls, Cunliffes, Leylands and Fildarts created a merchant community based on cotton imports and cotton goods exports, sugar and slaves.

Perhaps the most valid criticism of the Old Colonial System is that it operated too exclusively in favour of England. In the short term, this helped English manufactures and increased the supply of cheap raw materials. Later, it restricted the growth of trade and precipitated the clash with the American colonies that brought the Old Colonial System to an end. On the other hand, the high labour costs of the early colonies prevented any real competition except in shipbuilding and it is likely that the colonists would have turned to England for manufactures without compulsion. Attempts were made to prevent the export of raw materials from this country and manufactures from the colonies. Bounties were paid to encourage both exports and imports which would contribute to a favourable balance of trade. Thus, naval stores, which came mainly from the Baltic, remained in foreign hands after the passing of the Navigation Acts. An attempt by Sir Matthew Dudley to found a company for their importation failed in 1688. In 1704 bounties were given for tar, pitch, turpentine, masts, cordage and sailcloth and in 1766 for timber. Attempts were made to control colonial shipbuilding in order to ensure an adequate supply for ourselves. Export of wool was forbidden but an attempt to control leather failed between 1662 and 1675. The colonial cloth industry was restricted in 1699, 1707 and 1719. Even such trivial items as beaver hats were controlled in 1732. Calico imports rose from 240,000 yd a year (1663–9) to 862,000 (1699–1701) and were then destroyed by a ban in 1721. Colonial iron manufactures were forbidden in 1731. However, it is easy to exaggerate the effectiveness of these prohibitions. For example, wool-smuggling continued on a widespread scale. By the 1770s, the New England colonies had developed manufacturing industries including 750 ironmills and one in three ships trading with England was American built. Trade between the colonies was difficult to stop, although direct trade with Europe was small in extent and had clearly been restricted by the Acts.

Restrictions of shipping and commodities under the old colonial system were on a national scale, and in the same period as regulation became more intense, the older companies began to decline. The later Stuart period saw a rise in the amount invested in joint-stock companies which rose from £5 million in 1695 to £10 million in 1707, £20 million in 1717 and to a peak of £50 million in 1720. Joint-stock companies were given the protection of limited liability for shareholders by an Act in 1662, provided they were incorporated. By 1695 there were some 140 companies trading on joint-stock principles, but they were sometimes unchartered and often unstable. Two-thirds of the companies in existence in 1695 failed to survive to 1698 during the economic crisis. The crash of 1720 was more spectacular and was followed by the Bubble Act which imposed restrictions on their formation. Three joint-stock companies, however, were of great significance. The Royal African Company has already been referred to. The other Caroline foundation was the Hudson's Bay Company. With the East India Company, these two controlled half the capital invested in joint-stock companies in Anne's reign.

France had secured the northern part of the American continent, controlled the fur trade and had a large share in the fishing trade. Quebec had been founded by Champlain in 1609, and the region slowly developed under the Company of One Hundred Associates. In 1663 royal government was established and between 1665 and 1672, Jean Talon reorganised the colony, whose population doubled to 7,000 under his intendancy. He was succeeded by Count Frontenac who, with Iberville, started an aggressive policy. Explorers were sent out, such as Radisson and Grosseilliers to Lake Superior, and Joliet and La Salle to the Mississippi in 1673 and 1682 respectively. Radisson and Groseilliers took service under Charles II in 1668 and the *Nonesuch* entered Hudson Bay. In 1670, under pressure from Prince Rupert, the Company of Adventurers of England trading into Hudson's Bay was Chartered. In 1690–2, Henry Kelsey was sent by the company into the Prairies. The French reacted by seizing the company's forts in 1682 but they were returned. In 1686 all the forts were seized by Iberville, although they were restored by the Peace of Ryswick in 1697. The struggle between France and England was renewed during the War of the Spanish Succession and Port Royal was taken by a combined English-colonist fleet in 1710. The Treaty of Utrecht recognised the rights of the Hudson's Bay Company, secured Newfoundland, which had been captured three times by the French during the War, and ceded Nova Scotia without Cape Breton Island. France was left in command but Britain had secured a foothold. The company secured a renewal of its Charter in 1690 and did not surrender its exclusive trading rights until 1869. Its profits, however, were small.

Attention was more closely focused on the third of the great joint-stock companies, the East India Company, which underwent a severe challenge to its authority in this period. The general stock had been established in 1657 and paid 18 per cent until 1682. After a rise in the 1680s to 20 per cent, the rate fell in the 1690s. Moreover, the price of stock fluctuated widely. It was £500 in 1685 and £33·25 in 1698 and this made investment somewhat hazardous. The forts in India cost some £100,000 to maintain in 1681, and the company was menaced by a wide variety of enemies at home and abroad. In 1668 in the case of *Skinner* v. *East India Company*, an interloper was awarded heavy damages against the company and a further judicial opinion against the company's monopoly was given in 1684. The company possessed forts at Surat and Madras and in 1668 obtained Bombay. In ten years, the population had risen from 10,000 to 60,000 under pressure from Gerald Aungier, President of Surat. In 1674 Madras was refortified. In 1690 the site of Calcutta was occupied and in 1697 Fort William was founded.

This vigorous policy in India was reflected in the firm defence of the company at home by Sir Josiah Child, who was a director from 1674 until 1699, and Governor from 1681 to 1690. Child consolidated his interest at Court, giving bribes and receiving a baronetcy. He fought off proposals for a rival company and secured the renewal of the Charter in 1686. After the Revolution, Whig interests urged the curtailing of the monopoly and although the Charter was renewed in 1693 pressure mounted. In 1698 a new East India Company was founded, conferring the right to trade in India on those who subscribed to a loan of £2 million at 8 per cent interest. The clash between the two companies was sufficiently important to be one of the election issues in 1701 but it was clear that two companies could only weaken our position. Agreement was reached between them in 1702; in 1708 they were amalgamated. The Royal African Company, Hudson's Bay Company, and the East India Company all survived, although with considerable difficulty and, in the first two cases, very little profit. Older companies were even less successful. The Merchant Adventurers' monopoly ended in 1689. An Act of 1673 threw open the Baltic trade and weakened the Eastland Company. The Russian Company became a regulated, instead of a joint-stock, company in the 1660s. Nor were some Late Stuart foundations of long duration. The Council of the Royal Fishing became a company in 1664 and was reconstituted in 1677. A company for trading in the Canary Islands lasted only two years (1665–7). The South Sea Company, set up in 1710 and strengthened by the Asiento in 1713, collapsed in 1720.

Trade was now much more a national than a company matter and its regulation was dictated by commercial treaties, rather than the privileges given to companies. The success of non-regulated trades and the association of monopolies with royal tyranny helped to seal the fate of the companies. In particular, trade with Portugal was regarded with great favour by contemporary critics as having always flourished without a company. The wealth of Exeter as third port of the land was largely explained by this trade. England's links with Portugal were political as well as economic. Elizabeth had backed Don Antonio against the Spanish in 1580 and English volunteers had fought in Portugal from 1660 to 1665. In 1662 Charles II married Catherine of Braganza and England secured Bombay and Tangier. A trading consul had been established in the time of James I and exports to Portugal were valued at £350,000 by 1671. There were a series of commercial treaties in 1642, 1654 and 1661, and then a clash over duties on sugar and wine imposed by England's colonial system aggravated the Portuguese, who forbade the import of English cloth. Demands were made for a treaty but it was not until the political pressure of the Spanish Succession War that John and Paul Methuen were able to negotiate one. English cloth was to be admitted freely and Portuguese wines were admitted at rates less by one-third than those charged on French wine. Port now became an English drink and gout an English complaint. The treaty brought considerable benefits. The value of exports rose from £355,000 in 1698–1702 to £610,000 in 1701–5 and £914,000 in 1726–30. Our imports rose from £200,000 in 1698–1702 to £242,000 in 1701–5, and £359,000 in 1726–30, thus maintaining a very favourable balance. A trading consul was established at Madeira in 1705. Brazilian gold was found "in the Fairs, markets, shops and amongst the gentlemen's Stewards" in the West Country.

With France, our trading relations were inevitably less amicable due to dislike of Popery, the ambitions of Louis XIV, colonial disputes and, later, to the accession of William III. Under Foucquet and Colbert, the French introduced a similar policy of protection to that of England and there were a number of trade wars. Trade between the two countries had been suspended between 1648 and 1657 and after its renewal, the French increased duties on imports. They rose from 30 livres in 1654 to 40 livres in 1664 and 80 livres in 1667. Fortrey and others maintained that £$\frac{1}{2}$ million was lost in trade with France and advocated a trade war. The clamour was increased when the French put a tax of 50 sols on our ships in retaliation for the navigation laws. Attempts to conclude a commercial treaty failed in 1670, and in 1678 an embargo was placed on French trade which lasted until 1685. It was renewed in 1689 and lasted until 1697 and it was in operation again from 1703 to 1710. Attempts to secure a commercial treaty with France were made by the Tories after 1710 but they were defeated by the Portuguese interests and it was not until 1786 that the Eden Treaty at last relaxed relations for a short while.

It remains to examine the effects of these events on England's trading pattern. The major effect was to increase the total volume and value of our trade. Thus, imports rose by a third and exports by a half between 1663 and 1701 and since calculations ignore the profits of the Newfoundland fisheries and the slave trade, they underestimate the gains. The balance of trade had become favourable and as the increase of shipping and insurance was also considerable, it is likely that invisibles also showed a favourable balance. This situation had been brought about largely by a rise in the proportion of re-exports. In the 1660s these were under a quarter of our total trade and by the 1700s they had become a third. Thus, in the 1700s two-thirds of our sugar and calico imports were exported again. A shift away from European markets was discernible and this trend accelerated in the eighteenth century. Between 1700 and 1760, imports from Europe fell from 53 to 44 per cent and exports fell from 78 to 63 per cent. Colonial imports rose from 33 per cent in 1700–1 to 60 per cent in 1772–3; exports rose from 13 per cent to 46 per cent. West Africa and the West Indies declined as markets during the early eighteenth century, whereas North America and later Canada and Bengal were of increasing significance with the development of manufacturing exports. The rise in total trade was sustained throughout the period (*see* Table 23).

Table 23—Imports and Exports, 1660–1760

	Imports	Exports
1660	£4·4m	£4·1m
1710	£4·0m	£6·3m
1730	£7·8m	£8·5m
1760	£9·8m	£14·7m

Of this trade, colonial produce was a high proportion in value. The figures do not represent the total colonial contribution because the commodities concerned were particularly prone to smuggling. The figures for the total value of colonial trade were: imports, £786,854 in 1698 and £4,443,443 in 1774; exports, £871,832 and £5,020,936. Shipping underwent great expansion during the period— from 323,000 tons in 1702 to 421,000 tons in 1751. This affected colliers, coastal, distant and home water fishing and foreign trade vessels. Ports developed so that Bristol had a population of 100,000

o

by 1750 and Liverpool had 35,000. Other western ports, such as Whitehaven and Glasgow, also developed.

The trading pattern was largely that of an advanced nation, importing raw materials and exporting manufactures. In particular, cloth exports recovered after the transfer to better-quality products had been achieved and although the proportion of our exports devoted to cloth fell from 57 per cent in 1700 to 45·9 per cent in 1750, the total value rose from £2 million in 1688 to £3·5 million in 1741. Thus, the figures for the percentage of manufactures were:

	Exports	Imports
1699–1701	55·9	31·7
1772–1774	54·1	16·9

and for food and raw materials:

	Exports	Imports
1699–1701	13·2	68·3
1772–1774	8·8	83·1

Colonial trading led to three developments. There was a rise in the re-export trade. There was an increase in the variety of products consumed at home. There was a rise in industries based on colonial imports. Thus, sugar imports rose as follows: 1615, 50,000 cwt; 1663–9, 148,000 cwt; 1699–1701, 371,000 cwt. Sugar-refining developed at Liverpool and Bristol and two-thirds of this import were re-exported. The price of sugar fell by half between 1630 and 1680. Imports of cotton rose from 1 million lb in 1700 to 6·7 million lb in 1775 before the development of the Industrial Revolution. Raw silk imports rose from 357,966 lb in 1700 to 697,529 lb in 1769. Coffee was first used in 1637 and was developed as a drink from the 1660s. Thus, retained imports of coffee were 4,763 cwt (1700–4) and 5,029 cwt (1720–4). The actual imports in the same period rose from 5,764 cwt to 13,648 cwt. Thereafter the drink lost popularity to tea which was first mentioned in 1660. Here the increase in retained import was from 26,000 lb in 1700 to 1704 to 685,000 lb in 1720–4. The total imports had risen from 0·07 million lb to 1·03 million lb in the same period. Tobacco had been the most valuable colonial import and its rise was spectacular. From 20,000 lb in 1619, it rose to 1,250,000 lb in 1640, 7,000,000 lb in 1662–3, and 22,000,000 lb in 1700. Thereafter, there was a decline in tobacco smoking, partially accounted for by the introduction of snuff after the capture of a Spanish consignment in 1702. There was a heavy loss from 1685 and Scotland took much in trade after 1707. Tobacco imports had fallen to 8·8 million lb by 1720 to 1724. Sugar similarly suffered some decline after France obtained Santo Domingo from the Spanish in 1697 and cut our re-export trade. National income increased considerably. Rough calculations by Petty (1664–5) and King (1668) indicate an increase of 28 per cent and for this trade was largely the cause. Between 1688 and 1760, the proportion of total incomes obtained by trade rose from 11·6 per cent to 23·3 per cent of the population.

The period 1660 to 1714, and even more so the next forty years, saw the creation of a closely controlled colonial empire providing an increasing focus for our exports and sending us, on profitable terms, imports and re-exports. Protected by the government in peace by the Old Colonial System, and in war by the Navy, the trading community grew rich and powerful. By the 1720s, residence in the country was no longer considered the only possibility for those with wealth and fashionable merchant quarters were established in towns like Liverpool. New industries developed such as chocolate making at Bristol in 1731. Fresh demands were made on inland transport facilities. Business required new forms of exchange and borrowing. National prosperity led to an ever-widening market for new products and diet was improved for many by tropical products. At long last, the dependence of England on the cloth trade was brought to an end and with it the dominance of London over the other ports. An ever-widening number of manufactures were required for the export trade. Bristol and Exeter, and later Liverpool and Whitehaven, overcame the supremacy of the Pool of London. Newspapers, journals and a postal service linked together a more widely divergent merchant community. Their money flowed into agricultural development. A national economic policy replaced the companies as arbiters of our future, except in the case of the East India Company, which was a political as well as an economic organisation. The commercial revolution, therefore, laid the basis for the Industrial Revolution, because it provided a two-fold stimulus to industry from increasing exports and import-based industries and also, by increasing wealth, developed the home market and brought about a rise in demand. It has been claimed that the Industrial Revolution evolved from a primitive economy similar to an underdeveloped nation of today. Any consideration of the busy ports of England under Anne and the early Georges, will show that theory to be false. The Industrial Revolution developed in a nation well nourished with trade, the possessor of a large empire, and the acknowledged naval power of the world; it was in the Treaty of Utrecht in 1713 that these foundations were first manifested to all Europe.

FINANCIAL AND BUSINESS ORGANISATION

A nation in which the trading community was increasing and becoming more widespread and, at the same time, taking on larger responsibilities in more and more parts of the world needed business facilities and financial institutions. Sir William Petty said that during Charles II's reign the postage of letters increased twenty-fold "which argues the increase of business." In 1572 Thomas Randolph had established the official post on a permanent basis and relays of horses were provided, so that up to 150 miles could be covered in a day. The right to seize horses for this purpose was restricted in 1603. In 1635 Thomas Witherings and Sir John Coke reorganised the Post Office and permitted private letters to be carried at the rate of 2*d.* for eighty miles and the cost of hiring a post-horse from the office. This public service collapsed during the Revolution, but the close supervision of correspondence by Thurloe led to the establishment of the Post-Master General's office in 1657. At the Restoration, this was given to the Duke of York. Net receipts increased from £20,000 to £50,000 during Charles II's reign. In 1680 William Dockwray started a daily post in London, which included four deliveries to the environs of the capital. The Post Office suppressed this service as an infringement of their monopoly, but provincial daily posts were soon established by the Post Office itself. In 1711 the Post Office Act established a general post for the whole country, and this was followed by a period of reform. Frauds were exposed in 1715, and from 1720, Ralph Allen of Bath was busy organising the farm of the provincial services. Menaced by highwaymen and restricted in speed, a service was maintained.

The Post Office carried personal mail, and from the 1690s, printed paper posts seem to have increased. Newspapers and commercial journals date from the Late Stuart period, and Addison's *Spectator* treated commercial affairs with a new respect. Weekly newspapers had appeared in Charles I's reign, when Nathaniel Butler produced a *Weekly News* (1622). During Charles II's reign, an official paper, *The London Gazette*, was started and a weekly paper, *The Public Intelligencer*, was produced from 1663 and another called *The Observator* in the 1680s. At this time, the press was subject to censorship, either through the operation of the Licensing Act (1662–79, 1685–95) or as a result of judicial decisions. Even when the press became free from direct censorship, it was still controlled by a number of "taxes on knowledge" which added to the cost. These were the paper duty (1694), the stamp duty (1712–14, 1725 onwards) and the advertisement duty (1701). However, in spite of these

restrictions, the press developed during Anne's reign. In 1702, the
first *Daily Courant* appeared and this was followed by daily papers
in various provincial centres, such as Liverpool and Exeter. Scotland (1690) with *The Edinburgh Gazette* and Ireland (1708) with
The Flying Post followed suit.

This daily press was accompanied by a number of specialist
journals which indicated the new concerns of the age. Perhaps the
first of these was *The Philosophical Transactions of the Royal
Society* (1665). Houghton's agricultural papers have already been
mentioned and it is significant that in those, from 1692 to 1702,
there appeared lists of share prices. In 1692 there were eight quotations; in 1694 as many as fifty. The shares of the trading companies,
the Bank of England and a few public stocks were included. A
London trade directory appeared in 1677. *Lloyd's List* developed
in the 1690s and was issued daily from 1726.

Edward Lloyd was the owner of a coffee house in Tower Street,
where underwriters met from about 1686 and he had issued
Lloyd's News in 1696. This was one indication of the importance
of the coffee houses, estimated to number 3,000 by 1708. Originally
set up by a member of the Levant Company for coffee drinking,
they had rapidly become important social centres. Various political
groupings met in some, and the government tried to suppress them
and failed in December 1675. Some were the forerunners of clubs,
so that Will's was famous for literature or Garraway's for medicine.
The oldest London club, White's, gives its foundation date as 1698.
Yet for the economic historian, the coffee houses' importance is to
mirror the growth of interest in commercial matters. It was in the
coffee houses that the earliest dealings in stocks and shares among
the public were started, and because they were unofficial strong
opposition was aroused. These dealings were condemned by the
Trade Commissioners and in 1697 stock-jobbers and brokers were
controlled by law, so that no more than a hundred were allowed.
The next year, the stockbrokers established themselves in coffee
houses in Change Alley. New companies were quickly floated, and
share prices rose to giddy heights. Heavy losses were inevitable
and the speculations of 1695–6 or 1720 were indications of the
precariousness of the situation. On the other hand, the existence
of such a share market showed that a new source of wealth besides
investment in land had come into existence. Even if shares did not
provide security, bonds with a fixed rate of interest were able to
do so.

Marine insurance was the earliest form of insurance to develop
and had its origins in Elizabeth's reign, although Italian *polizzas*
or policies had been comprehensive enough in the Middle Ages to

include shipping coverage. The Court of Admiralty, which had jurisdiction over naval matters, had referred to Lombard Street merchants and they had created the Chamber of Assurance (1575), whereby policies based on common benefits were to replace claims made under the Law Merchant. The position of these assurers was strengthened by an Act in 1601. Underwriting came to be done by individuals and business was gradually transferred from the United Provinces. Assurance companies were involved in heavy losses and by 1720 there were only two of note—the Royal Exchange and the London Assurance—and these turned to fire insurance, leaving the bulk of the business in the hands of the underwriters. Lloyd's was their centre; in 1760 the Society of Underwriters at Lloyd's was founded. This acted as a professional association to provide high standards of operation, and eventually in 1771 the underwriters entered the Royal Exchange.

Company insurance was more successful in the case of fire policies. The Great Fire of London in 1666 raged for three days and destroyed £3½ million of goods, 13,000 houses and 87 churches. Its effects on building in the City were small in regard to planning, since rebuilding took place on the same sites. The fire contributed little to sanitary improvements, since it left the liberties of Cripple-gate, Whitechapel and Stepney "in the same condition as they were before" (according to Defoe). On the other hand, many moved westwards and started a building boom. Sir John Reresby commented on the fire "that the dreadful destruction was not more extraordinary than the speed, regularity, and cost wherewith it was retrieved, and a new London, far exceeding the old, erected." Retail shops developed to some extent in place of street markets. In 1675 the Lord Mayor begged that these developments should stop, but the trend was not halted. The new houses were more often of brick and even of Portland stone, and the idea of insuring them was developed by Nicholas Barbon, a large property owner. In 1680, together with three others, he established the Fire Office, where timber houses cost twice as much to insure as brick houses. The City Corporation tried to found a rival organisation, but this failed in 1682. Barbon's organisation became the Phoenix Society in 1705. In 1696 the Hand-in-Hand fire insurance office started business in Tom's Coffee House in St Martin's Lane. The most important fire insurance business was established by Charles Povey and twenty-three other partners who founded the Sun Fire Office in 1710. Other organisations followed, such as the Union (1714) and the Westminster (1717). Fire insurance developed in the provinces, so that Bristol (1718) and Edinburgh (1720) were among the earliest in this field.

Life insurance was the third branch of the business to develop and was made possible by the collection of statistics on the probability of life expectancy. Observations of this nature had become possible with the work of John Graunt and William Petty. Such assessments were given added impetus by the plague of 1665. By 1693 Halley, the Astronomer Royal, was able to produce his *Mortality Tables*, and the government was the first in the field that year. In 1699 the Society for Assurance of Widows and Orphans was founded, and this was followed in 1705 by the Amicable Society for a Perpetual Assurance Office. The societies suffered badly in 1720 and the latter was the only one to survive. It was joined by the Equitable in 1762.

If insurance was an important prop for the business community, banking was even more significant, and during the period, both central and local banking came into existence. Banking was part of what Tories scornfully called "Dutch finance" and it took some time for writers such as Child and Petty to convince people of the need for banks. The functions of a bank as a place of deposit and of loans had developed with the scriveners or land agents, friperers or brokers and the goldsmiths. Scriveners concentrated on mortgages and Sir Robert Clayton, a leading scrivener, became Lord Mayor in 1679. Goldsmiths took property, particularly plate, and jewels as security for loans. They were willing to bank money from the 1640s, in return for which they paid interest. Clarendon said "bankers were a tribe that had risen and grown up in Cromwell's time . . . they were for the most part goldsmiths." By the 1660s, banking was in full swing. The interest obtained was 6 per cent and in 1664 Pepys was tempted to bank his new wealth with a goldsmith called Backwell, although in the end he decided against it and buried his money in the garden.

By 1676, when *The Mystery of the New Fashioned Goldsmiths or Bankers* was published, banking had become common practice and when Roger North's brother, Sir Dudley, returned from a long residence overseas, he was amazed by the dealings of bankers in bills, although he overcame his surprise sufficiently to bank with Sir Francis Child at Temple Bar. Bankers had developed cheques by 1675 and promissory notes soon afterwards. These were transferable and were thus in a sense banknotes. They were made legal in 1705. During the 1660s and 1670s, a number of bankers, such as Robert Viner and Edward Backwell, received London and provincial deposits, engaged in financing foreign trade with bills of exchange, and became indispensable to the Crown. Pepys used an inland bill for £50 from a deal merchant as early as 1664, although they were still comparatively rare. They were given some recognition by the courts in the 1670s and became fully legal in 1698.

The goldsmiths took over the role, once performed by international bankers and City merchants, of lending to the Crown and this was the cause of both their rise and fall. Charles II suffered from an inadequate and badly administered revenue and many avenues for taking taxes had been closed in 1640 to 1641. He resorted to a policy of acquiring money from abroad, including a Portuguese dowry and five loans from Louis XIV, but these only touched the edges of his problem. Administrative reform, such as that of Pepys at the Admiralty, the efficient work of the Treasurers, such as Danby and Godolphin, and of the Treasury Commissioners, such as Downing, helped a little more. Auditing and accounting, together with appropriation, was proposed in 1666 and opposed by Clarendon. However, they came about in 1689. Tax farming was done away with in 1671 and 1683–4. Yet the Crown still needed money. Charles II's debts rose to £2 million by 1670. Later, William III was faced with a war which produced £13½ million in debt between 1688 and 1702. Under these circumstances, the Crown turned to the goldsmiths and finally to the idea of a national bank.

Clarendon said that Charles always treated the goldsmiths "very graciously" and Martin Noell was knighted by him. With Backwell, Vyner, Meynell and Duncomb, they formed a close group, which advanced money on the hereditary revenues and in anticipation of Parliamentary grants, charging the king twice as much as the normal rate of interest. The bankers required that specific revenues or tallies on the farmers of customs and excise should be made. George Downing, Secretary to the Treasury Commissioners (1667–72) disliked the system and proposed an alternative in 1665–6 that included auditing of accounts, a direct appeal to the country to lend to the Exchequer, and the assignment of repayment orders, so that a creditor could take his order to a banker and cash it if he wished to before payment was due. This scheme was a failure. Auditing was eventually carried out in spite of Clarendon's opposition and revealed in 1669 the peculation of £1½ million. Thereafter, it was not used. The cost of the war led the king more deeply into indebtedness. In January 1672, it was announced that the government would not repay loans but only the interest over a period of twelve months. The goldsmiths were faced with serious difficulties and suspended payments to their customers.

It is not clear who was responsible for this move. Evelyn said that it was Clifford, but it was also attributed to Shaftesbury and Arlington. Arlington said "all concurred in it," but others maintained that the Council opposed the move. The immediate effect was the dishonouring of bills, and the collapse of five important goldsmiths. Sir John Reresby described the occasion as "the ruin of an infinite people, whose money they had borrowed at interest." The suspension of payments was continued until 1675, when the goldsmiths' creditors put their case to Parliament. It was agreed to devote the excise to the repayment of interest at 6 per cent, and this was paid until 1684. The remaining payments were eventually incorporated into the National Debt in 1705. But a decisive blow had been struck at the goldsmith-bankers and they continued to collapse—Backwell in 1682 and Vyner in 1684—so that as late as the 1690s, Lord Halifax thought that the repercussions of this would even prevent the government obtaining fresh credit.

However, the alternative of a national bank on the lines of that in the United Provinces, which was advocated as far back as 1627 and more frequently from the 1670s, still remained. The basis of the Bank of England was a loan made by a group of financiers led by William Paterson of £1·2 million at 8 per cent. In return, the subscribers obtained some allocations from the revenue and the right to found a bank. This was empowered to issue notes, buy and sell bullion, and deal in bills of exchange. Meanwhile the government had raised £1 million by either giving the subscriber an annuity of 4 per cent for life or 10 per cent until 1700 and then a growing share. The annuities were to be paid from a new excise on beer and spirits. This Act of January 1694 created the National Debt. In 1715 the Bank took over the management of the National Debt, and thus Whig subscribers to the war effort acquired a vested interest in the Bank, which they feared the Tories would repudiate. In spite of opposition from the goldsmiths, the Bank easily raised its capital and advanced it to the government. The Bank survived the perils of the 1690s and rapidly became an important financial organisation, disbursing payments for the troops and receiving foreign deposits which were previously handled at Amsterdam. Capital was encouraged to circulate. The rate of interest was lowered since the Bank paid 4 per cent and charged 6 per cent. In 1697 and 1708, the Bank was given the privilege of being the only joint-stock bank. This restricted banking in the provinces but it ensured stability. The Bank did not suspend cash payments until 1797, and it did not go bankrupt, as private banks frequently did.

The goldsmiths were still in business as London merchant banks, although the Bank of England (established in Threadneedle Street in 1734) remained the chief London bank. By 1725 there were only twenty-five goldsmiths left; there had been forty-four in 1677. They provided facilities in the City for overseas trade and in the West End for aristocratic finance. In the early years, firms such as the

o   *

Hoares and the Childs exemplified this transference from gold-smiths to private bankers. Both acquired landed property at Stour-head and Osterley Park respectively. In 1754 a Hoare became Lord Mayor. These banks were restricted by the monopoly of the Bank of England over joint stock banking and they could not extend their activities to the provinces. As a result, there was a lack of banking facilities in the provinces. Burke said there were only twelve country banks as late as 1750. During the seventeenth cen-tury, only one provincial banker, Thomas Smith of Nottingham, has been identified. Traders had to develop their own resources and the earliest country banks were established, not by goldsmiths, but by merchants. Smith was a mercer. The Gurneys were clothing manufacturers who performed banking functions in Norwich before the two parts of their business were divided in 1775. The first bank in Gloucester was founded by Wood, a chandler, and the first in Bristol by a bookseller. In Edinburgh, Coutts, a corn dealer, estab-lished a bank. These banks issued notes, but they were not widely accepted and some parts of the country, such as Lancashire, did without specific banks. However, merchants such as Finney of Manchester carried out banking functions and it is likely that these were widespread with the rising profits of trade, the receivers of taxes and the promoters of turnpike and waterway improvements having money to invest.

England did not supplant the United Provinces as the chief financial centre of western Europe until later in the eighteenth century. It took a long time for England to follow the Dutch example, so that, for example, the Central Bank of Amsterdam (1600) and the Bourse (1609) were not followed here until 1694 and 1774 respectively. On the other hand, the City emerged as an important part of the economy during the later Stuart period. Improved transport, better information, the post and the coffee houses made dealing in credit easier. It was a period of the last fling of the joint-stock companies, whose losses occasioned the anti-joint-stock Acts of 1708 and 1720. A national bank, a scatter-ing of merchant banks and a few country banks indicated how a banking system might evolve. Credit instruments such as the cheque, promissory note, inland bill and bill of exchange became commonplace. The national revenue at last left the precarious condition it had always been in and England was able to become the paymaster of Europe in the eighteenth century.

These changes were a response to the opportunities created by the growth of trade and the increased amount of money in circula-tion. After the currency reform of 1696 and the issuing of notes by the Bank of England, the availability of liquid assets was even more widespread. Two foreign influences played an important role in facilitating the developments already discussed. One was Dutch influence. A Dutchman, Houblons, was involved in the development of the Bank of England. Financiers, such as Van Neck and Van Notten, played an important part in eighteenth-century financing of the Bank and the Whig Party. Joshua and Gerard Van Neck were the sons of William III's Paymaster General, and they also brought other Dutchmen to England to settle near the Dutch church in Austin Friars, near to the Bank. The ideological contribution of the Dutch was equally great. Writing in 1668, Josiah Child had mentioned fifteen points in which the English might follow Dutch financial practice with advantage, including a central bank and a low rate of interest.

The other contribution was made by the return of the Jews to England. In the reign of Charles I, Carvajal had imported bullion into England, so it is clear that they had returned before the famous Whitehall Conference of December 1655. Cromwell was inclined to the Jews because of their sufferings under the Inquisition and their relevance to the Old Testament theology of the Puritans. Manasseh Ben Israel pleaded the case for a return before a conference of divines, lawyers and merchants and although no agreement was reached, it is clear that the Jews then began to settle. Thus, although it has been said that the Sephardic Jews from Spain and Portugal came to England after the Restoration, Pepys attended the Portugal Jews' synagogue in December 1659. The settlement of this group was followed by the Dutch and German Jews in the 1680s. Their importance was quickly recognised, for Sir Josiah Child recommended their naturalisation in the same way as that of the Dutch was quite often suggested in Parliament. Sir John Reresby said that Parliament debated the taxing of the Jews in 1675, and this proposal was renewed in 1689. However, they were too useful to the City community to permit discrimination, and were allowed to worship at the Bevis Marks' synagogue. Addison described the Hebrew merchants as "the instruments with which the most diverse nations converse with one another and by which mankind are knit in a general correspondence." In William III's reign, Solomon Medina was an army contractor and received a knighthood. His successor in Marlborough's wars was Sir Manasseh Lopez. They were the earliest members of a powerful group, later centred on Joseph Salvador and Sampson Gideon in the 1740s, on whom Walpole and Pelham much depended. Gideon's son was raised to the peerage as Lord Eardley. Trade and war together produced a wide variety of financial institutions and helped to nourish a business community which, on the one hand, was the carefully nurtured product of an exclusive trade policy and, on the other, was already caught up in the dextrous web of international finance.

THE DEVELOPMENT OF TRANSPORT

Tudor England did not witness any startling improvements in road transport and matters continued much as they had done in medieval times. Interest in travel was, however, more apparent and the age was marked by the reports of such travellers as John Leland and William Camden. Maps and even guides were provided and some attempt was made to be more scientific about travelling. John Norden produced *An Intended Guide for English Travellers* in 1625 and other works, such as one brought out in 1635, were often republished. The statute mile was fixed by law in 1593, although in the north it was long regarded as being 2,428 instead of 1,760 yards. William Harrison's *Description of England* in 1577 included lists of common ways and distances and Norden's work gave mileages between the principal towns. However, it was not until 1675, with the appearance of John Ogilby's *Britannia*, that a comprehensive set of maps was made available. Ogilby used a "waywiser" to measure accurately and his maps were to a scale of one inch to one mile. Other works useful to travellers appeared. In 1637 John Taylor produced his *Carriers Cosmography* giving details of the carters' services and the state of the inns. Chamberlain's work *Angliae Metropolis* (1690) gave a list of the waggon and stage-coach services leaving London. By the end of the Stuart period, a host of distinguished travellers had left accounts of their journeys and, in most cases, had commented on the poor state of the roads. Among these travellers were the diarists Pepys and Evelyn, Sir William Dugdale and Sir William Brereton, Ralph Thoresby, Daniel Defoe, and one lady, Celia Fiennes.

Government regulation had been tried in an effort to improve the roads, but for much of the Tudor and Stuart periods this amounted to little more than the enforcement of the medieval duty of labour on the roads. In 1531 the Statute of Bridges was passed, whereby corporate towns and the counties, through the justices of the peace, were made responsible for the upkeep of bridges. Inasmuch as there was soon to be an attack on the charitable endowments that were responsible for the upkeep of many bridges, this Act was a useful anticipation of public need. The Highways Act was passed in 1555 because "highways are now both noisome and tedious to travel in, and dangerous to all passengers and carriages." Decline in manorial organisation necessitated a new system and the Act made the parish the responsible unit. The justice of the peace was put in charge and a surveyor of the highway was to be elected by the parishioners. He was to carry out a survey three times a year but, since he was often unqualified, as Harrison pointed out, his work was often inadequate. Moreover, he was disliked by the village community. This was because they were required, if they had an income of less than £50 per annum, to work for four or five days on the roads. The Act of 1555 remained the basis of legislation until 1835 but it was subjected to a number of modifications.

In 1563 and 1586, it was re-enacted and the number of days' labour required was increased to six, but the laws seem to have had little effect. In 1630 an observer said that "the workdays appointed by the statute are so omitted or idly performed that there comes little good by them." Modification of the Acts occurred in two ways. In 1654 the surveyors were allowed to carry out assessments of the parish to pay for the necessary labour and materials. This system was developed by Acts in 1662 and 1670 and in 1691 the right to levy a road rate was definitely established. The difficulties encountered in collecting poor rates and the low total of rates collected suggest that little advantage was taken of this change. The other modification was made in 1691, when the surveyor was made the appointee of the justice of the peace. One group of roads came in for particular attention from the government; they were the Wealden roads affected by the heavy traffic of the iron and timber industries. Special laws were passed in 1581, 1584 and 1597 concerning the roads of Surrey, Kent and Sussex which were to be cinder-based for additional support. Once again, such measures seem to have had little effect. Oxen had to be used to drag coaches from the mud and Prince George of Denmark (husband of Queen Anne) spent six hours travelling 9 miles on his way to Petworth. In 1740 timber was so long on the roads of Sussex that it was said to decay on its journey.

By the middle decades of the seventeenth century, road conditions were appalling and the disruptions of the Civil Wars added to the shameful conditions. Travelling from Preston to Wigan, Cromwell said he crossed "twelve miles of such ground as I never rode in all my life." When Pepys travelled to the West Country in 1668, he and his wife were lost between Newbury and Reading and again on their way over Salisbury Plain, where "we were carried out of our way to a town where we would lie, since we could not go as far as we would. And there with great difficulty came about ten at night to a little inn." It was hardly surprising that Pepys indulgently gave 2s. to some roadmenders on his journey. It was a three-day journey from London to Bath. Macaulay's description of the perils of road travel in the 1680s was by no means an exaggeration. He cited particularly the diary of Ralph Thoresby, who had occasion to use the Great North Road and the roads of Yorkshire when travelling from Leeds to London. On one occasion, he was delayed at Stamford for four days and on another had to swim for his life at Ware. Macaulay's "perils and disasters as might suffice for a journey to the Frozen Ocean" were echoed by contemporaries. In 1751 Sir Francis Dashwood erected a land lighthouse near Lincoln and the Portsmouth coach was called "The Land Frigate." In 1685 the Lord Lieutenant of Ireland was five hours in travelling 14 miles from St Asaph to Conway and was forced to walk from Conway to Beaumaris. In 1722 Daniel Defoe described the road from Tonbridge to Lewes as "being so stiff and deep that no horses could go in it." As late as 1770, Arthur Young travelled the Lancashire roads "at the hazard of my neck."

Travellers faced other perils. Harrison had commented in 1577 that "no man travelleth by the way without his sword, or some such weapon with us, except the minister who commonly weareth none at all unless it be a dagger or hanger at his side." With more travellers and commerce, the risks of highway robbery increased rather than diminished and unemployed Cavaliers were among the first of the famous named highwaymen like Claude Duval, the French page of the Duke of Richmond, executed in 1670. Gangs haunted Shooter's Hill near Blackheath and Gadshill near Rochester and Evelyn was waylaid in 1671. To the north of London, Hounslow Heath, Finchley Common and Epping Forest were well-known perils to travellers. In the north, Thoresby only proceeded on one occasion because he had the company of fourteen Members of Parliament travelling together for protection. William Nevison, the original for Dick Turpin, was hanged at York in 1685. The Portsmouth mail was robbed at Hammersmith in 1757. Perhaps the rigours of the road were compensated for by the comforts of the inn, so well described by Harrison and highly spoken of by foreign travellers. But it can hardly be doubted that public communication was severely hampered by conditions that led to George II's coach overturning at Parson's Green in 1730 and to Lord Hervey's difficulties in getting from Westminster to Kensington in 1743.

The movement of goods was also severely inconvenienced in a number of ways. Agricultural produce fell in value on the drove roads, so that sheep lost 7 lb and bullock 28 lb on the journey from Norfolk to London. The posts were slow and often robbed. Speeds were inadequate. In 1706 it still took four days from London to York with only 14 lb of luggage. Movement by sea was sometimes quicker than by land. It was certainly cheaper. Heavy goods cost £7 a ton from London to Birmingham and £12 a ton from London to Exeter. Conveyance by stage wagon or packhorse was undoubtedly more expensive than movement by sea. Thus, in 1636 it cost 2*s*. a ton by water and £6 a ton by road to bring fuller's earth from Rochester to Ipswich. Cloth coming from Kendal to London in 1698 cost 28*s*. per pack by land and 12*s*. per pack by water. In winter, the roads were often impassable and the losses must have been great. As late as 1767, one writer said that "the trade of the kingdom languished under these impediments. . . . Except in a few summer months it was an almost impracticable attempt to carry very considerable quantities of it to remote places."

In spite of the difficulties, improvements began with the types of vehicles available. Walking remained common. Ben Jonson walked from Edinburgh to London and in 1600 William Kemp morris danced from the capital to Norwich. Riding was the normal method of movement and Mrs Pepys was quite willing to ride astride, although Celia Fiennes had a side-saddle. The first innovation was the coach, first developed in the United Provinces and which appeared in England during Elizabeth's reign, windowless and springless. In spite of a Parliamentary attempt to ban them in 1601, they gained in popularity and by 1615 Moryson could say "the streets of London are almost stopped up with them." Most coaches, such as that in which Evelyn travelled 700 miles, were cumbrous slow vehicles, slung between leather braces. It took Evelyn and Lord Treasurer Clifford a day to travel from London to Newmarket in 1671. By Charles II's reign, new forms of coach appeared, such as a glass coach owned by the Duke of York in 1661. Coach-building became one of the evidences of prosperity noticed by Sir William Petty and the Worshipful Company of Coach and Harness Makers was founded in 1677.

Public services were soon provided by the coaches; by 1637 there was a weekly coach between London and St Albans. In 1649 London stage-coaches were advertising journeys at a shilling for 5 miles and by 1658 regular services were scheduled. After the Restoration, these services developed more swiftly. A service between London and Oxford took two days, but in 1669 "The Flying Coach" ran from London to Oxford in thirteen hours. Cambridge followed suit and the idea spread rapidly, so that by the 1680s, a town like Windsor had six coaches a day and services were as frequent as three times a week from London. However, they were still comparatively slow, since the York, Chester and Exeter coaches took four days to reach London. The cost seems to have been about 3*d*. a mile on average. In London, other forms of public conveyance were developed. In 1634 Sir Saunders Duncombe obtained a monopoly over sedan-chairs, which became popular conveyances. In 1633 a Captain Bailey founded a hackney ("ambling horse") company in the Strand and a bitter dispute started between the hackneys and the London watermen. Restrictions were placed on their use in 1635, and the total numbers were limited to 50 (1637), 300 (1654) and 400 (1662), although with the help of considerable bribery, a great many more seem to have operated.

All writers on economic improvement agreed that the improvement of inland transport was essential. Roberts in 1641, Matthew in 1670, and Yarranton in 1677 were the first of many to make the points about increasing markets and reducing costs. Works such as R. Phillips's *Dissertation concerning the Present State of the Highroads of England* in 1737 illustrated the continued interest in the matter sustained by Arthur Young in his *Travels* in the 1760s. The rise of urban centres, the spreading of English trade more evenly through the ports, the increasing bulk of goods such as the products of Midlands mines and manufactures, the rising number of wheeled vehicles and the growing profit consciousness of farmers all contributed to pressure for road reforms. At first, the government responded by trying to limit the loads and wheel sizes in order to protect the road surface. Thus, in 1621 and 1629, no load weighing more than a ton was to be carried in one vehicle. In 1662 the Highways Act forbade the use of more than seven horses to one load, and wheels narrower than 4 inches. In 1753 the wheel dimension requirement was raised to 9 inches. Acts in 1710, 1741 and 1757 required the establishment of weighing machines at toll-gates, but the Acts were never enforced. As late as 1767 the Highways Act was passed to re-enforce the Tudor Acts, forbid nuisances, require parish roads to be at least 20 feet wide and require landowners to keep ditches open and prune hedges.

Government control of road-building never became as efficient as that in France. There all tax payers worked the *corvée* for thirty days on the roads, until this was replaced between 1774 and 1787. Louis XV established a body of road engineers and a training school in 1747; Pierre Tresaguet was responsible for important road improvements. In England, the government was only stirred to personal action when rebellion was possible. This accounts for the exceptional interest taken in north country and Scottish roads in order to facilitate troop movements against the Jacobites. Field-Marshal Wade built 250 miles of roads in the Scottish Highlands after the 1715 rebellion. In 1751 the Military Road from Carlisle to Newcastle was constructed "proper for the passage of troops, horses and carriages at all times of the year." Government concern was mainly confined to encouraging and protecting the turnpike roads which developed as a local response to the bad conditions.

Complaints had been forthcoming since 1656 about the condition of the Great North Road and in 1663 a Turnpike Act was passed to repair a 70-mile stretch of the road in Hertfordshire, Cambridgeshire and Huntingdonshire. A toll was to be levied on road users in order to maintain the road and a body of special commissioners appointed by the justice of the peace to organise the turnpike. The landowners were to provide a horse and cart and two men to labour for six days. In 1678 the first turnpike barrier was erected on the Great North Road. The system did not lead to an immediate improvement and the journey from York to London still took four days; it was not until 1776 that the turnpiking of the whole road was finished. At first, turnpike development was slow: two Acts under Charles II, six under William III and then in Anne's reign came a considerable expansion with twenty-eight. By 1748, there were 160 turnpike companies and these had increased to 530 by 1760. By 1774, the number had nearly doubled to 982. In 1706 an Act was passed whereby the commissioners were replaced by a board of trustees, but other legislation had little effect, although an Act of 1755 required men of substance to serve on the trusts. An Act for erecting signposts was passed in 1698, but it was not enforced on turnpike companies until 1773.

Turnpikes did not cover the whole country and most of them were built in the south-east. There were none in Scotland, Wales or the West Country for many years. Some of those built were little better than ordinary roads and Young complained about the one between Chepstow and Newport. The toll companies were usually small bodies of local landowners and other interested parties, whose legal rights were renewed every twenty-one years. They had little capital available and thus the turnpike roads were usually of short lengths. One at Warminster in 1727 was only 4 miles long. The toll roads from an important centre such as Manchester stretched for fairly short distances to Chapel-en-le-Frith (1724), Stalybridge (1732), Oldham (1733), Rochdale and Bury (1755). A multiplicity of toll-gates grew up and the rates charged varied greatly from one place to another. Collecting of tolls was often farmed out, bad toll-keepers wasted receipts, exemptions bore heavily on other road users and embezzlements were frequent. The companies tried to keep up their dividends and were only limited to 8 per cent in 1773. In that year, the same Act made the trustees answerable to the local justice. Few new roads were created by the turnpike trusts and "inefficient administration and financial malpractice" meant that little was available for repair.

Inevitably, the turnpikes became unpopular and Acts had to be passed in 1728 and 1735 to protect them. Riots against them were frequent and occurred in the south-west (1730), Herefordshire (1732) and Bristol (1749). In Leeds in 1753 there was a rebellion against them similar to the last anti-turnpike riots in Wales ninety years later. Nevertheless, the importance of the turnpikes must not be ignored. It is true that they failed to lower the price of goods carried by land, but they were responsible for improving mail-coach speeds when agreements were made to sound posthorns to open the toll-gates for regular coach services. Moreover, it was the turnpike companies who employed some of the earliest civil engineers. Perhaps the first of those was John Metcalfe of Knaresborough, who, although blind from the age of six, started in 1765 to construct 180 miles of road, linking places such as Huddersfield and Manchester, across the Pennines.

River transport was the alternative to road conveyance and England suffered disadvantages from the numerous navigable rivers, because for long attempts were made to concentrate water improvements on existing rivers rather than in constructing canals. General Acts dealing with river development had been passed with little effect in 1351 and 1371. The first Act specifically concerning improvement was passed for the Lea in 1424, creating a body of commissioners to borrow money and levy tolls to recoup their losses. During the sixteenth century, there were eight Acts including another for the Lea in 1571, which was so improved that Enfield was by-passed as a port. The seventeenth century did not at first see any rapid advance in river improvement, except for the Thames. Traffic had been regulated in 1514 and 1555 by statutes affecting London watermen. In 1606 navigation was to be improved from London to Oxford. A number of schemes were carried out elsewhere. William Sandys improved the Warwickshire Avon, John Mallett the Tone in the 1630s, and the Wey was made navigable from Guildford to London in 1651–3. Other schemes, such as Balk's to improve the Avon (1619) or Skipworth's for the Soar (1634), did not materialise. After this hesitant start, however, English river navigation entered a hundred years of slow but important improvement.

Bad roads, the development of coal and corn exports, building requirements, fuel supply and the supply of new consumer goods in a period when rising standards of living affected the home market were among the main factors accounting for this development. Two particular periods can be discerned. Between 1662 and

1665, there were nine Acts and between 1697 and 1700, eight Acts. Much interest was aroused by Andrew Yarranton who produced his work *England's Improvement* (1677) recommending river and canal development. He was concerned with improving the Severn from Stourport to Kidderminster, and the Avon from Stratford to Tewkesbury, which both enhanced the trade of Bristol. At the turn of the century, the Weaver, Sankey Brook, Aire, Calder, Don, Dee and Bedfordshire Ouse were being improved. In 1717 to 1720, improvements were being made on the Kennet, Derwent, Douglas, Idle, Mersey, Irwell and Weaver. The Mersey was navigable to Warrington, the Douglas to Wigan, the Aire to Leeds, the Severn to Droitwich, and the Medway to Maidstone. Clothiers advocating the Aire and Calder Navigation Bill in 1698 argued that it cost four times as much to move cloth by land as by river. Between Liverpool and Manchester, it was calculated that goods cost 40s. a ton by road and 12s. a ton by river. Coal supply was put forward as the reason for improving the Hampshire Avon in 1664-5 and the Somersetshire Tone in 1698. Some town corporations became involved in river improvements, such as Bath improving the Bristol Avon or Doncaster the Don.

Yet the amount of river development is apt to be deceptive. The 1,000 or so navigable miles of river noted by Defoe were subject to mills, such as those on the Irwell at Manchester, and to varying supplies of water. Their maintenance, free of sediment and sludge, was a never-ending task in days without dredgers. Such problems were partially solved by building canals, but here England lagged behind. In France, the Seine-Loire (1640), the Du Midi (1681) and the Orleans (1692) canals of Paul Riquet were part of an important network, which was greatly admired by English writers such as Matthew who wrote *A Mediterranean Passage by Water* in 1670 describing the French canals. Yet scarcely any attempts were made to build English canals, because of the nearness of highly developed coastal shipping and the possibilities of river transport.

One exception to this was to be found in the West Country. It will be recalled that Exeter had lost its position as a port to Topsham in the middle of the thirteenth century. Among numerous expedients to recover the City's position, the Exeter Canal (1564-6) was constructed to draw trade from Topsham. It was 3 miles long and contained pound locks and may be regarded as the first English canal. It was rebuilt in 1676 and 1698-1701 and contributed to Exeter's period of prosperity before she was displaced by Bristol as the leading western port. The only other canals to be found were those created to drain the Fens, such as the New Cut and the Bedford Level. It will be recalled that a canal had been in operation from Sawtree to Whittlesea Mere in Huntingdonshire in the twelfth century, so the concept of using drains for transport was by no means a new one. It is clear that the East Anglian waterways were used for transport. Even so important a person as the Bishop of Ely had a state barge, for travel between Ely and Cambridge, which was in use during the eighteenth century. No canals were built in England during the first half of the eighteenth century. Rather surprisingly, it was in Ireland that the first one was built. This was constructed by Thomas Steers for conveying coal from Newry in 1742 and it was 35 miles long with 15 locks.

Ports came under a twofold pressure—from the great increase in foreign trade and the consequences of internal communications improvements. The Late Stuart period saw the development of a large number of port towns. London was the most important of these; in 1660 the first dock east of London Bridge (Howland Wet Dock) was opened, and the development of the Pool had started. In 1711 the first dock at Rotherhithe was opened and it was clear that a vast new riverside city was growing with warehouses, tanneries, breweries and coffee houses. In 1760 the City gates were sold and finance and commerce joined hands in Wapping and Shadwell. Bristol developed to be the second port of the kingdom, overtaking Exeter and then, in her turn, being overtaken by Liverpool. A wet dock was built at Sea Mills in 1712 and another at Hotwells in 1765 but already by the 1750s Bristol was beginning to experience the difficulties of being some way up a tidal river. Whitehaven in Cumberland was developed by the Lowther family and profited from a connection between that family and the Penns. In 1750 Whitehaven took 100,000 tons (outward clearance) as compared with London's 180,000. Liverpool was then still the third port, although it matched Whitehaven's tobacco trade with slaving. Port improvements occurred in 1715, 1753 and 1771. Lesser ports on the east and south coasts continued to profit from fishing, the corn trade and shipbuilding. Sunderland, Grimsby and Great Yarmouth developed in the early eighteenth century and the great customs house (1683) at King's Lynn testified to that port's continuing importance. On the south coast, Itchenor, Lymington and Buckler's Hard shared in the great age of naval construction. Roads, rivers and ports had all responded in the sixty years 1660–1720 to the increase in trade resulting from a rise in home demand, the increase in re-exports and finally the rise of overseas demand. Yet technical improvements had been few and the available resources were ill-adapted to meet any great increase in traffic. More capital and more ingenuity were needed in order to bring about a revolution in road and water communications.

INDUSTRY AND THE SPIRIT OF INNOVATION

At first it does not seem as if the underlying conditions of the economy in 1660–1760 were favourable to industry until near the end of that period. Prices were not rising. Population increased only moderately. The main manufactured export still remained cloth. Yet in 1706, one observer said "industry was further advanced in England than in any other part of the world." This was an exaggeration, because the United Provinces had led in many respects in the middle years of the previous century and French industry, benefiting from a better transport system and a larger market, developed at the same pace and even more rapidly for a time after 1735. However, there was a wide variety of factors that contributed to industrial growth, and it seems likely that development during this period has been underestimated. Guild and apprenticeship restrictions declined and the fixing of wages and the outlawing of workers' combinations contributed to an improvement of the employer's lot. With food prices, wages were low and the possibility of buying non-essential goods was increased among the richer section of the community. The great rise in consumption of retained imports already mentioned was caused by a rise in demand and accompanied by a fall in price. One of the main causes of industrial growth was, therefore, a rise in domestic consumption. Where domestic industries were subject to foreign competition, legislative controls helped the manufacturers, as in such notorious cases as the banning of calicoes or imported beaver hats. In other cases, foreign craftsmen established their industries here; white paper, silk and linen manufactures all developed in this way. Colonial trade provided directly for new industries such as sugar-refining, transformed older ones such as cloth and cotton manufacture and gave rise to the growth of home industries such as the Midlands metal crafts to provide for expanding markets, particularly the Thirteen Colonies. Moreover, the wealth accumulated in foreign trade and the genesis of organised finance also contributed to the rise in demand and to the availability of resources.

The foreign contribution to the growth of English industry was considerable during the later Stuart period, not least in that the English were acutely conscious of Dutch superiority and French growth and imitated and reacted vigorously to both challenges. Dutch improvements in cloth manufacture were copied. The Saxony wheel, which added a flyer and a bobbin to the spindle, replaced the earlier spinning-wheel. Gig-mills which had been opposed in 1551 and 1633 were now allowed. Similarly, the narrow Dutch ribbon-loom which had been banned in 1638 was now steadily coming into use and they were known at Manchester by 1660. Innovation in the linen and silk industries was also important, and the introduction of the Dutch loom was welcomed in Manchester, where it was found in workshops containing half a dozen of them. Elsewhere, the loom met with the kind of resistance that the eighteenth-century inventions in the cotton industry faced. There were riots in 1675 in London against them. Louis Crommelin developed the Irish linen industry and perfected the finishing process. The silk industry had a complicated history, but the Huguenots helped a revival in the 1680s, and in 1719 Thomas Lombe set up the first silk throwing-mill, using a stolen Italian patent. In the Midlands hosiery industry, the stocking-frame which had been invented in 1583 by William Lee and had led to the creation of the hosiery industry was considerably improved by Strutt's frame, so that Leicester and Nottingham became important industrial centres. An Act of 1696 forbade the export of stocking frames and the numbers increased:

	London	Provinces
1660	400	250
1727	2,500	5,500
1750	10,000	12,000

There were riots against the stocking-frame in 1710.

The Huguenots contributed greatly to the increase of technical skills in English industry, in the same way as their predecessors had in Elizabeth's time. It was significant that the old Walloon tapestry works at Fulham were moved from there to Exeter and staffed with ex-Gobelins workers. In 1681 and again in 1689, the government issued appeals to the distressed Protestants of Europe to settle here, thus anticipating the policy of the Great Elector Frederick William of Prussia. The Revocation of the Edict of Nantes in 1685 gave an added bonus to this policy of attracting foreign workmen. The numbers of foreign immigrants rose steadily; 1687, 15,000; 1692, 30,000; 1718, 100,000. But it must be remembered that this figure excluded existing residents. Surprisingly the Dutch had been offered the opportunity of settling here in 1672. In 1709 Germans were received in large numbers, although many passed on to Pennsylvania. Individual employers also recruited foreign labour. Crowley the ironmaster imported metal workers from Liège. German swordmakers from Solingen settled at Shotley Bridge in Durham.

Technical improvements resulted from this influx of foreigners, particularly since the new consumer demand required a range of

more refined goods. Porcelain manufacture started. Glass manufacture was improved, although it seems that the French at
Saint-Gobain retained the market for the best-quality products. It
was significant, however, that, in the French industry, coal-burning
factories for bottles were resisted and the glass-makers' monopoly
confirmed in 1727. In England, the industry was widespread and
by the 1680s there were some eighty or ninety glass workshops in
the country. Papermaking also developed, because after 1700
England began to make an increasing amount of white paper, which
she had previously imported. The White Paper Makers' Company
was founded in 1686 and included a number of Huguenots, such
as de Portal, among its members. Precision instrument-making
was also facilitated by the Huguenots and in the reign of William III
the famous English clock-makers Thomas Tompion and George
Graham, helped to establish a craft whose standards were high
in the remotest village. Silk manufacture was, however, perhaps
the most significant of the new industries as the figures for imported
raw silk indicate. Early attempts to establish a native silk industry
had little success and it was not until the late 1680s, with Huguenot settlements at Spitalfields, Norwich and Canterbury, that the
industry revived with the perfecting of the lustrating process. The
manufacture spread to Macclesfield and Stockport and lesser towns,
such as Styal, Mellor and Cromford. Thomas Lombe's mill which
enabled thrown silk to be manufactured in considerable quantities
ran into a good deal of opposition but by 1760 there were seven
silk-mills in operation throughout the country. At Macclesfield by
1765, seven firms employed 2,470 hands and one of them as many
as 720.

Industries for the consumer market reflected the same trend as
foreign trade—an increasing demand for better quality and for
more variety. It is significant that a Jewish merchant, Michael
Levy, introduced the English to caviar in 1671. Coach-building
and snuff-taking have already been noticed. Watch-making started
at Coventry in 1710, and the products of the Clockmakers' Company of 1631 now increased in many parts of the country. Thus,
Trevelyan wrote: "I possess an eighteenth-century grandfather
clock, still keeping good time, which was made in the small Warwickshire village of Prior's Marston." Coffee was replaced by tea
and chocolate manufacture started in 1731. The Company of
Fanmakers was incorporated in 1709 and a London Tobacco-Pipe
Makers' Guild was established. Home timber shortages turned the
attention of furniture manufacturers to imported hardwoods such
as mahogany and the great age of furniture manufacture, in which
design and production were closely associated, began with the

publication of Thomas Chippendale's *The Gentleman and Cabinet Maker's Director* in 1754. His example was followed by George Hepplewhite and Thomas Sheraton. Pottery works at Chelsea, Bow, Derby and Worcester developed, and in 1749 the secret of china manufacture—the use of bone ash—was discovered. Within ten years, Josiah Wedgwood's works near Hanley were opened. In some ways, the Industrial Revolution grew out of a widening scope for craft industries which had to provide for a mass market among the middle class.

These new crafts remained subsidiary in their contribution to industrial growth to the cloth industry. Although cloth exports fell in relative importance as our major export from 75 per cent in 1660 to 50 per cent by 1700 and, still lower, to 45 per cent in 1750, it remained the chief industry. Moreover, since the total of exports rose, the increase in absolute value of cloth was considerable and after readjustments in the later seventeenth century, the industry experienced a new lease of life with the doubling in value of cloth exports between 1700 and 1740. The underlying strength of the cloth industry is shown by its defeat of calicoes which were cheaper and lighter. By the 1690s, technical improvements, such as Gillet's patent process and the use of Indian methods, had developed the home calico industry in counties such as Surrey and Essex. The Huguenots helped the industry at such places as Richmond. Pressure by the cloth interest started in 1696 when a Bill to ban imports of the raw material was debated and rejected. Defoe said "the general fancy of the people runs upon East India goods." When, in 1700, imported calicoes were stopped, the native calicoes developed apace, as the Committee for Trade admitted in 1702. After renewed agitation, the use of calicoes was forbidden in 1721.

Cloth was a protected industry with its raw material guaranteed to it and with regulations often passed to enforce the wearing of woollen cloth, since the county and merchant interests could agree on this matter. However, the improvement in the industry's fortunes after the lengthy depressions was due to the technical improvements already discussed and, in particular, to the mastering of the dyeing problem and the finishing process. By the end of the seventeenth century, nearly all exported cloth was finished and the age-long problem of inferior quality had been conquered. In this matter, the Royal Society played an important part, since Robert Hooke, Robert Boyle, and William Petty all presented papers on textile dyeing to the Society between 1660 and 1667. Influenced by Bauer, a Dutchman, the English at last solved the problem. Moreover, colonial commerce provided the alternative for the Dutch dyes obtained from the Indian trade. Logwood was one of the enumerated commodities and, together with cochineal, provided the source for English dyes.

Thus, the industry started on a period of revival, marked by the erection of cloth halls at Halifax (1700), Wakefield (1710) and Leeds (1711) in Yorkshire, and by the wealth of late-seventeenth-century Exeter in the West Country. On the other hand, the industry remained subject to periodic depressions, due more perhaps to shifts in the kinds of cloth produced or to the movement of cloth from one place to another. Thus, in 1681 the serge trade of Taunton was in difficulty and "other adjacent fanatic places of trade." Some 500 hands were said to be out of work and the people began "to be mutinous, flocking up and down . . . with insolent and peremptory resolves that they were ready to break out on their neighbour's rights before they would starve." Monmouth gained support from such troubles in 1685.

In the south-west, the kerseys were largely supplanted by the serges and Spanish cloths, which made Exeter the third port of the realm and the centre of the cloth market. This section of the industry remained under the gentlemen clothiers, of whom Sir William Petty had been one, and they were entrepreneurs rather than manufacturers. In 1706 it was estimated that a third of the clothiers had never been involved in making the cloth. *The Bristol Merchant* (1713) calculated that a clothier might buy fifty packs in the market and make a hundred broadcloths, the total cost being £1,000. Profits were clearly quite good, because at Bradford-on-Avon in Wiltshire, Defoe found clothiers worth £10,000 a year and commented that "many of the great families who now pass for gentry . . . have been originally raised from and built up by this truly noble manufacture." By 1700 the main area concerned stretched from Topsham to Taunton; Tiverton was the main industrial town. From there, the cloth was brought on packhorses to the Exeter fulling mills and dye "fatts," as Celia Fiennes called them. The clothiers had a firm control over the domestic industry and it has been maintained that there were low wages, long hours, exploitation of female labour, and irregular working for the cloth workers. Consequently, with the collapse of guild and statutory controls, there was a rise in industrial discontent. In 1707 the West Country clothiers complained of clubs among the weavers, "particularly at Taunton"; eventually, in 1726, combinations among cloth workers were forbidden.

In East Anglia, the situation was a little different, although here the transition from the clothier-domestic system to concentrated manufacturer control was more in evidence. Whereas West of England employers were usually clothiers, in the east they were largely master woolmen, who put out the wool to spinners scattered throughout the region and connected together by the packmen. Thus, if the initial capital was high, the working unit was small, particularly in the country areas of worsted manufacture. Spinning remained an antiquated process and Yarranton in 1677 advocated schools to teach it, but even the improvement of weaving in 1733 did not produce a noticeable change and Kay's flying shuttle (1733) was not widely used. Although Norwich specialised in stuffs and produced light finished cloths, the city remained exceptional, since, as Defoe observed, "when we come into Norfolk we see a face of diligence spread over the whole country." The calico imports and the rise of the Yorkshire industry both presented threats to the East Anglian industry but it survived and Norwich and Exeter together accounted for 60 per cent of the cloth exported.

Although cloth was still produced in small quantities in many parts of England, so that towns such as Newbury and Shrewsbury were still noteworthy, there was only one other main production area and that was Yorkshire. West Riding cloth towns had become famous by the time of the Civil War. By the 1680s, ports such as Hull were thriving on the products of Leeds, Halifax and Wakefield and the Midlands cloth industry in such traditional centres as Coventry declined to make way for small Yorkshire manufacturers. The same applied to east Yorkshire towns such as Selby and Whitby—although plague and war devastation temporarily halted advance, this was soon followed by a period of growth when the production of bays was encouraged by the Poor Law authorities. However, the Yorkshire industry profited from the opening of the northern trade with the ending of the Eastland and Merchant Adventurers' monopolies and found a market for bays and the poorer worsteds. Celia Fiennes reported favourably on the growth of Leeds and Defoe described Halifax in terms reminiscent of the Industrial Revolution, when he said, "the nearer we came to Halifax we found the houses thicker and . . . the sides of the hills, which were very steep every way were spread with houses and that very thick." However, the smallness of the working unit held back development and it was not until 1772 that the West Riding drew level with East Anglia in terms of production.

The recovery of the cloth industry was a matter for congratulation. Exports from Norwich to Spain alone rose in value from £23,000 to £112,000 between 1700 and 1721. This was achieved in spite of new fabrics, but it was also enhanced by protection. It will be recalled that the Irish cotton industry had been suppressed in 1699. Scotland tried to organise a cloth industry by forbidding the import of finished goods and the export of yarn in 1681, and by 1704 there were some nine Scottish manufacturers. However, the Union of 1707 presented them with stiff competition and by 1713 Scottish cloth manufacture had collapsed, except for the occasional blanket. Yet the recovery of export markets as a result of producing better cloth was probably the main reason for growth. Writing in 1695, John Cary, a Bristol merchant, philanthropist and Member of Parliament, who was linked with the cloth trade, said in *An Essay on the State of England* that "new projections are every day set on foot to render the making of our woollen manufacture easy."

Such projects were typical of the age and they were part of a wider movement involving scientific discussion, invention and, to a lesser extent, practical application. The number of patents issued rose from 31 in 1660–9 to 102 in 1690–9 and there was no comparable rise until the end of the eighteenth century. Modern science developed during the sixteenth century and bore fruit in the work of Sir Francis Bacon who wrote *The Advancement of Learning*, *Novum Organum* and *New Atlantis*. These works developed the scientific method of investigating problems, which was quickly adopted by such men as William Gilbert and William Harvey. In Europe, the United Provinces led in scientific discoveries and an Academy of Sciences was set up in France in 1635. Organised scientific discussion in England can be considered to have started with Gresham College in 1596 and to have developed in the 1640s and 1650s with the Wadham College Circle. The Royal Society was established between 1660 and 1662 and in 1665, imitating French example, it began to issue a journal. The Royal Society has been criticised on two grounds. Macaulay said that in Charles II's reign "chemistry, divided for a time with wine and love, with the stage and gaming table, with the intrigues of the courtier . . . the attention of the fickle Buckingham." Thus, the work of the Society has been stigmatised as the cursory pleasure of a few. Charles II had a laboratory but he also strongly supported John Graunt as a member of the Society, when he was opposed as a commoner. Prince Rupert attended—and invented mezzotinto. Statesmen such as Chief Justice Hale and Lord Keeper Guildford were involved, but Guildford is credited with the invention of the barometer. Secondly, the Society has been criticised for the incredible notions that it entertained and the impracticability of its inventions. The Marquess of Worcester in *A Century of Inventions* (1663) included a discussion of perpetual motion. Joseph Glanvill still investigated the mysteries of witchcraft. Bishop John Wilkins of Chester showed by careful measurement how the Ark could have contained all the animals mentioned and gave diagrams to prove it. Some of the projections were, however, only impracticable because they were far ahead of their time. Robert Hooke devised "flying telegraphy" in 1665. Cornelius Drebbel devised a submarine. Wilkins also considered that matter and commented on flight, even as far as the moon, which he suggested was inhabited. He wrote: "I do seriously and upon good grounds affirm it possible to make a flying chariot and give much motion into it as shall convey him through the air."

Other projects came closer to the realms of feasibility. Dr Clayton of Kildare devised a gas lamp in 1691, long before Dr Argand's more famous oil lamp of 1784. After the plague and fire, attention was turned to building, draining, ventilation and sanitation. Foreigners commented on the inhabitants of Late Stuart England: "the amount of water the English people employ is inconceivable, especially for the cleaning of their houses." George Sorocold of Derby developed the public waterworks and between 1692 and 1697 Derby, Macclesfield, Leeds and Bristol were equipped with them. Internal sanitation developed more slowly, but ball-cock water supplies were in use by the 1750s. In 1730 it could still be said of London that "every inhabitant before his own house did what was right in his own eyes," and it was not until 1775 that Alexander Cumming and Joseph Bramah developed the water-closet. London was properly lit as a result of a patent given to Edward Heming and employed in the 1690s.

Churchmen took an active role in the Royal Society, including Wilkins, another Bishop of Chester, Pearson, and Sprat, Bishop of Rochester, who wrote the history of the Society. Pearson was the author of a standard work on the Creed and Sprat supported passive obedience and served on James II's revived Court of High Commission, so that there was still an empathy between the various branches of knowledge. Descartes had made this possible by his attempt to reconcile faith and reason, and the active encouragement of the Church was important in forwarding the new movement. There were opponents in the Church, such as Robert Smith and Peter Gunning, but Sprat's view that scientific investigation was "to increase the powers of all mankind and to free them from the bondage of errors" predominated. Heresy and witchcraft were repealed as offences punishable by death in 1677 and 1736 respectively. Wilkins interested himself in an international language and Robert Boyle, the great chemist, served as a director of the East India Company and procured translations of the Scriptures into Malayan and Turkish. He founded the Society for the Propagation of the Gospel, together with John Eliot.

Mathematics was a principle concern of the new scientists, particularly of the Cambridge Neo-platonists, and their work by encouraging precision and developing statistics has a direct bearing on economic development. Aubrey's *Lives* often reported mathematicians who followed in the steps of Descartes, the inventor of co-ordinate geometry, and Leibnitz, who shares with Newton the fame of developing the infinitesimal calculus. Leibniz was a member of the Royal Society and was largely responsible for founding its German equivalent, the Prussian Academy. He invented a calculating machine. Other important mathematicians were John Wilkins, Isaac Barrow and John Wallis. The earliest statistical tables were composed by Graunt and Sir William Petty in 1662 and after that calculations concerning the balance of trade and the distribution of wealth were made. Gregory King, who worked as a secretary to the Committee of Public Accounts, produced his *Natural and Political Observations* in 1696, and his fellow writer Charles Davenant his *Discourses* (1698) and *An Essay upon . . . the Balance of Trade* (1699). In 1696 Edward Culliford was appointed as the first Inspector-General and was succeeded by Davenant. Moreover, calculations extended into the field of social welfare with attempts to estimate the cost of poor relief. A link was established by some writers between full employment and prosperity and this led to changes in the existing paternalist structure.

The progress of science ranged over a wide field, and the Mechanical Committee of the Royal Society had sixty-eight members. Medicine was advanced by Sydenham, botany by Sloane and Ray, geology by Woodward, chemistry by Boyle and Hooke, and physics by Wallis and Newton. The development of astronomy went forward, since it was believed that it would improve navigation. Thus, Edmund Halley developed knowledge of tide movements, and went to St Helena to map the stars of the Southern Hemisphere. John Flamstead was the first Astronomer Royal. These inventions introduced a new spirit into industry, because it now became possible to improve by definite experimentation rather than by chance, or as Josiah Tucker said in 1757, "the English are uncommonly dextrous in their contrivance of the mechanic powers." Cary had also referred to the improvements in coal, where "mines and pits are drained by engines and aqueducts instead of hands." The importance of the Georgical Committee to agriculture, and of the improvements in dyeing to the cloth industry have already been stressed, and it is clear that the development of science had a practical impact on late Stuart industrial growth.

Motive power was still largely water-power, and as late as 1770, the industry of Sheffield ran on 133 water-wheels. In the mines, drainage problems resulting from the use of chain-pumps were criticised in 1667 and the Marquess of Worcester had referred to the use of a steam-engine pump. Coal-mining continued to develop, although at a slower rate, so that the total of coal mined scarcely rose from 1660 to 1700. Thereafter, it doubled by 1750 to about 6 million tons; there is little doubt that this change was the result of the development of an effective steam-pump which enabled deeper mines to be sunk. Mine-owners such as Lord Dartmouth in Staffordshire and Wilkins in Leicestershire were sinking deeper pits; during Anne's reign, there were a number of colliery disasters in the north at Gateshead (1705), Chester le Street (1708) and Bensham (1710). The demand for coal was less from domestic consumers and more from developing industries such as brewing, sugar-refining, malting and Midlands metalworks. Eventually, the development of coke from coal was to prove decisive in putting the coal industry in the forefront of development. France had greater resources of timber and relied less on coal and it was this factor that weakened the eighteenth century development of French industry. Late Stuart England saw the establishment of the Midlands coalfields as being almost as important as those of the north-east. Nef calculated that there was a 150 per cent increase in coal production between 1700 and 1760. In 1698 Thomas Savery developed an engine which made use of atmospheric and steam pressure and in 1708 to 1709 Thomas Newcomen developed a more effective atmospheric pump. A company was formed in 1715 to exploit the new invention and by 1765 there were at least a hundred of these engines at work in the Northumberland and Durham area alone to improve drainage. Yet the mines still had ventilation problems. Moreover, their growth away from the coast created serious transport difficulties, which were only to be solved with the coming of the canals.

An examination of the iron industry, which by the eighteenth century was the second largest employer of industrial labour in the country, indicates both the great developments of the period and the limitations which still attached to industrial growth. The iron industry reflected a growth in the working unit and the amount of capital used but it was handicapped technically. Ambrose Crowley began as a working blacksmith and died in 1713 worth £200,000. He and his son John have been said to represent the precursors of the Owen-type model employer influenced by the work of John Bellers. Crowley started at Sunderland in 1682 and moved to Swalwell and Winlaton in 1690. His workers' regulations included a doctor and a schoolmaster, sick pay and arbitration of disputes. Thomas Foley came to control the Forest of Dean, north Staffordshire and Cheshire and appointed a managing director, John Wheeler. Foley sent Yarranton to Saxony to reintroduce tin-plate manufacture. By 1669 the Foleys were capitalised at £68,830, and by 1692 they had fourteen major works. They controlled smelting furnaces, refining forges and slitting and rolling-mills and provided the material for the new Midlands industries. Nor were such employers atypical. In 1711 four partners founded the Backbarrow Company at Furness which was capitalised at £6,000 and raised £3,850 profit a year by 1716.

However, the iron industry could not produce the best quality iron and found itself short of charcoal supplies for smelting. Something in the region of two-thirds of iron manufactures were made with imported iron, and the quantities of this rose greatly. Thus, from Sweden we received 12,000 tons in 1668 and 20,000 in 1714, and from that year Russian imports rose. In 1714 13 tons came in, but this had risen to 40,000 by 1732. The small amount of steel produced at Newcastle came from Swedish iron and it was not until 1740 that a Doncaster man, Benjamin Huntsman, started the development of the crucible process. Iron had to be protected by forbidding its manufacture in the colonies and encouraging the tin-plate industry. Using displaced Cornish tin-miners, Welsh merchants like Roger Lewis and landowners like Lord Mansel developed the industry at Aberavon and Kidwelly. The process was perfected by John Hanbury of Pontypool and Acts of 1703–4 placed heavy duties on imported plate. The major break-through came with the final realisation of an alternative fuel supply. Dudley's work in the 1620s had gone unnoticed, and it was not until 1709 that Abraham Darby, an ironmaster of Coalbrookdale in Shropshire, produced pig iron smelted with coke, but his process was not widely adopted. The industry achieved its main economies by increasing the capacity of furnaces from 200 to 750 tons, and the duration of hearth-fires from twenty to sixty weeks between 1660 and 1760. Iron production seems to have increased by 45 per cent over the same period.

Defoe noticed in his journeys in Anne's reign that "no particular manufacture can be named which has increased like this of hardware." In saying this, he drew attention to one of the two chief regions of growth in the Late Stuart economy—the Midlands manufactures. The other was the rise of the Lancashire cotton and linen manufactures, together with the great new ports of Liverpool and Whitehaven. The Midlands manufactures developed as more traditional occupations, such as cloth and leather, declined, transport was improved and the location of the coal and iron industries shifted to the west Midlands and Welsh border. Above all, they were stimulated by the demand from the expanding American market. The area was free from the relics of earlier guilds which had controlled manufacturers. Nail-making was the most important craft and Dudley was particularly renowned for it. This was a domestic industry, although it came under the control of the iron-mongers of Birmingham. Wolverhampton specialised in locks, Walsall in bridles and Sheffield in knives and scythes. Birmingham was particularly noted for guns, swords, buckles and buttons and by the 1760s there were large factories owned by men such as John Taylor and Matthew Boulton. Moreover, the metal industries were not only specialised in location but also practised division of labour. It was no coincidence that Adam Smith chose pin-making to illustrate the advantage of this method of production, for it was widespread. Button-making practised a similar specialisation. Such specialisation spread into non-metallic industries and there were sixteen different kinds of coal-miner in the mines. Moreover, in production, an increasing number of machines for slitting, cutting, stamping and pressing were used to provide for a mass market in the kitchenware, stable accoutrements and household embellish-ments, such as candlesticks, now regarded as antiques. In connec-tion with these two important developments, the watch-making craft has a special place. Both Kay of Lancashire and Huntsman of Yorkshire were watch-makers and this particular craft called for great precision. By 1747 the manufacture of watches was divided into twelve separate processes. Tucker observed in 1757 that "when we still consider that at Birmingham, Wolverhampton, Sheffield and other manufacturing places, almost every master manufacturer hath a new invention of his own, and is daily improving on those of others," the conclusion might well be that "few countries are equal, perhaps none excel, the English in the number of contrivances of their machines to abridge labour." As yet, the production unit was small but Boswell referred to "chief-tains" of industry who were to be the precursors of Carlyle's "captains" and Horace Walpole described Sheffield as "one of the foulest towns in England" which was to indicate the trend towards Blake's "dark, satanic mills."

Between 1660 and 1710, the population of Manchester doubled and in 1729 the Manchester Exchange was founded. The population of Liverpool rose from 1,800 (1660) to 6,000 (1708) and 34,407 (1773). Liverpool and Whitehaven were the main ports of England after London and the outward clearances by 1750 were 40,000 and 100,000 tons respectively. Although Norwich and Bristol were still larger than Manchester, Sheffield and Birmingham, each with about 40,000 people, the latter cities were growing at a faster rate. Liver-pool was described as "one of the wonders of Britain." These figures reflect the growth of a varied complex of industries in Lancashire, Cheshire and Derbyshire after 1660.

Derbyshire was the centre of the silk industry and Lombe's factory was working by 1724. John Lombe and his half-brother, Thomas Lombe, helped by George Sorocold, the waterworks engineer, established a water-driven factory which employed 300 people. The industry spread to Macclesfield and Stockport and it is generally agreed that it revealed the method of approach adopted later in the expansion of the cotton industry. Prices fell and Italian silk imports disappeared. Cheshire developed a salt industry to compete with the traditional salt-panning of the Firth of Forth and Tyneside. In 1692 Robert Steynor sank pits at Droitwich and, together with Nantwich and Northwich, the area soon became "full of smoke from the salterns on all sides." Cheshire had rock salt exploited a little later by William Marbury and, as this yielded much more than the brine evaporation, saltworks using iron-made coal-fired furnaces soon developed. Lancashire had a much more diversified industrial pattern, because of the imports to Liverpool. Sugar-refining was developed in Dale Street by 1667, although both Bristol and Glasgow eventually drew ahead in this particular field. Glasgow started production with the East Sugar House in 1669. The chief Lancastrian products were cottons and linens relying on imported "cotton-wool" and on a mixture of flax and wool. Linens concentrated on Manchester and towards Liverpool and Preston; fustians were made in the Bury-Bolton-Blackburn triangle; and the older-established woollens concentrated on places like Oldham and Rochdale. Cotton was used in the manufacture of both linens and fustians. Gradually cotton supplanted wool and flax as a cheaper and lighter material and the Manchester Act of 1736 allowed the free import of cottons in spite of the opposition of the cloth interest which tried to ban them as being similar to calicoes.

Cottons from the Levant and Cyprus were used at first, but after the passing of the Navigation Acts, the imports of cotton from the colonies rose steadily. Between 1700 and 1750, the total increased from 1·75 million lb to 2·75 million lb and the official value of exports rose from £23,253 to £45,986 in the same period. Famous Manchester merchants made their appearance, such as Humphrey Chetham at the beginning of the seventeenth century and Joshua Brown at the end. Linen manufacture had been encouraged by an Act in 1663 and by the presence of the Huguenots. A company was set up in 1690 to encourage manufacture. It was given an export bounty in 1742, but was gradually superseded by the growth of the Irish and Scottish linen industries which has

P

already been discussed, and England produced under a quarter of her linen requirements by the 1750s. Josiah Tucker, Dean of Gloucester, commented that, by the middle of the eighteenth century, the traditional clothing areas of East Anglia and the west were giving way to Lancashire and Yorkshire; the growth of river improvements and turnpikes in those regions was evidence for this change. This shift should not, however, be exaggerated. The returns for the land-tax and the excise in the Late Stuart period indicated that the preponderance of wealth was in the south in proportions of 5:14 and 1:4 respectively. The north contained, at most, only a quarter of the population. Norwich and Bristol were larger than Birmingham and Manchester. The slave trade of London and Bristol was more than that of Liverpool, and the clearance of shipping from London was still more than that of her two nearest rival ports. The richest counties were Middlesex and Surrey, which experienced the greatest growth in wealth in the seventeenth century. The agricultural home counties, East Anglia and the west were the next richest; the seven poorest counties were Cheshire, Derbyshire, Yorkshire, Lancashire, Northumberland, Durham and Cumberland. This distribution of wealth reflected the continued pre-eminence of the profitable wheatlands of the south and of cloth as the main earner of trading wealth.

With the cautions that the period concerned was nearly a hundred years in which the overall growth rate was under 1 per cent, although it rose to 1·9 per cent in trade, and in which the population barely added a million to its numbers, and in the later Stuart period was almost static, the advance of industry was remarkable. Difficult conditions, such as inadequate finance and lack of revolutionary changes, were compensated for by the rise of the middle-class consumer market and the widening colonial demand. Industry was still very much a craft and domestic affair, but guild and government restrictions were giving away to employers' controls, and manufacturers with considerable capital controlled the widely dispersed domestic workers. Costs were lowered, wages remained low and prices were kept down, and these factors enabled expansion to take place. Technical improvements in looms, frames, and furnaces helped in this development. It was an age which accepted but did not fully apply technical changes. With Sir Isaac Newton as Master of the Mint and John Locke on the Committee of Trade, Late Stuart government was clearly appreciative of the new scientific spirit. The pace of technical change in turnpikes or river improvements and in inventions quickened in Anne's and George I's reign, then slowed in the 1730s and 1740s, only to rise steadily in the 1750s. Change affected the traditional crafts, and the widening home market enabled brewing and paper-making, for example, to become industries rather than small crafts. Thus, industrial progress took place in a number of ways. Cloth, iron, coal, leather, silk, linen, cotton, paper, glass, salt, tin-plate and brewing—all expanded to provide for a wide market at home and abroad. Coach-building, watches and clocks, snuff, sugar, chocolate, fans, sedan-chairs, pipes and other luxury crafts and manufactures provided for a smaller market. Traditional industries such as tin-mining, lead-mining, copper-mining, shipbuilding and fishing also continued to expand. Manufactures of a wide variety of metal goods developed.

Total industrial output thus grew faster than population or agricultural production. Deane and Cole give an index from 100 to 114 for home industries' real output between 1700 and 1760 and Hoffmann gives figures of 100 and 157 for the same period for industrial production, including building. Industries moved from high-wage to low-wage areas, reducing costs. Crafts tended to move into larger units, which were more efficient in that they produced economies of scale and the benefits of specialisation. Nearly all the industries experienced technical innovations: the hollander in the paper industry; Strutt's stocking-frame, the ribbon loom for cottons and the flying shuttle for woollens, the silk-throwing process brought in by the Lombes; Savery and Newcomen's drainage improvements; and Darby and Huntsman's work in iron and steel. None of these changes was universally adapted but their advent affected costs and put a premium on capital, rather than on labour. Agriculture and trade supplied this capital. Transport was developed by tram-roads and wagon-ways, turnpikes, river improvements, harbour and dock construction and the improvement of coastal shipping. Wealthy capitalists existed in considerable numbers, so that according to Defoe "an ordinary tradesman now shall spend more money by the year than a gentleman of four or five hundred pounds a year can do, and shall increase and lay up every year too." Their wealth and that of the "substantial merchant magnates, princes of wealth, drawing their riches from all parts of the world" provided the large sums necessary for founding a business. Benjamin Truman's business was valued at £23,000 in 1740 and £92,000 in 1760. In that particular industry, Whitbread, Barclay and later Worthington could equal this achievement. The size of the workshop and factory also increased, so that figures between 300 and 600 employees were common in silk, sailcloth, salt-making, tobacco-rolling, lace-making, glass, paper and the small (toy) metal trades. Thus, the creation of an economy in which industry was as important as agriculture and trade preceded the Industrial Revolution; there was no sudden transition from the age of Sir Roger de Coverley to that of James Watt.

ECONOMY AND PEOPLE AT THE BEGINNING OF THE EIGHTEENTH CENTURY

As a counterpart to the ruthless determination of mercantilist nations to damage each other's trade for their own benefit, it has been argued frequently that social policies underwent a similar hardening of the heart, influenced by capitalist ideas. For example, one writer says that "Sir William Petty's will, not inappropriately, sums up the new attitude at its most enlightened." Petty stated that he had little sympathy for the poor who "should be put upon their kindred," but "to answer custom and to take the safer side" he left £20 to the poor in his parish. It is not difficult to find quotations to support the theory that charity was less influential after 1660. Daniel Defoe's *Giving Alms No Charity and employing the Poor a grievance to the nation* (1704) was typical of a number of criticisms of Tudor paternal relief systems, the rising costs and the uneconomic way in which authorities dealt with the problem. Individual cases of parish miserliness have been cited, such as the case of the pauper who slept in a house crossing a parish boundary and who was eventually assigned to the parish in which his head resided. Moreover, there was a decline in the average number of new charities founded to be dated from the period 1640–60, which was "barren of constructive effort" for the poor.

The first reason given for the change in attitude was the substitution of local for central administration. Thus, after 1660, "even the pretence of state regulation was abandoned, and each parish went its own way." Inasmuch as state regulation in the 1630s had proved to be of little value, this was not a dramatic change. Moreover, the amount of legislation concerning the poor did not noticeably decline. On the contrary, more attention was paid by Parliament to the poor after 1660 than previously. The elimination of the Privy Council was accompanied by an increase in legislative awareness, even if this was directed towards encouraging local initiative. In 1662 the Law of Settlement was passed, whereby two justices were empowered to remove any pauper from a parish in which he was not domiciled within forty days of his arrival and to convey him back to his parish of origin. This law was modified by Acts in 1685, 1691 and 1697 which excluded certain classes of persons, such as labourers hired for seasonal agricultural duties, and allowed justices to issue certificates of exemption. Cottages were destroyed in order to prevent paupers from establishing a residence qualification. Considerable numbers were moved under

this Act and it continued in force in the nineteenth century, modified by Acts in 1795, 1846 and 1876. By the end of the nineteenth
century, 12,000 a year were being moved under the settlement laws.

However, the operation of these laws was not as severe as is often
suggested and they hardly achieved their aim of restricting the movement of labour. It has even been suggested that the distribution
of paupers evenly among the poor parish authorities gave more
effective relief. The cost of litigation between parishes and of
removing the poor were deterrents to the operation of the Acts.
It was, indeed, Defoe that criticised the settlement laws in *Every-
body's Business is Nobody's Business* in 1728, and other critics such
as the writer of the pamphlet *Parochial Tyranny* in the 1750s were
concerned with the same theme.

Attempts were made by the central government to tighten the
administration of the Poor Law at a local level. In 1691 justices
were put in control of the granting of relief instead of the overseers of the poor. In 1697 a £10 fine was imposed on those that
refused to take apprentices. This Act also enforced the wearing
of a badge of pauperism. The demands of the armed services were
considered an outlet for the poor, so that in 1703 justices were
allowed to recruit for the Army and in 1704 to apprentice to
service in the Navy from the age of ten for an eleven-year period.
House of Commons committees investigated the boarding-out of
poor children in 1716 and 1767, and an Act followed in that year.
Although Mackworth's Poor Law Bill failed in 1704, Knatchbull's
succeeded in 1723. A resolution of the House in 1759 denounced the
harsh enforcement of the settlement laws. There was no major
reform in the sense of increased centralisation and co-ordination,
but, since contemporary thought on social problems is concerned
with encouraging local, more personal, care rather than state
uniformity, the eighteenth century may be judged less harshly. It
was still free from Benthamism, with its administrative efficiency
and utilitarian motives, which was to shape the famous Act of
1834. The poor were more savagely regarded towards the end of
the eighteenth century when the Reverend Joseph Townshend, a
friend of Bentham, could say, "hunger will tame the fiercest
animals, it will teach decency and civility, obedience and subjection to the most brutish." It is possible to contend that the other
face of mercantilism was not as harsh as has been suggested. The
harshness came when Adam Smith's "invisible hand" and "the
beneficent wisdom of Providence" combined to equate poverty
with sin and to reject collectivism in favour of individualist
ideals.

Dr Johnson said that "a decent concern for the poor is the

true test of civilisation." Concern was shown over a wide field including the Poor Law, education, prisons, child care, and medical facilities. Poverty was a serious and massive problem throughout the period. Gregory King's estimate was that there were 1,300,000 "cottagers and paupers" and 30,000 vagrants in the country in 1696. When it is recalled that unemployment or sickness could also easily cast a considerable number of the 1,275,000 "labouring people and out servants" and the 240,000 "artisans and handi-craftsmen" on to the Poor Law authorities, it is clear that mounting cost was a serious problem. About a quarter of the people was in abject poverty, and it was the cost of this situation, rather than heartless brutality, that motivated a stricter attitude to the poor. It might be added that a realisation that the poor were an unused resource, and that it would be better for them to be set to work to benefit the economy, was also apparent. This is the view adopted by Josiah Child in his *New Discourse on Trade* which reached its fifth edition in 1699. It was Defoe's contention that alms encouraged poverty and giving them made it impossible to con-tribute to the ever-rising poor rate. The arguments concerning the poor, which increased from the 1690s, were prompted by a wish to solve the problem not to ignore it. Inevitably, some critics blamed one factor as the prime cause of poverty. John Locke claimed that brandy and beer were responsible for poverty in a report to the Board of Trade in 1697. Drink was a serious factor in encouraging idleness, preventing thrift and encouraging crime and, during the eighteenth century, gin became a social evil. The consumption of gin rose as shown in Table 24.

Table 24—Consumption of Gin, 1710–60

	m. gall.
1710	2·20
1720	2·48
1730	3·78
1740	6·65
1750	6·61
1755	4·65
1760	2·32

It is significant that, although the distilling industry greatly bene-fited the agricultural interest, the Gin Act of 1751 was passed and clearly had a significant impact on one aspect of the problem of the poor.

It is hard to accuse the mercantilists of indifference to the poor in view of the rise in the poor rate during the period, proportional to the slow population increase. Some of this rise can be accounted for by the inefficient and corrupt administration, but in spite of this, there was a rise. Figures given vary immensely, since none of them were collected systematically, but a selection such as in Table 25 indicates at least the general trend upwards.

Table 25—The Cost of the Poor Law before 1720

1650	£250,000
1685	£665,000
1701	£900,000
1714	£950,000

The burden was increased by the demobilising of Cromwell's army of 50,000 and by the disruptions of trade and the fluctuation from the civil to the military sector caused by the wars of William's and Anne's reigns. Each determined effort to keep down the size of the standing Army led to a burden on the Poor Law. The Royal Military Hospital (1682) at Chelsea and the Royal Naval College at Greenwich (1705) made only a small contribution to solving this particular aspect of the problem. The latter institution, for example, catered for 2,800 men and rioting unpaid sailors besieged government departments during the period of the Dutch Wars. Thus, the Act of 1697 had to make an exception for discharged soldiers in the settlement laws. It must also be recognised, however, that the services provided a source for employment; between 1756 and 1815, 31,000 boys were found work in the Navy by the Marine Society. Press-ganging accounted for a very small percentage of the total naval intake; at the most some 3–5 per cent. More often, recruitment was carried out from the prisons and Poor Law institutions.

Workhouses were the main solution adopted to reduce the burden of the poor rates in this period. Private individuals urged the importance of industrial training in them and writers such as Thomas Firmin, a mercer, and John Bellers, a clothier, put forward proposals for colleges of industry. A proposal was made in 1691 to create a joint-stock company for the erection of workhouses. As in the past, it was eventually local initiative that led the way. In 1647 the various London welfare institutions had been united to form a Corporation of the Poor and in 1699 Bishopsgate Workhouse was opened by this organisation. By 1732, London had nearly fifty workhouses. John Cary, the Bristol sugar merchant, was the first, however, to secure an Act for setting up a workhouse in 1696.

The idea was adopted by the larger towns. In 1698 Acts for Colchester, Crediton, Exeter, Hereford, Hull and Tiverton were passed; in 1700, for King's Lynn and Sudbury; in 1701, for Gloucester; in 1704, for Worcester; in 1708, for Plymouth; in 1712, for Norwich. The poorer country districts found it more difficult to respond but in 1723 Knatchbull's Act allowed parishes to combine their resources to erect workhouses, and to deny relief to those who refused to enter. In 1756 another Act set up the Incorporated Guardians of the Poor to erect rural workhouses in East Anglia. By the middle of the century, there were some sixty to seventy provincial workhouses. They helped to cut the cost of the Poor Law so that it had fallen to £689,000 by 1750, but thereafter it rose again. By 1776, it had reached £1,530,000, due in part to the accelerating pace of population growth. The effect of the workhouses on costs may be examined by looking at two places in Kent before and after the erection of a workhouse.

Table 26—Poor Law Costs

Place	Date	Cost before	Cost after	Cost 1776
Maidstone	1720	£929	£53	£1,555
Tonbridge	1726	£570	£380	£1,114

Private charity continued to play its important part in helping the poor. The Act of 1601 regarding charities was further extended in 1696, as far as Corporations were concerned, and an Act of 1736 freed the Church from the restrictions imposed by the mortmain statute of 1279. Active merchants such as Child, Cary, Firmin and Bellers, contributed liberally. London had 1,000 charities, of which nearly a third were founded between 1660 and 1713, and the same proportion of Norwich's 160 charities were founded in the same period. Bristol was an exceptional city with 600 charities. Many charities were poorly capitalised and consisted of doles of food, clothing and fuel, and in 1782 it was estimated that the annual disbursement by charitable trusts in England and Wales was £258,000. Emigration was also seen as a way of helping the poor by William Penn and James Oglethorpe. The latter founded Georgia in 1732 for the purposes of social reform and, later in the century, philanthropists founded Sierra Leone for freed slaves. In Stuart times, black slaves were in use in this country. Sir John Reresby commented in 1675 that: "I had a fine black of about sixteen years of age presented to me by a gentleman who brought him over from Barbados." Somersett's Case in 1772 ended slavery in England.

Children received new and particular attention during this period. Jonas Hanway wrote no less than seventy-four works on social reforms and concerned himself particularly with the abuses of boarding out and apprenticeship. Commons' investigation found that many children boarded out were "inhumanly suffered to die by the barbarity of nurses." These revelations were followed by an Act in 1767. With the spread of industrialisation, the use of pauper apprentices became more common. Samuel Oldknow of Mellor had them brought from Clerkenwell and Chelsea. Acts passed in 1788 and 1802 had little effect and the system of parish apprenticeship was not finally abolished until 1844. Thomas Coram established a Foundling Hospital in London in 1739 but the pressures on its resources proved so great that the government had to intervene and provide aid in 1756–60. The charity school movement started in 1699 and the amount spent rose rapidly, so that by 1729, 1,419 schools in England catered for 22,503 pupils. By contrast, foundation of schools for the middle class declined and only 42 were established between 1660 and 1714. By 1712, there were 117 charity schools in London alone. Dr Bray established parochial libraries and in 1709 a Bill for their improvement was passed. This development occurred before the creation of the more expensive circulating libraries at Bath and Southampton in the 1740s. More characteristic of the age was the continuance of religiously orientated charity. This developed with the societies for the reformation of manners set up by Horneck and Beveridge from 1678. Their work included the founding of schools, visiting the sick and the prisons. In 1698 to 1699 Guildford, Mackworth, Hook, Colchester and Bray founded the Society for Promoting Christian Knowledge, which encouraged the distribution of Bibles. Marlborough insisted on all his troops receiving copies. In 1702 the S.P.C.K. drew up a report on the London prisons but it was not published. Such concern over prisons was a new phenomenon. Oglethorpe presented reports on the London debtors' prisons in 1729 and 1754, and John Howard published *The State of the Prisons* in 1777, preparing the way for the Benthamite prison reformers of the early nineteenth century.

Poverty and the inadequacy of the "police" remained the main reason for the power of the mob and the continuance of crime abated, if at all, by the savagery of the law rather than by refinements in criminology and penology. The earliest trade-union disturbances date from the "mutiny of the workmen" at Portsmouth dockyard in 1663. In 1676 a weavers' demonstration at Colchester

P *

was sufficient to call out the militia and there were riots at Trow-bridge in 1677. West Country clothing towns were disturbed in 1683 and these kind of disturbances in various crafts led to laws in 1721, 1726 and 1749, forbidding the combination of workers. In the countryside, Acts against agricultural property had been dealt with by law in 1671 but riots caused by turnpikes, enclosure and shortage of bread were numerous. Thus, there were corn riots in 1727, 1740, 1751-7, 1762, and 1766-7, and it has been calculated that a third of the 275 riots between 1735 and 1800 were due to poverty and lack of food. Smuggling disturbed the peace of the southern counties, and wrecking was a profitable occupation in the west. Large gangs could terrorise parts of towns, and Jonathan Wilde's organisation of London crime produced a special Bill in 1725. If one adds the depredations of poachers and the frequency of highway robbery, it is clear that crime was a serious social problem, about which little was done. By the 1760s, 260 offences carried the death penalty, including appearing armed in a deer park, setting fire to an outhouse, and stealing goods worth more than a shilling. Although Alsatia, the criminal district of London, was cleared up in 1697, the law remained fiercesome and ineffective in the country at large. Henry Fielding in his *Enquiry into the Causes of the Late Increase of Robbers* (1751) blamed gin-drinking, the rise of prostitution, bad poor relief and corrupt justice. In despair, many people turned against the law and Edmund Burke failed to get through a Bill to punish whole villages for shipwreck-ing, thus indicating that the small bands of law enforcement officers were not well regarded by ordinary people. Thus, a clergyman could record in his diary in March 1777: "Andrews the smuggler brought me this night about eleven o'clock a bag of Hyson Tea 6 pound weight." Bow Street runners, parish constables and revenue officers had little chance of success.

One small gleam of sympathy for the underworld may be seen in the foundation of the Loch Hospital for Prostitutes in 1746. Moreover, Bedlam was moved from the City to Moorfields in 1676, and the practice of going to see lunatics for pleasure brought to an end. The late seventeenth and the early eighteenth century saw considerable improvements in medical facilities and hygiene and some improvement in surgical work, as a result of the scientific impetus of the age. Medical improvements were few, although by Charles II's reign, individual surgeons such as Sydenham were becoming known. Thomas Sydenham wrote on fever, gout and dropsy. Real advances were made in the eighteenth century, either by surgeons working in the Scottish universities, or by those engaged to help the armed services. A Surgeon-General of the Fleet was appointed in 1664. The Edinburgh College of Physicians (1681) and the Royal Infirmary (1736), together with the Edinburgh Medical Society (1737), were the focus for Scottish developments. The first professorship of midwifery was established at Edinburgh in 1726 and there, and later in London, William Smellie improved techniques. Although midwives remained unsuitable and parish nurses abused their position, infant mortality was cut from nearly 75 per cent to 32 per cent between the years 1730–49 and 1810–29. Nevertheless, in some quarters the children still died young. A committee of 1767 found that 93 per cent of children born or received into London workhouses before they were twelve in 1763 were dead by 1765. Child labour under increasingly severe conditions tended to keep infant mortality high. Thus, a Manchester official reported in 1796 that: "the untimely labour of the night and the protracted labour of the day with respect to children . . . tends to diminish future expectations as to the general sum of life," and that children in cotton factories "are peculiarly disposed to be affected by the contagion of fever." This led to the passing of the ineffective Health and Morals of Apprentices Act in 1802.

Such a situation was not surprising in the earlier part of the eighteenth century during the gin-drinking epoch. One witness said of a gin shop in Holborn that "between the hours of seven and ten in the evening there went in and came out 1,411 persons excluding children. . . . I am shocked at seeing children intoxicated with their fathers and mothers, children of from seven to fourteen years of age." Estimates varied of the extent of the trade but in 1721 one in ten and in 1743 one in six houses in London was claimed to be a gin shop. By the 1740s, the net population of London was falling, if outside immigration is ignored. Later, beer was to take the place of gin as a social evil, since there were no restrictions on its sale until the Acts of 1830 and 1834.

Operative techniques were improved by the Hunter brothers, John and William. Coming from Scotland, John became house-surgeon at St George's Hospital, London, in 1756. Other improvements were made by Sir John Pringle, who developed a cure for dysentery, and James Lind, who traced the cause of scurvy. Perhaps the most famous medical advance was made by Edward Jenner who studied under Hunter and in 1796–8 perfected vaccination. In earlier years, Lady Mary Wortley Montague had set up an Inoculation Hospital in London, but the idea had not spread and smallpox remained a serious killer. For many years, vaccination remained suspect and it was only in 1840 and 1851 that it became compulsory. Techniques were therefore limited and only adopted slowly. Moreover, in spite of the recognition of fresh air, cleanliness and iron beds with cotton sheets, as medically beneficial, their adoption was slow and hospital fevers were a serious risk to users. John Howard's report on the London hospitals in 1789 found that the death-rate was higher inside than outside hospitals and that, in one case, patients were required to pay a deposit on their funeral expenses before admission.

In the light of this situation, the spate of eighteenth-century hospital building is less impressive. St Bartholomew's was rebuilt in 1729 and a large number of new London hospitals founded. Thomas Guy started Guy's in 1721–4, St George's was founded in 1733. The London Hospital, Whitechapel Road, was founded in 1740 and building began in 1752. The Middlesex Hospital was founded in 1745. A number of specialist hospitals were also established in London. Three lying-in hospitals were founded in 1749, 1750 and 1752—the last becoming Queen Charlotte's on the South Bank. A Jewish hospital was founded in 1747. It has sometimes been stated that the building of hospitals was confined to London, but this was not so; for example, Bristol (1732) and Manchester (1752) Royal Infirmaries were founded in this period. Trevelyan gave the ambivalent statistic of 154 new hospitals and dispensaries between 1700 and 1825, but the inclusion of dispensaries makes it difficult to say whether hospitals became available to a greatly increased section of the population. In 1687 after a struggle, the free treatment of patients was allowed and in 1769 the first free dispensary was opened in Red Lion Square, London.

Life expectancy increased during the eighteenth century. Thus, whereas only 40 per cent of the marriages of peers contracted between 1675 and 1700 completed the full child-bearing period, this figure had increased to 63 per cent by the last quarter of the eighteenth century. For this there were a wide variety of reasons—cleaner houses, carpets instead of rushes, the use of soap, less salted meat, a more varied diet, improved internal sanitation and the seasonal varying of clothes. Many of these improvements were not confined to the upper classes and it is likely that the improvement in the standard of living was a vital factor in prolonging life, increasing resistance to disease and improving the birth-rate. The rise in the population was not due to improved fertility or fecundity, or to earlier marriages, but to the increasing number of child-bearing families having more children who in turn survived to child-bearing age. It is clear, therefore, that the fall in the death-rate was more important than the rise in the birth-rate, because one had to precede the other. Trevelyan claimed that the change in population "represented a rather larger birth rate and a very much reduced death rate."

Table 27—Birth- and Death-rates, 1700–60

	Birth-rate		Death-rate
1700	31·1	per 000	26·0
1710	27·5		26.7
1720	30·5		29·7
1730	32·0		33·4
1740	33·3		31·7
1750	34·1		28·2
1760	33·3		26·7

During the first half of the eighteenth century, the two traditional ravagers of the population died away—widespread starvation and the incidence of plagues. This is not to say that there were not years of dearth, or that various kinds of plague did not still occur. Jail fever carried off some hundreds during the Assizes at Taunton. In 1750, at the famous Black Assize, forty-four people, including the Lord Mayor of London and two judges, were wiped out. Howard said more died of jail fever than were executed. The Army and Navy were subject to frequent outbreaks of plagues. There was "relapsing" fever and "putrid" fever in various parts of the country in the late 1720s. Yet when the plague swept into Europe in 1720, the government took swift action and Richard Mead, in *A Short Discourse concerning Pestilential Contagion*, recommended various health measures. The elimination of the black rat during the 1720s ended the threat from bubonic plague, but typhus, smallpox and dysentery continued to take their toll. Even if the rise in population started before the middle years of the century, the total growth rate is 5 per cent (1700–50) and 49 per cent (1750–1800) respectively for the two halves of the century. The relationship between population and industrial growth is a complex one. Here, it is suggested that the steady if unspectacular change before 1750 was due more to the improvement of the standard of living and hygiene than of midwifery and surgery, more to better housing than better hospitals, and that, although the death-rate rose in the 1720s, in the 1730s and 1740s there was a significant fall. This was followed by a rise in the birth-rate which was to cushion the effect of the rising death-rate of the 1760s and 1780s. Thereafter, it seems likely that Ashton's contention that the death-rate fell more rapidly than the birth-rate is the main reason for growth.

The net increase between 1696 and 1760 was in the region of a million which, according to Pollard and Crossley, "was no faster

Table 28—Birth- and Death-rates (selected years)

	Birth-rate	Death-rate
1730–40	33·30 *per 000*	31·70
1780–90	35·44	25·65
1800–10	33·84	19·98
1820–30	32·36	21·65

than has been recorded in earlier centuries and among other traditional societies." Thus, wealth and output per head rose more
rapidly, prices and interest rates remained low, and expansion was
achieved without inflation and with only one notable depression
until the late 1750s, when prices began to rise. *Per capita* income
increased by roughly double between 1688 and 1770, from £8
(King) to £18 (Young).

It has been said that "by the end of the seventeenth century
England had already developed a fairly complex exchange
economy." In 1696 only 40 per cent of the national product was
agricultural, although the dependence of other sections of the
economy on agriculture and the large amount of available capital
tied up in land would tend to increase agriculture's overall importance. Moreover, agriculture was not in a state where new ideas
were merely "anticipated and discussed" rather than practically
applied. Enclosure by agreement is not included in enclosure figures
and 300,000 acres had been enclosed by Act alone before 1760.
Thus, later enclosure developments marked the culmination of a
process which had been resumed after the Restoration. It has been
shown that the main agricultural improvements were not confined
to newly enclosed regions. In Oxfordshire, field strips were consolidated by agreement, convertible husbandry was followed by
the adoption of *sainfoin* as early as 1673 and turnips by 1727.
Fodder crops were grown on the fallow field by "hitching," and
the county, influenced by the London market, increased wheat
supplies and the average size of flocks. This clearly disproves Lord
Ernle's view that "in the existing system of openfield farming there
was no room for either crop," that is, clover or turnips. It helps
to explain resistance to enclosure, which in many cases was more
concerned with units of ownership than units of production.

Because the population rise was not steep, agriculture was able
to respond to its requirements, provide more of the products for
industry, such as barley and wool, and also expand the export of
wheat. Improvement was not centred on the eastern half of the

country and it has already been stressed that Wiltshire was as progressive as Norfolk. Andrew Yarranton of Astley in Worcestershire wrote *The Improvement Improved . . . by Clover* (1662) and sold seeds to his neighbours. The Dutch introduced clover seeds at Topsham in Devon. Moreover, although wheat expanded at the expense of barley and spread into new lighter-soiled areas, so that Defoe remarked " 'tis more remarkable still how a great part of these downs come by a new method of husbandry to be . . . made arable," wheat prices fell, so that on average prices for 1717–24 were 25 per cent lower than for 1660–9. Animal farming was thus far more important than used to be conceded when Lord Ernle pointed out that Worlidge in his work on agriculture in 1669 devoted only three pages to animals.

It has been suggested that developments in horse-breeding facilitated interest in cattle and sheep. As early as 1674, Anthony Wood commented that meat was rarely spiced and it is clear that winter feed was becoming widespread. Among the early cattle-breeders were John Franklin of Cosgrove in Northamptonshire and Sir Thomas Gresley of Drakelow in Derbyshire. From his estate, improvements spread to Canley, Warwickshire, and it was from there that Bakewell obtained his stock. A commentator remarked in the 1730s that "of late years there have been improvements made in the breed of sheep by changing of rams." Sheep feeding and lambing techniques were partly responsible for the increase in average flocks, which doubled in size on the Yorkshire Wolds between 1700 and 1743. The by-products of the brewing and distilling industries were used to fatten pigs and, to a lesser extent, cattle. Moreover, the use of dairy produce increased during the period, so that one commentator on Nottingham in 1751 said that "even a common washer-woman thinks she has not had a proper breakfast without tea and hot buttered white bread."

Domestic consumption of home and colonial produce rose steadily in both the agricultural and industrial sectors of the community. The consumption of gin and beer was one indication of this, as was the sizeable increase in tea-drinking. Sugar consumption increased and, to a lesser extent, coffee, rum, chocolate and tobacco became part of the diet of the middle classes. Wheaten bread largely replaced barley or rye bread. Although much income went on food, there was an expansion of consumption in other ways. The metal industries expanded with the increasing use of cutlery. Wood of Burslem and Elers of Astbury produced crockery "cheap enough to find a place in the houses of farmers and cottagers." In textiles, the cloth industry recovered to provide "the labourer with cheaper and better clothing." Attention has already been drawn to the

widespread manufacture of "many agreeable and convenient pieces
of household furniture," which Adam Smith said were to be found
in labourers' cottages. If, on absolute standards, England was a
poor country, she was clearly drawing ahead with an increase in
average real income matched by an increase in output per man.
Thus, her rate of growth was in comparison with, for example,
France, relatively greater. France's total trade was greater in value
than ours, but our rate of increase was more rapid and the volume
of foreign trade per head of the population increased at the rate
of 13 per cent a decade between 1720 and 1760.

Already by 1697 to 1701, 80 per cent of our exports were manufactured goods, and thus, although it may well be true that the
rate of domestic consumption was rising faster than overseas
demand, it is clear that exports of cloth and other manufactures
were of great importance particularly to the American colonies
whose population rose from ½ million to 2½ million between 1715
and 1775. Estimates for increases in production show that the cloth,
linen, cotton, silk, textile and hosiery industries expanded. The
figures for cloth are: 1688, £7·9 million and 1772, £10·2 million.
Manufactures concerned with the metal trades showed an equally
large rise. Thus, to take the export of three products: iron increased
from 2,385 tons (1715–19) to 8,710 tons (1748–52); wrought brass
from 1,742 (1700) to 33,211 tons (1775); and wrought copper from
1,636 tons (1700) to 32,314 tons (1775). When the wide range of
consumer industries and new industries based on colonial products,
and the continued expansion of fishing, shipping, building and
mining are all considered, it is clear that English industry was
expanding on a wide front before the Industrial Revolution. Thus,
by comparison with France, England was behind in total production
of cloth, linen, silk and iron but ahead in coal, shipping and cotton
by 1760, in relation to a country whose total population and trade
were greatly in excess of our own.

Recently, the mercantilist and Old Colonial economy period has
undergone a refurbishment by historians. It used to be regarded
by *laissez-faire* and free enterprise writers as a time when restrictions on industry and trade combined with an outdated, carefully
protected, agricultural system to hold back development. Now a
rather different view has been taken and for this there are a number
of reasons. The simplest has been the increase in knowledge of
economic development. Statistics of some accuracy are available
back to 1696, and, for some aspects, even before that time. Another
reason has been the application of economic analysis to history in
order to reveal patterns of growth and trends of development, rather
than the older sharply defined changes in events caused by equally

sharp changes in opinion and techniques. Evolution has replaced revolution as the basis of much economic history thinking. This does not prevent acceptance of booms and slumps, but it makes it practically impossible to date major economic changes with precision. Perhaps there is a third reason why opinion about the possibilities of economic development before the Industrial Revolution has changed and this is that the wheel has come full circle. We have passed through the individualistic capitalist stage into the mixed and collectivist economies. We are more at home with government control of industry and trade and paternalist welfare policies than our immediate predecessors. One writer has summarised this change by saying:

> "the present day Socialist would be perfectly at home in the France of Louis XIV, where officials decided what industries should be created and located in what parts of France and her colonies, minutely regulated the imports and exports, subsidised and controlled prices, and managed the economy even down to prescribing the patterns which were to be woven in the state-owned tapestry works at Aubusson."

It is unfortunate that the deep contemporary concerns of some writers have led them to write economic history with what Wilson has called the "rough justice and intellectual shallowness of a standardised political conflict." Good examples of this, which we have already noticed, are the attempts to relate capitalism and Protestantism and to discredit both with the failings of each other; and the attempt to turn the Civil War into a standardised model for a class war. The deliberate attempt to confuse the gentry and the bourgeoisie and the calculated underplaying of factors such as religion have been two by-products of this latter political attempt to rewrite history. Now the same sleights of hand are being applied to the Industrial Revolution. The traditional Marxist theory of capitalist evolution was challenged by Rostow. Since then, discussion on the causes of the Industrial Revolution has been increasingly clouded, rather than clarified, as the relative role of capital and entrepreneurs and economic "evolution" as causes of the Industrial Revolution has been debated. If the Industrial Revolution was not the product of free trade, free operation of demand and supply in an open market, the growth of capital under favourable circumstances and the initiative of individual businessmen and inventors, then a convincing argument is ready to hand for those anxious to develop African, Asian and South American economies as planned economies today. If industrial growth occurred in a period of state control of consumption by taxation, partial regulation

of wages, restrictions by law on company and banking development
and a host of paternal and mercantilist laws affecting industry
and social policy, the case for the planned economy as a vehicle
of change is thereby greatly strengthened.

Economic history has, therefore, entered a stage in which evolution is more acceptable than revolution as an explanation of change.
It is said that agricultural improvements spread slowly at the rate
of a mile a year. Technical innovations come only "to the mind
that is prepared." They are anticipated by a series of earlier
experiments and very often the finished product is the effort of
several men. It is no longer possible to state precisely when the
first canal, railway, steam-engine or mechanised factory started.
However, at the same time as this development, historians have
been perplexed by the appearance of new "revolutions." Nef
suggested one between 1540 and 1640. Coleman disputed this, but
suggested another at the end of the seventeenth century. A commercial revolution between 1660 and 1760 has reappeared. Rostow
has stated that there was a decisive revolution from 1782 to the
end of the eighteenth century. Depressions have also made their
appearance in the 1690s, in the 1730s and 1740s and in the 1760s.
These developments mark an advance in the right direction, in
that they show that economies evolve by expansion and contraction
not because particular economic systems or policies prevail at
different times. It is recognised now that the exaggerated claims
made for the Industrial Revolution as a sharp break with the past
were incorrect. Clearly, the Industrial Revolution was always in the
making as long as industrialisation increased. There was no period
of pre-conditions, because the English economy had evolved by
boom and slump towards a position where domestic demand based
on rising incomes, foreign demand based on widening markets, and
the supply of raw materials based on home exploitation and foreign
importation, combined to produce accelerated production. A rising
population, more capital, greater inventiveness, and, above all,
agricultural development enabled this situation to be exploited by
the 1780s. A large, protected empire with a powerful navy and an
impressive merchant fleet, a government permeated by agricultural,
industrial and commercial interests, the growth of science and
education—all were stimulants to this response. It was what enterprise had achieved, not what the economy lacked, that led to the
Industrial Revolution. The pre-conditions were not slow growth,
dependence on agriculture and other phenomena associated with
today's underdeveloped economies. As R. M. Hartwell says,
"England in the century before the industrial revolution was not
underdeveloped." Thus, although "the United Kingdom, as the

first of the countries of the world to become highly industrialised, might be expected to provide a case history of peculiar interest," it does not do so if it is implied that there is some model, capitalist or otherwise, which operated at this time. Even if it is true that the Industrial Revolution was in the making in the mercantilist period, this gives little comfort to those who wish to discredit the earlier theory that it was a free-enterprise revolution. The change occurred because economic circumstances made it possible and not because either mercantilism or free trade prevailed.

Two considerations which may help to clarify the discussion of causes in economic history seem to have emerged in considering the period up to 1750. The first is that the economic writers of the day were usually wrong in their diagnosis of causes and, even when writing with tolerable factual accuracy used biased arguments. This is true even of the more practically minded mercantilists, who persisted in believing in the bullionist theory long after it had been refuted. If the producers and consumers had responded to the views of the medieval Church, the bullionists or the mercantilists, and if governments had then had the power to enforce such views, economic development would have been retarded. Secondly, it is clear that economic ideas and policies evolved from age to age, and they were more honoured in the breach than to the letter. Wage and price control in the fourteenth century, Tudor paternalism, the suppression of colonial industry, or attempts to restrict consumption by customs and excise, failed. Where government policy worked, for example, in suppressing the English tobacco industry, it worked in accord with a simple economic law—supply and demand. Therefore, growth has never been the specific product of a particular economic system and the reasons for it are only partially to be found in an examination of formal economic works and government pronouncements. For example, commenting on the growth of Anglo-Portuguese trade in the eighteenth century, H. E. S. Fisher said "it is unlikely that the Anglo-Portuguese commercial treaties . . . had much effect" in developing a trade, which was due more to "general movements of trade." Not the least of these general movements was a recognition of the law of comparative advantage, long before Smith proclaimed it as vital to trade expansion. The Anglo-Portuguese trade grew with little attention to mercantilist principles during the mercantilist epoch; supply and demand were more important, in the end, in creating trade.

Thus, although models for a guild economy or mercantilism do not explain growth, there are simpler explanations. Demand and supply have always ultimately conditioned the development of the economy, whatever the degree of government intervention, provided that it has been a capitalist economy. Only where the government is prepared to destroy general freedom can economic development be determined or planned against market forces. Thus, rationing may suppress inflation and limit consumer demand. Heavy duties raise prices and attempt to restrict luxury imports. But the black market and smuggling were the respective responses to those two particular attempts to plan demand. Once the economy of a country depends upon imported food-stuffs and raw materials, it is also virtually impossible to plan supply. It is difficult to do so, because restricting others imports is the beginning of a vicious circle leading to a fall in one's own exports. Moreover, individual nations can have little effect on world price levels, unless they are the chief creditor nation. Tariffs such as the excise were not the main reason for mercantilist developments. They provided a framework for industrialists, shippers and merchants to take advantage of, and if they had not done so, tariffs would have stultified growth. Demand and supply in a free economy are only marginally affected by government intervention. This is because they make up the life pattern of ordinary people, who remain free to choose to buy and sell goods and to labour where they will. To speak of controlling imports, encouraging exports, and restricting demand, is to speak of controlling ordinary everyday life. In the eighteenth century, the administrative resources and economic expertise of the government were so restricted that it is unlikely that they had as much effect as a modern government might seek to produce.

Economic growth has been sustained in the past by the wishes of individuals and their will to attain them. It has been fostered or retarded by successive governments because other issues have seemed more important. For example, to the mercantilists and paternalists, state security and a favourable balance of trade were all important. This is understandable. Economic growth without reference to general policies and plans will be wasteful, and if demand and supply operate quite freely, grave social injustice will mark the path towards a theoretical state of economic equilibrium. Thus, a dilemma faces historians of the Industrial Revolution, because there were economic benefits and social disadvantages as a result of the changes. Yet there were also the reverse of these circumstances. Ruthless capitalists made phenomenal profits; others went bankrupt. Some villagers lost their land and their domestic employment; others bought smallholdings and prospered. It is an insoluble dilemma inasmuch as it is surely impossible to value the economic advantages and social disadvantages one against the other. Without an agrarian and an industrial take-off at the end of the eighteenth century, there would have been either a longer period with a low standard of living or a political revolution produced by population pressure on limited resources, such as occurred in France. The social evils of the industrial epoch would have come later rather than sooner, and there would have been no compensating advantage from being the first industrial nation in terms of low prices, higher wages and more employment opportunities. Clearly, western Europe had to choose whether to atrophy or to develop. In the eighteenth century, Turkish and Chinese empires atrophied and the English and French expanded. All four had experienced periods of technical advance, intellectual ferment and political power, but it was the Western nations, and particularly England, that took advantage of what has been described as the most important economic change in history.

Samuel Smiles once said "nations have their character to maintain as well as individuals." It is clear that historical evolution produced in England a nation which was capable of creating political, social and economic institutions unlike those of other nations. One or two general examples will indicate this. National unity proceeded more rapidly here than elsewhere, and was copied in Europe, with the ideal of the nation state in the sixteenth century. Modern science received its inspiration from many sources, but none was so important as the English contribution in the seventeenth century. Limited forms of responsible government, individual liberty and universal justice were formulated here and adopted later by the European Enlightenment movement and during the American and French Revolutions. Our eighteenth-century contemporaries acknowledged the uniqueness of our position. Voltaire said that:

> "The English nation is the only one on earth which has succeeded in regulating the power of its kings by resisting them; and which after repeated efforts has established that wise government under which the prince all powerful for good is restrained from doing ill; in which the nobility are great without insolence and without vassals, and in which the people share in the government without confusion."

Eighteenth-century England had many imperfections, as we have seen, but it had also distinguishing features which helped economic development.

A Parliament had met every year since 1689. The Army had always been subordinated to the civil power since the same year. *Habeas corpus* had operated since 1679. Although limited by taxes, libel laws, and occasional government intervention, the press was freed from official censorship after 1695. After 1701, judges were independent of political influence. Juries had secured their freedom in 1670. Feudalism had largely been eliminated. Apart from toll-gates, freedom of internal trade prevailed. Taxation was in the hands of those who had to pay. Guilds had largely disappeared. The nobility and the gentry were active in agricultural improvement, and industrial development. Parliament hastened laws for river improvement, turnpikes, canals, enclosures and to repeal old restrictions. The rich had developed sufficient social conscience to administer and pay for a Poor Law as well as to dispense charity. Class barriers were broken by marriage and entail encouraged younger sons to work. Dean Tucker said the profession of merchant was "full as honourable as that of an officer." After 1685, there was no pitched battle on English soil and after 1745, no serious foreign invasion. When these political, economic and social circumstances are contrasted with the prevailing conditions in Europe, it becomes clear that in the eighteenth century "nations, like individuals derive support and strength from the feeling that they belong to an illustrious race, that they are the heirs of their greatness and ought to be the perpetuation of their glory." England was justified in thinking in this way at the time, if for no other reasons than her imperial expansion and naval supremacy.

Business depends upon confidence. Inasmuch as a nation has to be a going concern, it also depends upon that quality, and the economic changes of the eighteenth century were produced in a society with a rising population, better standards of living and a sense of uniqueness and purpose. Thus, Tucker said, "few countries are equal, perhaps none excel, the English in the number of contrivances of their machines to abridge labour." In this type of sentiment, as Wilson has remarked, there is much of Macaulay. Writing his famous chapter on the state of England in 1685, Macaulay said: "This progress, having continued during many ages, became at length, about the middle of the eighteenth century, portentously rapid, and has proceeded, during the nineteenth, with accelerated velocity." He described the long peace, lack of revolutions, survival of law, the preservation of public credit, civil and religious freedom, and the effects of science, as the factors most closely affecting this development. More ominously he finished the chapter by saying, "we too shall, in our turn be outstripped . . . and yet it may then be the mode to . . . talk of the reign of Queen Victoria as the time when England was truly merry England."

There was much that was xenophobic and much that was complacent about the prevailing mood of the eighteenth century, but in comparison with what was to come, it is hard to judge it harshly. Colbert's economic policies in France had little success and when chided by Louis XIV with the example of the Dutch, he replied, "the greatness of a country does not depend upon the extent of its territory, but upon the character of its people. It is because of the industry, the frugality and the energy of the Dutch that your Majesty has found them so difficult to overcome." Economic historians tend too often to explain the lives of men in terms of trends and logical models. It is more likely that events have been altered by individual determination or lack of it. An analysis of economic development that leaves aside the rich texture of historical evolution in all its facets will be unlikely to arrive at a satisfactory explanation of the great changes in economic life that preceded the Industrial Revolution. It may not be inappropriate to end this account of England's economic development with the words of the Marquess of Halifax:

"We are in an island confined to it by God Almighty, not as a penalty but a grace, and one of the greatest that can be given to Mankind. Happy confinement, that hath made us free, rich and quiet; a fair portion in this world, and very well worth the preserving; a figure that ever hath been envied, and could never be imitated by our neighbours."

BOOK LISTS

The book lists given below are meant to give a selective guide to further reading. They are neither a list of sources for this book nor a complete bibliography. Works have been included which develop a detailed picture of economic history and illustrate particularly interesting aspects, rather than those of a narrow academic nature. The lists are divided as follows:

1 *Standard works* These are given with some remarks on their usefulness.

2 *General works* Listed here are books which have a particular bearing at some point on economic development.

3 *Specialised works* These are divided under the following headings: Agriculture; Industry; Communications; Trade and Finance; Social Policy.

Each section is divided; A giving books and B giving articles. All the divisions are to some extent arbitrary and, therefore, it has been thought best not to include any further chronological division. Place of publication is not given, unless it is abroad.

Abbreviations

The abbreviations of journal titles used in the lists of articles are self-explanatory, except for the following:

Ec.H.R.	*Economic History Review*
E.H.R.	*English Historical Review*
P. and P.	*Past and Present*
T.R.H.S.	*Transactions of the Royal Historical Society*

1 STANDARD WORKS

A. Birnie, *An Economic History of the British Isles* (1935).
   Books I, II and III deal with this period. It is a readable survey and since this book is confined only to England Chaps. XIII, XIV, XV, XX and XXI dealing with the economies of Scotland, Wales and Ireland are useful.

M. Briggs and P. Jordan, *Economic History of England* (6th ed. 1954).
   Part I deals with the period to 1760 and perpetuates a number of errors about the economic history of the period, such as the

BOOK LISTS

existence of manorial and guild systems, the rise of "a money economy" and the bad effects of enclosure.

Sir John Clapham, *A Concise Economic History of Britain* (1949).
Although the course of lectures on which this book was based was by all accounts superb, the book is confused and now outdated in many places.

E. Lipson, *The Economic History of England* (Vol. I 1915, Vols. II & III 1931).
Although this work was written before much statistical information was available and is based too much on literary sources, it remains the only detailed coverage of the whole period to 1750. The chapters on the craft guilds, the Navigation Laws and the trading companies are of particular use.

S. Pollard and D. W. Crossley, *The Wealth of England 1085–1966* (1968).
This is a pioneering work in that it attempts a basically statistical approach to national income growth, and some of the facts gathered in it are useful. However, the book is badly composed, highly selective and fails to relate its selection of statistics to any recognisable pattern.

M. W. Thomas (ed.), *A Survey of English Economic History* (1957).
Parts I (K. G. T. McDonnell) and II (D. C. Coleman), although brief, are full of ideas and use their factual material well.

G. M. Trevelyan, *English Social History* (1942).
Although this book is little more than a random collection of Trevelyan's previously published work together with some additional chapters and is outdated in its economic analysis, the insight it gives into the relationship of economic history to social development remains unrivalled. It has the rare quality of immense readability.

C. Wilson, *England's Apprenticeship, 1603–1763* (1965).
An excellent modern account of the period which, if a little weak on the Early Stuarts, is particularly illuminating on the later period.

2 GENERAL WORKS

A: Books

M. Altschul, *A Baronial Family in Mediaeval England. The Clares, 1217–1314* (Baltimore, 1965).

T. S. Ashton, *An Economic History of England: The Eighteenth Century* (1955).

M. W. Beresford and J. K. St Joseph, *Mediaeval England: An Aerial Survey* (1958).

M. W. Beresford, *New Towns of the Middle Ages* (1967).

M. W. Beresford, *The Lost Villages of England* (2nd ed. 1965).

A. E. Bland, P. A. Brown and R. H. Tawney (eds.), *English Economic History, Select Documents* (1914).

E. M. Carus-Wilson (ed.), *Essays in Economic History* (3 vols. 1954–62).

E. M. Carus-Wilson and O. Coleman, *England's Export Trade, 1275–1547* (1963).

J. D. Chambers, *The Vale of Trent, 1679–1800* (n.d.).

D. C. Coleman (ed.), *Revisions in Mercantilism* (1969).

H. C. Darby, *An Historical Geography of England before 1800* (1936).

N. Davis (ed), *The Paston Letters* (1958).

P. Deane and W. A. Cole, *British Economic Growth, 1688–1959* (1964).

N. Denholm-Young, *Seigneurial Administration in England* (1937).

D. E. C. Eversley, *The Home Market and Economic Growth in England 1750–1780 in Land, Labour and Population in the Industrial Revolution* (1967).

F. J. Fisher (ed.), *Wilson's "The State of England"* (1936).

F. J. Fisher (ed.), *Essays in the Economic and Social History of Tudor and Stuart England* (1961).

M. D. George, *England in Transition* (1931).

J. R. Green, *The Conquest of England* (1883).

J. R. Green, *The Making of England* (1885).

J. H. Hexter, *Reappraisals in History* (1961).

J. W. F. Hill, *Mediaeval Lincoln* (1948).

J. W. F. Hill, *Tudor and Stuart Lincoln* (1956).

G. A. Holmes, *The Estates of the Higher Nobility in 14th Century England* (1957).

W. G. Hoskins (ed.), *Essays in Leicestershire History* (1950).

C. L. Kingsford, *Prejudice and Promise in 15th Century England* (1925).

C. L. Kingsford (ed.), *Stonor Letters and Papers, 1290–1483* (1919).

E. Lamond (ed.), *Walter of Henley's "Husbandry"* (1890).

E. Lamond (ed.), *Hales' "A Discourse of the Common Weal of this Realm of England"* (1893).

G. T. Lapsley, *The County Palatine of Durham* (1900).

W. T. MacCaffery, *Exeter, 1540–1640* (1956).

P. Ramsey, *Tudor Economic Problems* (1965).

R. R. Reid, *The King's Council of the North* (1921).

J. C. Russell, *British Mediaeval Population* (Albuquerque, 1940).

A. L. Rowse, *Tudor Cornwall* (1941).

G. A. C. Sanderman, *Calais under English Rule* (1908).

B. E. Supple, *Commercial Crisis and Change in England, 1600–1642* (1959).

G. Talbot Griffith, *Population Problems in the Age of Malthus* (1926).

R. H. Tawney and E. Power, *Tudor Economic Documents* (1924).

G. F. Warner (ed.), *The Libelle of Englyshe Policye* (1926).

J. A. Williamson, *The Ocean in English History* (1941).

E. Wingfield-Stratford, *The History of British Civilisation* (1928).

B: Articles

J. E. Baldwin, "Household Accounts of Henry de Lacy and Thomas of Lancaster", *E.H.R.* XLII (1927).

J. N. Bartlett, "The Expansion and Decline of York in the Later Middle Ages", *Ec.H.R.* 2nd S XII (1955).

M. W. Beresford, "The Six New Towns of the Bishops of Winchester", *Med. Arch.* III (1959).

F. J. Fisher, "Influenza and Inflation in Tudor England", *Ec.H.R.* 2nd S XVIII (1965).

H. J. Habakkuk, "English Population in the Eighteenth Century", *Ec.H.R.* VI (1953).

B. F. Harvey, "The Population Trend in England, 1300–1348", *T.R.H.S.* 5th S XVI (1966).

W. G. Hoskins, "English Provincial Towns in the Early 16th Century", *T.R.H.S.* 5th S VI (1956).

A. V. Judges, "The Idea of a Mercantilist State", *T.R.H.S.* 4th S XXI (1939).

T. McKeown and R. G. Brown, "Medical Evidence Relating to English Population Changes in the Eighteenth Century", *Pop. Studies* IX (1955).

E. Miller, "The English Economy of the Thirteenth Century", *P. and P.* 20 (1964).

J. U. Nef, "The Progress of Technology and the growth of large-scale industry in Great Britain 1540–1640", *Ec.H.R.* V (1934).

J. U. Nef, "A comparison of industrial growth in France and England from 1540 to 1640", *J. of Pol. Ec.* XLIV (1936).

M. M. Postan, "The Fifteenth Century", *Ec.H.R.* IX (1938).

M. M. Postan, "Some Economic Evidence of Declining Population in the Later Middle Ages", *Ec.H.R.* 2nd S II (1950).

P. Sawyer, "The Wealth of England in the Eleventh Century" *T.R.H.S.* 5th S XV (1965).

J. Z. Titow, "Some Evidence of the 13th Century Population Increase", *Ec. H.R.* 2nd S XIV (1961–62).

G. S. L. Tucker, "English Pre-Industrial Population Trends", *Ec.H.R.* 2nd S XII (1963).

3 SPECIALIST WORKS

Agriculture

A: Books

H. S. Bennett, *Life on the English Manor* (1937).

M. Campbell, *The English Yeoman under Elizabeth and the Early Stuarts* (1952).

E. C. Curwen, *Air Photography and Economic History: The Evolution of the Corn Field* (1929).

H. C. Darby, *The Medieval Fenland* (1940).

F. G. Davenport, *The Economic Development of a Norfolk Manor* (1906).

Lord Ernle, *English Farming Past and Present* (1961).

G. E. Fussell, *The Old English Farming Books from Fitz-Herbert to Tull* (1947).

G. E. Fussell (ed.), *Robert Loder's Farm Accounts, 1610–1620* (1936).

R. C. Gaut, *A History of Worcestershire Agriculture and Rural Evolution* (1939).

E. C. K. Gonner, *Common Land and Enclosure* (1912).

N. S. B. Gras, *The Evolution of the English Corn Market* (1915).

H. L. Gray, *English Field Systems* (1915).

W. G. Hoskins, *The Making of the English Landscape* (1955).

A. H. Johnson, *The Disappearance of the Small Landowner* (1909).

R. Lennard, *Rural Northamptonshire under the Commonwealth* (1916).

C. S. Orwin, *The Open Fields* (1938).

F. M. Page, *The Estates of Crowland Abbey* (1934).

T. W. Page, *The End of Villeinage in England* (1900).

J. A. Raftis, *The Estates of Ramsey Abbey* (Toronto, 1957).

N. Riches, *The Agricultural Revolution in Norfolk* (1937).

E. J. Russell, *A History of Agricultural Science in Great Britain* (1966).

F. Seebohm, *The English Village Community* (1883).

R. A. L. Smith, *Canterbury Cathedral Priory* (1943).

R. H. Tawney, *The Agrarian Problem in the 16th Century* (1912).

J. Thirsk (ed.), *The Agrarian History of England and Wales*, Vol. IV, 1500–1640 (1967).

R. Trow-Smith, *A History of British Livestock Husbandry to 1700* (1957).

P. Vinogradov, *The Growth of the Manor* (1905).

B: Articles

K. J. Allison, "Flock Management in the 16th and 17th Centuries", *Ec.H.R.* 2nd S XI (1958–9).

W. H. Beveridge, "Wages on the Winchester Manors", *Ec.H.R.* VII (1936).

D. C. Coleman, "Labour in the English Economy of the Seventeenth Century", *Ec.H.R.* 2nd S VIII (1956).

R. A. Donkin, "Cistercian Sheep Farming and Wool Sales in the 13th Century", *Ag. Hist. Rev.* VI (1958).

R. A. Donkin, "Cattle on the Estates of Mediaeval Cistercian Monasteries in England and Wales", *Ec.H.R.* 2nd S XV (1962).

J. S. Donnelly, "Changes in the Grange Economy of English and Welsh Cistercian Abbeys 1300–1540", *Traditio* X (1954).

J. L. Drew, "Manorial Accounts of St. Swithun's Priory, Winchester", *Ec.H.R.* 62 (1947).

F. R. H. Du Boulay, "A Rentier Economy in the Later Middle Ages: the Archbishopric of Canterbury", *Ec.H.R.* 2nd S XVI (1964).

G. E. Fussell, "Low Countries' Influence on English Farming", *E.H.R.* 74 (1959).

G. E. Fussell, "Farming Methods in the Early Stuart Period", *J. Mod. Hist.* VII (1935).

G. E. Fussell, "Agriculture from the Restoration to Anne", *Ec.H.R.* IX (1938–9).

H. L. Gray, "Incomes from Land in England in 1436", *E.H.R.* XLIX (1934).

H. J. Habakkuk, "English Land Ownership 1680–1740", *Ec.H.R.* X (1939–40).

H. J. Habakkuk, "The Market for Monastic Property", *Ec.H.R.* 2nd S X (1957–8).

M. A. Havinden, "Agricultural Progress in Open-field Oxfordshire", *Ag.H.R.* IX (1961).

R. H. Hilton, "Peasant Movements before 1381", *Ec.H.R.* 2nd S II (1949–50).

R. H. Hilton, "Freedom and Villeinage in England", *P. and P.* 31 (1965).

W. G. Hoskins, "The Reclamation of the Waste in Devon, 1550–1800", *Ec.H.R.* XIII (1943).

W. G. Hoskins, "Harvest Fluctuations and English Economic History, 1480–1619", *Ag.H.R.* XII (1964).

W. G. Hoskins, "The Leicestershire Farmer in the 17th Century", *Agric. Hist.* XXV (1951).

A. H. John, "The Course of Agricultural Change, 1660–1760", in *Studies in the Industrial Revolution*, ed. L. S. Presnell (1960).

N. Kenyon, "Labour Conditions in Essex in the Reign of Richard II", *Ec.H.R.* IV (1933).

E. Kerridge, "Turnip Husbandry in High Suffolk", *Ec.H.R.* 2nd S VIII (1956).

E. Kerridge, "The Sheepfold in Wiltshire and the Floating of the Water Meadows", *Ec.H.R.* 2nd S VI (1954).

E. Kerridge, "The Movement of Rent, 1540–1640", *Ec.H.R.* 2nd S VI (1953–4).

E. Kerridge, "The Revolts in Wiltshire against Charles I", *Wilt. Arch. and Hist. Mag.* (July 1958).

R. Lennard, "Agriculture under Charles II', *Ec.H.R.* IV (1932).

P. Mathias, "Agriculture and the Brewing and Distilling Industries in the 18th Century", *Ec.H.R.* 2nd S V (1952).

G. E. Mingay, "The Agricultural Depression 1730–1750", *Ec.H.R.* VIII (1956).

D. Oschinsky, "Mediaeval Treatises on Estate Management", *Ec.H.R.* 2nd S VIII (1955–6).

R. A. C. Parker, "Coke of Norfolk and the Agrarian Revolution", *Ec.H.R.* 2nd S VIII (1955).

J. H. Plumb, "Sir Robert Walpole and Norfolk Husbandry", *Ec.H.R.* 2nd S V (1952).

M. M. Postan, "The Chronology of Labour Services", *T.R.H.S.* 4th S XX (1937).

G. E. Russell, "Crop Nutrition in Tudor and Early Stuart England", *Ag.H.R.* III (1955).

J. Schreiner, "Wages and Prices in the Later Middle Ages", *Scandinavian Ec.H.R.* II (1954).

R. H. Tawney, "The Rise of the Gentry", *Ec.H.R.* 2nd S XI (1941).

J. Thirsk, "Sale of Royalist Land during the Interregnum", *Ec.H.R.* 2nd S V (1952).

F. M. L. Thompson, "The Social Distribution of Landed Property in England since the 17th Century", *Ec.H.R.* 2nd S XIX (1966).

B. Waites, "The Monastic Settlement of North-East Yorkshire", *Yorks. Arch. Jour.* XL (1959–62).

B. Waites, "The Monastic Grange as a Factor in the Settlement of North-East Yorkshire", *Yorks. Arch. Jour.* XL (1959–62).

Industry

A: Books

W. H. Chaloner and A. E. Musson, *Industry and Technology* (1963).

D. C. Coleman, *The British Paper Industry*, 1495–1860 (1959).

W. H. B. Court, *The Rise of the Midland Industries*, 1600–1838 (1938).

R. Davis, *The Rise of the English Shipping Industry* (1962).

P. Deane, *The First Industrial Revolution* (1965).

W. H. Dickenson, *A Short History of the Steam Engine* (1938).

M. B. Donald, *Elizabethan Copper* (1955).

M. W. Flinn, *Men of Iron: The Crowleys in the Early Iron Industry* (1962).

A. Friis, *Alderman Cockayne's Project and the Cloth Trade* (1927).

J. W. Gough, *The Mines of Mendip* (1930).

H. Hamilton, *The English Brass and Copper Industries to 1800* (1926).

H. Heaton, *The Yorkshire Woollen and Worsted Industries* (re-issued 1965).

G. H. Kenyon, *The Glass Industry of the Weald* (1967).

G. R. Lewis, *The Stannarles* (1907).

W. A. Lewis, *The Theory of Economic Growth* (1955).

E. Lipson, *The History of the Woollen and Worsted Industries* (1921).

G. I. H. Lloyd, *The Cutlery Trades* (1913).

P. Mathias, *The Brewing Industry in England, 1700–1830* (1959).

T. C. Mendenhall, *The Shrewsbury Drapers and the Welsh Wool Trade* (1953).

J. U. Nef, *The Rise of the British Coal Industry* (1932).

B. Rackham, *Early Staffordshire Pottery* (1951).

A. Raistrick, *Dynasty of Ironfounders: The Darbys of Coalbrookdale* (1953).

G. D. Ramsay, *The Wiltshire Woollen Industry in the 16th and 17th Centuries* (1965).

W. W. Rostow, *The Process of Economic Growth* (1960).

W. W. Rostow (ed.), *The Economics of Take-off into Sustained Growth* (1963).

L. F. Salzman, *English Industries of the Middle Ages* (1923).

L. F. Salzman, *Building in England down to 1540* (1952).

H. R. Schubert, *A History of the British Iron and Steel Industries to 1775* (1957).

E. Straker, *Wealden Iron* (1931).

G. Unwin, *Industrial Organisation in the 16th and 17th Centuries* (1957).

A. P. Wadsworth and J. de L. Mann, *The Cotton Trade and Industrial Lancashire, 1600–1780* (1931).

B: Articles

K. J. Allison, "The Norfolk Worsted Industry in the 16th and 17th Centuries", *York. Bull. of Ec. and Soc. Res.* 12 (1960), 13 (1961).

F. A. Bailey, "Early Coalmining in Prescot, Lancashire", *T.H.S. of Lancs. and Ches.* 99 (1947).

J. B. Black, "The Medieval Coal-Trades of North-East England: Some 14th Century Evidence", *Northern History* II (1967).

E. M. Carus-Wilson, "The English Cloth Industry in the late 12th and Early 13th Centuries", *Ec.H.R.* XIV (1944).

E. M. Carus-Wilson, "An Industrial Revolution of the 13th Century", *Ec.H.R.* XI (1941).

E. M. Carus-Wilson, "Trends in the Exports of English Woollens in the 14th Century", *Ec.H.R.* 2nd S III (1950).

E. M. Carus-Wilson, "Evidence of Industrial Growth in Some 15th Century Manors", *Ec.H.R.* 2nd S XII (1959).

G. L. A. Clarkson, "The Organisation of the English Leather Industry in the late 16th and the 17th Centuries", *Ec.H.R.* 2nd S XIII (1960).

D. C. Coleman, "Technology and Economic History, 1500–1750", *Ec.H.R.* 2nd S XI (1958–9).

J. G. Edwards, "Edward I's Castle-Building in Wales", *Proc. Brit. Acad.* XXXII (1946).

M. W. Flinn, "The Growth of the English Iron Industry 1660–1760", *Ec.H.R.* 2nd S XI (1958–9).

H. L. Gray, "The Production and Consumption of English Woollens in the 14th Century", *E.H.R.* 39 (1924).

G. G. Hopkinson, "The Charcoal Iron Industry in the Sheffield Region, 1588–1775", *Trans. Hunter Arch. Soc.* VIII (1961).

W. G. Hoskins, "The Rebuilding of Rural England", *P and P* 4 (1953).

B. L. C. Johnson, "The Foley Partnership", *Ec.H.R.* 2nd S IV (1952).

D. Knoop and G. P. Jones, "The English Medieval Quarry", *Ec.H.R.* IX (1939).

E. Miller, "The Fortunes of the English Textile Industry in the 13th Century", *Ec.H.R.* 2nd S XVIII (1965).

R. A. Mott, "English Bloomeries, 1329–1589", *Jnl. Iron and Steel Inst.* (1961).

J. U. Nef, "The Industrial Revolution Reconsidered", *J. of Ec. H.* III (1943).

R. A. Pelham, "The Migration of the Iron Industry towards Birmingham during the 16th Century", *Trans. Birm. Arch. Soc.* 66 (1950).

J. E. Pilgrim, "The Rise of the New Draperies in Essex", *Univ. Birm. Hist. Jnl.* VII (1961).

A. Raistrick and E. Allen, "The South Yorkshire Ironmasters", *Ec.H.R.* IX (1939–40).

A. Raistrick, "The South Yorkshire Iron Industry, 1690–1756", *Trans. Newcomen Soc.* 19 (1938).

Q

G. V. Scammell, "Shipowning in England *c*. 1450–1550", *T.R.H.S.* 5th S XII (1962).

H. R. Schubert, "The First Cast-Iron Cannon Made in England", *Jnl. Iron and Steel Inst.* 148 (1942).

P. J. Thomas, "Calico Printing in England", *E.H.R.* 39 (1924).

C. Wilson, "Cloth Production and International Competition in the 17th Century", *Ec.H.R.* 2nd S XIII (1960).

Communications

A: Books

R. G. Albion, *Forests and Sea Power* (Harvard, 1926).

R. and R. C. Anderson, *The Sailing Ship* (1926).

C. W. Bracken, *History of Plymouth* (1931).

G. Connell-Smith, *Forerunners of Drake* (1954).

D. Defoe, *Tours of Great Britain* (1724).

L. A. Harper, *The English Navigation Laws* (New York, 1939).

H. A. Innis, *The Cod Fisheries* (Toronto, 1940).

J. J. Jusserand, *English Wayfaring Life in the Middle Ages* (1889).

R. G. Lounsbury, *The British Fishery at Newfoundland, 1634–1763* (Yale, 1934).

C. M. MacInnes, *A Gateway of Empire* (1939).

I. D. Margary, *Roman Roads in Britain* (1955).

K. M. E. Murray, *Constitutional History of the Cinque Ports* (1935).

C. N. Parkinson, *The Rise of the Port of Liverpool* (1952).

P. Russell, *Dartmouth* (1950).

C. F. Savage, *An Economic History of Transport* (1959).

W. B. Stephens, *Exeter in the Seventeenth Century, a Study of industrial and commercial development, 1620–1688* (1958).

T. S. Willan, *River Navigation in England, 1600–1750* (1936).

T. S. Willan, *The English Coasting Trade, 1600–1750* (1938).

J. A. Williamson, *The English Channel* (1959).

B: Articles

F. W. Brooks, "The Cinque Ports", *Mariners' Mirror* XV (1929).

F. W. Brooks, "The Cinque Ports Feud with Yarmouth", *Mariners' Mirror* XIX (1933).

D. C. Coleman, "Naval Dockyards under the Later Stuarts", *Ec.H.R.* 2nd S VI (1953).

R. Davis, "Merchant Shipping in the Economy of the late Seventeenth Century", *Ec.H.R.* 2nd S IX (1956).

C. E. Lee, "Tyneside Tramroads of Northumberland", *Trans. New-comen Soc.* 26 (1949).

W. E. Minchinton, "Bristol—metropolis of the west in the 18th Century", *T.R.H.S.* 5th S IV (1954).

G. V. Scammell, "English Merchant Shipping at the end of the Middle Ages: Some East Coast Evidence", *Ec.H.R.* 2nd S XIII (1960–1).

F. M. Stenton, "The Road System in Medieval England", *Ec.H.R.* VII (1936).

W. M. Stern, "The First London Dock Book", *Economica* XIX (1952).

J. E. Williams, "Whitehaven in the Eighteenth Century", *Ec.H.R.* 2nd S VIII (1956).

Trade and Finance
A: Books

K. R. Andrews, *Elizabethan Privateering* (1964).

R. Ashton, *The Crown and the Money Market, 1603–1640* (1960).

D. G. Barnes, *A History of the English Corn Laws, 1660–1846* (1930).

S. B. Baxter, *The Development of the Treasury, 1660–1702* (1957).

A. R. Bridbury, *England and the Salt Trade in the Later Middle Ages* (1965).

P. J. Bowden, *The Wool Trade in Tudor and Stuart England* (1962).

J. Carswell, *The South Sea Bubble* (1960).

E. M. Carus-Wilson, *Medieval Merchant Venturers* (1954).

Sir John Clapham, *The Bank of England* (1944).

P. G. M. Dickson, *The Sun Insurance Office, 1710–1760* (1960).

P. G. M. Dickson, *The Financial Revolution in England* (1967).

F. C. Dietz, *English Public Finance 1558–1641* (1932).

M. B. Donald, *Elizabethan Monopolies* (1961).

A. E. Feavearyear, *The Pound Sterling* (1931).

N. S. B. Gras, *Early English Customs System* (1918).

A. S. Green, *Town Life in the Fifteenth Century* (1893–).

F. W. Maitland, *Township and Borough* (1898).

W. E. Minchinton (ed.), *The Growth of English Overseas Trade in the 17th and 18th Centuries* (1969).

S. K. Mitchell, *Studies in Taxation under John and Henry III* (1914).

R. L. Poole, *The Exchequer in the Twelfth Century* (1912).

E. Power, *The Wool Trade in Medieval English History* (1941).

E. Power and M. M. Postan, *Studies in English Trade in the Fifteenth Century* (1933).

W. H. Price, *The English Patents of Monopoly* (Harvard, 1906).

G. D. Ramsay, *English Overseas Trade in the Centuries of Emergence* (1957).

H. G. Richardson, *The English Jewry under the Angevin Kings* (1960).

A. A. Ruddock, *Italian Merchants and Shipping in Southampton, 1270–1600* (1951).

L. F. Salzman, *English Trade in the Middle Ages* (1931).

W. R. Scott, *The Constitution and Finance of English, Scottish and Irish Joint-Stock Companies to 1700* (1910–12).

A. L. Simon, *The History of the Wine Trade in England* (1906).

C. Stephenson, *Borough and Town* (1933).

J. Tait, *The Medieval English Borough* (1936).

S. B. Terry, *The Financing of the Hundred Years War* (1914).

A. P. Thornton, *West India Policy under the Restoration* (1956).

T. S. Willan, *Studies in Elizabethan Foreign Trade* (1959).

T. S. Willan, *The Early History of the Russia Company, 1553–1603* (1956).

B: Articles

Y. S. Brenner, "The Inflation of Prices in Early 16th Century England", *Ec.H.R.* 2nd S XIV (1961–2).

Y. S. Brenner, "The Inflation of Prices in England, 1551–1660", *Ec.H.R.* 2nd S XV (1962–3).

E. M. Carus-Wilson, "The Medieval Trade of the Ports of the Wash", *Med. Arch.* VI–VII (1962–3).

G. N. Clark, "War Trade and Trade War, 1701–1713", *Ec.H.R.* I (1927).

W. A. Cole, "Trends in Eighteenth Century Smuggling", *Ec.H.R.* X (1958).

D. C. Coleman, "The Scriveners", *Ec.H.R.* 2nd S IV (1951).

R. Davis, "English Overseas Trade, 1660–1760", *Ec.H.R.* 2nd S VII (1954).

R. Davis, "English Foreign Trade, 1700–1774", *Ec.H.R.* XV (1962).

D. A. Farnie, "The Commercial Empire of the Atlantic, 1607–1785", *Ec.H.R.* XV (1962).

F. J. Fisher, "The Development of the London Food Market, 1540–1640", *Ec.H.R.* V (1933–4).

F. J. Fisher, "Commercial Trends and Policies in 16th Century England", *Ec.H.R.* X (1940).

H. E. S. Fisher, "Anglo-Portuguese Trade, 1700–1770", *Ec.H.R.* 2nd S XVI (1963).

P. Grierson, "The Relations between England and Flanders before the Norman Conquest", *T.R.H.S.* 4th S XXIII (1941).

R. C. Jarvis, "Illicit Trade with the Isle of Man, 1671–1765", *Trans. Lancs. and Ches. Ant. Soc.* LVIII (1945–6).

A. H. John, "War and the English Economy, 1700–1763", *Ec.H.R.* VII (1955).

D. M. Joslin, "London Private Bankers 1720–1785", *Ec.H.R.* VII (1954).

H. F. Kearney, "The Political Background to English Mercantilism, 1695–1700", *Ec.H.R.* 2nd S XI (1959).

B. B. Parkinson and S. Marriner, "The Nature and Profitability of the Liverpool Slave Trade", *Ec.H.R.* V (1953).

M. M. Postan, "Credit in Medieval Trade", *Ec.H.R.* I (1928).

T. K. Rabb, "Investment in English Overseas Enterprises, 1573–1630", *Ec.H.R.* 2nd S XIX (1966).

R. D. Richards, "The Pioneers of Banking in England", *Ec. Hist.* I (1929).

R. D. Richards, "Early English Banking Systems", *J. Ec. and Bus. Hist.* I (1928).

A. Rive, "A Short History of Tobacco Smuggling", *Ec. Hist.* I (1929).

L. Stone, "Elizabethan Overseas Trade", *Ec.H.R.* 2nd S III (1949–50).

L. Stone, "State Control in 16th Century England", *Ec.H.R.* XVII (1947).

C. H. Wilson, "Treasure and Trade Balances", *Ec.H.R.* 2nd S II (1949).

Social Policy

A: Books

J. J. Bagley, *Life in Medieval England* (1960).

M. Beloff, *Public Order and Popular Disturbance, 1660–1714* (1938).

H. N. Brailsford, *The Levellers and the English Revolution* (1961).

J. Clayton, *Robert Kett and the Norfolk Rising* (1911).

G. N. Clark, *Science and Social Welfare in the Age of Newton* (1949).

C. Creighton, *History of Epidemics in Britain* (1891).

A. Fletcher, *Tudor Rebellions* (1968).

W. M. Frazier, *A History of Public Health* (1951).

D. George, *London Life in the 18th Century* (1925).

E. W. Gilboy, *Wages in Eighteenth Century England* (Harvard, 1934).

E. Griffiths (ed.), *The Diary of Celia Fiennes* (1888).

E. M. Hampson, *The Treatment of Poverty in Cambridgeshire* (1934).

F. Haverfield, *The Romanisation of Roman Britain* (1912).

C. Hill, *Puritanism and Revolution* (1958).

C. Hill, *Reformation to Industrial Revolution* (1967).

C. Hill, *The English Revolution* (1940).

C. Hill, *The Century of Revolution, 1603–1714* (1961).

C. Hill, *Intellectual Origins of the English Revolution* (1965).

C. Hill, *Society and Puritanism in Pre-Revolutionary England* (1964).

J. H. Hutchins, *Jonas Hanway, 1712–1786* (1940).

M. James, *Social Policy during the Puritan Revolution* (1930).

M. G. Jones, *The Charity School Movement* (1938).

W. K. Jordan, *Philanthropy in England, 1480–1660* (1959).

R. K. Kelsall, *Wage Regulation under the Statute of Artificers* (1938).

A. F. Leach, *English Schools at the Reformation* (1896).

E. M. Leonard, *The Early History of English Poor Relief* (1900).

H. MacLachlan, *English Education under the Test Acts* (1931).

B. Mc. Clenaghan, *The Springs of Lavenham* (1924).

D. Marshall, *The English Poor in the Eighteenth Century* (1926).

D. Mathew, *The Social Structure in Caroline England* (1948).

W. Notestein, *The English People on the Eve of Colonisation 1603–1630* (1954).

D. Owen, *English Philanthropy, 1660–1960* (1965).

V. Pearl, *London and the Outbreak of the Puritan Revolution* (1961).

E. Powell, *The Rising in East Anglia* (1896).

E. Power, *The Paycockes of Coggeshall* (1920).

B. H. Putnam, *The Enforcement of the Statute of Labourers* (1908).

J. Rogers, *The Old Public Schools of England* (1938).

H. Shaw, *The Levellers* (1968).

Sir John Simon, *English Sanitary Institutions* (1890).

A. Simpson, *The Wealth of the Gentry, 1540–1660* (1963).

F. M. Stenton, *The First Century of English Feudalism* (1932).

L. Stone, *The Crisis of the Aristocracy, 1558–1641* (1965).

G. S. Streatfeild, *Lincolnshire and the Danes* (1884).

G. Taylor, *The Problem of Poverty, 1660–1834* (1969).

J. E. Thorold Rogers, *Six Centuries of Work and Wages* (1884).

S. L. Thrupp, *The Merchant Class of Medieval London* (1948).

G. M. Trevelyan, *England in the Age of Wycliffe* (1909).

P. Vinogradov, *English Society in the Eleventh Century* (1908).

P. Vinogradov, *Villeinage in England* (1892).

S. and B. Webb, *English Poor Law History* (1927).

B: Articles

T. S. Ashton, "Changes in the Standards of Comfort in 18th Century England", *Proc. Brit. Acad.* XLI (1955).

A. L. Beier, "Poor relief in Warwickshire, 1630–1660", *P and P* 35 (1966).

J. P. Cooper, "The Counting of Manors", *Ec.H.R.* 2nd S VIII (1956).

R. K. Field, "Worcestershire Peasant Buildings, Household Goods and Farming Equipment in the later Middle Ages", *Med. Arch.* IX (1965).

J. L. Fisher, "The Black Death in Essex", *Essex Review* 52 (1943).

E. F. Gay, "The Midland Revolt and the inquisitions of depopulation of 1607", *T.R.H.S.* XVIII (1904).

J. H. Hexter, "Storm Over the Gentry", *Encounter* (May 1958).

W. K. Jordan, "Social Institutions in Kent, 1480–1660", *Arch. Cant.* LXXV (1961).

K. B. McFarlane, "England and the Hundred Years War", *P and P* 22 (1962).

K. B. McFarlane, "Bastard Feudalism", *Bull. Inst. Hist. Res.* XX (1945).

P. Mathias, "The Social Structure of the Eighteenth Century", *Ec.H.R.* 2nd S X (1951).

E. Mercer, "The Houses of the Gentry", *P and P 5* (1954).

E. H. Phelps Brown and S. V. Hopkins, "Seven Centuries of Building Wages", *Economica* NS 22 (1955).

E. H. Phelps Brown and S. V. Hopkins, "Seven Centuries of Consumables Compared with Builders' Wage Rates", *Economica* NS 23 (1956).

M. M. Postan, "Some Social Consequences of the Hundred Years" War", *Ec.H.R.* XII (1942).

M. M. Postan, "The Costs of the Hundred Years' War", *P and P* 27 (1964).

J. F. Pound, "The Social and trade structure of Norwich, 1525–1575", *P and P* 34 (1966).

L. Stone, "Social Mobility in England, 1500–1700", *P and P* 33 (1966).

L. Stone, "The Educational Revolution in England, 1560–1640", *P and P* 28 (1964).

L. Stone, "The Elizabethan Aristocracy, a Re-Statement", *Ec.H.R.* 2nd S IV (1952).

G. H. Trupling, "The Causes of the Civil War in Lancashire", *Trans. Lancs. and Ches. Ant. Soc.* LXV (1955).

C. H. Wilson, "The Other Face of Mercantilism", *T.R.H.S.* 5th S IX (1959).

INDEX

A

Aaron, of Lincoln, 77
Abbeville, 139
Abbey Dore, Herefordshire, 105, 140
Aberavon, Glamorganshire, 437
Aberystwyth, Cardiganshire, 156
Abingdon, Berks., 47, 62, 175, 215, 220, 342
Abraham, the Tinner, 201
Acca, of Hexham, 61
Acciouli, 138
Acontius, Jacobus, 302
Acts of Parliament (including statutes and assizes) (*see also* Proclamations) 70
   Act of Apprentices, 227, 296, 339, 344, 390
   Act of Frauds, 396
   Act of Retainer, 213, 252
   Act of Villeins, 190
   Aliens Act, 209
   Articuli Super Cartas, 89
   Assize of Arms, 70, 177
   Assize of Woodstock, 89
   Aulnager Acts, 252
   Bank of England Act, 415
   Bills of Exchange Act, 414
   Bubble Act, 404
   Chantrys Act, 339
   Charter of the Forest, 89
   Conventicle Act, 394
   Edict of Grateley, 43
   Enclosure Acts, 283–5, 382–3
   Fenland Act, 302
   Game Laws, 190, 315, 381
   Gin Act, 444, 449
   Health and Morals Act, 449
   Highways Act, 48, 422
   Joint Stock Act, 416
   Laws of Hlothere, 39
   Laws of Ine, 38, 39
   Licensing Act, 410
   Limited Liability Act, 404
   Magna Carta, 89, 100, 113, 124, 130, 132, 137, 157, 203
   Manchester Act, 439
   Navigation Acts, 209, 314, 328, 335, 396
   Ordinance of Andover, 53
   Ordinance of the Hundred, 43
   Partition Ordinance, 209
   Poor Relief Acts, 293–4, 381, 442
   River Improvement Acts, 425
   Smuggling Act, 398
   Staple Act, 396
   Statute de Falsa Moneta, 78, 135
   Statute de la Jeuerie, 77
   Statute of Acton Burnell, 78, 139, 157
   Statute of Bridges, 418
   Statute of Labourers, 164, 166, 171–2, 181, 190–1
   Statute of Labourers (1390), 172
   Statute of Marlborough, 100
   Statute of Merton, 89, 111, 150, 284
   Statute of Mortmain, 95
   Statute of the Staple, 213
   Statute of Westminster, 100
   Statute of Winchester, 177, 220
   Statutes of Inmates, 282, 288
   Statutes of Livery and Maintenance, 179
   Tillage Act, 283
   Timber Acts, 341
   Wantage Code, 43, 53
   Weavers Act, 343
   Wine Act, 399
Adams, Robert, 254
Adams, William, 333
Addison, Joseph, 410, 417
Administration, central, and economic affairs, 42ff, 53, 117, 177–78, 243–44, 329, 394, 414
Adulterine guilds, 129, 225
Aelfric, 57, 60, 63
Africa (*see also* individual countries), 321
Aggas, Ralph, 254
Agricola, 24, 27
Agricultural labourers, 21, 39–41, 111ff
Agriculture, methods of cultivation, 8–9, 11–12, 17, 20, 33, 36–37, 249–50, 304, 306ff, 307, 359, 383ff, 452–54
Agriculture, methods of tenure, 9, 12, 42ff, 105ff, 250–51, 276–77, 369–71, 386–87
Aids, feudal (auxilia), 100, 137
Aire, River, 155, 425
Alabaster production, 155, 196, 237
Alard, Gervase and William, 92
Albigensians, 159
Alcuin, 46, 175
Aldeborough, Suffolk, 310
Aldworth, Thomas, 334
Ale (*see also* Beer), 42, 206
Aleppo, 332

Cavendish, Sir John, 186
Caxton, William, 251
Cecil, Sir William (Lord Burleigh), 267, 273, 279, 299, 311, 338
Cecil's Fast, 299
Celts and Celtic influence, 2, 5, 32, 54
Ceorls (including consetlas, geneats, geburs), 39–41, 111
Ceylon, 255
Chagford, Devon, 201
Chamber, 53
Chamber of Assurance, 338, 412
Chambers, Richard, 374
Champagne Fairs, 133, 186
Chancellor, Richard, 326
Chapel en le Frith, Derbyshire, 423
Chapmen, 39, 57, 222
Charcoal production and use, 4, 199, 340–41
Charity and relief (see also Church and Paternalism), 173ff, 177, 226, 297, 362, 442, 446
Charlcote, Warwickshire, 315
Charlemagne, 57
Charnwood Forest, 34, 88
Charters, town (see also Towns), 48ff, 128–29, 136, 156, 352
Chaucer, Geoffrey, on social conditions, 71, 116, 160, 180, 206,
Cheese, 142, 212, 309, 399
Cheke, Sir John, 268
Chelmsford, Essex, 173, 190, 238
Chelsea, London, 56, 445
Cheltenham, Gloucestershire, 247, 388
Cheriton, Walter de, 217, 218
Cheshire, 4, 82, 119, 202, 436
Chester, 1, 24, 27, 46, 50, 55, 60, 98, 119, 133, 194, 223, 268, 352, 376
Chesterfield, Derbyshire, 125, 129
Chetham, Humphrey, 352, 439
Cheviots, 3
Chevisances, 138
Chichele, Robert, 224, 231
Chichester, Sussex, 23, 47, 91, 115, 121, 143, 236, 378
Chieftains of industry, 438
Chigwell, John de, 217
Child, Francis and Josiah, 393, 395, 405, 413
Chilterns, 417, 444
China, 18, 132, 255
China manufacture, 430, 453
Chippendale, Thomas, 430
Chippenham, Wilts., 164, 305
Chipping Campden, Gloucestershire, 216, 238
Chipping Norton, Oxon, 216

Chivalry, economic importance of, 97, 159–61
Chocolate, 429
Christ Church Priory, Hants, 238
Christ's Hospital, 294
Church and the economy, in agriculture, 103, 122, 140, 166, 236–37
  in capital formation, 138
  in industry, 60–61, 140, 142, 152–53, 360ff
  in political and economic influence, 17, 25, 45, 46–47, 75ff, 94, 118, 139–45, 156ff, 223, 360ff,
  in social policy, 434
  (see also Charity), 56, 115, 181, 183–84, 188, 235ff
Cider (and perry), 206
Cinque Ports (see also individual names), 2, 51, 91, 124, 157, 160, 203, 341
Ciompi, 159
Cirencester, Gloucestershire, 24, 165–66, 216, 219, 238
Cissbury, Sussex, 13
Cistercians, 88, 105, 122, 141
Civil War, economic significance of, 260, 316, 355ff, 369, 378–79, 419
Clarendon, Lord (Edward Hyde), 305, 357, 359, 360, 364, 367, 372, 377, 413
Class, development of (see also the main social groups), 363
Classical writers, allusions to economy, 10, 18, 19, 20, 22
Clayton, Sir Robert, 388, 413
Clement V, 175
Clerkenwell, London, 122, 189
Cleveland, Yorkshire, 55, 62, 199
Clifford, Henry, 275
Clinker building, 32, 204
Clock Makers Company, 429
Clothes, 12
Cloth manufacture (see also Broadcloth, and the individual processes), 4, 7, 21–22, 130–31, 151–53, 206, 208, 215, 342, 344ff, 360, 430–432
Cloth trade, 138, 148, 208, 241, 272, 317, 328, 359–60, 408
Cloudesley, William of, 179
Clough, Clym of the, 179
Clubmen, 356, 380
Cnut, 33, 50, 56, 58, 62
Coach building, 421–22
Coalbrookdale, Shropshire, 437
Coal production, 4, 23, 198, 337, 346, 436
Cobbler, Captain, 283, 292
Cobham, Lord, 306

Crowley, Ambrose; John, 428, 436
Crowley, Robert, 269, 276, 284, 384
Crowmarsh Gifford, Oxon, 384
Croydon, Surrey, 189
Crusades, economic importance of, 77, 131–32, 137, 156, 199
Cullompton, Devon, 237
Culliford, Edward, 435
Cumberland, 6, 23, 135, 202, 275, 283, 380
Cumming, Alexander, 434
Curach, 8
Customary rent (redditus), 110, 275,
Customs, organisation, 132, 210, 397
yield, 14, 137, 247, 319, 335–36, 398
Cutlery manufacture, 349
Cuxham, Oxon, 85, 161, 164
Cyprus, 132, 321, 439

D

D'Acre, Richard, 303
Dade, Henry, 360
Da Gama, Vasco, 255
Dalderby, Lincs., 103
Dale, Sir Thomas, 333
Damascus, 17, 132
Damask, 209
Danelaw, 106
Danes (including Vikings), 2, 32, 56, 62–63, 119
Dantzig, 321
Darby, Abraham, 437
Darenth, Kent, 22
Darien Scheme, 399
Darlington, Co. Durham, 130
Dartford, Kent, 349, 350
Dartmouth, Devon, 118, 208, 217, 247, 256, 321
Dashwood, Sir Francis, 420
Davenant, Charles, 301, 311, 335, 393, 435
Davis, John, 328
Day, Francis, 334
Dean, Forest of, 2, 13, 59, 198, 199, 436
Debasement (including deflation, devaluation) (see also Money), 74, 167, 170, 265–66
Debateable land, 6
Debts (including fines, payment, size), 137–38, 236, 415
De Dominio Civili, 80
Dee, River, 60, 425
Defoe, Daniel, 2, 262, 337, 341, 381, 389, 412, 418, 425, 441, 442

Dekker, Thomas, 296
De La Poles (John, Richard, William), 138, 162, 218
Deloney, Thomas, 70, 221
Demesne (including arrangement, alienation, consolidation, usage), 43, 108, 114, 150, 161, 249
Denmark, 63, 252, 328
Denmark, George of, 419
Dennage (dene and strand), 203
Denshiring, 308
Deorham, Gloucs., 6
Depopulation (see also Migration), 282
Derby, 48, 59, 119, 434
Derbyshire, 23, 119, 134, 202, 338, 439
Dergate, William, 109
Dersingham, Norfolk, 385
Derwent, River, 119, 425
Despenser, Henry; Hugh, 180, 190
Devizes, Wilts., 248
Devonshire, 3, 58, 88, 134, 201, 202, 216, 262, 390
D'Ewes, Sir Simonds, 359, 364
Dialogus de Scaccario, 73, 118
Difficlatio, 95, 96
Diggers, the, 356, 380
Digges, Dudley, 328, 329, 334
Diptych, Wilton, 197
Docks, 397, 426
Dockwray, William, 410
Domerton, South, Wilts., 105
Domesday Book, economic importance of, 41, 59, 62, 68, 71, 81, 83, 111, 117ff, 119, 123, 141
Dominion, theory of, 183
Domestic System (including putting out, cottage industry), 153
Don, River, 425
Dorchester, Dorset, 119, 161
Dordrecht, 325
Dorset, 34, 59, 110, 167, 216
Douglas, River, 425
Dover, 11, 23, 27, 49, 126, 186
Downing, Sir George, 393, 414
Drainage, land, 19, 90ff, 302
mines, 202, 347, 436
Drake, Sir Francis, 249, 333, 343
Drapers' Guild, 176, 218
Drebbel, Cornelius, 303, 434
Droitwich, Worcestershire, 59, 128, 425, 439
Drokensford, Bishop, 177
Dudley, Warwickshire, 438
Dudley, Dud and Edmund, 348
Dudley, Sir Matthew, 403
Dugdale, Sir William, 418
Duncombe, Sir Saunders, 422
Dungeness, Kent, 35

Pastons, 71, 160, 234, 251
Pasture (see Cattle, Sheep, Agriculture), 8, 105, 110, 275, 279, 308–9, 385
Paternalism (see also Charity), 268ff, 291–92
Paterson, William, 399, 415
Patten, Thomas, 402
Pay, Harry, 245
Payens, Hugh de, 122
Peacham, Henry, 315
Peak District, 3, 105
Pecock, John, 215
Pegolotti, 140, 211
Pembrokeshire, 104
Penda of Mercia, 57
Penn, William, 446
Pennington, Alderman, 376
Pennines, 3, 125
Penpons, Richard, 245
Penshurst, Kent, 195, 315
Pennsylvania, 428
Peppercorn, William, 202
Percys, 162
Perkins, William, 362
Persia, 255, 327
Persian Gulf, 255
Peruzzi, 138
Peterborough, Northants, 34, 95, 154, 189, 246
Petersham, Surrey, 60
Petham, William, 237
Petty, Sir William, 262, 390, 409, 410, 421, 430
Petworth, Sussex, 388, 419
Pevensey, Sussex, 23, 27, 35, 399, 442
Pewter (including latten), 22, 205, 351
Philpott, John, 186, 187, 204, 217
Phoenicians, 10
Physicians, Royal College of, 290
Piacenza, 138
Picard, Henry, 218
Picardy, 208
Pickering, Vale of, 82, 119
Pigg, 113
Pigs, 20, 33, 110, 309
Pilchards, 203
Pilgrimage, economic impact of, 33, 174–75, 222
Pindar, Sir Paul, 329, 336, 374
Pipe Rolls, 136
Pisa, 320
Pit disasters, 436
Pinks, 397
Plaice, 203
Plague (see also Black Death), 81, 83, 86–88, 247, 261–62, 288, 330, 360

Planning, town, 70, 82, 91–92
Plat, Sir Hugh, 306
Plough development (see also Agriculture), 3, 8, 12, 20, 37, 106–7, 108
Ploughland (measure), 37
Plymouth, Devon, 245, 247, 256, 260, 321, 446
Plympton, Devon, 201
Poitiers, William of, 39, 63
Polaroon, 333
Pole, Reginald, 291
Poleye, Robert de, 215
Poll tax, 81, 186
Pontage, 220
Pontefract, Yorks., 193
Pontife brothers, 220
Pontypool, Monmouthshire, 437
Poole, Dorset, 168, 245, 321, 323, 399
Population, changes in, distribution of, 3, 81ff, 88, 125, 168, 224, 257ff, 280, 402, 438, 450–52
Porchester, Hants, 27, 91
Porlock, Somerset, 304
Port, 406
Portland stone, 143
Portsmouth, Hants, 24, 91, 204, 324, 397
Portugal, 208, 254, 406, 457
Postal services, 410
Potash, 208
Pottery manufacture 13, 14, 22, 60, 429, 430
Poverty (see Charity, Agricultural labourers), 173ff, 282, 291–92, 390
Poverty, Captain, 292
Powell, Edward, 361
Powys, Marquess of, 390
Praemonstratensians, 122
Prayer Book, 283, 376, 377
Prefabrication, 196, 238
Press, development of, 410–11
Press-gang, 445
Preston, Lancs., 419, 439
Prices (see also Money), 71, 78–79, 148–49, 166–67, 170–71, 263ff, 274–75, 278, 301, 347, 359, 385
Priddy, Somerset, 351
Pring, Martin, 328
Pringle, Sir John, 449
Prisage, 132
Prison, 447
Privy Council (see also Administration, Acts), 243, 254, 269–70, 296, 299–300, 362, 381, 442
Proclamations, 171, 396

Providence Island Company, 329, 331, 373
Pulci, 138
Pultenay, John, Thomas, 167, 195, 218
Pumping mechanisms, 198, 347–48
Purchas, Samuel, 329
Puritanism, and relation to economic development, 331, 372
Purveyance, 52
Pym, John, 329, 363, 376, 379, 397
Pytheas, 13

Q

Quadraterius, Peter, 193
Quarr, Isle of Wight, 144
Quarrying, 60, 155, 196
Queenborough, Kent, 355
Queensferry, Flintshire, 352
Quebec, 404
Quern, 41
Quixley, Simon, 189

R

Radisson and Grosseilliers, 404
Ragusa, 329
Rainborough, Colonel, 375
Ramsey, 34, 90, 106, 109, 114, 120, 140, 142, 161, 165, 189, 191
Ramsey, John of, 193
Randolph, Thomas, 410
Raynham Park, Norfolk, 385
Rastell, John, 256, 269
Reading, Berkshire, 419
Rectitudines, Singularum Personarum, 38, 40
Reculver, Kent, 24, 27
Regenbald, 53
Reeves, 108
Re-exports (see also Foreign trade), 334, 394, 407
Reformation, and economic development, 219, 263–64, 356
Relief (see Poor relief)
Reliefs, feudal, 100
Remigius of Fecamp, 121, 144
Rents (see also Landowners), 52, 106, 276
Renegar, Robert, 257, 320
Repton, Derbyshire, 62, 297
Reresby, Sir John, 381, 412, 414, 417, 446

Revolutions (including revolts) (see individual names), 115, 173ff, 179–80, 190, 244, 250, 280–82, 287, 292, 353–54, 356ff, 390, 424, 448, 456
Reyce, Robert, 315, 365
Rhee Wall, 19
Rheims, 154
Rhineland, 20
Rhuddlan, 156
Riccardi, 138
Richard I, 2, 76, 89, 91, 100, 117, 120, 127, 138
Richard II, 69, 91, 92, 139, 172
Richborough, Kent, 20, 24, 27, 30
Rich, Lord, 329
Richmond, Surrey, 430
Ricquet, Paul, Yorks., 119, 268, 425
Rienzi, 159
Rievaulx, Yorks., 122, 142, 194
Ripon, Yorks., 237
Rivers, craft use, 424
Roads, 8, 11, 28–29, 57, 132, 220, 296, 341, 418ff
Roar, River, 35, 91
Roberts, Lewis, 396
Robertsbridge, Kent, 348
Rochdale, Lancs., 339, 352, 423, 439
Rochester, Kent, 33, 189, 420
Rockingham Forest, 34, 88, 89
Roe, Sir Thomas, 271, 334
Rogerus, Theophilus, 197
Rokesley, Gregory of, 92, 138
Rolle, John, 374
Rolle, Richard, 184
Rolls, 71, 181, 185
Romans, 2, 158
Romans, Humbert de, 133
Rome, 17, 54, 58
Romney, Kent, 19, 92
Romney Marsh, 19, 90, 398
Romsey, Hants, 61
Root and Branch Petition, 366
Rotation, crop (see also Agriculture), 384–85, 452
Rother, River, 34, 91
Rotherham, Yorkshire, 221
Rouen, 117, 145
Royal forests, 89ff
Royal Adventurers Trading into Africa, 393
Royal Africa Company, 401
Royal Exchange, 338, 412
Royal Society, 346, 383, 430, 433
Royston, Herts., 350
Rugby, Warwickshire, 298, 309
Rudyerd, John, 397
Run-rig (see Two-field system), 105
Rupert, Prince, 393, 433

Russells (Earls of Bedford), 218
Russia, 382, 405, 437
Rye, Sussex, 35, 92, 186, 195, 206, 214
Rymington, William of, 184

S

Sac and Soc, 44
Sadler, Sir Ralph, 270, 279
Saewulf, 131
Saffron Walden, Essex, 238
St. Albans, 15, 23, 24, 71, 113, 114, 142, 143, 153, 157, 165, 175, 236, 421
St. Aldhelm, 62
St. Anthony's Fire, 175
St. Antoninio, 79
St. Augustine's, 54, 61, 71, 90, 140, 237
St. Bartholomew, 127, 175
St. Bernard, 175
St. Boniface, 33, 61
St. Botulf, 47, 246
St. Briavel's, 199
St. Calais, William de, 121, 144
St. Cross, 127, 174, 237
St. Cuthbert, 41, 133
St. Giles, 127, 133
St. Godric, 63, 131
St. Helena, 333, 435
St. Hugh, 137, 194
St. Ives, Hunts., 47, 125, 130, 133, 204, 246
St. James of Compostella, 118
St. Jerome, 75
St. Martin, 178
St. Mary Redcliffe, 194, 238, 248
St. Mildred, 46
St. Neots, 66
St. Olav, 46, 62
St. Omer, 117, 139, 213
St. Oswald, 45
St. Patrick, 54
St. Paul's, 51, 88, 194, 196, 359, 388
St. Peter's, 174, 175
St. Swithun, 127, 174, 194, 222
St. Thomas, 175, 194
St. Werburgh, 46
St. Wilfrid, 56, 61
St. Wulfstan, 56, 61
Saladin tithe, 137, 138
Salford, Lancs., 202, 377
Salisbury, Wiltshire, 121, 154, 189, 194, 211
Salmon fishing, 60, 203
Saltpetre, 384
Salt production, 4, 14, 41, 59, 202, 350, 439

Salvador, Joseph, 417
Salzburg, 202
Sampson, Abbot, 76
Sanctuary, economic importance of, 178
Sandwich, Kent, 35, 46, 92, 139, 211, 310
Sandys, Sir Edwin, 329
Sandys, William, 424
Sankey Brook, 425
San Juan D'Ulloa, 322
San Lucar, 320
Santo Domingo, 257, 409
Santoft, Lincolnshire, 303
Savery, Thomas, 436
Sawtre, 105, 155
Saxons, 2, 6, 32
Saxony, 262
Saxony wheel, 427
Saye and Sele, Lord, 329
Scarborough, Yorks., 13, 133, 156, 189, 193, 247
Schutz, Christopher, Jaspar, 343, 351
Science (see also Innovation Royal Society), 435
Scot, Reginald, 306
Scotland, 3, 13, 16, 57, 159, 258, 290, 326, 351, 399, 433
Scriveners, 338, 413
Scutage, 99, 136
Seacourt, Berks., 87, 168
Seaford, Sussex, 91
Sedgemoor, Somerset, 90
Seeds, 307, 383
Seigniorial jurisdiction, 44
Seizin, 96, 100
Selby, Yorks., 194, 432
Selden, John, 338
Seliens (including doles), 110
Selsey, Sussex, 56, 91
Selwood Forest, 34
Seneschausie, 108
Sens, William of, 145
Serges, 345, 431
Serjeanty, 99
Serle, Abbot, 122
Services (money, kind, predial) 40, 109–10, 112, 150, 164–65
Sevenoke, William, 231
Severn, River, 2, 34, 60
Seville, 252, 255
Shack, right of, 106
Shalbourne, Wilts., 384
Shareshull, Sir William, 171
Sheep (see also Pastoral Farming, wool production), 4, 8, 20, 104, 142, 161, 280ff, 304, 453
Sheffield, Yorks., 309, 349, 435, 438
Shelford, Isle of Ely, 166